An
INTIMATE
CHRONICLE

The
JOURNALS
of
WILLIAM
CLAYTON

An

INTIMATE
CHRONICLE

The

JOURNALS
of
WILLIAM
CLAYTON

Edited by

George D. Smith

Signature Books
in association with
Smith Research Associates
Salt Lake City
1995

To
Camilla

12 11 10 09 08 07   8 7 6 5 4 3

Library of Congress Cataloging-in-Publication Data
Clayton, William, 1814-1879
  An intimate chronicle: the journals of William Clayton /
    George D. Smith
  p.   cm.
  ISBN: 0-941214-90-7 (limited editon)
  ISBN 10: 1-56085-022-1 (trade edition)
  ISBN 13: 978-1-56085-022-9
  1. Clayton, William, 1814-1879–Diaries. 2. Mormons–
    United States–Diaries.
I. Smith, George D. (George Dempster), 1938-   II. Title.
BX8695.C35A3   1995
289.3'32'092–dc20
[B]
                       89-27572
                       CIP

Table
of

CONTENTS

PREFACE

to the Trade Edition

Since the limited edition of *An Intimate Chronicle: The Journals of William Clayton* was published in 1991, new research has enhanced the significance of Clayton's six journals. Two works have appeared on Samuel Brannan (Mormon newspaperman and California pioneer) and Lansford W. Hastings (western trails promoter) and their influence on American westward migration: Will Bagley, "Lansford W. Hastings: Scoundrel or Visionary?" *Overland Journal* 12 (Spring 1994): 12–26; and Roderic Korns and Dale L. Morgan, eds., *West from Fort Bridger: The Pioneering of Immigrant Trails across Utah, 1846–1850,* revised and updated by Will Bagley and Harold Schindler (Logan: Utah State University Press, 1994). David John Buerger has published his documentary historical research on the development of ceremonies that began in the Kirtland, Ohio, and Nauvoo, Illinois, temples (*The Mysteries of Godliness: A History of Mormon Temple Worship* [San Francisco: Smith Research Associates, 1994]). Lyndon W. Cook has published two books: one on William Law, a Nauvoo leader who openly confronted Joseph Smith over his plural marriages (*William Law* [Orem, UT: Grandin Book Co., 1994]) and a compilation of Nauvoo vital statistics (*Nauvoo Deaths and Marriages, 1839–1845* [Orem, UT: Grandin Book Co., 1994]). D. Michael Quinn has authored the first of a comprehensive two-volume analysis of *The Mormon Hierarchy* (Salt Lake City: Signature Books in association with Smith Research Associates, 1994). His perspective on Mormon institutional development complements Clayton's "intimate" journal. Since completing my own research on Clayton four years ago, I have treated in greater detail the extent to which plural marriage was practiced in Nauvoo from 1841 to 1846, how it related to Joseph Smith's death in June 1844, and how its practice accelerated prior to the Mormons' forced departure across the frozen Mississippi River, eventually into Mexican territory (see "Nauvoo Roots of Mormon Polygamy, 1841–1846: A Preliminary Demographic Report," *Dialogue: A Journal of Mormon Thought* 27 [Spring 1994]: 1–72).

In the last few years the reaction of the Church of Jesus Christ of Latter-day Saints to historical research has been cautious. On occasion, official disciplinary measures have been imposed on scholars who felt that free inquiry was compatible with church membership. Some concern was even voiced from church headquarters over publishing William Clayton's journals, a portion of which remain officially sequestered. In fact, the limited edition of *An Intimate Chronicle* itself is currently held on restricted status at the LDS church library, although it was readily available in bookstores while in print and can still be found on the shelves of most public libraries.

From today's perspective, this collection of William Clayton's journals from 1840 in England, to Nauvoo, along the pioneer trail to Utah, and back to England in 1852–53 conveys a contemporary nineteenth-century view of the Mormon role in American history. I believe this personal record continues to provide an important window into that chapter of the past.

May 1995

ACKNOWLEDGEMENTS

An Intimate Chronicle: The Journals of William Clayton is the fifth volume in a limited edition series of early Mormon journals and autobiographies which was conceived in 1985. Signature Books finished releasing its nine-volume limited edition typescript of the journals of Wilford Woodruff (1832-98), fourth president of the Church of Jesus Christ of Latter-day Saints, when the decision was made to inaugurate the present series in association with Smith Research Associates. The journals of Joseph Smith, Heber C. Kimball, the correspondence of Martha Hughes and Angus M. Cannon, and the journals of John Henry Smith have thus far been completed and published.

An Intimate Chronicle has been a rewarding work to edit, accomplished only with the prolific contributions of many friends and associates. First, I wish to acknowledge the assistance of Janet Visick whose command of English and perception of nineteenth-century social and political relationships contributed form and coherence in annotating often cryptic journal entries. I gratefully acknowledge the strategic intervention of Gary J. Bergera and Ronald L. Priddis whose cogent and expansive questions breathed life into the historical record.

I also greatly appreciate the thoughtful comments and criticism offered by the following scholars of American and Mormon history: Thomas G. Alexander, Ian G. Barber, Lyndon W. Cook, Everett L. Cooley, Paul E. Dahl, Robert B. Flanders, Lawrence Foster, John E. Hallwas, Marvin S. Hill, Dean C. Jessee, Stan Larson, Linda K. Newell, Mario S. de Pillis, D. Michael Quinn, Harold T. Schindler, Gregory Thompson, Malcolm R. Thorp, and Nancy Young.

I wish to thank Madeline T. Hovland for her analytical reading and editing of the manuscript, to Joanna George for her thoughtful reading and recommendations, to Susan Staker for her careful evaluation and preparation of the manuscript for publication, to Brent Corcoran and Jani Fleet for their proof-reading, and to Maxine Hanks for her assistance. I also appreciate the research and advice of Linda Thatcher.

Thanks are also due to the following repositories of early American history without whose care and concern it would not have been possible to present with immediacy and candor this unique chapter in our past: the Bancroft Library at the University of California, Berkeley; the Harold B. Lee Library at Brigham Young University, Provo, Utah; the Chicago Historical Society; the Huntington Library, San Marino, California; the historical department of the Church of Jesus Christ of Latter-day Saints, Salt Lake City, Utah; the Marriott Library at the University of Utah; the New York Public Library; the Utah State Historical Society; and the Yale University libraries.

Special gratitude goes to Wanda Clayton Thomas, great-granddaughter of William Clayton, and to James L. Clayton, great-great-grandson of William Clayton, for their support.

Finally, I would like to thank my wife, Camilla, who read and criticized the introduction and annotations at various stages of completion, and our children — Sarah, George, Benjamin, Geoffrey, and Andrew — who, during the past four years, tolerated with curiosity and some concern the increasing commerce of paper throughout the house.

INTRODUCTION

William Clayton was personal secretary to Joseph Smith, who founded the Church of Jesus Christ of Latter-day Saints (Mormon). Over the course of thirteen years, Clayton kept extensive journals which provide an intimate portrait of the Mormon prophet and his new church in several contexts: in English factory towns; in Nauvoo, Illinois, a midwestern frontier community; in Salt Lake City, from the time of its founding; and on nineteenth-century pioneer journeys by wagon, riverboat, and ocean vessel.

Clayton joined the Mormons in England in the late 1830s during the Industrial Revolution. After immigrating to the United States, he traveled to Nauvoo to join the cooperative "Kingdom of God," which Joseph Smith had established. Clayton subsequently became one of Smith's closest confidants.

Clayton's remarkable diaries record early Mormon dealings in land and politics, millennialist expectations, and the secret practice of plural marriage. Clayton documents the two major Mormon migrations that took place during the period of westward American expansion prior to the Civil War: from Britain to America and from Illinois to the Great Salt Lake Valley. A decade after he came to America, Clayton returned to England as a Mormon missionary to explain and defend the controversial doctrine of polygamy. Because of Clayton's unquestioning belief in Joseph Smith and in the Mormon faith, his journals present a reliable and literal account of these unusual events. Most of Clayton's journals have appeared in print before; here, for the first time, they are collected and abridged into a single volume that spans the years, 1840–53.

An Intimate Chronicle: The Journals of William Clayton is composed of six journals and three appendices. Journal 1, "England and Emigration," begins in 1840 in England and concludes in 1842 in Nauvoo, Illinois. Journal 2, "Nauvoo, Illinois," reflects life on the Illinois frontier from 1842 until the Saints departed for the Great Salt Lake in 1846. Journal 3, "Nauvoo Temple," was written in 1845–46, during the final weeks of the "Nauvoo, Illinois" journals. Journal 4, "Pioneer Trek West," begins at Nauvoo in 1846 and ends at the Great Salt Lake Valley in 1847. Journal 5, "Visit to Utah Settlements," records a three-week journey to southern Utah in spring 1852. Journal 6, "Polygamy Mission to England," starts in Salt Lake City in 1852 and concludes in England in 1853. The appendices comprise writings attributed to Clayton and his own retrospective narratives. Appendix A, "Extracts from William Clayton's [Private] Book—Keys," was copied by L. John Nuttall; Appendix B, "An Interesting Journal," is a narrative on the construction of the Nauvoo Temple published in 1886; and Appendix C, "William Clayton's Testimony," is Clayton's 1874 notarized statement on plural marriage. Together, these nine documents record events that were of manifest importance in the second decade of Mormon history.

The Founding of the Mormon Church

In 1830, Joseph Smith, a twenty-four-year-old farmer's son in western New York state, founded the Church of Christ with six family members and friends.[1] Its adherents soon became known

---

[1] Smith organized the Church of Christ on April 6, 1830, with his brothers Hyrum and Samuel; two Whitmer brothers, Peter and David; and Oliver Cowdery, a third cousin to the Smiths and future brother-in-law to the Whitmers. All six initial members were Book of Mormon witnesses. In 1834 in Kirtland, Ohio, the name was changed to "The Church of the Latter-day Saints," and in 1838 in Far West, Missouri, the present name was adopted, "The Church of Jesus Christ of

as "Mormons," after the title of the new scripture Smith had recently published, the Book of Mormon. Smith said that he translated the book from ancient records kept by Hebrew tribes which migrated from Jerusalem to the Western Hemisphere long before the time of Jesus. Presented as a New World companion to the Bible, the Book of Mormon identified Native Americans as a newly-discovered remnant of Old Testament families. Similar explanations of where the Indians came from had been popular since Columbus in an effort to integrate the Indians into a biblical world view and answer skeptics who dismissed Genesis as a parochial Old World myth.[2]

During the fervor of the "Second Great Awakening" when nineteenth-century religious sects contested their authority to speak for God, Smith's claim was unique. He declared that the Mormon church was the "only true church" restored from ancient times in "these latter days." His dramatic visions and his translations of mysterious hieroglyphics captured the imagination and allegiance of 20,000[3] followers drawn from the "burnt-over district"[4] of the American frontier as well as from foreign countries.

Latter-day Saints" (The Doctrine and Covenants of the Church of Jesus Christ of Latter-day Saints [Salt Lake City: Church of Jesus Christ of Latter-day Saints, 1981], 21 and 115; James B. Allen and Glen M. Leonard, *The Story of the Latter-day Saints* [Salt Lake City: Deseret Book, 1976], 47).

[2] See Dan Vogel, *Indian Origins and the Book of Mormon: Religious Solutions from Columbus to Joseph Smith* (Salt Lake City: Signature Books, 1986); Brigham D. Madsen, ed., *B. H. Roberts: Studies of the Book of Mormon* (Urbana: University of Illinois Press, 1985).

[3] The *Times and Seasons*, November 15, 1845, quotes a Nauvoo census report in the *St. Louis Evening Gazette*, showing 11,057 within Nauvoo city limits and about 4,000 in the surrounding countryside. M. Hamlin Cannon, "Migration of English Mormons to America," *American Historical Review* (1946-47) 52:441, cited in Robert B. Flanders, *Nauvoo: Kingdom on the Mississippi* (Urbana: University of Illinois Press, 1975), 58, shows 8,518 total English conversions through 1844, after subtracting emigrants to the New World. Allowing for 80 percent retention (32,894 English members remained in the church from 41,331 conversions net of emigration by 1851) an estimated 6,800 English members would bring the total Mormon population to about 21,860 at the time of Smith's death in 1844. Compare Philip A. M. Taylor, "Mormon Emigration from Great Britain to the United States 1840-70," Ph.D. diss., University of Cambridge, 1950, cited in Leonard J. Arrington, *Great Basin Kingdom: An Economic History of the Latter-day Saints, 1830-1900* (Cambridge: Harvard University Press, 1958), 447.

[4] The "burnt-over district" refers to an area of intense revivalist activity in central upstate New York, where eternal fires of hell were threatened as punishment for disobedience to the commandments of God. The First Great Awakening of the 1740s began a period of revivalist reaction against the secular influence of the

The Mormon English Mission and
Migration to America, 1840–42

In 1835 Joseph Smith organized a group of his most trusted
followers into a Quorum of Twelve Apostles. Like the apostles of
the New Testament, Smith's apostles served as missionaries to
spread the message that the true church had been restored. On
July 20, 1837, the six members of the first Mormon foreign mission landed in Liverpool amid both economic recession and national excitement; England's newly-crowned Queen Victoria was
preparing to name her cabinet. The mission went directly thirty
miles northwest to Lancashire, the scene of the textile mills which
were an early expression of the Industrial Revolution. The missionaries began preaching in the church of Reverend James Fielding in the large factory town of Preston.[5] Twenty-three-year-old
William Clayton, who lived across the river in the area of Penwortham parish, became an early convert to the new church. On
October 21, 1837, mission leader Heber C. Kimball baptized
Clayton in the River Ribble.[6]

---

scientific revolution. A renewed period of religious revivals called the Second Great
Awakening began in the 1790s and proceeded intermittently toward a "grand climax
between 1825 and 1837." See Whitney Cross, *The Burned-Over District: The Social and
Intellectual History of Enthusiastic Religion in Western New York, 1800–1850* (Ithaca, NY:
Cornell University Press, 1950), 3–13.

[5] One of the Mormon missionaries, Joseph Fielding, was a British emigrant
who had been invited by his brother, Reverend James Fielding, to return there to
preach. The Reverend cancelled his welcome to the Mormons: "With regard to your
robbing me of my flock . . . I do not believe at all that you were sent of God to
rend my little church to pieces. Were I to speak as 'plain' as you do I should boldly
declare that it was not God but Satan as an angel of light sent you here" (James
Fielding to Joseph Fielding, August 27, 1838, cited in James B. Allen and Thomas
G. Alexander, eds., *Manchester Mormons: The Journal of William Clayton: 1840 to 1842*
[Salt Lake City: Peregrine Smith, 1974], 6–7; see also Paul E. Dahl, *William
Clayton: Missionary, Pioneer, and Public Servant* [Cedar City, UT: Author, 1959], 4, 5).
The 1841 census tabulated the population of Preston as a little more than 50,000
persons. Information about populations and place names in Lancashire gathered
with the assistance of the Harris Library, Preston, Lancashire, England.

[6] Penwortham parish predated the Norman conquest. Originally administered
by the church, parishes later evolved into civil governments. The northern boundary
of the Penwortham parish was the River Ribble, which empties into the Irish Sea
off the northwest coast of England. The British mission, formed in Kirtland, Ohio,
on June 1, 1837, was led by Apostle Heber C. Kimball with counselors Orson
Hyde (also a member of the Twelve) and Willard Richards, a recent convert. With
Joseph Fielding, originally from England, were Canadian converts John Goodson,
Isaac Russell, and John Snyder (Joseph Smith, Jr., et al., *History of the Church of*

The eldest of the fourteen children of Thomas Clayton and Ann Critchley, William Clayton was born within the parish at Charnock Moss on July 17, 1814.[7] William was not among the impoverished child laborers of the early Industrial Revolution but was part of the skilled working class. He was tutored by his school-teacher father and learned to play the violin and piano.[8] He belonged to the Church of England and worked as a bookkeeper in Bashall's textile factory. At the time of his conversion to Mormonism he had been married to Ruth Moon Clayton for about one year and they had an infant daughter.[9] Much later in life, Clayton

---

Jesus Christ of Latter-day Saints, ed. B. H. Roberts, 2d ed. rev., 7 vols. [Salt Lake City: Deseret Book, 1963], 2:489, 490n, hereafter *HC*; Dahl, 7).

[7] Clayton referred to his birthplace, "Charnock Moss . . . the old house where I was born and raised" (Journal 6, "Polygamy Mission to England," January 7, 1853). Named for a sixteenth-century landowner, Charnock Moss was a hundred-acre farmland, drained and enclosed from an extensive peat lowland called the Penwortham Moss (Alan Crosby, *Penwortham in the Past* [Preston, England: Carnegie Press, 1988], 91–92). By Clayton's time Charnock Moss comprised about a square mile in area and a third of Penwortham township. Charnock Moss appears on the 1846 Ordnance Survey map, about a mile southeast of St. Mary's Church and near both the Cuerdon textile mill (see n9) and Farington railway station, which Clayton used when traveling home from Manchester.

[8] Wanda Clayton Thomas to George D. Smith, August 25, 1990; Orson F. Whitney, *History of Utah* (Salt Lake City: George Q. Cannon and Sons, 1904), 4:58. In 1825 Thomas Clayton resided in Farington township, Penwortham parish, and was listed as a schoolmaster (Edward Baines, *History and Directory and Gazetteer of the County Palatine of Lancashire*, Vol. 2 [Liverpool, 1825], 650). Prior to 1870 school attendance was voluntary, and he may have run a private school in his home. A typical curriculum of the day included "absay (ABC), catechism, primer, accidence, perveley" (*Preston District and Leyland Hundred Directory, 1851,* 137).

[9] In 1853, during his return to England, Clayton took a taxi from Preston to visit Bashall's factory, where he met with "some of the Old Reelers who were there when I left" (Journal 6, "Polygamy Mission to England," January 7, 1853). Before he left for America in 1840, Clayton had tried to sell a "bass vial" to William Bashall (Journal 1, "England and Emigration," September 3, 1840). Clayton may well have worked at the Cuerdon Mill at Bamber Bridge, just east of Penwortham parish. William Bashall operated Cotton Manufacturers and Cotton Spinners in Bamber Bridge as early as 1818 ("The Preston Directory," *Lancashire General Directory* [Manchester, 1818], 13; David Hunt, *The History of Leyland and District* [Preston: Carnegie Press, 1990], 91). The Cuerdon Mill appears at Bamber Bridge on the 1846 Ordnance Survey Map. Clayton's journal indicates familiarity with the Cuerdon factory, where he preached "to a full house" after he quit work to become a Mormon missionary (Journal 1, "England and Emigration," March 26, 1840). See also "Clayton Family Records," Utah Genealogical Society Library, Church of Jesus Christ of Latter-day Saints, Salt Lake City; "Clayton Family History," in the possession of June M. McDonnel, Van Nuys, California, cited in Dahl, 7, 13; and Rose Marie Hart Clayton, "History of Ruth Moon Clayton," January 13, 1976, Marriott Library, University of Utah, Salt Lake City.

reflected on the consequences of his conversion, saying that it seemed to have made him a "Mormon outlaw" among some of his English relatives; but his immediate family, including his wife, numerous members of her family (the Moons), his parents, and all of his ten surviving siblings became Mormons and emigrated, as he did, to America.[10]

American novelist and historian Wallace Stegner has called him "the clerkly Clayton," and Clayton's love of order and methodical habits suited him well for his career among the record-keeping Mormons. Long after his death, Clayton was remembered as "the soul of punctuality"; his daughter remembering his "love for order, which he believed the first law of heaven . . . he would not carry a watch that was not accurate." Though she recalled him as not tending to "frivolity or mirth but rather seriousness and earnestness," she also remembered him as "witty [with] a keen sense of humor."[11] But the Clayton of the journals was a serious man.

The young Clayton readily accepted responsibility in his new church. Although he had been a member of the LDS church for less than six months, on April 1, 1838, Clayton was named second counselor to assist Joseph Fielding, the newly-appointed president of the British Mission, and first counselor Willard Richards. A few months later, on October 19, he resigned from his job at the mill in order to labor full time as an unpaid missionary. He sent his wife and child to live with her parents in Penwortham while he went to work among the converts in Manchester; in his journal, he scrupulously records their support of him in food,

---

[10] Clayton commented in 1852 that when Dinah Ann and Joseph arrived in Salt Lake City, "I shall have the satisfaction of knowing that my brothers and sisters who are living are in the Vallies of the mountains, except Sister Ellen who is yet in St. Louis" (Journal 6, "Polygamy Mission to England," September 17, 1852). Nearly two decades later he wrote, "I would be much pleased to learn something of my relatives in England, if possible. It is many years since I had any positive news from any of them. Of course, my being a Mormon outlaws one in their estimation, but their not being Mormons does not have that effect on me" (William Clayton to John Gillibrand, July 24, 1869, Bancroft Library, Berkeley, California). See also Victoria Clayton McCune's introduction to the Clayton Family Association's publication of *William Clayton's Journal* (Salt Lake City: Deseret News, 1921), v, vi.

[11] Whitney, *History of Utah*, 4:58; McCune, *William Clayton's Journal*, vi, vii. Whitney also commented: "In his youth and early manhood, Mr. Clayton was of a jovial and lively turn, but as he advanced in years he became serious and even solemn in mien and deportment" (58).

lodging, money, and small gifts. Three months into his new role, Clayton wrote to Willard Richards, expressing his bookkeeper's sense of accountability: "I feel I am not my own. I am bought with a price, even the blood of Jesus Christ, and as a servant I must soon give up my account. I desire and strive, brethren, to keep my account right with the Lord every day that I may meet him with joy. Lea could get away from his master but I feel always in the presence of mine, and my desire is to live nearer still that I may be ready in the hour to give up my accounts."[12]

Clayton was a man of simple faith and was drawn to the mystical and occult. Wilford Woodruff,[13] describing their first meeting in Manchester, wrote, "I here first met with Elder Wm. Clayton. As soon as I had an introduction to him, he informed me that one of the sisters in that place was possessed of the devil, and he asked me to go and cast it out of her, thinking that one of the Twelve Apostles could do anything in this line he might wish to."[14]

Never swerving from his belief in the church and its leaders, Clayton viewed the world in terms of right and wrong; he saw the Mormon church as a means to line people up on the right side and provide order in the world. He wrote: "The Lord . . . has given us the laws and order of His Church and He requires of us as officers to see that those laws are enforced. We shall have peace and righteousness only in proportion as the laws are enforced."[15]

---

[12] Clayton to Willard Richards, January 28, 1840, cited in James B. Allen, *Trials of Discipleship: The Story of William Clayton, A Mormon* (Urbana: University of Illinois Press, 1987), 1. See Clayton's Journal 1, "England and Emigration," January 1, 1840, for the story of James Lea.

[13] Wilford Woodruff (1807-98) joined the Mormon church at age twenty-six in New York. He was a member of the pioneer company to the Great Salt Lake Valley in 1847, was appointed Church Historian in 1856, and became the fourth president of the church in 1889. In 1890, after the church was disincorporated and its property was confiscated by the federal government, Woodruff issued a proclamation to end plural marriage. He married eight women and fathered thirty-three children.

[14] Woodruff's first attempt with Clayton to cast out the "devil" was prevented by "the unbelief of the wicked present"; a second attempt after clearing the room succeeded, and when the woman's child became "possessed," Woodruff reports that the two missionaries "cast the devil out of it, and the evil spirits had no power over the household afterwards" ("British Mission History," cited in Dahl, 14-15; Scott G. Kenney, ed., *Wilford Woodruff's Journal* [Midvale, UT: Signature Books, 1983], 1:408).

[15] Clayton to Willard Richards, January 30, 1840, cited in Dahl, 15-16.

Wilford Woodruff, who was in Manchester in January 1840, described the city in his journal as having a population of about 320,000, a little larger than New York City, and beautiful but troubled: "About 3,000 souls is flung out of employ at the factories because of the pressure of times & the lowering of the wages & they are standing in every corner of the Streets in groups counciling what to do, & their are at the present time (I have been informed) thousands of Souls are almost in a State of uter starvation."[16] Victims of the Industrial Revolution found it easy to believe that the end of the world was imminent. Farmers and craftsmen had left their ancestral villages to find employment in large cities. Factory workers lived in crowded tenements with poor sanitation and rampant disease; unemployment and homelessness were prevalent.

Latter-day Saint missionaries to England brought the good news that Jesus would soon introduce a glorious new kingdom over which he would rule for a thousand years. Nineteenth-century ministers of several faiths preached the Millennium which would close out the history of the world (Rev. 20:1-5), but the Mormons offered a concrete plan of action. Regardless of class distinction, members were invited to "gather" to help build the Kingdom of God, first in Illinois and then in Utah.

In his journals Joseph Smith had recorded a vision telling him that "the great and dreadful day of the Lord is near, even at the doors."[17] Unlike other millennialists Smith avoided the pitfall of predicting an exact date for the end of the world. However, when he resided in Missouri the prophet designated a spot on the Grand River in the northwest part of the state as the location of the biblical Garden of Eden and the place where Jesus Christ would return.[18] In 1835 he said that "fifty-six years should wind

---

[16] Kenney, 1:407, 409. Conditions were "so bad that it is not too much to say that in the Manchester of the 1830's we see the Industrial Revolution at its ugliest" (Frances Collier, *The Family Economy of the Working Classes in the Cotton Industry 1784-1833*, ed. R. S. Fitton [Manchester: The Chetham Society, 1965], 53).

[17] Scott H. Faulring, ed., *An American Prophet's Record: The Diaries and Journals of Joseph Smith* (Salt Lake City: Signature Books in association with Smith Research Associates, 1987), 158.

[18] While walking along the Grand River in Daviess County, Missouri, on May 19, 1838, Smith identified a place which he called Adam-ondi-Ahman, where "Adam shall come to visit his people" at the end of the world: "I saw Adam in the valley of Adam-ondi-Ahman . . . the Son of Man will descend, the Ancient of Days

up the scene" and eight years later added "there are those of the rising generation who shall not taste death till Christ comes."[19] Mormon apostle Parley P. Pratt even wrote to England's Queen Victoria to tell her that the end of the world was at hand, that governments and churches would vanish, and that God was about to establish "a new and universal kingdom, under the immediate administration of the Messiah and his [Latter-day] Saints." Pratt reflected the general feeling in the Mormon British mission during the 1840s that the millennial kingdom would be on the earth by the end of the century.[20]

On January 1, 1840, about two years after joining the Mormon movement, Clayton began to record the events which his church taught would culminate with the end of the world. He does not explain why he started to keep a journal, but the person who baptized him, Heber C. Kimball, kept journals for himself and for Joseph Smith. In addition, since October 19, 1838, Clayton had been working in the British mission presidency with Joseph Fielding and Willard Richards, two other prominent Mormon diarists.

Joseph Smith strongly advocated that his followers keep journals. Smith saw himself as the retriever of the ancient records of the Nephites and the Lamanites, the Hebrew peoples of the Book of Mormon, and he insisted that his followers keep a record of their own religious history. When Smith organized his church in 1830 he proclaimed a revelation in which the Lord said: "Behold, there shall be a record kept among you" (D&C 21:1).[21]

[Adam] sit . . . judgment was given to the Saints of the Most High from the Ancient of Days; the time came that the Saints possessed the Kingdom" (*HC* 3:34-40, 386-91; D&C 107:53-57).

[19] The 1835 prediction was made as Smith chose apostles who would convert Clayton while serving as missionaries to England (*HC* 2:182; 5:336).

[20] Parley P. Pratt, *To Her Gracious Majesty, Queen Victoria* (Manchester, England, 1841), 5, cited in Klaus J. Hansen, *Quest For Empire: The Political Kingdom of God and the Council of Fifty in Mormon History* (Lincoln: University of Nebraska Press, 1974), 3-4; Robert L. Lively, Jr., "Some Sociological Reflections on the Nineteenth-Century British Mission," in *Mormons in Early Victorian Britain*, eds. Richard L. Jensen and Malcolm R. Thorp (Salt Lake City: University of Utah Press, 1989), 26.

[21] Later, Clayton would keep other people's records for remuneration. He explained to Brigham Young on September 8, 1846, that he was "willing to engage in any common kind of clerking business for one dollar per day. But if it is to be copying letters or other documents I would rather have a dollar and a quarter for

Clayton's first extant journal consists of two parts. The first was written while he lived in Manchester and describes his experiences there as a missionary: visits to the members and religious experiences such as prophetic dreams, healings, and miraculous speaking in "tongues." The second begins with his journey as one of the 38,000 Mormons who migrated from Britain to America between 1840 and 1870.[22] With meticulous detail that was the hallmark of his writing, Clayton takes his reader on a thirty-three-day ocean crossing to New York, a boat trip up the Hudson River and west on the Erie Canal, a lake steamer ride from Buffalo to Chicago, and finally a horse-drawn wagon and river boat to the Mississippi River town of Commerce, Illinois.

Joseph Smith had come to Illinois after years of adversity. In 1839 he escaped from jail in Liberty, Missouri, where he had been imprisoned by his enemies. Hiram Kimball, a land speculator and non-Mormon cousin of church leader Heber C. Kimball, suggested Commerce, Illinois, as a Mormon refuge. The prophet brought about 5,000 followers to Commerce, which he renamed Nauvoo, his Hebrew translation for "beautiful plantation."[23] Due mostly to the influx of British converts, the population doubled in ten years (1837-46). Before the Mormons were forced to leave in 1846, Nauvoo had become the largest city in Illinois.

---

this is very tedious business and the fairest way to work is by the price" (Clayton to Young, September 8, 1846, in Dahl, 76–77). Two days later he and Young settled on "writing at a dollar a day or 3 cents on Every 100 words copying" (Journal 4, "Pioneer Trek West," September 10, 1846). The following year Clayton calculated the value of the 124 pages he wrote in Heber C. Kimball's journal as "over $110" (ibid., August 10, 1847).

[22] Philip A. M. Taylor, "Why Did British Mormons Emigrate," *Utah Historical Quarterly* 22 (1954): 249–51. The Mormon emigration was a segment of a much larger exodus from Great Britain, totaling 17 million persons during the century preceding World War I (Wilbur S. Shepperson, "The Place of the Mormons in the Religious Emigration of Britain, 1840–1860," *Utah Historical Quarterly* 20 [1952]: 207). The emigration from Britain represented a major portion of Mormon European emigration to the United States: between 1840 and 1890, the year Mormon polygamy was officially banned, 80,000 European Mormons migrated to America (Samuel E. Morison, *The Oxford History of American People* [New York: Oxford University Press, 1965], 479–86, 768, 813).

[23] King James Bible and Hebrew scholars have translated the Hebrew word "nah-voo" in Isaiah 52:7 as "beautiful" (*Soncino Books of the Bible: Isaiah* [with Hebrew text and English translation], ed. A. Cohen [London: Soncino Press, 1967], 258). Hebrew scholar Kenneth Zwerin helped to identify and pronounce the Hebrew characters in Isaiah.

When Clayton arrived in Nauvoo on November 24, 1840, he found a small frontier town with an economy built on land speculation. Hancock County, in which Nauvoo was located, was part of the Illinois Military Bounty tract, a region between the Illinois and Mississippi rivers which Congress had set aside for War of 1812 veterans in lieu of pay. Speculators had purchased most of the original land warrants from the veterans and were dealing for turnaround profits until the recessions of 1837 and 1839 diminished available capital. When the Mormons began arriving in Commerce/Nauvoo, they found a sprawl of unfinished rail lines and canal ditches.

Soon after the Mormons were welcomed to Illinois in 1839, the LDS church became one of the major land dealers in the state.[24] On October 20, 1839, the Nauvoo High Council of the LDS church made Joseph Smith treasurer of the church and empowered him to set prices and to sell lots. The thirty-three-year-old prophet bought a great deal of land in the name of the church. Newly-arrived Saints such as Clayton were then urged to buy their lots and farms from the church. Later, when Clayton assisted Smith with his land business, he wrote in the *Nauvoo Neighbor*: "To Emigrants and Latter-day Saints generally: . . . Let all the brethren . . . when they move to Nauvoo, consult President Joseph Smith, trustee in trust, and purchase their lands of him; and I am bold to say that God will bless them . . . We hold ourselves ready at any time to wait upon the brethren and show them the lands . . . and can be found any day, either at President Joseph

---

[24] In addition to his purchase of 500 acres of the Military Bounty tract in Illinois from Horace Hotchkiss, and several hundred more acres south of Nauvoo, Joseph Smith contracted with Isaac Galland for 20,000 acres from the "Half Breed" tract on the Iowa side of the Mississippi, which Congress had reserved for the offspring of Indian women and their soldier or trapper husbands. The ownership of these lands was in dispute, as Clayton himself experienced. No deeds were transferred in the Galland purchase, and deeds were obtained for only 90 of the 500-acre Hotchkiss purchase. No down payments were made either. Such land deals usually lacked surveys and adequate records; without clear titles, buyers often secured their land by paying the property taxes. For a time Illinois gave title to owners who paid the property taxes for seven years. Land was often sold at public auction for unpaid property taxes. When Smith stopped paying taxes on the Hotchkiss land, disputes with tax collectors ensued (Clayton's journals, May 3, August 1, 1843). In 1842 Smith filed for bankruptcy under the new federal bankruptcy law and put his personal assets into church name. See Flanders, 28-42, 115-43, 174; Journal 1, "England and Emigration," March 19, 20, 1841.

Smith's bar-room, or the Temple Recorder's office at the Temple."[25] Eastern members were urged to transfer their existing property to a seller of Nauvoo land and to accept Nauvoo lots in exchange.[26] Joseph and his brothers, Hyrum and William, dominated the land business, which flourished in Nauvoo more than either manufacturing or marketing activities.

Clayton wrote in his "England and Emigration" journal for over a year after his migration, until February 18, 1842. One week earlier Heber C. Kimball had asked him to assist Willard Richards in managing the Temple Recorder's Office, accounting for contributions and expenditures toward construction of the Nauvoo Temple. For the next nine months, as Clayton's managerial responsibilities continued to increase, he did not keep a personal journal. On September 3, 1842, Joseph Smith appointed Clayton to succeed Richards as Temple Recorder and to be Smith's secretary. Smith declared: "When I have any revelations to write you shall write them."[27]

The intimacy of Clayton's portrait of Joseph Smith stems from his involvement in all of Smith's activities at Nauvoo. Clayton's biographer, James B. Allen, wrote, "As a diarist and historian, he described what he saw around him. Beginning early in 1842,

---

[25] *Nauvoo Neighbor*, December 20, 1843, quoted in Flanders, 124.

[26] William A. Linn, *The Story of the Mormons* (New York: MacMillan, 1902), 220. Joseph Smith at this time was supporting himself primarily from land profits. Arriving at Illinois without money, he developed business enterprises with the capital value of lands he deeded himself using whatever credit he was able to obtain therefrom. But his trade in real estate was his main business (Flanders, 122, 160). The prophet associated his land dealings with his religious calling and suggested that people should buy land from him since he was sent by God. In his *History of the Church*, Smith remarked: "Suppose I sell you land for ten dollars an acre, and I gave three, four or five dollars per acre, then some persons may cry out, 'you are speculating.' Yes. I will tell how: I buy other lands and give them to the widow and the fatherless. If the speculators run against me, they run against the buckler of Jehovah. I speak to you as one having authority . . . that you may have faith and know that God has sent me . . . Those who have money, come to me, and I will let you have lands; and those who have no money, if they will look as well as I do, I will give them advice that will do them good, I bless you in the name of Jesus Christ, Amen" (*HC* 5:356; Flanders, 121; Allen, 85). Joseph also said: "Those who come here having money and purchased without the Church and without council must be cut of[f]" (Faulring, 304).

[27] "Journal History of the Church of Jesus Christ of Latter-day Saints," October 23, 1842, microfilm, Marriott Library; and Appendix B, "An Interesting Journal." In Appendix C, "William Clayton's Testimony," Clayton cites October 7, 1842, as the date on which these events occurred.

William Clayton found himself involved in nearly every important activity of Nauvoo, but especially the private concerns of the
prophet. For two and a half years," Allen continued, "until Joseph
[Smith's] death in 1844, they were in each other's company almost daily."

Allen explains that Clayton was not only Smith's trusted employee and associate but also his personal friend and confidant.
He wrote letters for the prophet, recorded his revelations, ran his
errands, and helped prepare the official history of the church.
Clayton received tithes collected for building the temple, kept its
construction records, and met frequently with the temple committee.[28] He was appointed city treasurer, city recorder, clerk of
the Nauvoo City Council, and secretary of the Nauvoo Masonic
Lodge. He was a member of the secret ruling body, the Council
of Fifty, which was designated to govern when Jesus returned to
establish the "Kingdom of God," and he was a member of Joseph
Smith's private prayer circle, where Smith introduced the temple
ceremonies of washings, anointings, key words, signs, tokens, and
penalties. "In this unique combination of the secular and the
religious," Allen summarized, "his life probably represents as well
as that of anyone, other than Joseph [Smith], the totality of the
Nauvoo experience."[29]

Polygamy and Secret Ceremonies
in Nauvoo, 1842-46

Clayton's "Nauvoo, Illinois" journal, which he began on November 27, 1842, reflects Mormon doctrines and religious practices, administrative and financial affairs, and political and legal
relationships. Since Clayton attended virtually all meetings, from
general church conferences to Joseph Smith's private prayer circle, and was often appointed to take minutes, he was usually present
when Smith delivered prophecies and revealed new doctrines.

---

[28] Clayton recorded contributions toward the construction of the Nauvoo
Temple in the "Book of the Law of the Lord" and kept a journal of temple
committee meetings. Neither of these documents is included in the present
compilation. See Appendix B, "An Interesting Journal," n1.

[29] Allen, 71, 81.

Many of Clayton's journal entries, changed to first person as if Joseph Smith had written them, have been published in the *History of the Church*.[30] When George A. Smith and other church historians compiled the *History of the Church*, they incorporated the writings of Willard Richards, Wilford Woodruff, and other diarists, including William Clayton. For example, on January 22, 1843, an entry of the official history begins with Clayton and concludes with Woodruff. The March 7, 1843, entry is another example. Clayton wrote in his journal: "Evening I went to Brother Kimballs Meeting. The house was crowded to suffocation." The official history is an edited version of Clayton's entry: "In the evening, a meeting was held in the house of Elder Heber C. Kimball, which was crowded." The official history omits some of Clayton's entries, such as those of March 7 and 9, 1843, which discussed plural marriage. Entries which recorded the words of Joseph Smith were often incorporated verbatim into the history, such as the message Smith related on April 2, 1843: "Joseph my son, if thou livest until thou art 85 years old thou shalt see the face of the son of man," which was also canonized as Mormon scripture (D&C 130).[31] Clayton's journals even contain Smith's "translation" of ancient characters from metal plates dug up near Kinderhook, Illinois, and discovered later to have been forged by Smith's detractors.[32]

---

[30] The official history of the church incorporates Joseph Smith's journals as well as those of his scribes. These edited journals were published serially in the Nauvoo *Times and Seasons* in 1842–46 and in the Salt Lake City *Deseret News* in 1851–58. This material was edited again by B. H. Roberts and published as the official seven-volume *History of the Church* in 1902–12. See Dean C. Jessee, "The Writing of Joseph Smith's History," *Brigham Young University Studies* 11 (Summer 1971): 439–73; "The Reliability of Joseph Smith's History," *Journal of Mormon History* 3 (1976): 23–47; ed., *The Personal Writings of Joseph Smith* (Salt Lake City: Deseret Book, 1984), xiii–xix, xxiii–iv; Howard C. Searle, "Early Mormon Historiography: Writing the History of the Mormons, 1830–58," Ph.D. diss., University of California, Los Angeles, 1979. Compare Journal 3, "Nauvoo Temple," December 29, 1845.

[31] Here Smith's own journals go further than Clayton's. On April 6, 1843, he recorded: "I prophecy in the name of the Lord God, and let it be written, that the Son of Man will not come in the heavens till I am 85 years old, 48 years hence or about 1890" (Faulring, 349).

[32] In his "Nauvoo, Illinois" journal, May 1, 1843, Clayton writes that he has seen "6 brass plates which were found in Adams County," Illinois, and that "President Joseph has translated a portion and says they contain the history of the person with whom they were found and he was a descendant of Ham through the

Clayton's Nauvoo journals are unique in preserving a detailed account of the practice of plural marriage, even before the doctrine was officially revealed in 1843. Although he eventually married more than forty women, Joseph Smith never publicly acknowledged that he had practiced polygamy. In response to a grand jury indictment for polygamy, Smith announced from the pulpit in 1844, "What a thing it is for a man to be accused of committing adultery, and having seven wives, when I can find only one."[33] Even while the prophet issued denials Clayton recorded his secret marriages.

Rumors about the practice of plural marriage in the Mormon church first circulated in Kirtland, Ohio. In 1835 Joseph and his wife Emma employed a girl who helped Emma with her housework. This girl, Fanny Alger, was later described as Smith's first plural wife.[34] Joseph Smith's secret marriage to Louisa Beaman in Nauvoo on April 5, 1841, was his first officially-recorded polygamous marriage. By the time Smith dictated his revelation on

---

loins of Pharaoh king of Egypt, and that he received his kingdom from the ruler of heaven and earth." See also *HC* 5:372–76. As late as 1962, upon rediscovery of one of the "Kinderhook Plates" at the Chicago Historical Society, the church cited Joseph Smith's translation of the plates as "reaffirm[ing] his prophetic calling" (*Improvement Era*, September 1962, 660). However, tests subsequently performed by a materials engineer showed that the plates had been forged. Mormon scholar Stanley B. Kimball concluded that "the time has come to admit that the Kinderhook plate incident of 1843 was a light-hearted, heavy-handed, frontier-style prank or 'joke' as the perpetrators themselves called it" (*Mormon History Association Newsletter*, June 1981). The tests were published in Kimball, "Kinderhook Plates Brought to Joseph Smith Appear To Be A Nineteenth Century Hoax," *Ensign* 11 (August 1981): 66–74.

[33] *HC* 6:405, 411. Polygamy was a criminal act under Illinois 1833 Antibigamy Laws (*Revised Laws of Illinois 1833* and *Revised Statutes of the State of Illinois 1845*, secs. 121, 122, University of Chicago Law Library).

[34] *Salt Lake Tribune*, October 6, 1875. Smith's scribe, Warren Parrish, said that "he himself and Oliver Cowdery did know that Joseph had Fannie Alger as wife, for they were spied upon together" (recounted by church patriarch Benjamin F. Johnson in a letter to George F. Gibbs, 1903, 10, archives, Church of Jesus Christ of Latter-day Saints; hereafter LDS archives). After an 1838 letter in which Book of Mormon scribe, Oliver Cowdery, characterized Joseph's relations with Fanny Alger as a "dirty, nasty, filthy affair," Cowdery was excommunicated on charges that included "seeking to destroy the character of President Joseph Smith jr by falsly insinuating that he was guilty of adultry &c." (Donald Q. Cannon and Lyndon W. Cook, eds., *Far West Record: Minutes of The Church of Jesus Christ of Latter-day Saints, 1830-1844* [Salt Lake City: Deseret Book, Co., 1983], 162–63 [April 12, 1844]; *HC* 3:16). Alger was later married by proxy to Smith, and assistant church historian Andrew Jenson listed her as "one of the first plural wives sealed to the Prophet" ("Plural Marriage," *Historical Record*, 6 [May 1887]: 233).

celestial or plural marriage to William Clayton on July 12, 1843, the prophet had taken at least twelve plural wives. Those marriages were kept secret from all but a few trusted members.[35] Although Smith continued to deny that he had more than one wife, his revelation read: "If any man espouse a virgin, and desire to espouse another," the prophet announced, "he cannot commit adultery for they are given unto him . . . if he have ten virgins given unto him by this law he cannot commit adultery, for they belong to him." The revelation adds that if a wife is taught by her husband "the law of my priesthood . . . then shall she believe and administer unto him, or she shall be destroyed" (D&C 132:61–62, 64).

For some of Smith's followers, plural marriage "was a very heavy thing for us to meet, for we generally professed to be and were pure men."[36] Clayton's journal captures the reaction of the prophet's first wife to the new doctrine. On the day of the revela-

---

[35] Jenson, *Historical Record* 6:233–34. Aware that Joseph Smith took plural wives before 1843, church leaders have concluded that he received earlier instructions to practice polygamy. In an August 12, 1861, letter to Brigham Young, William W. Phelps recalled a July 17, 1831, revelation of Joseph Smith's directing seven married elders to take Indian women as wives "that their posterity may become white, delightsome and just," thus fulfilling a Book of Mormon prophecy ("the scales of darkness shall begin to fall from their eyes; and many generations shall not pass away among them, save they shall be a white [pure] and delightsome people" [2 Ne. 30:6]). Although this revelation was not published, church president Joseph F. Smith also concluded that the principle of plural marriage must have been revealed to Joseph Smith in 1831 (*Deseret News*, May 20, 1886). Nevertheless, Joseph Smith's journal on July 12, 1843 contains a contemporary account: "Received a Revelation in the office in presence of Hyrum and W[illia]m Clayton" (Faulring, 396). On that date, the *History of the Church* reports the same in the first person: "I received the following revelation in the presence of my brother Hyrum and Elder William Clayton," and continues with a text entitled, "Revelation on the Eternity of the Marriage Covenant, including the Plurality of Wives; Given through Joseph, the Seer, in Nauvoo, Hancock County, Illinois, July 12th, 1843" (*HC* 5:500–501). Clayton reaffirmed the 1843 date of the revelation: "I testify again that the revelation on polygamy was given through the prophet Joseph on the 12th of July 1843" (Clayton to Madison M. Scott, November 11, 1871, LDS archives). See also Van Wagoner, *Mormon Polygamy*, 3–4. LDS president John Taylor later recalled hearing of plural marriage for the first time when Smith presented his 1843 revelation: "Joseph Smith was the first I ever heard mention that principle. Presidents Young and Heber C. Kimball were present at the time.. ... He gave us the full details of that doctrine, showing us the revelation" (*Deseret Evening News*, December 9, 1879).

[36] LDS president John Taylor in the *Deseret Evening News*, December 9, 1879.

tion, Clayton wrote as follows: "After it was wrote Prests. Joseph
& Hyrum presented it and read it to E[mma] who said she did
not believe a word of it and appeared very rebellious." Shortly
before the revelation, Clayton had recorded a domestic dispute
between Joseph and Emma, which threatened to draw him into a
triangle, the prophet warning Clayton that Emma wanted to "lay
a snare" for him and "indulge" herself with him. Clayton worried
that he might be cut off from celestial glory if he accepted any
advances from Emma.[37] In the month following the revelation,
Smith told Clayton that he was afraid Emma might divorce
him.[38] On August 21, 1843, Clayton was again drawn into the
Smiths' domestic problems when Emma questioned him about
two letters from Eliza Roxcy Snow, Joseph's plural wife for over a
year.[39] Clayton assured Emma that he had not delivered the letters that she had found in her husband's pocket.

Clayton had learned of plural marriage at least by March 7,
1843, when Joseph Smith told Brigham Young to give Clayton a
"favor" regarding priesthood instruction. The word "favor" in
Clayton's journal refers to the granting of an additional wife.
Clayton and his first wife, Ruth Moon, were in their seventh year
of marriage and had three children. The prophet personally visited the family in their Nauvoo home and suggested that Clayton
participate in plural marriage. On March 9 Smith offered Clayton
the money to send for Sarah Crooks, a woman Clayton had be-
friended when he was a missionary in England.[40]

---

[37] Journal 2, "Nauvoo, Illinois," June 23, 1843. Emma Smith's reaction to her
husband's revelation on plural marriage is also described in Appendix C, "William
Clayton's Testimony."

[38] Journal 2, "Nauvoo, Illinois," August 16, 1843. Emma Smith's biographers
comment that "by late summer 1843 most of Emma's friends had either married
Joseph or had given their daughters to him." They note, however, that he
"apparently did not take additional wives after November 1843" (Linda K. Newell
and Valeen T. Avery, *Mormon Enigma: Emma Hale Smith* [Garden City, NY:
Doubleday, 1984], 147, 179).

[39] Eliza R. Snow was married to Joseph Smith on June 29, 1842. See *Historical
Record*, 222.

[40] See Clayton's 1874 statement on plural marriage, included as Appendix C.
Clayton had become close to Sarah Crooks who had "bath[ed] my forehead with
rum," and about whom he once acknowledged, "I certainly feel my love towards her
to increase" (Journal 1, "England and Emigration," February 27, March 3, 1840).
At the time of this conversation Clayton had already sent a letter to England which
prompted Crooks to depart immediately for America. See Journal 2, "Nauvoo,
Illinois," May 31, 1843, the date she arrived in Nauvoo.

However, it was not Sarah Crooks but Margaret Moon, his legal wife's sister, who became Clayton's first plural wife. The marriage was recorded on April 27, 1843, three months before Smith dictated his plural marriage revelation. In support of Clayton's second marriage, Smith assured him: "You have a right to get all you can."[41] Shortly afterward the prophet refused Clayton permission to marry Lydia, the third Moon sister, citing a revelation "he had lately, [that] a man could only take 2 of a family." Smith then asked if Clayton would "give L[ydia] to him." Lydia Moon refused Smith's offer because she had promised not to marry while her mother lived.[42]

Surprisingly, Emma joined with Joseph to manage the crisis when in October 1843, six months after Clayton's plural marriage to Margaret Moon, Margaret became pregnant. On the road to the western Illinois town of Macedonia, after consulting Emma, Joseph offered their collective advice to resolve Clayton's predicament: "Just keep her at home and brook it and if they raise trouble about it and bring you before me I will give you an awful scourging and probably cut you off from the church and then I will baptise you and set you ahead as good as ever."[43]

Orson Whitney, an early historian of Utah, characterized William Clayton as "silent and secretive";[44] Clayton's biographer found him interesting because of the "secrets he shared with the prophet": In Nauvoo "Clayton semisecretly courted, married, and lived with four young women" besides his first wife.[45] Though a Victorian Englishman, he embraced plural marriage without hesitation. After polygamy was made public, Clayton wrote: "I have six wives,

---

[41] Journal 2, "Nauvoo, Illinois," August 11, 1843. In Appendix C, "William Clayton's Testimony," Clayton quotes Joseph Smith as saying, "It is your privilege to have all the wives you want." Smith also once reportedly explained: "The result of our endless union will be offspring as numerous as the stars of heaven or the sands of the seashore" (*HC* 5: 391–92). Compare Journal 2, "Nauvoo, Illinois," May 16, 1843.

[42] Journal 2, "Nauvoo, Illinois," September 15 and 17, 1843. At Clayton's memorial services Apostle Joseph F. Smith reflected that of those "who had an intimate acquaintance" with the prophet Joseph Smith, "few, if any of them, were so closely identified with him in this matter [plural marriage] as Brother Clayton" (*Deseret Evening News*, December 9, 1879).

[43] Journal 2, "Nauvoo, Illinois," October 19, 1843.

[44] Whitney, 58.

[45] Allen, 143, 188.

whom I support in comfort and happiness and am not afraid of another one. I have three children born to me during the year, and I don't fear a dozen more."[46] He eventually married ten women and fathered forty-seven children.[47]

Clayton lived during the height of Mormon plural marriage, a time in which as many as two-thirds of some local populations resided in polygamous households.[48] The journals reveal how Clayton allocated his attentions among his plural wives and also courted other women. After dreaming that he "had received Miss [Emily] Cutler in addition to those I had already got," Clayton awoke and pleaded "God if it be thy will give me that woman for a companion."[49] Six weeks later, when Brigham Young consented to Clayton's fifth marriage with Diantha Farr (just sixteen years old), Clayton again turned to God and asked, "give me favor in her eyes and the eyes of her parents that I may receive the gift in full."[50] His prayers were answered. In early 1846 he wrote about bringing three wives to the Nauvoo Temple to be sealed (united with him forever) in a ceremony of eternal marriage. He "then took Ruth and Diantha home, but Margaret tarried till morning."[51] Another time he cryptically noted that "Diantha was at my house when I got home and tarried with us all night."

---

[46] Clayton Letterbooks, November 7, 1869.

[47] Dahl, 214-20; Allen, 218n33. In 1941 one of Clayton's great-granddaughters, Wanda Clayton Thomas, asked his last-surviving wife, Anna Elizabeth Higgs, "how a girl only 17 years old could marry a man in his early 50's who already had so many wives and children." Higgs replied that she "fell in love with him before he ever knew her" and "just had to follow him from church to church to hear him speak. I wanted to be with him in the hearafter. I courted him" (Thomas to Smith). Anna's attraction was shared by Clayton's fifth wife, Diantha Farr. Pregnant in Nauvoo, Diantha wrote to her husband in Keosauqua, Iowa: "I dream about you almost every night . . . I never shall consent to have you leave me again" (Diantha Farr Clayton to William Clayton, March 10, 1846, in Dahl, 68B).

[48] Study of an 1880 census — a peak year of Mormon plural marriage that marked the end of the Brigham Young era and preceded a decade of federal raids on polygamous households — showed that 33 percent of the Mormon population in the St. George, Utah, stake lived in plural families. The highest incidence of polygamy was 67 percent in the town of Orderville, Utah (Lowell "Ben" Bennion, "The Incidence of Mormon Polygamy in 1880: 'Dixie' Versus Davis Stake," *Journal of Mormon History* 11 [1984], 27-42).

[49] Journal 2, "Nauvoo, Illinois," October 19, 1844.

[50] Ibid., December 5, 1844.

[51] Ibid., January 26, 1846.

Then, "this A.M. I had some talk with Diantha in bed. All things seemed to go right."[52]

Though according to his daughter he was "not demonstrative," Clayton nevertheless had "great love for his home and family and provided well for their comfort."[53] He took his domestic life quite seriously: he left England earlier than expected at the behest of his mother-in-law; he battled Aaron Farr for Margaret Moon; he maintained concurrent conjugal relations with his wives, as their childbirth records demonstrate — five of his children were born in 1857; he comforted himself when he was lonely by reflecting on his family; when Maria Louisa Lyman divorced him, Clayton declared she would not find a better home than the one she had left.[54] His journals contain no trace of irony about his complex marital life. Having lived under the guidance of three polygamous leaders (Joseph Smith, Brigham Young, and John Taylor), he did not live to see the fourth (Wilford Woodruff) reverse the practice under the pressure of court decisions and congressional acts.

While depicting the drama of plural marriage, the Nauvoo journals also describe how the religious government of Nauvoo operated in other areas. One of Clayton's administrative duties was to oversee the building of the temple. In January 1841 Joseph Smith presented a revelation to his followers requiring them to build a place dedicated to the baptism of the dead and to other sacred ordinances. Clayton chronicled the financing, construction, and use of the Nauvoo Temple.

As Smith's personal assistant, Clayton witnessed the rising tensions between Mormons and the non-Mormon community in Hancock County, Illinois. Nauvoo had been organized as an independent political entity, separate from state influence. Nauvoo functioned as a quasi-sovereign city-state without separation of

---

[52] Ibid., January 13, 1845.

[53] McCune, vii.

[54] Clayton to Francis M. Lyman, July 24, 1871. Ever faithful to the doctrine of plural marriage, Clayton throughout his later years continued to call "Celestial Marriage or plurality of wives, the Most important principle ever revealed from the Heavens to man" (July 19, 1874, to F[rancis] M. Lyman) and the doctrine which Joseph Smith "died to establish" (July 25, 1869, to Karl Maeser), Clayton letter collection, Bancroft Library and University of Utah.

powers; it was a theocracy in which the civil government was a proxy for the church hierarchy. The office of mayor was adjunct to Smith's position as president and prophet. An unusual feature of the Nauvoo charter allowed the municipal government to free those arrested by state or federal officers by issuing a writ of habeas corpus. Thus state or federal law could be enforced in Nauvoo only if the city government concurred.[55]

When, in the winter of 1843–44, the Nauvoo City Council ruled that no writ issued from any other place than Nauvoo should be honored for the arrest of anyone, Illinois governor Ford characterized the public reaction as one of "general astonishment." He observed that "many people began to believe in good earnest that the Mormons were about to set up a separate government for themselves in defiance of the laws of the State." About that time, according to Ford, "the Mormons openly denounced the government of the United States as utterly corrupt, and as being about to pass away and to be replaced by the government of God, to be administered by his servant Joseph."[56]

---

[55] Flanders, 92–93, 97–101. Governor Thomas Ford observed that the Nauvoo charter "seemed to give [Mormons] power to pass ordinances in violation of the laws of the state." The charter established a local militia, the Nauvoo Legion, which was "entirely independent of the military organization of the state." He noted that the effect was for the Mormons to set up "a government within a government, a legislature with power to pass ordinances at war with the laws of the state; courts to execute them with but little dependence upon the constitutional judiciary; and a military force at their own command." Such a charter seemed to Ford to be "capable of great abuse [such that] the great law of separation of powers of government was wholly disregarded" (Thomas Ford, *History of Illinois from Its Commencement as a State in 1818 to 1847* [Chicago: S. C. Griggs, 1854], 2:64–67). The previous governor of Illinois, Thomas Carlin, wrote to Emma Smith on September 7, 1842, expressing surprise at the assumption of power in the Nauvoo charter, that to release persons in custody of the state courts was "most absurd and ridiculous . . . a gross usurpation of power that cannot be tolerated . . . a burlesque upon the city charter itself" (*HC* 5:153–55). See also Edwin B. Firmage and Richard C. Mangrum, *Zion in the Courts: A Legal History of the Church of Jesus Christ of Latter-day Saints, 1830–1900* (Urbana: University of Illinois Press, 1988), 110; James L. Kimball, Jr., "A Wall to Defend Zion: The Nauvoo Charter," *Brigham Young University Studies* 15 (Summer 1975) 4:491–97.

[56] See Ford, 2:155–56, 159. After petitioning for U.S. protection from further attempts to extradite him to Missouri, Joseph Smith recorded in his journal on December 16, 1843, his prophecy before the Nauvoo City Council: "I prophecy by virtue of the Holy Priesthood vested in me in the name of Jesus Christ that if Congress will not hear our petition and grant us protection they shall be broken up as a government and God shall damn them. There shall nothing be left of them,

Clayton documented Smith's claim that the power of the Nauvoo Municipal Court was not limited by the state of Illinois.[57] After employing the habeas corpus mechanism to escape arrest on a treason charge, Smith said to his followers: "Relative to our city charter, courts, right of habeas corpus, etc., I wish you to know and publish that we have all power; and if any man from this time forth says anything to the contrary, cast it into his teeth."[58]

Joseph Smith anticipated that the Saints would have to leave Illinois. Leaving the country itself was not a new idea to the Latter-day Saints. In 1839 Henry Clay had advised the Mormons that the best way for them to solve their problems was to move to Oregon, a vast territory north of Mexico, claimed by both the United States and Britain. In the early 1840s Joseph Smith had designated exploration companies to "select a location for the settlement of the Saints" in the West.[59] The most sweeping recommendation for migration had come from Lyman Wight and George Miller. They proposed Mormon kingdoms in "the south and western part of North America, together with the Floridas, Texas, West Indian Islands, and the adjacent islands of the Gulf of Mexico, together with the Lamanites [Indians] bordering on the United territories from Green Bay to the Mexican Gulf." It was on March 11, 1844, the day after receiving these proposals, that Joseph Smith set up his secret leadership organization, the "Council of Fifty," which included Wight and Miller.[60]

The Council, "conceived as the nucleus of a world government for the Millennium,"[61] planned to "direct the expected vast influx of converts and to establish Mormon colonies in the West

---

not even a grease spot" (Faulring, 432; see also *Latter-day Saints' Millennial Star*, 22:455 and *HC* 6:107). Compare Journal 2, "Nauvoo, Illinois," May 18, 1843.

[57] Journal 2, "Nauvoo, Illinois," June 30, 1843.

[58] *HC* 5:466 (June 30, 1843). Smith went on to challenge, "I wish the lawyer who says we have no powers in Nauvoo may be choked to death on his own words. Don't employ lawyers or pay money for their knowledge, as I have learned that they don't know anything. I know more than they all." In his own diaries Joseph Smith announced, "I'm a big lawyer and comprehend heaven, earth, and hell" (*HC*, 5:467 [June 30, 1843]; Faulring, 313 [February 25, 1843]).

[59] *HC* 5:393; *Latter-day Saints' Millennial Star* 26:327.

[60] *HC* 6:255-61.

[61] Andrew F. Ehat, " 'It Seems Like Heaven Began on Earth,' " *Brigham Young University Studies* 20 (Spring 1980): 274.

and Southwest, and in Central and South America." Joseph Smith
described the function of the Council of Fifty as "to take into consideration the subject matter . . . in the [Miller/Wight] letter, and
also the best policy for this people to adopt to obtain their rights
from the nation and insure protection for themselves and children: and to secure a resting place in the mountains, or some
uninhabited region."[62]

The Council of Fifty was also designed to govern the political
"Kingdom of God" on earth at the end of the world. A shadow
government for the city of Nauvoo, the Council of Fifty planned
strategy and finances, provided bodyguards for church leaders,
dealt with enemies, secured obedience to church directives, and
planned for the growth of the kingdom. Its members were "princes
in the Kingdom of God."[63] Clayton writes that on April 11, 1844,
Joseph Smith was ordained "King in the Kingdom of God"; Clayton
was appointed "Clerk of the Kingdom." The council planned Joseph
Smith's campaign for the United States presidency in 1844.[64] It
took responsibility for the political and economic development of
Nauvoo and later of Salt Lake City until it was replaced by the
"State of Deseret" which was formed in 1849.[65]

By 1844 Smith knew that his sovereign theocracy was becoming increasingly incompatible with the state of Illinois. Rumors of
polygamy were circulating and inciting public outrage. Antipathy
toward Mormon plural marriage would eventually be expressed
in the 1856 Republican platform in a plank to eradicate the "twin

---

[62] Juanita Brooks, *John Doyle Lee: Zealot, Pioneer Builder, Scapegoat* (Glendale, CA: Arthur H. Clark, 1972), 81; Arrington, 31–32.

[63] Flanders, 292–96. The Council of Fifty continued to exert power until the 1880s (Hansen, *Quest for Empire*, 92–96, 123–46, 173–76, 180–82). Some Mormon scholars argue that the Council of Twelve Apostles in fact has always exercised the powers attributed to the Council of Fifty (D. Michael Quinn, "The Council of Fifty and Its Members, 1844 to 1945," *Brigham Young University Studies* 20 [Winter 1980]: 163–97).

[64] In order to obtain federal support for the Mormons in conflicts with hostile state governments, Joseph Smith wrote to five presidential candidates in 1843. John C. Calhoun responded that within the limited specific powers of the federal government the Mormon grievances against Missouri were beyond its jurisdiction; Henry Clay sympathized with the Mormons but could "make no promises." Receiving no satisfactory replies, Joseph Smith decided to run for president himself in the next year's election. See *HC* 6:63–65 (November 4, 1843), 155–60 (January 2, 1844), 376–77 (May 13, 1844).

[65] Arrington, 31–32.

relics of barbarism," slavery and polygamy. But in 1844 Joseph Smith's most serious problems came from insiders. In that year Clayton's journals tell us about conflict within the Mormon community that contributed to events which led to Joseph Smith's murder and the expulsion of his followers from Illinois.

In the spring of 1844 Clayton recorded that several prominent persons — local businessmen, military officers, and members of the Nauvoo High Council — withdrew from the Mormon church. In an opposition newspaper called *The Nauvoo Expositor*, these reformers charged Smith with secretly teaching, yet openly denying, the practice of plural marriage, and with suppressing civil rights.[66] After the first and only issue of the *Expositor* was published on June 7, 1844, Smith convinced the city council to order the press destroyed. Clayton describes the nighttime gathering of Nauvoo police at the temple before they set off to demolish the *Expositor* press. The editors fled and swore out a complaint asking for Smith's arrest.[67]

On June 12 Clayton reported that when a constable came from Carthage, Illinois, with a writ to arrest the prophet and his associates for destroying the press, the Nauvoo Municipal Court intervened with a writ of habeas corpus. Following threats of state military action by Governor Ford, Smith submitted to the custody of an Illinois posse and was escorted to jail in the hostile community of Carthage, Illinois. At Smith's request, on June 23 Clayton buried the "Records of the Kingdom," the minutes he had kept for the Council of Fifty.

---

[66] June 7, 1844. In the preamble of the *Expositor*, the reformers declared that having "sought a reformation in the church, without a public exposition of the enormities of crimes practiced by its leaders," their "petitions [were] treated with contempt." Consequently, while affirming the truth of "the religion of the Latter Day Saints, as originally taught by Joseph Smith," they made public fifteen resolutions objecting to plural marriage, abuse of "political power and influence," and the introduction of "false doctrines" such as "the doctrine of many Gods." They also attached affidavits of their knowledge of the teaching and specific practice of plural marriage, which gave rise to "whoredoms" and were "not consonant with the principles of Jesus Christ." See also Journal 1, "England and Emigration," n84, and Journal 2, "Nauvoo, Illinois," June 10, 1844, ns 78, 81–83; and Appendix B, "An Interesting Journal."

[67] Questions about the legality of suppressing the *Expositor* are discussed in Dallin H. Oaks, "The Supression of the *Nauvoo Expositor*," *Utah Law Review* 9 (1965): 862–903; Firmage and Mangrum, 106–13.

On June 27 a large gathering of angry vigilantes overwhelmed the inadequate force guarding the jail and shot to death both Joseph Smith and his brother Hyrum. After the prophet's arrest and murder, violence continued between Mormons and non-Mormons. On October 1, 1845, a congress representing nine Illinois counties assembled at Carthage and resolved that the Mormons must either leave voluntarily or be expelled.

Brigham Young, who as head of the Quorum of Twelve Apostles assumed leadership of the church on August 8, 1844, considered the advice of Illinois governor Thomas Ford to emigrate from the United States:

> If you can get off by yourself you may enjoy peace . . . I was informed by General Joseph Smith last summer that he contemplated a removal west; and . . . I think if he had lived he would have begun to move in the matter before this time . . . Why would it not be a pretty operation for your people to go out there [in California], take possession of and conquer a portion of the vacant country, and establish an independent government of your own subject only to the laws of the nations? . . . if you once cross the line of the United States territories you would be in no danger of being interfered with.[68]

As a member of the Council of Fifty and keeper of its records, Clayton witnessed each step in the planning and preparation for the pioneer trek to the Great Salt Lake Valley. He recorded their meetings throughout 1845 when the council expressed interest in alternative westward relocation sites: on February 14 and March 1 they discussed Texas; on March 4 and August 31, Oregon; on April 15 and August 28, California. Brigham Young's plan on August 28, 1845 to send 3,000 men to Upper California that next spring was later revised; he chose the Great Salt Lake Valley as their specific destination.[69]

---

[68] *HC* 7:396–98 (April 8, 1845).

[69] As late as year-end 1845, the specific location was open to question. On December 31, 1845, Clayton records that he and Brigham Young examined maps "with a reference to selecting a location for the Saints west of the Rocky Mountains" (Journal 3, "Nauvoo Temple").

The Nauvoo Temple, 1845–46

While Clayton was finishing Journal 2, he was invited to assist Heber C. Kimball in keeping a record of the Nauvoo Temple. In Journal 3, "Nauvoo Temple," December 10, 1845, to January 7, 1846, Clayton recorded some five thousand ordinances that were performed day and night in hurried anticipation of the forced Mormon departure to the West. Clayton described the temple endowment, a ritualized drama of the creation, fall, and redemption of Adam, during which its participants promise obedience and loyalty to the church, and repeat passwords and signs they believe will enable them to enter into the Celestial or highest kingdom of heaven. He wrote about washings and anointings, preparatory rituals for the endowment ceremony, and described dramatic role-playing in which church members act out the Garden of Eden story of Adam, Eve, and the serpent.[70]

As church members rehearsed this celestial drama, they wore special clothing and volunteered the necessary words and signs to enter the highest heaven, the Celestial Kingdom. Clayton recorded that "The tokens and covenants are . . . the key by which you approach God and be recognized." In this ceremony, each husband escorted his wife through a veil, calling her by a "new temple name."[71] The woman's salvation would depend upon her husband's priesthood authority. Clayton reported Brigham Young saying that "the man must love his God and the woman must love her husband," adding that "woman will never get back, unless she follows the man back."[72]

In his Nauvoo journals Clayton described some elements of

---

[70] On December 12, 1845, in the "Nauvoo Temple," Brigham Young acted as "Eloheem," the Father, Parley P. Pratt as Jehovah, regarded as Jesus, Orson Hyde as Michael, or Adam, and W. W. Phelps played the role of the serpent. The next day Clayton described the duties of these three deities to create the earth, plant the Garden of Eden, and create man. See Journal 3, "Nauvoo Temple," ns 10, 11.

[71] Journal 3, "Nauvoo Temple," December 21, 1845. Brigham Young declared that this new name should be after some ancient person (ibid., December 28, 1845).

[72] Journal 3, "Nauvoo Temple," December 28, 1845. This particular example of dependence on male authority evokes a familiar religious theme. Within a few years of this entry, Elizabeth Cady Stanton, a leader of the women's movement, would begin to reexamine the traditional interpretation of biblical texts that were widely used to define the role of women. See Carol P. Christ and Judith Plaskow, eds., *Womanspirit Rising: A Feminist Reader in Religion* (San Francisco: Harper and Row, 1979), 85.

the temple ceremonies which had been practiced earlier in Joseph Smith's prayer circle. Beginning in 1842, Smith led the prayer circle in the office above his Red Brick Store on Water Street and at the home of Willard Richards. Later the ceremonies were performed at the Nauvoo Masonic lodge. The prophet had become a Mason in 1842 and quickly assumed the role of an officer in the Nauvoo lodge. The temple ceremonies were first conducted on a large scale at the Masonic lodge.[73] Similarities between Masonic and Mormon rites have been observed in clothing, signs, tokens, hand grips, spoken ceremonies, and oaths.[74] Mormon leaders have identified the temple ceremony as a restoration of ancient Masonic rites. In 1842 when Smith initiated these ceremonies, Heber

[73] On May 4, 1842, nine Masons met "in Joseph's private office, where Joseph taught the ancient order of things for the first time in these last days, and received washings, anointings and endowments." In these early prayer circles, participants learned certain signs and tokens and wore special robes (D. Michael Quinn, "Latter-day Saint Prayer Circles," *Brigham Young University Studies* 19 [Fall 1978]: 79-105; see Journal 3, "Nauvoo Temple," n5). See also the *HC* for that day: Joseph Smith "spent the day in the upper part of the store . . . instructing them in the principles and order of the Priesthood, attending to washings, anointings, endowments and the communication of keys. .. setting forth the order pertaining to the Ancient of Days [Adam] . . . In this council was instituted the ancient order of things for the first time in these last days" (5:1-2). Editor of the Nauvoo *Times and Seasons* Ebenezer Robinson elaborated: "As early as 1843 a secret order was established in Nauvoo, called the HOLY ORDER, [in which] scenes were enacted representing the garden of Eden, and that members of that order were provided with a peculiar under garment called a robe" (*The Return* 2 [April 1890]: 252). B. H. Roberts noted that the Red Brick Store was used as a "temple" for newly-instituted "sacred ceremonies," and it was "also the place of meeting for the Nauvoo Lodge of Free Masons" (*Comprehensive History of the Church of Jesus Christ of Latter-day Saints, Century I*, 6 vols. [Salt Lake City: Church of Jesus Christ of Latter-day Saints, 1930], 2:135-36). Wilford Woodruff observed that there were "meetings held in the Masonic Temple" in Nauvoo and "there were certain ordinances performed there" because "there was no [LDS] temple built at that time" (*Complainants Abstract of Pleading and Evidence In the Circuit Court of the United States, Western District of Missouri, Western Division at Kansas City. The Reorganized Church of Jesus Christ of Latter Day Saints, Complainant, vs. The Church of Christ at Independence, Missouri.* [Lamoni, IA: Herald House, 1893], 299).

[74] For example, on October 15, 1911, the LDS first presidency issued a statement that acknowledged these similarities: "Because of their Masonic characters, the ceremonies of the temple are sacred and not for the public." James R. Clark, ed., *Messages of the First Presidency of the Church of Jesus Christ of Latter-day Saints*, 6 vols. (Salt Lake City: Bookcraft, 1965-75), 4:250. For a comparison of Mormon and Masonic symbols, see Jack Adamson, "The Treasure of the Widow's Son," David C. Martin, ed., *No Help for the Widow's Son: Joseph Smith and Masonry* (Nauvoo, IL: Martin Publishing Co., 1980), 1-12; Jerald and Sanda Tanner, *Evolution of the Mormon Temple Ceremony: 1842-1880* (Salt Lake City: Utah Lighthouse Ministry, 1990), 16-22, 28-32, 142-51.

Kimball noted: "[T]hare is a similarity of preast Hood in Masonry. Br. Joseph Ses Masonry was taken from preasthood but has become degenerated. But menny things are perfect."[75]

Joseph Smith characteristically regarded the most sacred aspects of his new religion as secret, with doctrines and practices known only to a select few. Secret truths were to be shared among intimates and kept from enemies. On December 21, 1845, Clayton recorded George A. Smith's admonition "whatever transpires here ought not to be mentioned any where else." A week later Clayton reported Heber C. Kimball's recollection: "Joseph said that for men and women to hold their tongues, was their Salvation."[76] Clayton's description of the ceremonies is reticent: dissidents have at times

---

[75] Heber C. Kimball to Parley P. Pratt, June 17, 1842, quoted in *Brigham Young University Studies* 15 (Summer 1975): 456–59; see Journal 3, "Nauvoo Temple," n19. Although Masonry draws upon biblical and other ancient sources, historians of Masonry dismiss assertions of antiquity according to traditional lore. Masonic rites actually developed within Scottish stonemason "lodges" during the seventeenth century. Stonemason lodges originated at sheltered work places temporarily constructed at building sites. These transient communities of working masons restricted entry to those properly trained in the skills of stonemasonry. Since masons traveled from wide areas to temporary worksites, the lodges devised secret means of identification, such as handshakes, secret names, and passwords. These craft guilds evolved into a religious brotherhood with rituals and secret greetings. Over time, they developed an elaborate mythical trade history which identified its origins with secret crafts used in building the Tower of Babel, Solomon's temple, and crafts of ancient Egypt. By 1600 recitation of this legendary history was part of a secret lodge ceremony. As non-craftsmen began to join this brotherhood in the seventeenth century, spiritualistic influences of the Renaissance, namely Hermeticism and Rosicrucianism, reinforced the secret rituals. This "rebirth" of ancient knowledge assimilated astrology, magic, and alchemy. Untranslatable hieroglyphics, regarded as a preordained system of concealing sacred truths from the profane, enhanced the meaning of legendary Masonic ties to ancient Egypt. The knowledge claimed by the Rosicrucians of a long-hidden secret brotherhood in possession of ancient knowledge seemed to validate Masonic legend. All of these Renaissance influences enhanced the mystery and secrecy of medieval mythology already incorporated into Masonic ritual. See David Stevenson, *The Origins of Freemasonry* (Cambridge: Cambridge University Press, 1988), 1–23, 77–105, 129–53; and Douglas Knoop and G. P. Jones, *The Genesis of Freemasonry* (Manchester: Manchester University Press, 1947), 62–86.

[76] Journal 3, "Nauvoo Temple," December 21 and 28, 1845. The prophet conveyed his feelings about secrecy in a meeting of the Twelve: "Some people say I am a fallen prophet, because I do not bring forth more of the word of the Lord . . . the reason we do not have the secrets of the Lord revealed unto us is that we do not keep them, but reveal [them] to the world, even to our enemies, then how would we keep the secrets of the Lord?" (*HC* 4:478–79 [December 19, 1841]).

broken the ban of secrecy, and following recent changes in the ceremonies, some details of their content have been publicized.[77]

The Nauvoo Temple was the site for social gatherings as well as sacred ceremonies. At the end of a long day, the Saints danced in the temple "and Sister Whitney sung in tongues."[78] Clayton, a talented musician, composed songs and often played various instruments with a band that performed for dancing. Brigham Young advocated dancing in the temple for those "shut out from . . . amusement among the wicked" and invited the Saints to covenant not to "mingle with the wicked any more in their amusements."[79]

It became apparent that the temple could not be maintained after the majority of the Saints had abandoned Nauvoo, but the Mormons did expect to return someday to reclaim the building. Efforts to sell or lease the temple to local Catholics, who, it was thought, would preserve the structural integrity of the edifice, failed. Two years after the September 1846 expulsion of the last Saints from Nauvoo, the temple was set afire.[80]

---

[77] Since its inception, the LDS endowment ritual has undergone a number of changes. See David J. Buerger, "The Development of the Mormon Temple Endowment Ceremony," *Dialogue: A Journal of Mormon Thought* 20 (Winter 1987): 33-76. The most recent modifications occurred in April 1990. The news media reported that the "central temple ceremony has been altered to eliminate the woman's vow to obey her husband . . . Two other features dropped were a dramatization suggesting that Satan beguiles Christian clergy to teach false doctrine and the requirement that members make throat-slitting and disembowelling gestures as signs that they will not reveal the ceremony's contents . . . Also dropped is an 'embrace' of a man representing God, who stands behind a ceiling-to-floor veil. Reaching through a slit in the veil, the church member puts his or her hand to the back of the deity and presses against him at the cheek, shoulders, knees and feet with the veil between them. The contact at 'five points of fellowship,' including the hand to his back, has been omitted, although the member must still give a secret handshake and repeat a lengthy password" (John Dart, "Mormons Modify Temple Rites," *Los Angeles Times*, May 5, 1990, F20). A good overview of early LDS temple activities is Andrew F. Ehat, "Joseph Smith's Introduction of Temple Ordinances and the 1844 Mormon Succession Question," M.A. thesis, Brigham Young University, 1982.

[78] Journal 3, "Nauvoo Temple," December 30, 1845. Dancing was also held in the temple on January 1, 2, 5, and 6, 1846. On January 9, Brigham Young asked that all dancing cease, "lest the brethren and sisters be carried away by vanity" (*HC* 7:566).

[79] Journal 3, "Nauvoo Temple," January 1-2, 1846.

[80] November 19, 1848 (*HC* 7:617-18). Clayton notes reports of the expulsion from Nauvoo in his "Pioneer Trek West" journal, September 23-25, 1846. See also *HC* 7:214.

Escape from the United States, 1846–47

On February 27, 1846, after a week of waiting, William Clayton with three of his wives, four children, and a mother-in-law crossed the Mississippi River in wagons, beginning the 1,350-mile overland trek to the Great Salt Lake Valley. Clayton was "clerk of the camp" from Nauvoo to Winter Quarters, Nebraska, where several thousand Saints waited to resume the trip to the Rocky Mountain Great Basin beginning the following spring. He was among the 148-member advance party which left Winter Quarters on April 14, 1847. Clayton assisted Thomas Bullock, the official scribe, in recording the remaining journey to the valley. His journal of the trip provides a contemporary record of the Mormon contribution to the westward expansion of the United States.[81]

The circumstances were, of course, unique. In the tradition of Manifest Destiny the United States was attempting to acquire land from both Britain in the Northwest and Mexico in the Southwest.[82] The Mormons were not interested in extending the frontier of the United States but in leaving it for a new land. Even as they faced the necessity to move westward, the expanding boundaries of the United States were about to engulf them.

In 1845 Brigham Young had considered establishing a separate state within the independent Republic of Texas along the border of Mexico. Texas had separated from Mexico in 1836. By this time, however, the United States government itself was interested in Texas and annexed it as a state in 1845.[83]

---

[81] See Journal 4, "Pioneer Trek West," n11. On October 21, 1847, of his "Pioneer Trek West" journal, Clayton calculates the distance from Winter Quarters, Nebraska (near Omaha), to the Great Salt Lake Valley as 1,032 miles. The distance from Nauvoo to Omaha is about 320 miles. He counts all of the passengers in his company on April 16, 1847. .

[82] Both the United States and Britain claimed "Oregon," which then included present-day Washington, Idaho, Wyoming, and part of Montana and British Columbia. The territory had been ruled under joint occupation since 1818 (Samuel Eliot Morison and Henry Steele Commager, *The Growth of the American Republic* [New York: Oxford University Press, 1937], 464). The Transcontinental Treaty of 1846 settled the boundary dispute with Great Britain and divided the territory at the 49th parallel (John D. Unruh, Jr., *The Plains Across: The Overland Emigrants and the Trans-Mississippi West, 1840–60* [Urbana: University of Illinois Press, 1982], 32).

[83] See Lyman Wight's February 15, 1844, letters on migrating to Texas (*HC*

California, which belonged to Mexico in 1845, was another possible destination. On September 15, 1845, Brigham Young wrote to Samuel Brannan, publisher of an LDS paper in New York, "I wish you together with your press, paper, and ten thousand of the brethren, were now in California at the bay of San Francisco, and if you can clear yourself and go there, do so."[84] Next spring, Brannan took 138 Mormons aboard a chartered ship from New York to San Francisco. He then traveled east to meet the emigrant train in Wyoming in 1847 and tried to persuade Young to bring the Saints to the foothills of the Sierra Nevada in California; but the presence of many adventurers and explorers—even before the discovery of gold in 1848—diminished California's attraction to Young.

During the 1840s the rich Oregon country beckoned many settlers and interested Mormon planners. But the U.S. Senate was concerned that Britain might misunderstand a Mormon migration into Oregon territory, so it rejected an 1845 Mormon petition to go to Oregon. After negotiating with the British government to place settlers on Vancouver Island,[85] on September 9, 1845, Brigham Young considered a more cautious plan to move the Saints to the less popular Great Salt Lake Valley.[86] When the Mormons arrived there in 1847, the land belonged to Mexico. In 1848, at the end of the Mexican War, the valley became part of the United States under the Treaty of Guadalupe Hidalgo.[87]

6:255–60) and Dale L. Morgan, *The Great Salt Lake* (New York: Bobbs Merrill, 1947), 176, 188.

[84] *HC* 7:444–45.

[85] Hansen, 109.

[86] See *HC* 7:439. The Great Salt Lake Valley is located in the Great Basin of North America, a 200,000-square-mile region between the Sierra Nevada and Wasatch Mountains, from which rivers have no outlet to the sea. Although this relatively isolated area had been explored and mapped, it remained sparsely settled and thus was attractive to the Mormons.

[87] When Mexico won its independence from Spain in 1821, it controlled a region called "Upper California," which extended northward to Oregon and eastward to the Rocky Mountains. Under the terms of Guadalupe Hidalgo, Utah (including present-day Utah, Nevada, and parts of Wyoming and Colorado) became a United States possession but was not granted territorial status for two years because Congress was trying to maintain a delicate political balance among the thirty states of the union, half of which were free and half slave-holding. With the Compromise of 1850, Congress decided to admit California as a free state and allow Utah and New Mexico (including Arizona) to decide locally whether or not to allow slavery.

In preparation for their journey westward, the Latter-day Saints gathered information about trails and settlements between Illinois and the Pacific Ocean. Missionaries, trappers, and mountain men — such as Jedediah Smith, who explored the Rocky Mountains in 1822 — laid the groundwork for the emigrant trains which began in 1840.[88] By the time the Mormons reached the Great Salt Lake Valley over 12,000 emigrants, from 1840 to 1847, had traveled to California and Oregon.[89] While in Washington, D.C., exploring the option of settling Oregon, Orson Hyde obtained a map of Oregon from Stephen A. Douglas and also John C. Fremont's description of the Far West and the Platte River-South Pass route to Oregon. Fremont's journals from 1843 contain an extensive description of the isolated valley of the Great Salt Lake.[90] The Saints also got information from travelers they met along the trail, including Jim Bridger, near the fork to California; Oregon men on their way back, who described the Great Salt Lake Valley; and Samuel Brannan, whom they met at the Green River in Wyoming. Some of Bridger's men had been around the Great Salt Lake in canoes.[91]

---

[88] Jedediah Smith joined General William Ashley's expedition to the Rocky Mountains in 1822. By 1825, Smith, Etienne Provost, Peter Skene Ogden, John Weber, Jim Bridger, and William Sublette all had explored the Great Salt Lake Valley. See Dale L. Morgan, *Jedediah Smith and the Opening of the West* (Lincoln: University of Nebraska Press, 1953), 7, 26–29, 147–53, 170, 182–83, 189.

[89] Unruh, 84.

[90] See Orson Hyde's April 26, 1844 letter from Washington, D.C., on the probable route west (*HC* 6:373–75). Fremont had explored the Great Salt Lake in 1843, 1844, and 1845, in part to acquire military intelligence for President James K. Polk. For a narrative of exploring parties through that region from 1841 to 1846, see Morgan, *The Great Salt Lake*, 135–75; for more information about the early explorations of John C. Fremont, see Donald Jackson and Mary Lee Spence, eds., *The Explorations of John Charles Fremont: Travels from 1838 to 1844* (Urbana: University of Illinois Press, 1970). Other explorers who had mapped the west included James Mackay and John Evans, British leaders of a Spanish exploration group from the 1790s; Hudson's Bay and the North West fur companies' surveyors, whose maps of the upper Missouri River were published in London by Aaron Arrowsmith; Vancouver, who charted the lower Columbia River; Canada's Alex Mackenzie, who negotiated the Continental Divide in 1793; Alexander von Humboldt, the renowned European scientist and explorer, who explored western North America for the Spanish government and published his maps in 1808; and William Clark, who published a map in 1814 based upon his exploration with Meriwether Lewis (David Lavender, *The Great West* [Boston: Houghton Mifflin, 1987], 81, 89).

[91] Clayton reports that they met Jim Bridger on June 28 and Sam Brannan on June 30, 1847.

Clayton's journal portrays camp life on the westward trail. His days often began at five a.m., with a breakfast of fish and coffee, or one time "goose and mouldy bread." The Saints frequently broke camp by seven a.m. In order to calculate how far they went, Clayton proposed to Apostle Orson Pratt that wooden cog wheels be fixed to a wagon wheel hub. Clayton found that the 14-foot-8-inch wheel circumference made precisely 360 turns per mile. He was thereby able to keep fairly accurate record of miles traveled—approximately twenty miles a day—and was able to project the time required for a particular trip.[92] Clayton describes the territory along the trail. In one entry he found the prairie on both sides of the Platte River "literally black with buffalo," over fifty thousand "at a moderate calculation." On the return trip to Winter Quarters, he "counted" 200,000 buffalo.[93]

In the evenings Clayton would often play violin in a Mormon band and sing—sometimes given money, groceries, and on one occasion cake and beer. Although Brigham Young participated to some extent in singing and dancing on the trip west, Clayton recorded Young's admonition: "The moment I stoppt in the middle or the end of a tune, my mind was engaged in prayer." In a reprimand to the merrymakers, Young talked of "yielding to the evil spirit," exclaiming, "I have let the brethren dance, and fiddle . . . night after night to see what they will do . . . but I dont love to see it." He inveighed against dancing, cards, joking, and profane language, adding, "If you cant tire yourselves bad enough with a days journey without dancing every night, carry your guns on your shoulders." He warned, "if you dont stop it, you shall be cursed," and called a fast meeting to pray and ask forgiveness. "Every knee shall bow . . . and observe the laws of the kingdom," he stipulated.[94]

---

[92] Journal 4, "Pioneer Trek West," April 19, May 16, and August 10, 1847. Clayton first used the "roadometer" in 1847 going west from Winter Quarters. Every ten miles he marked the distance on stakes placed along the trail. Clayton checked the figures on his return trip later that year.

[93] Ibid., September 28, 1847. In 1806, Meriwether Lewis estimated 10,000 buffalo at Great Falls, Montana, shaking the air with "tremendous roaring"; see the first authentic history of the Lewis and Clark expedition: Nicholas Biddle, *History of the Expedition, 1803*, Paul Allen, ed. (Philadelphia: Bradford and Inskeep, 1814), quoted in Lavender, 91.

[94] Journal 4, "Pioneer Trek West," May 29, 1847.

On a smooth boulder in western Nebraska where he viewed Chimney Rock twenty miles to the west, Clayton recorded his presence with red chalk: "Wm. Clayton, May 22, 1847." Near the Weber Fork in Utah he found the scenery "wild and melancholy." Climbing across Donner Hill at the mouth of Emigration Canyon, he described his first view of the Salt Lake Valley:

> While the brethren were cutting the road I followed the old one to the top of the hill and . . . was much cheered by a handsome view of the great Salt Lake . . . 30 miles to the west . . . There is an extensive, beautiful, level looking valley from here to the Lake which I should judge from the numerous deep green patches must be fertile and rich . . . [The] valley appears to be well supplied with streams, creeks and Lakes . . . The ground seems literally alive with the very large black crickets crawling round, up grass and bushes. They look loathsome but are said to be excellent for fattening hogs.[95]

He also saw soil that "looks indeed rich, black and a little sandy, . . . grass [which] looks rich and good . . . [and] many rattlesnakes of a large size."

Upon arriving in the Great Salt Lake Valley, Clayton was assigned to compile a record of distances traveled along the Mormon trail from Winter Quarters to Salt Lake City. Here Clayton reveals his pride in inventing and using his measuring device. When Appleton Harmon claimed credit for developing Clayton's "roadometer," Clayton complained that Harmon only "made the machinery after being told how to do it," remarking, "what little souls work." Clayton also compared his accuracy with that of explorer John C. Fremont's map, which "does not agree with my scale," and he proposed making a new map.[96] From August 17 to October 21, 1847, Clayton went back to Winter Quarters for his family. In February 1848 he followed the Missouri River down to St. Louis where he published his *Latter-day Saints' Emigrants' Guide*, which made his mileage calculations available to many forty-niners

---

[95] Ibid., July 22, 1847.
[96] Ibid., May 14, 18, 1847.

and other travelers along the overland trail.[97]

After Clayton's December 6, 1847, entry concluded Journal 4, five years passed before he began Journal 5, "Visit to Utah Settlements." During that five years the Saints worked to establish viable communities for emigrants from the Missouri River Valley and Europe. After planting potatoes and turnips for an immediate supply of food, the advance party planted grain crops that could be harvested to feed the Saints who would arrive later from Winter Quarters. About 1,600 came the first year, 2,400 the second, and by 1852 the population was 20,000.[98] In 1849 the Perpetual Emigrating Fund was established to assist converts in gathering to the Great Salt Lake from every part of the world. The funds were to be repaid after the converts arrived in Salt Lake. That same year the Council of Fifty formed the provisional "State of Deseret," comprising "all of present-day Utah and Nevada, most of Arizona, parts of Idaho, Wyoming, and Colorado, and enough of southern California to provide an outlet to the sea."[99] The U.S. named Brigham Young as territorial governor but did not grant statehood for another forty-seven years, and then for a much-reduced area.

The event that insured the Saints' survival in the Great Basin was the discovery of gold in January 1848 and the ensuing California gold rush. As one historian put it, "Contemporary records leave no doubt that the most important crop of 1849-51 was harvested, not in the Salt Lake Valley, but at Sutter's Mill, near Coloma, California."[100] About 40,000–50,000 persons journeyed overland to California in 1849–50, and an estimated 10,000–15,000 went through Salt Lake City during each of those years, buying food, clothing, and implements. While publicly advocating homesteading in the Salt Lake Valley over seeking gold in California, Brigham Young privately advised the hundred members of the Mormon Batallion in the San Francisco Bay Area and those working at Sutter's sawmill to remain to acquire gold for the Kingdom

[97] William Clayton, *The Latter-day Saints' Emigrants' Guide* (St. Louis: Chamber & Knapp, 1848), original and facsimile at Marriott Library; see also the reprint by Stanley B. Kimball, ed. (Gerald, MO: Patrice Press, 1983). The original edition appeared in a printing of 5,000 copies and retailed for $5.00 apiece.
[98] Arrington, 47, 50, 97; see also Journal 4, "Pioneer Trek West," n87.
[99] Ibid., 50; Lavender, 310; see Journal 6, "Polygamy Mission to England," n11.
[100] Arrington, 66.

of God and to sell goods and services to the thousands of gold-seekers, who were creating boom markets.[101]

Also during the gold rush year, the Great Salt Lake Carrying Company was formed to carry freight and passengers from the Missouri River to the Great Salt Lake and California. Brigham Young began a colonization effort in 1849. He sent families on "missions" to plant Mormon communities throughout the West: a "heartland" centered in the Great Salt Lake Valley, and an outer ring of communities for defense and support—including Carson Valley, Las Vegas, San Bernardino, and part of the Salmon River in Idaho. Young conceived of a "Mormon corridor" of twenty-seven communities between the Salt Lake heartland and the California coast at Los Angeles.[102]

A Visit to the Settlements
in Southern Utah

In the spring of 1852 Clayton kept a three-week journal of a survey of settlements in southern Utah.[103] He served as historian for a seventy-nine-member camp led by Brigham Young and counselors Heber C. Kimball and George A. Smith. They visited Provo, Springville, Spanish Fork, Payson, Nephi, Manti, Parowan, and Fillmore—the capital of Utah from 1851 to 1856, all settlements along the corridor that Young wanted to develop between Salt

---

[101] In 1850, to help Brigham Young dissuade those who wanted to dig for gold in California, Clayton wrote a six-stanza ode to "The Gold Diggers" for the Pioneer Day Celebration. Part of it went: "Now, ye Saints, my advice I will give without price, Don't be tempted to worship the dust; But stick close to your farms, and build up your good barns, For the grain is much better, I trust" (*Deseret News*, September 7, 1850, quoted in Brigham D. Madsen, *Gold Rush Sojourners in Great Salt Lake City 1849 and 1850* [Salt Lake City: University of Utah Press, 1983], 47; see also Journal 5, "Visit to Utah Settlements," n11). Clayton's musical contributions are summarized in Dahl, 190–97.

[102] Eugene E. Campbell, *Establishing Zion: The Mormon Church in the American West, 1847–1869* (Salt Lake City: Signature Books, 1988), 57–91; Russell L. Elliott, *History of Nevada* (Lincoln: University of Nebraska, 1987), 50–61, 107–8, 379; Leonard J. Arrington, *The Mormons in Nevada* (Las Vegas: Las Vegas Sun, 1979); *Brigham Young: American Moses* (New York: Knopf, 1985), 167–91; *Great Basin Kingdom*, 84–89; and Andrew Jenson, "History of the Las Vegas Mission," *Nevada Historical Society Papers* 5 (1925–26): 115–284.

[103] Journal 5, "Visit to Utah Settlements," April 21, 1852.

Lake City and the seaports of San Pedro and San Diego. This camp took an inventory of timber, mineral, and farmland resources and selected civil court and church officers. They took a census and held dances as they visited "the southern settlements, exploring the country, ascertain[ing] the situation of the Indians, making roads, building bridges, killing snakes, preaching the gospel."[104]

When the camp arrived at Provo, the future home of Brigham Young University, Clayton wrote on April 23 that the "town looks dirty. The houses look miserable, and many young men idling in the Streets. It seems there is not much energy here." Two days later he found nearby Springville "one of the most handsome locations we have seen on the route. The land is beautifully situated, plenty of water. The houses all look clean and neat, and the hand of industry is clearly manifested throughout the village."

At Fillmore, Dimick Huntington, former Nauvoo constable, addressed the local Indians and told them to quit "stealing from the Mormons and go to work as Mormons do. . . . to cease killing Indians . . . to cease trading children to the Spaniards, but if they will trade children let the Mormons have them that they may be taught to read and write and be clothed like Mormons are."

For many years a slave trade in Indian children, especially from the poor Shoshonean tribes, had flourished along the Spanish Trail.[105] Since Mormons regarded Indians as "Lamanites" of the Book of Mormon who were cursed with dark skin but were destined to be redeemed, they were sympathetic to their cause. Brigham Young advised the Saints to "buy up the Lamanite children as fast as they could, and educate them and teach them the gospel, so that not many generations would pass ere they would become a white and delightsome people."[106] On March 7, 1852, the legislative assembly of the Utah territory had passed an act legalizing Indian slavery. Ironically, as a result of this act, Mormons themselves indentured Indian children.[107]

---

[104] Dahl, 155.

[105] Morgan, *The Great Salt Lake*, 40; Lavender, 171.

[106] Indians purchased into freedom: "Journal History," May 12, 1851.

[107] Campbell, 107. Missionary interest in the Indians began in 1831, when Joseph Smith sent Mormon elders to marry Indian women with the hope of producing "white and delightsome children" that would assist in fulfilling Book of Mormon prophecy (see n35). A modified practice of inviting Indian children to take

Return to England
to Explain Polygamy, 1852–53

Later that year, on August 28, Clayton was called on a mission to England to "sustain the Revelation on Celestial Marriage, given by our beloved Prophet [on] July 12, 1843."[108] The following day Orson Pratt for the first time introduced the doctrine of plural marriage to the church as a whole, and on September 14, 1852, the Salt Lake City *Deseret News* announced the doctrine to the world. By this time Clayton and thirty-eight fellow missionaries were on their way back to England to explain plural marriage to the English Saints.

Like the earlier pioneer trip westward, this eastward continental crossing on the way to England evoked colorful descriptions. Amidst their practical concerns over provisions, night watches, and the weather, the travelers concluded that angels were watching over them when an unseen power unhooked four horses from a broken hitch. On the way they met a Mormon company hauling machinery to Salt Lake to manufacture sugar. The company's tired-looking cattle provoked Clayton's observation that "inexperienced Englishmen or Frenchmen are not the men to drive teams across the plains as heavily loaded as these are." He also concluded that, if Mormons raised sugar beets, they would be "independent of Gentile merchants for sugar, molasses or spirits [and] the hearts of the Saints will be made to rejoice when this company . . . arrives in the Valley."[109]

After traveling by wagon to St. Louis and then by boat and train to Pittsburg, Philadelphia, and New York City, on December 17, 1852, the Mormon missionaries sailed to Liverpool, England, at $22.50 a person. On the way they experienced the worst gale recorded in twenty years, which probably accounted for their relatively fast seventeen-day voyage.

---

temporary residence in Mormon homes continues today. Former church president Spencer W. Kimball justified Indian home placement by suggesting that the resident Indians were becoming lighter skinned (*Improvement Era*, December 1960, 922–23).

[108] Journal 6, "Polygamy Mission to England," August 28, 1852.

[109] Ibid., September 27, 1852. This initial sugar beet venture failed, but a successful sugar beet factory was built in the 1890s. See Arrington, *Great Basin Kingdom*, 116–20.

Clayton's commentary of two ocean crossings and several trips across the American continent by land and water provides a first-hand description of nineteenth-century travel. Steam travel had begun early in the century. By the time Clayton wrote, steam locomotives prevailed in the eastern part of the North American continent, and steam boats plied seacoasts, rivers, and lakes. Although the first propeller-driven steam ship was built in 1845, transatlantic steam travel was not prevalent until the 1860s, and Clayton's ocean crossings in 1840, 1852, and 1853 were all by sail.[110]

Clayton recorded Orson Pratt's enthusiasm to preach and disseminate the celestial marriage revelation; but in England the reaction to polygamy was adverse. The Mormon elders were placed in the awkward position of having to defend the once-secret practice which they had denied for a decade. Clayton found that British Mormons had "heard many false reports concerning our customs in the [Salt Lake] Valley, such as taking a man's wife from him and giving her to another, without her consent; and taking young women and giving them to men contrary to their feelings &c."[111]

Shortly after his arrival in England, Clayton's discussion of polygamy was turned by an "apostate Mormon" into a charge of Clayton's "having had unlawful intercourse with women."[112] Mis-

---

[110] Conway B. Sonne, *Ships, Saints, and Mariners: A Maritime Encyclopedia of Mormon Migration, 1830–1890* (Salt Lake City: University of Utah Press, 1987), 35, 41, 155.

[111] Journal 6, "Polygamy Mission to England," February 2, 1853. British opposition to plural marriage arose even before the August 1852 official announcement in Salt Lake City. Mission president Richards wrote: "Much opposition has existed in this country for a few months past and much still continues. The report of the [clergy] in relation to polygamy etc. in the Valley has been one great cause of it. Many are turned out of employment for embracing the work and . . . attempts are made to poison elders, etc. . . . Women in this country are shamefully abused with language if they will not leve this church. They are told that polygamy is practiced by it and every other filthy thing the wicked can imagine" (Samuel W. Richards to Mary Richards, April 25, 1852, LDS archives). These reports of taking a man's wife could have referred to the giving of a married woman to someone of a higher priesthood rank or to the giving of a missionary's wife to another man during the husband's absence (Journal 3, "Nauvoo Temple," n32; S. George Ellsworth, ed., *The Journals of Addison Pratt* [Salt Lake City: University of Utah Press, 1990], 515).

[112] William Clayton to Brigham Young, November 17, 1856, and Clayton to

sion president Richards advised Clayton not to preach for a week or two "until the excitement and prejudice had subsided." A week later, Clayton read in the *Latter-day Saints' Millennial Star* that he had been suspended from his missionary duties.[113] Although he was reinstated a week after that, Clayton was sent back to Salt Lake City on April 6, 1853, only three months after his arrival in England.

The mission to teach plural marriage to the British Saints was a failure. Regarded as an objectionable practice in America, polygamy encountered similar resistance in England after its public announcement in the *Millennial Star* on January 1, 1853. British membership declined 60 percent from a nineteenth-century high of 33,000 in 1851 to 13,000 at the end of the decade. Although part of this decrease can be attributed to emigration, baptismal rates fell by 88 percent during the 1850s and excommunications from 1853 to 1859 totalled almost 18,000. According to a recent study of Mormon missionary efforts in early Victorian Britain, many apostasies occurred shortly after the introduction of "controversial teachings about plural marriage and about Adam as God."[114] Clayton's experience illustrates the difficulties of advocating this peculiar marital practice overseas. Clayton later described this episode in his "unfortunate mission of 1852-3" as "the most unpleasant, and bitterest period of my life."[115]

The last entry in Clayton's extant journals was written on March 2, 1853, when he was still in England. Just as Clayton began his first journal without a frame of reference, he abruptly concluded this last journal without summing up or even indicating that he would not continue.

Thomas Bullock, February 5, 1853, LDS archives; Journal 6, "Polygamy Mission to England," January 8 and 26, 1853.

[113] Journal 6, "Polygamy Mission to England," January 8, 26, 27, and February 2, 1853.

[114] Richard L. Jensen, "Church Councils and Governance," in Jensen and Thorp, 179-93. For information on British mission statistics, see Lively, 16-30, and Richard D. Poll, "The British Mission During the Utah War, 1857-58," in Jensen and Thorp, 226.

[115] Clayton to Young, November 17, 1856; Journal 6, "Polygamy Mission to England," January 8, 1853. This entry, though dated at the beginning of these events, reflects back from a later time upon the aftermath of Clayton's visit with the "apostate Mormon," whose charges precipitated his travail. For other instances of Clayton's retrospective journal-writing, see his September 26, 1852, entry and Journal 4, "Pioneer Trek West," April 5, 1846.

Return to Utah

Clayton returned to America and lived in Salt Lake City until his death in 1879. Although he was highly respected, his position in the church was less prominent than when he had served as Joseph Smith's private secretary in Nauvoo. When Brigham Young replaced Smith as church president, Clayton grew less intimate with the Mormon power structure. After the pioneer trek west he apparently had no official journal-keeping assignments for five years. After his doomed mission to explain polygamy in England, Clayton stood even further apart from the church hierarchy. His difficulties on the British mission, an alcohol problem, his absence from Salt Lake City — all served to distance him from the inner circle. In an 1856 appeal for reinstatement Clayton wrote to President Brigham Young: "I have no expectation of ever gaining your confidence as formerly . . . but if I am wanted, be assured that it will give me joy and consolation to do any thing I can that you wish of me; for I feel and have felt as tho' I was sadly out of my place."[116]

Privately, Clayton was drawn to a mystical interpretation of the world. In his later years in Salt Lake City he acquired occult objects which were promised to give the user spiritual power. Religion and unseen forces were ever part of his life. On the trail he had attributed successful Indian trades to God's intervention.[117] He later portrayed the stirrings of civil war not as products of sectionalism and slavery, but as divine retribution for mistreatment of the Mormons, perhaps leading to the end of the world.[118]

---

[116] Clayton to Young.

[117] Journal 6, "Polygamy Mission to England," October 9, 1852.

[118] In the last three decades of his life Clayton's personal letters show that he continued to worry about cataclysmic events — social, which he experienced in England and Nauvoo, and apocalyptic, which the church had always anticipated. During the American Civil War Clayton urged creditors to "lose no time" in collecting their due because of "certain indications of . . . a desolating war soon to break out in Europe" (December 11, 1863, to George Q. Cannon). Seeing sickness, cold, and scarce money, he asked "Are not the prophesies fulfilling fast, signs in the sun, earthquakes, hurricanes, storms and floods" (January 3, 1870, to Bro. Jessee). In response to his missionary son's complaints that the English people were unwilling to listen to the Mormons, Clayton wrote: "The hand of God . . . the judgements are being rapidly poured upon the nations. The severe storms on the coast of England, causing numerous shipwrecks and loss of life; the cattle distemper, potatoes disease, and the very high price of meat and fuel, are severe

Clayton saw social change through the lens of his unshakable belief in the Mormon faith.

Clayton also led an active public life. He and his sons built a
three-story red brick home called the "Big House" on the northwest corner of North and West Temple streets. There the children
of William and Ruth played several instruments to accompany
dancing in their large living room. In the Salt Lake City community, he participated in business, local government, and church
affairs; he ran a bookstore and a boarding house. He also maintained extensive correspondence. He apparently read widely and
had an insatiable interest in what went on around him. He carried his collection of books across the plains under his wagon
seat, including the works of Frederick the Great and the letters of
Voltaire; he brought back several plays from his 1852–53 missionary trip to England. He subscribed to the "best English newspapers all his life in Utah," as well as to several periodicals: *Harper's
Monthly* and *Weekly*, *Atlantic Monthly*, *Godey's Lady's Book*, *Author's
Magazine*, *Ballou's Dollar Monthly*, *Ballou's Novelette*, *New York Ledger*,
London Punch, and *Reynolds Miscellany*. Chronicler Orson F. Whitney
described Clayton as "a deep thinker, a clear writer and an impressive speaker." For a time Clayton and Brigham Young were
speaking companions at Sunday meetings at the Bowery.[119]

---

afflictions on the peoples of England. The famine in Persia; the overflowing of the
Po and the destruction by wind storm of Palazzo in Italy; the destruction of
Chicago and Boston by fire, the cholera in different parts of Europe and Asia . . .
and the dreadful increase of immorality among all nations are, to me, prominent
signs that the Lord is fulfilling the prophesies" (November 25, 1872, to Newel H.
Clayton). And Clayton referred to Brigham Young's talk about returning to Jackson
County, Missouri, associated in Mormonism with the world's end (Dec. 4, 1860, to
George Q. Cannon). He further wrote to ask Miles Romney to store his belongings
"when many of us will have to leave this region . . . in a hurry . . . There are
many ominous signs" (March 9, 1865).

Perhaps associated with his concern with mysterious signs of the end, Clayton
found new interest in the occult, expaning upon spiritual experiences in Nauvoo.
He mail-ordered the following esoteric items: "$1. for certified membership for
myself as member of the British Metallic Mutual Assn.; 1.00 for copy of the Guide
'cabala', and $3.00 each for Two of the Mysterious Elictical and Weird rings and
Secret Talisman of the Ancient Hebrews and Egyptians" (March 1, 1864, to Wm.
Freeman) and a subsequent order for a "sacred charm compound" (March 7, 1864),
letter collections, Bancroft Library and University of Utah.

[119]Thomas to Smith, August 25 and November 20, 1990; R. M. H. Clayton,
"History of Ruth Moon Clayton"; William Clayton to J. S. Bettinger, July 23, 1864,
in Dahl, 197; Whitney, 58; "Journal History," May 12, June 24, 1850. Clayton also

After he returned from his polygamy mission to England, Clayton assisted in cutting the dies for new Mormon money minted in Salt Lake City, was elected assistant secretary of the Territorial Council of Utah in the 1853–54 session, and was elected secretary of the territorial legislature in the 1854–55 session.[120] He was a partner in Cronyn and Clayton, a mercantile store on Main Street specializing in "Fancy Dry Goods and Notions, A Splendid Lot of Boots, Shoes, Hats and Caps, Ladies' Dress Goods and Trimmings, Porcelain, Queensware and Glasswares, Hardware, Groceries and Dye Stuffs." He subsequently founded Clayton and Dotten (another mercantile business), was a bookkeeper and debt collector, and engaged in mining enterprises and farming. He was also treasurer (cashier) of Zion's Cooperative Mercantile Institution, Recorder of Marks and Brands, Receiver of Weights and Measures, and Public Auditor for the Territory of Utah.[121]

Victoria Clayton McCune recalled her dignified father: "He was methodical, always sitting in his own armchair, having a certain place at the table . . . his person was clean and tidy; his hands small and dimpled. He wore very little jewelry but what little he had was the best money could buy . . . and his clothing was made from the best material. His children remember him best in black velvet coat and grey trousers and, in cold weather, a broad-cloth cloak in place of overcoat . . . his home was open always to his friends who loved to gather there for social hours. Civic affairs always interested him. He was a musician and played

owned ranch property in City Creek Canyon, north of Salt Lake City. Rose Marie Clayton accurately identifies the intersection at which the Clayton home was built on West Temple Street, and Nicholas G. Morgan, Sr., comp., *Pioneer Map: Great Salt Lake City: Great Basin — North America* (Salt Lake City: Compiler, n.d.) locates the house on the correct corner (northwest). Wanda Clayton Thomas, great-granddaughter of William and Ruth, recalls two other Clayton houses on adjacent lots. William Clayton recorded his choosing lots 1, 2, and 3 on Block 95 (Journal 4, "Pioneer Trek West," August 16, 1847).

[120] Dahl, 157.

[121] *Deseret News*, September 30, 1863; Dahl, 189–95; letters March 13, and 23, 1869, Bancroft Library; McCune, *William Clayton's Journal*, viii. The *Deseret News*, July 4, 1855, described Clayton's alphabetical list of 1,000 marks and brands arranged in thirty-nine "neatly printed" pages, "stitched and paper covered," available at the Post Office and Deseret Store to the owners of animals (Dahl, 158; originals at Utah State Historical Society, Salt Lake City).

in the pioneer orchestra and that of the Salt Lake Theater."[122] The Clayton name is still known and respected throughout Utah.

Clayton's journals are valuable because of the time and place in which he lived. He draws together familiar nineteenth-century themes: the aftermath of the Industrial Revolution, transatlantic emigration, settling the frontier, and politics before the Civil War. His journals provide valuable insight into the antebellum period of American history.

Appendices

The appendices differ from the journal documents in that they are extracts, narratives, or statements rather than contemporary journals. Appendix A, "Extracts from William Clayton's [Private] Book — Keys," includes Clayton's record of what he identified as the "Key[s] of the mysteries of the Kingdom [of God]," lectures from Joseph Smith's private prayer circles. These "keys" were apparently taken from Wilford Woodruff's notes, from Willard Richards's "Pocket Companion," from John Taylor's writings, as well as directly from Joseph Smith's comments after Clayton arrived in Nauvoo. L. John Nuttall, secretary to later church president, John Taylor, made extracts from Clayton's private book in 1880 and thus preserved some of Clayton's writings which are no longer available. Some of these "keys" may be found in other writings.[123]

Appendix B, "An Interesting Journal," a retrospective narrative composed by Clayton, focuses mainly on the construction of the Nauvoo Temple. This narrative complements Journal 2, "Nauvoo, Illinois," and Journal 3, "Nauvoo Temple."

Appendix C, "William Clayton's Testimony," is a notarized statement from 1874 in which Clayton documents the introduction of plural marriage in Nauvoo as he remembered it. This brief statement was evidently intended to assert the reality of plural

---

[122] McCune, *William Clayton's Journal*, vii–viii. William Clayton was fifty-two years old when Victoria was born.

[123] See Andrew F. Ehat and Lyndon W. Cook, comps. and eds., *The Words of Joseph Smith: The Contemporary Accounts of the Nauvoo Discourses of the Prophet Joseph Smith* (Provo, UT: Religious Studies Center, Brigham Young University, 1980).

marriage and to justify its practice at a time when Joseph Smith's surviving family denied that the prophet had ever practiced it.

Sources and Locations of
William Clayton's Journals

This abridgement of the William Clayton journals is based upon scrutiny—either my own or that of others—of the holographs of five of the journals. The text of the sixth, the "Nauvoo, Illinois" journal, has been compiled from published and unpublished transcripts of the holograph, and checked against the *History of the Church* and other contemporary sources for thematic and chronological consistency. The six documents which comprise Clayton's journals and the three appendices which include additional writings come from the following sources:

Journal 1, "England and Emigration," January 1, 1840, to February 18, 1842, was first published by Clayton family members in the early 1970s and then in James B. Allen and Thomas G. Alexander, eds., *Manchester Mormons: The Journal of William Clayton 1840-1842* (Santa Barbara, California: Peregrine Smith, Inc., 1974). The original manuscript, a notebook measuring four-and-one-half inches long, three inches wide, and five-eighths inches thick, written in "metallic pencil," was donated by Comstock Clayton (grandson of William and Augusta Braddock Clayton) and his wife to Brigham Young University after it was published by the family, and typescript copies were deposited at the University of Utah Marriott Library and Utah State Historical Society. Journal 1 records events both in England and in Nauvoo, Illinois. During the former, Clayton wrote virtually every day. Following his arrival in Nauvoo on November 24, 1840, there are gaps as long as four and five months between entries. There then appears to be an eight-month hiatus between Journals 1 and 2.

Journal 2, "Nauvoo, Illinois," is comprised of three notebooks measuring about six inches tall by four inches wide, which Clayton kept from November 27, 1842, to January 30, 1846.[124] This jour-

---

[124] The first notebook extends from November 27, 1842, to April 27, 1843, and then from September 24, 1844, through March 31, 1845; the second notebook,

nal was included in an inventory of LDS archives in 1858 as the "Journal of William Clayton, 1843–1844, 1842–1845, 1845–1846."[125] Subsequently, Clayton's "Nauvoo, Illinois" journal was transferred to the LDS first presidency's office, which has restricted access to it.[126]

This abridgment of the "Nauvoo, Illinois" journal draws together available typescript and published texts.[127] Material from the sequestered portions of the originals, not included in the present compilation, contains: references to the Masonic Lodge and Council of Fifty meetings, related minutes, and discussion of new members; legal and political conversations, including those with Henry Clay, James Buchanan, and Stephen Douglas; events concerning Joseph Smith's U.S. presidential candidacy; financial concerns

---

from April 25, 1843, to September 24, 1844, includes a separately-bound journal dated June 14 to June 22, 1844, which is inserted in the second volume; the third notebook extends from April 1, 1845, to January 30, 1846. Portions of this journal were kept concurrently, a typical practice of Clayton. See *Trial Record*, Ehat vs. Tanner, U.S. District Court, Salt Lake City, Vol. 1, March 21, 1984, 30.

[125] "Contents of the Historian and Recorder's Office G[reat] S[alt] L[ake] City, July 1858," 7, LDS archives. The two diaries written mostly during Joseph Smith's lifetime, 1842–45 and 1843–44, were also listed on page two of this inventory as part of Smith's journal.

[126] In January 1979, Clayton's Nauvoo journal was transferred from the LDS first presidency's office to church archives. During this period historians James B. Allen and Dean C. Jessee obtained permission to examine the journal, at which time they typed a 300-page, double-spaced transcript, which they have not shared with this editor. Several other scholars, including Andrew F. Ehat, at the time a graduate student at Brigham Young University, also examined the journal and compiled their own selections. One of these other researchers used his notes to corroborate Ehat's extracts within this compilation as well as to aid in identifying excluded entries. In 1981 a lay Mormon official, who worked in the same office as an associate of Ehat and with whom Ehat had shared his extracts, copied almost all of the extracts for friends without Ehat's permission. This copy, composed of eighty-eight pages of mostly single-spaced selections from the Allen-Jessee typed copy, comprised approximately one-half of the original holograph journal. The following year Modern Microfilm Company of Salt Lake City published a photo-reproduction of the copied extracts. During an unsuccessful lawsuit to enjoin their publication, the judge indicated that the extracts were not copyrightable (see *Trial Record*, 20).

[127] Lengthy selections from these three Nauvoo notebooks have been published in the following: the *History of the Church*; Ehat, "It Seems Like Heaven Began on Earth," 253–74; Ehat and Cook; Lyndon Cook, ed., *The Revelations of the Prophet Joseph Smith* (Provo, UT: Seventies' Mission Bookstore, 1981); James B. Allen, "William Clayton's Experience in Mormon Illinois," *Journal of Mormon History* 6 (1979): 37–59; Jerald and Sandra Tanner, *Clayton's Secret Writings Uncovered* (Salt Lake City: Modern Microfilm Company, 1982); and Allen, *Trials of Discipleship*.

such as Smith's bankruptcy, his borrowing and paying back money, and related subpoenas; land title disputes and the sale of land for taxes owed; temple construction; controversies about tithing; Joseph Smith's debate with a socialist lecturer and other arguments over his exercise of authority in personal and money matters; discussion of new theology, the anticipated Millennium and afterlife kingdoms; courtship, including Clayton's unsuccessful proposal of plural marriage to Sarah Ann Booth; Nauvoo social life, shared dinners, and carriage rides; the *Nauvoo Expositor* and its destruction; confrontation with Illinois troops, threatened arrests, prophecy of U.S. destruction, preparing the Nauvoo Legion for combat; hearing from Orrin Porter Rockwell of the assassination at Carthage; the threats of Mormon vigilantes, including women and the youthful "whittling and whistling brigades," against reformers in their number; the revocation of the Nauvoo Charter and feeling "cut off from the nation" comparable to the plight of the American Indians; writing history; and learning shorthand. Many of these subjects are represented in this abridgment of Clayton's journals. Furthermore, most are present in edited form in the *History of the Church*, primarily in the entries for 1843–45.

Within the time frame of the "Nauvoo, Illinois" journal is Journal 3, "Nauvoo Temple," that portion of Heber C. Kimball's diary which Clayton wrote from December 10, 1845, to January 7, 1846. This journal complements the sense of religious commitment expressed in the "Nauvoo, Illinois" journal and portrays the urgency of the Mormon departure for the West. As such, it serves as a bridge between the Latter-day Saint community in Illinois and that which the Saints would establish in the Great Salt Lake Valley.

In the 1880s significant portions of the "Nauvoo Temple" journal were published serially by Heber C. Kimball's daughter, Helen Mar Kimball Whitney, as "Scenes in Nauvoo and Incidents From Heber C. Kimball's Journal" in the *Women's Exponent* 12 (July 1, 1883), 3; 12 (September 15, 1883), 8; and 12 (October 15, 1883), 10. The Kimball journal material, including Clayton's portion, was deposited by the Kimball family with LDS archives in 1903 "until further notice." In 1982 Modern Microfilm Company of Salt Lake City published a photographic reproduction of the entire journal. Four years later Stanley B. Kimball published the Kimball portion of the journal as *On the Potter's Wheel: The Diaries of Heber C. Kimball* (Salt Lake City: Signature Books in association with Smith Research Associates, 1987). The Clayton portion of the journal is included in the present compilation. The temple record, the lists he kept of persons participating in temple ceremonies, is omitted here but may be found in the photographic publication cited above, as well as in typescripts on file with LDS archives, the Utah State Historical Society, the University of Utah Library, and the Harold B. Lee Library at Brigham Young University.

Just a few days after the last entry of Journal 2, "Nauvoo, Illinois," and a month after Journal 3, "Nauvoo Temple," Clayton began Journal 4, "Pioneer Trek West," covering the pioneer trip out of Nauvoo, Illinois, to the Great Salt Lake Valley and the return to Winter Quarters, from February 8, 1846, to October 21, 1847. Comprised of two notebooks, this detailed pioneer record was published in 1921 for the Clayton Family Association by the *Deseret News*,[128] republished in 1973 by Taylor Publishing Company of Dallas, Texas, and again in 1974 by Arno Press of New York City. The original manuscript resides in LDS archives, and the University of Utah's Marriott Library has a typescript. Again, by editorial policy, lengthy and repetitious descriptions have been abridged.

An uncharacteristic five-year gap in Clayton's known writing separates Journals 4 and 5. The original of Clayton's Journal 5, "Visit to Utah Settlements," written from April 21 to May 16, 1852, found in the back of the same three-and-three-fourths-by-five-and-three-fourths-inches volume that contains Edward Hunter's "Account Book: 1857–1897," is located in LDS archives. Typescripts are housed there and at the University of Utah's Marriott Library, the Utah State Historical Society, and the Lee Library at Brigham Young University.

With entries from August 28, 1852, to March 3, 1853, the original manuscript of the sixth journal, "Polygamy Mission to England," was published by the Clayton family in the early 1970s.

---

128 William Clayton's second son, Newel Horace Clayton, paid $500 to have the *Deseret News* print 500 copies of the "Pioneer Trek West" journal for the Clayton Family Association. Newel's son, Brigham Moroni Clayton, prepared a typescript of the journal, using a magnifying glass. After the journals were printed, Newel Clayton deposited the original handwritten notebooks with the LDS church (Thomas to Smith, August 25, 1990).

Julie Summers, a great-granddaughter of Clayton, typed an eleven-by-fourteen-inch copy to fit a "Book of Remembrance" family history binder. The original now resides at LDS archives, and copies of the family's published typescript are held by the Marriott Library at the University of Utah and the Lee Library at Brigham Young University. Clayton kept a corresponding "Camp Journal" which he sometimes used to update his own (see Journal 6, "Polygamy Mission to England," February 3, 1853). This "Camp Journal" is also located in the archives of the LDS church.

Appendix A, "Extracts from William Clayton's [Private] Book—Keys," comes through Leonard John Nuttall, who emigrated from England in 1852 and died in Salt Lake City in 1905. In 1879, the year of Clayton's death, Nuttall was appointed secretary to his father-in-law, John Taylor, who became LDS church president following Brigham Young. The year after his appointment, Nuttall wrote "Extracts from Wm. Clayton's [Private] Book—Keys," a collection of Joseph Smith's doctrinal discourses. Nuttall's manuscript is at the special collections division of BYU's Lee Library. Excerpts were published in Andrew Ehat and Lyndon Cook's edition of *The Words of Joseph*. Clayton's private book, the source of Nuttall's record, is either not extant or is sequestered.

Appendix B, "An Interesting Journal," essentially a history of the construction of the Nauvoo Temple, is located in LDS archives as "William Clayton's Journal, etc." It was published in an edited form in the *Juvenile Instructor* 21 (January 15–May 15, 1886), 2-10: 23, 47, 60-61, 79, 86, 106-107, 122-23, 141-42, 157-58.[129]

Appendix C, "William Clayton's Testimony," was recorded on February 16, 1874, in the form of a notarized statement in Salt Lake City, published in the *Deseret Evening News*, May 20, 1886. This statement was included in Andrew Jenson's "Plural Marriage," *The Historical Record* (May 1887): 224-26.

The ultimate source of much of Clayton's writings is Joseph Smith. Smith's ideas, practices, and occasionally his very words permeate Clayton's journals, which now stand as a firsthand con-

---

[129] Under the same title, "An Interesting Journal," the *Juvenile Instructor* then combined this temple history with a rewritten portion of Clayton's Journal 4, "Pioneer Trek West," January 1–April 27, 1847. See *Juvenile Instructor* 21 (June 15–October 15, 1886), 12-20: 186-87, 202-203, 230-31, 246, 258-59, 281, 290-91, 310-11. See Appendix B, "An Interesting Journal," n6.

temporary history of the Mormon community from 1840 to 1853. After Clayton's death on December 4, 1879, LDS official Joseph F. Smith memorialized his achievements as follows:

> He was a friend and companion of the Prophet Joseph Smith, and it is to his pen to a very great extent that we are indebted for the history of the Church . . . during his acquaintance with him and the time he acted for him as his private secretary, in the days of Nauvoo. We have the journals which he kept during that time, in the Historian's Office, from which — in connection with those of Elders Willard Richards and Wilford Woodruff and the Times and Seasons, a publication of the Church at that time — we have obtained the history of the Church during that period.[130]

Editorial Procedures

The primary goal of this abridged compilation of William Clayton's six journals is the faithful presentation of the records in a readable format. Careful examination and comparison of the holographic journals and of the original mansucript to Appendix A, "William Clayton's [Private] Book — Keys," have produced new renderings of some passages which differ from those of previously-published documents and collections.

In the interest of clarity for the reader, some aspects of form have been standardized. These include the format for dates at the beginning of each journal entry, which follows Clayton's month-day-year order, and for personal titles which have been spelled out and capitalized, such as Brother, Sister, Elder, and President. In particular, Clayton often referred to Mormon church founder and president Joseph Smith as "Prest J." These references now read "President Joseph." Typically Clayton abbreviated people's names. The names have been completed at their first mention in each journal and whenever, in the editor's judgment, spelling out the names enhances clarity or uniformity, such

---

[130] *Deseret Evening News*, December 9, 1879; *Journal of Discourses*, 26 vols. (London: Latter-day Saints Book Depot, 1854–86), 21:9.

as in comprehensive listings of participants of an organization. Brackets are used to indicate added letters. The ampersand (&) is uniformly rendered as "and"; the ampersand in "&c," which Clayton used consistently to indicate "etc.," remains.

Grammar and diction are presented as in the original. Capitalization is also that of Clayton's, except that the beginning letters of sentences and of personal names have been capitalized. Punctuation, or its absence (Clayton frequently omitted possessive and contractional apostrophes), is replicated from the original, but ending punctuation has been supplied to sentences. Clayton's original spelling has been generally retained, except when the correction of simple misspelling, such as that of an article, improves the readability of the passage.

Redundant material has been deleted. Abridgement within an entry is indicated by ellipses — three points for any omission, regardless whether it comes in the middle of a sentence or between sentences. Where an entire entry has been silently removed, the gap between the dates indicates abridgement. Occasional lapses in Clayton's writing are noted.

Conjectural readings are enclosed within brackets. Empty brackets [] indicate words that are missing or illegible. Editorial comments, including definitions and the location of place-names, are placed in footnote annotations.

A
William
Clayton

CHRONOLOGY

1814

July 17   Born at Charnock Moss,
               Penwortham Parish, Lancashire
               County, England, the first of four-
               teen children born to Thomas and
               Ann Clayton.

1836

October 9   Marries Ruth Moon.

1837

October 21   Baptized into Mormon church three
               months after missionaries arrive in
               England.

1838

April 1   Appointed second counselor to Brit-
               ish Mission president.

October 19   Quits clerking job at Bashall's textile
               factory and becomes a full-time mis-
               sionary for the LDS church.

1840

January 1   Begins Journal 1, "England and
               Emigration"; writes last entry on
               February 18, 1842.

	September 8	Sails, with two hundred of the second company of Mormon emigrants, from Liverpool, England, to New York City, arriving in thirty-four days on October 12.
1841	November 24	Arrives in Nauvoo, Illinois. Joins Nauvoo Riflemen
	April	Joins High Priest quorum Replaces Erastus Snow on High Council
1842	January 12	Appointed to assist Willard Richards as temple recorder and as scribe to Joseph Smith.
	February 10	Begins work as assistant to Willard Richards.
	June 29	Takes over temple books during Willard Richards's short trip to the East.
	September 3	Appointed "private clerk" to Joseph Smith, as well as temple recorder.
	September	Appointed city treasurer of Nauvoo, recorder and clerk of the Nauvoo City Council, and secretary pro tempore of the Nauvoo Municipal Lodge.
	November 27	Begins Journal 2, "Nauvoo, Illinois," which extends through January 30, 1846.
1843	March 7	Invited by Brigham Young to receive instruction in plural marriage.

	April 2	Performs plural marriage of Almera Johnson to Joseph Smith.
	April 27	Enters into plural marriage with Margaret Moon, sister to his first wife.
	May 1	Marries Lucy Walker to Joseph Smith.
	July 12	Records Joseph Smith's revelation authorizing plural marriage.
	October 19	Records first "second anointing" ceremony, which was received by Joseph and Emma Smith.
1844	January 22	Voted into the "Quorum," Joseph Smith's private prayer circle.
	March 11	Included in the formation of the Council of Fifty; next day made "Clerk of the Kingdom."
	June 10	Witnesses destruction of the *Nauvoo Expositor* printing press.
	June 28	Views the bodies of Joseph and Hyrum Smith.
	July 7	Named as temporary trustee-in-trust for the church.
	September 13	Marries third wife, Alice Hardman.
	November 20	Marries fourth wife, Jane Hardman, Alice's sister.
1845	January 9	Marries fifth wife, Diantha Farr.
	May 23	Commissioned by the Council of Twelve Apostles to document the

construction of the Nauvoo Temple.
This was later published in the
Juvenile Instructor as "An Interesting
Journal" (see Appendix B).

	November 30	Attends first meeting in Nauvoo Temple.
	December 10	Commences recording Nauvoo Temple-related activities (see Journal 3).
1846		
	January 26	Receives "second anointing" with three of his five wives.
	February 8	Begins Journal 4, "Pioneer Trek West," which he keeps until October 21, 1847.
	February 27	Leaves Nauvoo, following the first Mormon emigrants who had crossed the Mississippi River on February 4.
	April 15	Writes traditional Mormon hymn "Come, Come Ye Saints."
1847		
	April 14	Delivers Council of Fifty records to Brigham Young prior to leaving Winter Quarters for the Great Salt Lake Valley.
	April 21	Begins writing Heber C. Kimball's diary of the pioneer trip to the Great Salt Lake.
1848		Publishes *The Latter-day Saints' Emigrants' Guide.*
1849		Appointed public auditor for the provisional State of Deseret.
1850		Opens a bookshop and boarding-house for emigrants in Salt Lake City.

	October 5	Marries sixth wife, Augusta Braddock.
	December	Appointed secretary for the General Assembly of the State of Deseret.
1852		Appointed auditor and recorder of marks and brands for the newly organized Territory of Utah.
	April 21	Records expedition with Brigham Young to Fillmore, the territorial capital, and other southern Utah settlements. Account ends May 16, 1852.
	August 28	Appointed to visit England and explain plural marriage, a trip recorded in Journal 5, "Polygamy Mission to England," which he concludes on March 3, 1853.
1853	February 5	Relieved of responsibility in the British mission, as announced in this issue of *Latter-day Saints' Millennial Star*.
	February 12	Receives letter of reinstatement from mission president Samuel W. Richards.
	April 6	Sails from Liverpool on the *Camillus* to return to America.
	December 5	Granted United States citizenship.
1853-54		Elected assistant secretary of the Territorial Council of Utah.
1854-55		Elected secretary of the territorial legislature.

1855		Publishes the *Book of One Thousand Marks and Brands, Alphabetically Arranged*.
1856	November 30	Marries seventh wife, Sarah Ann Walters.
1858	December 13	Divorced from Alice Hardman.
1862		Elected alderman of Salt Lake City; re-elected two years later.
1866	October 3	Marries eighth wife, Maria Louisa Lyman, who divorces him in 1871.
1867		Becomes treasurer of Deseret Telegraph Company.
1869		Becomes secretary to just-formed Zion's Cooperative Mercantile Institute; later promoted to treasurer (cashier); resigns in 1872.
	December 19	Marries ninth wife, Elizabeth Ainsworth.
1870	December 30	Marries tenth wife, Anna Elizabeth Higgs.
1871		Divorced from Maria Louisa Lyman
1874	February 16	Defends practice of polygamy in a notarized statement.
1879	December 4	Dies, leaving four wives and thirty-three children.

The
William
Clayton

FAMILIES

A.
THE WIVES

NAME AND AGE AT MARRIAGE	DATE OF MARRIAGE	AGE OF WILLIAM CLAYTON	NUMBER OF CHILDREN
1. Ruth Moon, 18	Oct 9, 1836	22	10
2. Margaret Moon, 23	Apr 27, 1843	28	6
3. Alice Hardman, 28	Sep 13, 1844	30	4
4. Jane Hardman, 39	Nov 20, 1844	30	0
5. Diantha Farr, 16	Jan 9, 1845	30	3
6. Augusta Braddock, 16	Oct 5, 1850	36	8
7. Sarah Ann Walters, 18	Nov 30, 1856	42	11
8. Maria Louise Lyman, 17	Oct 3, 1866	52	1
9. Elizabeth Ainsworth, 45	Dec 19, 1864	55	0
10. Anna Elizabeth Higgs, 17	Dec 30, 1870	56	4

B.
THE CHILDREN

NAME	DATE OF BIRTH	MOTHER
1. Sarah Lucretia	Aug 1, 1837	Ruth Moon
2. Margaret Normandy	Apr 25, 1839	Ruth Moon
3. Henrietta Lucretia	May 6, 1841	Ruth Moon
4. William Heber	Feb 28, 1843	Ruth Moon
5. Daniel Adelbert	Feb 18, 1844	Margaret Moon
6. Vilate Ruth	Dec 8, 1844	Ruth Moon
7. William Adriel Benoni	Mar 30, 1846	Diantha Farr
8. Joseph Thomas	Jan 10, 1847	Margaret Moon
9. Newell Horace	Jan 12, 1847	Ruth Moon
10. Olive Diantha	Aug 7, 1848	Diantha Farr
11. Lydia Arabelle	Mar 28, 1849	Margaret Moon
12. David Hyrum	Sep 17, 1849	Ruth Moon
13. Rachel Amelia	Aug 18, 1850	Diantha Farr
14. James Leroy	Jun 8, 1852	Margaret Moon
15. Clara Agnes	Aug 5, 1852	Alice Hardman
16. Lydia Ann	Nov 22, 1852	Ruth Moon
17. Walter Alfred	Apr 1, 1853	Augusta Braddock
18. Algena Moon	Nov 21, 1854	Ruth Moon
19. Isabella Alice	Dec 16, 1854	Alice Hardman
20. Lovinia Tercilla	Dec 17, 1854	Margaret Moon
21. Nephi Willard	Oct 8, 1855	Augusta Braddock
22. Moses	Jan 15, 1857	Alice Hardman
23. Aaron	Jan 15, 1857	Alice Hardman
24. Brigham John	Mar 15, 1857	Ruth Moon
25. Don Carlos	Oct 31, 1857	Margaret Moon
26. Daniel John	Dec 29, 1857	Augusta Braddock
27. Archer Walters	Apr 10, 1858	Sarah Ann Walters
28. Athalia Rose	Mar 10, 1860	Sarah Ann Walters
29. Mary Adelaide	Mar 14, 1862	Sarah Ann Walters
30. Albert Cassius	Jul 3, 1862	Augusta Braddock
31. Harriet Lilly	Dec 19, 1863	Sarah Ann Walters
32. Carrie Gladys	Feb 2, 1865	Augusta Braddock

33. Julia	Jan 12, 1866	Sarah Ann Walters
34. Victoria Helena	Jan 24, 1867	Sarah Ann Walters
35. Isaac Ambrose	May 3, 1867	Augusta Braddock
36. Charles William	Feb 19, 1869	Sarah Ann Walters
37. Amasa Marion	Aug 12, 1869	Maria Louisa Lyman
38. Annie Matilda	Sep 11, 1869	Augusta Braddock
39. Rose Read	Nov 22, 1870	Augusta Braddock
40. Sarah Walters	Jun 9, 1871	Sarah Ann Walters
41. William	Sep 26, 1871	Anna Elizabeth Higgs
42. Lucy Loretta	Aug 23, 1874	Sarah Ann Walters
43. Thomas Higgs	Sep 11, 1874	Anna Elizabeth Higgs
44. Levi Murdock	Aug 14, 1876	Anna Elizabeth Higgs
45. Alma Carlos	Oct 8, 1877	Sarah Ann Walters
46. Helaman	May [?], 1878	Anna Elizabeth Higgs
47. Irene	Dec 23, 1879	Sarah Ann Walters

C.
MARRIAGE AND CHILDBEARING YEARS

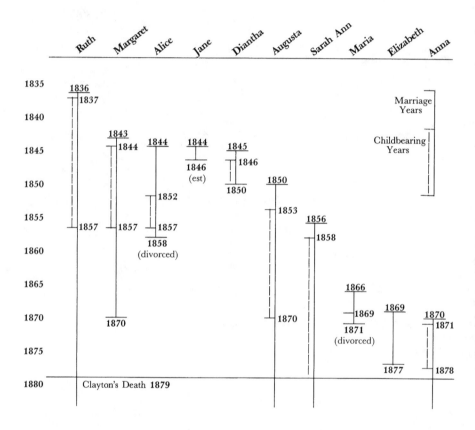

William Clayton practiced plural marriage from 1843 to 1879. Although he married a total of ten women, he typically had four or five wives at one time, except for parts of 1869, 1870, and 1871, when he had six. In 1857, Clayton fathered five children. Three of the mothers, who were his first three wives, bore him no more after that. Forty-seven children were born to Clayton during his forty-three years of marriage. His last child, Irene, was born nineteen days after Clayton died at the age of sixty-five.

PHOTOGRAPHS

and

MAPS

Penwortham, England, 1855, viewed from Preston across the River Ribble, about a mile downstream from a shallow area where the 1837 baptisms were performed. (Courtesy Harris Library, Preston, with special assistance of Terry Shaw; from Charles Hardwick, History of Preston *[Preston: Worthington & Co., 1857].) Ptolemy, a geographer in the second century, knew of the River Ribble by the name Belisama, apparently a Phoenician word for "the Moon" or "Goddess of Heaven." The Saxons contributed "Rhe," a prefix meaning river. Eventually Rhe Belisama became Ribble (Stephen Sartin,* The People and Places of Historic Preston *[Preston: Carnegie Press, 1988], 58).*

Preston Marketplace, site of early Mormon missionary meetings in England. (Engraving by John Ferguson, 1844.)

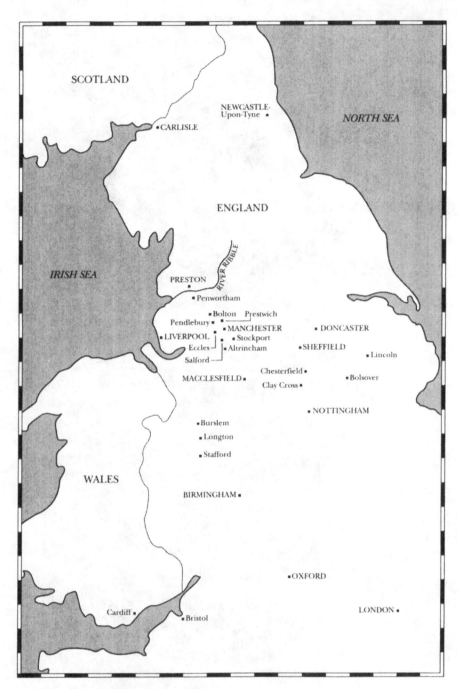

The English Mission of William Clayton.

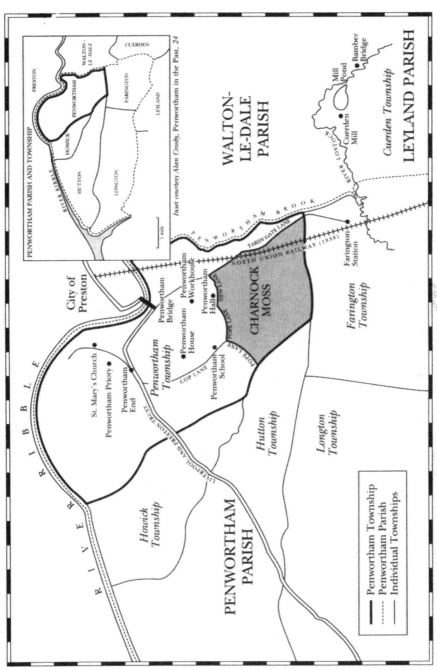

Penwortham area, ca. 1840. Penwortham Parish comprised five townships: Penwortham (which included Charnock Moss where Clayton was born and St. Mary's Church where he was married to Ruth Moon); Farington (where Clayton lived from the age of five and where his father taught school); Longton, Hutton, and Howick. Within adjacent parishes were Cuerden Township near Bamber Bridge (where Clayton apparently worked in a textile mill) and the city of Preston (named Priest-town in the tenth century) north of the River Ribble. (Research by Janet Visick)

*Old Cock Pit in Preston,
England, drawn and etched
by C. E. Shaw, 1882 (from
A. Hewitson,* History of
Preston, *1883), site of early
conferences of the LDS British
Mission.*

MARRIAGES solemnized in the Parish of ....
in the County of *Lancaster* .... in the Year 18*36*

William Clayton .... of *this* Parish
and .. *Ruth Moon* .... of *this* Parish
were married in this *Church* by *Banns*
with Consent of
this *month*
Day of
October in the Year one Thousand eight Hundred and *thirty six*.
By me. *W. Harrison Curate*
This Marriage was } *William Clayton*
solemnized between us { *Ruth Moon's X mark*
In the Presence of { *Wm. Wignall*
Margaret Moon's X mark
No. *684*

*Copy of the marriage certificate of William Clayton and Ruth Moon. Note
"banns" (notice of intention to marry read publicly at church), with X
marks of Ruth Moon and witness Margaret Moon. (Obtained by Janet
Visick; courtesy Lancashire County Records Office, Preston, England.)*

St. Mary's Church in Penwortham, England, where William Clayton and Ruth Moon were married on October 9, 1836. (Photograph by Nigel Morgan, Preston, 1991.)

Ruth Moon Clayton

Margaret Moon Clayton

Alice Hardman Clayton

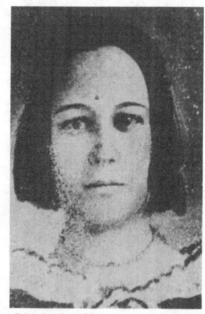

Diantha Farr Clayton

Augusta Braddock Clayton

Sarah Ann Walters Clayton

Maria Louisa Lyman Clayton

Anna Elizabeth Higgs Clayton

Nauvoo, Illinois, with Mormon temple on the horizon. (Daguerreotype, circa 1846; courtesy LDS photo archives.)

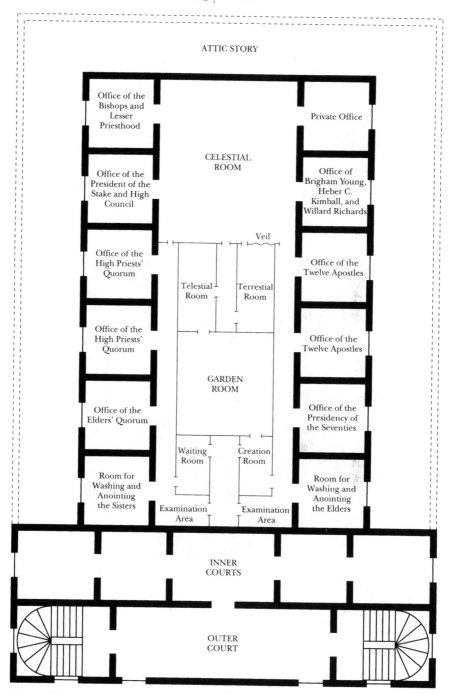

ATTIC STORY

Office of the Bishops and Lesser Priesthood

Private Office

CELESTIAL ROOM

Office of the President of the Stake and High Council

Office of Brigham Young, Heber C. Kimball, and Willard Richards

Veil

Office of the High Priests' Quorum

Office of the Twelve Apostles

Telestial Room

Terrestial Room

Office of the High Priests' Quorum

Office of the Twelve Apostles

GARDEN ROOM

Office of the Elders' Quorum

Office of the Presidency of the Seventies

Waiting Room

Creation Room

Room for Washing and Anointing the Sisters

Room for Washing and Anointing the Elders

Examination Area

Examination Area

INNER COURTS

OUTER COURT

Nauvoo Temple, interior design of top or attic floor.

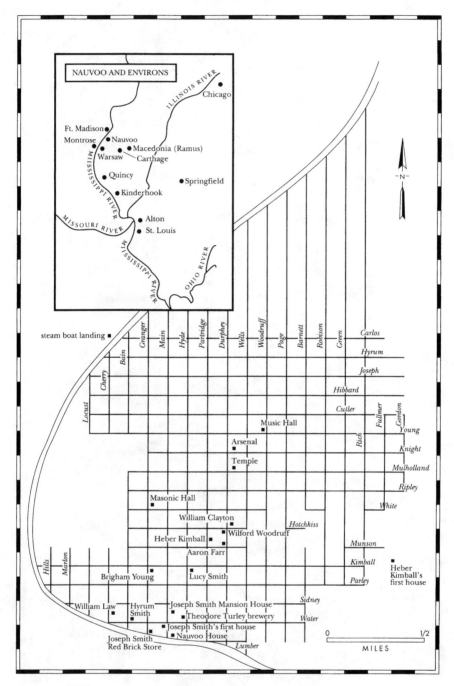

Nauvoo, Illinois, street map and environs (inset), circa 1844

Joseph Smith, the Mormon prophet, from a painting by Majors. (Courtesy LDS photo archives.)

Emma Hale Smith, wife of Joseph Smith. (Courtesy LDS photo archives.)

SUPER HANC PETRAM ÆDIFICABO.

FOR PRESIDENT,
GEN. JOSEPH SMITH
OF NAUVOO, ILLINOIS.
FOR VICE PRESIDENT,
SIDNEY RIGDON,
OF PENNSYLVANIA.

Broadside of Joseph Smith's U.S. presidential candidacy in 1844. (Courtesy LDS photo archives.)

The carved sunstone, originally a capitol of one of the pilasters of the Nauvoo Temple, erected in 1841.

The Mormon Trail Across the Prairies of Iowa from Nauvoo, Illinois.

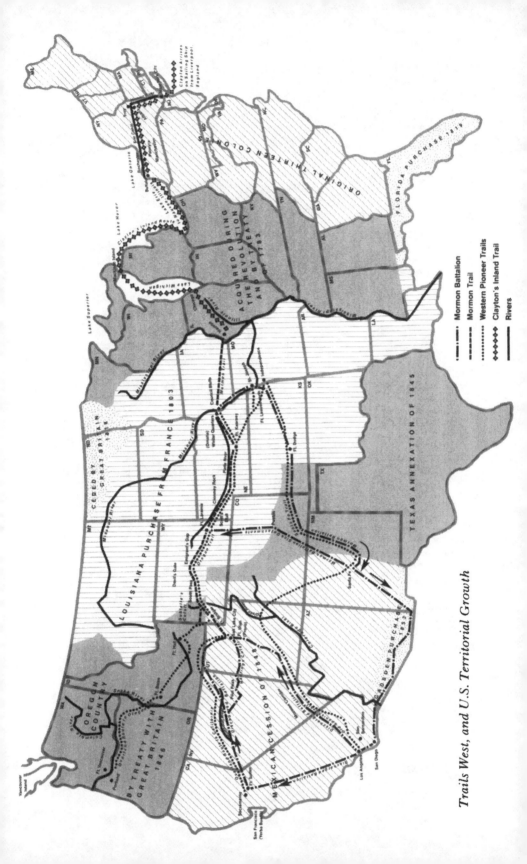

Trails West, and U.S. Territorial Growth

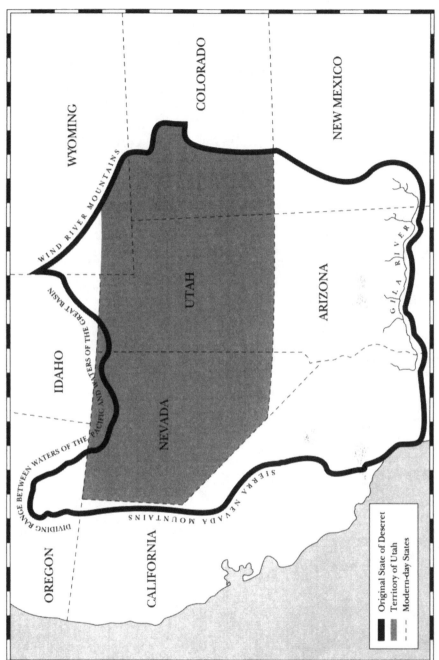

State of Deseret, 1849-51, and Territory of Utah.

"The New Wife," an engraving appearing in Frank Leslie's Illustrated Newspaper, circa 1880.

Brigham Young, daguerreotype, circa 1851. (Courtesy LDS photo archives.)

Salt Lake City, Main Street, looking northeast. (Photograph by C. R. Savage, circa 1865; courtesy LDS photo archives.)

Salt Lake City, Main Street, looking southwest. (Photograph by C. R. Savage, circa 1865; courtesy LDS photo archives.)

Sarah Ann Walters Clayton with Lily Clayton and Victoria Clayton (infant). (Courtesy LDS photo archives.)

Pioneer house of Sarah Ann Walters and William Clayton. (Courtesy LDS photo archives.)

Maria Louisa Lyman and William Clayton. (Courtesy of LDS photo archives.)

I feel determined to do all
I can to keep a journal of this expedition
which will be interesting to my children in after
days and perhaps to many of the Saints.

WILLIAM CLAYTON
May 24, 1847

The
DOCUMENTS

1840-1842

An *early convert to Mormonism in England, William Clayton records his missionary activities, his sea voyage to America, and his eventual resettlement in Nauvoo, Illinois. In Nauvoo Clayton meets the Mormon prophet Joseph Smith and becomes his private clerk.*

[January 1, 1840. Wednesday.][1] Brother James Lea from Bedford has called in at T[homas] Miller's and I have been with him to see his wife and children. One child is sick. He states that they left Bedford on the 22nd June on [account] of his master wanting him to go to Leicester at about two hours notice, to keep open a Inn until his master could let it. After being there some time, his wife came to him and they remained at the Inn untill December when he determined to leave because he thought his master[2] was trying to keep him there and he was loosing ground

---

[1] Two years after his conversion, the twenty-five-year-old missionary-diarist began the first of at least six journals. Clayton writes here in the large factory town of Manchester, England, where he served in the Mormon British Mission as second counselor; Joseph Fielding was mission president and Willard Richards was first counselor.

[2] Employer.

almost daily. He wanted to be amongst the saints. He states that when he entered the Inn it was merely as steward hence the Liquors &c was not judged and he did not know anything about untill he sent his master word that he would leave. Then his master brought in a heavy Bill against him which involved him in great difficulty. He was obliged to sacrifice his goods to get to Manchester. They both seem very humble. He acknowledges having been unfaithful.

[January 2, 1840. Thursday.] Bro[ther] [Joseph] Jackson acknowledges to having told a many things to a brother from Stockport[3] which he ought not. He says he will do so no more. Brother Jackson says that Brothers [William] Broome and [Thomas] Bateman are about £46[4] in debt which was contracted at the time of the community. The house is 150 debt. They have tried to sell it but cannot. Broome is likely to have the Bailiffs and wants Ann Criskersley to go and live with him. I have the house in her name. Ann is since gone. He did not ask our council at all.

[January 3, 1840. Friday.] Sister Mary Powell acknowledges to having said to Sister Walker, "John and I am one." At the same time she had a ring on her finger. She told Sister [Jane] Rigby she was not married. She [is] determined to be married. She knows it is of God. If we attempt to hinder we shall deny her. She says we want to forbid to marry and she has not a good spirit.

[January 4, 1840. Saturday.] Brother [Joseph] F[ielding] and I have been with [Sarah] Isherwood to her mothers and learn as follows. That Sarah and her sister has been disagreeable with each other. Sarah has been impudent and saucy with her mother. Has cleaned her shoes on the Sunday. Would not help to do any thing for her mother. She was out late at nights &c. We had a talk with her sister and bro[ther] in law. They both manifest a very

---

[3] Stockport is a town in Cheshire, six miles southeast of Manchester. Situated on the Mersey River, it is the site of an 1,800-foot long railroad viaduct built over the valley in the early nineteenth century. Identification of this town and other geographical references are taken from *Columbia Lippincott Gazetteer of the World*, ed. Leon E. Seltzer (New York: Columbia University Press, 1952).

[4] In the nineteenth century a British pound was valued at about $5.00 and, considering inflation from 1840 to 1991, would be worth about $20.00 today. The current pound is valued at about $2.00.

bitter spirit and we have reason to believe they are more to blame than Sarah although she is much to blame. She promises to do better.

[January 10, 1840. Friday.] Brother F[ielding] and I went to Stockport to enquire respecting Brother [Samuel] Heath. Found that Brother [Nye] had told them we should not come till Saturday under mistake. We saw a few of the saints and found much bad feeling against Brother Heath. My [feet] was sore when we got to [Elizabeth] Princes at []. Went to see Mr. Stowell. Found him full of frayed lies, a good deal of ignorance &c. [].

[January 13, 1840. Monday.] Have been with Sister [Sarah] Perkins this P.M. at Millers. After took supper at T. Millers. Sarah Crooks is grieved at S[arah] Perkins being hurt at a little thing. Sarah Crooks gave me 20/-10[5] of her own, 5 Rebekas and 5 Betsy Crooks, towards new trousers. I felt an object to taking it because they have given me considerable before this. Sarah was grieved because I objected and said if I did not take it I must speak to her no more. She seemed grieved.

[January 14, 1840. Tuesday.] This A.M. we received a letter from Brother [Willard] Richards stating the arrival of Brothers [John] Taylor, [Apostle Wilford] Woodruff, and [Theodore] Turl[e]y requesting Brother F[ielding] to go. We concluded to send Brother Clark. He went by Railway.

[January 15, 1840. Wednesday.] Received another letter from Brother Richards requesting Brother F. to go to Preston[6] and a letter from Brother David [Clayton's][7] wife stating she was sick and the youngest child. Brother David went off to Preston immediately and I wrote a letter to my wife and another to Sister Morgan.

---

[5] 20 shillings, 10 pence. A British pound was composed of twenty shillings, each of which contained twelve pence (plural for penny). Since 1971, "new" pence have been issued at a value of 100 to a pound, five to a shilling. There are still twenty shillings to a pound.

[6] The major port city on the River Ribble, twenty-eight miles northwest of Manchester, Preston was the site of Lancashire's first cotton mill built in 1791. It was also the birthplace of Richard Arkwright, known as the inventor of the spinning machine, whose story Clayton tells on February 24, 1853.

[7] Twenty-one-year-old David was one of William Clayton's thirteen younger siblings.

[January 16, 1840. Thursday.] Went with Brother F[ielding] to Bolton railway from thence to T. Millers to dinner. Attended books at meeting at night. Bought cloth for trousers [].

[January 17, 1840. Friday.] Was called up this A.M. at 3 oclock to Sister [Ann] Lea. I found her very ill, insensible. Prayed with her and she appeared better. Sent a letter to F[ielding] and R[ichards]. Went to see Brother [] Heath. Did not get to talk to him. Came back to Sister Lea. Found her worse. Stayed with her untill 1/2 p[as]t 7. Left her a little better. Went to council meeting. Brothers Miller and [Thomas] Green took Brother [Henry] Royle to Dukinfield.[8] Agreed that Sister [Sarah] Duckworth should go to Brother Jacksons for 2 weeks[9] and after meeting had talk with Brothers Heath and Featherstone respecting money which had been collected at Manchester for Joseph Millwood during his illness. There was 18/-[10] collected which Brother Green gave to Brother Heath who sent 13/-, to Jane [Millwood] and gave 3/- to Featherstone but did not give the other 2/- to Jane [which] has caused [].

[January 18, 1840. Saturday.] Had conversation with Brother Heath who says as follows. That once he drank a little wine which was for Joseph [] and several other things. The statements made by Brothers Heath and Featherstone was very contradictory. I told him he had better remain at M[anchester] untill I had wrote to my brethren. I received a letter from my brethren and wrote them another back. Went to Railway and met Brothers Clark, Woodruff and Turl[e]y. I rejoice to see them. Brought them to old Sister Hardmans.[11] Went to see Sister Lea and found her quite insensible. Brother Woodruff prayed and rebuked the fowl spirits. We anointed her head and gave her some oil inwardly. I then prayed and rebuked the pain. After washing her forehead with rum she appeared better and we left her. We [then went to]

---

[8] A cotton milling town on the Tame River, seven miles east of Manchester.

[9] Sarah Duckworth lodged with Joseph and Ann Jackson for only one week because Ann found her an imposition (see January 23, 24).

[10] 18 shillings, about $4.50.

[11] Clayton had converted the Hardmans and stayed in their Manchester boardinghouse. The two Hardman cousins, Jane and Alice, later became Clayton's plural wives in Nauvoo, Illinois.

Sister Perkins who had met with an accident by a fall. We prayed with her. Returned to T. Millers where we took supper.

[January 19, 1840. Sunday.] Brother Turley spoke this A.M. I spoke a little after. The wicked spirit seemed to disturb David Crooks. I led this afternoon meeting and spoke on the necessity of the Saints dealing honestly with each other and showed the order of the church with regard to cases of poverty. I also introduced Brother [James] Lea to the church who forgave him his transgression and offered him the right hand of fellowship. Brother Woodruff spoke after. Prayed with a number of sick and confirmed Jane Millwood. Elizabeth Mills manifested a bad spirit. I talked to her and she appears better. Brother Woodruff preached at night. Full house. He spoke plain. Good effect []. Distributed timely warnings[12] and prayed [with] many sick. Went to Brother [] Burgess and told him plainly about tale bearing &c. Prayed with child and blest his family. There has been several dreams in the church concerning my wife during the last 10 days. First I dreamt I was in the middle of a garden full of ripe fruit and after bringing some home was going out again and my wife run up a hill before me and vanished out of my sight. Another night I dreamed that I was at Hodsons, Penwortham, amongst ripe gooseberrys as above. I felt like a single or unmarried person. Sister Dewsnup dreamed that she saw me at Hardmans with one child in great trouble and the child was crying for bread. I asked her to get it something to eat. While I went somewhere Sarah Crooks dreamed that one of the American brethren was talking and joking me about having a second wife and Sarah joked &c. She thought I had then a second wife.[13] Sister C. [] says today she dreamed that I was [stopped] in the greatest trouble. My wife was either dead or near to dying

---

[12] *Timely Warnings* was a tract written by Orson Hyde. See Joseph Smith, Jr., et al., *History of the Church of Jesus Christ of Latter-day Saints*, ed. B. H. Roberts, 2d ed. rev., 7 vols. (Salt Lake City: Deseret Book, 1963), 2:495, hereafter *HC*.

[13] The dreams reflect Clayton's personal concerns. Back in October 1838, when Clayton quit his job in Bashall's factory to work for the British Mission full time, he left his twenty-one-year-old pregnant wife and year-old daughter with his mother-in-law while he boarded in Manchester for two years. This working separation put him in the position of a single man, and he was often in the company of Sarah Crooks and several other young women who were recent converts to the church. Clayton's feelings for Sarah Crooks continued to concern him. See his entry for February 27, 1840.

and I had one child with me. Sister Jones dreamed same as Sister Dewsnup.

[January 20, 1840. Monday.] Br[eakfast] at T. Millers. Dinner at Sands and tea. Wrote a letter to Burslem. Sup[per] at T. Millers. Have prayed with 8 sick today. Have been much gratified with the brethrens conversations. S. Green gave me 2/- towards brethrens coach fare. Last week Sister Bewsher gave me new drawers. Have had a little talk with Brother Berry on teetot[alers].[14]

[January 21, 1840. Tuesday.] Breakfast at Princes. Got a letter from Brothers F[ielding] and R[ichards] and answered it. A letter also from Brother Moon[15] at Walkers. Have been with the brethren to see them off per coach. Have had some conversations with Brother Berry upon the duty of the officers. Brother Woodruff laid hands on my head and spoke to this effect. Dear Brother Wm. I lay my hands upon thy head. [Six illegible lines.] Brother, thou art of the blood of Ephraim. Thou art one of the house of Joseph.[16] Thou art one of those who will stand upon the mount Zion with the 144,000. God shall give thee great wisdom. He shall make thee a wise councillor to council the saints of God. Thy life has been hid up with Christ in God and thou hast known it not, and I seal thee up with eternal life and while thou remainst faithful no power shall prevail against thee nor be able to take thy life. The Lord shall yet give thee many souls in Manchester over whom thou shall preside. God seal these blessings. &c &c &c. Took cocoa at Brother John Smiths after I had some conversation with Brother Arthur [Smith] the Deacon. I could get no satisfaction from him. He told me he had not partook of the sacrement and he was brought before the council Nov. 22. He stated that it

---

[14] The Teetotal (T for Total abstinence from alcohol) pledge, said to begin in Preston in 1832, was also found in New York (Stephen Sartin, *The People and Places of Historic Preston* [Preston: Carnegie Press, 1988], 73; *Brewer's Dictionary of Phrase and Fable* [New York: Harper and Row, 1959]).

[15] Clayton's wife Ruth was the oldest daughter of Thomas and Lydia Moon (Rose Marie Hart Clayton, "History of Ruth Moon Clayton," January 13, 1972, Marriott Library, University of Utah, Salt Lake City, Utah).

[16] Mormons place themselves within the Jewish tradition of "the chosen people" through lineage, or adoption into the house of Joseph through the tribe of Ephraim, one of Joseph's sons. Here Woodruff gives Clayton a "patriarchal blessing" which anticipates Clayton's fruitful service to the church.

had been told by some of the Elders to the members that his project for marriage was from hell.[17] And if it was he was determined it should return. But he would wait untill God showed him &c. I showed him that the Lord designed his servants to council in such cases but he said he should not look to man. He should look to God. He had seen enough of men. I said every soul must be subject to the higher powers. He said he should be subject to God and when God showed him that he had done wrong he would repent. I asked if Paul said so when he said let every soul be subject &c. He answered Paul said something else. He said men would rise up forbidding to marry and commanding to abstain from meats &c. I said we did not forbid to marry but the scriptures forbid to commit adultery and forbid us to covet our neighbours wife &c. I told him I had heard he was about to be [married]. He answered he had not said so. I told him I was informed it was known at [All] Saints Church. He said [] would not marry him. He said he should not partake anymore until God had shown him &c. I told him I could not see that we should be justified in suffering him to remain in office while he did so. He said I might take the office if I thought proper. He would not give it up untill required. Here expressed his union with the saints and his love [toward] the officers &c. But would tell me nothing conclusive with regard to his reasons or []. He said he could see a good deal. There was so much partiality in the church &c. He believed the gospel. He had no condemnation and if God showed him that he did wrong he would repent. After several other similar things passing I left him. He seems to manifest a kind of stubborness and insubordination. We came back to Hardmans. I wrote a letter to S[arah] Crooks and gave it to her. There was several of the Sisters present. Went after taking s[upper] to Crooks St. to sleep. Found them in bed. Prayed with sick.

[January 22, 1840. Wednesday.] Breakfast at Brother [] Wests. Seems comfortable. Desired Brother Davis to tell his class to pray for a revival &c. Dinner at Brother [James] Bewsher. Sarah Duck-

---

[17] Smith proposed to marry Betsy Holden, whose husband was missing-in-action in India, possibly still alive. Britain invaded Afghanistan in 1839 to secure its borders from Russia which threatened Britain's empire in India.

worth came and said Brother Jacksons wife told her she must seek lodgings &c. I have talked to her about being clean and submissive and to try to get something to do. Sister Bewsher says she can lodge with her a little while. We went to see Sister [Mary] Gill and found her about as usual. We administered sacrement. Took cocoa at Bewshers and came to see Sister Dewsnup. Found her some better. Went to see Brother [Thomas] Booth and told him concerning an accusation brought against him by Brother [] Jackson. He had borrowed 1/- from Brother Broome and promised to pay it back in a given time but had not done according to promise. Brother [Thomas] Owens had given him a suit of Cloths and he had pawned the coat and told a falsehood about it. He does not deny. There seems great grievance between him and his wife. Both are guilty. I spoke plainly to both of them shewing the consequence of their conduct and told them we should expect to see different conduct manifested for the future and should watch them more narrowly than we had done. Went to meeting at Grundys. But few attended. Supper at Sister Hardman's.

[January 23, 1840. Thursday.] Breakfast at John Hardmans. Received a letter from Brother Richards and answered it. Sent one also to my wife and writ one for Mary Hardman to Nottingham.[18] Sister Mary Hardman has dreamed about seeing my wife with her hair down upon her back all in disorder. She seemed in distress and was come to Manchester to seek me but I was gone to Burslem. No children with her. Took C[19] at Brother [William] Broomes. Find them comfortable. Went to Brother [Joseph] Jacksons to preach. About 9 stayed. I preached above 1 hour and Brother Clarke near 1 hour. Good attention. Some seemed affected. Gave out for another meeting. Saw Sister [Ann] Jackson after meeting. Seemed to have a bad feeling. Quite bitter against Sarah [Duckworth]. Is determined not to have her only tonight. I felt it would be best to say little to her. I think kindness will do best. She had given Sarah 1/6 which had been given for her. I talked to Brother Jackson about driving his wife and cautioned him not to do so. Brother Jackson has lent [] Stowell the Book of

---

18 Nottingham was the site of textile milling and lace making; according to legend, it was also the birthplace of Robin Hood.

19 Clayton sometimes uses the initial C to refer to cocoa or coffee.

Mormon. I told him he should not have done so.[20] He said he was sorry. Sister Whiss sick. Took Supper at Jacksons and returned.

[January 24, 1840. Friday.] Brother Heath has called this A.M. and I have told him our feelings about him and that we totally disapprove of his conduct in some instances. I told him the only way to make things right was to shew better conduct in future. He is going with Brother Clarke tomorrow to Peover and from there he will go to Southwick. Brother Bateman has come in and says he has given his watch for P[aul] Harris' debt and he owes £4 for Choutler. He has paid £2 and the man wants the other. He has heard about some work about 17 miles from Manchester and wants to know if it will be wisdom to go. He can get little to do here and I can hardly say nay. I feel on account of his office. He states that Sarah Duckworth has been telling the saints about Brother Jackson and wife and is causing trouble. Took breakfast at Sister Hardman's house. Sent a letter yesterday to Brother Richards. I have received a letter from Brother Woodruff and he states they got to B[urslem] at 1/2 past 9 after a cold windy ride. Gives a good account of the saints there. They have baptized 22 since I was there about 1 month since. Have writ a letter to Sister Dewsnup. D[inner] at Walker's. Brother [John] Walker is much troubled about his situation in work. Called at Brother Paul [Harris's]. Find him much grieved at Brother Jacksons conduct. It seems Brother Jackson has spoken false concerning him. He (Paul) still says that he put nothing in the wine after I had reproved him. He has only little work. But seems humble &c. Called at Sister M[ary] Ann Johnsons. Found her comfortable but very poor. Will try to do something for her. Called at Sister Whiss's. Find her better. Eliz[abeth] poorly. Took cocoa with Eliza. But I would rather not because they have it not to spare. If we did not Eliza would be grieved. Went to Sister Wm. Millers and saw Sister [Sarah] Perkins. All pretty comfortable. Came to T. Millers and writ 2 letters, 1 to Burslem and 1 to Brother Jackson. Sister Dewsnup came in, in deep trouble and Mary Wood says things are more comfortable at home. Took supper and came to Mother

---

[20] On January 10, Clayton found Stowell "full of frayed lies, a good deal of ignorance, &c." Perhaps this is Clayton's reason not to lend him the Mormon scripture.

Hardmans. Have heard that E[lizabeth] Clayton sent for us at 8 [1/2] oclock. Prayed with 4 sick.

[January 25, 1840. Saturday.] Went to Brother Jasners to breakfast. Brothers Clark and Heath are gone to Peover. To John Hardman's for dinner. R[obert Williams] is very sick. John tells me of something remarkable which took place yesteday viz. He has during the week had fears respecting Roberts Honesty and instead of leaving his waistcoat with silver in carelessly hung on a chair he has been impressed to conceal on account of suspicion. Yesterday afternoon John and Brother Lea was set together in the house and Brother Lea expressed his fears to John but they seemed stronger fully than John's. Whilst they were talking on the subject Mary [Hardman] came in and wanted to know what they were talking about. They would not tell her but she said she knew they were talking about Robert. She had the same feeling with them but fully stronger. Soon after Sister Lea who had been busy upstairs came down and expressed herself precisely the same not knowing that they had said anything about it. She had looked round the room to see if there was anything he could take and she knew not why she felt so. She did not like it. But after all her striving against it, it still followed her. John says that R[obert]'s conduct has been very different these last few days. He seems hasty and undependable. There had not a word been said with regard to suspicion untill the above circumstances took place. Took C. with Brother Clayton. I have had Brother Paul [Harris] and [Joseph] Jackson together. Find them both faulty. J[ackson] told me on Thursday night that P[aul] told him that I had told P[aul] all that passed at the council respecting him Friday before. P. says he never told him anything about it. They contradicted each other and both was positive that they were correct. J. threatened in my presence he would bring P. before the church for telling a lie. J. owned to having stated several things about P. before 2 or 3 of the members in such a manner as to hurt his character. Such as he had lost 3 or 4 pound by P. and had given him 6/6 towards leather for new shoes and P. had spent the money. I ascertained with regard to this that J. had given P. 6/6 to buy leather and at the time said that P. might spend 1/- for bread, he having neither money nor bread at the time. While P. had the money Jane [Harris] was brought to bed and having nothing to subsist on spent the money intending to make the shoes as soon as possible. P. has now got the leather and begun to make the shoes. Brother Jackson also acknowledged to having said to the leather cutter to the effect that he was afraid he would not get his shoes which caused the leather cutter to say to Sister Davies one of your L[atter] D[ay] Saints has turned L D Sinner. Jackson accused P. of being idle when at the shop. Paul says he went to bed once in the day time that he recollects. May have been more than once. He had to rise about from 2 1/2 to 4 oclock in the morning and keep the shop open until 11 at night. J. did not contradict this but still seemed to think he should not have gone to bed in the day time. Brother J. manifested a bad spirit some part of the time. I told him so. Then charged him with having said to P. he was determined P. should have nothing to do with the office of teacher and that it if came before the church he would raise his hand against him. I showed J. that he could not prevent P. having his office again but said he was determined &c and said he would bring P. before the church. I told him I should stop him. There was then something said between them about the money and after some conversation they mutually agreed that P. should give 10/- besides paying for a load of coals. I then asked them if they would both agree to forgive each other and be friendly with each other and never speak of these things again. They both said yes and so did Sister Jane. I then told them if ever I heard either of them having said anything about these things I should consider them guilty. We then parted on good terms. Went from there to Brother Greens. Found them troubled about the pox. I prayed with Brother G[reen] and wife and H[enry] Royle and felt to rebuke the disease in the name of the Lord. Brother G[reen] says that E[llen] Battersby went to the Doctor last night. I should have said that I had conversation with Brother Jackson after this and showed him he had been transgressing &c and cautioned him to mind. Took Supper at Sister Hardmans. She saw several of the sisters. Saw E[lizabeth] Gladson. Had no conversation with her.

[January 26, 1840. Sunday.] Took Breakfast at Hardmans. Preached from Daniel 2 dream. Spoke about 1 1/4 hour. Went to Bewshers to Dinner. Brother Green has told me something about S[arah] Duckworth not pleasant. Received a letter from my wife, another from Brother R[ichards]. Brothers Green and Berry spoke some time this P.M. Brother Berry speaks too much about his own works and other sects. I confirmed 2 gone to be baptized by Brother Berry. Spoke to the saints about being faithful and praying [eight illegible lines].

Sarah [Crooks] and Rebecca [Partington] brought cocoa to the services for me. I was much grieved at the church for being talking and confused just before meeting time. Preached about 1 1/4 hour on the Kingdom and baptism. Prayed with 4 sick. Brother Wm. Whitehead gave me 6 pence and Sarah Crooks gave me 1/- towards postage besides 2 oranges and some raisins. Sister Dewsnup very low. Took supper at Sister Hardman's.

[January 27, 1840. Monday.] Took Breakfast at Hardman's. Brother Lea wants me to write a note for a situation and as soon as I had wrote it Brother Berry came and said he was wanted at the shop where Brother [William] Garner works. So he went and was engaged. Went to see Brother [Joseph] West sick. Took dinner at T. Millers. Went to see Brother [Peter] Mottram and told him about manifesting a bad spirit during singing in service and also different reports which I had heard concerning him. His wife says she will be baptized as soon as her eye gets better. Is blind under Doctors hands. Been at Hart Street meeting. Spoke freely and felt well. Saints seemed affected. After meeting Brother Green proposed subscription for Sarah Duckworth and Brother Arthur [Smith] got up before the members and opposed him. Apparently in bad spirit. I talked a little to Sarah about her conduct. Prayed with Susan [Miller] at T. Millers. Susannah says she will be more diligent. Supper with Sister Battersby. She fetched 1 pint porter.[21]

[January 28, 1840. Tuesday.] Received a long letter from Brother [John] Taylor, Liverpool.[22] Answered it and sent one to Preston to Brother R[ichards]. Got 2 letters from Bedford concerning Brother Lea. Took Dinner at Wm. Millers &c. Spoke to Brother Berry about talking against the sectarians. Saw Sister Elizabeth in a very bad state []. Have been to see Sister Mary

[21] Abbreviation of "porter's ale," dark brown beer resembling a light stout and made from charred or browned malt.
[22] Located 180 miles northwest of London near the mouth of the Mersey River, Liverpool was the site of the first wet dock in Britain and a great industrial port city.

Becket is working till near 9 oclock. John Wytch married today. He nor she have said nothing to me about it as to when &c. Joked a great deal with []. Supper at Sister Hardmans []. Brother Berry came [] with me.

[January 29, 1840. Wednesday.] Spoke to Brother Berry this A.M. about being to rash in his preaching, speaking of the sects &c. Took Breakfast at Hardman's. 1 letter from Alston, 1 from Brother [John] Moon. Took dinner at Bewshers. Sent the Alston letter to Liverpool. Went to meet Brother Clark. He did not come. Preached first time at John Hardmans. About 5 strangers. Went from thence to see Sister Margaret Jones sick. Saw Sister S[arah] Perkins. She says Elizabeth Booth told her that Mary Powell and the Elders are abominable liars. Took Supper with Sarah Crooks. She is troubled about Susannah again being grieved for little.

[January 30, 1840. Thursday.] Breakfast at Hardman's. Went to see Burgess' child is very poorly. Received a letter from Liverpool and one from Preston. Sent answer to P[reston] and a letter for my wife. Dinner at Sister Greens. Ellen Battersby fetched me a pint of porter. Sister Green is troubled. She says Brother Heath has told at [Thomas] Owens that Jane Millwood took 2/- of his away with her. Sister Smith is very distant with her &c. Took C. at Brother Jacksons. Preached on Christs reign on earth for about 1 1/2. A full house. Supper at Brother Jacksons. Sister B[attersby] tells me that Arthur Smith has said a great deal to her about me. He has lost the confidence in me &c. Ellen Battersby gave me /6d,[23] Sister Green /2d, Sister Broome 1d.

[January 31, 1840. Friday.] Breakfast at Hardmans. Dinner at Rigby's. Saw Sister [Mary] Powell and Sister Booth and Elizabeth Booth, Booths are very ill. Grieved about reports told of me. Mary Powell acknowledges to having called me or the Elders abominable liars and said that if she had plenty to give me I should go and see her often. This was said before [Henry] Royle and Eliza[beth] Booth. Elizabeth Booth [] if this was so she would come no more to [five illegible lines]. I showed them the wickedness of such conduct. Sister Powell begged pardon and promised

---

[23] "d" refers to pence and is found to the right of the slash, which separates pence from shillings.

to satisfy those who had heard of her saying those things. Sister Booths were both satisfied and they all promised to mind better and guard against evil speaking. Brother Burgess' wife and child poorly. I anointed her breasts and prayed with them. Told P[aul] Harris that Brother Fielding said in his letter he never did say he might have his license. Brother Clark has returned from Peover []. Before the council meeting I took Brother Arthur Smith the Deacon alone and asked him if he was determined not to partake of the sacrement. He said he was untill he had obtained satisfaction from God that the thing came from hell. It had been told to the members by the Elders that it came from hell and he was determined if it did it should return thither. I told if he was determined thus to act I had orders from my brethren to take his license. He said if I did he would never take the office into his hands again. He said had seen a great many things. I asked what they were. He said I shall not say. They will come from hell to and I will say no more. The following subjects brought before council: H[enry] Royle and J[ohn] Wytch go to Dukinfield on Sunday. [] to Stockport. Brother Green and T[homas] Miller to visit Brother [John] Dunn who had not been seen lately. Agreed that the meeting in Bank Street be changed from Wednesday to Tuesday night for convenience of some of the members. The next subject was about the subscription made on the Monday night previous, Brother T. Miller stated that from what passed at the meeting on Monday night he had prevented James Mahon from making a subscription [] of £1. I then called upon the officers to state their feelings on the subject. Brother Bateman said when his sisterinlaw came from the meeting and heard what had passed he was very much grieved and thought we were breaking the order which I had spoke upon the meeting before. Brother Green said it was by the instructions of the Elder (Wm. Clayton) that he had done it and whatever the Elders told him to do he would do it if he knew it to be wrong and the blame should fall upon the Elder &c. Brother Arthur [Smith] said Brother Wm. [Clayton] has said in the council tis not meet for us to leave the word of God and serve tables. The brethren had spoken against having subscriptions in the meetings. Was like Babylon but one thing was spoken or advised at one time and contradicted another. The world had taken hold of it. We had collections &c. He understood that the higher powers had nothing to do with the Deacons office but he had found it to the contrary. There had been collections before that and the Deacons knew nothing of it and the Deacon ought to have been informed of it but he was not. I then stood up and said that I had not intended it be understood that the order of money being put into the box was so exclusive as to forbid the idea of making subscriptions in cases of absolute emergency. The case alluded to was one of this nature. Sarah should have lived at Brother Jacksons 2 weeks but his wife was not willing. Sarah [Duckworth] had been at Bewshers a few days but B[ewsher]'s could not do with. I had talked with Sister Bewsher about it. Sarah had no place to go, no bed to sleep on and something must be done immediately. The subscription was to purchase a bed and she might have Mary Ann Johnsons room and the church pay the whole rent of the house. I had it not in my untill I came to the meeting and then told Brother Green just before the meeting. Brother Arthur came forward at the meeting and publickly opposed Brother Green before he asked a word about either what it was for or who had ordered him &c. Arthur manifested a bad spirit &c. Arthur acknowledged to having done wrong in opposing and asked forgiveness. Granted. I told them the money was intended to be given to the Deacon but when offered to him he refused to take it. The council was satisfied it was not a breach. I showed them it was impossible to have such a case as J[ane] Millward's settled from the box and must be by subscription. I then stated that the clothing had been purchased and they might please themselves wether it should be done at Powell Street or not. It was finally agreed not. Brother Bateman then said he was satisfied when he had heard both sides of the question but he believed that if any of the Elders saw him go down and baptize they would stop him and he should watch that none of the officers took the Deacons business for time to come. I then stated to the meeting the case of Arthur. I showed that it was not because he had not been diligent in his office, not been kind to me. He had done both for which I felt thankful but it was for not partaking sacrement and because he was opposed to all the other officers and was determined to follow his own views independant of council &c. He again stated his determination not to partake untill he had the matter proved by revelation &c which proved his insubjection. He ultimately agreed to partake of the sacrement.

17

Brother Green stated that he had heard from Smith that he and Betsy was about to be married at all Saints and live at John Smiths and he believed the courtship was not broken up. I then stated as follows. Betsy Holden was a married woman. Her husband was a soldier. Had left England to India about 4 years since. Was 3 years since she heard from. No evidence had been given but that he was still living &c. Arthur had had a vision and it was shown to him not the person but the features and that begun the union &c. I had advised him when I first heard of it not to engaged in courtship but let it rest untill proper evidence could be obtained. I expected he would have done so but I found he acted quite to the contrary and seemed determined to pursue his own course. I asked Arthur if this statement was correct. He said it was not. I asked him to state wherein it was not and after being pressed upon he said that it was 4 years since she heard from Holden and that the features was not shewn to him but the []. The council then agreed that it was necessary he should make acknowledgement to the church and satisfy the church that he had broke off connexion with Betsy. He said positively he would not satisfy another individual any more about it. The council then seeing that he was determined to pursue his own course independent of council unanimously agreed to take his office from him. He said if they did he would never more take it again. The council was agreed in all their conclusions and a very solemn feeling pervaded the meeting. We separated at 12 oclock. Met at 8. Took supper at Sands. I went to see Brother Dunns child who was sick. We did not see it.

[February 1, 1840. Saturday.] Took Breakfast at Sister Jane Brown's. Went to see Brother Dunn's child. I think it will die. Took Dinner at Sands. Writ a letter to Brother F[ielding]. Sister Perkins grieved because her father scolded much on account of James staying out untill 12 1/2 oclock. Mr. Perkins got up and went to great lengths. James went away and slept at Green's. James did not intend to go to live there any more but I advised him to go back and ask forgiveness and try to do better, this partly because Sarah wanted him to stay. Went to see Elizabeth Prince. She had resolved not to come near the [world] any more. Had found herself with worldly company. Felt herself entirely drawn from us. I begged she would consider her ways. I knew she

had had much said about her by some of the saints without cause
&c. Her mother has been cross with her &c. She wept much. I
felt to weep. R[ebecca] P[artington] gave me 2 oranges. M[argaret]
Jones, A[nn] Jackson at Claytons.

[February 2, 1840. Sunday.] Breakfast at Sister Hardmans.
Went to Stockport. Preached the resurrection. Dinner at Brother
Staffords. Talked to him about chastizing his children and train-
ing them &c. P.M. spoke about evil speaking. Showed the saints
their duty. Talked about sufferings in America. [Three illegible
lines.] Christiana Crooks behaved bad on her return home and
quite stupid and sulky. Till finally when Sister D[ewsnup] crossed
the street to speak to her she crossed opposite and when they
came back again she also went from them to the other side. I felt
disgusted at her conduct and determined not to take any notice of
her. I had considerable talk with Eliza[beth] Prince. I believe she
has been used badly both at home and in church. She loves the
Elders and believes all we have told her. She has not a friend
in the church but all seemed to stand against her untill she has
determined to leave the church and turn to the world again. I
reasoned a good deal with her and advised her to stand to the last
and God would make it manifest who had done wrong. She acknowledges to having done wrong &c. I feel much on her account.
Her mother is very cross with her and unkind. Took supper at
Hardman's. My foot very sore. Felt weary.

[February 3, 1840. Monday.] Have dreamed that I was going
to baptize my father where the water was very muddy and soon
as we got into it it arose almost to our heads and I could not
baptize him. I also dreamed that a raging fever was making desolation in the towne. I saw carts come to the fever [ward?] [] with
afflicted people in. Took breakfast at Hardman's. Got a letter
from my wife. Well. Fatherinlaw tempted. Dinner at Brother Blacks.
Went to Prestwich thence to Thatchley. Saw Brother Barlow. His
wife very sick. Prayed with her and child. Returned to P[restwich].
Brother Clark preached us 2 hours. Full house. After meeting
I told Barlow what we had heard of him going to the churches
and telling falsehood. He denied telling falsehood and promised
to go no more to the churches. I said if he did we should warn the
church &c. I was very foot sore. Supper at Hardmans. Got home
about 11 3/4.

[February 4, 1840. Tuesday.] Breakfast at Hardman's. Received a letter from Brother F[ielding], one from Brother R[ichards], one from A[gness] Patrick. 4 went to see E[lizabeth] Holden but could not find her. Dinner at T. Millers. Went to see Brother Davies. Found him some better. Sister Rigby gave me 1/-, Sister Walker /6d, Brother West /6d. Went to post office to see for a letter from [Agness] Patrick. Will get it in the morning. Water at T. Millers. Talked with Sussanah Miller. She has no faith in the word of wisdom[24] and has not kept it. She has not the same degree of knowledge which the other saints have. Loves her acquaintance in Babylon &c. She seemed better when we parted. Brother Lea gave me 2/-, Sister Poole /4-, Chris[tiana] Crooks 2/-. Sarah Crooks gave me a pint of porter. Supper at T. Millers. Went to see Brother Burgess child. Very sick. Not very likely to recover. Let considerable matter out of my head. Brother Green rather sick. A[lice] Hardman sick.

[February 5, 1840. Wednesday.] Took breakfast at Hardman's. Went to seek Betsy Holden again but cannot find her. Have sent a small note to her. Dinner at Brother Bewshers. Have been to the clerk at Saint Saviours who says that Arthur and Betsy was married last Sunday morning at 9 o'clock. Went to Hart Street and prayed with 5 of Brother Greens family. Left Book of Covenants[25] till I return. Went to Brother B. [] Sister Perkins gave me

---

[24] On February 27, 1833, with the temperance movement gathering strength in the United States, Joseph Smith dictated a revelation now commonly known as the Word of Wisdom, which counselled church members to avoid meat, tobacco, alcohol, and "strong" and "hot" drinks. In the nineteenth century the Word of Wisdom was considered less a commandment than a guide to healthy living. In his diaries Joseph Smith himself expressed pleasure with the wine being served at one wedding celebration: "our hearts were made glad, while partaking of the bounty of the earth which was presented untill we had taken our fill" (January 20, 1836). He later approved Theodore Turley's request to build a brewery in Nauvoo (March 10, 1843). See Scott H. Faulring, ed., *An American Prophet's Record: The Diaries and Journals of Joseph Smith* (Salt Lake City: Signature Books and Smith Research Associates, 1987), 105, 117, 329. During the 1920s, the period of national legislation prohibiting alcohol, abstinence became a requirement not only for holding office in the church but for participating in temple ordinances. See Thomas G. Alexander, "The Word of Wisdom: From Principle to Requirement," *Dialogue: A Journal of Mormon Thought* 14 (Autumn 1981): 78-88.

[25] The canonized collection of Joseph Smith's revelations, first printed in 1833 as A Book of Commandments (incomplete), was published in 1835 as The Doctrine and Covenants. The first European edition was published in 1845 in Liverpool, England.

a tea cup full of Red Wine. C. at M[ary] Miller. Went to P[aul] Harris', Mary Ann Johnson and [Elizabeth] Prince's. Brother Burgess child appears worse. Many of the sisters at Hardman's. Sister Poole gave me 1/-, E[lizabeth] Mills 2/-, R[ebecca] Partington 1/6, John Smith 1/-, J[ames] Mayon /8, Sarah Crooks 3/-, for Brother Richards. She gave me some raisins and some articles for my wife. Brother Sands gave me optical die for my Sarah.[26] Sister E[llen] Battersby has had an interview with Arthur and Betsy. Arthur very bitter and independent. Received a letter from Brother Heath and one from Brother [Alfred] Cordon. Sarah Crooks gave me [].

[February 7, 1840. Friday.] Took breakfast at [George] Kannon's. Went with Brother Taylor to see Brother Gills daughter Park Lane. Found her comfortable ready to be baptised. Returned from the Docks to Norfolk for Brother F[ielding] has wrote a letter to A. Patrick and one to Brother Clark. Dinner at Kannons and then Brother Taylor gave me his blessing. He blessed me with wisdom and utterance so that I should be a wonder to myself and others. By the spirit. Ministering angels. He blessed Brother Fielding and then Brother F. blessed Brother Taylor. Brother T[aylor] afterwards give an address in tongues and interpreted.[27] We then started to go by the Docks to the Railway station. Started at 2 1/2. Through the tunnel and then by Eugene at 2/3. Instead of stopping at Farington went through to Preston but they brought me back to F[arington] by 5 o'clock coach. Went to my Fathers and thence home about 5 1/2.

[February 8, 1840. Saturday.] Writ a letter to Mr. James []. Went to Preston to Brother Richards. We entered into conversation respecting a letter which Brother R[ichards] had sent to Brother F[ielding]. Brother F. sent a letter to Brother R. asking some questions and it seems Brother R. had misunderstood the meaning of Brother F's letter and writ rather severely &c. Brother R. sees into the subject and purposes to write to Brother F. and satisfy him. Took water at Brother R's lodgings. Went to council.

---

[26] This refers to Clayton's two-year-old child, Sarah.
[27] Speaking in tongues was sometimes regarded as an expression of the true Adamic language with the speaker acting as a passive medium for the Holy Spirit. It was practiced in the early Mormon church but was eventually abandoned.

Several things, part of no particular moment. When I addressed the council upon the necessity of attending to order such as seeking council from the highest officer present, the necessity of being united and upholding each other, not speaking of anything passed at the council &c Brother R. bore testimony to the same effect. After the council had concluded we entered into conversation with Brothers Walmsley and Miller and Halsale upon Sister Walmsleys case. We advised that it should be stated to the church that it was never intended to be understood that Sister W[almsley] was a liar &c but that she acknowledged to having circulated reports. Brother Halsale opposed the council we gave and said there was partiality in the case. Brother R[ichards] stated last sabbath that Sister W[almsley] had reported that Sisters F[ielding] and R[ichards] could not agree. That two of the Elders had been to Sisters F. and R. and they both testified that they could not recollect ever quarrelling but (added Brother Richards) it does not prove that they may not hereafter recollect something neither does it matter for the charge is for circulating reports. Wether true or false is no matter. It seems from this statement that some understood that Sister W. had told lies and she was determined not to make satisfaction untill this proved. We considered it would be best to say as little as possible and let the matter drop. Brother H[alsale] thought we ought to state in public that Sister W's statement was true &c and unless this was done it was partiality. He would not give his assent to it. We reasoned much upon the matter to little purposes. It was concluded that Brother [Peter] Melling should state that the church was not to understand that Sister W. had told a lie but for circulating reports. I fear that something else will arise out of this subject for it is almost 6 months since the circumstance took place. Sister W[almsley] has manifested a bad spirit, quite rebellious, and I think she has hardly been fairly used. Home about 10 1/2.

[February 9, 1840. Sunday.] Wrote a letter to Sarah Crooks, Manchester. Preached in the A.M. on the resurrection, in the P.M. on perfection, gifts of the spirit and how to obtain these things. Spoke upon the armour and charity. After meeting went to see Sister Sumner and child. Sick. Preached at night up Daniel 7 chapter the restoration of the earth. House not full. Wet.

[February 11, 1840. Tuesday.] Went to Preston to see Brother Richards. Bought a memorandum book at Walkers for 1/6. Took at Liptrots. Went to Mechanics Institution[28] about 4 hours. Returned home a little before 8 P.M. Saw Brother John Moon. He had been to see about preparing for Zion.[29] I told him that I could see no reason why they may not go this season, that Brother [Heber C.] Kimball had said let the gathering alone till we come and that some of the Saints would go to Kirtland when he came. Have not been in the prayer meeting. Prayed with Father Moon.

[February 12, 1840. Wednesday.] Having been writing the whole of the day. My mother[30] came this A.M. to say that she thought my wife was dissatisfied on account of my being from home and it was hard for Moon's to keep her and children.[31] Brother R[ichards] came to dinner. Went to see Brother Romney and prayed for him. Was troubled with temptation about the gift of tongues &c. Prayed with Sister Sumner.

[February 13, 1840. Thursday.] Went to Preston. Saw Sister Morgan and then went to Brother Walmsleys. Had considerable talk with Sisters W[almsley] and F[ielding]. Sister W. promised to try to live better and let the matter rest. Saw Brother Richards and wife. Took cocoa with Sister Morgan. Conversed a good deal on the order of the church after I returned home.

[February 15, 1840. Saturday.] Took breakfast at Hardman's. Went to Cookson Street. Prayed with Brother Davies. Went to Brother Burgess. Had a good deal of conversation with two of Brother Burgess's brothers. Wm. [Burgess] rejected our testimony. The other would seek [after] it. Prayed with and anointed his wife

---

[28] A self-improvement society for working men which began about 1825; its most popular classes were in literacy.

[29] Many Mormon converts in the Moon family (Clayton's in-laws) were planning to emigrate to the United States. Gathering to Zion symbolized a return to the Kingdom of God, once centered in Jerusalem, and subsequently defined by Joseph Smith as "the whole of America" (HC 6:318). For a discussion of the religious and economic motivations of the "gathering" from Britain, see Philip A. M. Taylor, "Why did British Mormons Emigrate," Utah Historical Quarterly 22 (1954): 249-59.

[30] Clayton apparently refers either to his mother or to his mother-in-law, Lydia Moon.

[31] William Clayton and his wife, Ruth Moon, had two children, Sarah and Margaret.

and child. Went to Matthew Claytons. Eliz[abeth] very poorly. Prayed with her and anointed her. She received instant relief. Went to see Mary Ann Johnson and prayed with and anointed her. Came to see Brother Rob[ert] Williams. Prayed with and anointed him. Brother Clark went to []. I went to Wm. Millers. Took Water with S[arah] Perkins. She is very poorly. Went to T. Millers. Took supper and staid till 10 1/2. Susan very sick. Rebecca fetched a pint of Porter into the street. Read a letter today from Brother Woodruff. Wrote on Tuesday. Have heard today that there has been 14 baptised at Manchester since last Sabbath and 4 at Stockport. E. Miller gave me a half crown.

[February 16, 1840. Sunday.] Went to breakfast at Matthew Claytons. Elizabeth went up stairs and would not let me see. Went to the room and Brother H. Royle preached a while and then I spoke about 35 minutes. During the service William Smith and another went to be baptized. Prayed with Sister Jones. Was sick. Went to Bewshers to Dinner. Had conversation with Sister Bewsher's cousin. She seems quite convinced of the truth. Had a considerable conversation with Arthur [Smith] and told him what the church would have to do &c. He cautioned me to justly &c. He said they was intending to live together &c. His case was brought at the meeting in the P.M. I stated it from first to last and put it to the church if he must be cut off. Many held up their hands. I then put it to the contrary and Sister C[atherine] Beates held up her hand. I called upon her to give her reason and she spake considerable but nothing to shew cause why he should not be cut off. She wanted to be merciful. I then put it again if the church would rather suspend him and Sister Usherwood and P[e-ter] Mottram held up their hand. I considered it conclusive and closed the case. Sister [Elizabeth] Holden was suspended. I spoke about 1 hour to the church. Confirmed 13 blessed 1 child, anointed 3 and prayed with 6. Tarried in the room and R[ebecca] Partington fetched some cocoa. She is a loving soul. Preached at night about 1-10 on the gifts of the spirit. Several given us their names to be baptized on Tuesday night. Had considerable talk with C. Beates after meeting. Had 14 oranges and about a dozen sweet cakes given to me. Sister Bewsher gave me a pint of Porter.

[February 17, 1840. Monday.] Brother C[] returned from Stockport. Took Breakfast at Hardman's. Wrote to B[urslem] and

Liverpool. Took dinner at Wm. Millers. Sister Perkins gave me a pint porter. Went to Thomas Millers to Cocoa. Wm. Miller went with me, from thence went to Prestwich. Wm. and I waited on the road for Sarah Crooks and Henry Royle. Sarah was waiting near the old church through a misunderstanding. Wm. returned and I went on alone. Arrived about 7 o'clock. Waited a few min-[utes] and Henry came in and a little while after Sarah came. The people seemed slack at coming up and we waited awhile. One of the brethren came from another house and said there was a congregation waiting for us so I went and left Henry at Eckersleys. Sarah went with me. Found a full house. I preached something more than 1 hour and the people was attentive. Some few were unruly. Had talk with some of them and think they will some be baptized. Gave out another meeting in 2 weeks. Sarah gave me a orange and ginger losenges. Got home at 12 o'clock. Supper at preaching house.

[February 18, 1840. Tuesday.] Breakfast at Hardman's. Wrote a letter for R. Williams to his father in London. Had conversation with Wm. Garnett. He seems to received it gladly. Anoi[nted] Sister Margaret Hardmans leg. Went to Sand's to dinner and thence to Brother Green's. Sister Green very low. Gave them each some oil inwardly and prayed with them. Had conversation with some hardened females at Sands. Took water there. Returned to Hardman's, to meet some to baptize. Had a house full of saints. Went to the water and baptised 3 females. Got my cloths changed and then Gilford came up I baptised him and changed my cloths again and another female said she would go and I went into the water a third time 5 baptised in all. Supper at T. Millers. Sister Dewsnup has left home.

[February 19, 1840. Wednesday.] Breakfast at Hardman's. Got a letter from Brother Heath. Sister Poole has been and says Susan is jealous of Thomas [Miller]. He wants her out of the way. If she was to die he would be married again in 3 months &c. Thomas wanted to know who he would be married to &c. She would not tell him. He says he will not go to his work untill she does tell him and she says she will not. Thomas is very much troubled &c. Thomas has practiced kissing all in the house before he goes to bed &c. Went to Bewshers to dinner. She gave me a pint of Porter. Brother James was with us a little while. Went

25

from thence to see Brother Gills wife. She is much the same. Have learned that all the family is baptized. We administered the sacrement and went to Brother John Smiths to C. Prayed with Brother John and 2 of the children. Came back to Brother Burgess and anointed and prayed with his wife. Went to Pollard Street to preach. Brother Clark talk some time and after he had done two of the Owenites[32] opposed but would not say much to them. They left the house and then I talked a little to the others. Came home and found Sarah Crooks here and Christiana who was sick. We prayed with her. [Three and one half lines crossed out.] Supper at Hardman's. Writ a letter

[February 21, 1840. Friday.] . . . Supper at T. Millers. Susan wept because she heard that Tho[ma]s had intended to buy S[arah] Isherwood a new cloak. Susan is yet troubled with jealousy. Sarah Crooks gave me 1/- and some raisins.

[February 22, 1840. Saturday.] . . . Matthew put me some buttons on my shoes. Went to see some of the Town missions at Pollard Street. Met 2 of them. They wanted to see a sign. I proved that signs were not a sure evidence. Acknowledged. Told them the order of the gospel. They assented to it. I then said if you preach that — so then it is a proof that you are not the servants of God. They turned from their acknowledgment. We bore testimony and asked them did they reject our testimony. Yes. So we parted. Went to T. Millers to Supper. Susan yet grieved. B[etsy] Crooks very low. She has given way to her temper &c. Margaret Jones gave me two oranges and cleaned my shoes. Home about 11 1/2. R[ichard] Hardman gave me a few figs.

[February 24, 1840. Monday.] Breakfast at Hardman's. Received a letter from Sarah Flint. Wrote a letter to Brother F[ielding]. Went and anointed and prayed with Sister Jane Browns child. Went to seen R. Williams. Prayed with and anointed him. Dinner at T. Millers. Brother Clark came and is gone to Pendlebury. John Wytch to Prestwich. Went to see Wallace in Salford. Not at home. Water at T. Millers.[33] Susan has been much

---

[32] Followers of Robert Owen, a British socialist who opposed organized religion and was a strong supporter of education.
[33] Sources of good water were important because of widespread contamination.

grieved at a many things. Thomas struck her this morning. He repented at it and desired that they both might begin anew. Susan has forgiven him. Margaret Jones is grieved with Betsy Crooks and is for leaving T's. Betsy Crooks is grieved at them all. She says they use her unkindly call her a hypocrite &c. She says she has made up her mind to leave the church. I feel to weep over her. Their seems to be a spirit of contention amongst them. Prayed with little Ann and Sarah Isherwood. Supper at T. Millers. Have advised the Saints to give up the practice of kissing.

[February 25, 1840. Tuesday.] Breakfast at Hardman's. Sent a letter to Sarah Flint. Went to Brother Sand's to Dinner and C. Went to visit also Paul Harris [] and Burgess. Went with Brother Bowman to see some of his acquaintances. Preached the gospel to them. They were kind and invited me to go again. Brother Bowman wanted advice concerning his property and I gave such as I had given me. He says he will have nothing to do with property that is not pure &c. He [said] a small estate was left to his father sometime since by some of his father's relatives (brother) and when his father became entitled to it their was other relatives who had more need of it than his father had. Did his father wrong in claiming the property. I answered no again. In the year 1825, his father began to build a range of houses in a very pleasant situation and while they were in building he was solicited [through] an agent to sell the houses. His mother was very much opposed to selling them and used her influence to prevent them being sold. After repeated solicitations his father very unwillingly set a price on them £2800. The agent in a day or so returned and offered him £2700. But he being still very unwilling to part with them would not abate any thing. The agent then asked if he would not allow something as commission. His father asked what he would want. He replied it was usual to have 1/4 per cent. Bowman said he did not mind that. Therefore the deed was drawn up and Bowman was desired to sign it &c. He begged they would wait and consider a few days longer thinking the man would be willing to rue of his bargain. However at the time appointed the contract was signed and a deposit of £2 given as earnest. The purchaser had 1500 in bank and promised to pay the other in a given time. Before the time expired their began to be a great pressure in trade. Money grew scarce and property was of very little value.

27

Said he could purchase many houses at about 12 ea. The purchaser then came and wanted to know what Bowman would accept of as the bargain. Bowman did not want the bargain to be broke as at that time. The money was of far more value to him than the property. After repeated solicitations he agreed for 400, which was given. Brother Bowman wanted to know if his father done right. I told him to let it rest and if any thing was necessary to do the Lord would make it known. He next stated that he had assisted in building a chapel for [] and had £420 lying invested in it. He dared not to sell the chapel because he considered it as given to God. I told him if he would get all his money in and sell the chapel the Lord would not be displeased but would bless him because such places were of no use to the Lord. We parted at 10. Went to Sarah Perkins to supper and to sleep there. Sister Jones told me her trouble. I recommended mercy and charity and said [].

[February 26, 1840. Wednesday.] Breakfast at Perkins. Sister Poole has bound my stock with leather. Had conversation with Mrs. Miller (old). Told her that she should see a day when she would desire to escape out of England unless she dies soon. I warned her of the jury reports &c. But she said Ninevah repented and the Lord was merciful &c. Susan is poorly. Prayed with R. Williams. Very poorly. Prayed with Brother Green. Got a letter from Brother Woodruff B[]. Dinner at Bewshers and C. Answered Brother Woodruffs letter. Sent 1 to Brother [Alfred] Carden. 1 to my wife. Brother Bewsher gave me a pair of twezers. Preached at Pollard Street to about 12 on the Kingdom &c.

[February 27, 1840. Thursday.] A letter from Brother R[ichards]. Breakfast at Hardman's. Went per packet[34] to Ashley to see Brother George Woolstencroft. Found him in a bad state. He believes the Bible is all truth and because Brother Berry said there was errors in it he said he had inbibed infidel principles. I told him I could prove that there were contradictions in it and therefore could not all be true. I referred him to Acts 9 ch. and 22 ch. I told him I had heard he could preach. Yes, he said, Jesus Christ had sent him to preach and no man should stop him. I

---

[34] A packet boat, one that travels a regular route along a river or coastline carrying passengers, freight, and mail.

said it was contrary to the order of the church. He said he would not be led by man and he had often thought that the order of the church was like priestcraft &c. He said Jesus Christ had spoke to him. Had he heard him? Yes. How did he speak to him? In such a manner that satisfied him. I asked him if he believed we were the servants of God. He said he believed that sometimes Satan had sent men with a design to do good. I answered I believed that for Satan had deceived him &c. He answered if I said that Christ had not sent him. He would look upon me like unto the lying prophet &c. I told him he never could be saved if he did not abide in the church &c. He said his determination was to do the will of God and he new he should be saved. I told him that the will of God was that he should be subject to the higher powers and he was not subject &c. He was subject to God &c. I asked him what evidence he had for believing that the order of the church was priestcraft. He referred to the Mass book. I showed him that was no criterion — the Bible. I asked him if he was determined to continue preaching. He said Christ had sent him to preach and he should stop him. He would not be stopped by any man. I then told him he could no longer hold an office in the church and must be suspended from fellowship &c a few weeks so that if he repented he might acknowledge it, if not he would be cut off. He seemed to speak with great confidence and was very stubborn in spirit of subjection. I said I wanted to do him good. He does not believe the Book of Mormon. I walked back to the Boat about 3 miles. Took dinner with Brother [James] Johnson. Got back to Manchester about 4 o'clock. Took C. at Hardman's. Went to T. Millers. Susan is determined to have a less family and break up house. They would go to old Mrs. Miller. She was weary in consequence of having to much work. She could not bear it &c. I went to Wm. Millers to meeting and spoke much on the tribulation which is at hand. The Saints seemed moved. I had great liberty in speaking. Prayed with one sister. Sarah [Crooks] and Rebecca [Partington] brought me home. I told them what Susan was intending to do. Rebecca seemed much troubled and Sarah appeared rather tempted to get married. I felt to sorrow on this account. I don't want Sarah to be married. I was much [] and tempted on her account and felt to pray that the Lord would preserve me from impure affections. She gave me an orange. I certainly feel my love towards her to increase but shall strive against

29

it. I feel too much to covet her and afraid lest her troubles should cause her to get married. The Lord keep me pure and preserve me from doing wrong.

[February 28, 1840. Friday.] Was called up before six to Brother Batemans wife. She was in labour. She was delivered before I got there. A girl. Prayed with her. Took Breakfast and returned and wrote a letter to Brother Richards. Went to Wm. Millers to Dinner. Sarah Perkins gave me a pint of Porter and some Raisins. Sarah Crooks gave me 1/-. I objected but she would make me have it. Rebecca went a little on the way with me. [One line crossed out.] I went to see Brother Owens. I had heard there was disturbance between him and wife. It was so but I was glad to find that the matter was settled between them. They gave me 1/-. I went to Wm. Millers to C. and talked to Sister [Ellidge] about the judgements. She over[heard] me talk last night and was troubled and seemed short of faith. I gave scripture testimony for what I had said. I felt to prophecy last night and fully believe that the troubles are very nigh at hand. Went to see Brother R. Williams. Anointed him and Brother Clark prayed. I prayed with Brother Green this A.M. He is better a good deal to night. Sister Burgess says that the 2 Missionaries whom we conversed with Saturday evening says that we are two of the worst devils that ever came from hell. They are coming next Wednesday evening to bring a map of America &c. At council meeting 1. I introduced Brother Lea as a worthy member of the council. Shewed in few words why we had kept him back &c. The council voted him in &c. 2. Stated Brother Woolstencrofts case and he was voted out of office. I applied the case to their benifit. 3. George Butterworth and wife at Edgerly disagree. Are to be visited by Brothers T[homas] Miller and J[ames] Lea on Sunday. 4. Brother Berry to Dukinfield and T. Miller and Lea to Stockport. 5. Brother and Sister Booth, Brother Bailey and Brother Mottram don't attend class meeting. M[ary] Becket will as soon as she gets better of her health. Brother Featherstone proposed Adam Lee for a teacher at Stockport [four illegible lines].

[March 1, 1840. Sunday.] Breakfast at Hardman's. Went to Brother Greens to meet E[lizabeth] Keithly. He did not come. Was tired. From thence to the room. Brother Davies preached about 35 minutes on the doctrine of Christ. I spake after about same time on infant baptism. After meeting had some conversation with a man I think a Wesleyan. He asked could he not be saved without baptism. Was it not awful to teach that one man could be saved by being baptized and another damned for not being. Was it essential to believe in the personal reign of Christ. Did faith always include obedience. I answered his questions and bore testimony and told him he could not be saved unless he was baptized. He said he had searched much of mans works but could get little light of the scriptures. He was in darkness, but had a hope of heaven and with that he would be satisfied. I said if he would obey the gospel he should have the light of God &c. We parted. To Bewshers to Dinner. Brother Davies was there. I talked some time in the P.M. on the judgements &c. We ordained Brothers Green and H. Royle, Elders, and Brother Sands, Teacher. Brother J[ames] Royle was voted Priest but he was not present. 4 was confirmed and Brother C[harles] Miller's child blessed. 4 sick prayed with. Brother Clark cried with a loud voice and commanded the evil spirit to depart from Sister Mary Warburton. She seemed better immediately. Sister Booth gave me -/6d. 3 baptized. Sarah and Rebecca gave me Cocoa. Rebecca gave me 2 oranges. Sarah gave me 1. Sister Birch gave me 1/-. I preached on the judgement. Prayed with a number sick. Went to see Brother Matthew Clayton. Prayed with him. Supper at Prince's. Sat with Alice and Hannah till 2 o'clock.

[March 2, 1840. Monday.] Breakfast at Hardman's. Went to see Sister Booth. Better. To Sister Jane Browns. Some better. Got a letter from Brother Richards. Prayed with Brother R[obert] Williams and with Brother Burgess wife and []. Went to Brother Paul [Harris's]. Sister Warburton was jawlocked. Brother Clark cried with a loud voice and rebuked the fowl spirit and immediately her mouth opened. He anointed her and I prayed. Sister Jane Harris says she has been disobedient to Paul. They have not been very comfortable together. She feels to repent and do better. We prayed with her. To Brother Owen's to dinner. I wrote him a letter to his sister in Somersetshire. He gave me 1/-. Saw Wm. Millers wife and family Sarah Perkins and Brother Browns. Sister Brown says she enquired what time Brother [C.] Miller told us about her sickness and says at the same time she began to amend. She says if she had sent a pocket Handker-

31

chief and we had touched it she would have been well &c. To T. Millers to water. From there to Prestwich. Alice Hardman with me. Found Brother A[mos] Fielding there and 2 brethren from Ratcliff. I preached 1-40 on baptism. Attentive audience. Sarah and Rebecca came to the workhouse to meet us. To T. Millers to Supper. Home soon after 12.

[March 3, 1840. Tuesday.] Breakfast at Hardman's. Went to see Brother Burgess wife and child. She has been disobedient. She seems very penitent. She has a cow dung plaster on her breast. We promised her in the name of the Lord that if she felt to repent and begin to live faithful she should receive a blessing. We anointed and prayed with her and []. Went to Newton to Sister Booths to Dinner and Water. Sister White and Mary Aspin was there. To T. Millers to Pancake. There was too much lightness. I had little to do with it. Sarah Crooks bath my forehead with rum and gave me some mint drops. Sister Booth gave me some raisins. Sarah is anxious to know where to go to lodge. I told her I preferred Rulingtons.

[March 4, 1840. Wednesday.] Breakfast at Hardman's. Sent a letter which came yesterday to Preston and a pamphlet written in Peover. To Brother Burgess. She is some better. We prayed with her and anointed her again and M. To Bewshers to D[inner]. Got a letter from Brother F[ielding], [and] from Brother [Moon] and from Brother Alfred [Cordon?]. Sent one to Brother Alfred. Went to [] Street, full house. I preached 1 1/2 hours on baptism. Before I had got properly through one of the town Missions (3 were present) interrupted and threw the meeting into confusion. They disproved nothing but manifested a bad spirit, railing and saying the doctrine was a doctrine of damnation &c. [William?] Jordan the writer was present and what he heard made him tremble. He said the devils which was in the cellar are come here. Some I think will be baptized. Supper at Hardman's.

[March 6, 1840. Friday.] Breakfast at Hardman's. Went to see Sister Burgess. Prayed with her and anointed her breast. Prayed with Maria. Prayed with R. Williams. Went to Sister Cath[erine] Beates to dinner [sixteen lines crossed out]. She also saw in a dream Brother Richards and Robert Williams and one of Hardmans Sons and old Richard Hardman sitting in a room together. Brother Richards seemed sick and in trouble. The room opened above their heads and she saw 12 small children dressed in white. One of them was Brother Richards child. She knew it. It came down and sat on his shoulder and bending down looked in his face. The scene closed. She says Brother R[ichards] will not live long. He is expecting a many things but in some he will be disappointed. She says she foresaw all that has taken place concerning Arthur Smith. And she prophecies bad concerning Sister Mary Wytch &c. Took tea with her. Called at Hardman's. Brother John Moon is come. Went to have conversation with Sister Mary Aspen's sister and brotherinlaw. He is a unitarian. I proved to him that Christ was a divine being, God &c and preached the gospel to him. He seemed to believe. Will consider of it. Called at T. Millers. Took supper. Mary Aspin gave me some ascive drops. Sarah and Rebecca has been at Rulingtons but they cannot take them in yet. Sarah is much troubled. She says Susan keeps hinting that she is tired of them. She cannot bear it. Gave me some raisins.

[March 7, 1840. Saturday.] [] Went to see Sister Burgess. Anointed and prayed with her and Maria. Went to Cookson Street. Prayed with and anointed Sister Jones, Rigby's 2 children and Brother Davies. Prayed with Brother Walkers son. Dinner at Walkers. Talked to Brother Davies on the divinity of Christ. Sister C[atherine] Beates gave me new pocket Handkerchief. To Prince's to C. Went to Coach office for Brother John Moon's Box. Paid 1-8 for it. Received a pie from Sister Mary Miller. A letter from Brother Alfred Corden. To T. Millers to Supper. While here I recollected a dream which I had a few nights before. I thought I was shooting and a number of men with me. I thought some who charged lightly killed almost every shot. I charged heavy. Shook almost everything around me but stunned the bird did not kill it. Sarah [Crooks] and Rebecca [Partington] are in trouble. They cannot go to P[rince]'s. They came up with me to Sister Hardman's and engaged to come next week end. They tarried till 12 o'clock. M[argaret] Jones gave me 2 oranges.

[March 8, 1840. Sunday.] Sister Burgess came. Her breast is very bad. I prayed with her . . . Supper at Hardman's. Used great liberty toward Alice Hardman.

[March 9, 1840. Monday.] Breakfast at Hardman's. Wrote a letter to Brother Fielding. Went to see Sister Burgess. Very bad. Prayed with her and daughter. Prayed with Mary Ann Johnson and Robert Williams. T. Millers to Dinner []. Went with John Moon to railway. Called at Paul Harris'. Prayed with him and child and S[arah] Isherwood. Mary Warburton strives to hide her pipe &c. Last week Sister Betsy Crooks bought a fur collar for my cloak and on Saturday put it on. Sisters Poole and Jones has left T. Millers this A.M. Gone to Richard Hardmans. Brother H[enry] Royle baptised 3 at Dukinfield yesterday. I baptized at Stockport. Water at T. Millers. Went to Pendlebury to preach on the resurrection. After preaching a socialist proposed some questions. I answered him till he was almost speechless. He showed a mild temper &c. After I had conversation with a professor. She was very stubborn and would not believe baptism would do her any good. T[oo]k Supper returned 11 1/2.

[March 10, 1840. Tuesday.] Breakfast at Hardman's. Saw Sister Burgess. Some better. Prayed with her and daughter and R. Williams and Hardmans child. To T[homas] Mayors to dinner. Went to see Sister Booth. Very ill. Prayed with her. To H[ardman]'s Street. Sister Smith sick. I told about circulating [reports]. She denies all except telling Isaac Royle and Brother Bateman that Brother Greens had the Itch.[35] Isaac was intending to sleep there had she not told him. Prayed with her. To Brother Batemans. Prayed with Sister [Nancy] Street and a knee and hand. Went to Eccles.[36] Preached the gospel to a full house. Had a few words with a Wesleyan. He said Paul was not sent to baptize. I prayed with the woman of the house. She was sick. Took water at Sister [Ann] Williamsons. Supper at Hardman's. Got home at 11. Received a letter from Sister Ravenscroft.

[March 12, 1840. Thursday.] Breakfast at Hardman's. Received a letter from Brother Fielding. Sent one to my wife. Went to Smiths for Timely Warnings. To Wm. Millers to dinner. To

---

[35] Possibly scabies, a skin disease caused by a parasitic mite.

[36] Eccles, also known as Eccleston, was a textile and milling town on the Manchester Ship Canal and the origin of Eccles cake, a rich cake with fruit filling, which Clayton received as a present.

Sarah Perkins to water. Went to Leighs in Salford. Preached to him near 1 hour. He sent for an old woman named Campon. She was very stubborn and prejudiced. She said I was one of the false prophets. Leigh and wife seems to believe. Sister Mary Aspen offered me a soverein[37] to buy a polyglot Bible.[38] But I refused to take it. She pressed much. Supper at Leighs. Sarah Crooks gave me some raisins. Mary Aspen gave me 2 oranges.

[March 13, 1840. Friday.] Breakfast at Hardman's. Found 4/- amongst the raisins. Was sent for to Princes. E. Dewsnup keeps bad hours. Burgess family improving. Sister Booth better. Went to Newton Dinner and Water. Sister Booth and Brother Whitehead gave me 2 oranges each. Prayed with Sister Booth and read her Brother Fieldings words in his letter. Conversed with 2 females and they promised to be baptized tonight. Brought a dress to Sister Burgess. Went to see for Brother Henry Royle to baptize. Could not find him. But Brother Green is gone. Sister Sands gave me 1/2 a quire of papers.[39] Agreed that Brother John Gill should take charge of Hart Street Meeting, Brother Sands Bank Street, Brother T. Miller Cornet Street, Brother Lea Newton, the priest &c. to visit the members who cannot attend the room on a Sunday and administer sacrement. Brother C[harles] Miller to assist the Deacon. I read the officers their duty and exhorted a little. Supper at Brother Greens. Brother Green only baptized one. T. Miller gave me 1/-. I wrote a letter to Sarah Perkins. One to E. Dewsnup. 1 to Mr. Williams London. Some trouble between Sisters Green and Gilford and Battersby. Sister Battersby is very low. Brother Gill gave me a pence cash.

[March 14, 1840. Saturday.] Breakfast at Hardman's. Sister Poole says that E[llen] Battersby intends to go to her mother's. Sister Galeford complains that B. does not do enough for G[aleford]. Yet she has pawned nearly all her cloths for them even to her Sunday dress. Got a letter from Brother D[avid] Wilding. He says he had to sell some of the goods out of the house to pay me that 7/- referred Feb. 14. I have given A[lice] Hardman

---

[37] A British gold coin worth one pound sterling.

[38] A Bible printed in several languages arranged in columns for textual comparison.

[39] A quire of papers is a set of twenty-four sheets, a twentieth part of a ream.

3/- to give him back together with 50 Timely Warnings which he may have the benefit. I find at Cookson Street that there is a hard feeling against Brother Davies. Brother West says they want another leader or else must they go to another meeting. He says Brother Davies hints that it is their duty to support him and is grieving the saints minds every week. He has not said that it is himself that he wants them to relieve but says the poor in their own class &c. Brother West is quite bad tempered over it. Seems to manifest a bad spirit trembled with hard feelings. Sister Black and West and Walker and Rigby quite grieved. They state that Brother Davies had said something about meeting together so much and they only meet to read the scriptures. When I had seen them all and learned all the grievances I went to Brother Davies and asked how was the meeting attended. He said very well. Not many strangers. How did the saints appear. Very comfortable. What had he been teaching of late? On Thursday night he was speaking about the members relieving each other &c. Brother Walker had given 1/2 load of potatoes to Brother Barlow who lived in the country and poor old Joseph West had scarcely bread sufficient to eat and this was why he said so. I saw at once that Brother Davies had been speaking for Brother Joseph and it had been universally understood that he was hinting at his own case and Joseph said to me that there was members in the street as bad off as they (Davies) were. I then went and explained it to them all and the prejudice began to abate and they looked more cheerful. I last went to see Joseph but he would hardly speak to me. Was quite overcome with bad feelings but I begged he would be patient and I would give him some evidence that he was mistook. He would hardly listen but I showed him what passed and he began to see into it and he presently looked more cheerful but it was with difficulty that I could persuade him that it was a mistake. I trust things are comfortably settled. Came home with Brother Green and Lea to [] St. Brother Green was in a little difficulty concerning his club. I gave him 1/ to set him at liberty. He is troubled about the disease which is troubling the family. I told him I thought there was something wrong and I intended to find out if possible. I told him about Sister Battersby's cloths being pawned &c. I anointed him and prayed with him and advised him to go and pray with his family. We anointed inwardly and prayed with Sister Jane Brown. She was troubled with []. I finished writing a letter to Brother Dunns Father and then Brothers Garner and Bowman came and tarried after 10 o'clock. Betsy Crooks gave me some figs. Sarah Crooks and Rebecca Partington are come to live at Hardmans. I should have gone to R[ichard] Hardmans to see the child but did not get away. Supper at Hardman's. Sarah and Rebecca seem low.

[March 15, 1840. Sunday.] Breakfast with Sarah and Rebecca. Preached this A.M. about 1 1/4 on Isaiah Chapter 40. To Bewshers to Dinner. Gave me 2 oranges and a pint of Porter. Spoke a while in the P.M. Confirmed 3 and Brother T. Miller baptized 3. C[hristiana] Crooks gave me 2 oranges and 1/-. Sarah Crooks 2 oranges. M[argaret] Jones 2/-. Sister Birch gave me 1/-. Preached at night on Isaiah 24-5,6 and made some remarks on a pamphlet. I baptized after another gave in his name for Thursday night. C[harlotte] Grundy gave me a apple from Derbyshire. J[ames] Mahon gave me /6. Went to Prince's and found the devil busy around them. The family finds fault with Sister Dewsnup. Elizabeth called her a little wasp, a bad dispositioned girl and many other things. Elizabeth says she will never come near the church again. I did not say much to them. I thought it would be best for them to leave &c. Took C. with Sarah and Rebecca. Supper at Prince's. Prayed with many sick.

[March 16, 1840. Monday.] Breakfast at Hardman's. Received a letter from Brother Woodruff. He has baptized 32 in 6 days. Been to see P[aul] Harris. Sick. Got a letter from my wife. Sent a letter to Brother Fielding. 5 was baptized at Stockport yesterday. E[lizabeth] Booth says that those whom Brother David baptized at Bury are nearly all turned against. J. Loffe whom he lodged with reported that David was £10 in his debt. David went to ask him about it and took a man with him (not a saint). He asked for a correct statement of what he owed him. He reckoned for 3 weeks at 8/- per week 24/-. David said he had only been 17 days from the first and 3 of them 17 he spent in Manchester. The man then made out a bill for 2 weeks 16/-. The man who went with David paid down the money. He confirmed 8 yesterday. Water at Sarah Perkins. Prayed with [Sarah] and little C. Miller. Went to Narrow lane 1 mile beyond Prestwich. Preached on Revelations 20-1 to 6. Full house. I gave his name. Several believing. Supper at

37

preaching house. Got home at 11 o'clock. Rebecca [Partington] gave me some egg milk.

[March 17, 1840. Tuesday.] Breakfast at Hardman's. Received a letter from Brother Heath and one from Mr. R[obert] Williams stating that he had previously sent two pounds which I had not received. The letter was an order for 2 pounds which I got but could [find] nothing of the other two. I sent him another letter . . .

[March 18, 1840. Wednesday.] . . . R[obert] Williams sent me 2/6. I would have refused it but must take it . . .

[March 19, 1840. Thursday.] . . . Went to post office to enquire after R. Williams letter but [could hear nothing of it]. Told R. about it and he seemed much troubled and wanted me to write immediately for more money. I said I would rather wait a while lest his father should be vexed. After I went out he began to murmur and John Hardman said it was like robbery &c. to expect more so soon. R[obert] gave way and rose up as if to strike John but fainted back in the chair. They came for me and I found them apparently full of the spirit of the devil. I cautioned R[obert] and told him if he did not be patient and humble he would die. He wept aloud. I advised him to go to bed after cautioning. Baptized 2. Supper with Rebecca . . .

[March 20, 1840. Friday.] . . . Rebecca gave 1/6 and Sarah gave me 10/- towards a new pair of Boots. I was resolved not to have it. She has done so much for me but she persisted and I must take it. I received a letter also which she had wrote. Brother T[homas] Mayer gave me 1/-. Sister Poole would have done to but I would not take it. We went and prayed with Burgess' family. Took the Railway at 2 1/4 and got home about 5 o'clock. Found the children rather poorly. Wife and rest of the family well. They rejoiced to see me. Dinner at home.

[March 22, 1840. Sunday.] Went to Cock Pit.[40] Miles [] preached. Dinner at Brother Partington's. Brother Richards oc-

---

[40] The Cock Pit in Preston was built around 1800 as an enclosed amphitheater for cock fights. Mormon meetings were held there after the missionaries arrived in 1837 (Richard L. Evans, *A Century of "Mormonism" in Great Britain* [Salt Lake City: Deseret News Press, 1937], 45).

cupied the P.M. I preached at night on Isaiah 46. Preached 1 1/2 hour. Full house and very attentive. 3 confirmed.

[March 25, 1840. Wednesday.] Went to Eccleston to Sister Alice Moons Sale. They had fixed upon me to write for them. We commenced at 2 o'clock and I finished writing after 11. Dinner and supper at Moon's. The auctioneer gave me 2/-for copying list &c. Got home at 2 o'clock.

[March 26, 1840. Thursday.] Brother Richards has been here this P.M. Brot me a letter from Burslem stating that Brother Turley was in prison. I preached at night at Cuerden Factory. Full house. Isaiah 24-5, 6. Nancy Riley gave me 1/-.

[March 27, 1840. Friday.] Brother Hugh Moon gave me 2/- for timely warnings. He asked what I should charge for writing at sale. I said I should make no charge so he said no more about it. But seemed satisfied. I started at 2 1/2 per Railway from Far- ington and arrived at Manchester at 4 1/2. Took Water at Hardmans. Saw Brother Clark. Found Sisters Alice [Hardman] and Hannah [Walker] very low. David Wilding has grieved Alice with something. Went to council meeting. Nothing particular. 5 has been baptized at Stockport since I left. Brother David Wilding says that Brother Green's family has the Itch. I sent a letter to Brother Fielding to know what to do &c. Sarah [Crooks] and Rebecca [Partington] gave me supper. Sarah washed my head with [rum].

[March 28, 1840. Saturday.] Breakfast at Hardman's. Bought a new pair of Boots for 18/-. Went to Pendleton. Dinner at Sister [Ann] Williamson's. Went to Brother [Thomas] Jennings. Met him on the road. He said his wife had not been fairly. Brother [Joseph] Jackson had not acted scripturally. I asked how. He an- swered the scriptures say if thy brother sin against thee tell him his fault alone &c. Yes I said but a public transgression required a public acknowledgment. He said he could not find it in scrip. I answered Paul says them that sin rebuke before all that others also may fear &c. He seemed rather stubborn and hard against Brother Jackson. His wife has been drunk and calling in the street in a very disgraceful manner. She had said to the effect that the L D S were L D devils &c. Brother J[ennings] wanted to cover it up and was not willing that his wife should make acknowledgment to the church. I went forward to see Sister J[ennings] and when I had been in a little while Brother Jackson came in. She seemed quite bitter against him because he had exposed her before the church and told all the subject in [plain words]. I reasoned considerable with her and she seemed to grow milder. She said she had never had so much of the spirit since she joined the church as she had when among the ranters[41] &c. I had a good deal of talk with her and Sister Jackson. They are in a poor state. I afterwards told Brother Jackson I thought he was to rash with the saints &c. Prayed with Sister Jackson's son and returned home. Water with Sarah and Rebecca. Bought a Satin Stock for 3/6. Went to see E[liza] Prince. Prayed with several at night and after was taken very poorly. Marg[aret] Jones gave me 2 oranges. 4 has been baptized at Dukinfield since the 24.

[March 29, 1840. Sunday.] Breakfast at Sarah and Rebeccas. Went to Stockport. Sarah and Rebecca went with me [four lines crossed out]. Brother Green preached. Dinner at Brother Stafford. In the P.M. we confirmed 11 and I ordained Brother Adam Lea, Priest, Thomas Howarth, Teacher, and James Hawkins, Teacher; I preached upwards of 1 hour in the evening on John 10-1 to 8. Sarah gave me 2 oranges and another sister 1. Got home at 11 in the P.M. Robert Crooks stood up previous to confirmation to shew why he suffered himself to be cut off and how he had felt since. He said he was sincere and believed it was false, through reading a tract against the Book of Mormon. He had prayed much that he might be right. But never could get peace not even as much as before he joined the church. He prayed that the Lord would let him die sooner than let him go astray &c. He was standing by the fire one night lately and was suddenly taken very ill almost lost the use of his limbs. He prayed and said if the Lord would raise him again he would go and be baptized. He found immediate relief and his former peace returned to him. He rejoiced and soon got better. He says if this church is not right there is none right in the world. He feels to love all the saints and

---

[41] In the nineteenth century members of the Primitive Methodist and Quaker sects were sometimes called "Ranters." Like the seventeenth-century Ranters, a pantheistic sect that the Puritans had suppressed, religious Ranters believed that Christ may speak to anyone (by means of the "inner voice") and they denied the authority of the Bible.

wherever he sees them he rejoices. Those Elders which he railed the most against he feels to love the most &c. He spake to me but said he felt ashamed to do so. He seems very humble and comfortable with Sarah. He has had a deal of hard feelings against her. But all seems to be gone. After all I feel to have little hopes that he will hold out to the end. I believe he will again turn against us and be cut off &c. [seventeen lines crossed out].

[March 30, 1840. Monday.] Rebecca brought me raw egg in some red wine. Went to T. Millers to Dinner. Received a letter from Brother Fielding and one from Brother Woodruff. Sent one to Brother Alfred Cordon. Water at Hardmans. Went to Prestwich on Narrow lane. Preached on Revelations 14.6. Several are ready to be baptized. Sarah at the preaching house. Eliza Prince and Ann Jackson came to meet us and walked behind. Eliza seemed to be in a fret. Betsy Crooks and Dewsnup went with me. 6 baptized at Dukinfield yesterday, 5 at Manchester. My feet were very sore to[night]. Sarah washed them and gave me a pint of warm Porter. I lent her Book of Doc[trine] and Cov[enants].

[March 31, 1840. Tuesday.] Breakfast at Hardman's and Dinner with Sarah and Rebecca. Went to Cookson []. Brother Clark is gone to Macclesfield.[42] I went to Sister Williamsons to Water and thence to Eccles. Preached on Isaiah 24-5,6, attentive house. Got home about 11. To night Jones' Machine shop was burned to the ground. Supper with Sarah. She was waiting for me. Brother Jackson gave 1/-.

[April 1, 1840. Wednesday.] Breakfast at Hardman's. Rebecca and Alice very poorly. Went to see a lame lad. Prayed with and anointed his leg. Prayed with Brother Burgess and family and Alice. To Bewsher's to Dinner. Brother Bewsher gave me more than a pint of Porter. Betsy Crooks gave me some figs. Got a letter from Brother Richards and one from Brother Heath. Went to see Sister Heath. Water with Rebecca. From thence per Railway to Patricroft[43] and to m[eetings]. Preached at Row Green to a very full house. After a Ranters travelling opposed. Nothing

---

42 The center for England's silk milling after it was introduced into the country in 1756; fifteen miles from Manchester.
43 A cotton and silk milling town near Manchester.

very particular. Preached the gospel. He said children were born in sin &c. Walked home very quick about 7 or 8 miles. Mother and Sarah was waiting. Supper with Sarah. She washed my feet. She had a dream last night something like this. She thought a man brought a young man before her and said he was to be her companion. Wh[ich] I had told her was not true &c. about eternity and he said we were of different dispositions. She was troubled and thought in her own mind she would not be in a hurry &c. [five lines crossed out]. She gave me a new pair of slender shoes. Christiana gave me raisins.

[April 3, 1840. Friday.] Breakfast at Hardman's. Have seen Brother Booth and told him about respecting pledging his bible. He denies it. I warned about other things which I had heard going from house to house, abusing his wife idling &c. Dinner at Sister Booth's Newton. She gave me 3 oranges and 6 pence, Sarah Ann 7 oranges. I have had some conversation with Sister M[argaret] Townsend. She is quite calvinistic in sentiment. Will not hear of keeping all the commandments. Says I was going to Sinai &c. I read several passages and told her those opinions would be her ruin if she did not repent. She said I had no charity. She could not do with me. I should have to repent &c. I was like the Pope and many such things. She said we might cut her off. She told me I had a bad spirit. My blood boiled when she began to talk to me &c. Dinner and Coffee at Sister Booth's. Sister Mary Aspen gave me £1 for a Bible and some raisins. Bought a Bible and Crud[ins] concordance for 25/. Betsy Crooks gave me an orange and Christiana gave me one and some mint cake. Brother H[enry] Royle baptized 3 at Dukinfield on the 1st. Supper with Sarah Crooks.

[April 4, 1840. Saturday.] Went to pray with Brother Davies child. To C[atherine] Beates to Breakfast and Dinner. Sister Catherine says her mission is nearly done in England. She thinks of going to America &c. Saw Brother Bowman and Green &c. Brother Fielding came in from L[iverpoo]l about 10. Supper with Sarah. [ ] gave me 2 oranges, B[etsy] Crooks some drops, Rebekah is grieved at something.

[April 6, 1840. Monday.] Breakfast at Hardman's. Sent a letter to D[avid] Wilding. Dinner at T. Millers. Brother Fielding has been very sick. Water at T. Millers. Went to Pendlebury. Preached near an hour on the destruction of the gentiles &c. Got home at 11 o'clock. Supper with Sarah and Rebecca. They gave me a pint of Porter. Sarah washed my feet.

[April 7, 1840. Tuesday.] Breakfast at Hardmans. Got a letter from Brother Richards. Sent a letter to Alfred Cordon. Dinner with Sarah and Rebecca. Had some conversation with Sarah. It seems that the saints generally appear to envy her and feel a little jealous for some cause which they will not make known. Rebecca has seemed very much grieved at her, but I think she is mending of it [twenty-one lines crossed out]. I went with Brother Alston to Garner's and thence to the Post office. Came home for oil and went to see the lame boy in Islington. Thence to Brother Bateman's to water. Brother Fielding went to Eccles and I to Cookson Street. Brother Lea preached and I said a little after. One woman ready for baptism. Supper with Sarah.

[April 8, 1840. Wednesday.] Breakfast at T[homas] Mayors. Wrote a letter to Brother Richards. Met Brother Fielding at Bewsher's to Dinner. Elizabeth Mayor seems somewhat careless. She says the saints don't love her. She has observed a great difference since her mother died &c. Brother Bewsher gave us some Porter. Went to see Sister Birch. She gave me an orange. To Brother Bewshers to C[]. From thence I went to Worsely and preached on Revelations 20. Was opposed by a Methodist, Daniel Bradshaw. Took something to eat with Mary. She gave me a glass of Porter. I got to Manchester about 11 o'clock, nearly through. Sarah had some egg milk ready and she washed my feet and I then went to bed.

[April 9, 1840. Thursday.] This morning Rebecca brought some red wine and a raw egg in it. She also gave me 2 oranges. Breakfast at Hardman's. Received a letter for Brother Fielding stating that Brother [Heber C.] Kimball and 5 others were in Preston. They landed in Liverpool on Monday and left P[arley] P. Pratt at Liverpool with Brother Taylor. Dinner at Wm. Miller's. [William] gave me 2/6 for Brother Turly. Went with Brother Fielding to the Railway from thence to Sister Bewshers to Tea. Saw Sister Plant. She expects they are about to move into Derbyshire. Went to Princes to Supper.

43

[April 10, 1840. Friday.] Breakfast at Hardman's. Received a letter from Brother Fielding. 1 from A[lfred] Cardon. 1 from Mr. Williams. Went to see Benson's boy. Called at Cookson Street. Dinner with Sarah and Rebecca. To Brother T[homas] Owens. He and wife have been quarelling again. The boy is very disobedient. Brother Owens says he had better be cut off. His wife is upstairs but does not seem inclined to come down. Brother Owens gave me 1/-. Water at Hardman's. To council meeting appointments supplied &c. Lectured on faithfulness and true to each other. Supper with Sister E[llen] Battersby. She gave me a pint of Porter. She is much troubled about the Itch &c. Betsy Crooks gave me some raisins.

[April 11, 1840. Saturday.] Breakfast at Hardman's. Went to Bank and received 25/- for [Robert] Williams. Saw Sister C[atherine] Beates at Paul Harris's. She was very ill. She has brought me another fruit. Received a letter from Brother Woodruff. 1 from D[avid] Wilding. 1 from Brother Clark. 1 from Sister C. 1 from Brother Booth. Water with Sarah and Rebecca. Elizabeth Mills has been grieved on account of having lent money and clothing to some of the saints such as [] Harris and Mary Becket and they have not returned it according to promise. Sister H[anna]h Walker has been sitting upstairs 4 or 5 hours. There is something matter with her but she appears to stupid to tell what is matter with her. Margaret Jones gave me 2 oranges. Supper with Sarah and Rebecca. Brother Lea gone to baptize. 7 baptized tonight.

[April 12, 1840. Sunday.] This morning have had some conversation with Sister Hannah. She has had much trouble at the Mill and with her father. She is grieved because Alice is shy with her. Has been tempted to go and live with Mather's again. She has been tempted to leave the church. Does not think of going to meeting today. Wants Alice to speak freely to her again &c. I reasoned with her and tried to encourage her, but she is very stupid. She will have no breakfast. When I asked Alice to speak to her she seemed unwilling because she has done it so often. Breakfast with Sarah and Rebecca. Brother [Charles] Miller preached about 1 1/2 hours this A.M. Had a good meeting. P.M. confirmed 4. Went to Brother M. Greens to Dinner. Had conversation with Mr. Goodson. I took a little beer. Sarah Crooks gave me a orange and a sweet cake. Preached on John 10 chapter about 1 1/4. H. Whitehead gave me -/6. Brother Birch -/6. Sister Booth -/6. J[ohn] Smith 1/-. Brother Bewsher 1/- and about 3/- besides from others. Supper with Sarah and Rebecca.

[April 13, 1840. Monday.] Breakfast at Hardman's. Dinner with Sarah and Rebecca. Sarah Crooks gave me 2/6. Betsy Crooks 2/-. C[hristiana] Crooks 1/-. Rebecca Partington 1/6 and []. Brother Woodruff and Clark came in from the Potters and we started at 2 3/4 for Preston. Found Brother Kimball and Brigham Young at home. My family well.

[April 14, 1840. Tuesday.] Came this A.M. to Preston and found Brothers Taylor, P[arley] P. Pratt, [Orson] Pratt, G[eorg]e Smith &c. at Brother Richards. Dinner with Brother Fielding. Met in council with the twelve. C. at George Greenwoods and again met in conference at Brother Fieldings room. I bought a voice of warning 2/6. History of the persecutions []. Poems on Millennium 3/-.[44] Brother Richards ordained [].

[April 15, 1840. Wednesday.] Met in the cock Pit for conference. Brother Kimball was chosen president and I was chosen clerk. Total members 1677. Dinner at Sister Morgans. Brother Clark appointed in the place of Brother Richards. Ordained 2 priests. C. at George Greenwoods. Brother Woodruff and Taylor preached at night to an overflowing congregation.

[April 17, 1840. Friday.] This day the brethren have come from Preston. Brigham Young, P. P. Pratt, Orson Pratt, Heber C. Kimball, George A. Smith, Willard Richards, Willford Woodruff, Ruben Hadlock, H[ira]m Clark and J[osep]h Fielding. We have each had a glass of wine which my brother in law made 40 year since. We spent the day together and I wrote a minute of the conference for Brother Kimball to send to America. Brother Hadlock preached in my father in laws barn this night on John 15. Brothers Bradbury and Bourne from Burslem came and Brother Stafford from Stockport. They slept at our house.

---

[44] These three works by Parley P. Pratt were entitled *A Voice of Warning* . . . (1837); *The Millennium and Other Poems* (1840); and *History of the Late Persecutions* . . . (1839), cited in Chad J. Flake, ed., *A Mormon Bibliography, 1830-1930* (Salt Lake City: University of Utah Press, 1978), 522, 524, 525. First issued in 1837, Parley P. Pratt's *Voice of Warning* is considered to be the first doctrinal work published by church elders (*HC* 2:518).

[April 18, 1840. Saturday.] Went to B. Budge with Brother Stafford &c. Returned home and got dinner. Borrowed 4 of my wife to pay my Coach fare. Went to Preston and took Railway at 2 1/2. Got to Manchester 2-12 in company with brothers Clark and Smith. Saw Sister E. Ravenscroft. She gave me a new watch guard and brought a letter from E. Bromley. Sister H. Parkinson gave me 3 oranges. Margaret Jones gave me 2. Sarah and Rebecca gave me water and supper. Sarah gave me 1 pint of Porter and told me that C[atherine] Beates had told her that great trouble was coming upon her and she must keep herself single for she would scarce have an inch of ground to stand upon. I felt poorly tonight. My limbs and [head] ached very bad.

[April 19, 1840. Sunday.] My head still very bad. Sarah brought me some wine and a egg in it. Breakfast with Sarah and Rebecca. Brother Clark preached this morning. To B to dinner. Had a pint of Porter. I led meeting in P.M. Brother G[eorge] Smith spake a good deal. We confirmed 9, blessed 1 child and prayed with a number sick. Sarah gave me an orange. Sarah wept this morning much on account of what Sister Catherine said to her. Brother Lea baptized 4 this A.M. 5 has been baptized at Manchester this past week. Sarah gave me an orange. Brother Smith gave a lengthy detail of the rise of the church to a very full house. Good attention and good feeling. A man stood up and wanted to ask questions. I told him to wait till the meeting closed. But he did not come forward. Brother R[ichards] [gave] me 1/-, Sister Birch 1/-. Had conversation with Mary Darrah. She says she cannot believe the testimony. She has long seen baptism to be a duty. She asked if God was no respecter of persons why had he not sent an angel sooner &c. I talked a good deal to her. She wants to be baptised if she could believe, but she does not want to be an hypocrite. I told her she would be an L.D.S. She burst into tears and said if she thought she must not she would be miserable. I told B[etsy] Crooks that she should have her companion again. She is a loving young woman and desires to do right. I feel to love her much. Supper with Sarah and Rebecca.

[April 20, 1840. Monday.] Breakfast at Hardman's. Dinner at Sister He[rr]daker's. Went to see Bensons boy. From thence to the Railway to meet Brother P. P. Pratt. He arrived at 4 3/4. Took water with Sarah and Rebecca. Spent the evening at home with a many saints. Had [some] conversation with Mary Darrah. She feels more satisfied and feels to love the saints. E[lizabeth] Gladstone gave me oranges. Supper with Sarah and Rebecca.

[April 21, 1840. Tuesday.] Breakfast at Hardman's. Spent this A.M. with Brother Pratt in ascertaining the expense of printing a monthly paper. Dinner at Wm. Millers. Tea at old Mrs. Millers after which Brother Pratt and I went to [] fair. Went to see some wild animals. Brother Pratt went to preaching at Cookson Street. I remained at home. E. Gladstone [gave me an orange] and Sister Mary Wood a smelling bottle. Supper with Sarah and Rebecca. Alice is poorly and seems low.

[April 22, 1840. Wednesday.] Spent this A.M. with Brother Parley in seeking a suitable situation for a book establishment. Brother Bewshers to Dinner. Brother Clark is gone to Macclesfield. Went per Railway to Patricroft. Sarah Crooks went with me. Preached at Worsley on 2 Thessalonians 1-6 to 9. Had considerable questions to answer to some very ignorant men who professed to have a great deal of religion. I could scarce pray at the commencement they were so noisy. They dwelt much on the thief being saved without baptism. We got home about 1 o'clock. Took Supper with []. Sister Poole washed my feet. Sarah Crooks gave me an orange.

[April 23, 1840. Thursday.] This A.M. Brother Smith and Sister Ravenscroft are gone to the Potteries. Breakfast with Rebecca. Went with Brother Pratt to the Printers. He engaged with Mr. Thomas for 6-12 p[e]r thousand on good paper and to print a number of prospectus's gratis []. To Brother J. at Grundy's to Dinner and Wm. Millers to cocoa. Took a walk together to Knott Mill fair. Attended meeting at Wm. Millers at night. Sister Jemima Whittaker went into a kind of fainting fit she said through a blessing. Mary Darrah has been much tempted and feels her heart quite hard. Supper with Sarah and Rebecca. Sarah Perkins gave me an orange.

[April 24, 1840. Friday.] Breakfast at Hardman's. Sarah Crooks is at home short of work. Dinner at Thomas Mayors. Had some conversation with Elizabeth. She has felt hard against the saints. They have told falsehoods about her &c. She has not taken sacrament but 2 or 3 time since her mother died. Took water with

Sarah. Went to see the proof sheet for prospectus and thence to see Brother Lambert who is awfully afflicted with Small pox. Had council meeting with the officers. Supper at Hardman's with Sarah.

[April 25, 1840. Saturday.] Breakfast at Hardman's. Went to Cookson Street. Brother Richards came. Dinner at Brother West's. Went again to the printers. Brother Richards took coach for Burslem. To Princes to Cocoa. E[lizabeth] Crooks very full of trouble. Had a good deal of conversation with Mary Darrah. She had a many objections against the work and the bible such as contradictions and Jacob and David having more wives.[45] I reasoned with her and she was satisfied and said she would have been baptized had it not been late. She had something against Sarah Crooks for having taken Esther away from under the employment of her sister without giving a weeks notice. Sarah asked her forgiveness but she said she felt she could not. She wanted to do. Sarah was much grieved and seemed to fret. H. Parkinson gave me some oranges. Supper with Sarah and Rebecca.

[April 26, 1840. Sunday.] Breakfast with Sarah and Rebecca. Brother Pratt preached on Isaiah 24 ch. To Brother Bewsher's to Dinner. I opened meeting in the P.M. Brother Pratt spoke considerable. Sarah Crooks gave me an orange. Brother Pratt spake at night on Jacob have I loved but Esau have I hated. Sister Booth showed a very bad spirit on account of us not speaking to her on Thursday night. She said she came with a full determination to be cut off. She would hear no reason. Manifested []. Supper with Sarah and Rebecca [two illegible lines].

[April 27, 1840. Monday.] Breakfast with Sarah. To Brother Greens. Went to Printing office for prospectus's. To Wm. Miller's to Cocoa. From thence to Prestwich. Preached on I Cor. 3. To supper at Brother [Briersleys]. Sarah Crooks told me this A.M. something more that she was fretting of. When she was among the Methodists she began to keep company with George Buchanan. But on some account she took a kind of dislike to him. She went to Carlisle for 2 weeks and when she came back there had been

---

[45] This exchange occurred three years before Clayton learned of Mormon plural marriage and began to defend the doctrine.

some report about her. George came to her and humbled himself to her and when she still resisted him he said he would leave class again &c. She felt afraid and said if he would not leave class she would go with him again &c. The report spread abroad that she begged of George to go with her. She was to have been called before the school for it. But she never told them any other than that which they believed. When Mary Darrah spake to Sarah on Saturday night all these things came to her mind [ten lines crossed out]. I baptized at Rudleby.

[April 29, 1840. Wednesday.] Alice Hardman says her mother is very unkind to her and is almost about to break up house. Breakfast with Sarah. To Brother Bewshers to Dinner with Brother D[avid] Wilding and Pratt. Went to see Sister Jennings and found her in a bad state but she asked to be let alone a little longer. Called at the next house and there found her and 3 children sick. They have [scarce any] faith. He just came with medicine from the dispensary. I had some conversation and she appeared opposed in principle. I went on to roe Green. Waited till after 8 o'clock before any came. Preached on I Cor. 3. Slender house. Got home about 11 1/2. Sarah washed my feet and gave me supper.

[May 1, 1840. Friday.] Breakfast with Sarah. We went to Newton. Took Dinner at Sister Booths. Sarah and I took a walk into the fields. She appeared low and fretful. Water at Sister Booths. She gave me []. Went to Council meeting. Nothing particular. Supper with E. Battersby. She gave me a pint of Porter. Sister Sands was took very dangerously ill through miscarriage. She has been growing careless. Had hardness against me and was giving way to the world. She says she will be better.

[May 2, 1840. Saturday.] Breakfast at Hardman's. Dinner at J[ohn] Hardmans. Went to Oxford. Water with Sarah and Rebecca. Spent the evening upstairs with Sarah and Rebecca. Sarah has repaired my clothes and showed much kindness. Supper with Sarah and Rebecca. Mary Darrah is rather low. Sarah has fallen downstairs but is not much hurt.

[May 3, 1840. Sunday.] Breakfast with Sarah and Rebecca. Went to Dukinfield. Preached at [] on 1 Corinthians 3. Went to Dukinfield. Dinner with Sister Mary Burton. Spake on the kingdom in the P.M. Confirmed 6. Water with Royles. Preached D on Matthew 24, this gospel &c. Christiana Crooks gave me []. M. Parkinson gave me 1/- yesterday. On our way home I was disgusted in some measure with the conduct of Eliza Prince. She would not keep company with us but walked behind until Ann Jacson and her missed their way. Sarah and Rebecca, A[lice Hardman] and H[annah Walker] came to meet us. 4 baptized at Manchester 5 at Stockport on Friday. Sarah Ann Booth gave me a small sweet cake which came from France.

[May 4, 1840. Monday.] Alice Hardman and her mother is vexed at each other. Alice says her mother would soon break up the house if I was not there. Got a letter from my wife. Went to printing office to start the printer. Dinner at Sister Walkers. Spent the P.M. with Sarah and Alice. Water with Sarah then she went with me to Pendlebury. Preached on Matthew 24 this gospel &c. Full house. [] tea and returned. I found some oyster left by B[etsy] and C[hristiana] Crooks.

[May 5, 1840. Tuesday.] Breakfast with Sarah. Went to Sister Booths Newton. Sarah went with me. Dinner and Water at Sister Booth's. She gave me 3 oranges and -/6. We then went together to Eccles. Preached on Mark 16-15,16. Was much interrupted. One man asked me to lay aside my bible and preach without it. The enemies threw the meeting into confusion. Baptized 1. Supper at Harriss.

[May 8, 1840. Friday.] Got a letter from my wife saying that my mother is very ill. Breakfast at Princes. Dinner with Sarah and Rebecca. Sister Walker gave me 1/- Sister Black -/6. Water at Sister Green's. Sister Grundy has been slighting Sister Green because she had Itch and did not tell her. Nothing particular at council meeting. John Bailey has been drunk again. To be visited again and if he will not repent to be cut off. I spake to the officers to be faithful and set a good example. Teach the church unity &c. Supper with E[llen] Battersby. She gave me a pint of porter. C[hristiana] Crooks gave me 1/- Betsy Crooks 2/- and sweets.

[May 9, 1840. Saturday.] Sarah is rather grieved because she thinks she is to bold &c. She remembers the liberty which has been taken with her before time and how she suffered by it. She tarried till 7 o'clock. Breakfast with Hardman's. Sarah has returned from her work. Called at Jane Brown's. Alice and Jane was both weeping but would not tell me what for. H. Parkinson gave me 2 oranges. I left home at 10 1/2 for Knotts Mill. Started by boat at 11 1/2. Sarah came with me to Attrincham. I got to [] at 5 1/2. Set sail by steam Boat at 6 and arrived at Liverpool at 8 o'clock. The days was rather wet and gloomy otherwise it was a pleasant ride. Found Brother Taylor better. Supper with Cannons. Had a pint of warm Porter at R[].

[May 12, 1840. Tuesday.] Breakfast at Cannons. Went with Brother Taylor to see Sister Harrington. Took dinner and tea and returned to Brother Dumvills. We had a church meeting for the purpose of organizing the church. Brother Taylor spake considerable on the necessity of organization the nature and design &c. He then proposed Wm. Mitchell to be chosen as secretary for the church, Richard Harrison priest and John James priest Thomas Dumville and John Dixon T. which being elected unanimously Elder Taylor called upon the brethren to know if they accepted their offices which Wm. Mitchell said he would rather have nothing to do with money matters. He was told there was no money matters, but to keep a church record. But he refused to do it. Elder Taylor then proposed Brother George Cannon who accepted the office. We then proceeded with ordination after which I spake a little on the importance of having an office and the necessity of the prayers of the Saints and concluded the meeting. Supper at Dumvills. Brother Armstrong has made me a new vest and Brother Mitchell has repaired my Boots. Brother Taylor gave me 33/-0 for Brother Pratt.

[May 14, 1840. Thursday.] Breakfast at Hardmans. Spent the A.M. chiefly reading. Went to Wm. Millers to Dinner. Sent a letter to my wife and one to Brother Heath. Called at the printers. Went at night to Prince's. E. Dewsnup has again been railing and endeavoring to prejudice them against Elizabeth Crooks. Eliza[beth] says she can bear it no longer and says she will be cut off. I told her we would not do it on those reasons but I would emdeavor to get things right. Took supper with them and returned.

[May 17, 1840. Sunday.] Breakfast with Sarah and Rebecca. Preached on Ephesians 4, 1 to 16. To Mr. Patricks to dinner. Agness was married this week to a Mr. Bilbirene. I spake again

51

in the afternoon on evil speaking and hard feelings. There seemed to be a weight on the meeting. 2 was confirmed. I had some conversation with P. Grundy. She is grieved at Sister Green and grieved because she has heard that we intend to remove the meeting. Preached again on the same Chapter. After meeting 2 were baptized. 2 baptized from Eccles this A.M. Had some conversation with Alice' Cousin Jane Hardman. She is a very nice young woman and does not seem to object to anything. Sister Dewsnup came and I told her what had been said about her and what I thought but she denies all and seems to justify herself but I don't feel satisfied with her spirit. I had a letter from my wife this A.M. Brother Joseph Birch gave me -/6 H. Parkinson -/6 Jane Mahon -/6 and C[atherine] Beates -/6. Supper with Sarah and Rebecca. They gave me a pint of warm porter. 2 baptized at Pend.

[May 19, 1840. Tuesday.] Breakfast with Rebecca. C. with Sister Rigby. Rebecca went with me to Eccles. Preached on Ephesians 4 chapter. Full House and behaved well. Took a little refreshment. Supper with Sarah, 1 pint porter. She washed my feet. We sat together till 2 o'clock.

[May 20, 1840. Wednesday.] Breakfast with Rebecca. Went to Bewshers to Dinner. Had a pint of porter. Returned to fetch 200 stars[46] from office. C. with Rebecca. Brother Garner is gone to Liverpool this A.M. to start for America. 3/- was sent from Brother Clark. Left by a sister. [] On Monday night Alice and Hannah went to Brother Pratts and tarried til near 11. [Nineteen lines crossed out.] I took Railway at 5 o'clock and was at home at 7. Found all Matthias Moons family except John who was gone to Liverpool but he soon returned. Had a little made wine.

[May 25, 1840. Monday.] Brother Fielding came and his wife. Sent for Brother [Peter] Melling and he having previously been ordained to the office of Patriarch he proceeded to confer a patriarchal blessing upon Thomas Moon and then upon his wife. After he got through Brother Moon proceeded to bless his children in order according to their age. I also received my blessing under

---

[46] The *Latter-day Saints' Millennial Star* was the first foreign Latter-day Saint newspaper, a monthly periodical published in England beginning in 1840. Parley P. Pratt arrived in Manchester on April 20 and began planning the newspaper the next day.

his hands to this effect, that I should have a good memory, have strong faith in God, should be the means of bringing 100s and 1000s to God and to the truth of his gospel, should be preserved from the hands of wicked and ungodly men and should come forth in the kingdom of God.

[May 26, 1840. Tuesday.] Went with Brother Kimball to Preston. Dinner at Sister Morgans. Thence to Francis Moon's. Brother Kimball here gave me a most extensive and great blessing. Returned home and proceeded to writing.

[May 27, 1840. Wednesday.] After finishing writing I went to see my mother who is a little better. Came back and got ready for Manchester. Went to Preston. Met Brother Kimball at the Railway and we started. Arrived in 1 3/4 hours. Called at Hardmans and took Water and then went to the office[47] where we found Brothers Pratt, Young, and Taylor. Supper with Sarah and Rebecca. Brother Kimball slept with me. I had a fit of sickness tonight. I drank 6 pints of brandy which gave me ease.

[May 28, 1840. Thursday.] Took breakfast at Sister [Elizabeth] Pooles. Brother Kimball sent for a quart of Porter. Dinner with Sarah and Rebecca. I went to the office a little and in the P.M. my face began to be very bad. I had it washed with brandy and went to bed about 12 but was obliged to get up again about 1 and continued up untill 4 1/2. I suffered a great deal.

[May 29, 1840. Friday.] Dinner with Sarah and Rebecca. Went to the office to help in selecting hymns. At 5 1/2 met Brothers Heath, Berry and Wytch. They have been contending one against the other and has hard feelings against each other. We heard all their stories and Brother Wytch seemed to manifest in some degree a very bad spirit. I spake a little to them and advised them to be one &c. Brother Kimball and Young came to Hardman's and sung some and afterwards spake with each other in tongues. I had supper with Sarah and Rebecca. Brother Kimball went to Prince's.

[May 30, 1840. Saturday.] Breakfast at Hardman's. Dinner at P. Hams. Brother Taylor sick. He and Brothers Kimball and

---

[47] They went to the office of the *Millennial Star* on Oldham road in Manchester.

Young are gone to Liverpool. C. with Sarah and Rebecca. Read the vision[48] to some of the sisters. Felt it good. Supper with Sarah and Rebecca.

[May 31, 1840. Sunday.] Breakfast with Sarah and Rebecca. Preached on John chapter 17. To Bewshers to Dinner. Had a pint porter. Led the P.M. meeting. Brother Pratt spake some. Ordained Brother Wm. Parr Elder. John Lee Priest and William Black Teacher. Had a cake given me. Sarah Crooks tells me that she has been informed that James Mahon has a wife and 2 children living in Ireland that James was cut off from the Catholic church because of disowning her. His wife was sent for by the priest (who had got a certificate of their marriage) and she came to him but he denied her. She said if he would only own her she would not trouble him. She went back to Ireland. They separated because of poverty.[49] James was taken ill sometime after and thought he should die. He then acknowledged the fact. These things Sarah has heard from credible witness. James is about to be married to E[lizabeth] Mills. Brother Pratt preached on 3 chapter I Peter, restoration. I baptized 2 after. One was Jane Hardman. Sarah and Rebecca gave me each an orange and sweet cake [].

[June 1, 1840. Monday.] Breakfast at Hardman's and Dinner with Sarah and Rebecca. Went to Prestwich and preached on the Priesthood Hebrews chapter 7. After preaching I spake to the members on the words of wisdom and afterwards ordained Brother Walker Johnson priest. Took tea and returned. Met Sarah Crooks.

---

[48] This most likely refers to the vision which Joseph Smith proclaimed in 1832 of an afterlife of three kingdoms, now found in D&C 76. This was widely known as "The Vision." It is also possible that Clayton refers to the story of Joseph Smith's "First Vision" of 1820, which was unknown to most Latter-day Saints until Orson Pratt described it in his September 1840 missionary tract, *An Interesting Account of Several Remarkable Visions and of the Late Discovery of Ancient American Records*, published in Edinburgh, Scotland. Since Smith's account of an awesome confrontation with "the Father and the Son" was recorded in the manuscript history of the church the year before, Clayton could have heard that account circulating in the British mission before its publication. For a discussion of various accounts of the "First Vision" story, see Dean C. Jessee, "The Early Accounts of Joseph Smith's First Vision," *Brigham Young University Studies* 9 (Spring 1969); James B. Allen, "The Significance of Joseph Smith's 'First Vision' in Mormon Thought," *Dialogue: A Journal of Mormon Thought* 1 (Autumn 1966): 29–45.
[49] Many people fled to Manchester from widespread famine and poverty in Ireland.

She seems low and poorly. Supper with Rebecca. There was come thunder and heavy rain soon as I got home.

[June 3, 1840. Wednesday.] Breakfast with Elizabeth Mayor. To Bewshers to Dinner. Brother D[avid] Wilding says that Wilkinson or Worsley dare not let us preach. His master has got to hear and he is in danger of losing his work. Called at Sister Birchs. She is in much trouble on account of her husband. She gave me -/6. Supper with Sarah and Rebecca.

[June 4, 1840. Thursday.] Have been this morning to see Mr. Hearne and enquire concerning James Mahon. He says he knows nothing about him. Breakfast at Hardman's. Dinner and Water at Wm. Millers. Went to Pollard St. and entered into conversation with a man untill it was time to close the meeting.

[June 5, 1840. Friday.] Brother Pratt spake some at the council concerning the rise of the church, the visit of angels and many strange things &c.[50]

[June 6, 1840. Saturday.] Had conversation with Mr. John Hardman about 3 hours. He seems to have much false notion and tradition &c.

[June 8, 1840. Monday.] I have no reasons to believe that the reports concerning James Mahon are true but pretty clear evidence that they are false. Sarah Crooks and I went to Pendlebury. Spake on the priesthood authority &c. Sarah was taken very ill.

[June 12, 1840. Friday.] At Council meeting a number of the saints attended. Brother Green almost got the gift of tongues. Brother Young spake in tongues.

[June 13, 1840. Saturday.] About 2 o'clock this A.M. Elizabeth Crooks began in her sleep to sing in tongues. She spake and sung in about 7 languages occupying about 2 hours. During the day Betsy Pool got the gift of tongues.

[June 14, 1840. Sunday.] Brother Young preached on Matthew 9 he that heareth these sayings. In the P.M. Sister Pool spake in tongues then Rich[ard] Hardman James Mahon Sister Heath.

---

[50] Pratt's speech may anticipate the *Remarkable Visions* pamphlet in n48.

We confirmed 4. Christiana Crooks and Jemima Whittaker spake in tongues. I preached on Galatians 1 though we are an angel &c. After preaching I baptized William Hardman and a young woman.

[June 20, 1840. Saturday.] This evening I had considerable conversation with Mr. Bland who was once a member of the church. He was fully confounded in some of his favorite opinions and left without room to say a word. We talked about 3 hours.

[June 27, 1840. Saturday.] Very poorly all day. At night Brother Green spake in tongues. The power of Satan was powerfully manifested upon some of the Sisters. Sarah gave me a pint of porter.

[June 29, 1840. Monday.] Went to Hart Street. Found them all confusion. One blaming another &c. To Sister Booth's to Dinner. She gave me 1/6. Stayed at the meeting. 2 spake in tongues. I addressed them and tried to encourage them to dilige[nce]. My face was very bad.

[June 30, 1840. Tuesday.] Brothers Kimball and Richards came from Preston. We went together with E[lder]s Parley Pratt and Young to Wm. Millers to singing meeting. Took supper. My mind was very low because I thought the brethren looked shy.

[July 1, 1840. Wednesday.] Went to Sands to Dinner. Called at Sarah Perkins. Brothers Woodruff, Smith and Turley came in. I received a bonnet for my little Sarah from E. Ravenscroft. Had talk with Ann Darrah. Full of sectarian [notions].

[July 6, 1840. Monday.] This day we held our conference in Carpenters Hall members 2513, Elders 59 Priests 122 Teachers 61 Deacons 13. Elder Pratt was president. I was chosen clerk. Brother Green was suspended from office for giving way to a false spirit for accusing a young female of things which he could not prove (in a public meeting) and for abusing house and congregation at Dukinfield June 28, 1840. Brother John Taylor preached at night. Ordained 14 officers and 4 others to be ordained.

[July 7, 1840. Tuesday.] Held council at the Star office. It was voted that I should go to Birmingham as soon as my family were gone to America.

[July 19, 1840. Sunday.] Preached this A.M. in Carpenters Hall on the fall of the Gentile church and the judgements to be poured out on consequence.

[July 23, 1840. Thursday.] Returned to Penwortham by Railway to assist my family in making preparations for America. Found them all well and in good spirits. Sister C[atherine] Beates gave me a yellow silk Handkerchief and Sister Elizabeth Dewsnup gave me a red one. Sister Mary Wood gave me a new satin stock. Sarah Crooks has got me money for a new pair of boots 28/-. Sarah Ann Booth gave me a four penny pence to remember her by. Sister Hannah Walker gave me a Pocket handkerchief and I feel it hard to leave the saints at Manchester yet willing because it is for the best.

[September 3, 1840. Thursday.] Since July 23, we have been engaged in making preparations for America. On Tuesday the 18 of August we had our sale. I was writer. We had some difficulty in getting all our money in and especially some due from the Railway company for damages. We had after to go and did not get it untill a few days before we started. The time had been appointed for us to be in Liverpool on the 27th of August but the time was prolonged untill Sept[ember] 4 on account of some of the saints not being ready. It happened well it was so for we had hardly time to settle up our business by the 4 of Sept. During this time I preached occasionally on the sabbath. The first 3 or 4 days after I came home I spent in writing Brother Kimballs history which was lengthy.[51] I have got a pair of Boots which cost 27/6. On this day we have been very busy packing up and have taken one load of Boxes to the Railway. The brethren have collected 7/- towards carrying me to Birmingham. The parting scene was affecting. Elder Riley felt very much. He gave me 2/6. Elder Brigham Young has been over from Manchester. On Monday we went to Longton and returned same night. He returned to

---

[51] Heber C. Kimball, who had baptized Clayton, was head of the British Mission but had little formal education. A powerful speaker, he often turned to scribes such as Clayton to do his writing. Allen and Alexander suggest that Kimball's history was the "History of the British Mission," the first foreign mission of the church (1837–41), presented in *HC* 4:313–21. See James B. Allen and Thomas G. Alexander, eds., *Manchester Mormons: The Journal of William Clayton, 1840–1842* (Salt Lake City: Peregrine Smith, 1974), 169n177.

Manchester on Tuesday. I have spent one afternoon at Sister
Morgans in company with Brother Wm. Hardman. He made me
a present of a handsome knife. Several have been baptized while
I have been here and the work is in a prosperous state. The preaching will be held in future at [Edward] Martins. John Melling was
married to Mary Martin about 2 weeks ago. Some person on
Saturday evening last threw two notes into Brother Whiteheads
shop one for himself and the other for me. They both contained
the same matter namely a request that we would preach from
Ecclesiastes chapter 10 verse 1 signed a lover of Mormons.[52] I
went over to Manchester and walked all the way and in the morning went to Liverpool. I returned home in the P.M. having learned
that the ship which Brother Moon's sailed in arrived in New York
about the 18th of July. On Wednesday the 19th I received a letter
from Brother John Moon giving an account of their voyage. They
were 41 days on the water including 3 days quarantine. They had
3 storms and considerable sickness but all arrived safe and in
good spirits. I have endeavored to sell Brother Moons Base Vial
but without success. T. Pickering promised to buy it for the new
church in Farington but when I went to agree with him he declined taking it. I then went to Wm. Bashale but he would not
have any thing to do with it. I was obliged to leave it with Brother
John Melling for sale. I have received two letters from Brother
Kimball of London and one from Sarah Crooks.

[September 4, 1840. Friday.] We arose early this A.M. and
packed up our beds &c. and took the remainder of our goods to
Preston. All the company their came together to our house about
1 o'clock from whence we started to the Farington Railway station. Here an extra carriage had been left for us and we loaded
ourselves a little after two and waited the arrival of the Train. We
were 26 in number including children. The train soon came up
and our carriage being attached we started off in the presence of
about a dozen saints. We had a pleasant ride to Liverpool about 5
o'clock. When we got there I made a bargain with a carter to take
our boxes &c to Princes dock for 1/ 1 1/2. When we got to the
Dock another man professing to be the owner of the cart came

---

[52] This was a derisive request. The biblical verse cited refers to "dead flies" in
the ointment.

and demanded 1/6 pr box. We had a hard contest. He threatened to fetch a policeman &c. He then wanted 2/6. I told him that for his bad behavior I would not give him any thing more than the bargain. He refused to take it for sometime but at last he took it and went away in a rage. Several of the brethren who came had to pay extremely on account of hiring men and not making a bargain before they engaged them. I was aware of such things and therefore acted as stated above. We found Elder Turley and Young soon. All the company was confused and busy arranging their boxes. We slept in the ship this night or lay awake.

[September 5, 1840. Saturday.] This A.M. I bought a pair of trowsers having tore my others. I engaged the cart to fetch our other luggages and during the day we got them in some measure arranged. My motherinlaw seeing the toil and trouble there was in these things began to weep and wish me to go with them. She made her request known the brothers Young and Taylor who consented for me to go.[53] I immediately started for Railway to Manchester where I arrived about 1/2 past 7. When I got to Hardmans I found Sarah and Rebecca just making preparations to leave that night. I saw there was something rather unpleasant between them and it almost broke my heart. Almost as soon as I arrived here I was taken sick on account of being so long without meat and over exerting myself. I vomited much and felt very ill. I could eat nothing. I slept at Hardmans that night.

[September 6, 1840. Sunday.] This A.M. I was very sick and kept my bed till noon. Several of the saints came to see me. Went to Perkins in the P. M. Was obliged to go to bed again and remained in bed untill 10 o'clock. A many of the saints came to see me. Brother Grundy gave me 2/6. Sister Birch gave me some plumbs and 1/-. Some of them wept much at parting. Sarah Crooks has got some linnen and cut it to day for shirts. Arthur Smith has been today and bought cloth for my trowsers and cut my cloths [out].

---

[53] Although Clayton was originally designated to preside over the church in Birmingham, England (see July 7 entry), he now accompanies his families to America.

[September 7, 1840. Monday.] Breakfast at Perkins. Sister Jane Hardman sent me a watch guard and four penny box to remember her by. Brother T. Miller gave me a new hat. Left Perkins about 11 for Railway. Was obliged to get a cab in St. Anns Square. Was a few minutes to late at the office. Went to Mr. Thompsons where I took dinner. She gave me a glass of wine. Took first carriage at 2. Arrived at Liverpool a little after 3 o'clock. When I arrived at the ship I found Elder [Willard] Richards. He seemed to object to my going. This gave me some trouble. I was yet very poorly. At night preparations was made for sailing on the morrow. Ship North America captain [Alfred] Lower.[54]

[September 8, 1840. Tuesday.] This A.M. about 8 o'clock we was hauled out of dock and a steamer being attached we was tugged into the sea in the presence of many spectators. The company cheerful. Elders Young, Richards and Taylor went with us and returned by the steamer. About this time many began to be sick myself amongst the number. 2 brothers was obliged to be put back on account of being over number. We was 201 men women and children. One of those put back was Brother Heap from Preston. I had no knowledge of having to go yet until Saturday afternoon and I did not send any letters being so sick. Brother William Hardman promised to write for me and my brother David was at Liverpool. Soon after the steamer returned the mate came down and ordered all boxes fast as they expected a good rocking that night. It was even so. The wind blew hard the vessel rock and many were sick all night. This was a new scene. Such sickness, vomiting, groaning and bad smells I never witnessed before and added to this the closeness of the births almost suffocated us for want of air.

[September 9, 1840. Wednesday.] This A.M. Elder Turley ordered all the company on deck to wash as the weather was a

---

[54] Captain Alfred B. Lowber was shipmaster on this eventful thirty-four-day voyage of the *North America* which included gales, fire, disputes, and six deaths. His name was spelled different ways, including "Lower." Conway B. Sonne, *Ships, Saints, and Mariners: A Maritime Encyclopedia of Mormon Migration, 1830–1890* (Salt Lake City: University of Utah Press, 1987), 155–56.

little more calm.[55] We had a pleasant view of the North of Ireland as we sailed on that side. In the afternoon the wind increased and blew a gale until Saturday morning. I was in bed nearly all this time and very sick and so was many of the company. Elder Turley was sick a little, Brothers William and Robert and Nehemiah Greenhalgh, Sister Mary Moon and James Crompton was not sick. These were very kind in waiting upon those sick. During all this gale the whole of the company or nearly so was very ill and many confined to their beds. We were drifted back to the North and was 4 hours in one place and could not move. I have been told that we were in two whirlpools near to a rock and the captain expecting us to be dashed against it. We was in great danger but the Lord delivered us. On the Friday night a little girl belonging to a family in the second cabin[56] was frightened by the storm and lost her reason. The company was composed but we were ignorant of [our] danger. Some of the rigging was blown away. See September 21.

[September 12, 1840. Saturday.] The storm is somewhat abated and the company begin to brighten up a little. Myself remains very feeble.

[September 13, 1840. Sunday.] The captain requested Elder Turley to preach this P.M. He read John chapter I and preached about 3/4 of an hour. This night the child which was frightened died or rather in the morning.

[September 14, 1840. Monday.] At the request of the Captain, Elder Turley read the burial service and the body of the child was committed to the deep. The weather continues favourable.

[September 15, 1840. Tuesday.] We have had another storm and many has been sick.

[September 18, 1840. Friday.] [] the company continue very sick especially three of the children. Some have doubt concerning

[55] Theodore Turley presided over this second company of Mormon emigrants from Liverpool.

[56] Second Cabin was the designation for relatively comfortable private quarters, more expensive than Steerage Passage, where the Mormon company was lodged in open, dormitory-style, quarters with more than one person per bed. Best Cabin was first-class passage.

[] recovery. Brother and Sister [Holmes] of Herefordshire have given up their [] to die. Elder Turleys mind is much grieved in consequence of these things. At night he called the saints together in order to ascertain their feelings concerning the recovery of those sick. The sequel showed [] was some unbelief in our midst. He spake considerable on the subject and asked the brethren to state their feelings. One immediately said he believed Holmes's child would not recover. I said I did not believe it was the will of God we should lose one soul. Elder Turley said to the same effect. The saints then began to be more cheerful and the power of darkness was in some degree banished. We prayed with the children and desired all to hold them by faith. But after all our exertions Brother Holmes' child died same night. This was a grief to our minds, but it was so.

[September 19, 1840. Saturday.] Early this A.M. the mate came and ordered the child to be sewed up which was soon done and it was immediately thrown overboard without any ceremony. After the place was cleansed out gas was burned to sweeten the ship air and prevent disease. A head wind.

[September 20, 1840. Sunday.] We were not requested to preach today but Elder Turley called the saints together in the P.M. and we broke bread to the company. Many seem much pleased with our [meeting].

[September 21, 1840. Monday.] Good sail. At night Elder Turley spoke considerable on cleanliness and afterwards went round the births to see if all the company undressed. Some was found with their cloths on and some had never pulled their cloths off since they came on deck but had done their dirt in their cloths. Others had dirt in the corner of their birth. This made the most awful smell when discovered almost to much to bear. Elder Turley undressed and washed them and ordered the place cleaned out. [Some of the company] are filthy indeed.

Errata. See September 9th. On Thursday night during the gale when the sailors had close reefed all the sails except about 4 and were endeavoring to Reef these there came a gust of wind that took away 3 of the sails one maine sail. On Friday night we lost another sail and some of the blocks.

[September 22, 1840. Tuesday.] This A.M. we had a calm. About 11 o'clock I heard the chief mate cry out all hands on deck and buckets with water. It appears that some of the Sisters was sitting near their births watching what they considered to be the reflections through a glass [light] until sparks of fire began to drop. They then cried out the ship is on fire. The mate heard and sang out as above. This caused considerable alarm and bustle for some time. The sailors was speedily at work and water was poured on for sometime. It was soon discovered that there was not much danger. The fire originated in the galley or cooking house. The wood underneath the stove had caught fire by some means and burned through the deck. After the fire was put out the Captain ordered the stove removed and the place examined. It was cleaned out and repaired and some improvements [made]. Some of the saints smelled fire last night and told the mate but he could not discover any thing wrong. We look upon this circumstance as another attempt of the adversary to destroy us but the Lord kindly preserved us. Some of us had wished in the morning that the wind would blow but it was well we had a calm or the consequence might have been awful. As soon as the bustle subsided the wind began to blow and we were again on our way home. The Lord has been kind to us for which we feel thankful but [not] as much [as we might]. Same night also we had the painful task of casting overboard Mormon son of Paul and Jane Harris []. He was one of the three which has been sick for some days. He was thought to be dead sometime before he was and preparation was made to bury him. He died about 8 o'clock. Sister Jane Harris was very sick at the same time. There are several others also very sick. We attend to prayer every evening as well as our awkward circumstances will permit.

[September 23, 1840. Wednesday.] This A.M. the Captain called upon all the heads of families to give account of the number of Packages each one owned. He appeared vexed on account of some having so many boxes. Our family was one. We have reason to think that he is seeking some occasion against us from several expressions which dropped from his lips this A.M. We have had a little trouble on account of the peevish selfish actions of some of the second cabin passengers. We have some difficulty in keeping things [quiet] amongst us. Many things are lost and nobody finds them. Some are not saints who profess to be. But considering our situation all things have passed off pretty well through the blessing of God.

[September 26, 1840. Saturday.] To day being our turn to attend the sick I took it in hand. But the smoke made me very ill. My head and limbs ached much. Sister Naylor and I have had a few words concerning our boxes. They have tresspassed on our privileges a little. They are but one family and have two boxes out, we are two families and have but one. I desired them to move one about four inches but they would not. She railed a little at me and used some hard words.

[September 27, 1840. Sunday.] Fair wind. One of the cabin passengers read prayers out of the church prayer book. They requested us to preach but Elder Turley was not willing and I did not feel at all fit for it and so it was neglected. We had no meeting. Some sick [].

[September 28, 1840. Monday.] We have had a head wind but a good days sail. Myself very sick. The infant child belonging to Brother and Sister Corbridge of Thomly died this P.M. and was cast overboard. At night Brother Turley spake concerning some of the company having said he had a shilling a head for all the saints and other such things. He shewed his bills and accounts to satisfy them and [] them for their hardness of heart and unbelief.

[September 29, 1840. Tuesday.] This A.M. we have a perfect calm. The captain and some of the cabin passengers have been swimming and afterwards took a short voyage in a small boat. The weather is extremely hot to day almost to much for us to bear. Brother Samuel Bateman caught a young Shark during the calm near a yard long. The infant child belonging to Brother and Sister Green of Manchester died this evening and was buried in the deep. We have spent this P.M. in arranging for payment of potatoes. The whole cost is about £28 which amounts to 3/1 per head or adult persons. Elder Turley has from time to time spoken much concerning the sisters keeping themselves from the sailors. Sister Mary Ann Holmes from Herefordshire has made great freedom with them which has been a grief to us. This night Elizabeth Wilson, Elizabeth Lambert and Eliza Prince all from Manchester and Sister Crampton from Bolton was making very free with one of the mates and 2 of the cabin passengers. Brother Cope says they were drinking wine with them. Elder Turley sent Sister Poole to request them to come [away] but they returned very indifferent answers and said they could take care of themselves.

[October 1, 1840. Thursday.] The wind began to blow []. During the day we crossed the fishing banks. We saw about 20 fishing boats ankered on the banks while we were crossing the banks. We had a squal. The main Top sail was torn from top to bottom and the vessel rolled much. Many were sick last night. The Captain and cabin passengers spent the night in dancing to the violin.

[October 2, 1840. Friday.] The wind good this A.M. sailing about 9 to 10 miles an hour. We discover that the crew are mad with us and we judge it is because we are unwilling that the sisters should be so familiar with the mates and sailors. There has been some unpleasant feelings manifested from those who [] company with the mate and cabin passengers the other night. Philip the Captains brotherinlaw is proved to be an enemy to us and tells tales to the mates. He seems very kind to our face but it is to spy us. My little Margaret is very sick.[57]

[October 3, 1840. Saturday.] This A.M. the mate says some of our company has been stealing water the last night. We don't believe they have. We have reasons to believe they have not as we had a watch appointed to see that the sailors did not come down as they have done before in the dead of the night. They saw no one but must have seen them if anyone had been at the water. We look upon it as another instance of Phillips madness and seeking to injure us. About this time Elizabeth was passing the sailors cabin and one of the sailors asked her to go down and have breakfast. She would not. He then asked if she would have a piece of meat. She said she had no objections and accordingly took it. It appears the steward saw her and went and told the Captain who immediately came down and demanded it from her. He also asked who gave it her. She said she did not know. On account of this the sailors are to have a pound a day less each and they are mad and swear vengeance on the steward when they get to land. This

---

[57] Clayton's eighteen-month-old daughter.

afternoon Joseph Jackson entered into an argument with some of the second cabin passengers upon religious subjects. The Captain and some of the cabin passengers was listening. The Captain went to the side of the ship and called Jackson to him to ask if he has said that he would go and take the water by force. He acknowledged to saying that he believed it right to take it as many were suffering for want of water and also that he believed those childrens death was partly caused on account of being short of water. The Captain ordered him down and told him if he heard him say anything like it again he would bind him down in chains and feed him on bread and water. Jackson answered the Captain again that we were suffering for want of water. I rebuked him and got him to hold his peace. He said he would defend himself. The captain said he might preach his religion as much as he liked but say nothing more like that. He also said he would like to kill about a dozen of us. This myself heard. The Captain afterwards came to Elder Turley and asked if he understood the laws of mutiny. Elder Turley answered yes and the laws concerning water to. The Captain said "You must know we lost six barrels of water during the storm soon after we left Liverpool." It seems the Captain thought brother was ignorant concerning the laws but when he saw to the contrary he softened down and changed colour. He said he would bind Jackson if he heard him use the same expressions. Yes says Brother Turley and I will help you. It is more and more evident that Satan wants to destroy us or throw us into confusion. After dark the chief mate came to Elder Turley and said "some of your damb'd crew has up set the water tub." It was found to be some of the Scotch people in the second cabin.

[October 4, 1840. Sunday.] This A.M. we have a good wind. Are sailing from 9 to 11 miles an hour. We have also our full allowance of water again. We have only had 1 1/2 quarts since September 20th. We had no meetings to day only as usual at night. My mother in law is very poorly, also Eliz[abeth] Ravenscroft.

[October 5, 1840. Monday.] We are not sailing much today. I feel myself very poorly. Motherinlaw and my wife yet very sick. Elder Turley and some of the cabin passengers along with the Captain have had a long argument this night concerning the ministration of the angel to Joseph. They treat it with disdain, especially the Captain.

[October 6, 1840. Tuesday.] This day Elder Turley went to prove to the cabin passengers the rationality of prophecy and administration of angels. They will not admit of reasonable evidence. They found themselves confounded. At night Elizabeth and William Poole spoke in tongues. He prophesied of the death of his child.

[October 7, 1840. Wednesday.] Early this A.M. Wm. Poole's child died and was committed to the deep. Some at Penwortham had said it would die before it got over the waters and Betsy had been troubled on this account. I wish they would not do so for Satan takes advantage of such things to discourage the minds of the Saints when surrounded by trouble and difficulty. This A.M. the chief mate saw Cape Cod on the American coast. The line was heaved and found 55 fathom.[58] They tacked ship about 8 o'clock to near South and then found 44 fathom. We were a few hours becalmed. About 12 o'clock we was much pleased to hear the mate speak to a ships Captain. The Condor of Halifax bore down to us and they spake to each other. She was from Jamaica 24 days homeward bound. My motherinlaw yet very poorly.

[October 8, 1840. Thursday.] Last evening being my turn for [] ask the Lord for a fair wind and I rejoice to see he has answered my prayers [] the third instance of the Lord answering my prayer for fair wind in a calm.

[October 9, 1840. Friday.] Fair days sail. The crew are very busily engaged cleaning the ship and making preparations for landing. At night the anker chains was fastened to the anker.

[October 10, 1840. Saturday.] About 8 A.M. land was discovered by the sailors from the fire mast and in about 2 hours we had a pleasant view of Long Island. About 1/2 past eleven we spoke the Tuscany. New York, 56 days from Gibralter. About 5 o'clock the Pilot came on board. We saw lighthouses on the Island.

---

[58] A fathom is six feet, which here indicates a water depth of 330 feet.

[October 11, 1840. Sunday.] This morning early we cast anker and a little after 4 o'clock I went on deck and found that we were between two Islands. We had a pleasant view of the Sailors Hospital and a many beautiful white houses and fine trees. 'Twas indeed a pleasant sight. The Docter came on board about 8 o'clock and about the same time the child belonging to Brother Parry from Herefordshire died. All the rest passed the docter without difficulty. The docter ordered him to be sent on shore which was done in a small Boat. Here I may say that we struck a sand bar last night and had it not been calm we might have gone to pieces. This was off Sandy Hook.[59] After the boat returned the ship was turned land. In a short time we was on our way for New York. Considering the wetness of the morning we had a very pleasant sight of the fowls and Island. After about an hours sail we arrived in New York exactly at a quarter before twelve. It was truly delightful to see the multitude of shipping in the Harbour. There is no docks here but a very good harbour. The buildings look elegant. When our vessel came to harbour she pressed against a small schooner and stove in her bulwarks and broke some rigging. After the ship was made fast Elder Turley and me and Joseph Jackson left the ship and set our feet on land exactly at 10 minutes past 12 o'clock. This was another treat to us to set our feet on terra firma although the streets was dirty in consequence of rain. In taking a slight glance I must confess I was delighted to see the superior neatness and tastly state of the buildings many painted white others brick and some have the door steps painted yellow. We bought some large red apples for a cent each which was truly delicious. The streets are wide but not so well flagged and paved as in England. The first house we entered was Brother Delongs where we took dinner. From here we went to meeting at the Military Hall in the Bowery.[60] The first thing that struck my attention was all the men and women I saw sitting cross legged

[59] The Sandy Hook peninsula in northeast New Jersey lies between Sandy Hook Bay and the Atlantic Ocean and marks the south side of the entrance to Lower New York Bay. Henry Hudson explored Sandy Hook in 1609; the British held it during the Revolution. The Sandy Hook Lighthouse, built in 1763, is the oldest now in use in the United States.

[60] A section of lower Manhattan borough of New York City, the Bowery was the first country estate of Dutch Governor Peter Stuyvesant, who is buried in St.-Mark's-in-the-Bouwerie Church.

and all the left leg over the right. Elder Adams preached on the principles of the gospel. After preaching we took bread and wine. We went to Elder Fosters and took tea with Brother Simmons. After tea Elder Turley went on business and I went to writing. We slept on board the ship. Many of the Saints went to meeting and was much pleased. We learn nothing of Brother Hardman nor the other two brethren who were turned back at Liverpool.

[October 12, 1840. Monday.] This P.M. a lighter[61] came to the ships side into which we put our luggage. We slept on board the North America again.

[October 13, 1840. Tuesday.] Having finished loading our luggage those of the company who were present went on board a steamer (the Congress) and sailed to the Albany basin. We bid adieu to the North America at 12 o'clock. The Captain seemed very friendly and said he should wish to bring another company of us over. He enquired if we had a church in New York and where they meet. Elder Turley introduced him to Elder Foster. I gave Elder Adams 25 letters for England for which I paid 25 cent. The agreement which Elder Turley made with the proprietors of the Congress was that we should sail this day but they have broke their [bargain] and Elder Turley is much troubled. We slept on board the Congress. I feel struck to see the horses and carts even to see the light harness and small carts and light loads drawn by them. The drivers all ride. The fruit is quite delicious to English people. I slept in best cabin.

[October 14, 1840. Wednesday.] About 9 o'clock this A.M. H. C. Greenhalgh died after being ill 8 or 9 days. The city coroner came and sat over him. I was one of the jurors. Verdict, died from unknown [cause]. A coffin was provided and he was taken into the city to be buried. At 5 o'clock P.M. we had a very beautiful sight. 7 steam boats all left the harbour at one. It seemed as though the harbour was on a move. We left about 20 minutes after 5. The company was in good spirits. As we left New York we had a pleasant view of the North part of the city. The buildings chiefly white and very neat. The several spires towering towards the sky

---

61 An open barge used in loading or unloading larger ships that are unable to cross shallow water to shore.

bore a majestic appearance. On one part there was a large lot of wood which we was told was provided for [poor] folks against winter. We had not gone far before it began to grow dark and we could only discover by moonlight the lofty rocks on earth since the river which is Hudson River especially the west side which was indeed beautiful with here and there a beautiful white house scattered on the banks. Before we started from New York we learned that the Mary Kingsland was arrived in New York and the Brother H[ardman] and the other families was arrived. Some one went over to get them along with us but it found impossible. We left Brother Richard Tell at New York. He got work there and was likely to do well.

[October 15, 1840. Thursday.] This morning I arose to behold again the beautiful white houses and banks on the river's side. We passed the village Cantskill[62] which looked very beautiful and a little further we passed a village called Colonel Youngs village. He settled in this place and established a foundry and got a number of workmen along with him where they now have houses built which forms the village. As we proceeded we saw many fields of grain which was cut. We saw in one field a great number of pumpkins quite yellow and pretty. On one farm we saw about 140 cows and oxen and sheep in different places. After proceeding some time we passed the beautiful town of Hudson on the East side of the river. This seems to be a town of about ten thousand inhabitants. Still passing along we continued to be delighted with the houses and in some places we saw fruit on the trees. As we got higher up the river the land appeared to grow richer but get very rocky. Close to the banks of the river about 14 miles from Albany[63] we passed a coal wharf which is a scarce thing in this country. The fuel is almost all wood and this article is exceeding plentiful. About 1/2 past 5 we arrived at Albany. We left a boat with a number of passengers here. This is a large town on the west side the river containing perhaps 40 thousand inhabitants. We could see the court house and prison and the different churches interspersed here and there. Here is also a pleasant harbour for a

---

[62] Catskill, New York, is a town located on the Hudson River 100 miles north of New York City.
[63] The capital of New York State, Albany is situated at the juncture of the Hudson River and the Erie Canal.

few shipping. The coast is almost covered with timber. We saw a large iron foundry and workshops of different kinds. We soon left Albany and at 7 o'clock arrived at the city of Troy[64] where we now are stopped for the night. We also passed the City Athens a while before Albany.

[October 16, 1840. Friday.] This A.M. Elder Turley bought a sheep ready dressed for 1 1/2 dollars. This was divided amongst some of the company. We got our luggage off the steamer by 10 o'clock and soon after we were tugged to the canal.[65] We were obliged to hire another boat into which some of us got with much difficulty. It is evident Mrs. Benbow wants one boat for their company and they have made choice of one with a best cabin.[66] This has caused a little feeling. Elder Turley had again considerable trouble with the proprietor and had to pay more than he ought at last. About 1/4 to 4 we left West Troy.

[October 17, 1840. Saturday.] We are now passing through a very pleasant country. Many fruit trees loaded with fruit and loads scattered on the ground. I took up a large handkerchief full.

---

[64] A city just north of Albany, Troy was home of Samuel Wilson, known locally as "Uncle Sam" and who was still alive as Clayton passed through. During the War of 1812, Wilson had the job of stamping barrels of meat with the initials "U.S." for "United States." Originally a symbol of unfriendly satire, Uncle Sam became a popular American figure.

[65] The Erie Canal was a 350-mile toll waterway from Albany to Buffalo, New York, on Lake Erie. After it opened in 1825, the canal served as a major carrier of immigrants to the Midwest. British Mormon emigration began in 1840 from Liverpool to New York and used the Erie Canal en route to Nauvoo. However, from 1841 to 1844 British Saints disembarked at New Orleans and took river boats up the Mississippi to Nauvoo, a route which was cheaper than overland travel from New York. During the period of tension following the death of Joseph Smith in 1844, British emigrants were advised to land in New York where they could get jobs and await a better time to continue west. When the Saints left Nauvoo in 1846 British emigration was temporarily discontinued. It resumed in 1847, again from New Orleans up the Mississippi and Missouri rivers to the westward trailhead at Council Bluffs, Iowa. In 1854, the Mormon emigration route shifted back to New York because of health problems along the Mississippi River and because inexpensive railroad travel had reached the Midwest. By 1869 emigrants could go all the way from the Atlantic coast to the Great Salt Lake Valley by train. See Wilbur S. Shepperson, "The Place of the Mormons in the Religious Emigration of Britain, 1840-1860," *Utah Historical Quarterly* 20 (1952): 213-16; Philip A. M. Taylor, "The Mormon Crossing of the United States, 1840-1870," *Utah Historical Quarterly* 20 (1957): 320.

[66] The company traveled along the Erie Canal in three boats: the *Silver Arrow*, the *J. D. Hawks*, and the *Chautauqua*.

There are a great quantity of pigs kept in this region. We have passed the upper aqueduct which is a stupendous work. Soon after this we arrived at the beautiful town of Schenectady[67] seated close to the canal or rather the canal passed through it. Here there is a Railway. We buy our milk at the grocery shops for 4 cents a quart.

[October 18, 1840. Sunday.] We are now standing still as the owner of the boat is religious and will not allow it to run on Sundays. Some of our people went to washing as we had not had the privilege of washing since we left England. Last night Wm. Greenhalgh's family came into our boat. Not having room to sleep in the other ones. I and several others went to the top of a very large hill and George Foster and I went up in the topmost tree from whence we had a pleasant view. As we returned we met Elder Turley and some of the sisters going up the hill to pray. We returned with them and united our hearts together.

[October 19, 1840. Monday.] We passed a town called the little [Halls].

[October 20, 1840. Tuesday.] About 2 o'clock this A.M. we passed Utica in the midst of heavy rain. One of our horses fell into the canal and was near being drowned. A horse belonging to another boat was drowned a little before. We passed the city of Rome.

[October 21, 1840. Wednesday.] Before sunrise this A.M. we passed Syracuse,[68] a place where a great quantity of salt is daily made. I got to day a 2 Dollar Bill which I cannot pay also a coin for a quarter dollar which only pays for 17 cents. At night we passed a very pretty town called Montezuma. I have wrote a letter which I intend to send from Buffalo to Brother John Moon. 10000 Bushels of salt per day.

---

[67] Located thirteen miles northwest of Albany, Schenectady developed with the railroads in the 1830s and later, in 1886, became the home of Edison's electrical machinery, forerunner of General Electric Company.

[68] Located about mid-way between Albany and Buffalo, Syracuse was a major saltmaker before the Civil War.

[October 22, 1840. Thursday.] William Poole paid my 2 Dollar Bill loning 12 1/2 cts. We have passed the city of Palmyra[69] and soon after viz. about 11 o'clock Elder Turley and myself left the Silver Arrow and took packet for Tonnewonta fare 4.12 each. About 1/2 past 7 we landed at Rochester which appears to be a place of considerable business of different kind. Here we changed packets and in about 15 minutes started off again.

[October 23, 1840. Friday.] About 11 this A.M. we passed the town of Lockport. At this place there are 5 locks which raise the canal 60 feet. These locks as well as above from 1 to 2 miles of the canal westward is cut out of solid rock and present a stupendous appearance. The wind arose very high and in our place opposite the river from the lake drive us against the shore. Several were thrown down and somewhat frightened. As we passed along the side of the river we saw the large drifts of sand like mountainous drifts of snow. We arrived in Buffalo[70] about 6 o'clock and soon met with some of the brethren from the first boat the J. D. Hawks. We went to her and found that 3 children had died since we left them. Sister Benbow manifested a bad spirit as she has often done and has given Elder Turley many slight cants.[71] After this we went to meet the second boat Chatauqua which had been detained at the second bridge on account of the canal being high. In this boat all were pretty well but had been short of provisions. The first boat arrived here about 9 this A.M. and the captain immediately ordered the company to get their luggage out of the boat which they did to great disadvantage into a wharehouse. They had to pay 5 cents for this privilege.

[October 24, 1840. Saturday.] We got the luggage of two boats weighed and engaged to Chicago on board the Wisconsin [] at 10 Dollars each person. Some went on board same day. We

---

[69] Palmyra was a boom town on the Erie Canal between Albany and Buffalo. From 1816 to 1827 Joseph Smith lived in Palmyra, which he named as the site of his first vision in 1820, three years before reporting the discovery of the Book of Mormon plates in nearby Manchester.

[70] Named by the French for its position on the Niagara River, Buffalo ("beau fleuve," beautiful river) was a transfer point from canal boat to lake steamer, by which the Mormon immigrants continued their westward journay along Lake Erie to Chicago.

[71] The insincere use of pious words.

waited at night on the other boat untill 2 o'clock Sunday morning but did not come. Then I bought a pair of mittens for 5/6 York money. On this day Elder Turleys mind was much cast down in consequence of being obliged to leave some of the poor in our company at Buffalo. While he was reflecting upon the best manner of accomplishing this and when almost heartbroke the President Elder of the stake at Kirtland[72] [Hiram] Kellog came by and Turley knew him. After they had saluted each other he made his case known to Elder Kellog who immediately advised to take the company to Kirtland as they would winter more comfortable there than in Commerce.[73] This was a total deliverance to Elder Turleys mind and a relief of his burden. The reason why some must be left here was a want of money. Elder Turley had been given to understand that we might go from Buffalo to Chicago for 5 Dollars a head and had it been so all the company would no doubt have gone through. But when he enquired the fare it was found to be 10 Dollars a head instead of 5 and there was no privilege of altering it for there was only one boat appointed to go this season. The Wisconsin had lately come in and was not to go any more only short voyages. Elder Turley went to the captain and endeavoured to charter the boat but to no purpose. After some time consulting between Elders Turley and Kellogg it was concluded that all who wanted and could raise means should go to Commerce and the remainder to Kirtland which proved highly satisfactory to the majority of the company. The weather was at this time very cold as a large quantity of snow had fallen and whitened the streets. One boatload of the company went on board the Wisconsin expecting we should go on that boat. The other boat load having nowhere to go Mr. Proper's partner kindly offered them the Counting House to sleep in which they gladly accepted and immediately went there.

[October 25, 1840. Sunday.] This A.M. Elder Turley and my self went to meet the Silver Arrow which we came in sight of

---

[72] Kirtland, Ohio, was the headquarters of the Mormon church from 1831-38. During this period there were also several Mormon settlements in Missouri.

[73] The company's destination was Commerce, Illinois, renamed Nauvoo by Joseph Smith. Located on the eastern bank of the Mississippi River, it became the headquarters of the Mormon church from 1839-46. Portions of the town are presently maintained by the LDS church as historical sites.

after walking about 3 miles. When we went on board the saints rejoiced greatly. They had had some very ill treatment from the captain and crew since we left them and we found them with scarce room to stand. We arrived in Buffalo about 12 o'clock. I spent the remainder of the day in making up accounts for those who were going to Kirtland. Whilst I was doing this Sister Elizabeth Poole's son Edward fell into the canal and was near drowned when got out. This Mother fainted and was very ill some time. This evening the Greenhalgh's concluded either to go to Kirtland or stay at Buffallo which grieved me much.

[October 26, 1840. Monday.] The weather was very wet and cold. It was concluded that the Wisconsin Steamboat should not go. Consequently the company had to embark on board the Illinois captain Blake.

[October 27, 1840. Tuesday.] This A.M. the Boat should have left Buffallo but could not on account of storm. The Greenhalghs have took a house and two of them got work. I have bought a cap for 12 Dollars and a pair of Boots for 4 a Rifle for 16 powder 71. [I] also bought Saw and plane.

[October 28, 1840. Wednesday.] The weather continues stormy at night. We moved from amongst the shipping to the end of the Creek . . .

[October 29, 1840. Thursday.] About 1 this A.M. we left Buffallo for Chicago. The names of those who are gone to Kirtland are T[homas] Green and family, Josh West and family. Alice Whiss and family. M. Blake and wife. Josh Jackson and wife from Manchester. T. Featherston. Martha Shelmerdine and Jane Fyldes from Stockport. J. [Crompton?] and wife from Bolton. J. Hutchinson and family. John Craig and family. Ralph Thompson and family []. George Slater and family from []. Samuel Bateman and family from Pendlebury. T[homas] Hooper and family from Herefordshire. George Naylor and family from Bolton. Jane Harris from Manchester. These all had their names on a recommend except Thomas Hooper whose conduct has been very bad. This company generally appeared chearful and rejoiced in the prospect of soon having a place of rest. Some was inclined almost to wish they had not left England rather than be left short of Commerce. We proceeded on our way pretty well until we arrived at

Fairport partly to take in wood and part on account of strong wind. Here some of us went on shore and had we time Elder Turley and myself would have gone to Kirtland as we were then only 11 miles from that place. Sometime in the night we started forwards again.

[October 30, 1840. Friday.] We had a [place] sail. At night we anchored at the mouth of the river between lakes Erie and Huron.

[October 31, 1840. Saturday.] This A.M. about 7 o'clock we arrived at Detroit.[74] This is a very pleasant looking place of about 20000 inhabitants. Here we took in some more passengers which crowded us up very much. We left Detroit after taking on wood and proceeded [to] lake St Clair[75] where we saw many hundreds wild ducks. Some amused themselves by shooting at them with their Rifles.

[November 1, 1840. Sunday.] We are on lake Huron[76] in the P.M. we called at Pesqu Isle to take in wood. Here I picked us some curious pebble stones. The lake is bounded by gravel of the whitest and hardest kind. At night we arrived at Mackinau[77] where we again took in wood.

[November 2, 1840. Monday.] We are on lake Michigan[78] and for some time could not see land. We called at the Manitou Islands to take in wood. Here I took up some more pebbles. Some of the company shot a few rabbits and small birds. We continued here some hours on account of strong head wind.

---

[74] Detroit was settled first by the French, later by the British in 1760, and then by the Americans in 1796, through treaty provisions negotiated by John Jay in which Britain left fur trading posts along the frontier to the United States. America had to win it back from the British again in the War of 1812.

[75] An important water transit junction adjacent to Detroit, Lake St. Clair connects Lake Huron to Lake Erie by way of the Clair and Detroit rivers.

[76] Lake Huron is the second largest of the great lakes, 206 miles long and 183 miles wide, and is shared by Canada and the United States. The Great Lakes form the world's largest body of fresh water and with their connecting waterways the largest inland water transportation system.

[77] Mackinaw City, at the connecting strait between Lake Huron and Lake Michigan, a former trading center with the Indians of the Northwest; known for the heavy woolen blankets and coats by that name.

[78] Lake Michigan, 307 miles long and 118 miles wide, is the only one of the Great Lakes which is wholly within the United States.

[November 4, 1840. Wednesday.] About 1/2 past 1 this A.M. we arrived at Chicago.[79] Very early in the morning we moved our luggage from the boat and Elder Turley went to seeking teems to go to Dixons ferry as that was considered to be the best rout[e]. We engaged two teems for our family but after loading both and weighing one we found it necessary to have another. I went back to were the boat landed and after a little time met with another. We got loaded about 2 o'clock and proceeded on our way. After leaving Chicago we entered a wide prairie which was to us a new scene. We traveled about 12 miles and rested for the night. We made our fire and cooked our victuals out of doors. We slept on the floors of the tavern. We had no beds but some bedding.

[November 7, 1840. Saturday.] This day we arrived at Dixon after travelling about 100 miles. We saw a wolf on one prairie and many prairie hens. At one house we saw a wild cat which had been shot in the woods. It was as large as a common sized dog. We have several times had one of the teems fast in the sloughs. During this journey Brothers Cope and Benbow went with their teems foremost and thus secured to themselves the best accommodations and provisions &c. We was obliged to submit to it and take what we could get. When our teems viz. our 3 and Copes 14 and Benbows 2 and Walter Cran 1 arrived at Dixon the others being considerable behind we made inquiry as to the probability of boats going down the river. We was told that some boats had gone a week previous but it was not likely that any more would go this season. We then asked if there was any boat we could buy but of this we could get no satisfaction. We were advised to take our teams and go over to Fulton and there take steamboat. To this I objected on account of Turley not being arrived. S. Cope was disposed to go and would not unload his waggon. I engaged a house for the whole company at a Dollar 24 hours. We went to the house and unloaded our waggons myself being determined not to move until the others arrived. I paid the teamsmen 75 dollars for the 3 teams but desired them to wait till morning to see what course Elder Turley would pursue. It appears that at this

---

[79] In 1840 Chicago was a small lake town of about 5,000 people. Around the turn of the century, the railroad and steel industries turned Chicago into a metropolis of several hundred thousand.

place I offended Brother Cope from what he said afterwards. In the building was 3 rooms one a small room which would scarce hold our folks. Into this we moved our boxes and laid down our bedding (no beds). During this time Mr. Copes brought some of our luggage in saying they would go in their for they had as much right as any one else or something like this. But when they saw us lay our bedding down they took their things out apparently much grieved. But I would not submit to [] as we had submitted to the worst fare [on] the way from Chicago and I had took the house and considered myself at liberty to go into any part I choosed.

[November 8, 1840. Sunday.] This morning Walter Cran engaged his team and started for Fulton. Mr. Cope wanted to do likewise and asked my intentions. I told him I would not move any further untill the remainder of the company arrived. He seemed a little vexed and would rather have gone on. In order to pacify him and others I started back with our teams to meet the others. We met them about 7 miles from Dixon. I gave Turley a statement of things as I had found them and that I believed it was possible to go down Rock river. Brother Cope still desired to go by land to Fulton. I told him I had no disposition to go and leave the poor behind (as was evident we should have to do if we went that way). He then manifested anger and said he had not either &c. [We] arrived back about 2 o'clock.

[November 9, 1840. Monday.] This day Elder Turley purchased a boat bottom for 75 Dollars and engaged 2 men to fit it up ready for sailing.

[November 13, 1840. Friday.] During this week the boat has been got ready myself and many of the brethren assisted. We got our luggage on board to start but it being late and beginning to snow it was decided not to move [] untill morning. While loading the boat Brother Cope and I had a few words again. I had fixed some of our boxes in one corner of the boat and Cope brought his and was determined to have them fixed up to ours so that we could get no more of ours up to them. I told him what I had intended to do. He was vexed and said "You nasty scamp I pay as much as you." We had not many more words but seemed much vexed. I told him to use his pleasure and I would be satisfied.

[November 14, 1840. Saturday.] This A.M. Brother Cope declined going with us in the boat and would not pay his share according to his agreement. I paid down one half of the expenses and we got loaded and prepared to start. We left wood got at Dixon and started about 10 o'clock. We went about 12 miles and tarried overnight at Stirling. The weather was very cold.

[November 20, 1840. Friday.] This day we passed over the rapids. The greater part of us walked while the boat went over. It stuck fast once but was not damaged. Soon after this we entered the Mississippi River which caused us to rejoice much.

[November 21, 1840. Saturday.] This night we had to camp at a wood there being no houses near. We [had] some rain. Elder Turley and some others camped in the wood. He spake much to them and [called] upon those who had had quarrels to forgive each and manifest it. Many acknowledged their faults and asked forgiveness. Some spake in tongues and Wm. Poole interpreted. It was a time of rejoicing.

[November 22, 1840. Sunday.] We arrived at Burlington this evening and as we anticipated landing at Commerce on the morrow many of us washed ourselves and changed our cloths. Many of our family slept on a carpet on the floor.

[November 23, 1840. Monday.] This A.M. Elder Turley and my self had some unpleasant words in consequence of his taking the boat [] some Islands which appeared to me and others to be considerable out of our course. I spake to him about it but he would not listen. I then turned my conversation to C. Price. Elder Turley then said if I did not cease to agitate the minds of the company he would put to shore and leave the boat. This was said in an unpleasant spirit. In the P.M. we got the boat fast on a tree and lost considerable time. After Elder Turley had tried his own way to move the boat a long time but in vain I begged of him to let me have my plan. After much request he partially consented and finding it likely to answer he yielded to my plan and the boat was soon loosed. We sailed untill after dusk almost determined to go to Commerce that night. But seeing a light on shore we made towards it and hearing a man we asked how far we were from Commerce. He said 9 miles. At which report we concluded to stay for the night.

79

[November 24, 1840. Tuesday.] This A.M. Elder Turley having been in company with a man from Commerce said that if any choose to walk that man would conduct them at which Wm. Poole myself and several others went along with him by land to Commerce where we arrived at about 12 o'clock. We called at the Upper stone house and found Sister Garner from Manchester. They had arrived about one week previous having been 6 months on their way. We then went to Sister Hyrum Clarks and on our way called at Francis Moon's. After we had been here a little while we perceived Elder Turley and some others coming. Knowing then that the Boat had arrived we returned to the boat and after taking a little dinner we proceeded according to the appointment of Committee to move our luggage to a new house on the banks of the Mississippi River. Thus ended a journey of over 5000 miles having been exactly 11 weeks and about 10 hours between leaving Liverpool and arriving at our journeys end. We had been much exposed to cold weather and suffered many deprivations and disconveniences yet through the mercy of God we landed safe and in good health with the exception of [2] persons one of whom died soon after landing. We were pleased to find ourselves once more at home and felt to praise God for his goodness. We did not get all our luggage unloaded that night and having no fire we concluded to take the invitation of Brother Henry Moore and stay overnight at his house. He kindly gave us our breakfast the following Morning. We slept on the floor. On the morning of the 25th we proceeded to unload the remainder of our luggage. Brother Thompson lent us a small stove. The house being small for 14 of us viz. Wm. Poole and family, Richard Jenkinson and wife, Mary Ware and my father in laws family and my family. We was some crow[d] but we were pretty comfortable. We made our bed on hay on the floor and was obliged to move them every morning for the room. After a few weeks we made our beds upstairs and fill them with oak leaves. In a few days after we arrived at Nauvoo Elder Hyrum Smith[80] came for me to go on board the Steam Boat

---

[80] Hyrum Smith (1800-44) was Joseph Smith's older brother and his second counselor in 1837. He served many roles in the church. He was one of the eight witnesses to the Book of Mormon. He was one of Joseph's bodyguards and was appointed church patriarch, an office which included offering special blessings concerning the future role of a member's service to the church. Hyrum was killed with the prophet in 1844. His descendants provided significant leadership in the

Nauvoo. I spent one day on it and it was then concluded not to sail her any more this season. We remained at this house 7 weeks during which time we made enquiry concerning some land and after much consultation I went to Hyrum Smith for council. He said he had some land to sell in Iowa Territory for 3 dollars an acre and he counciled us to go. We finally concluded to move over the river into the Territory. The saints frequently told us that the devil was over the river &c. but this did not hinder us from going. I agreed with William Smith for 185 acres of land and was to pay for it out of my wages on the Steam Boat which he []. I was to give him 1/2 of my wages untill it was paid up. We also bought a Waggon of him for 60$ paying 1/2 down the []. We bought a Yoke of oxen and chain for 55$ and 3 Hogs for 8$ of Mr. Thomas Grover. We did not attend many meeting while on this side the river. We heard Joseph [Smith] speak twice and Sidney Rigdon[81] once. We attended singing meetings frequently and often had to sing "Gentle Gale" for Joseph and others.[82] On January 12th 1841 we began to move our luggage over the river on the Ice which occupied 4 days in the whole. I had previously taken a house a little from Montrose[83] at 18 pr month. This house smoked very bad and we had oftentimes to be without fire and cook out of doors. We found things in some measure as was told

major branch of the church which migrated to Utah while his brother Joseph's wife and children remained in Illinois to become active in the Reorganized Church of Jesus Christ of Latter Day Saints. See Richard S. Van Wagoner and Steven C. Walker, *A Book of Mormons* (Salt Lake City: Signature Books, 1982), 282–87.

[81] Sidney Rigdon (1793–1876), a prominent Baptist and Campbellite minister in Ohio, converted to Mormonism in 1830, convinced Joseph Smith to bring his church to Kirtland, Ohio, and became Smith's first counselor. After Smith's death in 1844, Rigdon was excommunicated when he organized a splinter group that denied the authority of the Quorum of the Twelve Apostles. See Van Wagoner and Walker, 232–38.

[82] Clayton had composed his first Mormon hymn, "Gentle Gale," aboard the *North America*. Having just met Joseph Smith, Clayton wrote of his confidence in the young prophet to his friends in Penwortham: "We have abundance of proofs that Joseph Smith Junior is what he pretends to be viz a Prophet of the most high God and this is the work of God and will roll forth to the ends of the earth and the Lord will gather His People . . . Last night many of us was in company with Brother Joseph, our hearts rejoiced to hear him speak of the things of the Kingdom, he is an affectionate man and as familiar as any of us. We feel to love him much and so will you" (Clayton to Edward Martin, November 29, 1840, LDS archives).

[83] Built upon a French trading post, Montrose is a town in Lee County in southeast Iowa, across the Mississippi River from Nauvoo, Illinois.

us viz. the saints to be in a very bad state and having no meetings, full of envy, strife and contention and in a very bad state. Soon after we arrived here the weather began to be extremely cold and having no wood for fire it seemed as though we must be froze to death. We were still 31 in number and all could not get to the fire. When the weather moderated we went to cutting logs and hauling them for building also making rails. We got our house part raised by the 8th of March Wm. Poole assisting us. At this time Wm. Poole moved over the river to seek employment and left us. We continued to labour preparing rails and house &c. untill about the 16 of March when we seemed to be all at once put under a cloud of trouble. In the night I was taken sick and could not go to work for a few days []. We had a hog which we set much store on and was very desirous to keep him to breed from. On the 15th he got out of the penn and did not come home at night. On the morning of the 16th he came home cut which was a sad grief to us [two lines partially crossed out]. On the same day about 5 o'clock while I was set doing a little something in the house a person called and said the new house was all on fire. I immediately sprang up and started off. Just as I got to the door I saw a waggon going that way and I got into it. Having 2/4 miles to go we was some time before we arrived. When we got there I found the lady who lived at Bosiers house had carried water from the house about a quarter of a mile and put the fire partly out. I soon put all the fire out and ascertained that the house had not sustained much damage but a large rope which cost $2.50 also a pair of Bed cords was entirely burned to ashes which in our circumstances was a considerable loss to us. We have during the winter had this chimney on fire 3 times. First on a cold day when Wm. Poole killed his hog. He made to large a fire and the chimney was turned [].

[March 19, 20, 1841. Friday, Saturday.] I commenced planting seed for the first time in this land. On the latter day while I was busy in the garden a person named Wm. Miller (who said he had a claim upon the land we bought from Hyrum Smith) came up and with him a constable and another man. The constable drew from his pocket book a paper and read it to me which was a notice to quit the land signed Wm. Miller. I felt some astonished at this but not many words passed between us. Miller said he had been to Brother Ripley who was somewhat saucy and told him he must fight it out, and that was the way he intended to do it. A few days after I took the notice paper to the river to Sister [Mary?] Smith who advised me to take no notice of it but proceed with our business, I however felt it would be wisdom to wait a while as we expected Hyrum at home in a few weeks.

[March 24, 1841. Wednesday.] This night the constable brought me a summons to appear before Justice Spain to answer to Wm. Miller for trespass on his premises.

[March 26, 1841. Friday.] I went over the river to see Brother Ripley and ask his council. I called at the store and made Joseph acquainted with the circumstance who ordered Brother Thompson to write a few lines to Brother Ripley in his name requesting him to take the matter into his own hands and appear with me before the justice. I saw Brother Ripley who said I need trouble myself no further he would see to it. I would here state that during the past few months I have had much trouble concerning the boat which was made at Dixonville. I have repeatedly endeavored to see Mr. Benbow who ownes one half of it and settle with him but have yet been disappointed. He has been for council to Brother Law and has divided the boat and taken away his share. Soon as I learned this I also went to Brother Law for council who advised me to get 2 men to value the portion of the boat which fell to us and then charge the whole company with the whole of the difficiency. This I immediately attended to and made out bills for all our own family taking an equal share of the loss. Some of the accounts I took in and the first man who complained was John Blezard. He did not believe it was a just debt and did not intend to pay except others did &c. His conduct since has fully proved that he does not intend to pay for he has been insolent both to myself and Lydia and her mother who have been to ask repeatedly for the money. But hitherto we can get no satisfaction wether he will pay or no.

[March 28, 1841. Sunday.] This day we met at Montrose. Uncle John Smith presided. He called upon all who had hardness and who had transgressed to confess and repent. He stated that about 12 months ago he had appointed them a person to take charge of the meeting and administer the sacrement which he had

83

only attended to once since that time. After many had confessed he called upon myself and Brother Nickerson to break bread and administer which was done and we hope it will be continued faithfully hereafter.

[March 30, 1841. Tuesday.] This day I made a contract for a cow with Abner Tibbetts for 20 dollars value to be cut out in cord wood at 75 cents pr cord. She calved on the morning after and seems to answer pretty well.

[April 2, 1841. Friday.] Brother Nickerson settled with Wm. Miller for his claim on the land and we can now pursue our improvements.

[April 6, 7, 8, 9, 1841. Tuesday-Friday.] These four days I attended the Conference. On the 7th I was organized with the High Priest Quorum and set with them during the conference. I was much pleased with the order of the meeting. When any case was to appear before the church it was first put by the Bishop to the quorum of the Lesser Priesthood. Then by the president of the Elders to that quorum, then the 70 then High Priests, then High Council and lastly to the presidency. If any objection arose it had to be tried by that quorum who objected but a majority of the quorums decided the matter. The names of the official characters are as follows Joseph Smith first president Sidney Rigdon and Wm. Law[84] councillor. Brother Law was appointed councillor at this conference in the stead of Hyrum Smith who was appointed a Prophet Seer and Revelator according to a revelation given January 19, 1841. Brother Law was objected to by our quorum but honourably elected after investigation. On account of the ill health of Sidney Rigdon John C. Bennett[85] was appointed in his stead

---

[84] William Law (1809–92) converted to the Mormon church from Canada in 1836 and became the prophet's second counselor. After Smith began to take additional wives in Nauvoo in 1841, Law opposed plural marriage and other financial and legal practices and was excommunicated in 1844. In a new newspaper called the *Nauvoo Expositor*, Law and other reformers voiced their opposition to "false doctrines" and what they considered illegal practices. After his experience with the Mormons, Law practiced medicine for forty years in Illinois and Wisconsin. See Lyndon W. Cook, "William Law, Nauvoo Dissenter," *Brigham Young University Studies* 22 (Winter 1982): 47–72.

[85] John C. Bennett (1804–67) was a Campbellite minister, physician, military man, and Mason. Bennett arrived in Nauvoo in August 1840, three months before Clayton, and while the apostles were on a mission to England. He became close to

until Brother Rigdons health improved. Names of the 12 or traveling high Council. Brigham Young, Heber Chase Kimball, Parley P. Pratt, Orson Pratt, Orson Hyde, William Smith, John Taylor, J[oh]n E. Page, Willford Woodruff, Willard Richards, George Albert Smith and Lyman Wight was appointed in the room of D[avid] W. Patten deceased. Standing High council Samuel Bent, Henry G. Sherwood, George W. Harris, Thomas Grover, Newel Knight, Lewis D. Wilson, Aaron Johnson, David Fullmer, Alpheus Cutler, W[illia]m Hunting[t]on Senior, William Alread, Leanord Sowby was appointed this conference. Presidents of the High Priest quorum Don C. Smith Councillors Noah Packard, A[masa] Lyman. President of Elders quorum J[oh]n A. Hicks, councillers Samuel Williams, Jesse Baker. Quorum of seventies Joseph Young, Isaiah Butterfield, Dan[ie]l Miles, Henry Heremond, Zerah Pulcipher, Levi Hancock and James Foster. Lesser Priesthood Priests Samuel Rolphe, Stephen Markham, Hezekiah Peck Counselors. Teachers Elisha Everett, James W. Huntsman, James Hendrick. Deacons P[hineas] R. Bird, David Wood, W[illia]m W. Lane. Bishopric Vincent Knights, councilors S[amuel] H. Smith and Shadrac Roundey. Newel K. Whitney, Coun[selors] Jonathan H. Hale, W[illia]m Felshaw. George Miller, Councillors Peter Haws and John Snider. Isaac Higbee, Coun[selors] Graham Coultrin and John S. Higbee. Alanson Ripley has had his Bishopric taken from him for frequently being drunk and not fit for business. President of the stake W[illia]m Marks, councillors Austin Coles and Charles C. Rich.

[April 6, 1841. Tuesday.] The Nauvoo Legion[86] was drawn up to exercise and afterwards proceeded to the Temple ground to

Joseph Smith and quickly rose to power. Bennett became the first mayor of Nauvoo, major general of the Nauvoo Legion, and secretary of the Nauvoo Masonic lodge. Then on April 8, 1841, he replaced the ailing Sidney Rigdon as assistant president of the church—two days after Smith took Louisa Beaman as his first recorded plural wife; ironically, the next year Bennett was excommunicated for "spiritual wifery." He later avenged himself by writing *The History of the Saints: Or an Expose of Joe Smith and the Mormons*. He helped found the Illinois State Medical Society, Indiana University at New Albany, and served as a U.S. army field surgeon in the Civil War. See *HC* 5:75-76; Van Wagoner, *Book of Mormons*, 10-14.

[86] A "body of independent military men" established by Section 25 of the Nauvoo Charter and "at the disposal of the Mayor" in executing the laws and ordinances of the city (*HC* 4:244). Nauvoo historian Robert Flanders discusses its independence from the military laws of Illinois (*Nauvoo: Kingdom on the Mississippi* [Urbana and Chicago: University of Illinois Press, 1975], 100-101).

lay the corner stones. The first Presidency proceeded to lay the South East corner stone. (The High Council laid the South West corner in the name of the travelling High Council. The president of High Priest quorum the North West and the Bishops the North East. See Times and Seasons April 15). Before the ceremony of laying the corner stones President Rigdon delivered an address for the occasion in his usual powerful manner.

[April 8, 1841. Thursday.] President Rigdon delivered a discourse on baptism for the dead, showing the propriety and absolute necessity of such an ordinance. After preaching a many were baptized for their dead relatives and many for the remission of sins. At this conference a Revelation was read (given January 19, 1841) containing instructions to build the Temple and a boarding house called the Nauvoo house and many other important items. A short revelation was also read concerning the saints in Iowa. The question had been asked what is the will of the Lord concerning the saints in Iowa. It read to the following effect, Verily thus saith the Lord let all those my saints who are assaying to do my will gather themselves together upon the land opposite to Nauvoo and build a city unto my name and let the name of Zarahemla be named upon it. And all who come from the east and West and North and South who have desires let them settle in Zarahemla that they may be prepared for that which is in store for a time to come &c. Brother Joseph when speaking to one of the brethren on this subject says you have [Haun's] Mill[87] for a sample. Many of the brethren immediately made preparations for moving in here but on account of its being so late in the season President John Smith advised to get through with planting and then proceed to move in.

[April 16, 1841. Friday.] Alice Moons family arrived from Pittsburgh state of Pennsylvania.

[April 25, 1841. Sunday.] Brother Clark arrived with a company of saints amongst whom was my sister Alice.

---

[87] In October 1838 near Far West, Missouri, a party of 200 armed men killed seventeen Mormons, including two children, at a small settlement called Haun's Mill (*HC* 3:326n).

[May 1, 1841. Saturday.] We finished cutting the 26 cord of wood for corn. Same day Brewetts company arrived amongst whom was Seth Cook and family.

[May 2, 1841. Sunday.] Elders W[illia]m Law and Hyrum Smith preached at Zarahemla. On the 6th my wife was taken poorly about 4 o'clock A.M. Her mother was on the other side the river. As soon as it was light she wanted me to go and fetch her. I went and got Brother Davis' skiff and went across as hard as I could and was about 2 hours away. When she got back she was delivered of a daughter who are both doing very well. She got up on the 8th and continued to mend without interupt[io]n. The child is named Henrihetta Lucretia Patten Clayton.[88]

[May 9, 1841. Sunday.] Joseph preached on his side on baptism for the dead (see Record).[89] Afterwards a number was baptized both for remission of sins and for the dead. I was baptized first for myself and then for my Grandfather Thomas and Grandmother Ellen Clayton, Grandmother Mary [Critchley] and Aunt Elizabeth Beurdwood.

[April 24, 1841. Saturday.][90] I was requested to attend meeting of the High Council at President John Smiths. I was appointed one of the number in the place of Erastus Snow who is gone preaching. At this council Willard Snow was appointed to get up a company of independent Rifle men. I have joined this company.

[May 16, 1841. Sunday.] I went over the river to hear Joseph. Election and eternal judgement (see Record).

[June 30, 1841. Wednesday.] We have continued to labour very hard in splitting rails up to the present time. The wether

---

[88] Clayton's third child, Henrihetta, died on August 20, probably of malaria.

[89] Mormons are baptized as proxies for their (or someone else's) deceased ancestors in a ceremony meant to enhance the station of the dead in the next world. Joseph Smith preached on his side of the river, in Nauvoo, as opposed to Clayton's side, in Lee County, Iowa. In their book *The Words of Joseph Smith*, Andrew Ehat and Lyndon Cook speculate that the record to which Clayton refers "may have been the private book" from which L. John Nuttall made excerpts, which are reproduced in the present compilation in Appendix A, "Extracts from William Clayton's [Private] Book—Keys" (Lyndon W. Cook and Andrew F. Ehat, eds., *The Words of Joseph Smith* [Salt Lake City: Bookcraft, 1980], 71 and 93).

[90] The entries for April 24 and August 8, 1841, are out of order here as they are in Clayton's original journal.

now begins to be very hot almost more than we can bear. We are yet very far short of completing the fence and in danger of having the corn spoiled by cattle every day.

[July 1, 1841. Thursday.] Early in the morning I was taken very sick with vomiting and purging which held me 5 or 6 hours very severely. I could not go to work. I felt a little better on Friday and Saturday. On Sunday I went over the river and saw Brother Kimball and went with him to Sister Pratts where we took a little dinner.

[July 5, 1841. Monday.] I attended the celebration of American liberty at Zarahemla. We was called to drill at 8 in the morning and continued untill about 4 o'clock at which time the company went to dinner which was set out in a field on account of so many being present. The provisions was done before all had had dinner. I was shure without and felt bad for want of meat.

[August 14, 1841. Saturday.] Alice Moon died.

[August 17, 1841. Tuesday.] Up to the present time I have been very sick after the 5th. As stated above I went to work on the 6th but was not able to do much. On the 7th I was seized with the bilious fever and after a few days suffering took an Emetic which gave me relief. Soon as I began to amend I was seized with the Ague[91] and Fever and shook every day. After about 10 days shaking I was advised by Dr. Rogers to take some Pills. I objected but Sister Taylor had bought some Quinine and I finally for her sake concluded to take it. These Pills broke the Ague for about 10 days during which time I had another attack of the Bilious Fever and took an Emetic which gave relief. After about 10 days' relief from the Ague I was seized with it again and had it every day for about 2 weeks. At this time we were near all sick and had been except young Lydia and on this day Thomas Moon died 1/4 before 11 A.M. after about 2 weeks sickness. On this day also the brethren went to haul Rails and put up a fence around our field but did not complete it on account of being short of Rails. Soon after there were many cattle in the field especially Mr. Copes sometimes to the number of 35 in one day. The brethren again went to

[91] Malaria.

haul more Rails and complete the fence but did not make it secure consequently cattle continually were eating up the corn untill they destroyed the whole both the corn and fodder. On the 19th Dr. Culbertson came and said he would cure us of the ague and charge nothing for his trouble. Accordingly 5 of us took each a dose of Calomel and Caster Oil. Afterwards 1 teaspoon full of Bitters every hour for 8 hours. This broke our ague for sometime. On the 20th our infant child Henrihetta Lucretia Patten Clayton died after being sick and having chills some time. During the last 2 days she suffered much at times and especially in the last hour of her life. When dead she was as pretty as I ever saw in my life. She died about 10 minutes after 3 P.M. This was a grief to us but we afterwards saw the hand of God in it and saw it was best to be so During this time.

[August 8, 1841. Sunday.] President John Smith[92] and several other brethren came and for the first time during our sickness we received the sacrament. Afterwards Pres[iden]t Smith asked particularly concerning our circumstances and being pressed I told him that had not a privilege of having many things which we greatly needed. After this the church helped us considerable. Being advised by Brother Kimball to buy 2 city lots and move into the city of Zarahemla (according to a previous revelation) on the 30th I went over to President John Smiths and bought two.

[September 11, 1841. Saturday.] Lydia Moon Senior was taken suddenly ill and remained very sick 3 or 4 weeks. On the 18th Richard Jenkinson died appearantly suffering much. About this time we suffered severely on account of having no fire in the house. The chimney was blown down in March and was not built up again untill George A. Smith one of the Twelve and Brother Montague came on the 29th with a load of wood and afterwards built up the chimney for which we felt thankful. The wether was wet and having no fire in the house our clothing were damp and we took cold. Consequently on the 21st I began to shake every day again. On the 28th Brother Tanner brought us some Beef. Oct. 6 Ellen Jenkinson died. She was never baptised nor believed in this work while she lived. We had about 1 acre of Potatoes

---

[92] John Smith (1781–1859) was Joseph Smith's paternal uncle and official church patriarch.

planted and the time now came that they should be dug. We sent over to Wm. Pool to come and help us also to Edd Whittbe. They both promised to come but were sick at the time. They did not come after they got better. Seeing this and after waiting untill the frost had destroyed about one half I began to dig them myself. I dug in the morning untill the Ague came on and afterwards as long as I could bear. I was soon reduced so that I was not able to dig any longer and then my wife and her sister Lydia dug the remainder and gathered about 1 1/2 acres of corn which we had on the farm we rented. About the middle of November I came over to Nauvoo and there Brother Kimball councilled us to move over the river into Nauvoo which we did on the 14th of December. We were still sick and occasionally shaking. We moved into a very bad house and suffered much from cold. We remained here 6 weeks and then moved to where we are now living viz lot South of the burying ground. During the 6 weeks above mentioned I proved that Wm. Pool (who had always professed to be my friend) had been striving to cause a separation in the family viz. to cause mother Moon to turn me out of doors and in order to accomplish this he had told Margaret many reports one of which was that I was the sole cause of her fathers death.

[February 10, 1842. Thursday.] Brother Kimball came in the morning to say that I must go to Joseph Smiths office and assist Brother Richards.[93] I accordingly got ready and went to the ofice and commenced entering tithing for the Temple. I was still shaking with the Ague every day but it did not much disable me for work.

[February 12, 1842. Saturday.] I was able to continue writing all day although I had the ague but not severe.

[February 13, 1842. Sunday.] We had a Singing meeting at Brother Farrs. Brother and Sister Kimball was present.

[February 17, 1842. Thursday.] I dined at Sister Hydes with Brother Joseph Smith, H[eber] Kimball, W[ilford] Woodruff,

---

[93] Clayton was appointed to keep records for the funding of the Nauvoo Temple. His responsibilities increased when he later served as Joseph Smith's scribe and secretary.

B[righam] Young and Willard Richards. At night saw W[oodruff] & S[mith].

[February 18, 1842. Friday.] Pained with tooth ache all day, heard Joseph read a great portion of his history.

1842-1846

As *Joseph Smith's secretary, William Clayton records the prophet's teachings and participates in plural marriage. After Smith dies in 1844, Clayton describes the transfer of leadership to the Quorum of the Twelve Apostles and to Brigham Young.*

[December 1, 1842. Wednesday.] Attended lodge at night.[1]

[January 20, 1843. Friday.] President Joseph Preached in the Temple on the Prodigal Son and showed that it did not refer to any nation, but was me[re]ly an answer to the remark "he receiveth the sinners and eateth with them." The Temple was crowded with people.

[January 22, 1843. Sunday.] This A.M. Joseph preached in the Temple. Subject arose from two questions proposed from a Lyceum. 1st Did John Baptize for remission of sins? 2nd Whether the kingdom of God was set up before the day of Pentecost or not till then? To the 1st Q he answered, "he did." It is acknowledged of all men that John preached the gospel and must have preached the 1st principles, if so he must have preached the doctrine of

---

[1] The Masonic Lodge; see also the Introduction, ns73-75.

Baptism for the remission of sins for that is the 1st principal of the Gospel and was ordained before the foundation of the world. I next give my own testimony because I know it is from God. On the 2nd question He said "Where the oracles of God are revealed there is the Kingdom of God. Wherever the oracles of God are and subjects to obey those oracles there is the kingdom of God. What constitutes the kingdom of God? An administrator who has the power of calling down the oracles of God, and subjects to receive those oracles no matter if there are but 3, 4 or 6 there is the kingdom of God &c."

[March 7, 1843. Tuesday.] A.M. at the office. Afterwards went to President Josephs and commenced settlement with those who have claims on city Lots. Elder Brigham Young called me on one side and said he wants to give me some instructions on the priesthood the first opportunity. He said the prophet had told him to do so and give me a favor which I have long desired.[2] For this again I feel grateful to God and his servant, and the desire of my heart is to do right and be saved.

[March 8, 1843. Wednesday.] . . . Evening I went to Brother Kimballs Meeting. The house was crowded to suffocation. He made use of the figure of the Potter and clay, and showed that O[rson] Pratt was stiff and had to be cast off the wheel and A[masa] Lyman put on it.[3] The discourse was good.

[March 9, 1843. Thursday.] At President Josephs office. Walked out in the P.M. He told me it was lawful for me to send for Sarah and said he would furnish me money.[4]

---

[2] The favor of which Clayton speaks is the invitation to enter the secret practice of plural marriage. In the previous sentence, Clayton speaks of "instruction on the priesthood." "The priesthood," "everlasting covenant," "celestial marriage," and "the principle" are all terms he uses in his journals to refer to plural marriage.

[3] Kimball frequently referred to the potter and clay metaphor from the Old Testament book of Isaiah. In 1841 while Orson Pratt was on a mission to England, Pratt's wife, Sarah, accused Joseph Smith of proposing that she become one of his "celestial wives." The following year Pratt refused an invitation to endorse Smith's moral character, and in August 1842 he was dismissed from the Quorum of Twelve Apostles. He was rebaptized in January 1843 (Richard W. Van Wagoner, *Mormon Polygamy: A History* [Salt Lake City: Signature Books, 1986], 27-37).

[4] In his 1874 statement Clayton recounted such a conversation which was probably about Sarah Crooks. After Smith made him his "private clerk" on October 7, 1842, Clayton recalled, "the Prophet Joseph frequently visited my house in my

[April 2, 1843. Sunday.][5] . . . P.M. Joseph preached on Revelations Chap[ter] 5. He called on me to open the meeting. He also preached on the same subject in the evening. During the day President Joseph made the following remarks on doctrine. "I was once praying very ernestly to know the time of the coming of the son of man when I heard a voice repeat the following. 'Joseph my son, if thou livest until thou art 84 years old thou shalt see the face of the son of man, therefore let this suffice and trouble me no more on this matter.'[6] I was left thus without being able to decide w[h]ether this coming referred to the beginning of the Millenium, or to some previous appearing or w[h]ether I should die and thus

company and became well acquainted with my wife Ruth, to whom I had been married five years. One day in the month of February, 1843, date not remembered, the Prophet invited me to walk with him. During our walk, he said he had learned that there was a sister back in England, to whom I was very much attached. I replied there was, but nothing further than an attachment such as a brother and sister in the Church might rightfully entertain for each other. He then said, 'Why don't you send for her?' I replied, 'In the first place, I have no authority to send for her, and if I had, I have not the means to pay expenses.' To this he answered, 'I give you the authority to send for her, and I will furnish you with means,' which he did. This was the first time that the Prophet Joseph talked with me on the subject of plural marriage" (Andrew Jenson, "Plural Marriage," *Historical Record* [May 1887]: 224-26, hereafter *HR*; see Appendix C, "William Clayton's Testimony").

[5] Before delivering the important address which Clayton records here, Smith, accompanied by Clayton and Orson Hyde, visited Benjamin F. Johnson's home in Macedonia (formerly Ramus), Illinois. That morning, as Johnson recounted, "Pres. Smith took me by the arm for a walk, leading the way to a secluded spot within an adjacent grove, where, to my great surprise, he commenced to open up to me the principle of plural or celestial marriage; but I was more astonished by his asking me for my sister Almera to be his wife." Johnson described a subsequent trip to Nauvoo where Hyrum Smith sealed his brother Joseph to Almera (*HR* 6:221-22). In a 1903 letter to George S. Gibbs, Johnson concludes the story somewhat differently, reporting that William Clayton performed the marriage (Benjamin F. Johnson to George F. Gibbs, 1903, 10, archives, Church of Jesus Christ of Latter-day Saints, Salt Lake City; hereafter LDS archives).

[6] This revelation later became Section 130 of that part of Mormon canon known as the Doctrine and Covenants. Millenialist William Miller, using biblical computations of time and the prophecies of Daniel and the book of Revelation, had predicted the end of the world during the prior month, March 1843. When the end did not occur, he recalculated to April 3, the day following this entry. Thousands of his followers sold their property and waited in ascension robes for Christ to come. The Seventh-Day Adventists were an outgrowth of his following. Joseph Smith said that Miller's error was due to incorrect translations of the Bible and that before Christ would return certain prophecies had to be fulfilled: "The sun must be darkened and the moon turn to blood" (Joseph Smith, Jr., et al., *History of the Church of Jesus Christ of Latter-day Saints*, ed. B. H. Roberts, 2d ed. rev., 7 vols. [Salt Lake City: Deseret Book, 1963], 5:272, 326; hereafter *HC*).

see his face. I believe the coming of the son of man will not be any sooner than that time." In correcting two points in Elder [Orson] Hydes discourse he observed as follows. "The meaning of that passage where it reads 'When he shall appear we shall be like him for we shall see him as he is' is this. When the savior appears we shall see that he is a man like unto ourselves, and that same sociality which exists amongst us here will exist among us there only it will be coupled with eternal glory which we do not enjoy now. Also the appearing of the father and the son in John c[hapter] 14 v[erse] 23 is a personal appearing and the idea that they will dwell in a mans heart is a sectarian doctrine and is false."

In answer to a question which I proposed to him as follows, 'Is not the reckoning of gods time, angels time, prophets time and mans time according to the planet on which they reside he answered yes. "But there is no angel ministers to this earth only what either does belong or has belonged to this earth and the angels do not reside on a planet like our earth but they dwell with God and the planet where he dwells is like crystal, and like a sea of glass before the throne. This is the great Urim and Thummim whereon all things are manifest both things past, present and future and are continually before the Lord. The Urim and Thummim is a small representation of this globe. The earth when it is purified will be made like unto crystal and will be a Urim and Thummim whereby all things pertaining to an inferior kingdom on all kingdoms of a lower order will be manifest to those who dwell on it.[7] And this earth will be with Christ. Then the white stone mentioned in Rev[elation] c[hapter] 2 v[erse] 17 is the Urim and Thummim whereby all things pertaining to an higher order of kingdoms even all kingdoms will be made known and a white stone is given to each of those who come into this celestial kingdom, whereon is a new name written which no man knoweth save he that receiveth it. The new name is the key word.[8]

---

[7] D&C 130. Joseph Smith's image of the earth becoming a great seerstone at the end of time is related to the Urim and Thummim, a crystal device he used to translate the Book of Mormon from "reformed Egyptian" (Richard S. Van Wagoner and Steven Walker, "Joseph Smith: 'The Gift of Seeing,'" *Dialogue: A Journal of Mormon Thought* 15 [Summer 1982]).

[8] In the emerging ritual of the Quorum of the Anointed, initiates would soon be given a secret name by which they would be recognized at the veil separating life from death.

"Whatever principle of intelligence we obtain in this life will rise with us in the resurrection: and if a person gains more knowledge in this life through his diligence and obedience than another, he will have so much the advantage in the world to come. There is a law irrevocably decreed in heaven before the foundation of this world upon which all blessings are predicated; and when we obtain any blessing from God, it is by obedience to that law upon which it is predicated.

"The Holy Ghost is a personage, and a person cannot have the personage of the H[oly] G[host] in his heart. A man receive the gifts of the H[oly] G[host] and the H[oly] G[host] may descend upon a man but not to tarry with him."

He also related the following dream. "I dreamed that a silver-headed old man came to see me and said he was invaded by a gang of robbers, who were plundering his neighbors and threatening destruction to all his subjects. He had heard that I always sought to defend the oppressed, and he had come to hear with his own ears what answer I would give him. I answered, if you will make out the papers and shew that you are not the aggressor I will call out the Legion and defend you while I have a man to stand by me. The old man then turned to go away. When he got a little distance he turned suddenly round and said I must call out the Legion and go and he would have the papers ready when I arrived, and says he I have any amount of men which you can have under your command.

Elder Hyde gave this interpretation. "The old man represents the government of these United States who will be invaded by a foreign foe, probably England. The U. S. government will call on you to defend probably all this Western Territory, and will offer you any amount of men you may need for that purpose."

Once when President Joseph was praying ernestly to know concerning the wars which are to preceed the coming of the son of man, he heard a voice proclaim that the first outbreak of general bloodshed would commence at South Carolina (see Revelation).[9]

---

[9] See D&C 87. Joseph Smith's Civil War prediction was made in 1832, when South Carolina had rebelled against federal authority, declaring a U.S. tariff null and void. The press carried speculations concerning a civil war, but when war did not follow, the prediction was withheld from the revelations in the 1833 Book of

The sealing of the 144,000 was the number of priests who should be anointed to administer in the daily sacrifice &c. During President Joseph's remarks he said there was a nice distinction between the vision which John saw as spoken of in Revelations and the vision which Daniel saw, the former relating only to things as they actually existed in heaven, the latter being a figure representing things on the earth. God never made use of the figure of a beast to represent the kingdom of heaven, when they were made use of it was to represent an apostate church.

[April 6, 1843. Thursday.] This day was a special conference. The saints assembled in the Temple soon after 9. I was appointed to take minutes. About 11 President Joseph arrived and proceeded to business. He first stated the object of this conference, viz. 1st. To ascertain the standing of the first presidency. 2nd To take into consideration the propriety of sending some of the Twelve into the branches abroad to obtain funds for building the Nauvoo House.[10] 3rd. To give a chance to those Elders who have been disfellowshiped or had their licenses taken away in the branches to have a re-hearing and settle their difficulties. He then spake on the importance of building the Nauvoo House stressing that the time had come to build it. And the church must either do it or suffer the condemnation of not fulfilling the commandments of God.

He next presented himself and was unanimously voted president of the whole church. Next his councillors Elders [Sidney] Rigdon and W[illia]m Law, and afterwards Elder Hyrum [Smith] who was voted with a hearty aye. He blessed the people in the name of the Lord.

The next business was appointing the Twelve on their mission &c. He showed the injustice of Elders collecting funds for the Temple in as much as they rarely brought them here. The conference must contrive some measures to put the Twelve under bonds, for a true return of monies received by them &c.

Commandments. Smith's prediction was first published in the 1851 edition of the Pearl of Great Price, then included among his other revelations in the 1876 edition of the Doctrine and Covenants.

[10] A hotel.

[April 7, 1843. Friday.] Various little items of business attended to and a discourse from the president on Rev[elations].

[April 16, 1843. Sunday.] Heard President J[oseph] preach on the resurrection shewing the importance of being buried with the saints and their relatives in as much as we shall want to see our relatives first and shall rejoice to strike hands with our parents, children &c. when rising from the tomb.[11]

[April 24, 1843. Monday.] . . . Sister Marg[are]t Moon went with me. She is a lovely woman and desires to do right in all things and will submit to council with all her heart. Got back at dark conversed some with President.

[April 27, 1843. Thursday.] At the Temple A.M. went to Presidents who rode with me to Brother H[eber] C. Kimballs where Sister Marg[are]t Moon was sealed up by the priesthood, by the president, and M[arried] to me[12] . . . evening told Mother in law concerning the priesthood.

[April 27, 1843. Thursday.][13] At the Temple A.M. at 10 Brother Kimballs was M[arried] to M[argaret] M[oon] . . . evening told Mother in law about the priesthood.

[April 29, 1843. Saturday.] Rode out to Prairie with President Joseph, W[illia]m [Smith] and Samuel H. Smith and John Topham.

[April 30, 1843. Sunday.] . . . P.M. at Sister [Ann] Booths where I learned that S[arah] Ann would obey her instructions.[14] Evening walked out with Margaret and accomplished a good object.

---

[11] Joseph Smith taught that resurrected bodies will all come out of their tombs at the same time (*HC* 5:360-62).

[12] In his 1874 statement, Clayton summarized this day: "On the 27th of April, 1843, the Prophet Joseph married to me Margaret Moon, for time and eternity, at the residence of Elder Heber C. Kimball: and on the 22nd of July, 1843, he married to me, according to the order of the Church, my first wife Ruth," to whom he had been civilly married for six years (*HR* 6:225, in Appendix C, "William Clayton's Testimony").

[13] The concurrent entries for April 27 indicate that Clayton has begun writing in his second Nauvoo journal. See Introduction, n124.

[14] Sarah Ann Booth would be married to John Needham on October 17, 1843, by Hyrum Smith.

[May 1, 1843. Monday.] A.M. at the Temple. At 10 m[ar-ried] J[oseph] to L[ucy] W[alker]. P.M. at President Josephs[15] . . . I have seen 6 brass plates which were found in Adams County . . . President Joseph has translated a portion and says they contain the history of the person with whom they were found and he was a descendant of Ham through the loins of Pharaoh king of Egypt, and that he received his kingdom from the ruler of heaven and earth.[16]

[May 2, 1843. Tuesday.] . . . Talked with Jane Charnock. She loves me and would sooner unite to me than R[][17] Joseph rode out today with Flora W[oodworth].[18]

[May 3, 1843. Wednesday.] . . . Diantha Farr went with me . . . Much use of the term "Joe Smith" and snearingly.[19]

[May 5, 1843. Friday.] President Joseph told the Temple com-mittee that he had a right to take away any property he chose from the Temple and they had no right to stand in the way. It

---

[15] Lucy Walker helped Emma with the housework and attended school with the Smith children. Clayton officiated at Joseph's wedding to Lucy while Emma was buying supplies in St. Louis (Linda King Newell and Valeen Tippetts Avery, *Mormon Enigma: Emma Hale Smith, Prophet's Wife, "Elect Lady," Polygamy's Foe* [Garden City, NY: Doubleday, 1984], 139). Lucy Walker was the twelfth plural wife on LDS historian Andrew Jenson's list of Joseph Smith's wives, the last before the revelation on plural marriage was recorded on July 12, 1843 (*HR* 6:233–34). Thirty years later Clayton repeated the story, spelling out the names: "On the 1st day of May, 1843, I officiated in the office of an Elder by marrying Lucy Walker to the Prophet Joseph Smith, at his own residence" (*HR* 6:225, reproduced in Appendix C, "William Clayton's Testimony"). See Journal 4, "Pioneer Trek West," n21.

[16] Photographs of the Kinderhook Plates, named after the Illinois town where they were buried, are found in *HC* 5:374–76. See Introduction, n32.

[17] Jane Charnock, whom Clayton evidently admired, could have been involved with any of several R-named persons, such as Reynolds Cahoon, Willard Richards, or Robert Booth. On October 17, 1843, she was civilly married to William F. Conner by Hyrum Smith.

[18] According to Clayton, Joseph Smith married sixteen-year-old Flora Woodworth in the spring of 1843 (*HR* 6:225; Fawn M. Brodie, *No Man Knows My History: The Life of Joseph Smith* [New York: Knopf, 1945], 458).

[19] The *History of the Church* relates that on this day Joseph Smith remained in Nauvoo to sit on a case at the mayor's court (*HC* 5:380). Meanwhile, Clayton, accompanied by Diantha, who would become his fifth wife on January 9, 1845, went to Carthage, the Hancock county seat, to settle a tax dispute. There, an abusive tax collector derided Joseph Smith. This was not the only time that Clayton represented Smith in tax questions. Later that month, Smith sent Clayton to Carthage to redeem city lots which had been sold for taxes (Clayton's journal entry for May 25, 1843).

was the people who had to dictate to him and not the committee. All the property he had belongs to the Temple and what he did was for the benefit of the Temple and the committee had no authority only as they receive it from him.

[May 7, 1843. Sunday.] . . . P.M. at Sister Booths with my wifes. Evening walked to Presidents with Marg[are]t.

[May 13, 1843. Saturday.] . . . Sister Desdemona Fullmer came to see if she could board with me.[20] I told her she could on Tuesday.

[May 14, 1843. Sunday.] . . . Walked out with Marg[are]t who promises to be true.

[May 15, 1843. Monday.] At the Temple office. Night my wife and Margaret slept together.

[May 16, 1843. Tuesday.] Went to see President Joseph who ordered me to prepare for Carthage. I returned home and got ready and started about 11 o'clock in the New Carriage with President Joseph. George Miller, Eliza Partridge, Lydia Partridge[21] and J. M. Smith. Lor[i]n Walker drove. We called at Carthage and saw [George P.] Styles, [Jacob B.] Backenstos and others.[22] Tarried about 15 minutes and started again for Ramus where we arrived about 3 1/2 o'clock. We stayed at W. G. Perkins.

---

[20] Desdemona Fullmer had become a secret plural wife of Joseph Smith in 1842 (*HR* 6: 235). By residing with the Claytons, she could maintain the confidentiality of her relationship with the prophet. After eight months, however, family disagreements caused Clayton to ask her to leave. See Clayton's journal entry for January 29, 1844.

[21] Lydia Partridge was the wife of Mormon bishop Edward Partridge. After Bishop Partridge's death in May 1840, Emma Smith took in the two eldest daughters, Emily and Eliza, to care for her baby Don Carlos; the younger children remained with their mother, Lydia. In 1887 Emily wrote in her autobiography that she became Smith's wife on March 4, 1843; a few days later, on March 8, her sister Eliza followed suit "also without the knowledge of Emma Smith." Emily further wrote that "two months afterwards she consented to give her husband two wives, provided he would give her the privilege of choosing them. She accordingly chose my sister Eliza and myself, and to save family trouble Brother Joseph thought it best to have another ceremony performed. Accordingly on the 11th of May, 1843, we were sealed to Joseph Smith a second time, in Emma's presence, she giving her free and full consent thereto. From that very hour, however, Emma was our bitter enemy" (*HR* 6:240; see entry for August 16, 1843, and Newell and Avery, 138-39).

[22] George P. Styles was the Nauvoo city attorney. Jacob Backenstos was the circuit court clerk.

President Joseph and I went to B[enjamin] F. Johnsons to sleep.[23] Before we retired the President gave Brother Johnson and wife some instructions on the priesthood. He put his hand on my knee and says "your life is hid with Christ in God, and so is many others." Addressing Benjamin says he "nothing but the unpardonable sin can prevent him (me) from inheriting eternal glory for he is sealed up by the power of the priesthood unto eternal life having taken the step which is necessary for that purpose." He said that except a man and his wife enter into an everlasting covenant and be married for eternity while in this probation by the power and authority of the Holy priesthood they will cease to increase when they die (i.e. they will not have any children in the resurrection), but those who are married by the power and authority of the priesthood in this life and continue without committing the sin against the Holy Ghost will continue to increase and have children in the celestial glory. The unpardonable sin is to shed innocent blood or be accessory thereto. All other sins will be visited with judgement in the flesh and the spirit being delivered to the buffetings of satan untill the day of the Lord Jesus." I feel desirous to be united in an everlasting convenant to my wife and pray that it may soon be. President J[oseph] said that the way he knew in whom to confide, God told him in whom he might place confidence. He also said that in the celestial glory there was three heavens or degrees, and in order to obtain the highest a man must enter into this order of the priesthood and if he don't he can't obtain it.[24] He may enter into the other but that is the end of his kingdom he cannot have increase.

---

[23] On this visit, according to Benjamin Johnson, Smith stayed with Almera "as man and wife" and "occupied the same room and bed with my sister, that the previous month he had occupied with the daughter of the late Bishop Partridge as his wife" (*HR*, 222; letter to George S. Gibbs). Almera confirmed her marriage to Smith: "I lived with the prophet Joseph as his wife and he visited me at the home of my brother Benjamin F. at Macedonia [Ramus]" (sworn statement cited by Joseph F. Smith, Jr., *Blood Atonement and the Origin of Plural Marriage* [Salt Lake City: Deseret New Press, 1905], 70–71). According to his letter to Gibbs, Johnson's eldest sister, Delcena, was also a plural wife of Joseph Smith.

[24] For nearly fifty years the order of plural marriage remained a requirement for Latter-day Saints who wanted to achieve the highest exaltation in the afterlife. The doctrine was officially rescinded in 1890 although practiced secretly until the Second Manifesto of 1904 (D. Michael Quinn, "LDS Church Authority and New Plural Marriages, 1890-1904," *Dialogue: A Journal of Mormon Thought* 18 [Spring 1985]: 9-105). The general membership began to practice plural marriage after

[May 17, 1843. Wednesday.] Breakfast at Brother [] Perkins, after which we took a pleasure ride through Fountain Green. At 10 President Joseph preached on 2nd Peter Chap[ter] 1. He shewed that knowledge is power and the man who has the most knowledge has the greatest power. Also that salvation means a mans being placed beyond the powers of all his enemies. He said the more sure word of prophecy meant, a mans knowing that he was sealed up unto eternal life by revelation and the spirit of prophecy through the power of the Holy priesthood. He also showed that it was impossible for a man to be saved in ignorance. Paul had seen the third heavens and I more. Peter penned the most sublime language of any of the apostles.

Dined at Brother [Almon] Babbits. President Joseph said to Brother Johnson and I that J[oseph] B. Noble when he was first taught this doctrine set his heart on one and pressed J[oseph Smith] to seal the contract but he never could get opportunity. It seemed that the Lord was unwilling. Finally another came along and he then engaged that one and is a happy man.[25] I learned from this anecdote never to press the prophet but wait with patience and God will bring all things right. I feel to pray that God will let me live so that I may come to the full knowledge of truth and salvation and be prepared for the enjoyment of a fulness of the third heavens.[26]

After dinner I took a pleasure ride with Lorain and the children. P.M. President Joseph attended the City council and afterwards rode out with B. F. Johnsons family. In the evening we went to hear a Methodist preacher lecture. After he got through President Joseph offered some corrections as follows. The 7th verse of C[hapter] 2 of Genesis ought to read God breathed into Adam his spirit or breath of life, but when the word "ruach" applies to Eve it should be translated lives. Speaking of eternal duration of matter he said There is no such thing as immaterial matter. All spirit is matter but is more fine or pure

---

1844 (Quinn, "The Mormon Hierarchy, 1832-1932: An American Elite," Ph.D. diss., Yale University, 1976, 60).

    [25] Brother-in-law of Smith's plural wife, Louisa Beaman, Noble had entered polygamy on April 5, 1843.

    [26] The "third heavens" refers to the Mormon concept of the "three degrees of glory" in the afterlife, of which the "Celestial Kingdom" is the highest followed by the "Terrestrial" and the "Telestial" (a word new to the English language). See D&C 76:81-119; HC 5:392, 402, 426.

and can only be discerned by purer eyes. We cant see it but when our bodies are purified we shall see that it is all matter.[27] The gentleman seemed pleased and said he should visit Nauvoo immediately.

[May 18, 1843. Thursday.] We left Macedonia about 8 1/2 and arrived in Carthage at 10. I asked the President w[h]ether children who die in infancy will grow. He answered "no, we shall receive them precisely in the same state as they died i.e. no larger. They will have as much intelligence as we shall but shall always remain separate and single. They will have no increase. Children who are born dead will have full grown bodies being made up by the resurrection."[28]

At Carthage we paid some taxes &c. Dined at Backenstos's with Judge [Stephen A.] Douglas[29] who is presiding at Court. After dinner the President and Judge had conversation concerning sundry matters. The President said "I prophecy in the name of the Lord God that in a few years this government will be utterly overthrown and wasted so that there will not be a potsherd left" for their wickedness in conniving at the Missouri mobocracy. The Judge appears very friendly and acknowledged the propriety of the Presidents remarks.

We left Carthage about 2 and arrived home at 5 1/2. My family all well.

---

[27] Joseph Smith taught that spirit and matter were two indestructible parts of existence (see the discussion in Appendix A, "Extracts from William Clayton's [Private] Book—Keys"). In his King Follett discourse Smith echoed contemporary writers in asserting that God did not create the world out of nothing but organized it out of existing materials which "had no beginning and can have no end" (*HC* 6: 308–309). In an 1839 treatise, "Regeneration and Eternal Duration of Matter," Elder Parley P. Pratt elaborated: "Matter and spirit are the two great principles of all existence . . . the elements are as durable as the quickening power which exists in them. Matter and spirit are of equal duration; both are self-existent, — they never began to exist, and they never can be annihilated" (ibid., 4:54–55n).

[28] Although Smith is reported here and in his King Follett sermon (April 1844) to have said that deceased infants would remain of the same stature as they held when they died, B. H. Roberts maintained that this was an erroneous report based on misunderstanding, and that the doctrine of the church assured that resurrected children would develop full stature (*HC* 4:556–57n).

[29] Stephen A. Douglas went on to become a U.S. senator from Illinois. When he ran for his third term in 1858, his Republican opponent was Abraham Lincoln. Though Douglas narrowly won the election, the Lincoln-Douglas debates of that year helped to create a national reputation for Lincoln, who defeated Douglas in the U.S. presidential election of 1860.

[May 20, 1843. Saturday.] . . . Rode on prairie with President Joseph, [Joseph H.] Jackson, Brother Oakley and others to look lands. P.M. rode out with Jackson to shew lands. President Smith tells me he has appointed Jackson to sell lands and relieve me of their burthen. He says Jackson appears a fine and noble fellow but is reduced in circumstances. The president feels disposed to employ him and give him a chance in the world. Jackson says he shall be baptized ere long.[30]

[May 21, 1843. Sunday.] President Joseph preached on 2 Peter chapter 1 to a very full house. P.M. we had sacrement administered. Evening I took a walk with my wife M[argaret] to H[eber] Kimball's and thence to the post office.

[May 22, 1843. Monday.] Went to President Joseph's. He received a letter from Sister [Sybella] Armstrong of Philadelphia complaining of slanderous conduct in B[enjamin] Winchester. The President handed the letter to Dr. [Willard] Richards saying the Twelve ought to silence Winchester . . . [31] In company with Jackson, President Joseph, Mr. Simpson and some others.

[May 23, 1843. Tuesday.] Conversed with H[eber] C. K[imball] concerning a plot that is being laid to entrap the brethren of the secret priesthood by Brother H[?] and others. Attended to much tax business with sundry brethren . . . President Joseph and lady rode to his farm. Evening President gave up lot 4 B 148 which he agreed to purchase of Asa Smith some time ago in consequence of Asas wanting to drag all money out of President and paying it for land else to here. President said such covetous minded men would be damned. President stated to me that he had had a little trouble with Sister E[mma]. He was asking E[liza] Partridge concerning [Joseph] Jackson['s] conduct during Presidents absence and E[mma] came upstairs. He shut to the door not knowing who it was and held it. She came to the door and called Eliza 4 times and tried to force open the door. President opened it and told her

---

[30] Jackson presented himself as a Catholic priest and gained employment selling land for the prophet. He later was a member of the mob at Joseph Smith's martyrdom in Carthage (*HC* 5:394; 7:146).

[31] See "Minutes of the Investigation of Benjamin Winchester" in Wilford Woodruff's journal, May 27, 1843 (Scott G. Kenney, ed., *Wilford Woodruff's Journal* [Midvale, UT: Signature Books, 1983], 2:234–36).

the cause &c. She seemed much irritated. He says Jackson is rotten hearted.

May the Lord preserve me from committing a fault to cause me to lose the confidence of my friends for I desire to do right thou Lord knowest.

[May 24, 1843. Wednesday.] . . . President Joseph bought 11 quarter sections of land of Gen. [James] Adams . . . President Joseph rode on the hill with Emma and also attended Court in the Ferry case.

[May 25, 1843. Thursday.] Started early to Carthage to redeem the city lots. Completed the business and returned home. I arrived about 8. Rained very heavy.[32]

[May 26, 1843. Friday.] A.M. went with A[lfred] Cordon to look [at] a lot. Also at the Temple office. The carpenters finished in my house. President Joseph came up in the afternoon and I went back with him. Settled with W[illia]m Ford by giving him 1/4 of lot and took up the due bill. President in meeting with the Twelve and Judge Adams. Hyrum received the doctrine of priesthood.[33]

[May 28, 1843. Sunday.] At Brother Kimballs who was blessing his children, he also blessed W[illia]m Heber Clayton.[34] At 2 I met with the wardens of the lodge. P.M. at home writing papers on settlement with the lodge. We are occupying our new house for which I feel thankful.

[May 29, 1843. Monday.] This A.M. President Joseph told me that he felt as though I was not treating him exactly right and asked if I had used any familiarity with E[mma]. I told him by no means and explained to his satisfaction.[35] At the store office.

---

[32] Smith sent Clayton to Carthage to redeem Nauvoo city lots on the Galland tract which had been sold for taxes. See Introduction, xxin; *HC* 5:409.

[33] After opposing plural marriage along with Emma Smith and William Law, Hyrum Smith accepted Joseph's teachings.

[34] William Heber Clayton was the fourth child and first son of Clayton and Ruth Moon, born February 28, 1843.

[35] Compare Clayton's journal entry, June 23, 1843.

[May 30, 1843. Tuesday.] At the Mayors office preparing papers for the Lawrence business.[36]

[May 31, 1843. Wednesday.] . . . This A.M. Sarah Crooks arrived at Nauvoo. She received word that I had sent to Brother [Hiram?] Clark on Feb[ruar]y 12th, and started immediately. She has been prospered and blest on her journey.

[June 1, 1843. Thursday.] This day I have been at President Joseph's office all day, preparing papers for the settlement of the Lawrence business with Brothers Whiting and Richards . . . Evening Joseph rode in the carriage with Flora [Woodworth]. He let Lorin Walker[37] have a knowledge of some things.

[June 2, 1843. Friday.] . . . wrote to Susan Conrad. This evening I talked with Sarah again and she appears willing to comply with her privilege.[38]

[June 3, 1843. Saturday.] This A.M. started for Quincey on the Steam Boat 'Maid of Iowa.' I took my wife and her child. Also Margaret Moon and Sarah Crooks. We had a large company of brethren and sisters on a pleasure voyage. We arrived at Quincey about 1 o'clock. I immediately went to the Probate Judge and presented the papers which we had made out pertaining to the Lawrence Estate. He said he could do nothing with them. Upon enquiring what he wanted I finally made a new account which he accepted. I then went to the boat and President Joseph returned with me to make oath to the accounts. Balance in Guardians hands was $3790.89 3/4. We soon got through and started back about 5 o'clock . . .

[June 4, 1843. Sunday.] Evening conversed with Sarah and Eliza[bet]h Brotherton.

---

[36] Joseph Smith served as executor for the $8,000 Lawrence estate, which benefitted Maria and Sarah, the daughters of Edward and Margaret Lawrence, young Canadian heiresses. Within a few months the sisters would both become Smith's plural wives (*HR* 6:223-34; 8:976; Newell and Avery, 143-144, 334n62; *Women's Exponent*, 14:38).

[37] Lorin Walker was the brother of Joseph Smith's plural wife, Lucy Walker.

[38] This cryptic entry could indicate Clayton's expectation that Sarah Crooks, who had arrived in Nauvoo two days earlier, would become his plural wife. Compare Introduction, n40. Note also the August 20, 1843, entry, which indicates Clayton's interest in Sarah Ann Booth, an alternative possibility.

[June 8, 1843. Thursday.] . . . Made deed to H[eber] C. and H[elen] M[ar] Kimball for N.E 1/4L 2 B 118.

[June 11, 1843. Sunday.] . . . Margaret received a letter from Aaron [Farr] which made her feel bad.[39] It also gave me unaccountable sorrow.

[June 13, 1843. Tuesday.] . . . President Joseph started North. I have had some conversation with M[argaret]. She promised she would not marry A[aron] if she can possibly avoid it. And if she ever feels disposed to marry she will tell me as soon as she thinks of it. She will seek my Council and says she will abide it. Last night S[arah] Crooks went away abruptly to Tho[ma]s Millers but came back this A.M.

[June 23, 1843. Friday.] This A.M. President Joseph took me and conversed considerable concerning some delicate matters. Said [Emma] wanted to lay a snare for me. He told me last night of this and said he had felt troubled. He said [Emma] had treated him coldly and badly since I came . . . and he knew she was disposed to be revenged on him for some things. She thought that if he would indulge himself she would too. He cautioned me very kindly for which I felt thankful. He said [Robert] Thompson professed great friendship for him but he gave away to temptation and he had to die. Also Brother [Newel] Knight he gave him one but he went to loose conduct and he could not save him. Also B[righam] Y[oung] had transgressed his covenant and he pled with the Lord to spare him this end and he did so, otherwise he would have died. B[righam] denied having transgressed. He said if I would do right by him and abide his council he would save my life while he lived. I feel desirous to do right and would rather die than loose my interest in the celestial kingdom . . . [40]

---

[39] Clayton's plural wife, Margaret Moon, had been engaged to Aaron Farr, who was absent on a proselytizing mission for the LDS church.

[40] Joseph Smith is reminding Clayton that the consequences of disloyalty could lead to a loss of the Celestial Kingdom. The Quorum of the Anointed performed symbolic sacrifice to represent the spiritual "death" that punished an unpardonable sin. See David Buerger, " 'The Fulness of the Priesthood': The Second Anointing in Latter-day Saint Theology and Practice," *Dialogue: A Journal of Mormon Thought* 16 (Spring 1983): 10–44.

[June 30, 1843. Friday.] . . . At 4 o'clock a large multitude were assembled at the grove and about 5 President Joseph made his appearance on the stand in company with Cyrus H. Walker Esqr. The general theme of his discourse tended to enlighten the minds of the public concerning the powers of the Municipal Court in relation to Habeas Corpus as granted in the Nauvoo Charter, plainly proving that the municipal court had more power than the circuit courts inasmuch as the latters power was limited while that of the former was unlimited.[41] He also said that he had restrained the saints from using violence in self defense but from henceforth he restrained them no more. The best of feelings prevailed during the whole meeting.

[July 4, 1843. Tuesday.] Today we had a meeting in the grove . . . in the evening President Joseph related a history of the Missouri persecutions and the late arrest in the presence of about 900 passengers and a very large multitude of saints.

[July 8, 1843. Saturday.] . . . Marg[are]t wrote a letter to Aaron [Farr] which I dictated informing him that she should not marry.

---

[41] A writ of habeas corpus (Latin: "you have the body") requires an arresting authority to bring a detained person into court to determine the legality of the detention. The Nauvoo Municipal Court claimed unlimited power to challenge the validity of arrest warrants originating from other or higher jurisdictions. When Joseph Smith was arrested by Missouri officers on August 8, 1842, on charges that he was an accessory to the attempted murder of Governor Boggs, the Nauvoo court granted him a writ of habeas corpus, effectively protecting him from extradition to Missouri. At that time, the city council passed an ordinance imposing a mandatory life sentence upon any officer of the law attempting to arrest Smith on "old Missouri charges;" the ordinance stipulated that such a party could only be pardoned by the governor with the consent of the mayor of Nauvoo. Here, on June 30, 1843, as Clayton records, Smith is again defending his right to protect himself with the habeas corpus provision. A week earlier, while travelling in Dixon, Illinois, he had been arrested at gunpoint by two Missouri sheriffs on treason charges dating back to 1838. A renowned Illinois criminal lawyer, Cyrus H. Walker, succeeded in getting Smith released from custody and agreed to defend him for $10,000 and Smith's support in the forthcoming congressional elections. "I have converted this candidate for congress that the right of habeas corpus is included in our charter," said Smith when he returned to Nauvoo accompanied by Walker and the Missouri sheriffs. "If he continues converted I will vote for him" (*HC* 5:465-66; 6:105-106; Brodie, 348-51; Robert Bruce Flanders, *Nauvoo: Kingdom on the Mississippi* [Urbana: University of Illinois Press, 1965], 104-105; and Kenney, 2:250-54, for Wilford Woodruff's account of Joseph Smith's defense of the habeas corpus on June 30, 1843).

[July 9, 1843. Sunday.] A.M. at the Grove. President Joseph preached.

[July 12, 1843. Wednesday.] This A.M. I wrote a Revelation consisting of 10 pages on the order of the priesthood, showing the designs in Moses, Abraham, David and Solomon having many wives and concubines &c.[42] After it was wrote Presidents Joseph and Hyrum presented it and read it to E[mma] who said she did not believe a word of it and appeared very rebellious. Joseph told me to Deed all the unincumbered lots to E[mma] and the children. He appears much troubled about E[mma].

[July 13, 1843. Thursday.] This A.M. Joseph sent for me and when I arrived he called me up into his private room with E[mma] and there stated an agreement they had mutually entered into. They both stated their feelings on many subjects and wept considerable. O may the Lord soften her heart that she may be willing to keep and abide by his Holy Law . . .

[July 15, 1843. Saturday.] Made Deed for 1/2 S[team] B[oat] Maid of Iowa from Joseph to Emma. Also a Deed to E[mma] for over 60 city lots . . .

[July 16, 1843. Sunday.] A.M. at home writing Brother [Heber] Kimballs lecture. P.M. went to the Grove and heard President Joseph preach on the law of the priesthood. He stated that Hyrum held the office of prophet to the church by birthright and he was going to have a reformation and the saints must regard Hyrum for he has authority. He showed that a man must enter into an everlasting covenant with his wife in this world or he will have no claim on her in the next. He said that he could not

---

[42] Clayton later wrote: "I did write the revelation on Celestial marriage given through the Prophet Joseph Smith on the 12th day of July 1843. When the revelation was written there was no one present except the prophet Joseph, his brother Hyrum and myself. It was written in the small office upstairs in the rear of the brick store which stood on the banks of the Mississippi River. It took some three hours to write it. Joseph dictated sentence by sentence and I wrote it as he dictated. After the whole was written Joseph requested me to read it slowly and carefully which I did, and he then pronounced it correct. The same night a copy was taken by Bishop Whitney which copy is now here and which I know and testify is correct. The original was destroyed by Emma Smith" (Letter to Madison M. Scott, November 11, 1871, William Clayton Letterbooks, Special Collections, Marriott Library, University of Utah). The revelation can be found in D&C 132.

reveal the fulness of these things untill the Temple is completed &c.

[July 17, 1843. Monday.] A.M. at the Temple and at President Joseph's conversed with Joseph and Hyrum on the priesthood . . .

[July 22, 1843. Saturday.] . . . M[argaret] and A[aron] had a long conversation together. She has stood true to her covenant with W[illiam] C[layton]. I also had some talk with him and although the shock is severe he endures it patiently.[43] And I pray the Great Eloheem to make up the loss to him an hundred fold and enable him to rejoice in all things. My heart aches with grief on his and M[argaret]'s account and could almost say O that I had never known h[er]. But Thou O God knowest the integrity of thy servant. Thou knowest that I have done that which I have understood to be thy will and am still determined to do so and I ask thee in the name of Jesus Christ either to absolutely wean my affections from M[argaret], or give me hers entire and then I am content. But to live in this state of feeling I cannot. If I have done wrong in this thing, show it me that thy servant may repent of it and obtain forgiveness. But O Lord have mercy on me and by some means release me from this grievous bondage of feeling and thy servant will praise thee. President Joseph came to see me and pronounced a sealing blessing upon Ruth and me. And we mutually entered into an everlasting covenant with each other.

[July 23, 1843. Sunday.] . . . M[argaret] appears dissatisfied with her situation and is miserable. O that the Lord will bless my house and deliver us from every evil principal and feeling that we may be saved. For I desire to do right. O Lord make my heart and my affections right and pure as it shall please thee that I may enjoy the blessing of peace and happiness even so Amen. Hyrum preached A.M. and Joseph P.M. Evening I had some more talk with M[argaret] and find she is miserable which makes me doubly so. I offered to her to try to have her covenant released if she desired it but she said she was not willing.

---

[43] Aaron Farr probably learned here for the first time that Margaret had secretly married William Clayton. Margaret was also now pregnant. In the ensuing entries, Clayton refers to her condition euphemistically as the "circumstances."

[July 24, 1843. Monday.] . . . M[argaret] is still miserable and unhappy and it does seem that my heart must burst. What shall I do? How shall I recompense? And how long must I thus suffer worse than death for that which I have always regarded as being the will of the Lord. By the help of the Lord I will do right. I have repeatedly offered to M[argaret] to try to get a release from the covenant and I have done all I know to make things comfortable but to no effect. She appears almost to hate me and cannot bear to come near me. O God if thou wilt give me M[argaret]'s affections, and cause things to be pleasant and happy between us, if thou will bless her and comfort her by thy spirit and cause her to rejoice in what she has done, and bring it to pass that I may secure her truly with all her affections for time and for eternity. I feel to covenant to try to serve thee with more diligence if possible and to do all that thou shalt require at mine hands. Wilt thou not grant me this blessing, and relieve my aching heart from this worst of all troubles which ever befell me in the course of my life? O God plead my cause and give me thine everlasting blessing, and do remember M[argaret] for good that she may be comforted even so amen amen and amen.

[July 25, 1843. Tuesday.] . . . M[argaret] much as usual.

[July 26, 1843. Wednesday.] . . . M[argaret] seems quite embittered against me in consequence of which I called her to me and asked her if she desired the covenant to be revoked if it were possible. To this she would not give me a satisfactory answer only saying if it had not been done it should not be. (meaning our union). I then asked if she would consent if A[aron] would take her under all circumstances; but she would not consent to have it revoked, saying she did it not for her sake but for the sake of the peace of my family. Under these circumstances I could not rest until I had ascertained w[h]ether the c[ovenant] could be revoked and although contrary to her wish I went to see President Joseph. I took A[aron] to talk with him and asked him some questions whereby I ascertained that he would be willing to take her under all circumstances. I reasoned considerable with him to prove that I had done right in all these matters so far as I knew it. I called the President out and briefly stated the situation of things and then asked him if the C[ovenant] could be revoked. He shook his head and answered no. At this conclusion my mind seemed for the moment to get relief for the twofold reason that I had done all I could and I did not want the C[ovenant] revoked. I came back and M[argaret] and A[aron] were together in Farrs garden. I told them the answer I had got and advised them to take the best measures to make all things right between them. I cannot help thinking that M[argaret] has treated me not only unkindly but meanly and cruelly, but I forgive her before the Lord for I sympathize with her in her grief, but can't console her for she will not speak to me. My earnest prayer to God is that all things may soon become right and pleasant and that the Lord may bless her and save her from sinning against him. And if I have done wrong in asking if the C[ovenant] could be revoked and seeking to have it done O Lord forgive me for I desire to do right in all things that I may be saved. I feel that I have done right in the sight of God and that he has abundantly blessed me for which I thank him and something tells me that the time will come when M[argaret] will love those who she ought and when she will feel perfectly satisfied with her situation and rejoice that things remain as they are. And now O God bless thy servant and handmaid and stamp th[y] peace upon us and fill us with the spirit of truth for Jesus Christs sake Amen.

[July 27, 1843. Thursday.] I went to see President Joseph in our conversation about M[argaret] and A[aron] he said if A[aron] went to making me any trouble he would defend me to the uttermost and stand by me through all, for which I feel thankful . . .

[August 1, 1843. Tuesday.][44] . . . Bagby said he had done more for Joseph than for any other man in the country. Joseph reiterated that Bagby was continually abusing the citizens here. Bagby called the prophet a liar . . . pick up a stone to throw at him which so enraged him that President Joseph followed him a

---

[44] Following a series of tax issues which Clayton handled (see his journal entries for May 3 and May 25, 1843), Joseph Smith here deals with the tax collector himself. The *History of the Church* records: "At 4 P.M. I rode up to the temple and complained to the clerks that Mr. Hamilton had got a tax title from one of my city lots. Mr. Walter Bagby, the collector, came up in the midst of our conversation, and when asked about it denied all knowledge of it. I told him that I had always been ready to pay all my taxes when I was called upon; and I did not think it gentlemanly treatment to sell any of my lots for taxes." After Bagby insulted him, the prophet got out of his buggy and started toward Bagby (*HC* 5:524). Clayton records the altercation that followed.

few steps and struck him two or three times. Esquire Daniel H. Wells stepped between them and succeeded in separating them. President Joseph told the Esquire to assess the fine for the assault and he was willing to pay it. President Joseph rode down to Alderman Whitney stated the circumstances and he imposed a fine which the prophet paid and then returned to a political meeting. Bagby stayed awhile muttering that Joseph was a coward.[45]

[August 3, 1843. Thursday.] A.M. at President Joseph's . . . Conversed about W[illiam] Law, Emma &c . . . [46]

[August 6, 1843. Sunday.] . . . President Joseph made some remarks on the election showing that he had taken no part in it. Stated that Hyrum had had a manifestation that it was for our interest to vote for Hoge.[47]

[August 11, 1843. Friday.] A.M. To the Temple office. P.M. President Joseph came to my house and I went home with him

---

[45] On August 13, 1843, Joseph Smith summarized the Bagby incident in his own journal: "Mr. Bagby of Carthage, who has exercised more despotic power over the inhabitants of this city than any despot of the Eastern country I met. He gave me some abusive language [and] took up a stone to throw at me. I siezed him by the throat to choke him off" (Scott M. Faulring, ed., *An American Prophet's Record: The Diaries and Journals of Joseph Smith* [Salt Lake City: Signature Books and Smith Research Associates, 1989], 405.) Smith's journals describe similar physical conflicts (ibid., 267, 307, 310). Joseph Smith's vulnerability to the tax collector is described in Introduction, ns24, 26.

[46] At this point, Emma Smith and William Law were formidable opponents of plural marriage (Van Wagoner, 52).

[47] The Congressional elections of 1843 demonstrated the potency of a Mormon voting bloc. In order to court their favor in Illinois' Sixth District, which included Hancock County, both the Whig candidate Cyrus H. Walker and the Democratic candidate Joseph P. Hoge supported the Mormons' controversial interpretation of habeas corpus included in the Nauvoo Charter. When Smith was arrested on June 23, Walker arranged for Smith's release after the prophet had "promised Walker that he should have nine out of every ten Mormon votes." But just before the August 7 election Hyrum Smith announced that he had a "revelation from the lord that the people should vote Mr. Hoge." In his journal on August 6 Joseph Smith wrote, "Bro[ther] Hiram tells me this morning that he has had a testimony that it will be better for this people to vote for Hoge. I never knew Hiram say he ever had a revelation and it failed." Although Smith cast his personal vote for Walker, Hoge got the bulk of the Mormon vote and won the election. Of both candidates, Governor Ford said, "The Mormons were deluded and deceived by men who ought to have known and did know better." See "The Law Review," *The Daily Tribune* (Salt Lake City), July 31, 1887; Faulring, 402; Flanders, 233-39; Brodie, 348-51; Thomas Ford, *History of Illinois from Its Commencement as a State in 1818 to 1847* (Chicago: S. C. Griggs, 1854), 2:316; Flanders, 235-36.

and took dinner with him. In our conversation about Judge [James] Adams Joseph made this remark "No man can put forth his hand to steady the ark but God and his servant Joseph."[48] By the ark I understood him to mean this work and that no man could dictate and govern it but Jehovah and he whom God had appointed viz. his servant Joseph . . . Judge Adams died about 10 o'clock P.M. None of his family are here having only been sent for a few days and they are at Springfield. It is truly afflicting to see the sickness which exists through the city and the loss of this man seems very grievous. He attended the polls on Monday last and was elected Probate Judge for this County but he is gone to receive his reward in the other world. Joseph told me to day that [William?] "Walker" had been speaking to him concerning my having taken M[argaret] away from A[aron] and intimated that I had done wrong.[49] I told him to be quiet and say no more about it. He also told me Emma was considerably displeased with it but says he she will soon get over it. In the agony of mind which I have endured on this subject I said I was sorry I had done it, at which Joseph told me not to say so. I finally asked him if I had done wrong in what I had done. He answered no you have a right to get all you can.

[August 13, 1843. Sunday.] Went to meeting heard Joseph preach on 2 Peter 3. 10 and 11 being a funeral sermon on the death of E[lias] Higbee. When speaking of the passage "I will send Elizah the prophet &c." he said it should read and he shall turn the hearts of the children to the covenant made with their fathers. Also where it says and they shall seal the servants of God in their foreheads &c. it means to seal the blessing on their heads meaning the everlasting covenant thereby making their calling and election sure.[50] When a seal is put upon the father and mother it secures their posterity so that they cannot be lost but will be

---

[48] According to the Old Testament, no one was permitted to touch the Ark of the Covenant, the vessel containing the Ten Commandments, except the Levite priests. When Uzza tried to steady the Ark as King David moved it, God became enraged and struck him dead (1 Chr. 13:7–10; 15:1–3).

[49] William Walker, who was married to Aaron Farr's sister, Olive, was naturally concerned about his brother-in-law Aaron's happiness. Ironically, Walker became Clayton's brother-in-law when Clayton married Aaron Farr's sister, Diantha, on January 9, 1845.

[50] Joseph Smith thus promises them a secure position in the Celestial Kingdom. Compare n58.

saved by virtue of the covenant of their father. P.M. President Joseph offered some complaints of the citizens of Nauvoo 1st because some young men sat on the ladies camp ground and laughed and mocked during meeting. He next spake of Walter Bagby and the little skirmish he had with him about a week ago. He spoke of Esq. [Daniel] Wells interfering when he had no business. He then spake of the abuses he received at the election by King and the board of Judges. Also of the Grog and Beer shops and said he should rip them up. He then showed that Sidney Rigdon had bound himself by an oath to Governor [Thomas] Carlin to deliver Joseph into the hands of the Missourians[51] if he could and finally in the name of the Lord withdrew the hand of fellowship from him and put it to the vote of the people. He was cut off by an unanimous vote and orders to demand his license... At night my wifes mother went into the garden to pray just as we were going to bed. Margaret and Lydia went out and found her on her knees. She was deranged. She came into the bed room trembling and seemed as though she had been frightened but was altogether delirious. Her feet and legs were cold and I feared she was going to die. She got into bed and we got some hot water to her feet and rubbed her legs and feet with flannel and went to bed. She soon seemed some better. From her conversation with Lydia this afternoon it seems she took President Joseph's remarks very deeply to heart and that with her fears for Margaret overwhelmed her. I feel as though I was in some measure a child of sorrow but am determined to try to do right in all things. May the Lord bless my family and my fathers house and save us with an everlasting salvation and let peace and intelligence beam upon us in the name of Jesus Christ Amen.

---

[51] Joseph Smith refers to the writ of extradition Illinois governor Carlin had received to try Smith for the attempted murder of Missouri governor Boggs on May 14, 1842. See n41; Gary J. Bergera, "Joseph Smith and the Hazards of Charismatic Leadership," *Journal of the John Whitmer Historical Association*, 6 (1986): 33–42. Orrin Porter Rockwell, Joseph Smith's bodyguard, was arrested that year and charged with attempted murder. Rockwell never denied shooting Boggs. General Patrick E. Conner reported that Rockwell told him, "I shot through the window and thought I had killed him, but I had only wounded him; I was damned sorry that I had not killed the son of a bitch." Neither the prophet nor his bodyguard was convicted of the crime. See Richard S. Van Wagoner and Steven C. Walker, *A Book of Mormons* (Salt Lake City, Signature Books, 1982), 250; *HC* 5:14, 15, 67; Appendix B, "An Interesting Journal"; Flanders, 104.

[August 16, 1843. Wednesday.] . . . We returned and met President Joseph and some of the family going to the funeral of Judge Adams. P.M. I went with A[lpheus] Young to look at a lot and called at Sister Booths who is in trouble. Robert [Booth] is gone away to work, Sarah Ann [Booth] is gone to Keokuk, and Elesabeth [] and husband is going to Chicago this evening. This A.M. Joseph told me that since E[mma] came back from St. Louis she had resisted the P[riesthood]⁵² in toto and he had to tell her he would relinquish all for her sake. She said she would [have] given him E[liza] and E[mily] P[artridge], but he knew if he took them she would pitch on him and obtain a divorce and leave him. He however told me he should not relinquish anything. O God deliver thy servant from iniquity and bondage.

[August 17, 1843. Thursday.] . . . Margaret seems friendly but not well satisfied yet she treats me very well and I pray God to bless her forever.

[August 18, 1843. Friday.] President Joseph instructed S[amue]l James in the order of the Holy Priesthood . . . I had some conversation with Brother [Newel] Whitney and have learned that Farrs family are conspiring with Walkers boys and girls and they with E[mma] to accomplish my downfall. I find they are my secret enemies but I fear them not for God who knows the secrets of all hearts knows mine also. I told M[argaret] of this and ascertained that she had acknowledged to A[aron] that I had slept with her and if it never had been done (our union) it should not be. This of course has given him a plea and a weapon against me. At night my wifes mother had another fit of delirium, which fills us all with sorrow, and I think we have a good share.

[August 19, 1843. Saturday.] . . . evening went to President Joseph's did not see him. M[argaret] says D[iantha] Farr said to day she believed M[argaret] and I was vexed at her and she almost felt disposed almost to go to every house in the city and tell all she knew and then come home and kill herself. I felt my heart ac[h]e to night when we lay down being down stairs and M[argaret] up. My soul loves M[argaret] and my desire is to see her happy and comfortable. Oh may the Lord bless her.

---

⁵² Refused to accept polygamy.

[August 20, 1843. Sunday.] M[argaret] came up stairs to me
. . . P.M. I went to Sister Booths and had some conversation
about S[ara]h A[nn] at Sister B's request. I have evidence that
S[arah] A[nn] is true to me and desire to receive her. I also had
talk with M[ary] Aspen who is in trouble. P[arley] P. P[ratt] has
through his wife made proposals to her but she is dissatisfied.
Sister P[ratt] is obstinate. When P[arley] went away Sister P.
cautioned A. against me and said the Twelve would have more
glory than me &c. I tried to comfort her and told her what her
privilege was.[53] Tarried till 8 1/2.

[August 21, 1843. Monday.] . . . E[mma] asked if I handed
2 letters to Joseph which she showed me. I had not done it. I
satisfied her I had not. They appeared to be from E[liza] R[oxcy]
Snow[54] and President Joseph found them in his pocket. E[mma]
seemed vexed and angry.

[August 23, 1843. Wednesday.] . . . President Joseph told me
that he had difficulty with E[mma] yesterday. She rode up to
Woodworths with him and called while he came to the Temple.
When he returned she was demanding the gold watch of
F[lora]. He reproved her for her evil treatment. On their return
home she abused him much and also when he got home. He
had to use harsh measures to put a stop to her abuse but finally
succeeded . . .
This evening I had some more conversation with Margaret
and find she is stubborn and disposed to abuse me. I feel resolved
to break my feelings from her if I possibly can.

[August 24, 1843. Thursday.] . . . At night I asked mother if
M[argaret] might sleep with Ruth and me. She appeared very
rebellious and would not consent but said we might do as we had
a mind. J[oseph] S[mith] through W[illiam] C[layton] pays D[avid]
D. Yearsley.

[August 26, 1843. Saturday.] . . . Hyrum and I rode up to
my house and Joseph met Mrs. W[oo]d[wor]th and F[lora] and

---

[53] This oblique reference may be to Alice Hardman, who became Clayton's
plural wife on September 13, 1844.
[54] Joseph Smith had married Eliza Snow on June 29, 1842.

conversed some time . . . President Joseph and I walked from my house to Sister [Elizabeth] Durfee's[55] and thence to his house.

[August 27, 1843. Sunday.] A.M. at the Grove. President Joseph preached on Hebrews c[hapter] 7. After reading a letter from Tho[ma]s Carlin to S[idney] Rigdon and making some remarks about it. He shewed the word "Salem" is a wrong translation it should be "Shalome" signifying peace. He prophecied that "not all the powers of hell or earth combined can ever overthrow this boy" for he had a promise from the eternal God. He spoke concerning the priesthood of Melchisedek shewing that the sectarians never professed to have it consequently never could save any one and would all be damned together. He showed that the power of the Melchisedek P[riesthoo]d was to have the power of an "endless lives." He showed that the everlasting covenants could not be broken, and by the sacrifice required of Abraham the fact that when God offers a blessing or knowledge to a man and he refuses to receive it he will be damned, mentioning the case of the Israelite praying that God would speak to Moses and not to them, in consequence of which he curse them with a carnal law. P.M. I went to Sister Booths and talked with her and Mary Aspen.

[August 28, 1843. Monday.] . . . President Joseph met Ms W[oo]d[wor]th at my house.

[August 29, 1843. Tuesday.] A.M. at the Temple. President Joseph at my house with Miss W[oo]d[wor]th.

[August 30, 1843. Wednesday.] A.M. . . . at President Joseph's. He and Hyrum told me that Mr. Brown of Rushville had arrived last night and had no where to go. They requested me to take them in for about 3 weeks and I consented.

---

[55] Elizabeth Davis Brackenbury Durfee (sometimes spelled Durphy) claimed to have married Joseph Smith in Nauvoo and was sealed to him by proxy on January 22, 1846 (D. Michael Quinn, "Latter-day Saint Prayer Circles," *Brigham Young University Studies* 19 [Fall 1978]: 88). Mrs. Durfee had been called a "Mother in Israel," whose "duty was to instruct the younger women in the mysteries of polygamy" (Joseph H. Jackson, *A Narrative of the Adventures and Experiences of Joseph H. Jackson* [Warsaw, IL, 1844], 14, cited in Brodie, 305).

[August 31, 1843. Thursday.] . . . I move Mr. Browns family to my house this evening.

[September 3, 1843. Sunday.] A.M. at home. Unpleasant feelings with M[argaret].

[September 10, 1843. Sunday.] . . . In the evening I went to Sister Booths.

[September 15, 1843. Friday.] A.M. at President Joseph's afterwards at the Temple Office all day. Evening President Joseph met me and I returned with him to O[rson] Spencers to borrow $1400. to clear his farm from an incumbrance laying on it which fact Esq. Skinner has ascertained on searching the Records. President Joseph told me he had lately had a new item of law revealed to him in relation to myself. He said the Lord had revealed to him that a man could only take 2 of a family except by express revelation and as I had said I intended to take Lydia he made this known for my benefit. To have more than two in a family was apt to cause wrangles and trouble. He finally asked if I would not give L[ydia] to him. I said I would so far as I had anything to do in it. He requested me to talk to her.

[September 17, 1843. Sunday.] At home all day with M[argaret]. I had some talk with Lydia. She seems to receive it kindly but says she has promised her mother not to marry while her mother lives and she thinks she won't.

[September 18, 1843. Monday.] A.M. at President Joseph's . . . Joseph and I rode out to borrow money, drank wine at Sister Lyons. P.M. I got $50 of Sister Lyons and paid it to D. D. Yearsley.

[September 19, 1843. Tuesday.] . . . J[oseph] and E[mma] rode to Woolleys &c.

[September 20, 1843. Wednesday.] . . . At the Temple office and Joseph's. He and Hyrum rode to his farm. M[argaret] and Sarah Ann Whitney[56] also rode to the farm but did not see him.

---

[56] Sarah Ann Whitney married Joseph Smith on July 27, 1842 (*HR*, 233–34).

[September 21, 1843. Thursday.] A.M. at the Temple Office. P.M. at the Boat and Joseph's settling with the hands. He says I must go on the Boat a month to regulate the Books. This A.M. he came to talk with Lydia but she won't yet consent. She wants to tarry with her sisters.

[September 23, 1843. Saturday.] . . . I went to Sister Booths but S[arah] A[nn] did not come.

[October 1, 1843. Saturday.] Had some meditation about home, Margaret &c. on the summit of the Hill above Peru.[57] Never did M[argaret] and my little family appear more lovely and endearing than while my anxious thoughts were pondering over their probable situation. At 12 we started out for St. Louis.

[October 7, 1843. Saturday.] . . . At 7 we started in the stage and arrived at Montrose soon after 9 got over the River at 10 and arrived at home at 1/4 before 11. All my family were gone to conference but M[argaret]. We had a joyful meeting, and she gave me a warm evidence of her love, and never did my affections glow more warmly than during our meeting embrace and untill 3 o'clock when the rest of my dear family returned home. My bosom heaved with joy to find them all well . . . P.M. went to Morrisons, Sister Booths, Burbanks &c. S[arah] A[nn] had been at home 2 weeks ago and had gone back. I felt very much disappointed.

[October 11, 1843. Wednesday.] A.M. at home sick. P.M. at President Joseph's. He is gone to Benbows to dine &c . . . Evening B[enjamin] F. Johnson came to meet Joseph and Hyrum. At about 8 W[illia]m Walker came to say Joseph and H[yrum] could not come untill morning.

[October 14, 1843. Saturday.] A.M. at President Joseph's. He was conversing with some strangers one of whom I believe is Dr. Turner the Phrenologist and another a mesmerist. They had a pretty warm debate. Joseph said they could not prove that the mind of man was seated in one part of the brain more than another &c . . . Evening I went to Sister Booths and saw S[arah] A[nn] but could not have a chance to converse any.

[October 16, 1843. Monday.] . . . P.M. at the Temple Office and Sister Booths. S[arah] A[nn] is to be married to John Needham tomorrow.

[October 18, 1843. Wednesday.] . . . P.M. went to Joseph's, did not see him. Spent 2 hours with lovely M[argaret].

[October 19, 1843. Thursday.] A.M. at the Temple Office comparing books and recording deeds. At 11 W[illiam] Walker came and said President Joseph wanted me to go to Macedonia. I went immediately to see him and he requested me to go with him. I went home and got dinner and got ready. He soon came up and we started out. After we had got on the road he began to tell me that E[mma] was turned quite friendly and kind. She had been anointed and he also had been a[nointed] K[ing].[58] He said that it was her advice that I should keep M[argaret] at home and it was also his council.[59] Says he just keep her at home and brook it and if they raise trouble about it and bring you before me I will give you an awful scourging and probably cut you off from the church and then I will baptise you and set you ahead as good as ever.

[October 20, 1843. Friday.] At B. F. Johnsons writing Deed. Evening Joseph gave us much instruction, showing the advan-

---

[58] On September 28, 1843, Joseph and Emma Smith initiated a new ceremony called the "second anointing." This ceremony confirmed one's place in the Celestial Kingdom, or made one's "calling and election sure." This promise is offered only conditionally in the first anointing. The second anointing consisted of two parts. In the first an officiator anointed the heads of a husband and wife with oil and then conferred upon them the "fulness of the priesthood," making the man a priest and king in the next world and the woman a priestess and queen. The second part was a private ceremony between the couple, where the woman washed the feet of her husband so that she would have claim upon him in the resurrection of the dead. See Andrew F. Ehat, "Joseph Smith's Introduction of Temple Ordinances and the Temple Succession Question," M.A. thesis, Brigham Young University, 1982, 76–84 and 94–96; David Buerger, "The Evolution of the Endowment Ceremonies," *Dialogue: A Journal of Mormon Thought* 20 (Winter 1987), 33–76; Buerger, " 'Fulness of the Priesthood.' "

[59] Although about a dozen of the Mormon elite had plural wives by this time, the practice was still secret, and pregnancies, according to Emily Dow Partridge, were uncommon. Partridge was a plural wife to Joseph Smith and later to Brigham Young; in an autobiographical account, she said, "Spiritual wives, as we were then termed, were not very numerous in those days and a spiritual baby was a rarity indeed" (Emily D. P. Young, "Autobiographical Sketch," quoted in Van Wagoner, 230).

tages of the E[verlasting] C[ovenant].[60] He said there was two seals in the Priesthood. The first was that which was placed upon a man and woman when they made the covenant and the other was the seal which alloted to them their particular mansion. After his discourse B. F. Johnson and his wife were united in an everlasting covenant.

[October 24, 1843. Tuesday.] A.M. at President Joseph's. Receiving Temple property from Sister Emma.

[November 21, 1843. Tuesday.] A.M. at the Temple office. P.M. went to Joseph's to ask him to come to my house and marry Marg[are]t Butterfield[61] to her first husband. He could not come but sent Hyrum. I learned from H[yrum] that E[mma] had power to prevent my being admitted to Joseph's Lodge[62] for the present for which I feel somewhat sorry but yet believe that innocence will finally triumph. I stood as proxy for Edw[ar]d Lawrence. . . . Evening I attended the Lodge.[63]

[November 28, 1843. Tuesday.] . . . Evening at home. My feelings have been harrowed up while reflecting on the disappointment A[aron] must have felt when he returned home and found he had lost M[argaret]. I would gladly recompense him if it were in my power. I pray that the Lord may bless him and give him a companion worthy of him.

[December 3, 1843. Sunday.] . . . Joseph was reading my letter.[64]

[December 6, 1843. Wednesday.] A.M. at President Joseph's. Went to see Q[uorum?] for E[verlasting Covenant?] and was well pleased with it.

---

[60] Eternal marriage involving polygamy.

[61] Margaret Butterfield, wife of Josiah Butterfield, was the mother of the prophet's plural wives, Maria and Sarah Lawrence. Smith would now seal his recent in-laws together in a ceremony of eternal marriage. See n36.

[62] Also known as the Holy Order of the Anointed. Clayton believed that he was denied a place in the inner circle of Mormon elders because Emma Smith held a grudge against him.

[63] Probably the Masonic Lodge, but since the Holy Order had adopted some rites similar to those used in Masonry, this reference to the Lodge is ambiguous.

[64] Clayton had written a letter to Smith on December 2 complaining of his exclusion from the Quorum of the Anointed.

123

[December 7, 1843. Thursday.] A.M. at President Joseph's went to see. After at the meeting at the Temple which was got up to petition the Gov[ernor][65] not to issue a writ to satisfy the demand lately made in M[iss]o[uri].[66] P.M. at the Temple office making 2 Deeds. After [] Evening Lodge.

[December 8, 1843. Friday.] At the Temple Office and Joseph's. P.M. with Joseph. [] Evening attended Lodge.

[December 17, 1843. Sunday.] At home all day. Mother in law in trouble which causes M[argaret] also to weep. Evening my feelings were insulted while hearing M[argaret] and her mother in conversation.

[January 9, 1844. Tuesday.] At President Joseph's settling with E[benezer] Robinson and Lawrence &c. P.M. Got Lawrence's account from [David D.] Yearsley . . . Joseph sent for me to make out Maria Lawrence account.

[January 10, 1844. Wednesday.] At President Joseph's all day. Finished settlement with E[benezer] Robinson and passed receipts in full. After posted Books and prepared accounts for settlement on the Lawrence Estate.

[January 15, 1844. Monday.] At President Joseph's all day. P.M. settled with the Lawrence estate.

[January 17, 1844. Wednesday.] At President Joseph's all day. Settled with John Lytel. Gave him a deed of L3 B123 and took his due bill for 28.93. Evening attended Lodge.

[January 22, 1844. Monday.] A.M. at President Joseph's commenced taking inventory of Goods, Groceries &c. for Joseph and settling with E. Robinson who has this day rented the "Mansion House" for $1,000. per annum and some other matters.[67] P.M.

---

[65] Illinois governor Thomas Ford.

[66] Along with this petition to refuse to extradite Joseph Smith to Missouri, the next day Smith suggested to his council that they petition the U.S. Congress to "receive the city of Nauvoo under the protection of the United States Government" (*HC* 6:107).

[67] The Smiths had recently converted their home, the Mansion House, into a bed and breakfast tavern complete with bar. They then leased the Mansion and its stables to Robinson, who intended to continue taking in boarders. The Smith family was guaranteed permanent lodging (*HC* 6:33, 42-43).

Brother [Reynolds] Cahoon came to my house to say that a vote had been taken on my being admitted into the quorum and I was accepted. This filled my heart with joy, and gratitude for truly the mercy of the Lord and the kindness of my brethren have been great to me.

[January 23, 1844. Tuesday.] At President Joseph's all day taking inventory and trying to conclude the transfer to E. Robinson . . . Joseph sent for me to assist in settling with Brother [John] Taylor about the Lawrence Estate.

[January 25, 1844. Thursday.] . . . P.M. Sister Durphy came to make my Robe and Garment.[68] I was at President Joseph's.

[January 29, 1844. Monday.] At President Joseph's in Council with the Twelve on the subject of running Joseph for President of U.S. Joseph said he would have to send me out on a mission. P.M. at his house. Evening attended lodge and after had some conversation with Desdemona C. Fullmer. She has treated my family unfeelingly and unkindly in various ways and I requested her to look out for another home. She said she would not untill she had council from Joseph.[69]

[February 3, 1844. Saturday.] . . . P.M. was permitted to the ordinance of washing and anointing, and was received into the Quorum of Priesthood. This is one of the greatest favors ever conferred on me and for which I feel grateful. May the God of Joseph preserve me and mine house to walk in the paths of righteousness all the days of my life and oh that I may never sin against him or displease him. For thou oh God knowest my desire to do right that I may have eternal life.

[February 4, 1844. Sunday.] At home all day. Evening attended quorum.

[February 10, 1844. Saturday.] At President's all day. Recording Deeds. Evening attended quorum.

---

[68] It was probably Elizabeth Durfee who made the ceremonial robe and undergarment that Clayton needed when he was admitted into the Holy Order.

[69] The next day Desdemona Fullmer complained to Brigham Young and to Heber C. Kimball that Clayton had threatened to "kick her." Clayton said she "lied" and accused her of having a "malicious disposition."

[February 11, 1844. Sunday.] At home all day. Evening I attended quorum but we did not organize.

[February 17, 1844. Saturday.] At President Joseph's all day. Evening with [Reynolds] Cahoon at Joseph's. Emma talked a good deal about B[righam] Young and others.

[February 18, 1844. Sunday.] About 12 A.M. M[argaret] began to be sick and continued to grow worse until 5 o'clock when she was delivered of a son. She did remarkably well for which I thank my heavenly father. Mother attended her. I was at home all day. M[argaret] seems to do very well.

[February 25, 1844. Sunday.] A.M. at the Temple. Heard President Joseph preach. P.M. met singers &c. Evening attended quorum. President Joseph gave some important instructions. We had an interesting season.

[March 3, 1844. Sunday.] . . . Evening attended Q[uorum].

[March 10, 1844. Sunday.] . . . Evening attended Council with the First Presidency and the Twelve on important business arising from a letter from the Pine Country.[70] Brother W. Richards was appointed Chairman and myself, was appointed Clerk.

[March 11, 1844. Monday.] In Council again all day, as last night many great and glorious ideas were advanced, we had a very profitable time. We organized into a Council[71] and I was admitted a member. I will here name whose names were put on the list of members of this important organization: Joseph Smith, Hyrum Smith, Brigham Young, W[illard] Richards, P[arley] P. Pratt, O[rson] Pratt, J[ohn] Taylor, H[eber] C. Kimball, G[eorge] A. Smith, W[illiam] W. Phelps, L[ucien] Woodworth, G[eorge] Miller, A[lex] Badham, P[eter] Haws, Erastus Snow, Reynolds Cahoon, Amos Fielding, A[lpheus]

---

[70] Writing from a church logging operation in Wisconsin, Apostle Lyman Wight proposed expanding the Saints into other parts of the North American continent. To formulate and execute these (and other) plans, a quasi-political body called the Council of Fifty was formed the next day. Clayton was appointed to his usual role, that of clerk.

[71] The Council of Fifty.

Cutler,[72] Levi Richards, N[ewel] K. Whitney, J[ohn] M. Bernhisel, L[orenzo] D. Was[s]on, myself . . .

[March 13, 1844. Wednesday.] . . . At 11 the Council was called together . . . P.M. in council again, also in the evening O. Hyde, W. Woodruff, and James Emmett were admitted members. The President appointed W. Richards Recorder, and me the Clerk of the Kingdom.[73]

[March 14, 1844. Thursday.] In Council all day again.

[March 19, 1844. Tuesday.] At the Council meeting. S[amuel] Bent, Uriah Brown, Samuel James, John D. Parker, O[rrin] [Porter] Rockwell, Sidney Rigdon, W[illia]m Marks and O[rson] Spencer were admitted members.

[March 22, 1844. Friday.] P.M. Met with the Twelve in prayer at B. Youngs.

[March 23, 1844. Saturday.] A.M. rode with President Joseph and brother Neibaur to Doctor [Robert] Fosters. He was gone to appanose[74] and his wife was at Mr. Gilmans. We went down there and saw her. President Joseph asked Sister Foster if she ever in her life knew him guilty of an immoral or indecent act. She answered no. He then explained his reasons for asking and then asked if ever he had used any indecent or insulting language to her, she answered, never. He further asked if he ever preached any thing like the spiritual wife doctrine to her only what he had preached in public. She said no! He asked her if he ever proposed to have illicit intercourse with her and especially when he took dinner during the Doctors absence. She said no. After some further conversation on the subject we left. Mrs. Gilman was present all the time.

---

[72] Alpheus Cutler (1784–1864) had been apppointed a member of the High Council in Nauvoo in October, 1839; he also designed the stone schoolhouse there (*HC* 4:12, 18). Earlier, he was, according to Brigham Young's biographer, "the master builder for the Far West Temple" (Leonard J. Arrington, *Brigham Young: American Moses* [New York: Knopf, 1985], 71). In later years he founded the Mormon "Cutlerite" church.

[73] The Kingdom of God or the Council of Fifty.

[74] Appanoose County, Iowa, about fifty miles from Nauvoo.

CONTENT

[March 24, 1844. Sunday.] . . . A.M. . . . went to the Temple heard President Joseph speak a little also O. Spencer and S. Rigdon.

[March 26, 1844. Tuesday.] In Council through the day . . .

[March 29, 1844. Friday.] . . . night clothed and offered up prayer for W[illiam] Heber [Clayton].[75]

[April 4, 1844. Thursday.] In Council of the Kingdom. Eleven Lamanites appeared and wanted council. We had a very pleasant and impressive interview.

[April 7, 1844. Sunday.] At the conference all day A.M. Elder Rigdon preached. P.M. President Hyrum talked on spiritual wives and after Joseph discoursed on the dead.[76]

---

[75] Clayton dressed in priesthood robes to bless his son, William Heber, who had the measles.

[76] Joseph Smith's address on "the subject of the dead" was presented as a funeral sermon for King Follett, a long-faithful church member who died while constructing a well in Nauvoo. Clayton was one of four scribes who recorded the King Follett sermon in which Joseph Smith spoke on the physical nature of God, an anthropomorphic concept he had been developing since 1832 when he wrote an account of his "first vision" of deities in human form: "First place wish to go back to the beginning of creation. There the starting point in order to fully acquainted with purposes decrees &c of the Great Eloheim that sits in the hev. for us to take up beginning at the creation necessary to understand something of God himself in the beginning . . . what kind of a being is God. Any man or woman that know, any of you seen him? heard him? communed with him? Here a subject that will peradventure occupy your attention while you live . . . What kind of a being was God in the beginning . . . 1st God that sits enthroned is a man like one of yourselves. That is the great secret . . . to know that we may converse with him as one man with another & that he was once as one of us and was on a planet as Jesus was in the flesh . . . Learned Doctors tell us God created the heavens & earth out of nothing . . . Element . . . may be organized and re organized equals but not destroyed . . . another subject the soul the mind of man they say God created it in the beginning. The idea lessens man in my estimation. Don't believe the doctrine know better God told me so Make a man appear a fool before he gets through if he dont believe it . . . the mind of man the intelligent part is coequal with God himself . . . Is it logic to say that a spirit is immortal and yet had a beginning because if a spirit have a beginning it will have an end good logic illustrated by his ring . . . But if I am right then I might be bold to say that God never did have power to create the spirit of man at all" (Andrew F. Ehat and Lyndon W. Cook, comps. and eds., *The Words of Joseph Smith: The Contemporary Account of the Nauvoo Discourses of the Prophet Joseph Smith* (Provo, UT: Religious Studies Center, Brigham Young University, 1980), 355-60; compare the edited composite in *HC* 6:302-17; see discussion of "first vision" accounts in Journal 1, "England and Emigration," n48).

[April 8, 1844. Monday.] Elder G[eorge] J. Adams preached P.M. attended Elders conference.

[April 11, 1844. Thursday.] . . . Afterwards in the Council.[77] We had a glorious interview. President Joseph was voted our P[rophet] P[riest] and K[ing] with loud Hosannas.

[April 13, 1844. Saturday.] A.M. at President Joseph's recording Deeds. He prophecied the entire overthrow of this nation in a few years.

[April 18, 1844. Thursday.] . . . Sarah Cook has been at my house to day and before she left again she shewed her enmity to Joseph and others in full. She has got a wicked spirit in her and will be cursed if she do not repent.

I also attended in council with the Twelve and High Council on cases of the Laws and R[obert] D. Foster, when W[illia]m Law and his wife Jane Law, Wilson Law and R[obert] D. Foster were cut off from the church by unanimous vote.[78]

At 9 met in Council. This day President Joseph introduced J[oseph] W. Coolidge and D[avid] S. Hollister and added L[yman] Wights name, and then declared the council full. The names as they now stand of those who have been called upon to form the grand Kingdom of God by revelation are as follows:[79]

1. President J. Smith, Standing Chairman	
2. Samuel Bent	65
3. John Smith	62
4. Alpheus Cutler	60
5. Uriah Brown	59
6. Reynolds Cahoon	54

---

[77] Council of Fifty.

[78] Serious business disputes arose between Joseph Smith and the Laws, who had been among Smith's ablest supporters. They were further divided by the practice of plural marriage. Reports from Illinois governor Ford and others indicate that Joseph Smith desired to make William Law's wife Jane his plural wife (Ford, *History of Illinois*, 2:322). The Laws and Robert Foster opposed polygamy and sought to reform the church. Joseph moved quickly to neutralize their opposition by holding a secret excommunication. See Lyndon Cook, "William Law, Nauvoo Dissenter," *Brigham Young University Studies* 22 (Winter 1982): 47–72. See Introduction, n66; Journal 1, "England and Emigration," n84.

[79] Members of Council of Fifty except Smith, Clayton, Richards, and Wight are ranked by age.

7. Ezra Thayre	53
8. W[illiam] W. Phelps	52
9. Amos Fielding	51
10. William Marks	51
11. Sidney Rigdon	51
12. John P. Green	51
13. Geo[rge] Miller	50
14. N[ewel] K. Whitney	49
15. Peter Haws	48
16. Jos[eph] Fielding	46
17. C[ornelius] P. Lott	44
18. Levi Richards	44
19. J[ohn] M. Bernhisel	44
20. J[ohn] D. Parker	44
21. H[yrum] Smith	44
22. L[evi] Woodworth	44
23. B[righam] Young	42
24. H[eber] C. Kimball	42
25. O[rson] Spencer	42
26. J[ames] Emmett	41
27. P[hilip] B. Lewis	40
28. Elias Smith	39
29. O[rson] Hyde	39
30. Sam[uel] James	38
31. W[ilford] Woodruff	37
32. P[arley] P. Pratt	36
33. Edw[ar]d Bonny	36
34. D[avid] D. Yearsley	36
35. D[avid] S. Hollister	35
36. John Taylor	35
37. Alex Badham	35
38. C[harles] C. Rich	34
39. G[eorge] J. Adams	33
40. Orson Pratt	33
41. M. G. Eaton	32
42. A[lmon] Babb[itt]	31
43. A[masa] Lyman	30
44. J[oseph] W. Coolidge	30
45. O[rrin] P. Rockwell	29
46. G[eorge] A. Smith	26

47. E[rastus] Snow   25
48. L[orenzo] D. Was[s]on   24
49. B[enjamin] F. Johnson   24
50. W[illiam] Clayton   Clerk
51. W[illard] Richards   Recorder
52. L[yman] Wight

During the day much precious instructions were given and it seems like heaven began on earth and the power of God is with us.

[April 25, 1844. Thursday.] In Council all day. Adjourned sine die.[80]

[April 28, 1844. Sunday.] . . . Sister Mary Wood came evening attended quorum. We united for President Joseph the Church, the presidency contests the Lawsuits. The apostates, the sick &c. &c. We had a good time. President Joseph was not there.

[May 2, 1844. Thursday.] A.M. preparing to go to Dixon. Went to President Joseph's and he desired me to go to Mr. Laws to find out why they refused to pay their note. I went with [] Moon and asked Wilson [Law] what he meant by saying he had got accounts to balance the note. He seemed to tremble with anger and replied that he had demands for his services when he was ordered to call out the Legion to go and meet Smith besides money which he expended at that time. I told him that was a new idea and that General Smith had had no intimation of any such thing. Wm. Law came in and mentioned $400 which was borrowed of Baily $300 of which I am satisfied was paid, and the $100 Wm. Law said he would pay and give it to help defray the expense of the persecution but he now demands the $100 and some more of the $300.[81] On the whole this is to me a certain evidence of the meanness of the men and a proof that they also are disposed to oppress and persecute those who have invariably befriended them and saved them from the public indignation. I returned and told

---

[80] To adjourn without setting a date for a following meeting.

[81] After William and Wilson Law had opposed the practice of polygamy, a complaint was initiated against them in the Masonic Lodge, and they were court-martialed by the Nauvoo Legion. Continuing this dispute, Wilson Law refused to pay a note, and he claimed offsetting obligations which Clayton believed were paid (*HC* 6:331-51).

Joseph what had passed and he ordered Dr. Richards to sue the notes and also gave Moore his own note for $200. payable 6 months after date.

[May 25, 1844. Saturday.] A.M. at President Joseph's. Also P.M. in council with the quorum.[82]

[June 10, 1844. Monday.] . . . The City Council passed a resolution declaring the Printing press on the hill a "nuisance" and ordered it destroyed if not moved in 3 hours notice. About sundown the police gathered at the Temple and after organizing proceeded to the office and demolished the press and scattered the Type.[83]

[June 12, 1844. Wednesday.] A.M. went to Temple office then to President Joseph's and walked with him, O. P. R[ockwell] and J[edediah] Grant to my house and then to Temple. P.M. at President Joseph's recording. [John] Saunders Died at 1 1/2 o'clock. David Bettisworth a constable from Carthage came with a writ for Joseph, Hyrum, Phelps, Jno. Taylor, L. Bennett and a number of others for riot, in breaking the press of the Nauvoo Expositor. After the officer got through reading the writ, Joseph referred him to this clause in writ "before me or some other justice of the peace of said County" saying we are ready to go to trial before Esqr. [Aaron] Johnson, for that was their privilege allowed by the Statute. The man said he should take them before [Thomas]

---

[82] On this day Joseph Smith received notice that he had been indicted for adultery, a charge that would be echoed by other dissenting Mormons and contribute to events resulting in Smith's arrrest and murder. Two days earlier William Law had charged him in the Circuit Court of Hancock County for living with Maria Lawrence in "an open state of adultery" from October 12, 1843, to May 3, 1844. On June 4, two weeks after Law's charges were filed, Smith was appointed legal guardian of the two orphan girls, Maria and Sarah Lawrence (Van Wagoner, 64; HC 6:403, 405; compare n36).

[83] On June 7, 1844, the Nauvoo Expositor published its only issue. Initiated by dissenting members of the Mormon community, the Expositor voiced a message of reform summarized in a letter from Frances M. Higbee: "The paper I think we will call the Nauvoo Expositor; for it will be fraught with Joe's [details of] peculiar and particular mode of legislation; . . . and above all, it shall be the organ through which we will herald his mormon ribaldry. It shall also contain a full and complete expose of his mormon seraglio, or Nauvoo harem —; and his unparallelled and unheard of attempts at seduction" (Frances Higbee to Mr. Gregg, May 1844, Nauvoo, Chicago Historical Society; also in the Hardin collection, in McQuown collection, Special Collections, Marriott Library).

Morrison[84] the man who issued the writ and seemed very wrathy. Joseph asked him if he intended to break the law, for he knew the privilege of the prisoners and they should have it. Joseph called upon all present to witness that he then offered himself (Hyrum did the same) to go forthwith before the nearest justice of the peace, and also called upon them to witness whether the officer broke the law . . . a writ of Habeas Corpus which was taken out and served on Bettisworth.[85] While this was going on and the Marshall summoning the Municipal Court Hyrum related the whole history of the difficulty with Wm. Law to the constable and a man with him, showing them what we believed on sealing of the covenant, that Law wanted to be sealed and Joseph told him he was forbid which begun the hard feelings. He talked about 2 hours, then Joseph came in and told about [Joseph] Jackson.[86] About 5 the court assembled in the 70s Hall, much testimony was brought to the point and the Court discharged Joseph from the writ and assessed the costs to F[rancis] M. Higbee the complainant.

[June 14, 1844. Friday.][87] A.M. conversing with a number of gentleman in the Bar room[88] concerning the proceedings of our enemies. He prophesied in the name of the Lord that if they did mob us it would be a precedent to come down upon their own heads with fury and vengeance.

[June 15, 1844. Saturday.] A.M. conversing with Dr. [Joseph] Wakefield and others in the Bar Room, telling a dream concerning his father killing a man who attempted to stab him. He also

---

[84] Thomas Morrison was Justice of the Peace in Carthage. See *HC* 7:66, 67.

[85] Though Justice of the Peace Morrison compelled them to appear before the Carthage magistrate, Smith overruled the authorities by instructing the Nauvoo Municipal Court to issue a writ of habeas corpus requiring Bettisworth to release them and the others and demonstrate why they should not be tried in Nauvoo.

[86] Jackson was a leader of those opposing the Mormons and declared that he had eighteen legal accusations against Joseph Smith (*HC* 6:569).

[87] Clayton's entries from June 14 to June 22, 1844, comprise a small separate journal which is here included chronologically within the second Nauvoo journal, 1843-44. The unspecified references are to Joseph Smith.

[88] The bar room was located in the Nauvoo Mansion and Orrin Porter Rockwell was the bartender, according to Joseph Smith III ("Memoirs of President Joseph Smith," *Saints' Herald*, January 22, 1935, 110, cited in Brodie, 332). On December 12, 1843, the Nauvoo City Council had passed an ordinance giving the prophet the sole right to sell liquor at his hotel (*HC* 6:111).

spoke concerning key words.[89] The g[reat] key word was the first word Adam spoke and is a word of supplication. He found the word by the Urim and Thummim.

[June 15, 1844. Saturday.][90] It is that key word to which the heavens is opened. A.M. at President Joseph's. 2 brethren came up from the Morley settlement saying that old Col. Williams' Company had been to demand their arms and they wanted to know if they must yield them. Joseph told them not to do it while they lived. Various reports have come stating that the Warsawites have ordered the Saints to leave forthwith and threatening pretty bad. P.M. at the Temple office.

[June 16, 1844. Sunday.] Preached at the stand. P.M. at the Masonic Hall laying the proceedings of the City Council before a number of Gentlemen from Fort Madison. 4 o'clock at the stand stated the design of the meeting and ordered the Major General to have the Legion in readiness to suppress all illegal violence in the city.

[June 17, 1844. Monday.] A.M. at President Joseph's wrote a letter for Hyrum to the Twelve requesting them to come home without delay.

[June 18, 1844. Tuesday.] This A.M. the Legion is ordered to parade . . . At 11 he rode to the parade ground and after staying a short season the whole legion marched down to the Mansion. Judge Phelps there read the preamble and resolutions of the mob in which they threaten extermination to the whole Church in Nauvoo. After Phelps got through General Joseph Smith addressed the multitude. He briefly explained the object of the mob and showed that they waged a war of extermination upon us because of our religion. He called upon all the volunteers who felt to support the constitution from the Rocky Mountains to the Atlantic Ocean to come with their arms, ammunition and provisions and defend the constitution. He called upon them as the Lieutenant General of the N[auvoo] L[egion] and Illinois Militia in the name of the Constitution of the U.S. The people of the State of Illinois

---

[89] By which to discern the mysteries of God.

[90] On June 15, 1844, Clayton wrote this concurrent entry in his second Nauvoo journal notebook, 1843–44.

and the citizens of Nauvoo. He called upon the Citizens to defend the lives of their wives and children, fathers and mothers, brothers and sisters from being murdered by the mob. He urged them in strong terms not to shed innocent blood, not to act in the least on the offensive but invariably in the defensive and if we die, die like men of God and secure a glorious resurrection.[91] He concluded by invoking the Great God to bless the people.

. . . In the above address he advised all to arm themselves those who had no rifles, get swords, scythe and make weapons of some kind. He informed them that he had 5000 Elders, minutemen would come with volunteers as soon as he would inform them. He said there were many from Iowa waiting to come when requested.

[June 22, 1844. Saturday.] Joseph whispered and told me either to put the r[ecords] of K[ingdom] into the hands of some faithful man and send them away, or burn them, or bury them. I concluded to bury them, which I did immediately on my return home.[92]

[June 23, 1844. Sunday.] At 5 A.M. [Albert] Rockwood and [John?] Scott came to ask advice what to do with the Cannon &c. I went to Joseph and got all the public and private records together and buried them.

[June 28, 1844. Friday.][93] . . . And all this brought upon us by those who have shared of the kind sympathies and generosity of Generals Joseph and Hyrum Smith and have received good at their hands. The names of these men are William Law who was one of Josephs Council and a member of the Quorum. Wilson Law Robert D. Foster, Charles A. Foster, Francis M. Higbee, Cha[u]ncy L. Higbee. Their associates in crime were Austin Cowles, Joseph H. Jackson a murderer, John M. Finch, W[illia]m A. Rolloson William H. J. [Marr], Sylvester Emmons,

---

[91] American historian Klaus Hansen has observed that the Mormons are the only group to have fought a holy war on American soil (*Mormonism and the American Experience* [Chicago: University of Chicago Press, 1983], xiii).

[92] Clayton dug up the records on July 3, 1844, and kept possession of them until April 14, 1847, the day he left Winter Quarters for the Great Salt Lake Valley.

[93] On June 24, Joseph Smith was arrested and taken to jail at Carthage, Illinois, where he and his brother, Hyrum, were assassinated on June 27, 1844.

Alexander Sympson S. M. [Marr] John Eagle Henry O. Norton
and Augustine Spencer. These had been aided and abetted by
Charles Ivins and family. P[]. T. Rolfe, N[]. J. Higbee, W[il-
lia]m Cook and Sarah his wife formerly Sarah Crooks of
Manchester England, James Blakeslee. And, finally, a band of
mobocrats scattered through the county, among whom are
Alexander Sympson, Tho[ma]s C. Sharp, Colonel Williams, Walter
Bagby, and O[nias] C. Skinner. Some of the aforesaid parties
were storekeepers here and have drawn a vast [amount] of money
from the place. David Bryant also joined in the clamor but did
not take any public measures.

. . . After the bodies were laid out I went in to see them.
Joseph looks very natural except being pale through loss of blood.
Hyrum does not look so natural. Their aged mother[94] is dis-
tracted with grief and it will be almost more than she can bear.

[June 30, 1844. Sunday.] . . . A few of the Quorum assembled and agreed to send G[eorge] J. Adams to bear the news to
the Twelve. [Lucien] Woodworth is bitter against Adams and said
many hard things against him.

[July 2, 1844. Tuesday.] A.M. went to see Emma. She is in
trouble because Mother [Lucy Mack] Smith is making disturbance about the property in Josephs hands. Mother Smith wants
Samuel to move into Nauvoo and take the Patriarchs office and
says the church ought to support him. There is considerable
danger if the family begins to dispute about the property that
Joseph's creditors will come forward and use up all the property
there is. If they will keep still there is property enough to pay the
debts and plenty left for other uses. I had much talk with Emma
on the subject.[95]

[July 3, 1844. Wednesday.] A.M. at the Temple Office. Emma
sent for me and A[lpheus] Cutler and R[eynolds] Cahoon. We
had conversation with Esquire [James W.] Wood on the subject.
Emma has councilled Esquire Wood on the subject. P.M. at the

---

[94] Joseph's and Hyrum's mother, Lucy Mack Smith, was sixty-seven years old.
[95] Much of Joseph Smith's property had been transferred into church name,
making it difficult to distinguish among the shares due Emma, Smith's creditors,
and possibly his plural wives. (Although there is some dispute as to the exact
number, there is evidence that Joseph Smith had about forty-five plural wives.)

Temple Office and after went to dig up the Records. Water had got into the place where they were and they were damaged.

[July 4, 1844. Thursday.] . . . I went to Emmas and assisted Esquire Wood to examine Josephs affairs. The situation looks gloomy. The property is chiefly in the name of the Trustee in Trust while the obligations are considered personal. Woods advised Emma to have all the Deeds recorded at Carthage for he says our Recorders office is not legal. This will cause trouble and much dissatisfaction. P.M. in Council with Brothers Marks, Cutler and Cahoon at Mark[s's] house.[96] It seemed manifest to us that brother Marks place is to be appointed president, and Trustee in Trust and this accords with Emma's feelings. Brother [John] Taylor is at Brother Mark[s's]. I saw some of his wounds which are bad but he is recovering.

[July 6, 1844. Saturday.] . . . Yesterday a raft of Pine Lumber arrived for the Trustee in Trust. [Lucien] Woodworth laid claim to it, but the brethren say it is my duty as agent for the Trustee to take charge of it. I have accordingly done so and ordered [Albert P.] Rockwood to Guard it till we can get it to the Temple. The greatest danger that now threatens us is dissensions and strifes amongst the Church. There are already 4 or 5 men pointed out as successors to the Trustee and President, and there is danger of feelings being manifest. All the brethren who stand at the head seem to feel the delicacy of the business. [W. W.] Phelps and Dr. [Willard] Richards have taken a private course and are carrying out many measures on their own reponsibility without council.

[July 7, 1844. Sunday.] At home writing this history which I now conclude again at 1 o'clock P.M. 5 o'clock went to council with the Quorum on the subject of appointing a Trustee in Trust. I was told on the way that R[obert] D. Foster is in Nauvoo having a permit from the Governor to come and settle business. O[rrin]

---

[96] William Marks was stake president, and all four men were members of the Council of Fifty. They met to consider the disposition of Joseph Smith's and the church's entangled estates. Smith left no will. Emma Smith favored Marks as trustee-in-trust, probably because he had not accepted the doctrine of plural marriage and would be less inclined than some to grant Joseph Smith's other wives equal inheritance.

P. Rockwell, M[erinus] G. Eaton and Theodore Turley are raging and threaten his life if he tarry here, consequently the City Council have sent a guard to take care of him. I reasoned with Rockwell and tried to show him the folly of his conduct inasmuch as the Governor had said that if one of those men were assassinated the whole city would be held responsible, and that President Joseph gave himself up into the hands of his murderers for the express purpose of saving the City from being Massacred. But no reasoning seemed to touch him. He swore bitterly he would have revenge and that Foster should not tarry here. I feel grieved at this conduct, for there is now a little prospect that the public sympathy will turn in our favor if we keep still. I was late at the Council. The brethren had agreed not to appoint a Trustee untill the Twelve came home, and that I should act in the place of Trustee to receive property &c. untill one was appointed.

[July 8, 1844. Monday.] At the Temple all day. Emma came up . . . She also objected to the conclusion of the Council last evening and says there must be a Trustee appointed this week on account of the situation of business.

[July 12, 1844. Friday.] A.M. at the Temple measuring Lumber. President Marks came up to enquire which was best to do about appointing a Trustee. We concluded to call a meeting of the several presidents of Quorums and their Council this P.M. at 2 o'clock. As I returned to dinner, Brother [Newel K.] Whitney came down with me and stated his feelings about Marks being appointed Trustee. He referred me to the fact of Marks being with [William] Law and Emma in opposition to Joseph and the Quorum. And if Marks is appointed Trustee our spiritual blessings will be destroyed inasmuch as he is not favorable to the most important matters.[97] The Trustee must of necessity be the first president of the Church and Joseph has said that if he and Hyrum were taken away Samuel H. Smith would be his successor.[98]

After dinner I talked with Cutler and Cahoon on the subject, and they both agreed in the same mind with Brother Whitney and myself. At 3 we went to meeting. Emma was present and

[97] Clayton indicates that William Marks, William Law, and Emma Smith each rejected the doctrine of plural marriage.
[98] Samuel Harrison Smith was the eldest surviving brother of Joseph Smith.

urged the necessity of appointing a Trustee immediately. But on investigation it was considered we could not lawfully do it. Another meeting was appointed for Sunday Eve. Dr. Richards and Phelps seem to take all the matters into their own hands and won't tell us anything what they intend or have thought to do.

[July 13, 1844. Saturday.] This A.M. [John A.] Forgens paid over $[] from L[yman] Wight and $1000 from Brother Kimball in paper money. He however requested payment of an execution against [Elbridge] Tufts amounting to $254.95 which President Joseph agreed to do. I consulted Cutler and Cahoon and they said I had better pay it which I did. Emma sent for me to enquire about the title to Snyders Lot. She talked much about Trustees being appointed and says if he is not a man she approves of she will do the church all the injury she can by keeping the Lots which are in her name.

[July 14, 1844. Sunday.] . . . At 6 went to the Council. Phelps and Richards and P[arley] P. Pratt stated that they had concluded to appoint 4 Trustees when a majority of the Twelve returned. These three brethren seem to keep matters very close to themselves and I and several others feel grieved at it. After meeting I informed Emma of the proceedings. She thinks they don't use her right.

[July 15, 1844. Monday.] . . . Emma sent for me. I went and conversed considerable with her. She feels dissatisfied with the conduct of Richard[s] and Phelps and says if they undertake to trample upon her she will look to herself. I conversed with Richards and Phelps and told them our feelings and they seem to feel more free. They told me the names of those they had thought of nominating for Trustees, Myself and A. Cutler are two of them. I told Emma of this and she seems better satisfied.

[July 30, 1844. Tuesday.] Emma sent for me early concerning the Lawrence business. She concluded that she and I had better go to Quincy to settle the business.[99] I went home and got ready and we started on the "Osprey." . . . We arrived at Quincy about 6 1/2 P.M. Went to the City Hotel. After supper I went to

---

[99] Here Clayton and the prophet's widow worked cooperatively to settle Joseph Smith's legal guardianship of Maria and Sarah Lawrence.

see Mr. Lawrence[100] concerning a tax title which he holds on some property in Lima belonging to Brother Marks. He wants $100 for it. I had much conversation with him. Emma stayed at Burr Riggs' and I went to the City Hotel.

[July 31, 1844. Wednesday.] Went to see Judge Miller and found that the Lawrence business could not be settled until another Guardian was appointed . . . At 12 at night a Boat came and we left for home on the "Waverly." Amasa Lyman and G[eorge] P. Dykes was on the Boat. We arrived at Nauvoo at 11.

[August 1, 1844. Thursday.] At 11 we arrived in Nauvoo, where we heard that Samuel H. Smith died on Tuesday evening.

[August 4, 1844. Sunday.] A.M. attended meeting. Brother [Sidney] Rigdon spoke on the words My ways are not as your ways &c. He related a vision which the Lord had shown him concerning the situation of the Church and said there must be a Guardian appointed to build the Church up to Joseph as he has begun it. P.M. at home. Brother [Newel] Whitney came. Evening Charles C. Rich came to my house to enquire about some revelations. He said Brother Marks had notified the public that next Thursday there would be a meeting to choose a Guardian inasmuch as Mr. Rigdon was in a hurry to go home again. I do not feel satisfied with this move because it is universally understood that the Twelve have been sent for and are expected here every day and it seems a plot laid for the saints to take advantage of their situation.

[August 5, 1844. Monday.] This last night I dreamed that Joseph and Emma came to me and appeared very much dissatisfied and displeased because I had kept back the money sent by Brother [Heber C.] Kimball. I thought I explained the reason and told them I had been councilled to do so.

[August 6, 1844. Tuesday.] . . . [W. W.] Phelps told me that they had a council and called upon Elder Rigdon to say why he was so much disposed to hurry matters &c. He said they should wait untill the Twelve returned.

---

[100] In all probability this Mr. Lawrence was not related to the Lawrence heiresses referred to above.

[August 7, 1844. Wednesday.] This morning the Committee and myself went out to Lots to take invoice of Josephs property. Brother [Alpheus] Cutler said that in the council yesterday he drew out from [William] Marks that Sidney Rigdon was to be president and Marks Patriarch.

5 of the Twelve got home last night viz. B[righam] Young, H[eber] C. Kimball, L[yman] Wight, O[rson] Pratt and W[ilford] Woodruff. This seems very providential and has given great satisfaction to the people. At 4 P.M. the Twelve and the High Council assembled in the 70s Hall when Elder Rigdon stated the object of his mission. He said he had a vision presented to his mind, not an open vision, but rather a continuation of the one mentioned in the Book of Covenants. It was shown to him that this Church must be built up to Joseph and that all the blessings we receive must come through Joseph. He had been ordained spoken to Joseph and he must come to Nauvoo and see that the Church was governed in a proper manner. The people could please themselves whether they accepted him or not. He said he had a conversation with Judge [] Pope on his way to Pittsburgh and that Pope told him that the U.S. Government were determined to deal with our Municipal Court for the proceedings in relation to Jeremiah Smith[101] and that Butterfield and Pope were very determined to prosecute &c. After Elder Rigdon got through B. Young said a few sentences. He said he did not care who lead the Church if God said so even if it was old "Ann Lee"[102] but he must know that God said so. He said he [] the keys and the means of knowing the mind of God on this subject. He knew there were those in our midst who would seek the lives of the Twelve as they had sought that of Brother Joseph. He should ordain some man and give him the keys so that if he was killed the church might still have the priesthood. He said the Twelve would not be permitted to tarry here long. They would organize the Church and then go away and they would baptize Mormons a great deal faster than

---

[101] For more information about this incident, see *HC* 6:416–25.

[102] Ann Lee was the founder of the Shakers or "Shaking Quakers," a celibate sect which separated from the Quakers in England in the eighteenth century and went to America. The Shakers believed in a dual godhead — Eternal Mother as well as Father; their popular name referred to their contortions during religious dances. See Lawrence Foster, *Religion and Sexuality* (New York: Oxford University Press, 1981), 21–24.

the mob would be able to kill them. Elder Lyman Wight followed in the same strain and said he knew there were those in our midst who were seeking his life. The meeting closed by appointing a conference for next Tuesday at 10 o'clock.

[August 8, 1844. Thursday.] A.M. I went to council with the Twelve. Brother Kimball concluded to pay the $1000 to Emma. I went home to get it and while there B. Young came and said they were going to have their conference this afternoon and wanted I should notify the brethren. I then went with Brothers Kimball and Richards to see Emma. Kimball paid her the $1000 and bore testimony to her of the good feelings of the Twelve towards her. She seemed humble and more kind. P.M. attended conference. The Church universally voted to sustain the Twelve in their calling as next in presidency and to sustain Elder Rigdon and A. Lyman as councillors to the Twelve as they had been to the First Presidency. The church also voted to leave the regulation of all the church matters in the hands of the Twelve.[103] There was a very good feeling prevailed, except amongst a few who were disappointed.

[August 11, 1844. Sunday.] A.M. had conversation with Diantha Farr[104] on various subjects. She seems to be true and faithful. Margaret is miserable and unhappy. P.M. attended meeting for prayer with Elders B[righam] Young, G[eorge] Miller, H[eber] C. Kimball, A[masa] Lyman, W[illard] Richards, L[evi] Richards, J[ohn] P. Green, L[ucien] Woodworth, N[ewel] K. Whitney, and G[eorge] A. Smith and W[ilford] Woodruff.

---

[103] On August 9, Newel K. Whitney and George Miller were appointed to settle the Joseph Smith estate and to serve as trustees-in-trust of the church (*HC* 7:247). When the Quorum of Twelve Apostles was put in charge, Brigham Young, who had been president of the quorum since 1841, became the de facto president of the church and later that year signed documents as such. The following winter, on February 4, 1845, Young was made president of the Council of Fifty and thereby directed the church's all-important function of planning the westward immigration, thus further consolidating his position of leadership. Two months later in April, he was sustained as "President of the whole Church." In December 1847 Young was sustained again by the Quorum of the Twelve and a general conference as "President of the Church," formally ending the "Apostolic Interregnum." See *HC* 7: 245–47; Clayton's journal, February 4, 1845; Van Wagoner and Walker, 406.

[104] Diantha was Aaron Farr's sixteen-year-old sister.

[August 12, 1844. Monday.] At the Temple Office and Emma's settling and preparing papers for her settlement as administratrix.

[August 15, 1844. Thursday.] . . . I went to see Sister Emma, as she had sent for me early this A.M. I found her very cross. Esquire [James W.] Wood told me what he wanted done with regard to settling up the estate. He wanted a "list of all titles in the name of the Trustee in Trust, and not conveyed away, whether deeded or bonded, and by whom conveyed to the Trustee. Also a list of all lands conveyed to him as Trustee and by him conveyed away and to whom conveyed. Also a list of lands in his individual name. Also a full list of such personal property as was in his name as Trustee at time of his death. Also a list of all notes and accounts and given their value and whether good or bad. Also a list of all property both real or personal belonging to the heirs." Besides this he wanted me to produce the papers pertaining to the transfers of the "Maid of Iowa" and recommended Emma to have the Boat included in the schedule. While he was talking I felt as though he was laying a deep plan to find out the situation of the private and public matters of the Church and to lay a trap for our ruin. I did not feel free to give him the papers of the Boat untill I could get council. Emma seemed very much dissatisfied because I did not go in the morning and because I yielded to do anything else untill she had her business settled. After dinner I went to see Elder B. Young and have his council. I laid the matter before him and he advised me not to give Wood any accounts pertaining to the business of the Trustee in Trust. We both went over to Brother Whitneys and stated the matter to him. He was also opposed to Wood's interfering with the business of the Trustee in Trust. I then went to see Emma. I found her alone and began to talk to her and tell her what I thought Wood's intended to do. She grew warm and said that all the business of the Trustee must be presented. We had no secrets that we must keep back from the public for she was determined to have everything settled now. I replied to her that there were many things which I was unwilling the world should know anything about and should not lend my hand to ruin the church. She then grew more angry and said I had neglected her and the business, and there was nothing that had President Smith's name to that should not be investigated. She said she had no secrets nor anything she was unwilling the whole world should know. I told her that there was some things which would be unwilling the public should know. She denied it. I said I knew things that she did not want the world to know. She said if I harbor'd any idea that she had ever done wrong it was false. I answered "what I have seen with my eyes and heard with my ears I could believe." She said, if I said she had ever committed a crime I was a liar and I knew it. I replied Sister Emma I know I don't lie and you know better what I know I know and although I never have told it to any soul on earth nor never intend to yet it is still the truth and I shall not deny it.[105] She then several times called me a liar and said she knew I was her enemy and she never had been so abused in all her life. I told her I was not her enemy nor never had been. She said I neglected her and spent my time in the secret counsel of the Twelve and it was secret things which had cost Joseph and Hyrum their lives, and says she "I prophecy that it will cost you and the Twelve your lives as it has done them." She repeated this two or three times in a threatening manner, and said it in a manner that I understood that she intended to make it cost us our lives as she had done by President Smith. I told her that I would rather die than do anything to ruin the Church. She raged very hard and used many severe threats and told me that she had now proved that I was an enemy to her and she did not want such persons about her to do business. I coolly replied that I was her friend and she would prove it so and I had done nothing but what I felt perfectly willing to meet her and Joseph together and answer for it. I also tried to show her that she had misinterpreted my words for I did not mean what she said I did. I told her I had run at her call night or day whenever I could get a chance and have suffered abuses which I never would have borne from any other woman in the world. She would not listen to anything I could say and I left her. I still feel to befriend her all I can but she will now try to destroy my character and influence no doubt but I have no enmity towards her and am determined I will not give way to it. She is blind as to her best interest and those who are her best friends she is the

---

[105] There have been repeated suggestions that Emma, in reaction to Joseph Smith's polygamy, might have herself encouraged relationships with other men. While this altercation between Emma and Clayton might be read as an allusion to such an indiscretion, no definitive evidence has been found.

most bitter against. She is cherishing and putting her life into the hands of traitors and murderers and they will use her up; for she will not listen to the advice of her friends nor be at peace with those who wish to do her good. I feel to pray that God will soften her heart and show her the danger she is exposing herself to and to bind her up that she may not have power to destroy thy servants O God. I went and told President Young the whole circumstances and he told me to fear not, but rejoice.

[August 18, 1844. Sunday.] She don't want to give up the money[106] and I suppose if she can ruin my character and hold on to the money she will accomplish a two fold object. God knows that I am innocent of the charge as the angels in heaven, and it is grossly wicked in her to give out this report. Elder Young recommended me to watch carefully, and in the morning go and get the secretary. I feel sorry to think that after I have served that family like a slave, having run at her call night and day, and never wronged them out of the first cent that she should thus abuse me, for I must say I never met with oppression and tyranny so cruel from any person in all my life as I have borne from that woman, but yet I will not be her enemy nor do her any harm, except it should be in the defence of my own life and character.

[August 27, 1844. Tuesday.] During last night D[aniel] A[delbert] grew much worse. The Canker in his mouth grew worse and turned quite black. About 7 this A.M. he was seized with a kind of fit which weakened him a good deal. He sank gradually . . . untill 2 o'clock P.M. he breathed his last. Thus has ended the earthly career of an innocent sufferer who has known no comfort in this life but has suffered since his birth to his death. The tongue of slander has swung freely against him and many which his death. He is gone to rest with the just and will come forth again to inherit thrones, kingdoms, dominions, principalities and powers in the mansions of his father[107] . . . She did this by means of a false key which will unlock it.[108] Her treachery

---

[106] Two hundred dollars which Clayton had taken from the estate to apply to a debt.

[107] Daniel Adelbert, born February 18, 1844, was the son of William Clayton and Margaret Moon.

[108] Although the church had retrieved Joseph Smith's secretary (desk), the

seems unbounded. Rigdon, Marks, Emma, and some others are trying to draw off a party. They say there is no church.

[August 29, 1844. Thursday.] At the Temple, A.M., at 10 met the Twelve at President Youngs. Elders Marks and Rigdon had been notified to attend (for whom the council was designed). Elder Rigdon said he was sick and should not attend. Elder Marks was present. President Young stated to Elder Marks that in consequence of rumors and reports of the proceedings of him and Elder Rigdon he had called them together that the thing might be talked over and if possible an union effected. Elder Young stated what he had heard and Elder Marks denied the charges in toto, and said he had been abused by the tongue of slander. He acknowledged that the course the Twelve had pursued was contrary to what he had expected but he did not intend to say anything. The meeting was beneficial to me and I though[t] I would never listen to reports again. Evening Elder Kimball called to see us. I had a long conversation with him. He advised me to take L[ydia Moon] for time.[109]

[August 30, 1844. Friday.] At the Temple all day. Talked with L[ydia] but she don't seem disposed to do what is councilled.

[August 31, 1844. Saturday.] At the Temple Office all day. P.M. went to see A[lice] Hardman who is getting better. She will do right and wants her sister Elizabeth to go with her.

[September 2, 1844. Monday.] At the Temple Office, had much talk with father about the gospel &c.

[September 3, 1844. Tuesday.] At the Temple all day Brother Whitney handed me the following:[110]
John Smith and wife 2
Hyrum Smith and d[itt]o 2
Mercy R. Thompson 1

---

papers which Wood had requested were missing from it. Clayton held Emma responsible.

[109] Heber C. Kimball advised Clayton to marry Lydia Moon only for their lifetimes, not "for eternity"; Smith had proscribed marrying more than two women from the same family (Journal 2, "Nauvoo, Illinois," September 15, 1843).

[110] A list of participants in "endowment" ceremonies while Joseph Smith was still alive, before the cermonies were held in the temple. See Introduction, n73, and Journal 3, "Nauvoo Temple," n5.

W[ilford] Woodruff and wife 2
G[eorge] A. Smith and w[ife] 2
N[ewel] K. Whitney and d[itt]o 2
R[eynolds] Cahoon and d[itt]o 2
A[lpheus] Cutler and d[itt]o 2
John Taylor and d[itt]o 2
O[rson] Hyde and d[itt]o 2
James Adams and d[itt]o 2
H[eber] C. Kimball and d[itt]o 2
B[righam] Young and d[itt]o 2
O[rson] Spencer and d[itt]o 2
O[rson] Pratt 1
P[arley] P. Pratt 1
W[illard] Richards and wife 2
J[ohn] M. Bernhisel 1
L[ucien] Woodworth and wife 2
W[illiam?] Law and wife 2
Sister [Elizabeth] Durfee 1
Mother [Lucy M.] Smith 1
Geo[rge] Miller and w[ife] 2
Jos[eph] Smith and w[ife] 2
W[illia]m Marks and w[ife] 2
Jos[eph] Fielding and w[ife] 2
C[ornelius] P. Lott and w[ife] 2
L[evi] Richards 1
W. W. Phelps and w[ife] 2
S[amuel] H. Smith 1
Isaac Morley and w[ife] 2
Agness Smith 1
Jos[eph] Young and w[ife] 2
W[illiam] Clayton 1
J[oseph] P. Green 1
S[idney] Rigdon 1
W[illia]m Smith 1
Almon Babbit 1
Lyman Wight 1

[September 4, 1844. Wednesday.] Last evening the Twelve and some others met together with Elder Rigdon to investigate his course. He came out full against the Twelve and said he would not be controlled by them. They asked him for his license, and he said he would give that if he must expose all the works of the secret chambers and all the iniquities of the church. The Twelve withdrew fellowship from him and James Emmett.

There is considerable feeling prevailing. Edward Hunter,[111] Leonard Soby, [] Cottier, B[] Coles are amongst those who have joined Elder Rigdon. Samuel James is one of his main supports. Every one of his followers as far as I can learn are ordained prophets and immediately receive the same spirit Elder Rigdon is of. In the evening the Twelve and a few others of us met at Elder Youngs and offered up prayers for our preservation and the preservation of the church, and that the Lord would bind up the dissenters that they may not have power to injure the honest in heart. We had a good time and we believe the Lord will answer our prayers.

[September 5, 1844. Thursday.] This evening I heard Elder [Orson] Hyde in the Masonic Hall. He proved very plain that Elder Rigdons course since he came here has been a continued course of deception and falsehood and that his object is to scatter the people and break up the foundation laid by our beloved prophet Joseph Smith. The people seem to feel indignant at Elder Rigdon for it is now reduced to a certainty that he is conspiring with the apostates to bring a mob upon us.

[September 6, 1844. Friday.] . . . A.M. Elder H[eber] C. K[imball] came up to say that I might take A[lice] H[ardman]. I went to the Temple office and also to see A[lice] H[ardman]. P.M. attended the High Council as clerk. Leonard Soby was disfellowshipped by the council for following Elder Rigdon. He spouted hard.

[September 8, 1844. Sunday.] At the meeting all day and acted as clerk. Elder Rigdon Samuel Bennett, Leonard Soby, George Morey, Joseph H. Newton and John A. Forgens were cut off from the church and Samuel James and Jared Carter disfellowshipped. There was a good feeling among the people and a bad feeling among the Rigdonites.

---

[111] Edward Hunter soon returned to the church body led by Brigham Young and became Presiding Bishop of the church. See *HC* 7:317; Andrew Jenson, *Latter-day Saint Biographical Encyclopedia*, 4 vols. (Salt Lake City: Andrew Jenson History Co., 1901-36), 1:227-32.

[September 9, 10, 12, 1844. Monday, Tuesday, Thursday.]
. . . P.M. at Phelps office comparing minutes.

[September 13, 1844. Friday.] . . . At 3 went to see Alice
Hardman who is sick and was united in the E[ternal] C[ove-
nant].[112]

[September 15, 1844. Sunday.] A.M. hear P. P. Pratt preach
on the priesthood.

[September 20, 1844. Friday.] . . . Also wrote a letter for H.
C. Kimball after he and I went to see A[lice] H[ardman] and
E[mmeline?] B[alos?].[113] The latter will obey his instructions.
He again earnestly told me that all the Twelve were my very
warmest friends and he will help me to accomplish all my desires
inasmuch as they are right. He says I shall yet have S[arah]
C[rooks].

[September 24, 1844. Tuesday.] [David D.] Yearsley has
wronged me and it is an evidence to me that he is about to deny
the faith. I feel that he has wronged me a second time. He refused to take a $5. bill a few days ago and said it was a counter-
feit, when it is well known that it is good.[114]

---

[112] Clayton here alludes to his marriage to Alice Hardman, his third wife.
Within two months of her marriage to Clayton, Alice married Austin Sturgess on
November 3, 1844, in a civil ceremony performed by Levi Richards. LDS records
do not indicate divorces until 1846. She is listed in the 1850 census in Salt Lake
City as Alice Sturgess, widow, immediately followed by six of Clayton's children by
other wives on the same page as Clayton. Perhaps this listing of Clayton's children
under the Sturgess name for the official census record was intended to minimize
Clayton's profile as a polygamist, two years before the church officially acknowl-
edged the practice. Not until 1852, eight years after their marriage and at least two
years after she became Sturgess's widow, did Alice begin having children by
Clayton; they had four children from 1852 to 1857. By 1858 they had divorced.
On November 20, 1844, about three weeks after Alice Hardman Clayton married
Austin Sturgess, William Clayton married Alice's cousin, Jane, who would also
divorce Clayton. See Lyndon W. Cook, ed., *Civil Marriages in Nauvoo and Some
Outlying Areas* (Provo, UT: Lyndon W. Cook, 1980).

[113] E. B. could have been Emmeline Balos, a woman Heber C. Kimball might
have been courting prior to her marriage to Newel K. Whitney on February 14,
1845. It is unlikely to have been Elizabeth Brotherton, because she was Parley P.
Pratt's first plural wife, married in 1843. See Van Wagoner and Walker, 218.

[114] This date concludes the second "Nauvoo, Illinois" journal notebook
(1843-44). Clayton now resumes recording events in the first Nauvoo journal
notebook (1842-45).

[October 1, 1844. Tuesday.] . . . Evening met the Twelve at Brother Kimballs and offered up prayer for the Governor and Emma and sundry other things. We had a very interesting season of conversation. A man has a right to be baptized for his acquaintances who are not relatives and sealed to them only by the consent and authority of him who holds the keys.[115]

[October 11, 1844. Friday.] . . . Evening at Heber C. K[imball]'s in company with President Young. H. C. K[imball] and G[eorge] A. S[mith] of the Twelve, the two Trustees and Sisters Kimball and Whitney. We offered up prayer for the sick and Sister Emma &c. and also that the enemies may have no more power over us. We had much conversation respecting the Temple Committee.

[October 16, 1844. Wednesday.] . . . At 12, married Lucius N. Scovil to Lucy Snow also Alice Harris to L[ucius] N. S[covil].

[October 18, 1844. Friday.] . . . I was at the office all day recording. P.M. Bishop [Newel K.] Whitney read much in the Book of the Law of the Lord.

[October 19, 1844. Saturday.] . . . Last night I dreamed I was in a rich building in a very pleasant place. I thought I was married to Brother [Alpheus] Cutlers youngest daughter[116] and she seemed as happy as an angel and I felt full of joy and peace. I thought I had received Miss Cutler in addition to those I had already got. When I awoke I felt disappointed and felt to pray in my heart O God if it be thy will give me that woman for a companion and my soul shall praise thee but thy will be done and not mine . . . Sister [Ann] Booth tells me that Sara Ann [Whitney] is very unhappy and wants to see me she says Jane Charnock is perfectly unhappy and if there is any way she can be loosed she wants me to take her. Mary Aspen is ready to unite to me as her savior and Sister Booth says she shall not risk her salvation in Roberts [Booth] hands and wants me to interfere. We had considerable conversation on many subjects and felt pretty well.

---

[115] Clayton refers to the nascent doctrine of adoption, whereby each leading patriarch establishes a "pyramid" of family connections. Lesser elders become associated with a patriarchal family through a sealing ceremony.

[116] Emily Cutler (1828–52), about sixteen years old.

[October 21, 1844. Monday.] . . . P.M. I went to see M[ary] Aspen. She has made up her mind to go with me. I also went to see A[lice] H[ardman]. She is better.

[October 27, 1844. Sunday.] A.M. went to fetch books from the office. Called at Brother Cutlers. Then went to George Millers, in council with N[ewel] K. Whitney, Orson Pratt, George A. Smith, George Miller, Amasa Lyman, Lucien Woodworth and John D. Parker. Brother Parker has been prying into the secret designs of the mob. He has professed to be an apostate and by that means got into their secret councils. He was told by the mob that all their plans to overthrow the church has completely failed, but they had one plan in view which they felt satisfied would accomplish the purpose and that plan was to obtain our sacred records and destroy them and also obtain testimony from them to our overthrow. They gave him to understand that this was to be accomplished by the means of a man in our midst who had free access to the records and who had agreed to put them in possession of them. They finally told Brother Parker that the man who was to do this was W. W. Phelps and Parker was told by several that Phelps was the man on whom they depended to get the records. I went over to Dr. Richards and found that all the records were safe in his hands. There was also considerable fears entertained that Brother [Reynolds] Cahoon is not true to us. A[lmon] Babbitt is suspected from good evidence of being treacherous and of conspiring with the mob to overthrow us.

[November 8, 1844. Friday.] . . . P.M. went to see Jane Hardman. She prefers me for a Saviour to anyone else, so she says.

[November 19, 1844. Tuesday.] . . . At night, I retired and prayed for him[117] according to the order of the priesthood.

[November 20, 1844. Wednesday.] . . . P.M. went with President Young to see Sister Jane Hardman. President Young blessed her with the blessings of the everlasting covenant and she was sealed up to eternal life and to W[illiam] C[layton] for time and for all eternity.[118]

---

[117] Clayton's son, William Heber Clayton.
[118] Jane Hardman became Clayton's fourth wife.

[November 21, 1844. Thursday.] . . . We moved into the new office in P[arley] P. Pratts [store] today. Evening I went to Brother H. C. Kimballs awhile and then to see J[ane] H[ardman] and prospered.

[November 22, 1844. Friday.] . . . Evening Brother Kimball sent for me to write two letters for him. We had considerable talk on the priesthood. Margaret don't seem happy, which makes my head ache.

[December 2, 1844. Monday.] . . . The brethren had a council at Dr. Richards but I was not permitted to be there, probably they did not think worthwhile to tell me. I feel sorry and grieved at heart, but don't intend they shall know it.

[December 5, 1844. Thursday.] . . . I was at the office all day. At noon we had some conversation concerning recorders for the Baptism of our dead &c. We feel very anxious on the matter but have little prospect of anything being done very speedily. I feel very anxious on the subject myself, inasmuch as the Records of our Baptisms for our dead have not been kept in order for near 2 years back. The minutes have been kept on loose slips of paper and are liable to be lost and they have not been kept according to the order of God. There is so much treachery in man that it is hard to find a man who can be trusted with those Records for they cannot be public property. Inasmuch as they will have to contain histories pertaining to the transactions of individuals which never must be public. Dr. Richards remains very sick and I fear if he do not change his mode of living he will die . . . Brother Kimball asked President Young concerning D[iantha] Farr. He gave full consent and ordered Brother K[imball] to attend to it. I feel humbly grateful for this grant. And feel to ask the father in the name of Jesus to give me favor in her eyes and the eyes of her parents that I may receive the gift in full.

[December 19, 1844. Thursday.] . . . Read 2 letters from Elder Woodruff to President Young concerning W[illia]m Smith and G[eorge] J. Adams showing that they are in opposition to the Twelve and have collected money in the east for the Temple and have used it. There are warrants out for them in N[ew] York and Boston and all seems confusion and sorrow wherever they go.

[December 22, 1844. Sunday.] Met with the brethren of the first quorum to pray and counsel. My wife and O[rson] Pratts wife, P[arley] P. Pratts wife and A[masa] Lymans wife was voted in. We have to use the greatest care and caution and dare not let it be known that we meet.

[December 24, 1844. Tuesday.] . . . Evening I went to converse with Brother [Winslow] Farr concerning D[iantha]. He and Sister Farr feels well towards me and are quite willing to give me what I ask. He wishes to converse with Brother Kimball and D[iantha] before he decides. Thus has my prayer been answered to the full, and my heart is full of joy and gratitude to God for his mercies to me and my house. If my heart was as pure as I desire it should be, no sin nor evil would ever be found there but I am subject to vanity.

[December 25, 1844. Wednesday.] . . . Afterwards I went with the Band to [Joseph] Collidges.[119] We had a very pleasant interview. President Young, H. C. Kimball, G. A. Smith, A. Lyman, and John Taylor and their Ladies were all there. After we got through playing President Young read some remarks expressive of his good feelings and love for the brethren. His remarks were very profitable. He said the Lord would never suffer us to overcome enemies while we cherish feelings of revenge. When we prevail over our enemies it must be from a sense of duty and not of revenge.

[December 27, 1844. Friday.] . . . After meeting I asked Brother [Winslow] Farr if he had come to a conclusion and he gave assent to my request and seemed to feel well.

[January 1, 1845. Wednesday.] . . . The organization of the Kingdom of God on 11th March last is one important event. This organization was called the Council of Fifty or Kingdom of God, and was titled by revelation as follows. "Verily thus saith the Lord, this is the name by which you shall be called, the Kingdom of God and his Laws, with the Keys and power thereof, and judgment in the hands of his servants, Ahman Christ."[120] In this Council

[119] Clayton played the violin, French horn, and drum.
[120] "Ahman" is a sacred term in Mormon lexicon, also used in Joseph Smith's

was the plan arranged for supporting President Joseph Smith as a candidate for the presidency of the U. S. President Joseph was the standing chairman of the Council and myself the Clerk. In this Council was also devised the plan of establishing an emigration to Texas, and plans laid for the exaltation of a standard and ensign of truth for the nations of the earth. In this Council was the plan devised to restore the Ancients to the Knowledge of the truth and the restoration of Union and peace amongst ourselves.[121] In this Council was President Joseph chosen our Prophet, Priest and King by Hosannas. In this Council was the principles of eternal truth rolled forth to the heavens without reserve and the hearts of the servants of God made to rejoice exceedingly. I was admitted a member of the first quorum and a member of the council of fifty. I have received two companions, received two children and buried one.[122]

[January 9, 1845. Thursday.] . . . We went over to Brother [Winslow] Farrs to spend a little season together. Winslow Farr was married to Olive H. Freeman for time and all eternity. After which the seal of the covenant was put upon Diantha.[123] The question was asked of each one present, did they freely give her up, and they all signified their willingness by saying they had no objections. There was present Winslow Farr her father and his wife. Also Loren Farr and Nancy his wife and William Walker and Olive his wife.

The blessings pronounced upon her head were great and one promise was that her seed should become numerous as the sands on the seashore. H. C. K[imball] gave her some very good advice afterward and she seems to feel well . . . She was born in the town of Charleston Orleans County State of Vermont on the twelfth of October 1828 making her 16 years old last October. May she

---

reference to the location of the "Garden of Eden" at "Adam-Ondi-Ahman" in Missouri. See Introduction, n18.

[121] "Ancients" refers to North American Indians. According to the Book of Mormon, the Indians had descended from the Lamanites, who were remnants of lost Hebrew tribes.

[122] In 1844 Clayton had married Alice and Jane Hardman and had fathered two children: Vilate Ruth, born of Ruth Moon on December 8, and Daniel, son of Margaret Moon, born February 18 and died August 27.

[123] On January 9, 1845, sixteen-year-old Diantha Farr became Clayton's fifth wife.

never violate her covenant, but may she with her companion realize to the full all the blessings promised. And may there never
the first jar or unkind feeling towards each other exist to all eternity is thy prayer of thy servant William O Lord and may it be
ever so Amen. We had a very pleasant interview and parted about
8 1/2 o'clock.

[January 12, 1845. Sunday.] At the Council Hall. Elder H.
C. Kimball preached. He used many figures to illustrate his ideas
amongst the rest when speaking of the unwillingness of the saints
to abide the laws of exaltation. He said that the church was like a
swarm of Bees, who when they want to increase the king and
queen go and seek a new location and when they have found it
they come back to the hive and persuade the young folks out but
as soon as they begin to fly the old women and young women run
with their old tin Kettles and pans and cow Bells, ti[n]kling to
drown the voice of the king and throw them into a confusion and
prevent their enlargement. Just so with the saints when any seem
disposed to enlarge their kingdom and godhead the old women
and young women run with their old kettles and pans and cow
Bells to drown the sound of the leaders and throw the saints into
confusion and keep them shut up in their old traditions. After he
got through, O[rson] Pratt added an idea on the extent and mag-
nitude of the planetary system and the beautiful adaptation to the
enlargement of the saints. It was a very interesting meeting.

P.M. attended the H[igh] P[riests] quorum with Aaron Farr.
I conversed with him some concerning D[iantha] in Margarets
hearing and she felt bad. President Young, Kimball and others
attended the quorum and selected 50 of the members to go on a
mission till about April 1st. Evening met with the first quorum at
Parleys. Joseph Young and his wife were annointed with the second ordinance. D[iantha] was at my house when I got home and
tarried with us all night.

[January 13, 1845. Monday.] This A.M. I had some talk
with D[iantha] in bed. All things seemed to go right.

[January 14, 1845. Tuesday.] . . . Evening rode out with Lot
to A[aron] Farrs. Talked to Aaron considerable also with D[iantha]
and was with her until 12 1/2 and accomplished the desire of my

heart by gaining victory over her feelings. May the Lord bless her until her cup shall run over and her heart be pure as gold.

[January 22, 1845. Wednesday.] . . . Bought two rings and gave one to S[ara] A[nn] Whitney for painting aprons.[124]

[January 25, 1845. Saturday.] . . . Aaron Farr seems to be working to get Marg[are]t away from me. We had a long talk together on the subject.

[January 26, 1845. Sunday.] Spent the day very pleasantly with D[iantha] F[arr] for I felt so bad about Marg[are]t. I did not like to go to meeting. Evening met with the quorum. John E. Page and J[oseph] C. Kingsbury[125] were received also Sara Ann Whitney, Hellen M. Kimball, Eliza R. Snow, [Mary] Page, [Sarah M.?] Pratt, Olive G. Frost, Lucy [Decker] Seeley, Louisa Beaman. Aaron Farr has been talking again to M[argaret] and has succeeded in alienating her feelings much.

[January 27, 1845. Monday.] . . . P.M. talked with S[ara] A[nn] and Brother Whitney who reminded me of some items of law which proves that M[argaret] cannot get away unless I break the covenant. I talked with M[argaret] again and told her these things and she seems more satisfied.

[January 28, 1845. Tuesday.] At the office all day. Talked with Brother Kimball, who confirmed Brother Whitneys remarks and is of the same mind. He said he will converse with A[aron] and show him that he is handling edge tools, for it cannot go down in as much as I hold more authority than he does.
    . . . At 11 o'clock President Young, H. C. Kimball, J. Taylor, N. K. Whitney, Geo. Miller, Elias Smith, R. Cahoon and myself (who are members of the Council of fifty) also John E. Page (not a member) went up into the council room . . . At noon I told M[argaret] what Brother Kimball said and she seems to feel much better.

---

[124] Ceremonial aprons.
[125] Kingsbury was clerk to Bishop Newel K. Whitney and the person who copied the July 12, 1843, revelation on polygamy. This copy remained in church possession when Emma Smith destroyed the original. See n42.

[February 4, 1845. Tuesday.] Met at the 70s Hall with the Council of the Kingdom.[126] There were only 25 members present viz: B[righam] Young, S[amuel] Bent, John Smith, Alpheus Cutler, R[eynolds] Cahoon, W[illiam] W. Phelps, G[eorge] Miller, P[eter] Haws, Josh Fielding, Levi Richards, J[ohn] D. Parker, L[ucien] Woodworth, H[eber] C. Kimball, O[rson] Spencer, P[hilip] B. Lewis, D[avid] D. Yearsley, C[harles] C. Rich, O[rson] Pratt, A[masa] Lyman, J[oseph] W. Coolidge, O[rrin] P[orter] Rockwell, G[eorge] A. Smith, E[rastus] Snow and W[illar]d Richards and myself. This is the first time we met since the massacre of President Joseph and Hyrum Smith. The Council was reorganized and President B. Young appointed standing chairman as successor to President Joseph Smith by unanimous vote. The vote then passed for absent members according to their ages and stations and resulted as follows viz. Ezra Thayer, Amos Fielding, N[ewel] K. Whitney, C[ornelius] P. Lott, J[ohn] M. Bernhisel, Elias Smith, O[rson] Hyde, W[ilford] Woodruff, P[arley] P. Pratt, D[avid] S. Hollister, John Taylor, W[illia]m Smith, A[lmon] W. Babbitt, J[edediah] M. Grant and B[enjamin] F. Johnson were unanimously sustained and received into the new organization. The following were rejected and dropped from the Council: Uriah Brown, W[illia]m Marks, Sidney Rigdon, Lyman Wight, James Emmett, Samuel James, Edward Bonny, Alexander Badlam, Geo[rge] J. Adams, Merinus G. Eaton and Lorenzo D. Wasson. President Joseph and Hyrum two of the members were martyred for the truth and John P. Green is dead, so that there is only 40 members left in the Council. It was voted to fill up the Council at some future time. The weather is extremely cold and the Council adjourned at 2 1/2.

[February 6, 1845. Thursday.] At the office all day recording minutes of Council &c. Evening clothed for to offer prayers for W[illia]m H. [Clayton] and Vilate R. [Clayton] who are both very sick.

[February 11, 1845. Tuesday.] At the Office all day copying records of the Kingdom.

---

[126] Council of Fifty.

[February 12, 1845. Wednesday.] At the office all day copying records of the Kingdom.

[February 14, 1845. Friday.] . . . In the evening the following brethren met together to pray and ask God to thwart the plans of the mob and deliver the brethren out of their hands viz. B. Young, H. C. Kimball, O. Pratt, G. A. Smith, Wd. Richards, N. K. Whitney, Geo. Miller, A. Cutler, R. Cahoon, Isaac Morley, O. Spencer, Joseph Young and myself. We have a very good time and the Lord blesses us and I believe we will have the desires of our hearts. After prayers it was voted that Father [Isaac] Morley move in to Nauvoo as soon as possible and that Solomon Hancock be appointed to preside over the Lima Branch in his stead. It was also voted that Dr. [John] Bernhisel be appointed a traveling Bishop to visit the churches. We had also some conversation on the subject of sending six brethren with brother Lewis Dana to the West, and especially to Texas.

[March 1, 1845. Saturday.] At 10 A.M. met at the Seventies Hall in the Council of Fifty. The following brethren were taken into fill up the Quorum viz; Joseph Young, John E. Page, David Fullmer, Theodore Turley, Albert P. Rockwood, Jonathan Dunham, and Lucien R. Foster. They subscribed to the laws of the Council and covenanted before God with uplifted hands to maintain all things inviolate agreeable to the order of the Council. Brothers Daniel Spencer, Isaac Morley, and Shadrack Roundy were selected to make up the number of 50 but they were absent and sick. Brother John Pack was admitted to sit in the place of Wilford Woodruff, John D. Lee in the place of Ezra Thayer, and Lewis Dana in place of Amos Fielding they being absent [] on business. Lewis Dana is a Lamanite of the Oneida nation and the First Lamanite who has been admitted a member of any Quorum of the Church.

The object of the Council was to decide whether we shall send out a company of men with Brother Dana to fill Josephs measures originally adopted in this Council by going West to seek out a location and a home where the Saints can dwell in peace and health and where they can erect the ensign and standard of liberty for the nations, and live by the laws of God without being oppressed and mobbed under a tyrannical government, without protection from the laws. Many able speeches were made on the subject and the Council finally agreed to send out a company with Brother Dana to accomplish this important object. The following brethren were selected and appointed by unanimous vote of the Council, for this mission, viz. Samuel Bent to be the first man and president of the Mission, Jonathan Dunham next, Cyrus Daniels, Daniel Spencer, John S. Fullmer, Charles Shumway, Albert Carrington and John W. Farnham. These brethren are expected to start immediately after Conference and proceed from tribe to tribe, to unite the Lamanites and find a home for the saints. The Council adjourned in the midst of the best kind of feelings.

[March 4, 1845. Tuesday.] . . . At 9 o'clock met with the council of the Kingdom. We had a very interesting meeting. The subject being Oregon Mission.

[March 6, 1845. Thursday.] At the office all day copying records of the Kingdom.

[March 7, 1845. Friday.] As above.

[March 10, 1845. Monday.] . . . While writing and copying the records of the Kingdom, I was writing these words dropped by Elder H. C. Kimball in the council on the 4th inst.[127] viz. "if a man step beyond his bounds he will lose his kingdom as Lucifer did and it will be given to others who are more worthy." This idea came to my mind. It has been a doctrine taught by this church that we were in the Grand Council amongst the Gods when the organization of this world was contemplated and that the laws of government were all made and sanctioned by all present and all the ordinances and ceremonies decreed upon. Now is it not the case that the Council of the Kingdom of God now organized upon this earth are making laws and sanctioning principles which will in part govern the saints after the resurrection, and after death will not these laws be made known by messengers and agents as the gospel was made known to us. And is there not a similarity between this grand council and the council which sat previous to the organization of this world.

[March 11, 1845. Tuesday.] In the Council of Fifty all day. Cyrus Daniels was admitted a member. The subject of writing

---

[127] Instant, meaning of the current month.

letters to the Governor's and a number of other subjects were discussed. The subject of the movements of the mob was talked over and it was considered best for those who are hunted with writs to go on Missions so that we may if possible evade the blow until we can finish the Temple and the Nauvoo House.[128] It was also decided that the workmen on the walls of the Temple commence tomorrow.

[March 12, 1845. Wednesday.] At the office all day copying records of the Kingdom.

[March 14, 1845. Friday.] At the office all day chiefly recording records of the Kingdom. Brother Whitney tells me today that he has notified Margaret to go and receive her washings and annointing at the same time Ruth does. This makes my heart rejoice. I had heard of it on Wednesday but not officially. Truly God is kind to me.

[March 15, 1845. Saturday.] A.M. at the office copying records of the Kingdom . . . P.M. at the High Council taking minutes. G[eorge] J. Adams had his trial. Presidents Young and H. C. Kimball were witnesses against him. Many hard things were proven against him which he confessed and begged for mercy. It was decided that he write a confession of his wickedness, and agree to be one with the Twelve and do right here after, which he agreed to. The property in his hands belonging to the Temple he promised to bring and have a settlement. It was a good and interesting season and will do Adams much good.

[March 17, 1845. Monday.] At the office all day chiefly copying records of the Kingdom.

[March 18, 1845. Tuesday.] In the Council of Fifty all day. D[aniel] Spencer was admitted a member. The subject of the Western Mission was most on hand, and all seemed interested fully in it.

[March 19, 1845. Wednesday.] P.M. copying records of the Kingdom.

---

[128] Joseph Smith declared it had been revealed to him that both the temple and the Nauvoo House should be built.

[March 20, 1845. Thursday.] At the office all day. A.M. recording tithings, afterwards copying records of the Kingdom.

[March 22, 1845. Saturday.] At the council of the Kingdom all day. The Western Mission occupied near all day. The subject of the Nauvoo House, Printing Office, Church History and organization of the City were talked over.

[March 24, 1845. Monday.] . . . Chiefly recording the minutes of the Council of Fifty.

[March 25, 1845. Tuesday.] At the Council of Fifty all day. The subject of the Nauvoo House, and organization of the City were the principle topics of conversation.

[March 26, 1845. Wednesday.] . . . I am a perfect slave to them all the while. I have as much work to receive the tithings for the Temple as an ordinary penman could keep up with, but more than this I spend about 3 and 4 days a week in council and recording records of the kingdom. I have also spent day after day writing brother Kimball's journal for the press, besides writing letters and attending to a multitude of contingent business. I have two dollars a day for six days in the week and spend near every sabbath for no compensation. Other men who don't do half the work have a great deal more money and good property for their comfort than I have and they seem to be extolled to the skies. The church has given me a poor lot for an inheritance but they have also given other men better lots who work no harder than I do and have more money to sport in.

[March 27, 1845. Thursday.] . . . At the office all day copying records of the Kingdom.

[March 28, 1845. Friday.] . . . Sister [Sara Ann] Whitney went to attend to anointing my wife and Margaret but was again prevented through Sarah Ann not being there in season.[129]

[March 31, 1845. Monday.] . . . On Saturday Ruth and Margaret received their anointing[130] for which I feel thankful. Margaret had some good instructions and she feels satisfied and

---

[129] "In season" is a British term meaning on time.
[130] Second anointing follows on January 26, 1846.

reconciled. She says she will never leave me on any consideration.

I still feel determined to do all I can and be as faithful as I know how for that is the desire of my heart, but my greatest desire is to so live that I may secure for myself and mine the highest degree of exaltation and glory which is possible for me to obtain, and to be with my friend Joseph Smith in the eternal world.[131]

[April 1, 1845. Tuesday.] At the office all day, quite unwell, recording minutes of the Kingdom.

[April 3, 1845. Thursday.] . . . Evening met with a few of the high quorum at Dr. Richards house for prayer. There were present B. Young, H. C. Kimball, W. Richards, John Taylor, O. Pratt, G. A. Smith, J. E. Page, G. Miller, Joseph Young and myself. Our prayers were that the plans of the mob might be frustrated that they might have no influence nor power to disturb nor trouble us. That the leaders of the mob especially [Thomas] Sharp may be visited with judgements, and that we may be preserved in peace to finish the houses and see the Elders endowed and fulfil all that the Lord commanded us in this place, also that Brother Whitney, A. Lyman and Uncle John Smith may be healed of their sicknesses, and that our families may be blessed &c. We had a good time.

[April 5, 1845. Saturday.] At 9 at the Seventies Hall with the Council of Fifty but on account of a multitude of business waiting the Council adjourned until without doing business to next Friday at 8 3/4.

[April 11, 1845. Friday.] With the Council of Fifty all day taking minutes. President Young appointed J[onathan] Dunham, C[harles] Shumway, Lorenzo Young to go with Brother [Lewis] Dana on the Western Mission. It was decided to move the printing office into three lower stories of Masonic Hall and commence the business on a larger scale. The Council all voting to do their utmost to sustain it.

---

[131] Here Clayton concludes the first "Nauvoo, Illinois" journal notebook, "Journal by Wm. Clayton 1842–5." Next follows the third and last Nauvoo journal notebook, "Journal of Wm. Clayton No 3 commencing April 1st 1845."

[April 15, 1845. Tuesday.] Dined at 12 o'clock with Brother George Miller and afterwards rode with him to meet with the Kingdom of God in the upper room of the Seventies Hall. Phineas Young was received into the Council and decided to go with Brothers Dana, Dunham and Shumway to the Indian Council at Council Bluffs and thence if they think best to the Pacific Ocean. It was also decided that Brother Solomon [Zundal] should go with them to his tribe the Delawares. A letter from Gov[ernor Thomas] Ford was read giving his advice relative to our policy in organizing the City. He advises to organize the City into corporations of a mile square so as to include the whole surface. He also recommends to go and establish an independent government in California.

[April 16, 1845. Wednesday.] . . . P.M. at the office mostly copying records of the Kingdom.

[April 17, 1845. Thursday.] . . . Part of the day I was copying records of the Kingdom . . . The following verses were composed by Elder John Taylor, the Apostle, and revised by him at the Council of the Kingdom on Friday 11th inst.
"The Upper California. O thats the land for me." &c.
Evening tarried at the office till 8 o'clock. Afterwards met at Dr. Richards' to pray in company with B. Young, H. C. Kimball, W. Richards, J. Taylor, G. A. Smith, A. Lyman, O. Pratt, of the twelve; N. K. Whitney and George Miller the two church bishops, John Smith, Patriarch and Joseph Young. The particular subjects asked for was father [Samuel] Bents mission to L[yman] Wights[132] company and the deliverance of the church from their enemies. At my suggestion the hands who labor on the Temple were remembered to be preserved from accidents, inasmuch as they are in danger all the while. We had a very good time.

[April 21, 1845. Monday.] . . . Recording minutes of the Kingdom.

[April 22, 1845. Tuesday.] A.M. at the office recording minutes of the Kingdom. P.M. attended the Council of the King-

---

[132] Bent carried "a plea for union" from the Council of the Twelve to Wight, who had evidently planned to go west on his own (*HC* 7:400–401).

dom. There was not much business done. The brethren are not
yet gone west and will probably not start for a day or two.

[April 27, 1845. Sunday.] . . . Evening met at Dr. Richards
with the Dr. President B. Young, H. C. Kimball, A. Lyman, G.
A. Smith, O. Hyde, J. Young and John Smith. Our object was to
offer up prayers for a number of subjects. The meeting broke up
about 10 1/2 o'clock with perfect peace and union.

[April 28, 1845. Monday.] . . . A.M. recording minutes of
the Kingdom.

[April 29, 1845. Tuesday.] . . . At 6 1/2 met the Council of
Fifty at Seventies Hall.

[May 1, 1845. Thursday.] . . . President Young told me that
he had learned that the Rigdonites are intending to have me taken
up and prosecuted for polygamy, especially George W. Robinson
and Samuel James . . . Evening met for prayer at Dr. Richards.
There were present B. Young, H. C. Kimball, W. Richards, A.
Lyman, O. Hyde, O. Pratt, G. A. Smith, John Smith, I. Morley
and Joseph Young and myself.

[May 3, 1845. Saturday.] . . . P.M. . . . Charles Ivins was
in the office and says that in conversation with [Austin] Cowles
he learned that Rigdons party is very much divided both in doctrine and sentiment. Law and Rigdon differed in fifteen points of
doctrine, Rigdon wanting to deny the book of Mormon which
Law could not do. [William] McLell[i]n and Rigdon also differ in
sentiment.

[May 6, 1845. Tuesday.] . . . Evening met with the Council
of Fifty in the Seventies Hall. The principal topic of conversation
was the movements of the mob. It appears their determination is
to get up an excitement at the Court and they are already trying
it by reporting that the Saints are going en masse to Carthage at
the Court, and if the Court does not execute the law on the murderers that we intend to destroy the Court and citizens of the
County. From reports which the brethren have brought which
have been at Carthage the mob are laying deep plans to bring us
into collision with the State, so as to bring about our expulsion or
extermination forthwith. It was agreed that none of the brethren
leave the City at the Court, only those who are required to be

there on business, so that we may prevent the mob from coming into the City and committing depradations in the absence of the brethren. An article was written by O. Hyde and W. Richards to publish in tomorrow's paper notifying the public of the designs of the mob and also the course we intend to pursue. The Council did not break up till 10 1/4.

[May 7, 1845. Wednesday.] . . . Evening met with the following brethren at Dr. Richards for prayer being clothed &c.[133] viz. B. Young, J. Taylor, W. Richards, G. A. Smith, A. Lyman, N. K. Whitney, L. Richards. Brother Kimball came in at the close of the meeting. We had a very pleasant time. The chief subjects were to pray that the Lord would hedge up the way of the mob so that they may have no power over us during court. Also that the Lord would hedge up the way of John Greenhow that he may not have power or influence to go to England and publish the book of Doctrine and Covenants.[134] Petitions were also offered for Brother [George] Miller and others who are sick. It was also agreed to send a letter to Elder [Wilford] Woodruff in England and warn him to forestall Greenhow and get out a copy right for the Doctrine and Covenants before him.

[May 8, 1845. Thursday.] . . . Evening met at Dr. Richards for prayer in company with President B[righam] Young, H[eber] C. Kimball, W[illard] Richards, J[ohn] Taylor, G[eorge] A. Smith, A[masa] Lyman, O[rson] Pratt, J[ohn] E. Page, N[ewel] K. Whitney, L[evi] Richards, Joseph Young. We had a very interesting time.

[May 10, 1845. Saturday.] . . . P.M. met with the Council of Fifty and adjourned sine die. The adjournment was about in consequence of the Conduct of D[avid] D. Yearsley of whom there is strong suspicions of treachery.

[May 11, 1845. Sunday.] At the office all day comparing account books with Brother [James] Whitehead. Evening met with Dr. Richards for prayer with B. Young, W. Richards, J. Taylor, O. Pratt, G. A. Smith, J. E. Page, N. K. Whitney and Levi

---

[133] Dressed in ceremonial undergarments, robes, and aprons.
[134] Greenhow, from Liverpool, published an unauthorized version of the Doctrine and Covenants (*HC* 5:9).

Richards. President Young advised me to keep closed up for a week or two inasmuch as the apostates, especially S[amuel] James and G[eorge] W. Robinson have entered into measures to take me with a writ to Carthage. The mob also want to get President Young, H. C. Kimball, J. Taylor, W. Richards, O. Hyde and W. W. Phelps and it is said they have taken out writs for them. They want twelve men out of Nauvoo but we are unable to learn who the others are.

[May 15, 1845. Thursday.] Evening met at Dr. Richards for prayer, in company with President Young, H. C. Kimball, G. A. Smith, O. Pratt, N. K. Whitney and L. Richards.

[May 18, 1845. Sunday.] . . . I went to meet with the brethren at Dr. Richards but felt too unwell to remain.

[May 23, 1845. Friday.] . . . W[illiam] Smith is coming out in opposition to the Twelve and in favor of [George J.] Adams. The latter has organized a church at Augusta, Iowa Territory with young Joseph Smith for President, W[illia]m Smith for Patriarch, Jared Carter for President of the stake and himself for spokesman to Joseph. Wm. says he has sealed some women to men and he considers he is not accountable to Brigham nor the Twelve nor any one else. There is more danger from William than from any other source, and I fear his course will bring us much trouble. Evening went with Brother Whitney to see the Twelve at Elder Taylors on Main Street. We tarried till near 10 o'clock. There were present B. Young, H. C. Kimball, J. Taylor, W. Richards, G. A. Smith, J. E. Page and N. K. Whitney. I presented to them a proposition to write a short history of the building of the Temple from its commencement, together with other matters and deposit the history in the corner stone about to be laid tomorrow.[135] They acquiesced with the plan. The case of Wm. Smith was also talked over. It appears he is determined to rule the church and monopolize the whole to himself. Samuel Brannan[136] came in while we were talking. I had an introduction

---

[135] This account by Clayton is catalogued in LDS archives as "William Clayton's Journal, etc." It was serially published in the *Juvenile Instructor* 21 (Jan. 15–May 15, 1886): 10–157, and is reproduced here in Appendix B, "An Interesting Journal." The capstone, or uppermost stone, was laid on May 24, 1845.
[136] Samuel Brannan (1819-89), born in Maine, converted to Mormonism

to him. J[onathan] C. Wright and Elias Smith also came in and stated that the court had got a jury empannelled and was to proceed to try the murderers at 8 o'clock tomorrow morning. They say there is no manner of doubt but the murderers will be acquitted.

[May 25, 1845. Sunday.] . . . At a little after 8 Brother Kimball called and I went with him to Dr. Richards to meet with the quorum for prayer. Present President B. Young, H. C. Kimball, W. Richards, G. A. Smith, A. Lyman, John E. Page and O. Pratt of the Twelve. N. K. Whitney, and G[eorge] Miller, Trustees, and Levi Richards, Patriarch John Smith, Joseph Young and myself. We had a good time and felt that our prayers would be answered. We broke up about half past eleven.

[May 29, 1845. Thursday.] . . . Evening met at Dr. Richards for prayer in company with President B. Young, H. C. Kimball, W. Richards, John Taylor, Amasa Lyman, G. A. Smith, O. Pratt, and O. Hyde of the Twelve, N. K. Whitney and George Milller, Trustees, Joseph Young and Levi Richards. The subjects prayed for were many, especially that the Lord would over-rule the movements of Wm. Smith who is endeavoring to ride the Twelve down, and also that the Lord would over-rule the mob so that we may dwell in peace until the Temple is finished. The Council broke up at half past 12 o'clock.

[June 1, 1845. Sunday.] . . . Evening at Dr. Richards with B. Young, H. C. Kimball, W. Richards, J. Taylor, J. E. Page, O. Pratt., G. A. Smith, A. Lyman, John Smith, N. K. Whitney, G. Miller, L. Richards and Joseph Young. It was decided that [Peter O.] Hanson translate the Doctrine and Covenants and Book

---

and went to Kirtland, Ohio, in 1833 to become a newspaperman. In 1844 Joseph Smith called his brother, William, and Brannan to found *The Prophet*, a Mormon periodical in New York City. After Joseph Smith died, Brannan, William Smith, and George J. Adams were accused by Wilford Woodruff of using *The Prophet* for personal gain. In April 1845 Brannan was disfellowshipped for practicing "spiritual wifery" in Massachusetts, was reinstated a month later, and with Parley P. Pratt established the New York *Messenger* and serialized Lansford W. Hastings's *Emigrants' Guide to Oregon and California*. Brannan helped expedite the pioneer trek west and became a California pioneer; in 1848 in the *California Star* he publicized the discovery of gold at Sutter's sawmill. Excommunicated from the LDS church, he later resided in San Francisco and built the resort of Calistoga in California's Napa Valley (Van Wagoner and Walker, 20-23; *HC* 7:395, 418; see Journal 4, "Pioneer Trek West," ns56, 63).

of Mormon into the Norwegian language and that Elder O. Pratt assist. Also decided that the Trustees give G[eorge] D. Watt a quarter of a Lot and build him a house and employ him as a reporter for the Church, and let his labors go towards paying for his house and lot. I read a part of the record which I prepared for a deposit, but it was not as full as President Young wanted and the council concluded to deposit all the Times & Seasons, to give a perfect history of the church in Nauvoo. Separated at 12 o'clock.

[June 5, 1845. Thursday.] . . . Evening met at Dr. Richards for prayer in company with B. Young, H. C. Kimball, W. Richards, J. Taylor, O. Pratt, A. Lyman, J. E. Page, G. A. Smith, N. K. Whitney, G. Miller and L. Richards. We separated at 12 o'clock.

[June 8, 1845. Sunday.] A.M. at the office, afterwards at home all day. At 4 met at Dr. Richards with B. Young, H. C. Kimball, J. Taylor, W. Richards, O. Hyde, O. Pratt, J. E. Page, G. A. Smith, A. Lyman, N. K. Whitney, G. Miller, L. Richards, and J. C. Kingsbury. We had a very interesting time and separated about [9] o'clock.

[June 12, 1845. Thursday.] . . . At 4 o'clock met at Dr. Richards[137] . . . We had a very interesting time and separated about half past 8 o'clock.

[June 15, 1845. Sunday.] At the office till 4 P.M. Afterwards at Dr. Richards . . .

[June 19, 1845. Thursday.] . . . Afterwards at Dr. Richards . . . Prayers were offered up for many things especially that the curse of God may fall upon Judge [?] Young and the Lawyers who have justified the murderers, and that they may not be able to hold court. Evening at home.

[June 22, 1845. Sunday.] . . . P.M. met at Dr. Richards.. . Sister Richards is yet very sick and it was agreed that four of the company should go down with Elder Richards to lay hands on her while the other remained to offer up prayers for her in the room. Elders J. Taylor, O. Pratt, J. C. Kingsbury, and myself

---

[137] This abridgement excludes repetitious listing of names in this and subsequent mention of the prayer circle meetings at Willard Richards's house.

were appointed to go with the Doctor. He anointed his wife and we then laid hands on her. After we returned to the room prayers were offered up for sundry matters, especially that God would overrule the movements of our enemies &c.

[June 24, 1845. Tuesday.] . . . Wm. Smith has given bail for another brother of the Hodges[138] who was in custody for robbing, and also beat Brother [Elbridge] Tufts shamefully yesterday for a matter of small consequence. Wm. Smith is railing against the movements of the Twelve and says he has authority here to do as he has a mind to and the people shall know it. It appears he is determined to cause us trouble.

[June 26, 1845. Thursday.] . . . afterwards at Elder Richards with President B. Young, H. C. Kimball, W. Richards, G. A. Smith, A. Lyman, O. Pratt, N. K. Whitney, G. Miller, J. Young, L. Richards, and John Smith. Brother Richards Rhoda Ann, Brother Kimball, Brigham Willard, and Brother Whitneys Mary Jane were blessed each with great blessings. The afternoon was spent in conversation and prayer till 8 o'clock.

[June 27, 1845. Friday.] . . . All things seem to go right according to our prayers . . . At 9 met at Dr. Richards with President B. Young, H. C. Kimball, W. Richards, J. Taylor, A. Lyman, O. Pratt, G. A. Smith, J. E. Page, George Miller and Joseph Young. Most of the day was spent in conversation on various subjects, and towards the evening we clothed and consecrated [eight] bottles of oil and offered up prayers for general matters. Afterwards I went to the mansion.

[June 28, 1845. Saturday.] . . . A new revelation has come to light from Mother Smith, corrected and altered by William Smith so as to suit his wishes by representing him as the legal successor of Joseph in the presidency.

[June 29, 1845. Sunday.] . . . At 4 met at Dr. Richards.. . Prayers were offered for a variety of subjects. Sister Richards is recovering.

---

138 A Brother Hodges was mentioned in Kirtland (*HC* 1:355), a Curtis Hodges was excommunicated in Nauvoo (ibid., 5:350), and an Amos Hodges was sent on a mission to Vermont in April 1844 (ibid., 6:336).

[June 30, 1845. Monday.] At the office till 4 P.M. council with President Young and the Trustees about buying lands lately owned by President Smith which will be sold by the administrator tomorrow. It was agreed that I should bid them off for the Trustees. At 4.P.M. went to visit Mother Smith in company with President Young, H. C. Kimball, John Taylor, W. Richards, O. Pratt, A. Lyman, G. A. Smith, N. K. Whitney, G. Miller and R. Cahoon. A long conversation was had between her and President Young pertaining to a vision she had last week, in which Wm. Smith is represented as president over the patriarchs to guide and council the church. I asked permission to copy it but she was unwilling. William Smith did not meet with us but sent a letter, the following is a copy.

"Correspondence. William Smith to Brigham Young and the Council of the Twelve. Nauvoo June 30th 1845. Elder Young. It has been my purpose from the first to do all I could for peace. I said in a short note to you the other day that I would stand by you till death. But it might be asked upon what principle? I will answer, on the principle that I am dealt justly by in the church. The next morning after our meeting I notice an article that appears under the head of Patriarch.[139] It is not so much the doctrine that I care about; it is the spirit of the article, a disposition that appears in the brethren to cut and shave me down to the last cent, every hour and minute in the day. I do not like it. And again, why was not the article shown to me as it was an article touching my office and standing in the church, nothing was said to me on the subject. This with other like circumstances since my return from the east, and for my hard labor there, have received no favor nothing but hints of abuse, whilst other men can be applauded to the skies, and that too for the fruits of other mens labors. I am sick and tired of such partiality. Only give me my just dues, that in truth, justice and honor demands, and all is well. I have often said and sufficient to satisfy all the saints that I was willing, it was my wish that you should stand as President of the church, but I claim to be patriarch over the whole church, this gives me my place and proper standing, and what I inherit; and as to works, I am ready to measure arms with any man; give

---

[139] *Times and Seasons*, June 26, 1845.

me what is due, then you know the understanding and the conversation we had on this subject when we met at Brother Taylors that I was Patriarch over the whole church. This is what I claim and must have, and now to conclude as I understand you are to meet at Mother Smiths today, the 12 &c &c. My proposition is my share of the kingdom and if you will publish in the Neighbor and Times & Seasons the true state of the case in regard to my office as patriarch over the whole church, this will give me a right to visit all branches of the church and intrude on no mans rights, and further to attend to all of the ordinances of God, no man being my head, I will reconcile all difficulties and Elder Young can stand as the president of the church, and by my most hearty wish and consent. This will settle all difficulties and restore peace and good order, and further than this I cannot say, only that I want all men to understand that my fathers family are of the royal blood and promised seed and no man or set of men can take their crown or place in time or in eternity. Brother Young the above is my proposition and will settle all difficulties at once and these are my avid sentiments and no equivocation. Wm. Smith."

To the foregoing President Young dictated an answer which I wrote, informing him that there could be no authority given to him, to place him in a situation where he would not be amenable to the quorum of the Twelve, and there are many ordinances which cannot be administered only here in this place &c (The copy is mislaid). The answer was read to Mother Smith and her daughters and they acknowledge they were satisfied with it. Mother Smith seems to feel well and said that although in her vision it was told to her that there was two men whose hearts were blacker than the rest, it was not any one who was then present. See July 4th. The company parted soon after six and Brother Whitney and myself returned to the office to prepare an order and get the money ready to send to morrow to St. Louis for the lead.

[July 3, 1845. Thursday.] At 4 met at Dr. Richards with President Young, H. C. Kimball, W. Richards, J. Taylor, A. Lyman, G. A. Smith, O. Pratt, N. K. Whitney, G. Miller, L. Richards and J. Young. We offered up our prayers for variety of subjects. I read a letter which I wrote for President Young to Brother Woodruff in England, which was accepted. It was decided to employ Brother [Isaac] Morley to make 100 barrels of wine for sacrament. Also to purchase a raft of Lumber laying at the w[h]arf of 150,000.

[July 4, 1845. Friday.] . . . The following is a copy of the answer to Wm. Smiths letter. Nauvoo June 30th 1845. D[ea]r Brother William. A Majority of the quorum of the Twelve, Bishops Whitney and Miller, and Brother Cahoon, one of the Temple committee, have met to hold a little conversation with Mother Smith at her house. We expected to have had your company but were disappointed. We however have received a note from you which we feel to answer before we separate so that it may be sanctioned or rejected by Mother Smith. We have had considerable talk with Mother Smith and find her possessing the best of feelings towards the church. As to your requests in your letter we would say that we are perfectly willing, and wish to have all things right, but there are some ordinances in the church that cannot be administered by any person out of this place at present, but must be done here. As to your having the right to administer all ordinances, in the world, and no one standing at your head we could not sanction, because the President of the church stands at the head of all the officers in the church, and each one of our quorum are amenable to the quorum, of which you are a member. But as to your right to officiate in the office of Patriarch, we say you have the right to officiate in all the world, wherever your lot may be cast, and no one to dictate or control you excepting the Twelve, which body of men must preside over the whole church in all the world.

We hope and trust there will be no feelings. Say nothing about matters and things. If you want peace, so do we; and let us walk together in peace, and help to build up the kingdom.

If this does not meet with your feelings Brother William, write me again or come and see me, and we will make all things right, for we surely want peace and the salvation of the people. We remain as ever, your brethren and well wishers. Brigham Young.

P.S. We have read this to Mother Smith, Catherine, Lucy and Arthur [Millikin][140] and they express their satisfaction with it as well as those of the council who are present.   B. Y.

---

[140] Joseph Smith's mother, two sisters, and brother-in-law.

[July 5, 1845. Saturday.] . . . At 4 P.M. met at Dr. Richards . . . We conversed till about 7 o clock and then clothed[141] and offered up prayers for general subjects. It was decided that the Trustees give to President Young a deed for the S.W. 25 7 N. 8 W and S.W. fr 10 7 N. 8 W. free of charge.

[July 8, 1845. Tuesday.] . . . President Young and Elder Richards came to the office and brought a bag containing $2599.75 in Gold. Joseph Toronto, an Italian, came to President Young and said he wanted to give himself and all he had to President Young. He had this gold which was carefully wrapped up in old rags, tin Books &c which he freely and voluntarily gave up saying he should henceforth look to President Young for protection and council.

[July 9, 1845. Wednesday.] . . . Sister Richards died this morning at about 1/4 after 10. She has suffered much for a long time back. We have held her by faith alone, but she is gone to rest.
At 2 P.M. went with the Band to the dinner given by the Trustees for the Smith's family at the Mansion. Near all the connexions of Brother Wm. either by birth or marriage were present, besides a number of Wms particular friends. The evening was spent cheerfully although the spirit of Wm. and his associates was very different from the spirit of the Twelve. The company broke up about 8 o'clock.

[July 13, 1845. Sunday.] . . . At home till 4 P.M. then met at Dr. Richards . . . Prayers were offered for general matters.

[July 16, 1845. Wednesday.] . . . Evening I went to see Diantha. We walked out some together. She seemed to feel very bad about something which passed during her visit this afternoon. When we returned to her home I saw that her mind was affected and she was likely to have another fit of mental derangement. I tried to persuade her to go bed but she was unwilling, but I finally got her mother to make her a bed down stairs and we put her to bed by force. Soon as she got laid down she began to toss about and rave as if in great pain which seemed to increase untill she was perfectly out of her mind and raging. She tore her hair

---

[141] Put on ceremonial clothing.

and I then held her which required all the force I had got to hold her hands. She continued about three quarters of an hour in this distressing situation and about half past 10 Sister Farr went and called Brother Farr. He came down and laid hands on her and rebuked the evil spirit and commanded it to leave her in the name of the Lord. She immediately calmed down and seemed to fall into a mild sleep. Soon after she commenced talking or rather answering questions. She seemed to be in the world of spirits on a visit, and about the first she conversed with was Brother Joseph and the conversation seemed to be on the subject of the massacre. She then appeared to go and visit a number of dead relatives who invariably enquired about their relatives on earth. The answers she gave were literally facts as they exist. She then enquired for William Smiths wife Caroline.[142] She was soon taken to her and entered into conversation. Caroline asked about William of course, how her two girls were and whether he had got married.[143] To all these interrogatories she answered in the nicest manner, avoiding carefully any thing which would wound Carolines feelings. She then enquired for Sister Richards and soon met with her. It seemed by her answers that Sister Richards asked how the Doctor felt when she left him, how his children were, and whether Lucy lived with him, all which she answered correctly. She then visited Wm. Snows first wife and conversed about Wm. and his daughter and father. She then appeared to go back to Brother Joseph and Hyrum Smith and Father Smith. Joseph asked about Emma and the children and how the Twelve and Emma felt towards each other &c. all which she answered wisely but truly. He also asked about Lydia [Moon] and gave her some instructions for Lydia. He asked about me and told her I was a good man. When she parted with her friends she always bid them "good bye" but when she parted with Joseph she said, "I am not in the habit of kissing men but I want to kiss you" which she appeared to do and then said "farewell." She then seemed to start back for home. She appeared all the time in a hurry to get back. She said she would

---

[142] The deceased Caroline Grant had been married to Joseph Smith's brother, William Smith, on February 14, 1833. See Jenson, *Latter-day Saint Biographical Encyclopedia*, 1:86–87.

[143] William Smith had remarried; on June 22, 1845, Brigham Young performed the civil marriage between Smith and sixteen-year-old Mary Jane Rollins.

like to tarry but she could not leave father and mother and another, but she would soon return and bring them with her and then she would tarry with them. She conversed about two hours in this manner and seemed overjoyed all the time. A pleasant smile sat on her countenance which continued after she awoke. It was one of the most interesting and sweet interviews I ever witnessed, and a very good spirit seemd to prevail all the time. I left about 1 o clock apparently much composed and comparatively free from pain.

[July 17, 1845. Thursday.] . . . I talked with Diantha at noon. She has not the least recollection of any thing that passed last night. She seems quite feeble and worn down with fatigue and exertion. At 4 P.M. met at Dr. Richards . . . It was decided in council that Dr. Richards have a barn built by the Trustees, also that the Masonic Hall and Arsenal be prepared for store houses for grain, also that the Trustees purchase the New York store[144] if it can be bought reasonable, also that Brother [John] Pack buy the Masonic Hall Tavern and that the Trustees rent or lease the Mansion for 3 or five years. Prayers were offered for the sick and a number of subjects and about 8 o'clock we separated.

[July 20, 1845. Sunday.] . . . at 4 met at Dr. Richards.. . It was decided that the Trustees furnish Orson Pratt $33. for his expenses East. Prayers were offered for general matters especially that the Lord would turn away the sickness now prevailing amongst the children in the City.

[July 24, 1845. Thursday.] . . . 4 P.M. met at Dr. Richards . . . Quite a number of sick were prayed for myself amongst the number. I felt immediate [relief].

[July 26, 1845. Saturday.] . . . Evening in council.

[July 31, 1845. Thursday.] At the office recording. At 4 P.M. met at Dr. Richards . . . It was decided in council that the Nauvoo House[145] committee get tithing teams to haul their wood, and

---

144 The so-called New York Store in Nauvoo.
145 The Nauvoo House, a hotel that was never completed, should not be confused with the Nauvoo Mansion, which was built for Joseph Smith and eventually transformed into an inn. See n67.

grain from the country. Also that they have 2000 feet of Lumber from the Trustees, also that they collect all the scaffolding poles and take them to the Nauvoo House. A letter was written to the Temple Committee rebuking them for abusing Brother [] Reese and teaching them their duty. During the conversation Brother [] Miller insulted Brother Whitney very meanly. Brother Whitney felt angry but governed his feelings and merely said he felt above such insinuations. Prayers were offered for a number of the sick and for several other general subjects.

[August 2, 1845. Saturday.] . . . P.M. rode in the new Church Carriage with President Young, H. C. Kimball, N. K. Whitney and George Miller to look out two Blocks of Emma's which she has agreed to give the Trustees for $550. They selected Blocks 96 and 97 and then went to Mother Smiths and took her into the Carriage to show her the Blocks and give her her choice which of the two she would have to be deeded to herself and her daughters. She selected Block 96. She wants a house building of the same pattern with Brother Kimballs. After we got through she asked for the new carriage saying that President Young and the Trustees promised it to her. She also wanted another horse and a two horse harness. Neither the Trustees nor President Young ever promised the carriage to Mother Smith, but they told her that when it was built they would ride her round in it. There is no doubt but Arthur Millikin, Lucys husband, or else William has prompted her to do this out of ill feelings and jealousy lest Brother Brigham should ride in it. Arthur idles his time away. He will do nothing either for himself or any one else, but out of respect for Mother Smith the brethren would rather indulge the whole family than to hurt her feelings. She is [old] and childish and the brethren strive to do all they can to comfort her. They have lent her the carriage while she lives but it is church property and when she dies it falls into the hands of the Trustees.

[August 3, 1845. Sunday.] . . . At 4 met at Dr. Richards . . . I read a letter from Wilford Woodruff giving a very cheering history of the progress of the work in England. Prayers were offered up for a number of sick.

[August 7, 1845. Thursday.] . . . At 4 P.M. met at Dr. Richards . . . It was decided to send John S. Fullmer and H[enry]

G. Sherwood with James Emmett to his company, to council and instruct them. The subject of Brother [George] Millers abusing [them] sometime ago was talked over. Brother Miller denies having done so, but his language is too fresh in my memory to forget it. It was decided to send out a number of the agents who went last spring to collect funds for the Temple and have them collect all the money and means they can so as to finish the Temple as speedily as possible.

[August 10, 1845. Sunday.] At 9 A.M. met at Dr. Richards . . . a letter was read from Pittsburgh from Amos Fielding dated July 25th, 1845 giving an account of Wm. E. McLell[i]n abusing him &c. Also that Sidney Rigdon has had a revelation requiring his followers to sell their property and give him the avails of it to purchase land in the East to build up the kingdom. This letter is published in the Neighbor of August 13th.

After reading the letter prayers were offered up.

[August 12, 1845. Tuesday.] At Dr. Richards . . . The subject under consideration was to prepare the brethren who are going west, and give them instructions for their mission. Their names are Henry G. Sherwood, John S. Fullmer and James Emmett. A letter of authority was written by Dr. Richards to Brother Emmetts company stating that Sherwood and Fullmer were sent by the authorities of the church here to council them according to their circumstances and when they leave to appoint whomsoever they think best to preside over them and council them. It is not the object of the council to send for the company back but to see how they feel and whether they are willing to abide council. Perhaps it will be best for them to tarry where they are untill they are joined by others in the spring and then either locate there or proceed west.

[August 17, 1845. Sunday.] . . . P.M. with D[iantha] till 5 o'clock, afterwards at Dr. Richards, with President B. Young, H. C. Kimball, W. Richards, J. Taylor, G. A. Smith, N. K. Whitney, G. Miller, O. Spencer, J. Young, J. C. Kingsbury and L. Woodworth. A. W. Babbitt and B. F. Johnson, called in to enquire whether it would be agreeable to the council to let Brother Johnson rent the Mansion. It was decided to call a council tomorrow at 2 o'clock to conclude on the matter inasmuch as Brother

177

[Ezra T.] Benson has been spoken to, to either take the mansion or Masonic Hall. After the conversation ended Babbitt and Johnson withdrew, and we then offered up prayers as usual for general subjects. Last Tuesday Brother [Lucien] Woodworth was discharged from the work at the Nauvoo House as Architect by [George] A. Smith one of the Trustees on account of incompetency and an unwillingness to listen to Council. He foamed considerable at the time but feels tolerably well now. At the stand today Wm. Smith preached to the saints "the first chapter of the gospel according to St. W[illia]m" as he termed it. It was just a full declaration of his belief in the doctrine of a plurality of wives &c. The people appeared disgusted and many left the ground. His object was evidently to raise an influence against the Twelve especially Brigham and Heber for he intimated in strong terms that they were practising such things in secret but he was not afraid to do it openly.[146] His course today will evidently hurt him in the estimation of the saints more than any thing he has done before.

[August 18, 1845. Monday.] . . . I then rode to President Youngs to council. It was there decided that B. F. Johnson can have the privileges of one of the Taverns, but he must pay the rent in cash. And in regard to his interest in the large Tavern in Macedonia we will [give] him property in Nauvoo for it, but not apply it on the rent.

[August 21, 1845. Thursday.] At the office recording tithings. P.M. met at Dr. Richards . . . A letter was read from Samuel Waldo of New Hampshire complaining of oppressive conduct and teaching doctrines calculated to break up the branch such as it being no harm for a man to sleep with a woman who was not his wife &c. in Nelson Bates. The Council decided that fellowship be withdrawn from Bates and he be called home forthwith to give an

---

[146] Most Mormons were still uninformed about polygamy and assumed it was an unfounded anti-Mormon charge. Only about fifteen families among Nauvoo Mormons were practicing polygamy in 1845. They were concentrated among Joseph Smith's closest associates and constituted less than 1 percent of the total population of about 20,000 (*HR* 6:219–40; Van Wagoner, *Mormon Polygamy*, 61, 77, 79, 85; Foster, *Religion and Sexuality*, 139–80). George A. Smith estimated that prior to Joseph Smith's revelation on plural marriage, July 12, 1843, only "one or two hundred persons" in Nauvoo knew that LDS leaders privately taught and practiced polygamy (*Journal of Discourses*, 26 vols. [London: Latter-day Saints Book Depot, 1854–86], 14:213).

account of his conduct. Elder W. Richards wrote a notice to the above effect for publication in the next Times & Seasons. He also wrote a letter to O. Pratt informing him of the same. A letter was then read from Samuel V. Searles requesting a license. It was voted to send him one and Elder W. Richards accordingly filled it out. The subject of the mansion and Masonic Hall again came up and it was decided that B[enjamin] F. Johnson take the Mansion and [John] Pack the Hall. These brethren then withdrew and the remainder clothed, offered up the signs of the Holy Priesthood and prayer for the usual subjects especially for the sick. There are a great many sick in the north part of town, so many that it is grievous to see their sufferings.

[August 27, 1845. Wednesday.] A.M. at the office recording. P.M. in council . . . On Sunday last the Council decided to let Wm. Smith go East by the authority of the church, to give Patriarchal blessings, but on the representation of Brother Parley [Pratt] today of Wms course and feelings of the people in the East towards him it was decided that he had better not go and Elder Richards wrote him a letter to that effect. A notice had been written me to publish in the next "Times & Seasons" informing the saints that Wm. would go East &c. but Brother Taylor was ordered not to insert the notice. It was also decided to pave the Temple floor with pressed brick instead of either stone or tile, to save expense and because they think it will be as good with brick. This morning Brother Parley came into the office to say that his women folks wanted the rooms over the store. This would deprive us of all but the one room for office, store and council room. I suggested to the Bishops to move to the New York store, inasmuch as that property belongs to the church and is much larger and we are paying $200. a year rent for this. The Trustees immediately went over and examined the premises and decided to enlarge the cellar and make the "New York Store" our office. They mentioned the place to President Young and he agreed to it at once. In council the matter was brought up and Brother Parley proposed to sell his whole establishment. They offered to give him 3 Lots and houses for it, viz. the one where Joseph Young lives, Mitchels house and Brother Lees. He wants $3000 but seems disposed to take the offer if the houses suit. After council I was at the office.

179

[August 28, 1845. Thursday.] . . . P.M. met at Dr. Richards . . . It was voted to select three thousand men who are able to bear arms to prepare this winter to start to California next spring with their families. Prayers were offered up for the usual subjects.

[August 31, 1845. Sunday.] . . . P.M. met at Dr. Richards . . . The subject of the Oregon expedition was again talked over and the Twelve seem to think it important that they should go with the company to select a location and plant the standard. They would leave their families here and return when they had succeeded in finding a place. Prayers were offered up for quite a number of sick, amongst whom is Hugh Riding, one of our best carpenters now laying at the point of death. It is truly grievous to see the many sick in our midst especially in the north part of Town. Last night the first load of Glass for the Temple arrived and to day another load. The last load is expected tomorrow . . .

[September 1, 1845. Monday.] Daniel Spencer has returned from the West. He brings word that Brother Jonathan Dunham died of a fever.

[September 4, 1845. Thursday.] . . . At the office all day. Foreman is sick and I had to tarry at the office instead of attending council.

[September 6, 1845. Saturday.] . . . Rode around with D[iantha] and notified the members of the council of fifty to meet next Tuesday.

[September 7, 1845. Sunday.] . . . At 5 met at Dr. Richards with President B. Young, H. C. Kimball, W. Richards, A. Lyman, G. A. Smith, J. Taylor, P. P. Pratt, G. Miller, L. Richards, I. Morley, and J. C. Kingsbury. Prayers were offered up for the usual subjects. Notified the members of the Council of Fifty to meet next . . .

[September 9, 1845. Tuesday.] At 2 P.M. met in the upper room of the Seventies Hall with the Council of Fifty. The subject of sending a company of Saints to the West next spring was talked over, and the following motion of by W. W. Phelps: "Moved that the President select such a portion of this Council as he may choose to remove west, and they select and organize the company subject to the final revision of the President." A vote was taken and the motion was carried unanimously. The following motion was also put and carried unanimously "That a committee of five be appointed to gather all information relative to immigration and impart the same to this council, and those about to emigrate when called upon."

Daniel Spencer has returned a few days ago from the West. He reported in substance as follows: Their mission was to the Seneca Indians. They proceeded to about 500 miles up the Missouri River. They there met brother [Lewis] Denay and from him learned that [Jonathan] Dunham was dead. They tarried five weeks with the Stockbridge tribe. This tribe manifested great kindness towards them and the Mormon people. They have considerable knowledge of the Mormons and of what is going on; their interest seems to be identified with ours. From Denay they learned that the Che[r]okees had given permission for any number of our people to settle near by them and were willing to lend us any assistance they could or to go west with us to explore the country. George Herring has been with several tribes and says they are all friendly and seem to understand what is going on and are ready to render us any assistance they can. Many of the Stockbridge tribe are joined in with the Baptists but are dissatisfied. Their chief expects to be here about the 6th of October. They preached to them and they seem satisfied with our doctrine. From what Brother Denay said they concluded it unnecessary to go to the Seneca tribe, they learned that Denay had accomplished what they were sent for.

[September 11, 1845. Thursday.] A.M. at the Office recording minutes of the Kingdom of God . . . P.M. met at Dr. Richards . . . It was decided to dispatch a messenger to the Lima Branch and advise the brethren to propose to sell their possessions to the mob, and bring their families and grain here. It was also decided to send a messenger to Michigan to advise the brethren to sell their farms for Stock, wagons, sheep &c. Also to send a messenger to Ottawa & advise the brethren to gather all the hay they can. Prayers were offered up for the usual subjects and also that the Lord would give us wisdom to manage affairs with the mob so as to keep them off till we can accomplish what is required. Also to give us wisdom to manage the affairs in regard to the Western emigration. A selection has been made by President

181

Young of those of the Council of Fifty who shall start west next spring. My name is included in the list. News has come in confirming the report of Gen. [Miner] Demings death, which was further confirmed in a letter from J[acob] B. Backenstos.[147] He died on yesterday at about 10 1/2 A.M. News has also come that the mob have burned eight houses belonging to the brethren in Lima. A letter was sent to Solomon Hancock by special messengers advising him to propose to sell out to the mob and also that we will send teams on Monday to fetch away the women and children & grain. A letter was also sent to J. B. Backenstos, informing him of the movements of the mob and requesting him to take prompt measures to quell them as Sheriff and also to inform the Governor immediately of the movement.

[September 14, 1845. Sunday.] Brother [George] Miller reported that he went to Carthage yesterday to attend to some business. While there he was arrested on a writ got up by the mob for the grave charge of Treason. He had a kind of trial and was admitted to parole bail till next Saturday. Col. [] William and [Thomas] Sharp were at Carthage with the mob. The writ is against President B. Young, H. C. Kimball, O. Hyde, O. Pratt, J. E. Page, L. Wight and several others. The treason is for colleaguing with the Indians, building an arsenal, and making Cannon. The Higbees[148] are very active with the mob, and there seems to be a desperate effort to break us up. All the families have got up from Lima and there are a great number of teams gone to fetch up grain. The last report gives 44 buildings burned and considerable grain, furniture, clothing &c. belonging to the poor Brethren. The Sheriff J. B. Backenstos has issued his proclamation warning the mob to disperse and calling upon all the Law and order citizens to act as "posse commitatus" to preserve the peace.

It was decided in the council to offer some of our best property in the City for sale to respectable merchants in Cincinna[t]i, Phi[l]adelphia &c. judging it better for the safety of the property to sell out to such men than to leave it to the destruction of the mob. A great many sick were prayed for and we also prayed that

---

[147] Backenstos replaced Deming as Hancock County Sheriff.
[148] Chauncey L. and Francis M. Higbee were Mormons associated with Joseph Smith's martyrdom in *HC* 7:144-46.

the Lord would preserve us from the mob till the Elders can get their endowment. It was also agreed to turn more force of hands to the Temple even if it have to hinder the Nauvoo House.

[September 16, 1845. Tuesday.] . . . A committee of five viz. Peter Haws, Andrew H. Perkins, Erastus H. Derby, David D. Yearsley and Solomon Hancock were appointed to carry a letter to Col. Levi Williams[149] stating to him that if the mob would cease their destructive operations, it is our calculations to leave the country in the spring, and requesting Williams to return a written answer, whether they would desist or not. The letter was signed by President Young and others. About 7 o'clock Backenstos with an escort of from fifty to one hundred men started for Carthage to fetch B[ackenstos]'s family and Demings family to Nauvoo.

[September 17, 1845. Wednesday.] . . . We learned this morning that the person killed yesterday was Frank Worrell, the person who stood at the jail door when Joseph and Hyrum were killed beckoning the mob and urging them on.

[September 19, 1845. Friday.] . . . At 5 evening met with some of the Twelve and others at Bishop Millers house . . . Before council broke up President Young and the company kneeled down and he offered up prayers that the Lord would preserve his servants and deliver those who had been active in the mob that killed Joseph and Hyrum into our hands that they might receive their deserts.

[September 24, 1845. Wednesday.] . . . It is very evident that the time is come for this people to separate themselves from all gentile governments and go to a place where they can erect the standard and live according to the law of God . . .

[September 25, 1845. Thursday.] . . . P.M. at Dr. Richards with some of the Twelve and others. We offered prayers for the sick &c. and especially that the Lord will preserve us in peace to finish the Temple and prepare to depart West in peace.

[September 30, 1845. Tuesday.] Met the Council of Fifty at the Seventies Hall. Elders [Samuel] Bent [Alpheus] Cutler and

---

149 Vigilante leader.

[Reynolds] Cahoon presented their lists of families selected by them to go west. They have each got their companies nearly made up of one hundred families each. Pres. Young also appointed S[hadrach] Roundy, J[oseph] Fielding, C[ornelius] P. Lott, P[eter] Haws and Daniel Spencer to select and organize each a company. Isaac Morley has got his company about full. While in Council report was brought in that two officers had just rode into town and had come to the Mansion. President Young sent B. F. Johnson to find out what they were after. He soon returned and stated that they called for liquor but could get none. They then went to [John] Packs but could get none there. They finally got some at [Benjamin L.] Clapps and then went off in different directions. Word was brought in that an armed company were outside the City. President Young sent C[harles] C. Rich to see what they wanted. He soon returned and reported that Gen. [John J.] Hardin, Judge [Stephen A.] Douglas[150] and the troops had arrived on the Square near the Temple, and that Douglas was at Elder Taylor's wanting to see the Twelve or the authorities of the place. The Council was immediately adjourned and the Twelve with one or two others went over to Elder Taylors . . . P.M. at the Office recording minutes of the Council of Fifty.

[October 4, 1845. Saturday.] . . . At 9 o'clock met with the Council of Fifty at the Seventies Hall and kept minutes of the Council.

[October 5, 1845. Sunday.] At the office all day recording minutes of the Council of Fifty. Recorded 43 pages of a small record like this. Evening met at Dr. Richards . . . A letter from Backenstos covering a copy of a dispatch from Hardin to the mobocrats was read, after which prayers were offered as usual.

[October 6, 1845. Monday.] . . . went to the General conference in the Temple and kept minutes all day.[151] W[illia]m Smith was disfellowshiped from his standing in the quorum of the Twelve and from the office of Patriarch. A vote was taken that this people move to the West en masse and carried, also that we all use our

---

[150] Douglas was a member of the Quincy Committee which advised the Saints to depart from Illinois (see *HC* 7:449–51).

[151] The first meeting in the Nauvoo temple was held on the previous day, October 5, 1845 (*HC* 7:456–57).

efforts to the utmost of our ability with our means and property to take all the poor with us.

[October 7, 1845. Tuesday.] . . . Evening met at Dr. Richards . . . We offered up prayers as usual especially that the Lord in his providence would cause the Governors troops to leave this County, and preserve the saints from the ravages of the mob.

[October 10, 1845. Friday.] . . . We councilled together on the best plan to be resorted to in the present emergency. It appears [General] Hardin has pledged himself to the mob that he will come to Nauvoo with his troops and either have O. P. Rockwell, and some others of the brethren or "he will unroof every house in Nauvoo." Three hundred of our enemies have volunteered to come with him from Quincy and they expect to be joined by others on the way. There seems to be no disposition abroad but to massacre the whole body of this people, and nothing but the power of God can save us from the cruel ravages of the bloodthirsty mob. We concluded to plead with our heavenly father to preserve his people and the lives of his servants that the saints may finish the Temple and receive their endowment, and that the Lord will soften the hearts of the Governor [Ford] [General] Hardin, [W. B] Warren and others like he did the heart of Pharoah that we may have peace this winter and depart in peace.

[October 11, 1845. Saturday.] . . . We had prayers in the forenoon and asked God to overrule the movements of the enemy and cause the Governor to withdraw his troops from this county, and preserve us in peace untill we can depart in the spring.

After prayer we went to prepare a circular for the agents to take abroad with them. P.M. President Young did not attend, being completely worn down with fatigue. At 4 we adjourned till 7. I went up to the office and attended to some little items of business. At 7 met again at Elder Taylors with the brethren. We offered up our prayers for the same subjects, believing that the Lord will defeat our enemies and preserve his people. After prayer we finished an extract from the conference minutes for the circular. Also appointed additional captains of hundreds, making Captains for twenty five companies.

[October 12, 1845. Sunday.] . . . At 7 met at Elder [John] Taylors with the brethren . . . We had prayers again as usual.

185

[October 14, 1845. Tuesday.] . . . At 8 went to Elder Taylors to write off the conference minutes with Brother [Thomas] Bullock . . . We offered up prayers that they might not be permitted to do any injury to any of the saints nor to interrupt our peace. They did not stay long, but returned accomplishing nothing, leaving us in peace.

[October 17, 1845. Friday.] . . . Evening met at Elder Taylors with the Twelve and others for prayer.

[October 19, 1845. Sunday.] At the office all day recording tithings. Brother [James] Whitehead and [John P.] McEwan told me that Bishop Whitney seemed very much dissatisfied because I had balanced up J[oseph] C. Kingsburys account without first asking them about it. I know of no reason why they should be dissatisfied unless it be because they don't like his account to shew on the book. He had been to work 10 months and has two dollars a day but is still $138. dollars in debt. Besides this he pays no rent, but this is paid by the Temple, neither does he pay anything for horse feed although his horse is kept on Temple feed and kept well. Besides this he has money when he asks for it and has the first pick at every thing that comes in on tithing. When we have sugar or honey he generally has more than twice as much as any other man and is treated as much better than any other man about the works as can be imagined. He has paid no tithing out of this years work and although he has work enough to keep him busy he can ride round when he has a mind to and all is right. He has no family, except Sarah Ann Whitney but he keeps an hired girl to wait on Sarah and a boy to wait on himself. Julia Durfee lives with him which makes the number of his family[152] and they take more to support them out of the Temple property than I have for my family although we are ten in number and I pay my own house rent and horse feed and pay for every thing I get. And when I asked for some flannel last week to make some flannel garments to wear this winter the Bishop hesitatingly said he supposed I could have it but finally said "wear cotton garments as I do." I have worked faithfully seven days in the week all this last season and frequently nights too, I have the same wages Joseph

[152] Kingsbury appears to have had five in his family.

has although I have been here near four years and when I recorded my tithing in full for my Sundays services which is one
seventh instead of one tenth day, the Bishop seemed some dissatisfied about this. Now on the reflection of all these circumstances, being virtually denied the flannel and found fault with
because I balanced Josephs account I could not help being grieved
and angry and I make this record that if ever the question should
arise in my absence as to the cause of my present feelings here it
is. Besides all this the Bishop has found great fault about the
Temple committee wasting property, but justice would bear me
out in saying that so far as I ever saw the Temple committee were
more prudent in this respect than has been practice for the last
year past. The Bishop's boys [Newel] Whitneys and [George]
Miller's have free access to every thing in the store and when
there is sugar in the store they eat it and waste it fluently . . . As
a general thing the bishops have treated me as well as any other
man but I confess they treat [me] more like a servant than a
brother. I have endeavored under all circumstances to take as
little notice as possible of all these things but they sometimes
force themselves on me and gall my feelings, especially to think
that Joseph who has only been here ten months can fare so much
better than the rest of us, and has a family of only himself and
Sarah except their hired hands to wait on them. I respect Bishop
Whitney as I do my own father but this does not make me insensible of feeling to see so much of what I consider to be unjust
partiallity and especially when I reflect that there has been so
much complaints of others for doing precisely the same things.

This morning Elder O. Hyde preached in the Temple afterwards Wm. Smith was cut off from the Church by unanimous
vote. He has published a pamphlet against the Twelve.

[October 20, 1845. Monday.] . . . General James Arlington
Bennett[153] from Arlington House Flat Bush Long Island arrived
today and met the Twelve and others at Elder Taylors in the
evening. I was present part of the time. It appears he was opposed to our selling out to gratify the mob, and would rather we
would fight them and maintain our ground, but when he was

---

[153] Joseph Smith's choice for running mate for the U.S. presidency in 1844,
disqualified by foreign birth and replaced by Sidney Rigdon.

informed of our ultimate plans and matters to be accomplished, he seemed to feel very different. I should judge him to be a very ambitious and a[s]piring man. After the interview, we retired upstairs and had prayers as usual.

[October 21, 1845. Tuesday.] . . . Brother Whitney told me (unasked) that I could go to Davis's and get the flannel I wanted. He seems to feel agreeable and I presume he don't know that his is the cause of my grief . . .

Evening met the brethren at Elder Taylors and had prayers. The council wrote a letter to Judge [James] Ralston inviting him to come here. He says he thinks he can bring a hundred Catholic families to buy out some of our propertys.

[October 22, 1845. Wednesday.] . . . Evening had a talk with Bishop Whitney and learned that he had not said the words as were told to me but the language he had used was altogether different and unexceptionable. He stated that he had had it in his heart for some time to raise my wages half a dollar a day. We had a long talk and I was satisfied his language had been misrepresented to me. Afterwards, went to Elder Taylors to counsel with the Twelve and others. Read a letter from R[euben] McBride in Kirtland stating that the Rigdonites, S. B. Stoddard, Jacob Bump, R[obert] D. Foster, Hiram Kellog, Leonard Rich [and] Jewel Raney are the leaders of the rioters.[154] They have broke into the House of the Lord and taken possessions of it and are trying to take possession of the Church Farm &c.

We also read a number of good articles from the New York Messenger relating to our troubles. After much conversation, we had prayers.

[October 24, 1845. Friday.] . . . Evening at Elder Taylors. We then had prayers as usual, and all felt that the Lord will deliver B[igelow] out of their hands. After prayer, it was decided that Mary Smith and Emma have all the wood they want off the church land. Also that we establish an agency over the river to receive and take care of tithing grain until spring so that when we move we can take it as we go. It was recommended that J[ohn] E. Page be appointed for that agency if he will do it. It was decided

154 Rioters in Kirtland, Ohio.

not to hire Pecks Mill, inasmuch as he wants $300 down for 6 months rent.

President Young seemed dissatisfied that Elder Taylor did not take more interest in our councils. We had to sit without a fire.

[October 25, 1845. Saturday.] . . . Evening met the brethren at Elder Taylors. Brother [Almon] Babbit related the circumstance of Father [Nathan] Bigelow shooting Lieutenant [] Edwards . . . We talked the matter over . . . and then offered up the signs and asked the Lord to overrule the matter and take it out of [Major] Warrens heart that he may not declare Martial law or otherwise let his hand be heavy upon him with judgment that he may not be able to bring trouble upon this people.[155] President Young seems quite unwell.

[October 26, 1845. Sunday.] . . . Evening met again at Elder Taylors, and had prayers as usual.

[October 27, 1845. Monday.] . . . About 4 P.M. Elder [Almon W.] Babbit returned and the council were immediately summoned together . . . The watchful care of our heavenly father in directing the matter last Saturday evening was plainly visible. .. We felt last night to return thanks to God for his kindness and ask him to overrule this matter also for the safety of his people and his servants.

[October 28, 1845. Tuesday.] . . . At 10 o'clock went to Elder Taylors and met to pray with John Smith, N. K. Whitney, W. W. Phelps, J. Young, O. Spencer, J. C. Kingsbury, and L. Woodworth. Afterwards at the office till 5 1/2 and then met again at Elder Taylors. After we got through with our prayers President Young came in and Elders Hyde and Babbitt . . . [Major] Warren[156] stated that when he came in with his troops on Saturday he had writs against the Twelve for "treason" but he considered it unjust to serve them, he considered that if the Twelve were to be harassed with writs, this people could not get away in

---

[155] Major Warren of the Illinois Militia sent five of his men to assist Nathan Bigelow in defending his house, which had been threatened. Bigelow shot a Lieutenant Edwards who had entered his house without announcing himself. Mormon leaders became concerned that Warren might use this incident as a reason to send in state troops to impose martial law (see *HC* 7:485-86).

[156] Major Warren was commander of the Illinois troops from Carthage (*HC* 7:487-488).

the spring, that from Elder Taylor's remarks, he understood that we meant that no writs of any kind should be served in Nauvoo but intended to resist. This was explained by President Young who told Warren that he was going to Springfield tomorrow and one part of his errand was to get his friends and relatives to come here and purchase some of our farms, for he was delighted with them. It appears that the Lord has softened his heart[157] in answer to our prayers for which we felt thankful.

[October 29, 1845. Wednesday.] . . . At 10 went to Elder Taylors. Soon after we arrived, President Young sent for Bishop Whitney and myself to go and see him as the Twelve are still out of sight. We went to where he was at A. P. Rockwoods and found him in company with H[enry] G. Sherwood and [Stephen] Markham, also George A. Smith and Amasa Lyman. Brother Sherwood and Fullmer returned from the West a few days ago. Brother S[herwood] reported their mission which was very satisfactory. He also gave us some very interesting information concerning our best route to the West which will be of service to us when we move.

There is a rumor that Wm. Smith and others are trying to get up an influence with the president of the United States to prevent our going West and has already wrote to him on the subject, revealing the acts of the Council of Fifty &c. and representing the council guilty of treason &c. . . . Evening at Elder Taylors with the Twelve and others . . . We had prayers as usual.

[October 31, 1845. Friday.] . . . Evening met the Twelve and others at Elder Taylors for prayer. The subject of the United States endeavoring to prevent our removal West by taking out U. S. writs for the Council of Fifty was talked over and plans devised to defeat them in case they undertake to do it.

[November 3, 1845. Monday.] . . . Evening met at Elder Taylor's with the Twelve and others . . . I was sick and did not stay long.

[November 6, 1845. Thursday.] . . . Evening attended council at Elder Richards.

---

157 Major Warren's.

[November 9, 1845. Sunday.] . . . Evening met at Dr. Richards with the Twelve.

[November 11, 1845. Tuesday.] . . . At 4 P.M. met at Dr. Richards with the Twelve.

[November 14, 1845. Friday.] . . . Evening met with the Twelve at Dr. Richards.

[November 17, 1845. Monday.] . . . My heart is grieved to see the difference of spirit, feeling and courses of Bishops [Newel] Whitney and [George] Miller. They appear to be at antipodes with each other in nearly all their operations. They have placed me as a mark for both to shoot at, and it has placed me in a very unpleasant situation. Miller seems angry with me because I appear to give preference to Whitney and which I consider I ought to do inasmuch as he is the Senior Bishop and is far more careful in his management than Brother Miller is. The latter is perfectly wasteful and wild in his business transactions and if he had the management of the Temple business alone he would soon wind it up and scatter it to ruin . . . At 5 met the Twelve at Dr. Richards.

[November 21, 1845. Friday.] . . . Evening met the Twelve at Dr. Richards and had prayers. Backenstos came in and stated that [Major] Warren has sworn he will have the men who murdered [Edmund] Durfee [Jr.] brought to justice.[158]

[November 22, 1845. Saturday.] At the office all day, made a deed from [William] Marks to the Trustees for the Kirtland property.

[November 23, 1845. Sunday.] . . . Afterwards I went to council. Received a letter from Uriah Brown saying that he sent the Encyclopedia to my house previous to his removal.

[November 29, 1845. Saturday.] . . . Evening at President Youngs with The Band. President Young, H. C. Kimball, Joseph Young and Levi W. Hancock danced a french four[159] together.

---

[158] Edmund Durfee was allegedly shot by an armed mob on Saturday, November 15, at Green Plains in Hancock County, Illinois, as he was trying to save burning homes. Major Warren was attempting to quell with his troops mob violence, which had begun in the latter part of 1845. See *HC* 7:145n, 523-31.

[159] "French four" is a colloquial reference to a Quadrille or square dance of

The two former are the only two of the first twelve apostles who have never wavered since their appointment and the two latter are the only two of the first presidents of seventies who have never faltered. During the day the Twelve, Bishops Whitney and Miller and some others met in the Temple and laid the carpet on the main floor of the attic story, and also on several of the small rooms ready for the first quorum to meet in.

[November 30, 1845. Sunday.] At 10 A.M. met in the attic story of the Temple with President B. Young, H. C. Kimball, W. Richards, P. P. Pratt, John Taylor, Orson Hyde, George A. Smith, and Amasa Lyman of the Quorum of the Twelve.[160] Also N. K. Whitney and George Miller presiding Bishops, John Smith Patriarch and President of the Stake. Joseph Young president of the Seventies. Alpheus Cutler, and [Reynolds] Cahoon Temple committee. Cornelius P. Lott, Levi Richards, Jos. C. Kingsbury, Orson Spencer, Wm. W. Phelps, Isaac Morley, L. Woodworth. Composed some verses to the tune "Here's a health to all good lasses" before the brethren assembled. At about 12 o'clock we clothed and sung "Come all ye sons of Zion &c." We then offered up the signs of the Holy Priesthood and repeated them to get them more perfect. I was requested to keep minutes. President offered up prayers and dedicated the Attic story, the male room and ourselves to God, and prayed that God would sustain and deliver from the hands of our enemies, his servants untill they have accomplished his will in this house. Elder Taylor then sang "A poor wayfaring man of grief &c." after which we again offered up the signs and Elder Kimball prayed that the Lord would hear and answer the prayers of his servant Brigham, break off the yoke of our enemies and inasmuch as they lay traps for the feet of his servants, that they may fall into them themselves and be destroyed, that God would bless his servant Joseph Young, heal his wife and bless his family, that God would bless and heal Elder Kimballs family and put the same blessings on all our families which he had asked for Joseph Young and himself.

Hans C. Hanson the door keeper reported that there were

French origin performed by four couples positioned to form the sides of a square: antecedent to the American square dance.

[160] First meeting of the quorum in the Nauvoo Temple.

two officers waiting at the foot of the stairs for President Young. The President concluded that he could bear to tarry up in the warm as long as they could stay in the cold waiting for him. Brother Amasa Lyman requested hands to be laid on him that he may be healed. Five of the brethren laid hands on him.

We again offered up the signs and Joseph Young prayed that our enemies may have no power over our leaders. He prayed for our brethren in England, on the Islands, Brothers Babbit, Turley and Reddins, also that the Trustees may have means to liquidate all the debts.

At 3 o'clock we undressed.[161]

The side rooms are occupied as follows. The 1st on the south side by President B. Young. The 2nd by H. C. Kimball. 3rd and 4th others of the Twelve. 5th Joseph Young and presidency of 70's. 6 is a preparation room. On the north side 1st Bishops and Lesser Priesthood. 2nd, President of the Stake and High Council. 3 and 4, High Priests quorum. 5, Elders Quorum. 6 Preparation room.

Hans C. and Peter O. Hanson are appointed to see to the fires, keep watch and guard the doors &c.

[December 4, 1845. Thursday.] . . . Went up into the Temple. The brethren are very busy preparing the room for work . . . Evening met with the first quorum in the Attic story of the Temple for prayer.

[December 6, 1845. Saturday.] . . . 5 P.M. met the brethren in the Temple for prayers.

[December 7, 1845. Sunday.] In the Temple all day. All the first quorum with one or two exceptions were present both male and female. About 1 o'clock we clothed.[162] Dressed in ceremonial robes and aprons. The meeting was opened by prayer by Joseph Fielding. After which Elders Taylor, Hyde, Phelps, Pratt and John Smith each expressed their feelings in regard to our present privilege of meeting in the Temple in spite of the combined opposition of men and devils. During the speaking, the Bishops having provided Bread and Wine, the bread was broke by Brother

---

[161] From their priesthood robes.
[162] Dressed in ceremonial clothing.

Kimball and then blessed by him and handed round by Bishop Whitney. Joseph Young then blessed the wine which was also passed around by Brother Whitney. President Young then addressed the company. He said the time would come when the Celestial law would be put in force and that law forbids any man taking the name of God in vain. But we have men in our midst who do not scruple to say by God, by Jesus Christ, God damn you &c. and the time will come when the law will be put in force on all such. He gave much good instruction and the spirit of God rested upon him. He stated "that a few of the quorum had met twice a week ever since Joseph and Hyrum were killed and during the last excitement, every day and in the hottest part of it twice a day to offer up the signs and pray to our heavenly father to deliver his people and this is the cord which has bound this people together. If this quorum and those who shall be admitted into it will be as diligent in prayer as a few has been I promise you in the name of Israels God that we shall accomplish the will of God and go out in due time from the gentiles with power and plenty and no power shall stay us." After the exhortation we offered up the signs and had prayers for the usual subject. Joseph Young being mouth.[163] We were then dismissed until next Sunday at 11 o'clock.

[December 8, 1845. Monday.] . . . At 5 went to the Temple and met the brethren for prayer, Geo. Miller being mouth.

[December 11, 1845. Thursday.] A.M. went to the temple. . . . I spent the forenoon writing the history of these proceedings in Elder Kimball's journal.[164] Also gave a description of the upper room.

At 12 President Young said I could go and fetch my wife if I had a mind to. I immediately went down and returned with her at 1 o'clock. I then went into the preparation room and was washed by Elder H. C. Kimball and George A. Smith, and then anointed a priest and a king unto the most High God by President Young and Amasa Lyman and pronounced clean from the blood of this generation. . . .

---

[163] The one who prays for the group, or prayer circle.
[164] Clayton began recording activities associated with the Nauvoo Temple the day before, December 10, 1845.

President Young then called the following persons into Brother Kimball's Room viz. H. C. Kimball, P. P. Pratt, O. Hyde, John Taylor, Amasa Lyman, George A. Smith, John E. Page, N. K. Whitney, George Miller and myself. The President stated that he had received a letter from brother Samuel Brannan stating that he had been at Washington and had learned [that] the Post Master General and Secretary of War were making preparations to prevent our going West, alleging that it is against the law for an armed body of men to go from the States to another government. They say the Mormons must not be suffered to remain in the States and neither will it do to let us go to California and there is no other way but to exterminate them and obliterate them from the face of the earth. We offered up the signs and asked our heavenly father to overrule them and inasmuch as the heads of this government are plotting the utter destruction of this people that he will curse them and let all the evil which they design to bring upon us come upon themselves.[165]

President Young said we shall go out from this place in spite of them. All the brethren felt agreed that God will deliver us from the grasp of this ungodly and modocratic nation.

[December 14, 1845. Sunday.] . . . Quite a number of the quorum assembled in the Temple and clothed at 11 o'clock. After singing and prayer the sacrament was administered by Isaac Morley and Charles C. Rich. President Young instructed the quorum concerning a number of items and proved that the office of seventies are higher than the office of High Priests or high Council. At half after one we offered up the signs and prayers, Elder Orson Hyde being mouth . . . At 2 o'clock also those new members who have been received into the quorum last week met in the Celestial room where they were instructed more fully into the Order of the Priesthood and their duty by W. W. Phelps and Parley P. Pratt.

[December 17, 1845. Wednesday.] . . . Brother Lucian R. Foster is now appointed to keep the Records of the endowment. Margaret came with me to the Temple this morning and received her washing and anointing. She was washed by Sister Patty

---

[165] United States reluctance to permit armed Mormons to enter Mexico or Oregon is further discussed in *HC* 7:544.

Sessions[166] and anointed by Sister Mary Ann Pratt wife of Elder Parley P. Pratt one of the Twelve. I conducted her through the remaining ceremonies and also received her through into the upper or Celestial department. I feel grateful for this privilege and for all the blessings I receive from day to day for the mercies of the Lord to me are great and many of them. I instructed Brother [Lucien R.] Foster in regard to keeping the Record and in the evening assisted Elder Young and Kimball to collect a list of brethren to come here on Saturday . . .

[December 21, 1845. Sunday.] . . . The brethren and sisters were instructed more fully into their duty by Elders A. Lyman, H. C. Kimball, George A. Smith and O. Hyde.

[January 11, 1846. Sunday.] . . . A.M. in the Temple with the Council of Fifty, arranging to make an early start West.

[January 18, 1846. Sunday.] In the temple with the Council of Fifty and also Captains of Companies.

[January 23, 1846. Friday.] . . . At 1 went to a council in the Temple with the Twelve, Bishops &c . . . Evening with [Newel] Whitney dividing goods purchased by [Erastus] Snow. [Bishop] R[euben] Miller reports that [J. J.] Strang is making heavy breaches in the church, and drawing many after him. In one place 30 families have left the church and gone with him. It is also rumored that many of the saints here are full of Strangism and talking [hard] in his favor. Among the rest are John Gaylord and Wm. A. Sangor who are openly advocating his rights to the presidency. I read a copy of a letter purporting to be wrote by President Joseph Smith on the 18th June 1844 in which he appoints Strang as his successor. The letter is a base forgery and is well calculated to deceive the simple minded and unfaithful.[167]

---

[166] A plural wife of Joseph Smith, whose daughter, Sylvia, also married the prophet (*HR* 6:234; Orson F. Whitney, *Life of Heber C. Kimball* [Salt Lake City: Bookcraft, 1945], 432; Patty Sessions's private journal, in Brodie, 445).

[167] J. J. Strang established a reorganized LDS church on Beaver Island in Lake Michigan. Denouncing polygamy as heretical, Strang was endorsed by the entire Smith family, except the prophet's widow, Emma. The Reorganized Church of Jesus Christ of Latter Day Saints separated out of the Strang movement, with Joseph Smith III, the eldest son of Joseph Smith, Jr., becoming its first president in 1860. See Van Wagoner, 74, 243–45.

It is also rumored that many are dissatisfied because the Twelve and some others are going West without taking the whole Church. This is a matter of impossibility and the saints have no cause for complaint. Amongst the rest are many of the Temple hands who are complaining much. The arrangements are made by which the whole church can go comfortably, but it is necessary that some men should go beforehand to prepare a place for the rest and the Twelve and some others have to go to save their lives, for there are plans laid for their destruction. My sister in law Lydia is in the way of apostacy. She went to Burlington last year but previous to her going she agreed to be sealed to me for time and eternity. She refused to be sealed to Joseph. While at Burlington she wrote pledging herself to her contract. When she came home she went out to fathers where she got entangled with my brother James and has resolved to marry him. She has lost her faith in the Church and is on the road to ruin, but so determined that no argument is of any use. The family feels sorry but cannot change her feelings. Her mother frets much about it.

[January 26, 1846. Monday.] . . . At 1 went to the temple with Ruth, Margaret and Diantha. We waited till about 8 o'clock before we could be waited on. We then dressed and then went into room No. 1 and were sealed to each other on the alter by President B. Young. Afterwards in No. 2 we received our annointing by H. C. Kimball and a number of others.[168] And afterwards Heber blessed us. I then took Ruth and Diantha home but Margaret tarried till morning.

[January 27, 1846. Tuesday.] . . . Evening with D[iantha].

[January 28, 1846. Wednesday.] . . . Evening at home.

---

[168] Here Clayton and three of his five wives receive their second anointings. As noted, his other two contemporary marriages, to Alice and Jane Hardman, would end in divorce (see n112).

Journal Three
Nauvoo Temple

1 8 4 5 - 1 8 4 6

O*n the day temple ordinances begin,*
Heber C. Kimball asks William
Clayton to help him keep a record of Nauvoo temple-related activities. Clayton
describes how the Saints hurry to perform the necessary rites prior to their
departure for the west.

[December 10, 1845. Wednesday.][1] This morning went up to
the Temple in company with my wife and sister [Sarah Ann]
Whitney.[2] The morning very fine and pleasant but cold. I arrived

---

[1] Heber C. Kimball began his journal of activities related to the Nauvoo
Temple on November 21, 1845. See Stanley B. Kimball, ed., *On The Potter's Wheel:
The Diaries of Heber C. Kimball* (Salt Lake City: Signature Books, 1987), xiii–xiv. On
December 10 the change in handwriting from Kimball to Clayton reveals when
Clayton begins to assist Kimball in keeping this record. Portions of this journal were
first published in 1883 by Helen Mar Whitney Kimball, "Scenes and Incidents in
Nauvoo," *Woman's Exponent*, 12 (1883-84): 26-74, and later in its entirety by Jerald
and Sandra Tanner, eds., *Heber C. Kimball's Journal: November 21, 1845, to January 7,
1846,* (Salt Lake City: Modern Microfilm Company, 1982).

[2] Clayton writes this entry in the first person, but he is describing Kimball's
visit to the temple with two wives. "My wife" refers to Kimball's first wife, Vilate.
"Sister" Sarah Ann Whitney, also Kimball's wife, secretly married Kimball on
March 17, 1845. She was formerly a plural wife of Joseph Smith. See Kimball,
111-12, n71. Continuing evidence of Kimball's voice appears in the subsequent list
of gentlemen invited to meet with Brigham Young in which separate references are

at 10 o clock and found a number of the brethren already present and some of their wives. President [Brigham] Young engaged himself, by fixing the curtains on the East Window. I assisted him with Sisters Kimball, Pratt and Whitney. About half after 10 o clock it was reported that priest [Hamilton] Tucker (Catholic) and his associates were below waiting an interview with the Twelve and Council. At 11 1/4 Mr. [Hamilton] Tucker and Mr. [] Hamilton were admitted into the upper room of the Temple accompanied by Bishop Joseph L. Heywood who gave the gentlemen an introduction to those present. The propositions of the council in regard to the sale of our property were presented to Mr. Tucker in writing who read them over and then handed them to Mr. Hamilton who also read them. The gentlemen were then invited into President Youngs room with myself, President Young, Willard Richards, Orson Hyde, John Taylor, Amasa Lyman, John E. Page, George A. Smith, P[arley] P. Pratt, George Miller, John M. Bernhisel, Joseph L. Heywood, W[illia]m Clayton. Mr. Tucker made some observations respecting the two Main Rooms of the Temple. He thought they were so high it would be difficult for a speaker. President Young replied and explained in regard to that matter, also the pulpits, place for the Organ &c. and also the side rooms. Mr. Hamilton asked a question as to the disposal of our public buildings. In answer to which Elder Hyde read aloud the written propositions and offered some explanations. A conversation then followed between Mr. Tucker, President Young and Elder Hyde on the subject. President Young remarked that we wish to realise from the sale of our property, sufficient to take all our poor with us in a comfortable manner.[3] If he was alone he could take his rifle and make his way to the Pacific with little difficulty but at the same time he don't wish to do it. He would rather have his wagons and go with all the rest of the Church comfortable.

Mr. Tucker said he thought it would be wisdom to publish our propositions in all the Catholic papers, and lay the matter plain before their people. He should also think it advisable for the Catholic Bishops to send a competent committee to asertain the value of our property &c. at the same time they will use all their

---

made to Clayton and "myself."

[3] The following spring Hyde reported an offer of $200,000 for the temple (Journal 4, "Pioneer Trek West," April 26, 1846).

influence to effect a sale as speedily as possible. He thinks they have men in St. Louis, New York and other Cities who could soon raise the amount we want, but the time is so very short, he dont know whether it can be done so soon. He then asked if we would be willing to have our propositions published in their papers. President Young replied we should have no objections providing it was understood that we reserve the right to sell when we had a chance. Elder P. P. Pratt thought it would be well to talk over the propositions and investigate them so as to have every thing perfectly and clearly understood. Mr. Hamilton wished to ascertain upon what conditions they could obtain two of our public buildings, one for a school and one for a Church. They intended to write to the Bishop and wished to be able to supply him with some information on this subject.

President Young said he was well aware that there were many men in the Catholic Church who could furnish all the money we want at once, but he supposed it was with them as it was with a Mr. Butler who owned a wealthy Bank and asked why he did not sign off more Bills. He replied it was a good deal of trouble to sign off the Bills. He supposed it was too much trouble for them to dig their money out of their vaults. But he wished it understood that while we make a liberal proposition to dispose of our property we must have the means to help ourselves away.

Mr. Tucker said their object was to write to the Bishop and enclose our propositions in his letter, at the same time advising him either to come himself or to appoint a committee of efficient men to come and value the property and enter into terms for a final agreement. He said the sum to be raised was large and the time very short to the first of April but he thinks it can be accomplished. He thinks they can be able to give us a decided answer by the 25th inst.

President Young said he would like to add a note to our proposals before it goes for publication to this effect that If they agree to our propositions we will lease them the Temple for a period of from five to thirty 5 years at a reasonable price, the rent to be paid in finishing the unfinished parts of the Temple, the wall around the Temple Block, and the Block West of the Temple, and keeping the Temple in repair.

The council agreed to the amendment which was accordingly added to the proposals and handed to Mr. Tucker.

Mr. Tucker seemed to give much encouragement that an arrangement would speedily be entered into, to accomplish what we want. Both the gentlemen seem highly pleased with the Temple and the City and appear to feel sanguine that the Catholics should get this Temple and vicinity.

About half past 12 they departed evidently feeling well towards us.

W. W. Phelps has been appointed door keeper this day in place of Elder George A. Smith who is engaged with matters of more importance. . . .[4]

At half past 3 o clock President Brigham Young, H. C. Kimball, John Taylor, P. P. Pratt, George Miller, Alpheus Cutler, Wm. Clayton, John M. Bernhisel and Lucien Woodworth retired to the Bishops room and consecrated 16 bottles of Oil which had been perfumed by Bishop Whitney for the purpose of anointing.[5]

---

[4] To preserve the continuity of Clayton's record, I have deleted the following text in Heber C. Kimball's handwriting: "At one o'clock Lucy Smith the Mother of the Prophet and Agness the wife of Don C. Smith, and Elizebeth Ann Whitney took dinner with me and wife being the first time that the Old Lady went in to the Attick. Mother Smith says that she eats very heartily. Sister Marry the widow of Hirum the Patriarch also Mercy R. Tomson, Robert Tomson's widow, took dinner with us."

[5] The Nauvoo Temple ordinances began on this date. These rites had been revised several times since the simple washings and anointings performed in 1836 in the Kirtland Temple, which has been called "a preparatory temple . . . built before the nature of temple ordinances was revealed" (Joseph Fielding Smith, "Temples and the Sacred Rites Therein," *Utah Genealogical Magazine*, 21 [April 1930]: 53–57). Joseph Smith introduced the first revision on May 4 and 5, 1842, in the upper story of his Nauvoo Red Brick Store. Nine men participated in this new ceremony: James Adams, Heber C. Kimball, William Law, William Marks, George Miller, Willard Richards, Hyrum Smith, Newel K. Whitney, and Brigham Young—all of whom were freemasons. Smith "instruct[ed] them in the principles and order of the Priesthood, attending to washings, anointings, endowments, and the communication of keys . . . " (Joseph Smith, Jr., et al., *History of the Church of Jesus Christ of Latter-day Saints*, ed. B. H. Roberts, 2d ed. rev., 7 vols. [Salt Lake City: Deseret Book, 1963], 5:1–2; hereafter *HC*; see also Introduction, n73). A year later the endowment was again revised to include the second anointing and celestial marriage for time and eternity. That same year, 1843, women were first included in this holy order or "Quorum of the Anointed." By the time of Joseph Smith's death, sixty-five persons had been admitted to this exclusive prayer circle. Most are listed in Journal 2, "Nauvoo, Illinois," September 3, 1844. See Andrew F. Ehat, "Joseph Smith's Introduction of Temple Ordinances and the 1844 Mormon Succession Question," M. A. thesis, Brigham Young University, 1981, 101; David John Buerger, "The Evolution of the Mormon Temple Endowment Ceremony," *Dialogue: A Journal of Mormon Thought*, 20 (Summer 1987).

At 1/4 to 4 Elder Hyde came into my room and brought tidings that our Sheriff J[acob] B. Backenstos was clear and acquitted.[6] The jury said if there had been no witnesses only on the part of the state it would not have required two minutes to have made up their verdict. They have got two of the mob witnesses in jail for perjury and Backenstos is gone to Springfield to request the Governor to withdraw his troops.

At 3 o clock Sister Mary Ann Young and Vilate Kimball, Elizabeth Ann Whitney, commenced washing and anointing each other being the first in this holy Temple of the Lord.[7] This was done in the preparation room in the North West corner of the Attic story. About the same time President Young put up the vail[8] in its place which things finish and complete the Celestial Room preparatory to the endowment . . . [9]

At 25 minutes past 4 o clock President Young and Heber C. Kimball commenced washing Elder Willard Richards.

About 5 o clock Isaac Morley and his wife Lucy Morley came in. And about half past 5, Joseph Fielding and Joseph C. Kingsbury, C[ornelius] P. Lott. We continued washing and anointing those present till about 7 1/2 o clock.

At 20 minutes to 8 o clock President Young announced that all things were now ready to commence and go through with the ordinances. He said that after we get properly organized and ready to go on without confusion, no person will be permitted to talk, nor walk about in the main rooms, neither would any person be expected to be in the Celestial room only those who were necessary to carry on the work. At the same hour he took the chair and appointed P. P. Pratt and John Taylor to assist him in taking those through who were now prepared. W. W. Phelps acted as serpent[10] . . . These went through all the ordinances untill they

---

[6] Backenstos was charged with having ordered Orrin Porter Rockwell to shoot Frank A. Worrell, leader of an anti-Mormon mob (*HC* 7: 541).

[7] Washing and anointing formed a preparatory ritual for individuals engaging in temple endowments for the first time.

[8] The "vail" (antiquated spelling of "veil") represents the transition between the present world and the one that is promised after death.

[9] The persons present at this first temple endowment ceremony are listed in *HC* 7:541-42.

[10] The temple ceremony began with a narration of the "Garden of Eden" story in Genesis. Shortly after the ceremonies were first administered in Nauvoo, actual participants published contemporary accounts. At that time the roles of Adam and

were passed through the vail at which time it was half past nine o clock.[11] President Young then called all present into the Celestial room where we kneeled down and Amasa Lyman offered up prayers.

Some of the brethren and sisters then retired home and the rest continued washing and anointing and taking through the whole ordinance until half past 3 o clock in the morning . . .

After all was lead through those present offered up the signs of the Holy Priesthood and offered up Prayers. Elder Orson Hyde gave praise to the Most High for his goodness. H. C. Kimball presides as Eloheem, Orson Hyde as Jehovah and George A. Smith as Michael and N. K. Whitney as the serpent. See 4 pages further.[12]

[December 11, 1845. Thursday.] I will now give a description of the way the attic Story is finished. The main room is 88 feet 2 inches long and 28 feet 8 inches wide. It is arched over, and the arch is divided into six spaces by cross beams to support the roof. There are 6 small rooms on each side the main room about 14 feet square each. The last one on the West end on each side is a little smaller. The first room on the South side beginning on the East end is President Brighams Room, the second Elder H. C. Kimball the third Orson Hyde, P. P. Pratt and Orson Pratt the fourth John Taylor, Amasa Lyman, J. E. Page and G. A. Smith the fifth Joseph Young and presidents of Seventies. The sixth is a preparation room for the male Members.

On the North side, the first from the East end is for Bishop

Eve were taken by those being initiated, while an officiating elder took the role of the serpent (Satan). See Increase McGee and Maria Van Dusen, *A Dialogue Between Adam and Eve, The Lord and the Devil, Called the Endowment* (Albany, NY: C. Killmer, 1847). Subsequently the theatrical part of the endowment ceremony was dramatized for the initiates to watch. Over a century later, in 1955, the dramatization was filmed for portrayal in endowment ceremonies (see Buerger).

[11] Names of those participating in the endowment ceremonies will be omitted and replaced by ellipses throughout this journal. Clayton recorded lists of the participants from December 10, 1845, through January 7, 1846. The *History of the Church* provides daily totals of endowments through February 7, 1847, about the time the Mormons began to leave Nauvoo and cross the Mississippi River. A comparison of Clayton's records and those in the *History of the Church* suggests a total of five to six thousand endowments performed in the Nauvoo Temple (*HC* 7:542–580).

[12] After the following description of the temple, the portrayal of temple ceremonies continues four pages ahead at the notation, "see 4 pages back."

Whitney and the lesser Priesthood; the second for the High Council. The third and fourth president George Miller and the High Priests quorum. The fifth the Elders Quorum and the sixth the female preparation Room.

The main room is divided into apartments for the ceremonies of the endowment. Beginning from the door at the West end is an all[e]y about 5 feet wide extending to about 3 feet beyond the first Beam of[f] the arch. On each side of the Alley is a small room partitioned off where the saints receive the first part of the ceremony or where the man is created and a help mate given to him. From these rooms to the third partition in the Arch is planted the garden, which is nicely decorated and set off with shrubs and trees in pots and Boxes to represent the Garden of Eden. In this apartment is also an altar. Here the man and woman are placed and commandments given to them in addition to what is given in the creation. Here also after the man and woman has eaten the forbidden fruit is given to them a charge at the Alter and the first and second tokens of the Aaronic Priesthood. They are then thrust out into a room which is dark being the one on the North side between the fourth and fifth division of the arch which represents the telestial kingdom or the world. Opposite to this is another apartment of the same size representing the terrestrial kingdom and between these two is an alley about 4 feet wide. In the telestial kingdom, after the man has proved himself faithful he receives the first signs and tokens of the Melchizedek priesthood and an additional charge. Here also he vouches for the conduct of his companion. They are then left to prove themselves faithful, after which they are admitted into the terrestrial kingdom, where at the alter they receive an additional charge and the second token of the Melchizedek Priesthood and also the key word on the five points of fellowship.[13]

There are words given with every token and the new name is given in the preparation room when they receive their washing and annointing.

After received all the tokens and words and signs they are led to the vail where they give each to Eloheem through the vail and are then admitted into the Celestial Room.

---

[13] This was modified in April 1990 (see Introduction, n77).

The Celestial room occupies the remainder of the main room being the space between two divisions of the Arch. This is adorned with a number of splendid mirrors, paintings and portraits. On the East wall are the following Portraits viz. in the centre President Brigham Young and next to the left H. C. Kimball, Orson Hyde. To the right, Willard Richards, John Taylor and George A. Smith.

On the East side of the first division of the Arch in the centre is the portrait of L. N. Scovil, next to the right is George A. Smith, next John Smith the Patriarch. To the left is Bathsheba Smith, and Mother Lucy Smith.

On the West side of this partition in the centre is the portrait of [] to the left H. C. Kimball and Caroline Smith. To the right [] William Collier, John L. Smith.

On the East side of the second division in the centre stands a brass clock over which is a splendid portrait of the late Hyrum Smith and next to the right C[harles] C. Rich, George Miller and Clarissa Smith. To the left Sister Rich, next Mary Catherine Miller and last Leonora A. Taylor.

There are also a number of maps. A large map of the world hangs on the North side wall, and three maps of the United States and a plot of the City of Nauvoo hangs on the West partition. On the South wall hangs another large map of the United States, besides a number of large mirrors and paintings.

In the centre and body of the Celestial Room are two splendid tables and four splendid sofas. Also a small table opposite the large Window on the East end of the room on which stands the Celestial and terrestrial Globes.

All the rooms are nicely carpeted and has a very splendid and comfortable appearance. There are a number of handsome chairs in it.

Brigham Young and wife, H. C. Kimball and G. A. Smith, also Sister Mary Smith, Mercy R. Thompson, W. W. Phelps and his wife tarried in the Temple all night. We only obtained about an hour and a half sleep. In the morning Sister Young and the other sisters went home. Brigham Young and myself went to Joseph C. Kingsbury's and eat breakfast. We there had an interview with Willard Snow who has just returned from his Mission to Boston. From thence we returned back to the Temple and found several of the brethren had come in with the expectations of

receiving their anointings . . . We commenced a little before one
o clock. George A. Smith and myself washed the brethren and B.
Young and Amasa Lyman anointed them assisted by George Miller.
Sister Vilate Kimball and Elizabeth Ann Whitney attended to
washing the females. At 2 o clock they also washed and anointed
Mercy R. Thompson.

At 1 o clock Elder Orson Pratt came up into the room while
we were attending to washing and anointing. He has just returned
from his mission to the East and brought with him $400 worth of
six shooters.

See 4 pages back. The men were washed by G[eorge] A.
Smith and John Taylor, and anointed by myself and B. Young.
The sisters were washed and anointed by Sister Whitney, Mary
Ann Young and Elizabeth Ann Whitney.

About half past 1 o clock mother Lucy Smith arrived. The
weather is cold and some inclined to snow.

A little before three Sister Elizabeth Ann Whitney and my
wife got through washing the sisters . . .

The first charge was given in the garden by President Young,
the other two charges by H. C. Kimball, who also received most
of them through the vail and Amasa Lyman received the remainder . . . It was about 5 o clock P.M., when they commenced
washing and anointing these.

A little before six we commenced taking them through the
ceremonies, Heber C. Kimball acting as Eloheem, George A.
Smith as Jehovah, Orson Hyde as Michael, W. W. Phelps as the
serpent. We were also assisted by P. P. Pratt . . .

President having gone out some time ago returned while we
were in the garden. The signs and tokens were all given by H. C.
Kimball. He also received them through the vail. It was about
half past seven when we got through. Those last who were taken
through were then instructed farther regarding the signs by Elder
Orson Hyde.[14]

The President then called all those who were present into the
Celestial room. We formed a circle, offered up the signs, and
then offered up prayers for the sick; for our families and that the

---

[14] For further discussion of temple rites, see James E. Talmage, *The House of the Lord* (Salt Lake City: Bookcraft, 1962); and Buerger.

Lord would frustrate the plans of our enemies. Elder John E. Page being mouth.

After we got through President Young called the following persons into Hebers Room viz. H[eber] C. Kimball, P[arley] P. Pratt, J[ohn] Taylor, O[rson] Hyde, John E. Page, George A. Smith, Amasa Lyman, Newel K. Whitney, George Miller and W[illia]m Clayton. The President then stated that he had received a letter from Samuel Brannan saying that he had been at Washington and had learned that the Secretary of War and the heads of the government were laying plans and were determined to prevent our moving West, alleging that it is against the Law for an armed body of men to go from the United States to any other government. They say it will not do to let the Mormons go to California nor Oregon, neither will it do to let them tarry in the States and they must be exterminated from the face of the earth.[15]

We offered up the signs of the Holy priesthood and prayed that the Lord would defeat and frustrate all the plans of our enemies and inasmuch as they make plots and lay plans to exterminate this people and destroy the priesthood from off the earth that the curse of God may come upon them even all the evil which they design to bring upon this people. And that the Lord would preserve the lives of his servants and lead us out of this ungodly nation in peace.

After we got through there was a unanimous feeling that the Lord would answer our prayers and defeat our enemies. President Young said we should go away from here in peace in spite of our enemies.

It was now a little after 9 o clock and we soon after retired to our homes. President Young and Amasa Lyman tarried in the Temple all the night.

---

[15] In a subsequent letter to Brigham Young, dated January 12, 1846, Brannan explained: "It is the intention of the government to disarm you after you have taken up your line of march in the spring, on the ground of the law of nations, or the treaty existing between the United States and Mexico, 'That an armed posse of men shall not be allowed to invade the territory of a foreign nation.' " Although war with Mexico was imminent, Brannan was able to report on January 26 that the Mormons "will be allowed to pass out of the States unmolested" (*HC* 7:587–88). Clayton's January 6, 1846, entry cites Governor Ford's December 29, 1845 letter, which expresses concern that the Mormons might join with the British in the Rocky Mountains.

[December 12, 1845. Friday.] This morning I again went up to the Temple with my wife. The morning is very fine but cold. We arrived at a quarter to 10 and found several of the brethren already arrived and preparing for the washings of others who have been notified to attend. At a quarter after 10 A.M. we again commenced the washings and anointings to the presidents of the seventies[16] and their wives and also to Elder Orson Pratt and his wife . . . He was washed and anointed by George A. Smith and Amasa Lyman who did the washing and President Young and H. C. Kimball attended to anointing.

Sarah Marinda Pratt was washed and anointed by V[ilate] Kimball.

At half past 12 o clock all things being prepared to take these through the remaining ceremonies they commenced President Young acting as Eloheem P. P. Pratt as Jehovah Orson Hyde as Michael Wm. W. Phelps as the serpent H. C. Kimball assisted through the whole. President Young gave all the charges and received Orson Pratt through the Vail. The remainder of the men were received through by O. Hyde, the females by their husbands . . .

At a quarter after 3 P.M. President Young, H. C. Kimball, N. K. Whitney and Vilate Kimball went to J[oseph] C. Kingsbury's to dinner . . .

After prayers the following took their blankets and lay down to rest on the floor of the Temple where they tarried over night, viz. President B. Young, Amasa Lyman, George A. Smith, Wm. W. Phelps, Charles C. Rich, John D. Lee, David Candland. Elder Joseph Young and his wife tarried in his own room over night.

During the whole of the three days already spent in the endowment, President Brigham Young presided and dictated the ordinances and also took an active part in nearly every instance except when entirely overcome by fatigue through his constant labors to forward the work.[17]

---

[16] The office of "Seventy" in the Melchizedek Priesthood, first organized on February 2, 1835, constituted "traveling quorums, to go into all the earth, whither soever the Twelve Apostles shall call them" (*HC* 2:202 and n).

[17] The temple ceremonies were performed from memory until 1877 when Brigham Young decided they should be written. Wilford Woodruff wrote in his journal March 21, 1877 "Presidet Young has been laboring all winter to get up a perfect form of endowments as far as possible. They having been perfected I read

Perfect peace and harmony prevail during the whole time, except in one case which happened this afternoon, wherein Phebe Woodworth interfered with business which did not belong to her, and in the presence of those who are higher in authority than her, and undertook to dictate and control those who were legally and righteously appointed to superintend and adminster the ordinance of washing and anointing of the females.

[December 13, 1845. Saturday.] This morning President Young and Elder Lyman left the Temple for a little season and returned about a quarter after 10 a number of the brethren being already assembled and preparing to continue the ordinances. About the same time Elder H. C. Kimball and Vilate Kimball arrived and soon after P. P. Pratt, O. Hyde, O. Pratt, N. K. Whitney, Sister Whitney and others . . .

Last evening an arrangement was made establishing better order in conducting the endowment. Under this order it is the province of Eloheem, Jehovah and Michael to create the world, plant the Garden and create the man and give his help meet. Eloheem gives the charge to Adam in the Garden and thrusts them into the telestial kingdom or the world. Then Peter assisted by James and John conducts them through the Telestial and Terrestrial kingdom administering the charges and tokens in each and conducts them to the vail where they are received by the Eloheem and after talking with him by words and tokens are admitted by him into the Celestial kingdom . . . [18]

About 7 o clock a report came up that a person just from Springfield states that Lucien B. Adams, son of the late Judge Adams has effected a complete revolution in the minds of the inhabitants of Springfield, so much so that Judge Pope is convinced that Elder [Theodore] Turley is imprisoned through persecution and says he shall discharge him the moment he arrives at Springfield.

---

them to the Company today" (Scott Kenney, ed., *Wilford Woodruff's Journal* [Midvale, UT: Signature Books, 1983], 7:340).

[18] Clayton's entries from the last three days list four participants in the drama: Elohim, Jehovah, Michael, and the serpent (Satan). In Joseph Smith's theology, Elohim was the supreme God of the universe under whom the lesser gods Jehovah and Michael served. On this date, the New Testament characters Peter, James, and John are added to the script.

President Young has superintended the days business, himself generally taking an active part in the ceremonies . . .

Perfect peace, harmony and good feeling prevailed through the day.

About 10 o clock most of the brethren and sisters retired home except the following who slept in the Temple over night, viz. Wm. W. Phelps, Erastus Snow, David Candland, Henry G. Sherwood, Benjamin S. Clapp, Henry Herriman and Aaron Johnson.

After the brethren had mostley left the Room, W. W. Phelps draughted the following to be observed in this House under the dictation of the President.

RULES OF ORDER

Rule 1st. No person allowed to enter these apartments without changing or cleansing shoes in the Vestry.

Rule 2nd. No person allowed to wear his hat or cap, while in these rooms.

Rule 3rd. No person allowed to enter further than the reception or washing and anointing rooms till he or she has been washed and anointed.

Rule 4th. No person allowed to pass from one room to another while receiving the ordinances without being conducted by a superintendant.

Rules for those who have received the ordinances.

Rule 1st. No person allowed in the rooms without an invitation while in the hours of labor, excepting at the hour of prayer.

Rule 2nd. All persons who are invited are requested to remain in their rooms during the hours of labor.

Rule 3rd. At the ringing of the bell, all walking about, and loud talking, must cease.

Rule 4th. No person allowed to remove things from one room to another without permission of the owner, and to be returned immediately when done with.

[December 14, 1845. Sunday.] . . . Soon after 11 o clock those who were present were ordered by the president to clothe themselves, which being done and seated at 20 minutes after 11 o clock, sang, "Adam Ondi Ahman" &c. After which we bowed before the Lord and President Young offered up prayers. We next sang "Glorious things of thee are spoken" &c. When bread and

211

wine having been provided by Bishop N. K. Whitney Elders Isaac Morley and Charles C. Rich were called upon to administer the sacrament. They broke the bread which was then blessed by Isaac Morley and passed round by Charles C. Rich, who also blessed the wine and passed it round likewise.

We then sang, "O happy souls who pray" &c. and "Come all ye sons of Zion." After which President Young introduced the subject of having rules of order to govern all who come here and to regulate our works, printed. He wished to know the minds of the quorum whether they thought it best. It was voted unanimously that we think it wisdom to have some rules printed for that purpose.

It was also unanimously voted that President Young introduce the rules.

He then explained that he had some rules draughted last evening, but they were now at the office to be printed ready for tomorrow, he however explained the majority of them explaining also the order he wished carried out, and then took a vote whether this quorum will sustain him in this regulation.

The vote was unanimous in the affirmative.

He then observed that he should henceforth have all the cloth, which was intended for robes, garments and aprons, brought and either cut or made in this Temple under the superintendance of those who know how to do it right. There are now scarcely two Aprons alike nor two garments cut or marked right, and it is necessary to observe perfect order in this thing and it never can be done unless we take this course.[19]

---

[19] Brigham Young's concern for performing temple rites correctly appears again in Young's reminiscences of his own endowment. L. John Nuttall recorded on February 7, 1877: "Prest Young was filled with the spirit of God & revelation & said when we got our washings and anointings under the hands of the Prophet Joseph at Nauvoo we had only one room to work in with the exception of a little side room or office w[h]ere we washed and anointed had our garments placed upon us and received our New Name. and after he had performed these ceremonies. he gave the Key Words signs, tokens and penalties. then after we went into the large room over the store in Nauvoo. Joseph divided up the room the best that he could hung up the veil, marked it gave us our instructions as we passed along from one department to another giving us signs. tokens. penalties with the Key words pertaining to those signs and after we had got through. Bro Joseph turned to me and said Bro Brigham this is not arranged right but we have done the best we could under the circumstances in which we are placed, and I . . . wish you to take this matter in hand and organize and systematize all these ceremonies with the signs tokens penalties and Key words I did so and

A conversation then ensued on the distinction of office or power, between a president of Seventies, and a member of the High Council or a High Priest. It arose in consequence of some of the High Council having been washed and anointed by some of the presidents of Seventies and inasmuch as there had been some considerable difference in the views of the brethern in regard to the difference of authority between the High Council and Seventies, President Young concluded it would be wisdom to have the subject understood at this early stage of business so as to prevent any feelings or dispute arising on the subject hereafter.

He stated that the Seventies are ordained Apostles, and when they go forth into the ministry, they are sent with power to build up the Kingdom in all the world, and consequently they have power to ordain High Priests, and also to ordain and organize a High Council.

Some of the High Priests have been ready to quarrel on the subject, supposing they had power and authority above the Seventies, and some in their zeal for power, have abused and trampled on the feelings of some of the Seventies.

There is too much covetousness in the Church and too much disposition amongst the brethren to seek after power and has been from the beginning, but this feeling is diminishing and the brethren begin to know better. In consequence of such feelings Joseph left the people in the dark on many subjects of importance and they still remain in the dark. We have got to rid such principles from our hearts.

He then referred to the manner in which the corner stones of this Temple were laid as published in the Times and Seasons and then stated that the perfect order would have been for the presidency of the Stake to lay the first or South East corner. The High Council the 2nd or South West corner. The Bishops the North West corner and the priests the North East corner, but added the High Priests laid the South West corner, but they had no right to do it.

---

each time I got something more so that when we went through the Temple at Nauvoo I understood and Knew how to place them there. we had our ceremonies pretty correct" (L. John Nuttall diary, Harold B. Lee Library, Brigham Young University, Provo, Utah).

He then introduced the subject of the brethren making objections to any person being permitted to receive the ordinances, and added that when objections were made he should feel bound to determine whether the person making the objections was a responsible person, if he was not he should do as he pleased about listening to the objections, but if he was a responsible person he should then listen to the objections.

To make a man a responsible man he must have the power and ability not only to save himself but to save others, but there are those who are not capable of saving themselves and will have to be saved if they are saved at all by those who are capable of doing it. An objection from such would have no weight on his mind.

When a man objects to another receiving the ordinances, he becomes responsible to answer to God for that mans salvation. And who knows but if he received the ordinances he would be saved, but if we refuse to give him the means he cannot be saved and we are responsible for it.

There is no law to prevent any man from obtaining all the blessings of the priesthood if he will walk according to the commandments, pay his tithes and seek after salvation, but he may deprive himself of them.

After much important instruction from the president the signs of the Holy Priesthood were offered up and prayers, Elder Orson Hyde being mouth after which the company were dismissed till next Sunday with strict orders to be here and dressed precisely at 11 o clock.

At 2 o clock P.M. agreeable to appointment nearly all those new members who have received the ordinances the past week assembled in the upper department to receive instructions in regard to the ordinances and their duty to be observed henceforth and forever.

At the same hour President Young, H. C. Kimball, P. Pratt, O. Pratt, O. Hyde, J. Taylor, G. A. Smith, A. Lyman, N. K. Whitney, G. Miller, W. W. Phelps, Wm. Clayton and P[hineas] H. Young retired into President Youngs Room. The President appointed W. W. Phelps and P. P. Pratt to instruct the brethren and sisters now waiting, which was done and much good instruction given by them. They were especially instructed more fully into the nature and importance of the blessings and powers of the

Holy Priesthood which they have received, and it was enjoined upon them not to talk out of doors, but to be wise and prudent in all things.

They were also informed that no one will be admitted into these rooms during the time we are to work except those who are called to assist, unless they are invited by those who have authority.

At a quarter to 5 they were dismissed by blessing from Elder Taylor.

At the same time this was going on those who were in President Youngs room were listening to a number of letters which were read together with the report of the trial of J. B. Backenstos as published in the Peoria Register.

About 5 o clock nearly all the company having left the house President Young and others of the Twelve went down to the lower story of the Temple to council together on the arrangements of the Pulpits. The following persons remained and slept in the Temple over night, viz. President Young, A[lbert] P. Rockwood, J[ohn] D. Lee and David Candland.

[December 15, 1845. Monday.] At 5 minutes to 9 o clock A.M. commenced washing and anointing . . .

At a quarter to 10 o clock the president called the brethren together who had Volunteered to assist in administering the ordinances this day and made the following appointments, Amasa Lyman, Orson Hyde, George A. Smith, Lucius N. Scovil, Erastus Snow and Franklin D. Richards to administer in the upper and middle department, W. W. Phelps to officiate as the tempter. Also Joseph Young and Jedediah M. Grant to anoint the seventies. Samuel Bent and Isaac Morley to anoint the members of the High Council and High Priests. Benjamin L. Clapp and Henry Herriman to wash the members of seventies. And Charles C. Rich and Phineas H. Young to wash the members of the High Council and High Priests, John D. Lee and David Candland as clerks and to attend to fires in the rooms and upper apartment &c. Aaron Johnson, Benjamin L. Clapp, Elijah Averett and Henry Herriman to attend to fires in the washing rooms, also heating and carrying in water and assisting when needed in the washings.

At a quarter to 11 o clock the bell was rung and commenced receiving those washed and anointed this morning through the lower and middle departments, the following persons officiating, viz. In the upper department John Taylor as Number 1 Amasa Lyman as number 2 Erastus Snow as number 3. In the middle department. Orson Hyde as number 1 Franklin D. Richards as number 2 Lucius N. Scovil as Number 3 W. W. Phelps as number 4 And George A. Smith as prompter . . .

About half after 8 o clock the president made a selection of men to assist in the ordinances tomorrow and also a list of brethren to be here on Wednesday to receive their endowment.

At 20 minutes to 10 President B. Young, H. C. Kimball, Orson Pratt, John Taylor, Amasa Lyman, George Miller, George A. Smith, John D. Lee and Franklin D. Richards retired to President Young's room being clothed and having offered up the signs of the Holy Priesthood offered up prayers President Young being mouth. At 5 minutes after 10 o clock they dismissed part retiring to their homes and the following tarried and slept in the rooms viz. Wm. W. Phelps, Wm. L. Cutler, Elisha Averett, Hans C. Hanson, Peter O. Hanson, Franklin D. Richards, Joseph Young, Jane Young, Agnes M. Smith and David Candland.

As on the days previous the most perfect harmony and good feeling prevailed. President Young superintended and directed all the movements of the day also selected those who should come on Wednesday assisted by Elder Kimball.

The names of those selected to work tomorrow are as follows. P. P. Pratt, O. Pratt, J. Taylor, O. Hyde, A. Lyman, G. A. Smith, O. Spencer, L. N. Scovil, F. D. Richards and Aaron Johnson for the upper department. W. W. Phelps as Tempter. P. H. Young and C. C. Rich to wash the High Priests, S. Bent and J. Murdock to anoint the High Priests, B. L. Clapp and H. Herriman to wash the seventies; J. Young and J. M. Grant to anoint the Seventies, Elijah Averett, Jesse D. Hunter and H. Stout to carry in water and keep fires in wash rooms Elisha Averett door keeper and D. Candland and J. D. Lee clerks &c.

[December 16, 1845. Tuesday.] 8 o clock being the hour appointed for meeting President Young, H. C. Kimball, George A. Smith and some others were here at the time appointed the morning being very fine but cold.

At a quarter after 8 o clock A.M. commenced washing . . . At 9 o clock President Brigham Young, Heber C. Kimball, Orson Pratt, George A. Smith, Amasa Lyman retired to President Youngs

Room, and without dressing consecrated and dedicated a new horn which has been prepared for the anointing, praying that we may be permitted to use it for this purpose for many years to come and that the spirit and power of God may attend it whenever it shall be used.

At 20 minutes after 10 o clock A.M. President Young, Heber C. Kimball, Orson Hyde, Orson Pratt, George Miller, Amasa Lyman and George A. Smith clothed themselves and retired to President Youngs room and consecrated 13 bottles of Oil which had been prepared and perfumed by Bishops Whitney and Miller. After consecrating the Oil a letter which had been written by Elder Hyde was dedicated to God with prayer that the desired object may be accomplished by it.[20] At half after 10 they got through and undressed . . .

During the day the 29th quorum of Seventies brought in 44 bottles of Oil for the anointing which was delivered into the care of Bishop Whitney.

President Young has been very busy through the day, dictating the order of business, appointing men to work in the various offices and giving much important and beneficial instruction, at different intervals, in connection with Elder H. C. Kimball who has also taken a very active part in conducting matters . . .

Sisters Whitney and Kimball have been very busy through the day overseeing the washings and anointings in the female department, and instructing the Sisters in cutting and making robes and garments.[21]

---

[20] On December 17, 1845, just a week after Samuel Brannan had written that Washington would try to prevent their westward move into Mexico, the Saints wrote to U.S. government officials to gain support for the planned move west (*HC* 7:544, 547).

[21] The temple garments were undergarments sewn with various markings designed to remind the wearer to live circumspectly. See S. H. Goodwin, *Mormonism and Masonry* (Salt Lake City: Grand Lodge, F. & A.M. of Utah; 1938), 45–46. They were originally cut from unbleached muslin by Nauvoo seamstress Elizabeth Warren Allred under the supervision of Joseph Smith. The garment was designed to reach the ankle and the wrist; Emma Smith reportedly introduced collars. The design was subsequently modified to shorten sleeve and leg, close the crotch, and eliminate the collar. The standardized markings remained. See Eliza Mariah A. Munson, "Early Pioneer History"; Rose Marie Reid, "Oral History"; Heber J. Grant, Charles W. Penrose, and Anthony W. Ivins to church leaders, June 14, 1923; all quoted in Buerger.

President Young retired at 5 minutes past 7, and Elder Kimball at 17 M[inutes] past 7.

[December 17, 1845. Wednesday.] At 35 m[inutes] past 7, President B. Young came in, and at 9, appointed each man his particular duty for the day.

At 9, commenced washing . . .

At 20 minutes past 2 o clock P.M. Bishop Miller perfumed 45 Bottles of Oil after which the following brethren, viz. Heber C. Kimball, Orson Pratt, Amasa Lyman, George A. Smith, W. W. Phelps, and Joseph Young clothed themselves and retired to Elder Kimballs room, where after offering up the signs of the Holy Priesthood they dedicated and consecrated the whole for the anointing in the following order, viz: the first 6 Bottles, Elder H. C. Kimball being mouth 2^d 6 Bottles Elder Orson Pratt being mouth 3^d 6 bottles G. A. Smith mouth, 4th 6 bottles W. W. Phelps mouth 5th 6 bottles Elder Amasa Lyman Mouth 6th 6 bottles Elder Joseph Young mouth 7th 6 bottles H. C. Kimball mouth remaining 3 bottles Elder Orson Pratt mouth, after which they consecrated 2 Bottles to the healing of the sick. They then offered up prayers for the sick and other subjects, according to our daily custom, Geo. A. Smith being mouth, at 3 o clock they undressed . . .

About 6 o clock, P.M. President Young selected the following persons to work on Thursday and notified them to be present . . .

He also selected a list of names of persons to be present on Friday to receive their washing and anointing; and put the list into the hands of John Pack to give notice to the individuals. About 20 minutes past 10, about 16 or 18 persons assembled in the east room and sung a hymn, and joined in prayer with President Young. He slept in the Temple, also his son Joseph and 10 or 12 other persons.

[December 18, 1845. Thursday.] At 14 minutes past 9 o clock commenced washing and anointing . . .

At a quarter past 6 o clock President Young left the Temple for the purpose of going a short distance to marry a couple.

The Weather this day has been very cold, it being very difficult to keep comfortably warm in the Temple the wind blowing very strong from the North . . .

At 6 o clock a report came to President Young that Theodore Turley had arrived in town, being liberated on bail of 250 dollars for his appearance at court next term, provided a bill of indictment should be found, report brought by Henry W. Miller . . .

The exercises of the day being over, President Young retired to bed about 12 o clock.

In consequence of the great pressure of business during the week past it has been decided to devote Saturday to the purpose of washing the robes and other garments, which had been used in the business of initiating those who had come in through the vail, but there being a general desire in the minds of all those who had officiated in the ordinances particularly the Sisters, that the work should not cease, it was afterwards determined that the clothes should be washed this night, and it was accordingly done, by the labors of several sisters, taking up the greater part of the night.

[December 19, 1845. Friday.] President Young having slept in the Temple was present at the appointed time for commencing preparations, and soon afterwards proceeded to appoint men to the various stations . . .

President Young left the Temple a short time at 12 min[utes] past 11, in company with Bishop George Miller, and Reuben Miller, the latter intending to return to his home in the Eastern part of the State on special business. He soon after took his departure . . .

At 7 o clock the following persons met in Elder Kimball's room, clothed in priestly garments, and offered up thanks to our Heavenly Father for the deliverance of Theodore Turley and others, that were in bondage by our enemies.

At 20 minutes before 8 the following persons met in council in Elder Kimballs room and made a selection of High Priests to be washed and anointed, viz. B. Young, H. C. Kimball, Orson Hyde, Orson Pratt, Amasa Lyman, George A. Smith and George Miller. President Young asked the question, Is it wisdom to send Hosea Stout and Jesse D. Hunter to England? Elder Hyde answered that the people in Eng[land] expected that any one sent from America would be expected to be something more than ordinary. The subject was dropped at this point.

[December 20, 1845. Saturday.] President Young having slept in the Temple last night, was early at his post, and dictating in

219

relation to the business of the day, and arranging the workmen in order &c. &c. after which he listened to a reading from Captain Fremont's Journal[22] by Franklin D. Richards . . . The morning was a very beautiful one, the sun shining clear and bright, through the east window of the room in which the party were assembled. President Young's son Joseph was present also having slept with his father. Amasa Lyman came in during the reading, also Elder H. C. Kimball, at a quarter to 10. The reading was finished at 10 o clock, at which time Miss Eliza R. Snow handed in a list of the females washed this morning, which lists she has taken for several days past . . . President Young left the Temple about half past 4 o clock to be absent for the night.

At 5 o clock a meeting was held in Elder Kimball's room, present H. C. Kimball, Orson Hyde, P. P. Pratt, Amasa Lyman, George A. Smith, John Taylor, W. W. Phelps and George Miller. Clothed in priestly apparel, they offered up thanks to God and asked for the health of Bishop Whitneys child, also Elder Kimball's, and that God would away the wrath of this government from us and overrule all things for our good. Elder Kimball being mouth.

564 Persons have passed through, 95 this day.

[December 21, 1845. Sunday.] According to appointment on Sunday last, a meeting was held in the east room this day of all those who could clothe themselves in the garments of Priesthood, 75 persons were present, Elder H. C. Kimball presiding . . .

At 5 minutes before 11, the song "Glorious things of thee are Spoken" was sung. Father John Smith then made a few remarks, blessed the bread and it handed round by Bishop Geo. Miller, the Wine was blessed by Geo. Miller and handed round by him. While the wine was passing round, Elder George A. Smith arose and addressed the congregation. He thanked God for the privileges this day enjoyed and spoke of the difficulties under which the church had labored to attain the blessings we now enjoy. Another thing he thanked God for, already had more than 500 persons passed through, and therefore if half of them should be like

---

[22] As a second lieutenant in the Army Topographical Corps, John C. Fremont had explored the Oregon Territory and the Southwest in 1843–44. His team of explorers included mapmaker Charles Preuss, who produced an improved map of the American West. See Introduction, n90; Journal 4, "Pioneer Trek West," May 20, 1847.

the foolish virgins, and turn away from the truth, the principles of the Holy Priesthood, would be beyond the reach of mobs and all the assaults of the adversaries of the Church. Order was one of the laws of Heaven, then ought to be no whispering here, no difficulty ought to be mentioned, whatever transpires here ought not to be mentioned any where else.

When we pray to the Lord we ought to come together clad in proper garments and when we do so, and unite our hearts and hands together, and act as one mind, the Lord will hear us and will answer our prayers. Our garments should be properly marked and we should understand those marks and we should wear those garments continually, by night and by day, in prison or free and if the devils in hell cut us up, let them cut the garments to pieces also, if we have the garments upon us at all times we can at any time offer up the signs. He then related an instance of some children being healed and cured of the whooping cough in one night, through the prayers of himself and Elder Woodruff, in Michigan, while they were there on a mission. Said that whenever they could get an opportunity they retired to the wilderness or to an upper room, they did so and offered up the signs, and were always answered. It would be a good thing for us to put on our garments every day and pray to God, and in private circles, when we can do so with safety.

We are now different from what we were before we entered into this quorum. Speedy vengeance will now overtake the transgressor. When a man and his wife are united in feeling, and act in union, I believe they can hold their children by prayer and faith and will not be obliged to give them up to death until they are fourscore years old.

Sometimes mere trifles destroy the confidence which each ought to have in the other. This prevents a union of faith and feeling. The apostacy of Thomas B. Marsh was caused by so small a thing as a pint of strippings[23] and his oaths brought the exterminating order which drove us all out of Missouri. The woman ought to be in subjection to the man, be careful to guard against loud laughter, against whispering, levity, talebearing. He expressed his unfeigned love for his brethren, and his confidence in their endeavors to keep these rules.

---

[23] See *HC* 3:166-72.

"The Spirit of God" was then sung.

Elder Kimball next addressed the meeting. He concurred in all that had been said, the observation of these things is most essential. About 4 years ago next May nine persons were admitted into the Holy order 5 are now living. B. Young W. Richards George Miller N. K. Whitney and H. C. Kimball two are dead, and two are worse than dead.[24] You have not got all you will have if you are faithful and keep your tongue in your mouth. You are pronounced clean, but were you pronounced clean from the blood of this generation? No! not all of you, only some few who have deserved it. Females were not received when we first received the Holy order. Men apostatized, being led by their wives, if any such cases occur again, no more women will be admitted. He spoke of the Necessity of Women being in subjection to their husbands. I am subject to my God, my wife is in subjection to me and will reverence me in my place and I will make her happy. I do not want her to step forward and dictate to me any more than I dictate to President Young. In his absence I take his place according to his request. Shall we cease from loud laughter and mirth? Will you never slander your brother or sister? I will refer your minds to the covenants you have made by an observance of these things, you will have dreams and visions. In the coming week we will take through 100 a day, we want no man to come in here unless he is invited, or on business. Let those having cloth to make up send it here and we will make it up and put it to good use. Women should be appointed to attend to the washing and anointings of the High Priests wives. There is a large lot ahead. You are not yet ordained to any thing, but we have the clay here, it is mellow and we shall soon put it on the wheel.[25] If any brother divulges any thing we shall cut him off. We shall not be with you long. We cannot rest day nor night until

---

[24] Of the nine persons admitted to Joseph Smith's private prayer circle on May 4, 1842, five remained active in the church. In addition to these persons which Clayton notes as "living," the two deceased members are Hyrum Smith and George J. Adams, and the two disfellowshipped persons ("worse than dead") are William Law and William Marks, both part of the 1844 reform movement. For a discussion and listing of those who had participated in endowment ordinances prior to the Nauvoo Temple ceremonies, see Ehat, 102.

[25] The potter's wheel (Jer. 18:3) was a favorite metaphor of Heber C. Kimball.

we put you in possession of the Priesthood. We want you now to make up garments for yourselves. I want my own robe back again. If we have made you clean every whit, now go to work and make others clean. We will have a screw put up before the vail, and will make an office of my room, and have a stairway leading down from it. No person will be allowed to take people through the vail but those appointed.

Let women wait upon women and let men wait upon men, then no jealousies will arise. He closed at 5 m[inutes] before one.

Elder P. P. Pratt approved of what had been said and said a few words about the fashion of our robes, his own robe, which was like those first used, was not sewed up at the sides, neither was it of more than one breadth.

Elder Kimball showed the right fashion for a leaf,[26] spoke of Elder Richards being protected at Carthage Jail, having on the robe, while Joseph and Hyrum and Elder Taylor were shot to pieces, said the Twelve would have to leave shortly, for a charge of treason would be brought against them for swearing us to avenge the blood of the anointed ones, and some one would reveal it and we shall have to part some say between sundown and dark.[27]

George Miller said that when near the camp of Gen[eral] Hardin, he was shot at, and the Sentinel who was near him was killed, but he escaped unhurt, having on his garment. He then spoke of the design and purpose for which all the Symbols in the garden were given &c. Paul said he bore in his body the marks of the Lord Jesus Christ, which was as plainly as he dare allude to these things in writing. But the marks Paul alluded to were just such as we now have on our garments. He spoke of the signs, tokens and penalties[28] and of the work in general, said it was the work of God, by which he designs to reinstitute man into his presence &c.

---

[26] The temple aprons were embroidered with fig leaves.

[27] The oath of retribution or vengeance remained part of the temple ceremony into the twentieth century. The issue of whether it compromised Mormon loyalty to the U.S. government arose in the hearings to confirm Reed Smoot as Senator from Utah in 1903. See U.S. District Court, *The Inside of Mormonism: A Judicial Examination of the Endowment Oaths Administered In All The Mormon Temples* (Salt Lake City: The Utah Americans, 1903).

[28] These are described in Goodwin, 46-47. In April 1990 they and other parts of the ritual were removed from the endowment (see Introduction, n77).

Elder John Taylor confirmed the saying that Joseph and Hyrum and himself were without their robes in the jail at Carthage, while Doctor Richards had his on, but corrected the idea that some had, that they had taken them off through fear. W. W. Phelps said Joseph told him one day about that time, that he had laid aside his garment on account of the hot weather.

Elder Kimball said word came to him and to all the Twelve about that time to lay aside their garments, and take them to pieces, or cut them up so that they could not be found.

The Sisters ought not to gather together in schools to pray unless their husbands, or some man be with them, every evening at 5 o clock the High Priests meet for prayer by themselves. Clothed in their robes of Priesthood. Also the High Council and the Seventies.

There are from seven to twelve persons who have met together every day to pray ever since Joseph's death, and this people have been sustained upon this principle. Here is brother [Theodore] Turley has been liberated by the power of God and not of man, and I have covenanted, and never will rest nor my posterity after me until those men who killed Joseph and Hyrum have been wiped out of the earth.

Elder [Reynolds] Cahoon had permission to speak at 20 m[inutes] past one. He bore testimony of the importance of those things which had been spoken. He rejoiced in the idea that the things he was taught in the beginning, were the same things now taught and remembered, and it is so because they are eternal things.

The whole assembly were then formed into 2 circles one within the other, the signs and tokens were given, the proper attitude for prayer assumed, and Elder Taylor being mouth, the whole congregation united with him in prayer to God, at 10 minutes past 2 the meeting was dismissed and all unclothed themselves of their robes and another congregation which had been waiting in the vestibule of the temple was admitted into the east room, not being clothed in the garments of Priesthood.

At 3 o clock sung Hosanna. Prayer by Elder Orson Hyde, after which by invitation of Elder Kimball who presided (President Young not having been at the Temple today, and the duty of presiding having devolved upon Elder Kimball as the next in succession) Amasa Lyman, addressed the assembly. He said Doubtless with the most of the present assembly it is the beginning of a

new era, in their lives, they have come to a time they never saw
before. They have come to the commencement of a knowledge of
things, and it is necessary they should be riveted on their minds,
one important thing to be understood is this, that those portions
of the priesthood which you have received are all essential matters, it is not merely that you may see these things, but it is matter of fact, a matter that has to do directly with your salvation, for
which you have talked and labored many years. It is not for amusement you are brought to receive these things, but to put you in
possession of the means of salvation and be brought into a proper
relationship to God. Hence a man becomes responsible for his
own conduct, and that of his wife, if he has one. It is not designed
that the things that are presented today should be forgotten tomorrow, but remembered and practiced through all coming life.
Hence it is a stepstone to approach to the favor of God. Having
descended to the lowest state of degradation, it is the beginning of
a homeward journey. It is like a man lost in a wilderness and the
means with which we are invested here are to direct us in our
homeward journey. You then see the reason why you are required
to put away your vain ties, cease to talk of all those things which
are not conducive to eternal life.

This is why you are required to be sober, to be honest, that
you could ask and receive, knock and it should be opened, and
that when you sought for things you would find them. It is putting you in possession of those keys by which you can ask for
things you need and obtain them. This is the Key by which to
obtain all the glory and felicity of eternal life. It is the key by
which you approach God. No impression which you receive here
should be lost. It was to rivet the recollection of the tokens and
covenants in your memory like a nail in a sure place,[29] never to
be forgotten.

The scenery through which you have passed is actually laying
before you a picture or map by which you are to travel through
life, and obtain an entrance into the celestial kingdom hereafter.
If you are tempted in regard to these things here, you will be
tempted when you approach the presence of God hereafter. You
have, by being faithful been brought to this point, by maintain-

---

[29] A phrase found in Masonic dialogue. Compare the term "sure nail" in
Goodwin, 48.

ing the things which have been entrusted to you. This is a representation of the Celestial Kingdom. It is not merely for the sake of talking over these things that they are given to you, but for your benefit, and for your triumph over the powers of darkness hereafter.

We want the man to remember that he has covenanted to keep the law of God, and the Woman to obey her husband and if you keep your covenants you will not be guilty of transgressions. The line that is drawn is for you to maintain your covenants and you will always be found in the path of obedience, after that which is virtuous and holy and good and will never be swallowed up by unhallowed feelings and passions.

If you are found worthy and maintain your integrity, and do not run away and think you have got all your endowment you will be found worthy after a while, which will make you honorable with God. You have not yet been ordained to any thing, but will be by and by. You have received these things, because of your compliance with all the requisitions of the law, and if faithful you will receive more.[30]

You have now learned how to pray. You have been taught how to approach God and be recognized. This is the principle by which the Church has been kept together, and not the power of arms. A few individuals have asked for your preservation, and their prayers have been heard, and it is this which has preserved you from being scattered to the four winds.

Those who have learned to approach God and receive these blessings, are they better than you? The difference is, they have been permitted to have these things revealed unto them. The principles which have been opened to you are the things which ought to occupy your attention all your lives. They are not second to any thing. You have the key by which if you are faithful, you will claim on you and on your posterity, all the blessings of the Priesthood.

Elder H. C. Kimball said, The ideas advanced by brother Lyman are good and true. We have been taken as it were from the earth, and have travelled until we have entered the Celestial Kingdom and what is it for, it is to personify Adam. And you

---

[30] A reference to the second anointing rite which promises a place in the highest kingdom of the next world (Journal 2, "Nauvoo, Illinois," n58).

discover that our God is like one of us,[31] for he created us in his own image. Every man that ever came upon this earth, or any other earth will take the course we have taken. Another thing, it is to bring us to an organization, and just as quick as we can get into that order and government, we have the Celestial Kingdom here. You have got to honor and reverence your brethren, for if you do not you never can honor God. The man was created, and God gave him dominion over the whole earth, but he saw that he never could multiply, and replenish the earth, without a woman. And he made one and gave her to him. He did not make the man for the woman; but the woman for the man, and it is just as unlawful for you to rise up and rebel against your husband, as it would be for man to rebel against God.

When the man came to the vail, God gave the key word to the man, and the man gave it to the woman. But if a man dont use a woman well and take good care of her, God will take her away from him, and give her to another.[32]

Perfect order and consistency makes Heaven but we are now deranged, and the tail has become the head.

We have now come to this place, and all your former covenants are of no account, and here is the place where we have to enter into a new covenant, and be sealed, and have it recorded. One reason why we bring our wives with us, is, that they make a covenant with us to keep these things sacred. You have been anointed to be kings and priests, but you have not been ordained to it yet, and you have got to get it by being faithful. You can't sin so cheap now as you could before you came to this order. It is not for you to reproach the Lord's anointed nor to speak evil of him. You have covenanted not to do it.

One other thing. You all want to get garments, and you need not wait to get fine linen or bleached cotton for your garments.

---

[31] Mormon doctrine holds that God developed from an ordinary man (Journal 2, "Nauvoo, Illinois," n76).

[32] Priesthood holders with a higher calling would occasionally choose the wife of someone of a lesser calling or of a nonbeliever. Both Joseph Smith and Brigham Young practiced this teaching. See Richard S. Van Wagoner, *Mormon Polygamy: A History* (Salt Lake City: Signature Books, 1986), 37-46; Fawn M. Brodie, *No Man Knows My History: The Life of Joseph Smith* (New York: Alfred A. Knopf, 1966), 304, 442-44; Linda King Newell and Valeen Tippetts Avery, *Mormon Enigma: Emma Hale Smith, Prophet's Wife, "Elect Lady," Polygamy's Foe* (Garden City, NY: Doubleday, 1984), 100-101.

Shirting or sheeting will do for garments. The women can cut theirs from the cuts on their husbands. We dont want you to come here and take up the time to cut your garments. Go to a good faithful sister, and secret yourselves, and make your garments. We have been crowded too much and we have got to stop it. And if you have cloth, and come here to get your cloth cut, we shall keep it here to make use of it till we get through. We dont want one person that has come into the order the week past, to come into this room during the coming week except those who are to work. If you want any thing let it come in writing.

Elder George A. Smith made a few remarks. He spoke principally in relation to the importance of keeping sacred those Signs and tokens and principles which we had received while passing along through the different degrees.

He was followed by Elder Orson Hyde who said a few words in approbation of what had been said by Elder Smith and followed up in the same matters.

The congregation was dismissed by prayer by Elder John Taylor, and soon departed from the Temple to their respective homes.

At 5 o clock P.M. the following High Priests met for prayer, clothed in their Priestly Garments, viz: Geo. Miller, Winslow Farr, Lucien Woodworth, William Crosby, Cornelius P. Lott.

David Sessions, Gilbert D. Gouldsmith and Elam Ludington volunteered to draw water from the river in barrels for the use of the Temple.

Elder Kimball spoke of the confusion which had been in the house hitherto. None will be permitted to stand at the vail but the one that may be appointed by the President. You have been washed and pronounced clean, but not from the blood of this generation.

[December 22, 1845. Monday.] This week has been assigned principally to the High Priests, for them to come in and receive their washings and anointing. President George Miller was early at the Temple making preparations for the day's work. President B. Young was at the temple, having slept there the last night. Each department and station having been filled by appointment of President Miller, at 17 minutes before 9, commenced in the male department washing and anointing . . .

At 5 o clock the following High Priests met in room No. 8 viz; President George Miller, William Snow, John M. Bernhisel, Simeon Carter, Lucien Woodworth, Daniel Spencer, Erastus Snow, Winslow Farr, William Felshaw, Stephen Markham, and F[ranklin] D. Richards Lucien Woodworth being mouth.

At 8 o clock P.M., President Brigham Young, John Taylor, Amasa Lyman, Geo[rge] A. Smith, Orson Hyde, Lucien Woodworth and George Miller met in President Young's room and consecrated thirty seven bottles of oil which had been prepared by Bishop Miller, for the purpose of anointing those who are prepared by washing.

At Twelve o clock P.M. all retired except President B. Young, H. C. Kimball, Amasa Lyman, John D. Lee, Lewis Robbins, David Candland, Theodore Turley, H[ans] C. Hanson, Peter Hanson, H[enry] G. Sherwood; these slept in the Temple.

At 10 o clock commenced receiving into the upper department company No. 4. Joseph Young being prompter. They were received in the following order . . .

Ended at 15 min[utes] past 11.

[December 23, 1845. Tuesday.] The dry house of Gen[eral] Charles C. Rich's emigrating company No. 13 was burnt to the ground early this morning and about 300 dollars worth of spokes, felloes and other timber consumed. It was situated near the Seminary building formerly the Arsenal. Gen. Rich came to the Temple and reported himself ready for the duties of the day, but on account of the accident above mentioned was excused for the day.

The High Council met this morning in room No. 4 for prayer, being clothed in the garments and Robes of Priesthood. They offered up prayer and thanksgiving to God . . .

At 5 minutes past one, Almon W. Babbitt entered the Temple, was invited by President Young into his room. He brings report that officers from Springfield are here and several of the State troops after some of the Twelve, particularly Amasa Lyman . . .

At 3 o clock John Scott informed George D. Grant that an officer and assistants were watching for President Young and others at the front door of the Temple. Brother Grant carried the information to President Young, who soon devised a scheme by which their intentions to carry him off might be frustrated.

229

He directed William Miller who was present at the time, to put on Elder Kimball's cloak, and go down with Geo. D. Grant to his carriage, at the door. They accordingly went down, and as Mr. Miller was about to get into the carriage, with Elder Grant, the officer and 5 or 6 of his assistants arrested him, supposing it to be President B. Young. They were about to drive away with him, having made their boasts that they would get as many of the Twelve as they could, take them down to Warsaw, and have a new Years frolic killing them, but were persuaded to drive to the Nauvoo Mansion and tarry until tomorrow morning when the validity of the writ would be tested.

They were kept in profound ignorance of their mistake all the time. Esquire Babbitt takes the legal management of the case, and when they have stopped long enough to make a good tavern bill they will probably get their eyes open and put off . . .

Esquire Babbitt came in at 5 o clock and reports that the Officer who arrested Wm. Miller (supposing it to be President Young) has left the city, and gone to Carthage, with the prisoner, continuing ignorant of his mistake. Mr. Edmonds, a partner of Mr. Babbitts, has gone with them to act as counsel for the prisoner. The Officer has writs for B. Young, P. P. Pratt, H. C. Kimball, John Taylor, Geo. A. Smith, Amasa Lyman and T[heodore] Turley who are all charged with counterfeiting the coin of the United States with President Young . . .

At half past 7 o clock P.M. the following persons met in President B. Young's room clothed in sacerdotal garments and offered up thanks to God for his preserving care over them, in delivering them from all the snares of their enemies, and prayers that he would continue to do so. Their names are Brigham Young, Heber C. Kimball, John Taylor, Orson Hyde, George A. Smith, Amasa Lyman, and George Miller. Orson Hyde being mouth.

At 20 minutes past 8 o clock, President Brigham Young, H. C. Kimball, P. P. Pratt, George A. Smith and Amasa Lyman left the Temple, nearly at the same time, disguised with other mens Hats and Coats. The reason of this is that their enemies are seeking their lives charging them with high crimes &c . . .

Besides the persons whose names appear in the record of the proceedings of this day there are many others who have been very efficient in forwarding the work, and have attended at the Temple not only to-day but several previous days. There is much labor to be done in keeping the utensils and garments in order.

Some of the names are as follows, viz; Cherizade Averett, Jane Sherwood, Mary Ann Turley, Priscilla Turley, Cynthia Durfee, Alcina Durfee, Amanda Rogers. Henry Herriman takes the names and ages of the men, who are washed and anointed. Miss Eliza R. Snow takes the names of the women. John D. Lee, David Candland and L[ucien] R. Foster act as Clerks. Brother Hanson has been sewing tent cloth to-day.

A Staircase has this day been put up by which we can pass out through Elder Kimball's room No. 3, which has been converted into an office, for the convenience of transacting business with persons from without.

[December 24, 1845. Wednesday.] At half past 6 o clock, the High Council met for prayer in the attic story of the Temple room No. 4, the following persons present: Samuel Bent, Alpheus Cutler, James Allred, Geo. W. Harris, Newel Knight, Thomas Grover, Charles C. Rich, David Fullmer, Aaron Johnson and Ezra T. Benson. And being clothed in the Robes of Priesthood, offered up prayers to God for our prosperity, the preservation of the Twelve, for means to remove from this place, for the welfare of all the honest in heart, our wives and children &c &c Alpheus Cutler being mouth . . .

At 20 minutes past 12, William Miller who was arrested yesterday, came into the Temple, having been liberated from arrest at Carthage last evening, when they found out that he was not Brigham Young. He was not ill treated . . .

At 5 o clock P.M. President Young came in, and shortly after George A. Smith, Amasa Lyman and Orson Hyde came in, intending to meet for prayer, but not meeting with others whom they expected, several persons being at the same time in prayer in another room they retired in a few minutes . . .

All the Twelve have been absent from the Temple the greater part of this day except Orson Pratt, who has spent the greater part of the day here.

In the evening President Brigham Young, Elder H. C. Kimball, Orson Hyde, Amasa Lyman and George A. Smith came in, but did not remain long. They soon retired, but at about 20 minutes past eleven, President Young and H. C. Kimball came

231

in and remained the rest of the night. The labors of this day have been very arduous 122 persons having been washed and anointed and received into the upper department. It was expected that troops would be in, with officers and writs, for the purpose of arresting the Twelve, who are mostly charged with counterfeiting the current coin of the United States, but no signs of troops, writs or officers have appeared to molest our peace. The day has been moderately cold, and in the evening a light flurry of snow.

Sister Huldah Duncan, whose name is among those who were washed and anointed did not go through the vail being obliged to turn back on account of the illness of her little child. See account of persons passed through January 20th.

[December 25, 1845. Thursday.] Present President Brigham Young, H. C. Kimball, George Miller and others who were here yesterday, with some others. The morning is fine, the sun shining clear and bright upon the light covering of snow which fell last night . . .

At a quarter past 12 o clock George D. Grant brings word that the United States Marshall is in the city again. Elder Kimball sent a message to him by Elder Grant, and at 15 minutes before one, Elders Young and Kimball left the Temple . . .

At 5 o clock, President Young came into the Temple and remained about an hour overseeing and directing in relation to business generally . . .

At 20 minutes before 6 came into the Temple Amasa Lyman, and George A. Smith, Orson Hyde, John Taylor. At 10 minutes past 6, P. P. Pratt and Orson Pratt, and at 18 minutes past 6 President Brigham Young and Heber C. Kimball came in.

At 20 minutes before 7 the Twelve met in President B. Young's room, which is No. 1 for prayer and council. The following persons present, President Brigham Young, Heber C. Kimball, Orson Hyde, P. P. Pratt, John Taylor, Orson Pratt, Amasa Lyman and George A. Smith. After considerable conversation about the western country they united in prayer, and offered up the signs and tokens of the Holy Priesthood, Geo. A. Smith being mouth, and afterwards laid hands on President Geo. Miller, who was in ill health. Closed at 8 o clock.

The High Council met for prayer at 6 o clock, in room No. 4. Present, C[harles] C. Rich, Thomas Grover, Samuel Bent,

Newel Knight, George W. Harris, David Fullmer, James Allred, Ezra T. Benson and H[enry] G. Sherwood. Prayed for the prosperity and deliverance of the Twelve, and of the whole church &c.

The High Priests met in room No. 8 at 6 o clock, for prayer, present, Freeman Nickerson, Stephen Markham, W[illiam] Felshaw, Winslow Farr, Joseph B. Noble, L[ucius] N. Scovil, Charles Allen, A[braham] O. Smoot, Willard Snow, William Snow, Erastus Snow, Joseph W. Johnson, and F[ranklin] D. Richards. Stephen Markham was mouth . . .

At 20 minutes before nine it was announced to the recorder by Elder Kimball that the Twelve had decided in council, that George D. Watt should be sent to Scotland to preach the Gospel, and take his family with him . . .

All the above mentioned persons have taken part in the business of the day, more or less, the females, many of them have been cutting out garments and sewing on them, for the use of those who are to receive their washing and anointing.

The business of the day closed at about 20 minutes past 10 o clock, notice was given that no more washings and anointings would be attended to at present. President Young and H. C. Kimball, with some few others, remained in the temple all night.

[December 26, 1845. Friday.] No persons having been notified to appear to day to receive their washings and anointings very few persons were present in the morning. President Young and H. C. Kimball were present also Orson Pratt, no others of the Twelve, a few of those who had officiated in the washing and anointing and as door keepers, fireman, Marshall clerks, and so forth, and several of the women were present; those were all called together in the east room at about 11 1/2 o clock, and addressed by President Young. He told them there would be no business done to day, and that they were all dismissed, except the two Brother Hansons, Lewis Robbins and Brother Averett, whom he wanted for door keepers and John L. Butler for fireman. Also Sisters M[ercy] R. Thompson and Eliza R. Snow whom he wanted to do some sewing. We shall have no more washings and anointings at present, and if the brethren do not get any thing more than they have already got, they have got all they have worked for

233

in building this house, and if there is any more to be received it is because the Lord is merciful and gracious. We shall not have any business done, except that the High Council and the High Priests will meet together once a day as usual for prayer. They will come in the back way, through the office door. Room No. 4 belongs to the High Council, No. 6 to the High Priests, No. 8 to the High Priests. No. 10 to the Elders. President Young asked President Miller how many High Priests had been washed and anointed. President Miller could not tell at the moment, but directed the clerk of the High Priests quorum to ascertain. The number was found to be 268.

President Young said when he began again he should pay no respect to quorums. Every man that comes in is washed and anointed by good men and it makes no difference. Every man that gets his endowment, whether he is High Priest or Seventy, may go into any part of the world and build up the kingdom if he has the keys, or on to any island. We have been ordained to the Melchisedeck Priesthood, which is the highest order of Priesthood, and it has many branches or offices. And those who have come in here and have received their washing and anointing will be ordained Kings and Priests, and will then have received the fullness of the Priesthood, all that can be given on earth, for Brother Joseph said he had given us all that could be given to man on the earth.

I feel disposed to rest a few days, and let the Temple rest, and when I commence work again I am going to make a selection of my hands, and shall select those that will stay all the time. We will have no more cooking and eating going on in those rooms. No person will be allowed to come in unless they are invited, and I shall take it as an insult if they come and stay. I felt it impressed upon me to rest a few days and make these regulations, and as we have run out of oil we can't do much any way. I shall not have any more cutting and sewing of garments going on in the Temple. I shall have houses selected where garments can be cut and made. It is my right to receive persons through the vail, and it does not belong to any one else unless I put him there. When persons come into this house and receive the tokens, and signs and the key words, they have got all they have worked for in building this house. President Young closed his remarks as the Temple Bell rung for noon.

234

All those who were not retained for door keepers, clerks &c. then departed and the rooms were cleared of those things with which they had been cumbered.[33]

There was a necessity for a reformation of this sort, for some men were doing things which ought not to be done in the Temple of the Lord. Some three or four men and perhaps more, had introduced women into the Temple, not their wives, and were living in the side rooms, cooking, sleeping, tending babies, and toying with their women. The men who were guilty of these things were H. G. Sherwood, B. L. Clapp, L. N. Scovil, and perhaps others. There was also a great many men introduced and passed through the ordinances who were not so deserving as some that were passed by. There were also many women and children passed through who were not well entitled to the ordinances, while none of the sons and daughters of the Twelve had been permitted to enter.

There were also many persons lounging about, who had no particular duty to attend to, but who thought they had a right to be present, because they had once passed through the Vail. There was also a number of men taking their stations at the vail without permission of the President; considering it their right to receive through the vail any female whom they might introduce into the washing and anointing room, while it is evidently the sole prerogative of the President to officiate at that place or any one that he may authorize to do so. Inasmuch as while there, the person stands in the place of the great Eloheim.

At a quarter past 3 P.M. President Young and George Miller confirmed by the laying on of hands Robert B. Barnes and Norman Barnes who had been baptized this day.

At about 6 o clock in the evening, the Twelve, the High Council, the High Priests, and the Presidents of Seventies met for prayer, each quorum in its own room.

At about half past 6 Sheriff Backenstos came to the Temple, was admitted to the office, Room No. 3, by the back Stairs, had a conference with President Young, H. C. Kimball, Orson Hyde, P. P. Pratt, John Taylor, Amasa Lyman, and George A. Smith. He gave an account of the occurrences at Carthage, when William

---

[33] Encumbered.

Miller arrived there, said the United States Deputy Marshall was in town with writs for the Twelve and President Geo. Miller. He remained about half an hour and retired.

President Young and H. C. Kimball left the Temple at 8 o clock and did not return again during the night. Sisters Snow and Thompson have been sewing and Sisters Barns, Margaret Moon and Sophronia M. Harmon have been washing garments in the evening.

[December 27, 1845. Saturday.] This morning was a very pleasant one, being moderately cold, and the Sun Shining clear and bright in the heavens. None of the Twelve present at the Temple except Orson Pratt.

At 15 minutes past 10 o clock the United States Deputy Marshall, from Springfield, by the name of Roberts, came to the Temple in company with Almon W. Babbitt. He was freely admitted to every part of the Temple, to which he desired access. He went into the tower, on the roof, and into the Attic Story, passed through the various departments into the east room, where he very intently examined the portraits, and made enquiries as to whose they were, severally but obtained no correct information on the subject. He was requested to take off his boots in the preparation room, which request he complied with.

After remaining about half an hour he departed. At about 2 o clock he returned in company with Sheriff Backenstos, and a gentleman whom the Marshall introduced as from New Orleans. They visited the Middle room and the tower, and departed after about half an hour.

Doctor Bernhisel came in at about One o clock, and borrowed the "New York Sun" of Dec. 9th, 1845, which contains a letter said to have been written by Emma Smith, to the Editor.[34]

Brother Candland has been so fortunate as to find at Lathrops store this morning, some crimson Damask cloth,[35] and some fringe

---

[34] In this letter, which is of doubtful authenticity, Emma Smith expressed her disbelief in her late husband's "apparitions and revelations." She repudiated this in a second letter which was printed in the *Times and Seasons*, January 15, 1846 (Newell and Avery, 222–25).

[35] Damask cloth is a lustrous silk or linen fabric in figured weave, often of rose-pink color, used as table linen.

for covering the new Altar that is to be used in the further ordinances of the Temple.[36]

Sisters Mercy R. Thompson and Eliza R. Snow are engaged in preparing the covering. Sister Barns is engaged in ironing the garments that were washed last night. Lewis Robbins is cleansing and putting in order the washing Rooms and apparatus, Hans C. Hanson is sewing tent cloth together. Peter Hanson is translating the Book of Mormon into the Danish language. E[lisha] Averett is door keeper, J[ohn] L. Butler, Fireman. David Candland and L[ucien] R. Foster, as Clerks. Orson Pratt has been engaged in making Astronomical calculations. From several observations, he makes the latitude of Nauvoo to be 40.35' 48".

In the evening several of the Twelve came in, viz; President Brigham Young, H. C. Kimball, P. P. Pratt, Orson Pratt, Amasa Lyman, and George A. Smith, these met for prayer in President Young's room at 15 minutes before 7 o clock. Bishop Whitney was with them also. All were clothed in priestly garments. Elder John Taylor came in just as they were commencing their exercises, and without having clothed himself united with them in prayer. Elder Kimball being mouth. Elder Orson Hyde came in after they had finished, and was asked by President Young what made him always so late. He replied that the officers had been watching his house. The High Council met in room No. 4 at 6 o clock . . .

Prayed for President Brigham Young and all the Twelve, that they might be preserved from their enemies, that all the faithful Saints may be permitted to receive all the ordinances of the Lord's house, that the Lord will bless all the different quorums, for Father Smith and wife, for sister Isabella Smith and child, and Eliphalet Rogers, for the High Council, their wives and children, for means to enable us to remove from this place, also for the restoration to health of Sister Slade and brother Lish . . .

After the meeting was over in the room of President Young, Bishop N. K. Whitney counted out Two hundred dollars, which came in as tithing from Brother [] through the hands of Elder Orson Pratt.

A general conversation ensued, in which President B. Young, and all the Twelve above mentioned, and Bishops Whitney and

---

[36] They were preparing to introduce the temple marriage ceremony.

Miller, L[ucien] Woodworth, J[edediah] M. Grant and one or two others took part. The visit of the Marshall and California were the prominent topics. Elder P. P. Pratt read from Hastings' Book . . . [37]

President Brigham Young, H. C. Kimball, Amasa Lyman, George A. Smith, N. K. Whitney and a few others remained in the Temple all night.

[December 28, 1845. Sunday.] Meeting at half past 10 o clock this day in the attic Story of the Temple, for those who could clothe themselves in the garments of Priesthood. A very large congregation was present, the side rooms were some of them filled, the curtain was withdrawn and the other rooms besides the east room were filled. About 200 persons were present, clothed in priestly garments. President Young addressed the meeting, it having been opened by prayer by P. P. Pratt, and singing the songs of Zion, "The morning breaks the shadows flee" and "Come to me" &c. President Young came into the room at 1/4 before 12 M.[38] He said he supposed those present were a part of those who had received their endowment, that they were those who desired to be wise and do honor to the cause they have espoused, and bring no reproach upon the character of him who has given us of the things of his Kingdom liberally. The keys or signs of the Priesthood are for the purpose of impressing on the mind the order of the Creation. In the first place the name of the man is given, a new name, Adam, signifying the first man, or Eve, the first Woman. Adam's name was more ancient than he was. It was the name of a man long before him, who enjoyed the Priesthood.[39] The new name should be after some ancient man. Thus

---

[37] See *HC* 7:500. Lansford Hastings is described in Journal 4, "Pioneer Trek West," n65.

[38] 11:45 A.M.

[39] Toward the end of his life, Joseph Smith had taught that human beings descended from a race of gods, who are born, die, and conceive children to people other worlds. Brigham Young elaborated on this theme to teach that Adam was a god from a previous world and that he was the father of Jesus. Young taught that Adam was God, who, after creating the world, descended from his immortal status to become the first earthly man. Speaking of Jesus, Young queried: "Who did beget him? — His Father; and his Father is our God, and the Father of our spirits, and he is the framer of the body, the God and father of Our Lord Jesus Christ. Who is he? He is Father Adam; Michael; the Ancient of Days" (Discourse by Brigham Young,

with your ancient name, your modern name and the name that was last given you, you enquire concerning things past present and future.

After his fall, another name was given to Adam, and being full of integrity, and not disposed to follow the woman nor listen to her was permitted to receive the tokens of the priesthood.

I wish you to cease talking about what you see and hear in this place. No man or woman has a right to mention a work of the appearance of this building in the least; nor to give the signs and tokens except when assembled together, according to the order of the Priesthood, which is in an upper room. There are not a dozen persons that can give the signs and tokens correct, and the reason is that person would run to that vail, one of the most sacred places on the face of the earth, that had not understood the right manner of giving the signs and tokens.

The order and ordinances passed through here prove the principles taught in the Bible. First men should love their God supremely. Woman will never get back, unless she follows the man back, if the man had followed the woman he would have followed her down until this time. Light, liberty and happiness will never shine upon men until they learn these principles. The man must love his God and the woman must love her husband. The love which David and Jonathan had for each other was the love of the priesthood. God is a personage of tabernacle, the Son is a personage of tabernacle, the Spirit or Holy Ghost is also a personage, but not a personage of tabernacle, but is a personage of Spirit. God dwells in eternal burnings puts his hand through the vail and writes on the wall.[40] Any persons that goes through these ordinances, unless they cleanse their hearts and sanctify themselves, and sanctify the Lord, it will damn them. When we

---

February 19, 1854, Brigham Young Papers, LDS archives). See also *Journal of Discourses*, 26 vols. (Liverpool: Latter-day Saints' Book Depot, 1855-86), 9:286, 327; L. John Nuttall diary, February 7, 1877; and Boyd Kirkland, "The Development of the Mormon Doctrine of God," in Gary J. Bergera, ed., *Line Upon Line: Essays on Mormon Doctrine* (Salt Lake City: Signature Books, 1989).

[40] Brigham Young's metaphor of God reaching through the veil alludes to the Old Testament where Yahweh breaches the separation between heaven and earth and writes with his finger (Deut. 9:10), but it also recalls the position of the initiate in the endowment, who hears instruction about the tokens of the priesthood from an unseen officiator on the other side of the curtain who could but does not penetrate the narrow opening.

begin again I shall select those that are worthy. We shall not be able to have another public meeting here on account of the weight on the floor, it has already caused the walls to crack, prevents the doors from shutting, and will injure the roof. I see here 200 persons, all clothed in their garments, and tomorrow I suppose we cannot find half enough to work with, unless we lay an embargo on your garments, and forbid any of you carrying away your garments. When we began we could dress a company of 30. Now we cannot dress 18. For my right arm I would not say that every body is honest, for I do not believe they are.

The names of those who would volunteer to furnish a suit of garments, to be used by those who were yet to go through the ordinances was then taken . . . 32 in all, each of these agreed to furnish one suit of garments for Temple use.

It was decided that when the High Priests were washed and anointed they should find the oil, and the lights, and the Seventies do the same when they occupied the rooms, and the wood is to supplied as follows; 1000 men, or as many as can be obtained, to go to the islands and cut wood, and teams to go and draw it to the Temple until 1000 cords have been obtained.

Sung the hymn "Glorious things of thee are spoken". Prayer by Amasa Lyman asking a blessing on the bread. Bread passed round by Charles C. Rich and George Miller. Blessing on the wine asked by P. P. Pratt. While the wine was passing, sung the hymn Adam Ondi Ahman.

Elder H. C. Kimball cautioned the brethren and sisters against telling that the Twelve were in the Temple. P. P. Pratt said a few words to the same point.

Elder Kimball moved that no man tell his wife what he has seen. President Young said "all that are in favor of this signify it by holding your tongues when you go away from here." P. P. Pratt, "Contrary mind by the same sign."

Elder Kimball continued his remarks, alluded to the stories in circulation that several persons had been killed on their way through the ordinances, and that men and women were stripped naked here. Joseph said that for men and women to hold their tongues, was their Salvation.

A circle was formed, composed of about 20 persons, most of whom had received the ordinances, and been admitted to the first quorum at a previous time. They united in prayer. Elder John

Taylor being mouth. A hymn was sung, being led by [] Goddard, [William?] Kay and [Reynolds] Cahoon, notice was given that no more meetings would be held in the Attic story, for the present, and the congregation dismissed after prayer by Elder Orson Hyde.

The people soon retired from the Temple and no other meeting was held . . .

Three of the Dragoons stationed at Carthage came in with a man named Noah Miles, whom they wished to deliver up to the proper officers. He was charged with swindling several persons out of their property, such as horses and a waggon, pistol &c &c. They brought a letter from Major Warren, the commanding officer, the tenor of which was as above, the letter is on file among President Young's papers. This occurred just at dark, President Brigham Young and his wife and child, Elder H. C. Kimball and his wife and child, and several other persons remained in the temple over night.

The High Council met for Prayer at the usual time, about 6 o clock. President Isaac Morley, David Fullmer, William Huntington, James Allred, Alpheus Cutler, George W. Harris, Aaron Johnson, Thomas Grover, Ezra T. Benson and Newel Knight. Prayed for the health of H. G. Sherwood, Wm. Huntington, James Allred's wife, and a boy in his family, and for all the sick among the saints. For President B. Young, that he might have wisdom, and bodily and mental strength, and be able to lead his people.

[December 29, 1845. Monday.] . . . The carpets were taken up to some extent and shook, and the floors swept, stoves blacked, trees and shrubbery arranged in the garden, and a general arrangement of matters attended to in the morning. Sisters Thompson and Snow engaged on the drapery and cushions for the new Altar, Sisters Moon and Harmon sewing garments, Sisters Kimball, Young, Cutler and Cahoon, engaged in arranging the Furniture &c. in the east room.

Several men presented themselves at the dwelling of President George Miller this morning, some came in the house and enquired for him while others remained outside. It was suspected they were after him with a writ, and although President Miller was present and before them all the time no one knew him, neither did any of the brethren, several of whom were present seem to know where he was, and the suspicious individuals soon left.

241

At 2 o clock word was brought that a company of Soldiers were in, from Carthage. Brother Willmer B. Benson, clerk in the office of Doctor Willard Richards, the General Church Recorder and Historian brought in a book for revision, it being part of the Church History.[41] Elders George A. Smith and Amasa Lyman attended to the revision. Half past 2 o clock P.M. President Young, H. C. Kimball and President George Miller have been listening to Elder P. P. Pratt, who has been reading from Captain Fremont's narrative of a journey to California.

At 15 minutes past 3 o clock P.M. Noah Rogers, just arrived from his mission to the Society Islands, in the South Pacific ocean came in to the office, room No. 3 of the Attic Story of the Temple. He brought with him a Mr. Tower, a fellow passenger on board ship, whom he baptized. He brings a favorable report of the progress of the gospel on those islands. He came on foot from Paducah,[42] on the Ohio River.

The soldiers above mentioned proved to be 4 Dragoons. They came up the hill, went around by the east end and north side of the Temple, out of the yard by the north gate, and drew up in front of the house of President Geo. Miller. They made some enquiries of the women at the door and after a few moments passed on . . .

At 10 minutes before 6, President Young ordered the lights taken out of the stair case, as the troops were endeavoring to get into the Temple. It was soon after ascertained to be a false alarm. They were searching for hogs said to have been stolen from Mr. Hibbard . . .

The Twelve met for prayer in President Young's Room No. 1 at about half past 10 P.M. Present President B. Young, H. C. Kimball, Orson Hyde, P. P. Pratt, Amasa Lyman, John Taylor, and George A. Smith. They were dressed in their garments of Priesthood, as were all the others who have met this evening. They prayed for deliverance from their enemies and that they might be spared to give all the faithful Saints their endowment,

---

[41] Here, Clayton records part of the process of revising Joseph Smith's *History of the Church*, prepared in the first person from Smith's scribes' records and his own writing.
[42] Kentucky.

that they might be clothed with the power and have the keys of Priesthood. Orson Hyde was mouth.

After prayer was over, P. P. Pratt, G. A. Smith, John Taylor and Orson Hyde went home, Amasa Lyman laid down on a sofa. President Young and Elder Kimball went into the Tower and on to the roof of the Temple spent half an hour, and returned. And President Young spent near an hour reading Capt. Fremont's Narrative, after which he retired for the night.

[December 30, 1845. Tuesday.] The morning was pleasant, and at an early hour a very large number were at the Temple waiting for the washing and anointing, they having been notified the day before to attend at an early hour . . .

At half past 9 o clock, 18 bottles of oil which had been prepared with perfume, were consecrated for the anointing in President Young's room, the following persons of the quorum of the Twelve being present, and clothed according to the Holy Order, viz; President Brigham Young, Elders H. C. Kimball, Parley P. Pratt, Amasa Lyman and George A. Smith, also President Joseph Young of the Seventies. President B. Young was mouth, for the first 12, and George A. Smith for the other Six . . .

At 10 minutes before 11, John M. Bernhisel brought in a suit of garments for the use of the persons receiving their endowments. Robe. Garment. Apron. Cap. Moccasins and Socks . . .

At half past 11, Almon W. Babbitt came in and reported that the Marshall had left Carthage for Springfield, and there would be no more danger from Writs . . .

At 4 o clock, President Brigham Young left the Temple and was gone until 25 minutes past 5 o clock.

Bishop Whitney has been engaged in arranging some business matters with Almon W. Babbitt Esquire as counsel for the Lawrence Estate.

Bishop George Miller has been in the Temple all day, considering it unsafe for him to be out much on account of the writ said to be out for him.

P. P. Pratt has been engaged part of the time in forming a schedule for a pioneer company of 1000 men, to preceed the body of emigrants, find a proper location and put in seed early in the summer . . .

The labors of the day having been brought to a close at so early an hour viz; half past 8, it was thought proper to have a little season of recreation, accordingly, Brother Hans Hanson was invited to produce his violin. He did so, and played several lively airs, among the rest some very good lively dancing tunes. This was too much for the gravity of Brother Joseph Young, who indulged in a hornpipe, and was soon joined by several others, and before the dance was over several French fours were indulged in. The first was opened by President B. Young with Sister Whitney and Elder H. C. Kimball with Sister Lewis. The spirit of dancing increased until the whole floor was covered with dancers. After this had continued about an hour, several excellent songs were sung, in which several of the brethren and sisters joined. The Upper California was sung by Erastus Snow. After which Sister Whitney being invited by President Young, stood up and invoking the gift of tongues, sung one of the most beautiful songs in tongues, that ever was heard. The interpretation was given by her husband, Bishop Whitney, it related to our efforts to build this House, and to the privilege we now have of meeting together in it, of our departure shortly to the country of the Lamanites, and their rejoicing when they hear the gospel, and of the ingathering of Israel. Altogether, it was one of the most touching and beautiful exhibitions of the power of the Spirit in the gift of tongues which was ever seen. (So it appeared to the writer of this.) After a little conversation of a general nature, the exercises of the evening were closed by prayer by President B. Young, and soon after most of the persons present left the Temple for their homes . . .

They united in prayer, for the preservation of President Brigham Young and his Council from all their enemies, for the protection of the Church of God from all our enemies, and that our enemies might be frustrated in all their plans, for all the sick in the Church, especially Brigham Willard Kimball, Sisters Hyrum Smith and Huldah Nickerson, Brother Scotts two children and Brother Daniels and Andrew Smith, for means for our removal, for the blessing of God upon all our possessions &c &c.

[December 31, 1845. Wednesday.] The morning cloudy and the ground soft and muddy . . .

President Young and myself are superinting the operations of the day, examining maps with reference to selecting a location for the Saints west of the Rocky Mountains and reading the various works which have been written and published by travellers in those regions, also making selections of names of persons to come in and receive their endowments . . .

[January 1, 1846. Thursday.] This day is the first of another year; the morning is rainy, the ground very soft, and the mud very deep. A heavy mist rests upon the low ground under the bluff, the sun light is very dim being nearly shut out by the dark heavy clouds which overspread the whole face of the Sky, and every thing around wears a gloomy and dismal aspect. But notwithstanding the unfavorable appearance of things, the brethren and sisters are assembling together to the house of the Lord to receive their Washings and anointings. President Brigham Young came in at an early hour, having left the Temple about 6 o clock last evening in company with Elder H. C. Kimball.

The plasterers have commenced this morning to plaster the arched ceiling of the lower hall of the Temple, the floor is laid, the frame work of the pulpits and surrounding seats for the Choir and band, is put up and the work of fitting the room for dedication and holding meetings therein progresses very fast . . .

At 15 minutes before 10, the following persons assembled in President B. Young's Room, clothed themselves, and consecrated 14 bottles of oil, which had previously been perfumed, viz; President Brigham Young, Amasa Lyman, and George A. Smith, of the quorum of Twelve, and Joseph Young, Orson Spencer, C. C. Rich, Erastus Snow and Benjamin L. Clapp, after which they united together in prayer to God that he would preserve us from all the snares and traps that were laid by our enemies, that he would paralyze their power, and turn away their wrath, that we might have means and power to remove from this place, and for the continued prosperity of the Church, &c &c &c.

After this was over President Young had a short conference with Father Isaac Morley, who had been waiting to see him, for half an hour in the Office . . .

At 10 minutes past 3 o clock P.M. in President Brigham Young's room No. 1 in the Attic Story of the Lord's House, Truman Leonard Jun[io]r and Ortensia White were united in the bonds of matrimony, by President Brigham Young, and were sealed for time and for eternity, in the presence of George A. Smith, and Parley P. Pratt, as Witnesses.

At 6 1/2 o clock, the High Priests met in room No. 8 attic Story of the Temple . . .

Meeting opened by singing "Come all ye Sons of Zion" then prayer by Winslow Farr. President Miller gave instruction most beautiful to the mind, explaining the signs, tokens and names of the Priesthood after which they all offered up the Signs and united in prayer with President Miller who was mouth.

Several members of the High Council came to the place of meeting but the number not being large, and No President being there no meeting was held . . .

After a little time had elapsed, the whole company were assembled together in the east room, in number about fifty and all kneeled down upon the carpet and united with Elder H. C. Kimball in thanksgiving to God for his great mercy, and goodness to us in granting us this opportunity of meeting together in the House of the Lord, and in prayer to him that he would continue to bless us, that he would bless President Brigham Young, with health and wisdom, that he might be able to lead and direct this people, and that the same blessings might be extended to all his brethren of The Twelve, and on all the Saints, and that God would bless our wives and give unto them strength of body, that they might live and administer to the servants of God that they might see three score years and ten, and behold the kingdom of God established in the earth. And that we might be enabled to continue in Nauvoo in peace, until all the faithful Saints had received their endowment, and that when the time to leave here should arrive, that we might have those things that we need to enable us to go away in comfort, that to this end our possessions might look good to those who are round about us that they may buy them and pay us gold and silver, and such things as we need.

Also that God would bless our children, and all that pertains to us, and dedicating the whole company to God, gave him the glory through our Lord Jesus Christ. Amen.

William G. Young and Adelia C. Clark were then married by President Brigham Young, in the following order, viz; chairs were placed for them near the west side of the room by Phineas H. Young in which they were seated, and Brigham H. Young and Cedenia O. Clark officiated as Groomsman and Bridesmaid. President Young then asked the Groom if it was the understanding that they were to be married for time and for eternity and receiving an answer in the affirmative, asked the Bride the same question, and received the same answer. He then asked Hazen Kimball and his wife if the Bride's parents understood their intentions and approved of them and received the same answer. He also asked the Bride how old she was, and was answered that she would be 20 years old the 28th of this month. These questions having all been satisfactorily answered, he requested them to stand up, and they did so, and by his direction joined their right hands together. He then said nearly as follows, William G. Young, you take Adelia C. Clark by the right hand to be your lawful wedded wife, and promise, in the presence of God and Angels, and these witnesses to observe all the laws and obligations and duties pertaining or belonging to this order of the Priesthood, do You? to which the Groom answered Yes Sir. He then asked the same question or nearly so of the Bride, and received a like answer. He then pronounced them Husband and Wife, and sealed them together as such for time and for all eternity, and also sealed them up to eternal life, against all sins, except the sin of the Holy Ghost, which is the shedding of innocent blood, and pronounced various blessings upon them, and when he had done, told William to kiss his wife.

Two or three songs were then sung, and President Young invited the company to supper, which had been prepared in another part of the hall, viz; the garden. Bishop N. K. Whitney and his wife led the way, and were followed by about half the company, the table not being extensive enough to accommodate more than that number. Supper was soon ended and the sound of Hanson's violin and Brother Averett's flute in the east room gave notice that business of a different nature would soon be attended to. The floor was cleared of chairs and tables, and filled up with two sets of dancers, one on each side of the stove. After dancing a few figures, President Young called the attention of the whole company, and then gave them a message, of this import, viz; that this temple was a Holy place, and that when we danced, we danced unto the Lord, and that no person would be allowed to come on to this floor, and afterwards mingle with the wicked. He said the wicked had no right to dance, that dancing and music belonged to the Saints, and he strongly impressed upon the mind of those present the impropriety of mingling again with the wicked after having come in here, and taken upon them the covenants which they had. He spoke pointedly to his daughter Vilate and told her that if she should do so after this, she might expect to meet the frowns of a father who held the keys of the Priesthood. He was followed by L. R. Foster, who concurred in the remarks of President Young, and said he would like to have the question put, that it might be known how many of those present were willing to make a covenant to this effect, that they would not mingle with the wicked any more in their amusements. Elder H. C. Kimball said before the question was put he wished to say a few words. He felt thankful that President Young had touched this subject, and also that we had this opportunity of meeting together in this manner. Said that those who were parents had become responsible for the conduct of their children, and for his part he should not be willing that his children should meet with the wicked, or have any thing to do with their amusements. He said to his own children that they had covenanted here this evening, that they would receive the instructions, and listen to the counsel of their father and mother, and he hoped they would remember it.

Erastus Snow, expressed his feelings in a few words, said he had never attempted to dance in his life, until he came on to this floor, and he must say that since he had commenced he had enjoyed himself very well in the exercise, and felt grateful to God that he had the privilege.

The question was then put, the President invited all those who were willing to covenant that they would keep themselves from mingling with the wicked to rise upon their feet, whereupon all rose up. L. R. Foster said again, that he was willing to serve the Lord, and look to him for the things that were unnecessary, and do the work he had for him to do, if the Lord would permit him to enjoy himself in the dance once in a while. Hans C. Hanson enquired if it would be permitted for him to speak a few words on this occasion and receiving an approving nod from the President, said he had been in the habit of playing the fiddle for mixed companies among the wicked, and that in such companies he had always seen very ungodly conduct, that on a certain occasion he played for some who were called saints, but they went down to a Steam Boat and got about 25 passengers to join them, and said he, they wanted to get away all our gals, and there was very bad talk there, and that when he saw the saints enjoying themselves in the dance as they did the last night here, he made a covenant with himself that he would no more play the fiddle for the wicked, but that saints should have the use of his fiddle, and that when he went on a mission he would leave the fiddle with the Saints, and asked them if they would take care of it. They answered Yes.

The Spirit of the Lord was present, and the spirit of meekness and humility and gratitude to God, for the great privileges we enjoy, that tears came into the eyes of many of those present. Love and union, peace and harmony prevailed, the utmost decorum was observed, not a loud laugh, nor a rude jest saluted the ear. All were in the most perfect subjection to the word of the President, and when he told them at about half past 2 o clock that it was time to quit and seek repose the whole company assented without a murmur, although many would have been glad to have continued the exercise longer.

The sisters retired to the side rooms, and the brethren stretched themselves on the floor, or on the sofas and all were soon in the embraces of "tired nature's sweet restorer, balmy sleep," with the exception of the Bridegroom and Bride, and a few of their friends who, being unable to close their eyes in sleep, from the abundance of their joy, passed the short hours of the morning, in agreeable conversation, in the office . . .

[January 2, 1846. Friday.] The weather was clear and cold this morning, and the mud which was very abundant yesterday, was dried up this morning. At an early hour those who slept in the Temple were stirring, and large company had assembled in the vestry, waiting for their washing and anointing, although it had been supposed the work must cease for a short time for want of oil, but several bottles had been brought in for Temple use by various individuals so that by the time it was wanted, there were 17 bottles. These were perfumed, and consecrated for washing and anointing those who were invited to the Temple. The oil was consecrated, by the following persons who assembled together in room No. 4, clothed in their robes and garments. Viz; Amasa Lyman, Geo. A. Smith, Joseph Young, William Crosby, A. O. Smoot, C. C. Rich and F. D. Richards, they commenced at 20 minutes before One and continued 10 minutes, after which they united in prayer to God for the welfare of the

249

Church in general &c. and for the restoration to health of a few sick persons . . .

After the regular exercises and business of the day was over, and the meetings of the High Council and the High Priests were closed, we have some excellent instrumental and vocal music. Several members of the Band having been invited in by Elder Kimball, viz; Wm. Pitt, Wm. Clayton, J. F. Hutchinson, and James Smithies. They performed several very beautiful pieces of music and at the request of Joseph Young, played Fishers Hornpipe, upon which brother Joseph broke the gravity of the scene by dancing a hornpipe by himself. He was soon joined by John L. Butler, Ezra T. Benson and A[lbert] P. Rockwood. These danced until they were weary and sat down.

President B. Young then invited some one to join him in the dance and found a partner in Brother Chase, a french four was indulged in by these and others. After a short time, spent in dancing Elder Hyde made a short address, and requested those present to unite with him in thanksgiving and prayer to God, which they did. A new song, composed by Wm. Clayton called "Come go with me" was first sung by Clayton and Hutchinson, accompanied on the violin by Pitt, and on the Bass Viol by Smithies. When this was over, the address was made by Elder Hyde, and after the address and prayer, the President gave permission to any one to speak or pray, or shout, or speak in tongues. No one seemed disposed to use the opportunity, where upon the President arose and made a short address to those present, himself. Some of the topics which he spoke upon are as follows. He alluded to the privilege which we now have of meeting in this house, and said that we could worship God in the dance, as well as in other ways. He alluded to the ordinances of the endowment, and said they must always be attended to in an upper room. When we see a temple built right, there will be places for the Priests to enter and put on their robes, and offer up sacrifices, first for themselves, and then for the people.[43]

The way for us to grow and thrive is for us to serve the Lord

---

[43] Early Mormons believed in a literal biblical promise that the sons of Levi — a hereditary Old Testament priesthood in charge of escorting the Ark of the Covenant, which contained the Ten Commandments — would reenter the restored temple and perform sacrificial offerings to observe their covenant with Yahweh.

in all we do, and as we have called upon the different quorums to meet together once a day, so it will eventually be with the whole Church. There will be houses for them to meet in. Remember the Covenants that we have entered into. No man is to be filled with lightness. No brother or sister will be allowed to speak evil of his brother or sister, or speak against them. It is the duty of the quorums to meet together. We cannot enjoy it but a short time.

No person is at liberty to reveal any thing that takes place here to any mortal upon the face of the earth, unless they know that person to be a good one, and one that the Lord is well pleased with. We have not the privelege of telling what we have seen here to night, but we will praise the Lord as we please.

Now as to dancing in this house. There are thousands of brethren and Sisters that have labored hard to build these walls and put on this roof, and they are shut out from any opportunity of enjoying any amusement among the wicked, or in the world, and shall they have any recreation? Yes! Where? Why in the Temple of the Lord. That is the very place where they can have liberty, and we will enjoy it this winter and then leave it. And we will go to a land where there are at last no old settlers to quarrel with us, where we can say that we have killed the snakes and made the roads, and we will leave this wicked nation, to themselves, for they have rejected the gospel, and I hope and pray that the wicked will kill one another and save us the trouble of doing it.

We cannot have another public meeting in this room, for if we do our roof is ruined. But this church have obtained already all they have labored for in building this temple, but before we leave here, (I feel it in my bones.) there will be thousands and thousands of men that can go into any part of the world and build up the kingdom, and build temples. If any want to faint let them faint. If there are any that dont want to go with us, dont urge them.

The U.S. Government says if we let the Mormons go out from this Nation they will give us trouble. Well perhaps their fears will come upon them. Where is there a city of refuge, on the face of the earth but this. They have tried to break us up. But with all their officers, all their troops, and all their power we are here yet. They have got writs out for me, but they have not got me yet, and when they do get me they will get some thing else, I

251

assure you. From Polk,[44] down to the nastiest Bogusmaker, or whiskey seller, it was resolved to break up the Mormons this fall. And if I had hearkened to Col. Backenstos we should have broken up, and all put out of the way. But when he received correct instruction he acted right, and the plan and trap which our enemies laid for us, worked so that it gave us the advantage over them, and when he went according to counsel he came off victorious every time. And we are hunted, and persecuted, and our enemies try to trouble us every way. And now brethren will it hurt your feelings any if we dance a little. We need a little recreation. My mind is continually upon the stretch, because I know that this church must be saved. The Gospel must be preached to all the world. Temples must be built, and then add to this all minor matters. I tell you no man knows nor can know, the burden and responsibility that rests upon my mind, unless he experiences it. One thing I will do. I will do my utmost to break down every thing that divides. I will not have divisions and contentions. I mean that there shall not be a fiddle in this church but what has holiness to the Lord upon it, nor a flute, nor a trumpet, nor any other instrument of music, and if they will not make music exclusively for the Lord's house, they shall not play at all.

If Joseph Smith had lived we should not have been here at this time. We should have been in some other country. We can't stay in this house but a little while. We have got to build another house. It will be a larger house than this, and a more glorious one. And we shall build a great many houses, we shall come back here and we shall go to Kirtland, and build houses all over the continent of N. America. Last night we had some of our young folks here, some of our children, and they all covenanted that they would no more mingle with the wicked.

After closing his remarks he gave permission for all that wished to retire to do so. Many of the High Council, and High Priests were present, in all as many as forty, some of whom were perhaps at first a little doubtful as to the propriety of praising the Lord in this way, but probably their prejudices were dissipated, or removed, when they heard the remarks of President Young.

---

[44]James K. Polk, U.S. president, 1845-49.

[January 3, 1846. Saturday.] This was a clear and beautiful morning, the air comfortably warm. President Young having been up late last night did not rise very early. Elder Kimball was up somewhat earlier . . .

At 5 o clock, President Young came out of his room into the Large Hall. He has been quite out of health to day suffering from chills and fever, and pain in his bones &c . . .

[January 4, 1846. Sunday.] No public meeting was held in the Temple this day, on account of the floor being not stiff enough to support so large a company as would have come in, without swaying too much.

There was a council in President Young's room No. 1 at which the following persons were present, in the morning, viz; President Brigham Young, Elders H. C. Kimball, Orson Hyde, P. P. Pratt, Bishops N. K. Whitney and Geo. Miller.

Sisters Mary Ann Young, Vilate Kimball, Elizabeth Ann Whitney, Eliza R. Snow, Mary Smith, Mercy R. Thompson, and Sarah Ann Kingsbury were employed most of the day in working at the cushions for the new Altar.

In the afternoon, at 20 minutes past two, at a council held in President B. Young's room at which the following persons were present, viz; President B. Young, H. C. Kimball, Orson Hyde, P. P. Pratt, and Joseph Young, it was decided that David Candland be sent to England to preach the gospel. Brother Candland was present at the council, and of course was officially notified.

A letter was received this day, from Samuel Brannan in New York, also one from Pittsburg, signed Wm. W. Salt, both of which were answered, the one to Brannan under the signature of Brigham Young, the other was signed Willard W. Pepper, by David Mustard Clerk, both written by Elder Hyde.[45]

A copy of the New York Sun of Dec. 19, 1845, containing a letter from James Arlington Bennett to the Editor, in which he refers to a letter bearing the signature of Emma Smith, published in that paper on the 9th of Dec. was also received by President Young.

---

[45] This levity suggests familiarity with "Wm. W. Salt" of Pittsburgh.

Bennett's letter to the Editor contained some things which were considered as evidences that he was also the author of the letter signed Emma Smith, at least that idea was advanced by L. R. Foster, and was generally concurred in by those present, and was referred to in President Young's letter to Brannon . . .

[January 5, 1846. Monday.] This was a pleasant morning, and many persons were early at the Temple to receive their washings and anointings. President Young's health is almost restored. He was ready for duty at an early hour, spent the morning in hearing letters, and newspapers, and giving directions as to the business of the day . . .

A letter from William Smith to George D. Grant, was read to President Young and 10 or 12 others, this morning, by Brother Grant's permission. The letter was dated at Cincinnati, and was very scurrillous and slanderous . . .

The High Council met at 6 o clock. Present Isaac Morley Samuel Bent, James Allred, David Fullmer, H. G. Sherwood, C. C. Rich, Thomas Grover, Lewis D. Wilson, Newel Knight, George W. Harris, and Ezra T. Benson prayed for the preservation of President B. Young and his Council, and all the quorums, and for blessings upon all the Saints, the overthrow of our enemies, the healing of the sick that are among us, for blessings upon the house of Israel, and for our reception among them, and for all the saints abroad.

After the labors of the day were over, which was soon after nine o clock P.M. the violin and flute, played by brothers Hanson and Averett, in the east room, enlivened the spirits of the saints that were present, and they soon joined in the dance, during which the High Council adjourned, and the members thereof came into the room, and some of them, viz; Isaac Morley, Samuel Bent, James Allred, C. C. Rich, E[zra] T. Benson, C. C. Pendleton, Thomas Grover, and L[ewis] D[unbar] Wilson joined in. Efforts were made to induce Brother George W. Harris to join in it also, but his great gravity and superior wisdom forbade him to do so, and he thought that as he had not yet danced in his life, he would not begin at the present time. After continuing the dance until about 12 o clock, all retired except the few who generally remain over night. President Young left the Temple shortly after 12 and went home in his carriage. Elder Kimball also with his wife and William took their departure about the same time, for home. Also Bishop Whitney and his family.

[January 6, 1846. Tuesday.] . . . Elder H. C. Kimball came into the temple at 5 minutes before 11 o clock and in a few moments called upon all the others of the Twelve to unite with him in consecrating some oil for the anointing. The following persons therefore retired room No. 9, clothed themselves in the Priestly robes and garments, and consecrated 17 Bottles of oil, viz; P. P. Pratt, Amasa Lyman, J. M. Grant, A. O. Smoot, John D. Lee, George Miller, W. W. Phelps, and Joseph B. Noble, after consecrating the oil, they united in prayer.

At 20 minutes past 11, President Young came in with Mrs. Young, his health not very good, but being quite comfortable. He slept at home and dreamed the same dream three times in the course of the night.

Elder Babbitt came in at 15 minutes before 12, bringing a letter, written by Gov. Thomas Ford, to J. B. Backenstos, dated Springfield, Dec. 29, in which he refers, among other matters to the probability that the U.S. Government would send a military force to Nauvoo to assist in arresting the Twelve, who are charged with counterfeiting . . . [46]

At 6 o clock P.M. President B. Young and Heber C. Kimball with their wives Mary Ann Young and Vilate Kimball left the temple, to go to Elder John Taylor's to attend a party to which they were invited . . .

The Quorum of Seventies, met in room No. 9 clothed, and offered up prayers for the preservation of the Twelve and all the

---

[46] The letter of Governor Ford to Sheriff Backenstos read, in part: "You know that the impression has become pretty general that no officer can go with safety unattended to Nauvoo to arrest any of their principal men . . . This indictment in the U.S. court against the leading Mormons puts a new face on the matter. It will bring them and the United States for the first time into collision. It is impossible for me to guess . . . as to the course of Mr. Polk in the matter . . . I also think that it is very likely that the government at Washington will interfere to prevent the Mormons from going west of the Rocky Mountains. Many intelligent persons sincerely believe that they will join the British if they go there, and be more trouble than ever, and I think that this consideration is likely to influence the government." With this intelligence, the Twelve prepared to cross the Mississippi River before the ice broke up and, with a party of about two thousand, began the westward exodus. See *HC* 7:562-63, including note.

different quorums, and for the continuation of the blessings of the endowment.

After the business of the day was over the brethren and Sisters, indulged in a dance. The musicians were Hans C. Hanson, Jacob F. Hutchinson and Levi W. Hancock on the Violin, James Smithies on the Bass Viol, Elizha Averett on the Flute. After dancing two figures, Joseph Young addressed the party at considerable length, and made a prayer in which all joined after which the music and dancing was continued to a late hour, say 12 o clock.

President B. Young returned to the Temple a few minutes after 10, and took part in the exercises. By his directions, Lucian R. Foster and Ann Maria, his wife, and Stephen Markham and his wife, danced a French four. This was the first time that L. R. Foster and his wife danced together.

[January 7, 1846. Wednesday.] This morning there was an immense crowd at the reception room waiting for admission into the washing and anointing rooms. The brethren as they came along bearing Baskets, Pails and other vessels filled with all kinds of provisions, for the use of those who are attending on the ordinances of the Lord's House. The supply is much greater than the consumption . . .

A letter was received this morning from Mr. Tucker, the Catholic Priest, informing us that the Bishop could not raise money enough to purchase our property, but would either purchase or rent one of our public buildings but would not insure it against fire or mobs. A council was held in President Young's room, and the letter was taken into consideration. The result of the deliberations was that they would not answer the letter, and that the Catholics might go to hell their own way.

President B. Young, H. C. Kimball, P. P. Pratt, Orson Pratt, William Clayton and Peter Haws, were present at the council . . .

The High Council met at 6 o clock in room No. 10 . . . Prayed as usual for President B. Young and his Council, for the defeat of our enemies, the continuation of the endowment, and for the general welfare of all the Saints.

The High Priests held three different meetings in Rooms No. 8 and 10 . . .

The three meetings were conducted by persons chosen in each one to preside and all the individuals in them were clothed in priestly apparel, and the greatest unanimity of feeling prevailed. The most prominent things prayed for were, the preservation of President B. Young and all the Twelve, and that the ordinances of the endowment might continue, until all the elders had received their washings and anointings and that the Saints might all be able to procure means by which they could remove from Nauvoo to the West in comfortable manner, and for the sick, that they may be healed and that God would disappoint our enemies in all their plans.

Mrs. Ann Maria Foster, wife of L. R. Foster, left the Temple about 6 o clock, and went home with her little boy, Lucian R. Foster Junr, having been in the Temple all the time since yesterday noon. Her little boy was quite sick when he came, but went away quite well. On Sunday last she brought him to the Temple also, and at the request of his Father, Elders H. C. Kimball, Brigham Young, and P. P. Pratt laid their hands upon him and asked the Lord to restore him to health, and pronounced upon him the blessings of life and health.

About 9 o clock this evening, Elders Heber C. Kimball, and his wife, Bishop Whitney and his wife, left the Temple and went to Joseph Kingsbury's, to remain until William Kimball should carry a load of persons, viz; L. R. Foster, Horace Whitney, and Mary Ellen Harris, to their respective homes, after which he returned and carried home his Father and Mother in the carriage, with the grey horses. Bishop Whitney and his wife went home also in the same carriage.

President Brigham Young left the Temple about 10 o clock, and went home, for the night.

This afternoon and evening the new altar was used, for the first time, and four individuals and their wives were sealed. The altar is about 2 1/2 feet high, and 2 1/2 feet long, and about one foot wide, rising from a platform about 8 or 9 inches high and extending out on all sides about a foot, forming a convenient place to kneel upon. The top of the altar and the kneeling

---

[47] Clayton refers to the dedication of the new altar. Different parts of the temple, such as the baptismal font and the attic rooms, had been dedicated at different times (*HC* 4:446, 7:534). The temple received its public dedication on May 1, 1846: "Enterance was $1 each to pay the Hands that had worked on the Temple" (Kenney, 3:42). This dedication occurred three months after the first company of pioneers began their westward trek.

place are covered with cusions of scarlet damask cloth. The sides of the upright part, or body of the altar are covered with white linen.

The Twelve and the Bishops with their wives, were present at the dedication this afternoon . . .

Journal Four
Pioneer Trek West

1846-1847

William Clayton accompanies Brigham
Young's advance party leaving
Nauvoo, Illinois, in search of refuge beyond the borders of the United States.
After wintering in Nebraska they settle the following year in the Great Salt
Lake Valley, which was then part of northern Mexico. Clayton assisted in
keeping the official camp record and begins by describing preparations for
departure from Nauvoo.

[February 8, 1846. Sunday.] At the office all day packing
public goods.[1] Evening at [Aaron] Farr's writing out a letter of
instruction to Trustees.

[February 9, 1846. Monday.] At the office packing. At 3 1/2
the Temple was seen on fire.[2] Women carrying water.

---

[1] Clayton packed the official records of the church, musical instruments, and
books, which together with his families' personal belongings amounted to five tons
of baggage loaded into six wagons (see this journal, May 12, 1846).

[2] As some of the Saints crossed the Mississippi River, a fire broke out in the
upper room of the temple and burned for half an hour. Ignited by an overheated
stovepipe used to dry clothing, this accidental fire was easily extinguished. On
October 9, 1848, the entire temple was destroyed by arson. See Joseph Smith, Jr.,
et al., *History of the Church of Jesus Christ of Latter-day Saints*, ed. B. H. Roberts, 2d
ed. rev., 7 vols. (Salt Lake City: Deseret Book, 1963), 7:581–82, hereafter *HC*.

[February 13, 1846. Friday.] Sent 4 loads of goods over Mis-s[issippi]. Loading and packing.

[February 15, 1846. Sunday.] Riding around to get teams and things together. Sent two teams over [].

[February 18, 1846. Wednesday.] Got about ready to go over the river. Evening Pres[ident] B[righam] Young, H[eber] C. Kimball, J[edediah] M. Grant and some of the pioneers came to hurry us over. N[ewel] K. Whitney also came in. We conversed together some. They state that the brethren have made a perfect waste of food and property in the Camp.

[February 19, 1846. Thursday.] This morning the ground is covered with snow. It is so windy they cannot cross the river. Continued to snow all day. Evening went to Elder [Almon] Babbits to supper with Elder Kimball. President Young was there, [Jacob] Backenstos, J[edediah] M. Grant and some others.

[February 20, 1846. Friday.] The weather is very cold and windy. Impossible to cross the river. Spent the day running after things to get ready, fixing wagons and chopping fire wood.

[February 27, 1846. Friday.] We have spent the past week waiting for crossing over the river. It has been hard frost and much snow. This morning I concluded to start over the river and began early to send my teams. About noon I crossed with my family and then [rested] the teams and soon after went on to the camp where we arrived a little before four o'clock. Bishop Whitney concluded to stay at the river until morning because some of his teams could not get over. When we got to the camp we were received with joy and formed in the company of the band. The weather was still very cold and during the night. The distance from Nauvoo to this place is called 7 1/2 miles.

[February 28, 1846. Saturday.] A.M. arranging my tents &c. At 12 was sent for to council and about 2 the band was requested to go and meet Bishop Whitney and his teams. We went and met him 5 miles from the camp. We played sometime and then returned to the Camp. President Young, H. C. Kimball, P[arley]

Robert Bruce Flanders, *Nauvoo: Kingdom on the Mississippi* (Urbana: University of Illinois Press, 1975), 196.

P. Pratt, O[rson] Pratt and others accompanied us. At night played with the band.

[March 2, 1846. Monday.] Started this morning for another camp about 8 miles where we arrived about 5 P.M., the roads being somewhat hilly and muddy. The band played at night. During the day the artillery company broke into our ranks several times and broke a number of our wagon boxes. At night they complained of us at headquarters, but after hearing our story the matter stood about right.

[March 3, 1846. Tuesday.] Proceeded on our journey through Farmington[3] about 8 miles to a place where Bishop [George] Miller was encamped and arrived in good Season. The band played at night.

[March 4, 1846. Wednesday.] This morning we concluded to stay a day and fix up some wagons which were broken. A number of the citizens from Farmington came to the camp and gave a very pressing invitation for the band to go to Farmington and play some. Accordingly about 3 o'clock, the band started and arrived at Farmington about 4 1/2. We played at the principal hotel and then went to the school house and played till near dark. The house was filled with men and women, the leading part of the place. We then returned to the hotel where they had provided us with a good supper. They also gave us five dollars in money. [John] Kay sang a number of songs. At 8 o'clock we returned and when we left they gave us three cheers. When we arrived at the camp we met 30 of the guard just starting out to meet us. The President felt uneasy at our staying so long and was sending the men to protect us.

[March 5, 1846. Thursday.] Proceeded on our journey. Crossed the Des moines river at Bonaparte and afterwards had a very bad road up the bluff for several miles which detained us [un]til late in the afternoon. We stopped awhile to feed the band teams inasmuch as they had none this morning. We then started and went to the next camping ground, making the days journey about sixteen miles.

---

[3] Iowa.

[March 7, 1846. Saturday.] Proceeded about eight miles to a camp ground near to a Doctor [] Elbert's where the band camped. President Young was behind and when he arrived he went on about 8 miles farther. The band went to work splitting rails for corn and made before dark, about 130. In the evening Dr. Elbert and some others came to hear the band play. [John] Kay sang some songs which pleased them.

[March 8, 1846. Sunday.] Waited for orders from head-quarters. Many of the citizens came to hear the band play and gave us a very pressing invitation to go to Keosauqua[4] and give a concert. About noon word came that we should follow on to the camp. We immediately struck tents and started and we arrived at the main camp about 5 o'clock. Some of the citizens from Keosauqua followed us waiting for an answer whether we would give a concert as soon as we arrived at the camp. I asked the President whether the band should go to Keosauqua to give a concert. He advised us to go and I immediately sent out the ap-pointment and then we pitched our tents forming a line on the road opposite to the Presidents company.

[March 10, 1846. Tuesday.] The weather still continues fine. Spent the morning preparing for the Concert and about 1 o'clock P.M. started in company with the Brass band for Keosauqua. I rode in Elder Kimballs wagon with W[illiam] Kimball, J[ames] Smithies and W[illiam] Pitt. The distance from the Camp to Keosauqua is about 10 miles the Camp being at a place called Richardsons point. We arrived at Keosauqua about 3 o'clock and being requested we went through the Town and played some. One of the Grocery keepers invited us to play him a tune which we did. He then invited us in and offered to treat us to anything he had. We each took a little and then the next grocery keeper sent an invitation for us to play him a tune. We did so and he also gave us anything he had. A beer keeper next sent word that he did not want us to slight him and we went and played him a tune and then took some of his cake and beer. We then marched up to the Des moines Hotel near the Court house where we had ordered supper and after eating we went to the court house to prepare for

[4] A town on the Des Moines River in southeastern Iowa.

the Concert. At 7 o'clock the House was crowded and we commenced playing and singing till about 9 1/2. The audience seemed highly pleased, and gave loud applause. About the close one of the citizens got up and said it was the wish of many that we should repeat the concert the following evening, and he took a vote of all who wished us to go again. The vote was unanimous. We made nearly $25.00 clear of all expenses. We started back for the camp soon after 10 and arrived about 1 o'clock all well and pleased.

[March 11, 1846. Wednesday.] In the morning I reported to President Young our success and the request of the citizens of Keosauqua and he advised us to go again. We accordingly started about 11 o'clock. I again rode with W[illia]m Kimball, Horace Whitney and James Smithies. When we arrived we were welcomed again with the same kind feelings as yesterday. Pitt had a severe chill all the way and when we got there it commenced raining and made it very unpleasant. The house was again filled but we only made $20.00 besides all expenses. We learned that there are a party of socialists[5] there, and they and the priests are much opposed to each other. We also learned that a man named McCully was in jail close by under sentence to be hung on the 4th of April for murdering a man and a child. I did not feel so well at the concert as on the night previous on several accounts. We started back between 11 and 12 and got to the camp about 3 o'clock.

[March 12, 1846. Thursday.] The band moved to better ground about one quarter of a mile further. The heavy rains had made it very muddy and unpleasant, all our bedding and things being wet.

---

[5] Reacting in part to the economic and social changes of the Industrial Revolution, American socialism in the 1840s assumed various forms of social experimentation. In 1825 the British socialist Robert Owen set up "villages of cooperation" in New Harmony, Indiana. At Brook Farm in West Roxbury, Massachusetts (1841-47), residents did approximately the same work for equal wages and paid the same for food and lodging. While seeking perfection through communion with God, John Humphrey Noyes's Oneida community in New York in 1848 shared all possessions and lived as one family. In 1848 Karl Marx and Frederick Engels wrote the *Communist Manifesto*, which provided socialism with a political framework. Mormon experiments with common ownership in the United Order comprised another socialist community. Rural socialist groups, such as those the Saints encountered in Iowa, were generally short-lived.

[March 16, 1846. Monday.] Some of the citizens of Keosauqua came again to request us to give another Concert. We agreed to go tomorrow evening.

[March 17, 1846. Tuesday.][6] Started for Keosauqua with [William] Pitt, [J. F.] Hutchinson, [John] Kay, [James] Smithies and [Howard] Egan.[7] I took my music box and China to try and sell them. We arrived in good season and soon learned that the priests had been hard at work preventing the sectarians from coming to the Concert saying that it was an infidel move consequently there were not many present. We had far the best concert which lasted till 9 o'clock. We then went over to the Hotel, took supper and played for a private party till about 3 o'clock. We only cleared from both, about $7.00 over expenses but were well treated.

[March 21, 1846. Saturday.] We started early in the morning and soon came up with the main body of the camp. I rode ahead about three miles to hunt my cow. We did not have her last night being with the main camp. We traveled 9 or 10 miles and then rested our teams. We started again and traveled three miles further where we found the president and Heber [Kimball] camped on the brink of a long bluff. We concluded to go to the other bank which we did and camped in a good place. In the evening the band went and played for the President and Heber and then went to a farm house at the owners request about 3/4 of a mile from camp to play for his family. He promised to give us some honey if we would play for him. We played about an hour and then left but saw nor heard anything of the honey. We learned afterwards however that [J. F.] Hutchinson had a pail under his cloak and got it full of honey after the rest had left the house and kept it to himself, very slyly.

[March 22, 1846. Sunday.] Started again and soon came to the Shariton bottoms[8] which is a very low land for about 4 miles. The road was bad and took us sometime to cross. While on the bottom [Henry] Root and [William] Davis came again. Root has asked permission of President Young to go back to his family

---

6 Clayton leaves with the band to perform in Keosauqua.
7 Howard Egan had been a policeman in Nauvoo (1843). See *HC* 6:150
8 Alluvial bottom land in southeast Iowa, off the Des Moines River near Keosauqua.

some days ago, but it seems things did not go to suit him and he followed his team again. It took sometime to go up the bluff. We had to let the teams down into the Shariton River by ropes and also helped them up again by the same means. Our company got over in good season but we concluded to camp after getting up the bluff as it would take till night for the whole to get up. I spent the day helping the teams till I was so sore and tired I could scarcely walk.

[March 23, 1846. Monday.] In council with Brigham [Young], Heber [Kimball], and others. We found that [George] Millers company had gone still farther about 8 miles instead of waiting till we overtook them so that we could organize. I wrote a letter to them saying if they did not wait or return to organize, the camp would organize without and they be disfellowshiped. We concluded to stay at this place a few days to buy corn to last to Grand River, distance [] miles, but we found corn scarce and 25c a bushel, the farmers having advanced on account of a disposition to speculate.

[March 26, 1846. Thursday.] Evening in council.[9] Wrote a long letter to send to [James] Emmet's company by John Butler and James W. Cummings. This morning wrote another letter to P[arley] P. Pratt, [Orson] Pratt, and [George] Miller [again] telling them they must wait for us or come back to organize. The letters were sent by E[lder James] Smithies. He met them on the way and about noon P. P. Pratt, O. Pratt, [John Kay] and G. Miller came into camp and at 1 o'clock P.M. the council met. The brethren plead that the charges in the letters were unjust. They had not [] to keep out of the way but had done all for the best. [] The whole camp accordingly was organized,[10] A[lbert] P. Rockwood over 1st 50; Stephen Markham, 2nd 50; [] Young, 3rd 50; Howard E[gan] Kimball, 4th 50; Charles C. Rich, 5th 50;

---

[9] When Clayton writes that he was "in council," he usually means that he met with members of the Council of Fifty, now the operational governing body of the church for secular matters, including supervision of the travel west.

[10] The pioneer "Camp of Israel" was organized by families into groups of one hundred, which in turn were divided into groups of fifty and ten, each led by a captain appointed by church officials. Responsibility for each family and each wagon thus followed a chain of command up to Brigham Young, the camp president (Leonard J. Arrington, *Great Basin Kingdom: An Economic History of the Latter-day Saints, 1830-1900* [Cambridge: Harvard University Press, 1958], 19-20).

Charles Crisman, 6th 50. Each fifty had also appointed a contracting commissary for the purpose of contracting for work and grain as follows: Henry [G.] Sherwood 1st 50; David [Yearsley] Kimball 2nd; W[illia]m H. Edwards 3rd; Peter Haws 4th; Joseph Worthen 5th; Samuel Gully 6th. It was understood that I continue to preside over the band and in the absence of Brother Haws over the whole fifty. After this there was appointed for each fifty a distributing commissary to distribute feed in camp as follows: Charles Kennedy for 1st 50; J[edediah] M. Grant 2nd 50; Nathan Tanner 3rd 50; Orson B. Adams 4th 50; James Allred 5th 50; Isaac Allred 6th 50. The brethren then gave the following instructions for the whole camp with orders that same be observed hereafter, viz. No man to set fires to Prairies. No man to shoot off a gun in camp without orders. No man to go hunting unless he is sent and all to keep guns, Swords and pistols out of sight. There was then appointed a clerk for each fifty as follows: John D. Lee Young, 1st 50; John Pack 2nd 50; Lorenzo Snow 3rd 50; Geo[rge] H. Hales 4th 50; John Oakley 5th 50; A[sahel] Lathrop 6th 50. The council then adjourned to meet at Shariton Ford camp on Monday at 10 o'clock. We then returned to our Camp where we arrived just at dark.

[March 30, 1846. Monday.] Met with the council. The guard and pioneers were divided and distributed amongst the several companies of fifties. It was also agreed that company No. 4 should go on to the next camp tomorrow and the remainder the day following. Jackson Redding sold one of Kellers horses for 1 yoke of Oxen leaving me as bad off for teams as before.

[March 31, 1846. Tuesday.] It was concluded we could not get ready to move until tomorrow. O[rrin] P[orter] Rockwell arrived with the mail. I received a letter from Diantha and from father.[11] President Young received one from the trustees, one from [W. E.] Matlock and one from [] Pratt which I read in council. I was ordered to write an answer to the trustees and

---

[11] Pregnant with her first child, Diantha remained at home in Nauvoo. Clayton took Ruth, Margaret, and Alice, along with four children, to Winter Quarters. En route, he returned to collect Diantha on the trail with her child and father on June 28, a few miles east of Mt. Pisgah (see n13). Letter from Diantha quoted, xxixn47.

Matlock's letter, but being late I left it till morning when I was quite unwell. I got two new teamsters, Levi Kendall and [] Swap.

[April 1, 1846. Wednesday.] President Young also sent me two yoke of Oxen, wagon and Brother [] Jones the owner to assist me. We divided the load out of the spare wagons putting a yoke of Oxen to each and about 11 o'clock started on our journey. Mother [] was very sick and could not bear to ride. She walked all the way. I felt very unwell myself having much pain in my limbs. The roads were bad, but we arrived in camp about 2 o'clock and got on good ground. After getting our tents fixed fires made &c I went to wrestling, jumping &c to try to get well. I over-exerted myself without any symptoms of perspiration and was so sick after I had to go to bed.

[April 2, 1846. Thursday.] I was very sick all day and unable to write the letters or meet with the council. O. P. Rockwell started back to Nauvoo with letters. One of the Brother Hales arrived to say to his brother who drives team for [William] Pitt that his family is very sick and wants him to go back but we cannot spare the team and he says it is no use for him to go back without it. At night I wrote again to Diantha and sent it by Brother Hale who returns tomorrow.

[April 4, 1846. Saturday.] This morning all our clothing, beds and bed clothing were drenched with rain and it has continued to rain all day. I have been very sick again especially towards night. I was so distressed with pain it seemed as though I could not live. I went to bed and put a bag of hot salt on my breast which seemed to give me some ease but I suffered much through the night, and it continued to rain until after midnight. We put an extra cover on our sleeping wagon, which kept out the rain. We have only slept in the wagon 3 nights but have slept under a tent on the wet ground. Peter Haws[12] company are now formed with us, making our fifty nearly compleat. A number of the company feel unwell on account of the rain and wet.

---

[12] Peter Haws, who had accompanied Joseph Smith to Springfield, Illinois, in 1842 for trial on Missouri warrants, in October 1845 was made a company captain for the westward migration. See *HC* 7:482.

[April 5, 1846. Sunday.] This morning I feel a little better and the day is fine and pleasant. I have spent the day writing in this journal, having wrote from memory all since the date of March 9th. Some of the dates may not be correct but the matters recorded are true. It is now 1 o'clock P.M. There is a meeting at Elder Kimballs camp but I am set here in this wagon to fetch up this record. My health is some better for which I feel thankful. Elder Kimball says we had better not attempt to move tomorrow. We can get corn within 10 miles of here and he will help us to means. We have now to lay in corn to last till we get to Grand River about 50 miles further, there being no farms on the road. On Friday evening I appointed Charles Terry captain of my ten and Henry A. Terry clerk and my brother James [Clayton] to attend on my family agreeable with the order of the President that I may be able to spend my time writing for the council and camp and attend Councils. Elder Kimball instructed the captains of tens to call their companies together at 4 o'clock. Agreeably with this, the band assembled in front of my tent and administered the sacrament. W[illia]m F. Cahoon and Charles A. Terry officiating. I spoke about 3/4 of an hour on various subjects touching on our journey and the policy we ought to use &c. After I had done Elder Haws spoke on some subjects and the meeting adjourned. The captains then went over to Elder Kimballs camp about sending for corn. We concluded to send 4 teams for our fifty, Captain Egan and Haws then went through the camp to see if they could obtain some money. Haws obtained $31.45 and Egan about $9. I sent $14 by Egan for [corn]. Wrote to Diantha.

[April 6, 1846. Monday.] It has rained again the last night and continued to rain all day very heavy. The camp is very disagreeable and muddy. I spent the day reading. About 5 o'clock the clouds began to break and looks more likely for being fair. In the evening Elder Kimball came over and the band met opposite [J. F.] Hutchinsons Wagon and played some. After that the quadrille band met in my tent and played on the violins. All the time we were playing the lightning occasionally broke forth from the N[orth] W[est]. At 8 o'clock we dispersed just as the storm approached. Before I got to my tent the wind arrived and soon blew a perfect gale with heavy rain, hail, lightning and thunder. It continued for an hour and then abated some. All the tents in our company except mine and [John] Packs were blown down. The rain beat through the wagon covers and drenched the families and effects. It was the most severe storm we have experienced and with such wind it seems impossible to preserve our little clothing and provisions from being spoiled. But in the midst of it all, the camp seems cheerful and happy and there are but few sick.

[April 7, 1846. Tuesday.] This morning it is fair but cold and windy. The ground is frozen stiff and considerable ice. Many of the tents are still laying flat and everything around shows that the storm was very severe. A number of the band have no meat and some no flour, nor in fact scarcly any provisions and several have had little only what I have given them out of the stock I laid in for my family. I have this morning given the guard the bag of flour [George] Miller left and a piece of Pork and also a piece to [Jackson] Redding. The day continued fine but roads almost impassable. Evening the band played some.

[April 10, 1846. Friday.] The weather is yet very wet and gloomy. I spent the morning talking to Margaret. At 7 o'clock a gale struck up and blew our tents over. We then concluded to move a few rods lower out of the winds. Before we got moved the wind moved to the west and it grew very cold. Our teams are gone back to fetch some of the wagons left last night. It rains and blows very badly and is very severe on our women and teams. Margaret [Clayton] and Lydia [Moon] are out all the time and continually wet both feet and all over. We expect Robert Burtons, one of Pecks, [Jacob] Pearts and my wagon in tonight. One of mine was fetch[ed] early in the morning. Our teams fare hard with wet and cold, having very little corn.

[April 12, 1846. Sunday.] This morning before I got up, P. P. Pratt called and said that President Young wants the council to meet at Hebers Camp at 10 o'clock. I started out with Captain Egan on foot and arrived in season. Had some conversation with Ellen Sanders Kimball and then went to Council. It was decided to change our route and take a more northern one to avoid the settlements. We will go to Grand River and there enclose a space of land about 2 miles square and put up some 20 log houses for a

269

resting place for the companies.[13] A company starts out in a day or two to seek out the location amongst whom are the President, Heber and others of the Twelve. A company will also be sent west to Judge [] Millers to go to work for feed, &c. After council I took dinner with Heber the President being with us. I then wrote a letter to the Trustees and returned with Captain Egan to our Camp and soon after went to bed. The day has been fine but cold.

[April 13, 1846. Monday.] Finished my letter to Diantha and then went over to Pecks Blacksmith shop. We had concluded not to leave till morning. While there a message arrived saying that Haws has sent 8 yoke of cattle to help us on. We then concluded to start forthwith being noon.

[April 15, 1846. Wednesday.] Last night I got up to watch, there being no guard. [Horses and cattle] breaking into the tents and wagons. I tarried up then called up S[amuel] Hales and Kimball. This morning Ellen Kimball came to me and wishes me much joy. She said Diantha has a son. I told her I was afraid it was not so but she said Brother [Samuel] Pond had received a letter. I went over to Pond's and he read that she had a fine fat boy on the 30th ult.[14] but she was very sick with ague and mumps. Truly I feel to rejoice at this intelligence but feel sorry to hear of her sickness. Spent the day chiefly reading. In the afternoon President Young came over and found some fault about our wagons &c. In the evening the band played and after we dismissed the following persons retired to my tent to have a social christening viz. W[illiam] Pitt, [J. F.] Hutchinson, [James] Smithies, [John] Kay, [Howard] Egan, [Edward P.] Duzett, [Jackson] Redding, W[illia]m F. Cahoon, James Clayton and Charles A. Terry and myself. We had a very pleasant time playing and singing til about 12 o'clock and drank health to my son and named him William Adriel Benoni Clayton. The weather has been fine but rains a little tonight. Henry Terrys horses are missing and have been

---

[13] Parley P. Pratt named this resting place, 150 miles west of Nauvoo on the Grand River (Iowa), after the Pisgah mountain area in ancient Moab (Jordan) where Moses surveyed the promised land (Num. 21:20, 23:14; Deut. 3:27). Mt. Pisgah served as a way station for the immigrant companies that followed. See entry on May 26 and *HC* 7:606–607.

[14] The 30th day of the previous month.

hunted today but not found. This morning I composed a new song, "All is well."[15] I feel to thank my heavenly father for my boy and pray that he will spare and preserve his life and that of his mother and so order it so that we may soon meet again. O Lord bless thine handmaid and fill her with thy spirit, make her healthy that her life may be prolonged and that we may live upon the earth and honor the cause of truth. In the evening I asked the President if he would not suffer me to send for Diantha. He consented and said we would send when we got to Grand River.

[April 19, 1846. Sunday.] While the rest are gone to meeting I turned to unpacking and took an inventory of church property. It took me till about 4 o'clock to get through. Daniel Spencer's company had arrived about 5 o'clock. [Porter] Rockwell and Edwin Cutler arrived with the mail. Received a letter from Diantha written confirming the birth of my son &c also a letter from A[lmon] W. Babbit on some business. Went to see the President to show him the inventory but could not find him. About dark he sent for me and I went again but he was gone and I did not see him. My mare got in a mud hole last night and is very badly strained. Evening went to council and read many letters and wrote one to Elder [Orson] Hyde.

[April 20, 1846. Monday.] At 9 o'clock went to council. Had to read some letters and several pieces from papers. A report was read of all those who are able to fit themselves for the mountains. A law was made on motion of President Young that any person who interrupts the council hereafter by talking or otherwise shall be deprived the privilege of the council till the council see proper to admit them. The public teams being brought together the bishops took a list of them to be disposed of at Grand River. After council I went to work to assort the articles to be sold &c. Wrote to Diantha.

[April 25, 1846. Saturday.] This morning started by daybreak fishing. About half past seven the president sent for me. I came back but he was gone. President [Peter] Haws is regulating the company to watch our teams, and also go to making rails &c.

---

[15] Composed for the birth of Diantha's son, this song became one of the best known Mormon hymns, "Come, Come Ye Saints." See n30.

The morning is fine. About 9 o'clock [Amos] Kendall, one of my teamsters brought one of the horses he drives into Camp which had been bitten by a rattlesnake. His nose had begun to swell badly. We got some spirits of turpentine and bathed the wound, washed his face in salt and water, and gave him some snakes' master root boiled in milk. He yet seems very sick. Our men have made a pen for the cattle at nights. I feel quite unwell today. Spent the day chiefly reading.

[April 26, 1846. Sunday.] The first news I heard this morning was that the horse was dead. This is a very unlucky circumstance for me for I am already very deficient of teams. Moreover 3 of my teams leave me here, viz. [] Horlick, Charles A. Terry and [] Jones with their wagons and teams. I shall then have about quarter team enough to draw the loads. I have about 3000 lbs of church property besides my own goods. I see little prospect of my moving from here at present. The morning is wet but about 9 1/2 o'clock it cleared off and continued so all day. I spent the day reading and writing while the rest went to meeting. Evening was sent for to Council. Read a letter from O[rson] Hyde stating that they had an offer of two hundred thousand dollars for the Temple. He writes very hard times in Nauvoo. The council selected 100 men to make rails, 48 to build houses; 12 to dig wells 10 to build a bridge and the rest to go to farming.

S[tephen] Markham, C[harles] C. Rich, L[ewis D.] Wilson, James Pace to oversee the rail cutting. B. Young, H. C. Kimball, P. P. Pratt and [John] Smith the house building. A[lbert] P. Rockwood to boss bridge building. President Young to boss him and the whole camp and Jacob Peart to Boss well digging. The council decided to wait till morning to decide relative to selling the Temple. After we adjourned I went into my wagon. I wrote a long letter to Diantha. It was about 1 o'clock when I got through.

[April 27, 1846. Monday.] Rained all day. At 6 A.M., went to meeting. The men were divided out to work and commenced operations but had to quit on account of rain. After breakfast went to council, when it was voted to sell the Temple, assigning as to the reason it will be more likely to be preserved. It is as lawful to sell it to help the poor saints as to sell our inheritances. We do it because we are compelled to do it. I was ordered to write an answer to Elder Hyde's letter which I did at some length, saying finally that if the temple was sold 25,000 dollars must be sent for the benefit of this camp. The balance to be left at the disposal of Elder Hyde, [Wilford] Woodruff and the Trustees and to be appropriated to help away those who have labored hard to build the Temple and the faithful poor of the saints. Spent the balance of the day packing up china and crockery to be sent by [Howard] Egan.

[May 3, 1846. Sunday.] The morning fair, windy and cloudy, S.E. wind. Spent the morning making a list of all the company who have made their reports, also fixing tents. At 10 went to meeting. O[rson] Spencer talked a while and was followed by President Young who exhorted the camp to diligence in getting in crops for that will be our salvation the next winter. He said no company should start from here until the South field was made and some houses built. It commenced raining as this meeting closed and about 3 o'clock came on a thunder storm which lasted till near 5 o'clock. I spent the afternoon reading []. Soon after 5 it cleared off some and the sun shone again. While at supper President Young called and stated that he wanted I should [go] to council with him. I started and the council met opposite his tent. It was decided that his fifty build the bridge tomorrow and all the rest go to making rails and also that [Henry] Sherwood and O[rson] Pratt go about 25 or 30 miles southwest to seek out another section.

[May 4, 1846. Monday.] Finished my letter to Diantha and sent it by John Richards. [John] Horlick has concluded to tarry till my wagons are fixed. I spent the day examining my flour and crackers and helping [Margaret] to fix the tent as considerable of my crackers and flour are damaged on account of having poor wagons. I dreamed last night that I saw Diantha and her babe. Her babe was dres[se]d in white and appeared to be [layed] down with its eyes closed. She was bent over it apparently in sorrow. When I went to her she flew to me earnestly but the babe seemed to be kept still and I awoke. This dream has troubled me considerable. Evening met the clerks of 50's in my tent and instructed them how to make their reports &c.

[May 5, 1846. Tuesday.] The weather is fine. I spent the day preparing to enter the reports on the record. Went over to J[ohn] D. Lees and learned that some of the clerks had been to the

273

president and told him that I had ordered that they should include in their reports each wife a man has got. I did not do any such thing, only requested each name should be in full according to the order of a previous Council. The President said it did not matter about the names being in full but I think [] after days it will prove it does. Dr. [Willard] Richards thinks as I do. The president I understand appeared quite angry. Many of the band are entirely destitute of provisions and my flour is so near down I have concluded to eat biscuit.[16] I have given the band considerable of my biscuit already. At 9 o'clock evening fixing my wagons. Expected a storm, which soon after commenced, thundered hard and rained very [] the night.

[May 8, 1846. Friday.] The weather fine and pleasant. Spent the day fixing wagon covers and wagons. Andrew Cahoon arrived from Nauvoo with the mail but no letter from Diantha or father. He says the troops arrested O. P. Rockwell last Thursday evening and took him to Carthage and thence to Quincy jail.[17] It is doubtful whether he will now escape their cruel vengeance. This morning the mare had a colt. I have felt quite unwell all day. Evening went to President Youngs to get records to look for a deed from Hiram Kimball to Ira S. Miles. Searched till near 10 o'clock but the deed is not on record. Kimball seems disposed to take all the advantages he can from everyone.

[May 12, 1846. Tuesday.] Sent [Alvah] Keller and [] Corbite to the mills to try to get 2 cows and some flour and meal. Weighing and packing. About 9 was sent for to council. I waited about 2 hours before anything was done. The vote for Ezra T. Benson to stay as counselor for Father [Samuel] Bent was rescinded and it was voted to take Aaron Johnson in his place. A letter of authority was written for Father Bent by Dr. [Willard] Richards but he made me copy it, and afterwards when the President spoke to him to write to O. P. Rockwell he favored me to do that although I left 3 men waiting to weigh my loading and load my wagon. The fact is I can scarcely ever go to council but Dr. Richards

---

[16] Biscuit was a stored provision to substitute for freshly baked bread.

[17] Rockwell was arrested for defending Sheriff Backenstos on September 16, 1845, from mobs he had tried to restrain from burning Mormon homes. See Nauvoo journal entries of September 16 and October 10, 1845.

wants me to do his writing although I have more writing to do as clerk of the camp than I can possibly do. Moreover I have to unpack the chests and wait on all of them with the public goods in my charge which keeps me busy all the time. President Young, Heber [Kimball], Dr. Richards and Bishop [Newel K.] Whitney have all made out to get lumber sawed to make their wagons comfortable but I can't get enough to make a hind board for one of my wagons, which has none. They are tolerably well prepared with wagons and teams but I am here with about 5 tons of stuff and only 6 wagons and 5 yoke of Oxen to take it. I have dealt out near all of my provisions and have to get more before I can go on. It looks as if I had to be a slave and take slaves fare all the journey for it has worked that way so far. After council I was weighing and loading &c until night. We had some rain at night.

[May 19, 1846. Tuesday.] Spent the morning reading, afterwards went fishing. Some teams returned from camp and said that some from Nauvoo had arrived there who started two weeks ago last Saturday and that Elder Hyde had advised all the saints to move over the river as fast as possible from Nauvoo, they have their ferry boats constantly employed and numbers are already on their way here.

[May 20, 1846. Wednesday.] This morning is very rainy and cold. Spun 20 yards of fish line and tied on 11 hooks. [] Swap and [] Conrad returned soon after 11 o'clock. They say the camp is about 30 miles ahead. They confirm the report of Some having arrived from Nauvoo and say they were told that my father is on his way here. The roads are lined with teams &c on the other road north of this . . . I cannot yet learn a word from Diantha but think she must be on her way. My family are yet in good health except Margaret who looks sick but doesn't complain.

[May 23, 1846. Saturday.] James [] started out early to meet the wagons. After breakfast we started on the road and while standing there [Alvah] Keller came up and said he thought we [had to] go on about 4 1/2 miles and meet the [] the main road. [] proceeded [] on foot [] and after traveling about 3 miles came up to the teams where they had [stopped] on the road. When I got up the guard seemed pleased to see me. Captain [Orville] Allen had bought about 36 bushels of meal and 200 lbs of bacon. They would receive no pay. They have been faithful and diligent and have done much. There is yet 12 dollars due them from the meal and they are determined I shall have that too. When my teams came up we put the meal in the wagons and started on. We went about a mile further to Peters bridge where we concluded to camp for the night. We arranged our loading and I concluded to let Brother Allen have the wagon and team in his hands which is church property to send back to Nauvoo for his family. The guard made out a list of provisions which they wished me to leave them which was indeed very little. I gave them 4 pairs of shoes and probably 3 bushels of meal which is all the remuneration they would accept for all they had brought. They seemed well satisfied.

[May 24, 1846. Sunday.] This morning I gave certificates of discharge to A[lvah] Keller, John Horlick, Orville Allen, M[ora] Dodge, [] Tolman, [] Starks, [] Mecham, [] Bartlet and P. R. Wright. Keller and Horlick started immediately for Nauvoo and Wright and Dodge soon after. I concluded to move on about 2 miles to where [J. F.] Hutchinson and [Sylvester] Duzett were in Camp. I started out on foot and most of my family soon after. It soon began to rain and rained till I was wet through. I traveled on about 4 1/2 miles but could see no camp near timber. I stopped to rest at a post put up by [] Stewart where the Raccoon fork road led off. While there Josiah Arnold passed on his way to Miller's. From him I learned that there was a camp ground about a half a mile further. [] Soon after news arrived that Swap had broke his wagon tongue. I sent James to help bring on the loads. We only started with 3 wagons and left 3 back with Corbitt and Martin. The teams worked hard all day and at half past 9 the last team arrived having taken all day to travel about five miles.

[May 25, 1846. Monday.] This morning I sent James and Corbitt to go and trade 3 horses and some harness for cows. About noon I started out with 2 wagons and left one and about 3 loads of stuff in care of two of the guard. After we had traveled about 3 miles I met a messenger from the Camp who handed me two letters one was from Diantha and one from Brother [] Whitaker concerning a piece of land. We went on about a mile and crossed a creek where we waited to rest our teams. When I read D[iantha]'s letter it gave me painful feelings to hear of her situation. After resting about an hour we went on about 4 miles further and camped near Father Baker's camp on a creek. It was night before we got supper over. I found several men going back to Nauvoo for their families.

[May 26, 1846. Tuesday.] Wrote an answer to Whitaker's letter and also one to Diantha. We started on about 8 o'clock and found the road bad and many bad creeks where the bridges had been washed away. After traveling 2 miles one of my wagons loaded with corn meal was upset in a hole, but after about an hour's labor we got loading again. The wagon was not much damaged. We proceeded about three miles further and met two men with six yoke of oxen which President Young had sent to meet us. This was a great releaf to us for we saw that we could not get to camp today our teams were so wore down. We rested our teams about an hour and then started on at a good pace. We found several more very bad creeks to pass but we did not have much difficulty. Duzett and myself drove the cows. Edward Martin drove his horses. About sundown we arrived in camp having travelled about 13 miles. This place is called Mount Pisgah and is a very beautiful situation; the prairie rolling and rich skirted with beautiful groves of timber on the main fork of Grand River. Soon after we arrived Elder Kimball came to welcome us to camp and then came Elder Richards and family and President Young, who all seemed glad to see us in camp.

[May 27, 1846. Wednesday.] This morning my horses and 1 cow and several of the oxen are missing. I went to see Bishop Whitney about getting teams to send back for the loads remaining but could get no satisfaction from him. I went back and unloaded two wagons on the ground and about the same time saw the President who said he would send for them. Elder Kimball sent one wagon and the President sent two. President Y[oung] said they intended to take the church property into their wagons and take it on to council bluffs[18] but I must go with them and

---

[18] Members of Lewis and Clark's expedition gave the name Council Bluff to the site where they announced to the Oto Indian Council that the land west of the Mississippi, earlier claimed by the Spanish and the French, had been acquired by the United States from Napoleon in the Louisiana Purchase of 1803. Later, the name "Council Bluffs" came to be applied to the whole region, including the city of Kanesville, Iowa, which was renamed in 1852. The Mormons had named Kanesville in 1846 when they settled there for the winter. Because of its northwestern

leave James, Corbitt, and [Howard] Egan to bring on the wagons they get &c. I cannot think they understand my situation in regard to the teams or they would make some definite move about it. They intend to start in a day or two and [tried to get the wagons fixed] in good order but had no chance to get even one fixed. Spent the day fixing up my tent and having to get a new pole. Heber [Kimball] took my other one. P.M. it commenced gathering for a storm and we had barely time to get the tent up and the things under it before it began to rain and continued till I went to sleep. George Herring and [Charles] Shumway arrived here last night. I spoke with them today.

[May 30, 1846. Saturday.] Went and borrowed A[aron] Farr's ornaments and robe. Then rode with Dr. Richards about 3 miles on the prairie. There were 5 others and carriages President Young [brought our two tents]. We fixed them up and then met and clothed.[19] There was President B[righam] Young, H[eber] C. Kimball, P[arley] P. Pratt, W[illard] Richards, O[rson] Pratt. J[ohn] Taylor, Geo[rge] A. Smith, A[masa] Lyman, John Smith, N[ewel] K. Whitney, D[aniel] Spencer, O[rson] Spencer, C[harles] C. Rich, E[zra] T. Benson, W[illia]m Huntington and myself. Clothed and having offered up the signs[20] offered up prayer H. C. Kimball being mouth. We then conversed a while and prayed again, G. A. Smith being mouth. A[lbert] P. Rockwood and W[illiam] Kimball were guarding the tent. Prayers were offered that we might be delivered from our enemies and have teams to go on our journey &c. About 2 o'clock we returned to camp. Many of the teams were coming in and among the rest the teams sent back for my loading which all arrived tonight.

[June 4, 1846. Thursday.] Again sent the men hunting cattle. The day was very cold and windy, almost as cold as winter. I

---

location Kanesville (Council Bluffs) became the dominant embarkation point for pioneers heading west. It is on the eastern banks of the Missouri River, across from Omaha, and about fifteen miles downstream from the meeting place (David Lavender, *The Way to the Western Sea: Lewis and Clark Across the Continent* [New York: Harper and Row, 1988], 114; John D. Unruh, Jr., *The Plains Across: The Overland Emigrants and the Trans-Mississippi West, 1840–60* [Urbana: University of Illinois Press, 1982], 39, 42–3).

[19] Put on priesthood clothes.

[20] Signs of the priesthood.

spent the day fixing a wagon for Diantha expecting her on in about 2 weeks. Lucy Walker[21] called in this afternoon and expressed sorrow on account of the treatment of Hebers family toward her. Amos Fielding called on his way to the President's Camp. Towards evening it rained and there was one of the most beautiful rainbows I ever saw in my life. We could see its brilliant reflections within a few rods of us. In the evening [Sylvester] D[u]zett came for his cow which had tarried with ours. He concluded to stay over night. My teamsters returned without finding the cattle.

[June 6, 1846. Saturday.] After traveling about seven miles we arrived at a piece of timber where the Patriarch John Smith was resting. We concluded to rest our teams here and stopped at half past 11. At 1 P.M. we started again and soon after had a heavy thunder shower. I was about a mile ahead of the wagons and having no shelter was soon completely drenched with rain. It got very cold while raining. As soon as the wagons came up we stopt till the shower was over which did not last long. We then pursued our journey till 6 o'clock camped on the open prairie a long way from timber having traveled about 16 miles. After the shower the day was fine. I was very tired and wet and after eating a little went to bed . . .

[June 9, 1846. Tuesday.] Weather fine and hot. Went fishing at daybreak with James had good luck. At 9 went on. I rode again. P.M. 3 Indians overtook us and begged some bread. We camped on a bottom beside [] Coleman and others, having travelled about 12 miles. 2 Indians are here and we have learned that their Camp is only three miles from us. President Young left word to go in companies from here to avoid being plundered by the Indians. We had our cattle tied up and a guard over them through the night.

[June 10, 1846. Wednesday.] Went fishing at daybreak and caught 36. Weather hot. We started about 9 o'clock and found the roads good but over hills and ravines all the day. At about 6 o'clock we came in sight of the Pottawattamie [Indian] village.

---

[21] Formerly a plural wife of Joseph Smith, Lucy Walker married Heber C. Kimball in 1845 and bore him nine children (Fawn M. Brodie, *No Man Knows My History: The Life of Joseph Smith*, 2d ed. [New York: Alfred A. Knopf, 1966], 456).

[Then] about 2 miles from it they discovered us coming and we soon saw a number of them riding towards us. Some had bells on their horses which frightened our horses and cattle. James and I took the horses and let the others take the Oxen the best way they could. Some of the Indians followed our wagons and enquired often for whiskey. We had to pass some timber and a river before we arrived at their village which is situated on a very beautiful ridge skirted by timber and beautiful rolling prairie. Before we arrived at the timber it seemed that the whole village had turned out, men, women and children, some on horses and many on foot. Their musicians came and played while we passed them. They seemed to escort our wagons and asked if we were Mormons. When we told them we were they seemed highly pleased. It took us some time to cross the bridge over the river and we were then perfectly surrounded by the Indians apparently from Curiosity and friendship. They watched us cross the bridge and they followed on with us. The boys seemed pleased to learn the words our teamsters used to drive the cattle and would run and in their way help to drive. They manifested every feeling of friendship and nothing unkind or unfriendly transpired. Soon after we passed the bridge we were met by Ja[me]s W. Cummings and the brethren from Shariton Ford with John L. Butler to bring [James] Emmets company to meet us. The Cattle have been with Emmets company from the time they left Nauvoo. The road led within about 200 yards from the [bark] houses of the Indians. I wanted to go about 3 or 4 miles further to save the necessity of having a guard but soon after we left the village we had to ford a stream which was deep and bad to cross. I then concluded to camp on the ridge above the ford and in sight of the village being about a half or three quarters of a mile from them. Many of them followed us men, women and children and watched all our movements but about dark all departed home in peace, seemingly well pleased with their visit. They certainly showed every mark of friendship and kindness imaginable and treated us as brethren. We learned that the chiefs daughter was buried today. We have traveled about 15 miles. From Cummings we learned that Emmett had left his camp and had taken seven horses and other things belonging to the company with him. Part of the company has crossed at St. Louis and are now on the line below here. The agent of U.S. refuses to let them pass. The other part of the co[mpany] are thirty miles below the bluffs expecting us to cross there.

[June 11, 1846. Thursday.] Many of the Indians again came to the camp with the same friendly feeling. Some of the Squaws came to trade. We started soon after 9 the weather very hot. We travelled over about 5 miles of very uneven road. The rest was good. We had to travel till late before we came to water. We camped on a small creek where [] Coleman and [] Tanner were camped, having travelled about 14 miles . . .

[June 14, 1846. Sunday.] The weather very hot and mosquitoes tremendous[ly] bad. This morning I weighed bread for each man at the rate of a half a pound a day. They seemed very much dissatisfied and growl to each other very much. I weighed for my family of ten as much as I weighed for six teamsters. They were dissatisfied but we had some left. They have hitherto had all they wanted three times a day and above this have eaten up a bag of crackers unknown to me which I had reserved for the mountains. The mosquitoes being so bad I concluded to go on a little piece. We started at 1 and traveled til 4 when we arrived at a single clear stream having traveled about 6 miles. I camped here and in the evening told the men a part of what I thought of their conduct . . .

[June 16, 1846. Tuesday.] Started at half past seven and traveled about 14 miles when we came in sight of the Missouri river and the main camp about 5 miles further. We soon learned that some of the camp were coming back to find water. There being no water where we were we moved back about 2 miles to a spring and there camped [] till we can learn what to do.

[June 17, 1846. Wednesday.] This morning [John] Kay and [Sylvester] Duzett rode up and said they were anxiously expecting us at the camp and wanted us to go immediately. I went to the camp with them to look out a place while my men yoked up and brought the wagons. When I arrived I saw Heber [Kimball]. He seemed pleased to see me and went with me to look out a place to camp. I fixed a spot between President Young's camp and Bishop [George] Miller's. Heber said the Twelve had an invitation to go to the village[22] to the agent's to dinner and they wanted the band to go with them. I went back to meet the wagons which had been detained on account of some of the cattle being missing. As soon as my wagons arrived I got ready and started in Hebers carriage with Heber, Bishop [Newel K.] Whitney, [James] Smithies and E[dward] Martin, [William] Pitt and Hutchinson, Kay and Duzett rode in other carriages. When we arrived at Mr. Mitchells the agent we were introduced to him one by one. We then played and Kay sang till about 5 o'clock when we returned. This village is situated but a little distance from the river, probably 50 rods. It is composed of about 12 or 15 blocks houses without glass in the windows and is the noted place where the Lamanites for years held their councils. The inhabitants are composed of Lamanites, half breeds and a few white folks. I had an introduction to Sarrapee the Indian trader. We arrive home just at dusk . . .

[June 19, 1846. Friday.] Fixing wagons and preparing to send off some things to trade. Evening went fishing.

[June 20, 1846. Saturday.] Went with the band to hold a concert at the village. Many went from the camp. The Indians and half breeds collected 10 dollars and 10 cents and gave it to us and the Agent Mr. Mitchel gave a dinner to all that came.

[June 22, 1846. Monday.] Fixing my wagons. The day was windy and cold. I was informed yesterday that Diantha is twenty miles back from Mount Pisgah with her father still further back. They have sent her chest on to Pisgah and she is with Lorin [Farr]. I partly made up my mind to start in the morning and fetch her.

[June 23, 1846. Tuesday.] This morning I got my food ready to start after Diantha but Vilate Ruth[23] seemed quite sick and I

---

[22] Mr. Mitchel, the federal Indian agent, lived in the village of Council Bluffs [Kanesville], Iowa. The U.S. had begun placing government-appointed agents among Indian tribes shortly after the Revolutionary War. As white settlement poured into Indian territory, the agents were expected to live among the tribes, report on events in their areas, and encourage the development of agriculture (David Lavender, *The Great West* [Boston: Houghton Mifflin, 1965], 71).

[23] Clayton's third living daughter, Vilate Ruth, was born to Ruth Moon Clayton on December 8, 1844.

concluded not to start. We took the teams and went to the village to pick gooseberries but it rained near all the time we were gone. I bought a Scythe and some other things and tried to trade a watch for a yoke of cattle. Major [] Mitchel offered me 3 yoke for the Gold watch. We got home about 3:00 o'clock. I then went and told the president about Mitchel's offer and he told me to sell it. It was so cold and wet and windy we went to bed early and soon after we got to bed Heber [Kimball] and Doctor Richards came to my wagon with two letters from Diantha one dated Nauvoo May 17, 1846 the other Big Prairie, June 18. She tells that she is sent on by her father and is with Lorin and is very anxious I should bring her or send for her. I made up my mind to start tomorrow. The night was very stormy with strong winds and heavy rains.

[June 24, 1846. Wednesday.] The morning wet and cold. I went over to President Young and told him where I was going and what for. He said he would get the cattle for me. I also spoke to Heber [Kimball] and he said: "Go and prosper." At 11 I went to council and President Young, [Heber] Kimball and [John] Taylor concluded also to go to Pisgah after the cannon. I started at 2 o'clock it then being fair. At 5 o'clock I passed Father [] Knowlton's company 13 miles from camp and at 7 passed the LaHarpe company and inquired of Brother [] Burgham and [] Freeman about Diantha but could not learn much from them . . .

[June 25, 1846. Thursday.] This morning arose at 4 o'clock and moved our wagon a little to fresh grass to let the horses feed they being tied to it. It is fair but cloudy. We started again at half past 5 and traveled till 12 then rested till 2 and then traveled till dark making 31 miles. We camped just beyond the Indian village in the midst of a severe thunder storm. It rained most of the day and the roads were bad.

[June 26, 1846. Friday.] Did not start till after seven. Morning fair roads bad. After traveling about 6 miles we found Horace Clark and other camped on the [one] side of a small stream and Orson Spencer on the other side. The creek was full of water to the bank and in the deepest place about 6 feet over the bridge and part of the bridge washed away. We tarried until 3 o'clock and then concluded to try to get over. Walter L. Davis, and W[illiam]

D. Huntington and others volunteered to help us over. We un-loaded [] the wagon box off and made use of the box for a boat, taking a few of our things over at a time. When we had got them all over we swam the horses over loaded up, and at 5 o'clock started again and went till near 9 having traveled about 16 miles.

[June 27, 1846. Saturday.] The day was fine and we traveled about 38 miles and camped on the prairie about 8 miles from Pisgah. During the day we passed some United States officers on their way to see President Young and the Council. We afterwards learned that they profess to be going to the authorities of the church by order of the president of the U.S. to raise 500 volunteer Mormons to defend Santa Fe, but the feeling amongst the brethren is that they are spies sent to learn our movements and watch us.[24] It is evident the U.S. are afraid of us and perhaps the serpent will send a flood after us but the earth will help us.

[June 28, 1846. Sunday.] At daybreak it rained again. We started at 4 o'clock and arrived at Pisgah at 8. Had some conversation with Father [William] Huntington and C[harles] C. Rich. We fed and at 9 started again. We soon saw Brother [Wilford] Woodruff. He was glad to see me. We conversed together some time. From him I learned that Missouri had sent up a committee

---

[24] The U. S. government was reluctant to allow a company of armed Mormons to go to the Great Salt Lake since it was a potential war zone; at this time it was a part of Mexico that the U. S. Army planned to take. In 1844 James Polk had run a successful presidential campaign on a platform to annex Texas, California, and Oregon — the very places the Mormons wanted to go. Following his declaration of war against Mexico on May 11, 1846, Polk decided that the problem might be resolved by authorizing Colonel Stephen Kearny "to receive into service as volunteers a few hundred of the Mormons who are now on their way to California, with a view to conciliate them, attach them to our country, & prevent them from taking part against us." Hosea Stout wrote in his diary that he was "uncommonly wrought up" by Polk's request and was "glad to learn of war against the United States and was in hopes that it might never end until they were entirely destroyed for they had driven us into the wilderness & now laughing at our calamities" (Juanita Brooks, ed., *On the Mormon Frontier: The Diary of Hosea Stout* [Salt Lake City: University of Utah Press and the Utah State Historical Society, 1964], 1:172). Brigham Young saw an opportunity for the Mormons to be "the first men to set their feet on the soil of California." Further, the soldiers' cash pay could be used to help finance the westward emigration. By July 18, 1846, Brigham Young had raised five companies of 526 men which would join Kearney's troops as the Mormon Battalion. See Dale L. Morgan, *The Great Salt Lake* (Albuquerque: University of New Mexico Press, 1973), 181-83.

to Pisgah to search for Forts and Cannon &c. He says the Missourians are terrified and many are moving from the back to the interior settlements. He also stated that we have got a friend in the British parliament and the British had held a private council in relation to the treatment of the U.S. towards us. Britain is making great preparations for war. They have sent 10,000 troops to Canada and a Fleet around Cape Horn to Oregon. They are intending to arm the slaves of the South and have their Agents in the Indian country trying to bring them in war to fight the U.S.[25] After we left Elder Woodruff we passed on and soon met Sister [] Durfee and Brother [Cornelius P.] Lott and his company. He said Diantha was back about [4] miles. Soon after we met Orvile H. Allen and from him learned that Diantha was back at least 12 miles. We continued on and at 2 o'clock fed. We arrived at Father [] Chases between 4 and 5 o'clock. Diantha was very glad to see me and burst into tears. My little boy is far beyond all my expectations. He is very fat and well formed, has got a noble countenance. They are both well and I feel to thank my heavenly father for his mercies to them and Father Chase and family for their kindness to them and may the Lord bless them for it. And O lord bless my family and preserve them forever. Bless my Diantha and my boy and preserve their lives on the earth to bring honor to thy name and give us a prosperous journey back again is the prayer of thy servant William. Amen. At night we had a heavy thunder storm. It rained very heavy. I slept with my dear wife and boy in father C[hase]s wagon . . .

[July 1, 1846. Wednesday.] P. P. Pratt passed about 6 o'clock. We afterwards learned that he was going on express to Pisgah to raise the 500 volunteers to go to Santa Fe. After traveling about 7 miles we rested with Brother [William?] Weeks and ate breakfast, then went on till 2 o'clock and stopped to feed. We continued on till dark . . .

[July 3, 1846. Friday.] Started early and went about 4 miles to a creek [] ate breakfast. The day very hot but we traveled about 25 miles. We met President Young, Heber Kimball, and Dr.

---

[25] As a slave state at the edge of the American frontier, Missouri might have feared British-supported insurrection of slaves and Indians, perhaps using alienated Mormons whom Missouri had brutally expelled in 1839.

Richards going back to raise volunteers. They feel that this is a good prospect for our deliverance and if we don't do it we are doomed. After [questioning] them we went on and camped near Hiram Clark and took supper with him.

[July 4, 1846. Saturday.] This morning my horses and 5 from Clarks company were missing. I went on this [] west [] eight miles []. Diantha having eaten nothing this morning I tried to buy some bread but could not get it till I got home. We arrived at 3 o'clock and found my little Vilate sick the rest all well. I went over to Council at Captain [] Allens tent.

[July 6, 1846. Monday.] Spent the day fixing wagons. Day very hot. Bishop Whitney called to see us. They are getting over the river as fast as possible but it is slow work . . .

[July 13, 1846. Monday.] Went to the general meeting played with the band and then kept minutes. They got 3 companies of 43 each and half of the fourth company. All my teamsters have enlisted. I am now destitute of help. Edward Martin is advised to go and leave his family in my charge. I have still four yoke of oxen missing and I dont know them. Last night James[26] was seized with a fit and is quite unwell today mostly insensible. Vilate Ruth is quite sick and on the whole my situation is rather gloomy. The meeting adjourned at 5 till tomorrow at 8, after which the company danced till dark . . .

[July 16, 1846. Thursday.] Hunting my horses to take Diantha to see her fathers folks who arrived yesterday. Afternoon we started out and went about 3 miles from here. They appeared very glad to see us. We got home again at dark.

[July 21, 1846. Tuesday.] This morning it rained very heavy. Went to council at Elder Pratts camp. The council appointed a council of twelve to preside here, viz. Isaac Morley, Geo[rge] W. Harris, James Allred, Tho[ma]s Grover, Phineas Richard, Heman [T.] Hyde, W[illia]m G. Peck, Andrew H. Perkins, Henry W. Miller, Daniel Spencer, J[onathan] H. Hale and John Murdock. I wrote a letter informing them of their appointment also instructing them not to let any pass over the river unless they

---

[26] Possibly William Clayton's twenty-two-year-old brother; note journal entry dated April 5, 1846.

could be in time to go to Grand Island[27] and cut Hay to watch over the church establish schools for the winter &c. I spent the remainder of the day at the creek. I asked the President what I should do but could get no answer. I have not been able to get any satisfaction from any of the council as to what I should do and am totally at a loss to know whether to prepare to tarry here or go on. My provisions are nearly out and my teamsters all gone and near all the cattle strayed away and no one to hunt them except James and Corbitt and they are sick . . .

[July 29, 1846. Wednesday.] Got the balance of the flour making 889 lbs most of it at $2.50 and about 200 lbs of it at $2.00. P.M. went to the village with Alice, Diantha, and Margaret. There saw President Young and Heber. They have just bought a pony and some cloth and seem to have money enough but there is none to buy me flour. I yet lack about a ton . . .

[August 2, 1846. Sunday.] Preparing to cross the river. Pelatiah Brown went aswimming all the forenoon and when Corbitt asked him to help with the teams he swore he would not if Jesus Christ would ask him. I told him if he did not feel like helping us, he could go somewhere else. I did not want him. He went and I am again left without a teamster . . . About noon we crossed three wagons and kept to work until we had got them all over which took us till dark. We had to crowd our wagons together in the road just above the river on account of its being stopped up by other wagons. We could not get our cattle to grass and they have had none since last night but having a few bushels of corn we gave them five ears a piece. After supper I went afishing with W[illia]m F. Cahoon and others until two o'clock but had very poor luck.

[August 3, 1846. Monday.] Started this morning to get our wagons on the prairie. The road is very narrow and bad, up steep bluffs and very muddy. It took 4 yoke of oxen to take a very light load. When we had got 4 of the wagons up 8 yoke of Bishop Newel Whitneys cattle came to help us and afterwards 9 yoke of

---

[27] The pioneers stopped at Grand Island, Nebraska, on the Platte River and operated a ferry boat to carry subsequent companies of Mormons and other emigrants.

President Youngs and Kimballs. We got to the prairie about noon and stopped to feed our cattle. I sent on 5 wagons with the teams sent to help us and after feeding about an hour started with the remainder. I drove the spare cattle and horses. We got the wagons to camp about 6 o'clock. One of President Youngs Oxen killed himself in going to drink, being so eager he pitched into the creek and broke his neck. When we got to camp we were all completely tired. My feet were sore and my limbs ached and had to go to bed. We camped on the north end of Heber's company. We have left 9 head of cattle over the river yet and there is little prospect of being able to find some of them . . .

[August 8, 1846. Saturday.] This morning we arose about 3 o'clock and while some took the cattle to graze the rest got the wagons loaded &c. ready to start. We got away soon after sunrise. I drove the cows on a mule. We traveled about 9 miles before we came to any water . . .

[August 16, 1846. Sunday.] Since Wednesday have scarcely even been out of bed, but kept with raging fever all the time. Twice Heber [Kimball] has rebuked my fever but it has returned. Through the fears and persuasion of my family I have taken some pills and medicine given by Dr. Sprague, but seem to grow worse all the time. Today I have been very sick all day. Towards evening my folks concluded to get me out of the wagon into the tent where they had prepared a bed. Soon after I got into the tent President Young, Dr. Richards, G. A. Smith, O. Pratt, Lorenzo Young and others called to see me. When they had been in a few moments President Young called O. P. Rockwell into the tent and the feelings we had on seeing him cannot be described. He has been in prison some time but when his trial came on there was no one to accuse him and the judge discharged him. The brethren all laid hands on me and rebuked my disease in the name of the Lord President Young being mouth. I immediately felt easier and slept well all night being the first sleep I had had of any account for three days and nights . . .

[August 24, 1846. Monday.] Reading some and fixing a little at my violin. Feel very little better but have a better appetite . . .

[September 10, 1846. Thursday.] I still continue very weak and troubled with pain in stomach &c. President Young and Dr.

Richards called and brought me a letter from David []. Also said they had got me employment writing at a dollar a day or 3 cents on Every 100 words copying.

[September 12, 1846. Saturday.] Still quite unwell. President Young brought me $8 in money, one half dollar bogus and soon after Dr. Richards sent me some letters to copy which I did . . .

[September 20, 1846. Sunday.] A little better. I have been told that President Young has virtually cursed all who have gone to Missouri or those who shall go hereafter.

[September 21, 1846. Monday.] This evening about ten o'clock all the men of the Camp were ordered up armed to meet in this square forthwith. I got up and after a very little while quite a company of the brethren got together. President [Jonathan H.] Hales informed them that the President had received a letter from Mr. [Peter] Sarpy[28] informing him that two gentlemen from Missouri had informed him confidentially that the Missourians had got out writs for the twelve and others and were coming with a large force on the west side of the river to attack the camp by surprise &c. He advised the brethren to have their arms clean and their ammunition ready at a moment's warning. To pray with their families. Keep dogs tied up at nights &c. &c. The company was then dismissed except a guard for the camp.

[September 22, 1846. Tuesday.] This morning the brethren were ordered to meet at the springs below here at 9 o'clock. At the sound of the drum the brethren met and here organized into four Battalions one of artillery and three of infantry. There were about 300 brethren present. The President then stated that he had received a letter from Sarpey informing him that two gentlemen (confidentially) from Missouri had informed him that the Missourians were collecting with the Sheriff of Missouri at their head designing to come up and attack the saints, that they had writs for the Twelve and others. He had ordered out the brethren that they might be ready in case of necessity and advised them to organize and be prepared. S[tephen] Markham was elected Col[onel] over the Battalions, Hosea Stout Lieut. Colonel over the B's

---

[28] The Sarpy fur trading post was the site of Bellevue, the oldest town in Nebraska, located near the mouth of the Platte River. See June 17 entry.

and over the first B of Infantry. John Scott was elected 1st Major and major over the Artillery. Henry Herriman 2nd major to take command of the 2nd Battalion of Infantry and John S. Gleason 3rd major over the 3rd Battalion of infantry. After organizing the president addressed the companies and then dismissed them. It was advised to quit leaving and move the encampment to the fort on the river. A number of teams moved this afternoon.

[September 23, 1846. Wednesday.] This morning President Young and many others have moved down to the river. Heber told me to wait till the lots were selected and he would let me know when to move. My health is improving.

[September 24, 1846. Thursday.] Very cold all day. I did not feel so well. I have been told that Daniel H. Wells and William Cutler have arrived in camp and brought report that there has been a battle fought in Nauvoo and some of the brethren killed.

[September 25, 1846. Friday.] I learned today that the mob had made it known that they were coming to drive the Mormons. The Governor sent an officer to raise volunteers to disperse the mob, but the mob learning this they came sooner than they had calculated. The brethren being apprised of the intentions of the mob prepared to meet them as well as their circumstances would permit. Some of the new citizens also made preparations to join the brethren. They made five cannon shot of an old steam Boat Shaft. They also filled some barrels with powder, old Iron &c. which were buried in the passes to the City which could be fired by a slow match but this was of no avail as some traitors informed the mob of it, hence they did not come into the settled part of the city. On Saturday the 12 inst. the mob made their appearance being about 1200 in number. The brethren and some of the new citizens in the whole about one hundred and sixty, went to give them battle, but many of the new citizens and some of the brethren when they saw the numbers of the mob fled and left about 100 nearly all brethren to fight the enemy. The mob had pieces of cannon. They met near Boscow's store on Winchester Street. The cannon of the mob were two blocks from the brethren and the other part or rifle men one block from them. The mob fired a number of times into Barlows old barn expecting many of the brethren were concealed there but in this they were disappointed, the brethren chiefly lay down on the ground behind some shelter and fired in that position. They fought one hour and twenty minutes, when the mob offered terms of compromise which were these, that all the Mormons should leave the City within five days leaving ten families to finish the unsettled business. The brethren consented to this inasmuch as they had been well informed that 1500 more were coming to join the mob and they had nothing to expect from the authorities of the state. Lyman [E.] Johnson, one of the old Twelve, headed a party of the mob from Keokuk, Iowa territory. Three of the brethren were killed, viz. W[illiam] Anderson, his son, and [] Norris, a blacksmith. 3 others wounded. The mob would not own to any of their party being killed but one person saw them put 16 men into one wagon and handled them more like dead Persons than wounded. The ground where they stood was pretty much Covered with blood, so that there is no doubt they had many slain or wounded. They had 150 baggage wagons. Esquire [Daniel] Wells took command of the brethren and rode to and fro during the whole battle without receiving injury, altho the balls whistled by him on every side. Amos Davis fought bravely. While running across a plowed field, he stumbled and fell on his left arm which formed a triangle with his head. As he fell a cannon ball passed through the angle of his arm between that and his head. Hiram Kimball [received] a slight wound with a musket ball on the forehead. The mob fired 62 shots with the cannon and 10 rounds with the muskets making 12,000 musket balls only killing 3 and wounding 3.

The brethren did not fire so much in proportion but did much more execution. Truly the Lord fights the battles of his saints. The cannon of the brethren was not of much service, they would not carry more than a quarter of a mile, whereas those of the mob would hold well a half a mile. They shot 9 balls through a small smiths shop, one through Esquire Wells barn and one at his house but the ball struck the ground in front of his house and glanced through the well curb. The mayor of Quincy watched the battle from the tower of the Temple and owned that history never afforded a parallel. The brethren then began to get their families and effects over the river where they remain in a suffering and destitute condition til wagons and means are sent from the Saints to their relief.

On the Thursday following the mob 1200 strong entered the City. Tis said from good authority that such is the distress and sufferings of the saints as actually to draw tears from this mob.

[September 26, 1846. Saturday.] [] Russell told me that he had selected 3 lots for us and we could go as soon as we had a mind to. He saw Heber on the subject. I made up my mind to start on Monday.

[September 27, 1846. Sunday.] This morning Brother [James] Smithies came with 6 yoke of Heber's Cattle and said we must be ready to start in five minutes while he went to water his cattle and although we had every thing unprepared we were ready before he got back. I felt well enough to drive a team. We took 6 wagons down and camped on the same block with Heber [Kimball] in Cape Disappointment. James and Pitt went back to wait for Corbit who was herding cows and in the evening returned with three more wagons.

WINTER QUARTERS[29]

[January 1, 1847. Friday.] A.M. at the store. At 2 P.M. went with Diantha to her fathers and partook of a roast Turkey for Dinner. At 4 met the band at the Basket shop and played about 1 1/2 hours. The basket makers made each of us a present of a new basket and showed their gratitude various ways. At 6 met with the band at Father [Heber C.] Kimballs and played for a party till after 1 o'clock. Presidents Young and Kimball danced considerable and all seemed to feel well.

[January 2, 1847. Saturday.] At the store regulating the books and making out [Newel K.] Whitney and [Edwin D.] Woolley's current [accounts]. About 2 o'clock Sarah [Whitney?] came and said her mother wanted me. Moroni[30] had fell into the fire and

---

[29] Clayton's title refers to the camp where the Mormons spent the winter just north of Omaha, Nebraska, in the Missouri River Valley. After a two-month hiatus during which he did not record any entries in the journal, Clayton begins 1847 by describing the Saints' preparation for departure from Winter Quarters. Leaving his four wives and families at Winter Quarters, he departed with the pioneers on April 14, 1847, "in half an hour's notice," for the Great Salt Lake Valley.

[30] Clayton's seventh child, the first by Diantha Farr. At the time of the boy's

burned himself very bad. I went home and found as she said. His face very badly burned, large blisters round his left eye. And burned all over the left side of his head and neck. I immediately applied some consecrated oil and ordered them to keep it on all the time. I then returned to the store. Evening President Young came and took his hardware bill, Domestic Drilling &c. About 8 o'clock I went home . . .

[January 4, 1847. Monday.] At the store all day. Evening waiting on Orson Pratt and Amasa Lyman. Paid my tax today $2.17-1/2 to J[onathan] C. Wright.

[January 7, 1847. Thursday.] At the store, the weather still colder than yesterday. Evening went to Sister Buel[l]s and took supper on a Turkey. Afterwards went to [] Leonards and played for them with [J. F.] Hutchinson and [James] Smithies till 12 o'clock . . .

[January 12, 1847. Tuesday.] This morning Ruth began to feel unwell.[31] I went to the store and continued settlements as usual. Brothers [John D.] Lee and [] Russell returned from Missouri having obtained change for the checks. About 4 P.M. President Young and J. D. Lee came to Bishop Whitney's and I received in Gold $496.17, and in silver $1080.52 out of 3 checks which Lee took value $2,447.32, the balance to be accounted for hereafter. Soon as I got through receiving the money I was informed that my folks had sent for me and I went home soon after and found that Ruth had brought forth a son 20 minutes after 5 P.M. She had a pretty hard time but feels comfortable as can be expected. The boy is named Newel Horace. Evening I met with the band at [] Johnsons and played till about 11 o'clock. The house was very much crowded and not much room to dance, but they kept it up freely . . .

[January 18, 1847. Monday.] At the store all day mostly paying money to the soldiers wives . . .

[January 22, 1846. Friday.] At the store paying money &c.

---

birth, March 30, 1846, Clayton and Diantha named him William Adriel Benoni, but he was called Moroni, which was the name of the angel Joseph Smith described from a vision. See April 15, 1846, entry.
[31] Ruth was about to give birth to Newel H. Clayton.

Evening went with Hutchinson to [] Packers party and played for the party in the smoke till near midnight . . .

[January 26, 1847. Tuesday.] At the store till 2 P.M. Afterward went with the Quadrille Band to the "Council House" agreeably to previous notice and played for a party of men (70s) and their families who had assisted in building the house. They danced till about midnight. We had plenty to eat and drink through the interview and a very pleasant party.

[January 27, 1847. Wednesday.] At the store again till noon. At 2 P.M. at the Council House with the Q[uadrille] Band and played for another company of those who had assisted in building the house. We had plenty of refreshments and a very sociable party as on yesterday. Broke up again about midnight. ..

[February 2, 1847. Tuesday.] At the store till noon. Afterwards at the Council House with the Quadrille Band playing for Brighams children and the children of the Youngs family generally.

[February 3, 1847. Wednesday.] At the store till noon. Afterwards at the Council House with the Q[uadrille] Band to play for a family meeting of the Youngs family. President B. Young was quite sick and seemed very low spirited. After the meeting had been opened by prayer, the President called on his brothers to stand up by him in the center of the room which they did according to age. John Young took his place at the head, then Phineas, Joseph, Brigham [Young] and Lorenzo. The president then called on Heber to take his place in the line inasmuch as he had been recognized about fifteen years as a member of the Young family. He took his place between Joseph and Brigham. The President then said this was the first time that father Young's boys had been together in the same capacity for a number of years &c.[32] After a few remarks the remainder of the evening was spent by partaking of a good supper and cheerful dancing till about two in the morning, when the party broke up in the best of spirits and good feeling[33] . . .

---

[32] At this time Brigham Young had eighteen wives and eleven children (Leonard J. Arrington, *Brigham Young: American Moses* [New York: Alfred A. Knopf, 1985], 420–21).

[33] The pages from February 9 to April 8, 1847, are missing; a gap in the

[April 11, 1847. Sunday.] At home and Farrs. I told Winslow Farr concerning Hosea Stouts threats to take my life after the Twelve are gone &c. He called at night on his return from the Council and told me to be on my guard[34] . . .

[April 13, 1847. Tuesday.] At home most of the day. Thomas and James started for the farm. Evening went to the store and told Brigham and Heber about Hosea Stout's calculations &c.

[April 14, 1847. Wednesday.] This morning severely pained with rheumatism in my face. At 11 o'clock Brigham and Dr. Richards came. B. told me to rise up and start with the pioneers in half an hour's notice. I delivered to him the records of the K[ingdom] of G[od] and set my folks to work to get my clothes together to start with the pioneers. At 2 o'clock I left my family and started in Heber's carriage with Heber and W[illia]m Kimball and Ellen Sanders. Bishop Whitney and [Amasa] Lyman went out with us in another wagon. We went about 19 miles and camped on the prairie. After supper Heber prayed and we retired to rest.

[April 15, 1847. Thursday.] After eating and prayers by Bishop Whitney started at half past 7 and got to the Elk Horn at 11 1/2. We were all across at 12 and there we overtook Brigham, G. A. Smith, E. T. Benson and Amasa Lyman. We arrived at the pioneers Camp about 3 P.M. This Camp is about 12 miles from the Elk Horn and about 47 from Winter Quarters. I spent the evening with Aaron Farr, Horace Whitney and Jackson Redding.

[April 16, 1847. Friday.] This day is gloomy, windy and cold. About 8 the Camp were called together and organized. 2 Captains of 100's viz. Stephen Markham and A[lbert] P. Rockwood were appointed, also 5 captains of 50s and 14 Captains of 10s. There are 143 men and boys on the list of the pioneer company 3 women and Lorenzo Youngs two children. 73 wagons. O. P.

---

binding suggests that they either became unglued or were pulled from the journal. Entries of February 4-9 and April 9-10, which I have omitted, contain repetitious phrasings like "at store all day."

[34] A bodyguard of Joseph Smith, Hosea Stout was in charge of the Nauvoo police. Mormon historian Juanita Brooks asked whether Clayton was the delinquent policeman mentioned in Hosea Stout's diary whom Stout had threatened because he had neglected to attend his duty on January 30, 1847, to protect one of the Twelve (Brooks, ed., *On the Mormon Frontier*, 1:232-33).

Rockwell has gone back to Camp with J[esse] C. Little. Bishop Whitney, Lyman, W[illia]m Kimball and J[oseph] B. Noble return from here to Winter Quarters. The following is a list of all the names of this pioneer company. To wit:

Wilford Woodruff, John S. Fowler, Jacob Burnham, Orson Pratt, Joseph Egbert, John M. Freeman, Marcus B. Thorpe, George A. Smith, George Wardle, 2nd 10 Thomas Grover, Ezra T. Benson, Barnabas L. Adams, Roswell Stevens, Amasa Lyman, Sterling Driggs, Albert Carrington, Thomas Bullock, George Brown, Willard Richards, Jesse C. Little, 3rd 10 Phineas H. Young, John Y. Greene, Thomas Tanner, Brigham Young, Addison Everett, Truman O. Angel, Lorenzo Young and wife, Bryant Stringham, Albert P. Rockwood, Joseph L. Schofield, 4th 10 Luke Johnson, John Holman, Edmund Elsworth, Alvarnus Hanks, George R. Grant, Millen Atwood, Samuel Fox, Tunis Rappleyee, Harvey Pierce, William Dykes, Jacob Weilar, 5th 10 Stephen H. Goddard, Tarlton Lewis, Henry G. Sherwood, Zebedee Coltrin, Sylvester H. Earl, John Dixon, Samuel H. Marble, George Scholes, William Henrie, William A. Empy, 6th 10 Charles Shumway, Andrew Shumway, Thomas Woolsey, Chancy Loveland, Erastus Snow, James Craig, William Wordsworth, William Vance, Simeon Howd, Seeley Owen, 7th 10 James Case, Artemas Johnson, William A. Smoot, Franklin B. Dewey, William Carter, Franklin G. Losee, Burr Frost, Datus Ensign, Franklin B. Stewart, Monroe Frink, Eric Glines, Ozro Eastman, 8th 10 Seth Taft, Horace Thornton, Stephen Kelsey, John S. Eldredge, Charles D. Barnham, Almon M. Williams, Rufus Allen, Robert T. Thomas, James W. Stuart, Elija Newman, Levi N. Kendall, Francis Boggs, David Grant, 9th 10 Heber C. Kimball, Howard Egan, William A. King, Thomas Cloward, Hosea Cushing, Robert Byard, George Billings, Edson Whipple, Philo Johnson, William Clayton, 10th 10 Appleton M. Harmon, Carlos Murray, Hoarace K. Witney, Orson K. Whitney, Orrin P. Rockwell, Nathaniel Thomas Brown,[35] R. Jackson Redding, John Pack, Francis M. Pomroy, Aaron Farr, Nathaniel Fairbanks, 11th 10 John S. Higbee, John Wheeler, Solomon Chamberlain, Conrad Klinenman, Joseph Rooker, Perry Fitzgerald, John H. Tippets, James Davenport,

---

[35] A note under his name in the journal reads "dead."

Henson Walker, Benjamin Rolfe, 12th 10 Norton Jacobs, Charles
A. Harper, George Woodard,[36] Stephen Markham, Lewis Barney,
George Mills, Andrew Gibbons, Joseph Hancock, John W. Norton,
13th 10 Shadrach Roundy, Hans C. Hanson, Levi Jackman,
Lyman Curtis, John Brown, Mathew Ivory, David Powell, Hark
Lay, Oscar Crosby,[37] 14th 10 Joseph Mathews, Gilbird Summe,
John Gleason Charles Burke, Alexander P. Chessley, Rodney
Badger, Norman Taylor, Green Flake Black Ellis Eames.

72 wagons 93 horses 52 mules 66 oxen 19 cows 17 dogs and []
chickens.

The names of the females in this Camp are Harriet Page
Young, Clarissa Decker, and Ellen Sanders.[38] The names of the
children Isaac Perry Decker Young and Sabisky L. Young, making a total of 148 souls who have started to go West of the mountains as Pioneers to find a home where the Saints can live in
peace and enjoy the fruits of their labors, and where we shall not
be under the dominion of Gentile governments, subject to the
wrath of mobs and where the standards of peace can be raised,
the Ensign to the nations reared and the Kingdom of God flour-
ish until truth shall prevail, and the Saints enjoy the fulness of
the gospel.

The following are the names of the Captains of 50's as appointed at this organization Viz. Addison Everett, Tarlton Lewis,
James Case, John Pack and Shadrack Roundy. The Captains of
10's are as follows:

Wilford Woodruff, Ezra T. Benson, Phineas H. Young, Luke
Johnson, Stephen H. Goddard, Charles Shumway, James Case,
Seth Taft, Howard Egan, Appleton M. Harmon, John S. Higbee,
Norton Jacobs, John Brown, Joseph Mathews.

Stephen Markham was appointed the Captain of the Guard
and ordered to select out of the Camp, fifty men for guard, such
as he had confidence in who are to be considered as a standing

---

[36] A note underneath his name in the journal reads "Cannon."

[37] "Blacks" is written above Oscar Crosby's name in the journal.

[38] The wife of Lorenzo Young, Brigham Young's brother, and the plural wives
of Brigham Young and Heber C. Kimball; Clayton listed the two plural wives
without their husbands' surnames. Brigham Young planned to take only men on the
trek from Winter Quarters to the Great Salt Lake Valley. However, he agreed to
bring his brother's wife, Harriet, because of her asthma, and her daughter, Clara,
and Ellen Kimball to keep Harriet company (Arrington, *Brigham Young*, 130).

guard, to attend to the wagons each night, 12 of them to stand at a time, and to have 2 sets each night, that is 12 each watch to stand half the night. In cases where the horses and cattle are tied some distance from the wagons at night an extra guard is to be selected from the balance of the company or Camps. The standing guard not being permitted to leave the immediate neighborhood of the wagons. After the organization was over I wrote a letter to Diantha, and put it into the hands of Bishop Whitney, together with the one I received yesterday from father and I[] McEwan, also the one from Ellen to James [Case]. Up to 12 o'clock M. I had no w[h]ere to put my Trunk and clothing, and did not know what to do with them. However soon after Heber told me to put them in Appleton M. Harmons wagon, which was done. At 2 the camp started out to proceed on the journey. I bid farwell to Bishop Whitney and his brother Lyman and son Joshua, who all returned from this place, also William H. Kimball and Joseph B. Noble. We traveled about 3 miles and encamped in a line about 600 yards from timber, where there is plenty of Cotton Wood and some rushes. This night I slept with Philo Johnson, but having only one quilt, and the night severely cold, I suffered much, and took a very bad cold. The country in the neighborhood of the Elk Horn is one of the most beautiful I ever saw. The bluffs on the East are nicely rolling and beautifully lined with timber, and some very nice Cedar groves. From these bluffs a little above the Ferry you can see the meanderings of the Platte River, and the beautiful level bottom on the north of it about 15 miles wide for many miles up the river. The Horn is a beautiful River about 150 feet wide and about 4 feet deep.

[April 17, 1847. Saturday.] This morning the weather is severely cold, with a strong wind from the North and North West. We started out at 9 o'clock and traveled till near 12 the distance being about 7 miles. We camped close by a cotton wood grove, and the brethren fell hundreds of them to feed their teams and save corn. There is a small lake close by but the water is not good and the brethren go to the river about a half a mile. At 5 P.M. the Camps were called together and organized in military order as follows:

Brigham Young, Lieutenant General
Stephen Markham, Colonel

John Pack and Shadrack Roundy, Majors.

The Captains of 10's to be captains of 10's in this order, except John Pack, who being appointed Major, Appleton M. Harmon was appointed captain in his stead.

Thomas Bullock, clerk of the camp. Thomas Tanner captain of the cannon with the privilege of choosing 8 men to manage it in case of necessity. The President then said after we start from here, every man must keep his loaded gun in his hand, or in wagon where he can put his hand on it at a moments warning. If they are cap locks, take off the cap and put on a little leather to keep wet &c. out. If flint locks, take out the priming and fill the pan with tw[ine] or cotton &c.[39]

The wagons must keep together when travelling, and not separate as they have previously done, and every man to walk beside his own wagon, and not leave it only by permission. A while before evening one of the traders wagons came from the Pawnee village, loaded with furs and peltry, and camped about 1/4 of a mile below us. At night [Ellis] Eames and [Hans C.] Hanson played some on their violins. All peace and quietness. At night I slept with [Howard] Egan in Heber's wagon, Heber being gone to sleep with President Young.

[April 18, 1847. Sunday.] This morning I wrote a letter for Heber to his wife Vilate which was sent by Brother Ellis Eames who has concluded to go back on account of poor health, spitting blood &c. He started back with the traders wagon about eight o'clock A.M. The wind this morning E. and S.E. and very cold, with a slight shower of snow. At 10 A.M. 7 more traders wagons came in and stopped about 1/4 of a mile below us, soon after 6 mules loaded with robes and furs. These traders say they have come from the Pawnee village in two days. Brother Roundy got some Buffalo meat from them and give me a little, which I thought tasted very good. I commenced writing Hebers journal and wrote

---

[39] Young is describing two types of muskets — smooth-bore, long-barrelled firearms used before the invention of the rifle. Each type employed a particular gunlock mechanism which ignited the primer, causing the main charge to explode and expel a projectile. The earlier flintlock variety used flint and steel to ignite a primer charge with a spark. In the more advanced caplock, a percussion hammer caused the primer to explode. In each case, it was necessary to keep the ignition powder dry.

considerable. He wants me to write his journal all the journey.[40] I also wrote considerable in this book. P.M. the weather more moderate and pleasant, the wind has changed near South and the sun shines . . .

At 5 o'clock, the officers of the camp met with President Young, and he told the order for travelling and camping hereafter, which was communicated to the companies by the Captains of 10's as follows.

At 5:00 in the morning the bugle is to be sounded as a signal for every man to arise and attend prayers before he leaves his wagon. Then cooking, eating, feeding teams &c. till 7 o'clock at which time the Camp is to move at the sound of the bugle. Each teamster to keep beside his team, with their loaded gun in their hands or in their wagon where they can get them in a moment. The extra men, each to walk opposite his wagon with his loaded gun on his shoulder, and no man to be permitted to leave his wagon unless he obtains permission from his officer. In case of an attack from Indians[41] or hostile appearances the wagons to travel in double file. The order of encampment to be in a circle with the mouth of the wagon to the outside, and the horses and stock tied inside the circle. At 8 1/2 P.M. the bugles to be sounded again at which time all to have prayers in their wagons and to retire to rest by 9 o'clock. Tonight I went to bed about 7 1/2 o'clock suffering severely with pain in my head and face. I slept with Philo Johnson.

[April 19, 1847. Monday.] At 5 A.M., at the sound of the bugle I arose, my face still paining me very badly. After eating breakfast I started out on foot before the wagons started with my rifle on my shoulder. At 7 1/4 the wagons began to move and at 7 1/2 were all formed in double file and proceeded on. After traveling about 8 miles we arrived at a number of small lakes, where

---

[40] Clayton wrote the entire "Pioneer Journal of Heber C. Kimball" from April 5 to June 25, 1847. This was serialized in the *Utah Geneological and Historical Magazine* from 1939 to 1940. See Stanley B. Kimball, ed., *On the Potter's Wheel: The Diaries of Heber C. Kimball* (Salt Lake City: Signature Books in association with Smith Research Associates, 1987), xiv–xv.

[41] Indian attacks accounted for only 4 percent of the deaths encountered on the overland trail from 1840 to 1860. Cholera was the primary killer, followed by drownings and gunshot wounds (Unruh, 345).

were many ducks. A number of brethren shot at them and killed several. At 1 1/4 we arrived at a bend in the river where a small stream runs around an island.

We stayed here to feed awhile, having traveled about 15 miles mostly a western course with the wind South. The roads very good and the country very level on these flat Bottoms of the Platte river which bottoms appear to be from ten to fifteen miles wide. Soon after the camp was formed O. P. Rockwell, Jackson Redding, and J[esse] C. Little came in from winter quarters. They arrived at 10 minutes after 2. They have found Dr. Richards mare which was lost east of the Elk Horn and brought her to camp. They brought me a line from Diantha and one from Ruth and Margaret. In the last was a very gentle piece of information which has caused me to reflect much, and proves to me that Ruth and Margaret's virtue and integrity have for the last year been far superior to mine. In my letter to them I requested them to attend to family prayer in my absence, a thing which I have neglected since leaving Nauvoo. They informed me that they had done that when I was at home but unknown to me, and they had then, and still continue to bear me up before their heavenly father. O what integrity, what faithfulness. I feel unworthy to possess two such treasures, but still feel to try to reward them for it, and may my Father in heaven bless them, and all my family and let his angels guard them, and me during my absence that we may all be permitted to meet again and enjoy each other's Society in this world for many years to come, and eternally in the world to come. O Lord, grant this prayer of thy unworthy Servant, and fill my family with peace and union, and open a way that they may have the necessaries and comforts of life, and thy Spirit to brood over them, and Thy name shall have the praise, even so Amen . . . I walked some this afternoon with Orson Pratt and suggested to him the idea of fixing a set of wooden cog wheels to the hub of a wagon wheel, in such order as to tell the exact number of miles we travel each day. He seemed to agree with me that it could be easily done at a trifling expense . . .

[April 20, 1847. Tuesday.] Arose at 5 1/2 . . . John S. Higbee, Luke Johnson, S[tephen] Markham, and some others, started ahead of the camp about noon, and went about 2 miles farther than this place to a lake with the boat and seine.[42] They took over 200 very nice fish, and arrived with them about the time the camp was formed. The fish were distributed around the Camp according to the number of persons in each wagon, generally two to a wagon, and the brethren enjoyed a good supper on fish. I went to the river and washed my feet which were very dusty and sore. I also washed my socks as well as I could in cold water without soap. After Brother Luke Johnson had got through distributing fish, I went and asked him to draw my tooth. He willingly agreed, and getting his instruments, I set down in a chair, he lanced the gum, then took his nippers and jerked it out. The whole operation did not take more than one minute. He only got half the original tooth, the balance being left in the jaw. After this my head and face pained me much more than before. I eat but little to supper and then lay down, but could not sleep for pain till near morning. The evening was very calm and pleasant.

[April 21, 1847. Wednesday.] Arose at 5, my face easier, but swelled and my gums raw. Took breakfast on fish and coffee, but ate no bread it being very dry and hard I could not bear to put it in my mouth. At 7 started on foot the ox teams being gone ahead. Some appearances of rain, and a slight shower fell. Wind North East and pretty cool. At 1/4 to 9 an Indian rode up to the first wagon and appeared very friendly. Soon after 6 or 8 others came running on foot. They came from the timber about a mile to the left. At 10 we arrived at a fork in the road, the one on the left leading to the new Pawnee Village, and the one to the right leaving the Village some distance to the South. A consultation was held by President Young with father [James] Case, relative to the roads crossing the river &c. when it was concluded to take the right hand road. We proceeded accordingly and at 12:00 came in sight of the new Pawnee village, in an open spot on the south bank of the Loop Fork, between two bodies of timber. The village appeared to be about three 3/4 mile South of the road we were on. At 12 1/2 we were opposite the village, and could then see distinctly upwards of 100 lodges, set pretty close together, and appeared to be ranged in several lines, and set in good order. We proceeded until we arrived at a long narrow lake by the side

[42] A fishnet.

of the timber and near to the river. At 1 P.M. the encampment was formed on the bank of the lake and a guard instantly placed at the passes, as many of the Indians had followed us, although they had to wade the river, but it is very shoal. One of the Indians presented several certificates from persons who had previously traveled through their village, all certifying that the Grand Chief of the Pawnees was friendly disposed, and they had made him presents of a little powder, lead, Salt &c. Heber gave them a little tobacco and a little salt and President Young gave to the chief some powder, lead, salt and a number of the brethren gave a little flour each. The old chief however did not seem to think the presents sufficient, and said he did not like us to go west through their country, he was afraid we should kill their Buffalo and drive them off. Brother [Charles] Shumway told him we did not like Buffalo, but this does not appear to give him much satisfaction. However there was no appearance of hostility. In fact, all that came to camp seemed highly pleased to shake hands with our brethren and would run from one side to another so as not to miss one. A number of the squaws were on the opposite side of the lake with mattocks[43] digging roots. Brother Shumway says there are about twelve thousand of the Pawnees in this neighborhood, and it is reported that there are five thousand warriors. We did not see many of them. [] Sarpy is at their village trading, and it is uncertain whether he will endeavor to use an influence for us or against us. We have no fear however, because their only object appears to be plunder, and it is the calculation to be well prepared by night and day. During the resting hour I spent the time writing in my journal. At 2 1/4 P.M. the ox teams started out again and the horse teams soon after. The weather had been calm and pleasant for a few hours, but about 2 or a little before, some heavy clouds began to gather, and thunder was heard at a distance. About 1/2 after 2 the rain began to descend heavy, accompanied by heavy peals of thunder and vivid lightning which continued till about 4 o'clock. A strong north wind blew up, the rain and thunder ceased and the weather grew very cold. We traveled till 5 1/2 and the encampment was formed on the Loop fork of the Platte river. After the encampment was formed and teams turned out the brethren were all called together and some remarks

---

[43] A digging tool sharpened like a pickaxe.

made by President Young advising them to have a strong guard around the camps tonight. He called for volunteers to stand guard and about 100 volunteered amongst whom were all the twelve except Dr. Richards. This guard were divided into two companies of fifty each, one company to stand the first half the night, and the remainder the last half. Those of the twelve who stood took the first watch till 1 o'clock. Brigham and Heber both stood on guard. Out of the companies a party were stationed as a picket guard some distance from the Camp, the balance stood near the camp. The night was very cold, with a strong wind from the north East, and in the middle of the night it rained considerable. Our course this morning was about west. This afternoon, north West, we are now within 3 miles from the bluffs on the north. We have travelled today about 20 miles, the roads being good and very level. This grass here is short but looks good. The Buffalo grass is very short and curly like the hair on a buffalo robe. The spring grass don't seem to be as early here as at the Elk Horn, [] and the last years growth not being burnt off, will be rather a disadvantage to the spring companies. I have noticed all the way on this bottom from the Elk Horn that the ground is full of wild onions which appear far richer and larger than any wild onions I ever saw. I have no idea that Corn would grow here for the land is very dry and loose and sandy, and appears poor. The country is beautiful and pleasing to the eye of the traveler, although you can only see one kind of scenery for several days.

[April 22, 1847. Thursday.] Arose soon after 5 o'clock, my face very painful again caused by the cold. There has been no trouble from the Indians and all is peace and safe. The cannon was prepared for action, and stood all night just outside the wagons. There was considerable joking this morning on account of two of the picket guard having their guns stole and Colonel [Stephen] Markham having his hat stole. The owners were found asleep while on guard and those who found them so, took their guns to be a warning to them, but it is difficult for men to keep awake night after night, after traveling 20 miles in the day taking care of teams, cooking &c . . .

At 12 1/4 we arrived on the East bank of "Be[a]ver river" having travelled about 10 miles. This stream is from 20 to 25 feet wide swift current, clear water and pleasanted tasted, the banks tolerably well lined with timber. Here we stopped to feed. Some of the brethren went to fix the fording place a little, the banks are steep on each side and the water a little over two feet deep. At 2 P.M. started again the ox teams first. When [passing] the river a number of the brethren stood on the west bank with a long rope which was hooked to the wagon tongue and they assisted the teams up the bank. The wagon I rode in crossed at 20 minutes after 2 and in a little while all were safely over. We proceeded on till half past 5 when we arrived at the Pawnee Missionary station which is about 7 miles from "Beaver River" . . .

The government station is a quarter of a mile below, or south where Father [James] Case lived as government farmer and received $300. a year for it, but when Major [Thomas] Harvey learned at the last pay day, which was last November that Father Case had joined the Mormons he very politely dismissed him from government service. The Sioux came down sometime ago and burned up the government station houses, blacksmith shop and every thing, but the missionary station they did not touch. This place according to my account is 134 miles from winter quarters, and a lovely place to live. Before dark the President called the camp together and told them they might use the fodder and hay for their teams but forbade any man carrying anything away, even to the value of one cent. He said he had no fears of the Pawnees troubling us here but we had better be prepared lest the Sioux should come down and try to steal horses. A guard was selected and a picket guard to watch the ravine to the north . . .

The variation of the compass is about 12 degrees at this place. The latitude []. I again introduced the subject of fixing machinery to a wagon wheel to tell the distance we travel, describing the machinery and the time it would take to make &c. Several caught the idea and feel confident of its success . . .

[April 24, 1847. Saturday.] . . . Evening I walked over to O. Pratts wagon, and through his telescope saw Jupiter's four moons very distinct, never having seen them previously. I went over to my wagon and looked through my glass and could see them with it, but not so distinct as with Orson's . . .

[April 25, 1847. Sunday.] Arose soon after five, shaved and changed some of my clothing. The morning very pleasant, wind west . . . P.M. Elijah Newman was baptized by [Tarlton] Lewis

305

in the Lake for the benefit of his health. Brother Newman has been afflicted with the black scurvy in his legs and has not been able to walk without sticks, but after being baptized and hands laid on him he returned to his waggon without any kind of help seemingly much better. Soon after 5 P.M. a meeting was called at the wagon of President Young and remarks made by several, and instructions by President Young, chiefly in reference to the guard and the folly of conforming to gentile military customs on an expedition of this nature. After dark the twelve and some others met together opposite the presidents wagon, to select men to go a hunting Buffalo &c. as we proceed on the journey. It was ascertained that there are 8 horses in the company which are not attached to teams. Then eight men were selected to hunt on horseback viz. Thomas Moulsey, Thomas Brown, John Brown, O. P. Rockwell, John S. Higbee, Joseph Mathews. Then there was selected 11 men to hunt also on foot viz. John Pack, Phineas H. Young, Tarlton [Lewis], Joseph Hancock, Edmund Ellsworth, Roswell Stevens, Edson Whipple, Barnabas S. Adams, Benj[ami]n F. Stewart, Jackson Redding and [E.] Glines.

It was also noted that all the twelve have the privilege of hunting when they have a mind to. After some remarks and cautions in regard to chasing the wild buffallo the company were dismissed, and I retired to bed soon after 9 o'clock, the evening being very fine and pleasant.

[April 26, 1847. Monday.] This morning about half past 3 an alarm was sounded. I immediately got out of the wagon and learned that three of the guard who were stationed to the North East of the Camp had discovered some Indians crawling up towards the wagons. They first received alarm from the motions of one of our horses, and noticing this they went towards the spot and listening heard something rustle in grass; they first suspected they were wolves and fired at them. Only one gun went off and six Indians sprung up and run from within a few rods of where they stood. Another gun was then fired at them and the Camp alarmed. A strong guard was placed all round, and a charge of cannister put in the Cannon. The day was just breaking when this took place and the moon had just gone down. The air being extremely cold and fires put out I retired into the wagon till morning and arose again at half after 5. After daylight, the footsteps of the Indians could be plainly seen, where they had come down under the bank and sometimes stepped into the water. No doubt their object was to steal horses, and they had a fair privilege, if the guard had been found asleep for the Camp was only formed in a half circle and some horses tied outside. However the prompt reception they met with will have a tendency to shew them that we keep a good watch and may deter them from making another attempt. Orders were given for the tens to assemble for prayers this morning instead of two in each wagon, which was done. President Young told me this morning that as soon as my health will permit, he wants me to assist Brother [Thomas] Bullock in keeping minutes &c as Brother Bullock is hard run, having to take care of a team and attend to other chores.

The camp started out about 8 o'clock. I started at 7 1/2 on foot and travelled four miles, then waited for the wagons. There no road here, Consequently, President Young, Kimball, G. A. A. Lyman and others went ahead on horse back to point out the road. The horse teams travel first to break the strong grass so that it will not hurt the Oxens feet. The hunters started out in different directions keeping only a few miles from the wagons . . .

About 8 o'clock Joseph Mathews came into Camp from seeking his horses and stated that an Indian had rode a horse off a little before and he supposed it was Brother [Jesse] Little's horse, which was missing. Dr. Richards mare was also missing. Brother Mathews stated that he went out to see for his Black man who was out watching his team, and as he arrived he saw Brother Little's horse as he supposed going towards the river. He ran towards it to turn it back to camp, but as soon as he commenced running the horse sprang to a gallop, which made him suppose there was an Indian on him, but he could not see the Indian. As soon as he gave the alarm 5 or 6 of the brethren mounted their horses, and pursued on the course pointed out to the river, but could neither see nor hear a horse nor Indian. When they returned, President Young and Kimball and a number of others went out on horseback and searched till near 11 o'clock, but likewise proved unsuccessful. The brethren have been repeatedly warned not to let their horses go far from their wagons, but every time we stop they can be seen around for more than 2 miles. These are 2 good horses and the owners feel bad enough, but it will be a warning to others to be more careful.

[April 27, 1847. Tuesday.] Arose soon after 5. The morning fine and pleasant. During the night the guard fired twice but they supposed they were wolves they fired at. I went back to old Indian village before breakfast, and also with O. P. Rockwell, to see if any tracks of the lost horses could be found. He followed one track some way into a bunch of willows, but having no arms we returned. At 1/4 to 8 the wagons commenced moving and travelled till 1/4 after 2 being about 12 miles, nearly a South course, the design being to go to the main branch of the Platte. President Young, Kimball and others went forward again to point out the road. O. P. Rockwell and some others started back to hunt the horses about the time we started . . .

At 1/2 after 6 O. P. Rockwell, Joseph Mathews, John Eldridge and Thomas Brown returned from hunting the 2 lost horses. They reported that they went back to within about 2 miles of where we encamped on Sunday and looking off towards the river they saw something move in the grass at the foot of a high mole. They proceeded towards it thinking it was a wolf, when within about 12 or 14 rods Porter stoppt to shoot at the supposed wolf. The moment he elevated his rifle 15 Indians sprang to their feet, all naked except the breech cloth, and armed with rifles and bows and arrows. Each man having a rifle slung on his back, and his bow strung tight in his hand and about 20 arrows. The Indians advanced towards them but the brethren motioned and told them to pucacher[44] and held there rifles and pistols ready to meet them. When the Indians saw this they began to holler, 'bacco' 'bacco.' The brethren told them they had no tobacco. One of the Indians came close beside J. Mathews horse to shake hands with Mathews but kept his eye on the horses bridle. When nearly within reach of the Bridle Brown cocked his pistol and pointed at the Indian shouting if he did not leave he would kill him. At which, the Indian seeing the pistol ready to fire retreated. The Indians made signs to get the brethren lower down the river but the brethren turned their horses to come to camp thinking it unsafe to go nearer to the timber where they expected more Indians lay in ambush. When the brethren turned to come back the Indians fired 6 shots at them with their rifles and the brethren immedi-

---

[44] The context of this term, perhaps Indian, suggests a warning to stop and put down their weapons.

ately faced about at which the Indians fled towards the timber below. The brethren did not shoot at the Indians, even when the Indians shot at them. They saw the tracks of the horses which are missing and returned satisfied that the Pawnees have got them, and no doubt intended to get the horses on which the brethren rode, but they met with too stern a reception to risk an attempt. Some of these same Indians were amongst those who came into camp when we stopped for dinner near their village, and proves that they eyed the horses pretty close, and also proves that they have followed us close ever since. The brethren run great risks indeed, but got back safe to camp without harm . . .

[April 28, 1847. Wednesday.] Morning fine and pleasant, no disturbance from Indians . . .

Our course for the first 7 miles was a little East of South over a very level prairie and green with grass. The largest wild onions grow here I have ever seen. After traveling about 7 miles we turned South West, being within a mile of the main Platte and opposite to Grand Island. We traveled till half past 2 and then stopped to feed having come about 11 miles today. The roads extremely dusty and the strong wind blows it into the wagons and everything is covered. We are now near to timber and a good chance for grass for the cattle. At 4 P.M. we moved again and traveled till 6, having travelled about 4 miles and during the day about 15 miles. We have camped about a quarter of a mile from the timber and there is plenty of grass to fill the stock tonight. The water is also clear and cool and good tasted. The evening is cloudy and very cool, which affects my head some. Suppered on some antelope and went to bed early.

[April 29, 1847. Thursday.] The wagons started at 5 o'clock this morning before breakfast to find more grass as this is all eat off. We traveled till 6 1/2 being about three miles, and then turned out the teams to feed. The morning very cool. There seems to be very little rain in this country and no dew. Breakfasted on Goose and mouldy bread . . .

[April 30, 1847. Friday.] . . . Having the privilege of copying from Brother Bullock's journal, I will now record the names of the standing guard as organized April 16, also the men selected by Brother Tanner to form the gun division as ordered Saturday, April 17[45] . . .

[May 1, 1847. Saturday.] The morning very cold indeed. Inasmuch as there is little grass for the cattle, the camp started out at 20 minutes to 6 and travelled till a quarter after 8 about 6 miles before breakfast. Soon after we started this morning three buffalo were seen grazing on the bluff about 6 miles distance. I could see them very plain with my glass. O. P. Rockwell, Thomas Brown and Luke Johnson started on horseback to try to kill some. Soon after they went, another herd of buffalo were seen to the North West at the foot of the bluffs about 8 miles off. I counted with my glass, 72, and Orson Pratt counted 74 . . .

[May 2, 1847. Sunday.] This morning is fine but cold. Ice about half an inch thick. Sometime in the night a buffalo and calf came within a short distance of the wagons. The guard discovered them and shot at the calf, wounding it in the hind leg. They caught it alive and tied it up near the wagons but concluded finally to kill and dress it. About 6 o'clock we were gladdened to see Joseph Hancock come into camp with a piece of buffallo meat. He reported that he Killed a buffallo yesterday back on the bluffs, and there being no one with him he concluded to stay by it over night. He made a fire and scattered a little powder round his buffallo to keep off the wolves . . .

[May 4, 1847. Tuesday.] At half past 7 the camp was called together and received instructions from President Young, especially in regard to leaving the wagons and scattering off hunting without counsel. He strongly urged the brethren not to do it any more and said if they did, some of them would be caught by the Indians and if not killed would be severely abused. The instructions and regulations given April 17th were read and enjoined upon the camp to be observed more strictly. It was decided that the cannon wagon should be unloaded, the box put on another wagon, so that the cannon can be always ready for action. An addition of 10 volunteers was made to the standing guard and ordered that all horses and mules should be tied inside the circle

---

[45] Here Clayton records a list of names which he apparently copied from the journal kept by Thomas Bullock, the official camp scribe.

at night, and cattle and cows outside within a few rods of the wagons. A guard to be placed around the cattle when turned out to graze. It is thought best to travel with the wagons four abreast and the cannon to go in the rear . . .

After travelling about half a mile the camp stopped some time waiting for some wagons behind. While stopping 3 wagons were discovered on the opposite bank of the river considered to be traders going back to Council Bluffs. The river is about 2 miles wide and no person here acquainted with it, consequently no one attempted to go over, which many desired. About 11 o'clock we proceeded five wagons abreast so as to be better prepared for defence should the Indians attack us. After traveling about two miles, one of men from the wagons on the other side the river overtook us and we halted to see him. He said there are only 9 of them. They have been to Fort Laramie[46] for furs and are going to counsel bluffs. This is the sixteenth day since they left the Fort with Ox teams. He says the road is good on the other side and the river easily forded, not being more than knee deep in the deepest place and a good bottom. He cheerfully agreed to carry letters back for us but could not wait long. I wrote one to my family and in about half an hour a pretty large mail was made up to send back to winter quarters, and may the Lord grant that it may arrive safe. Brother Johnson bought a buffalo robe of the man for about a pound and a half of coffee, and another brother bought one for a pound of sugar and a little Pork. I feel my mind relieved by this unexpected privilege of writing back to my dear family and hope they will have the pleasure of perusing the contents . . .

[May 6, 1847. Thursday.] . . . we discovered the horsemen coming back, and found that the president had lost his large spy

---

[46]There were four main trading posts along the western trail: Fort Laramie, Fort Bridger, Fort Hall, and Fort Boise. What is known as Fort Laramie was originally Fort William, located at the convergence of the Platte and Laramie rivers, operated by the American Fur Company. Over time the fur company rebuilt it of adobe, under the name of Fort John, though it was still commonly called Fort Laramie. In 1849, the American Fur Company sold it to the United States government. It was built around the early-nineteenth-century home of Jacques Laramie (possibly Lorimier or La Ramee), an American fur trapper of French descent who explored southeast Wyoming. Frances Parkman said that at Fort Laramie "the overland travellers were plundered and cheated without mercy" (Unruh, 198–204, 215).

glass while chasing the cows from the buffalo herd a second time.[47]

[May 7, 1847. Friday.] . . . About 8 o'clock the camp were called together and measures taken to raise more team to put to the Cannon, as some of the horses and even cattle have gave out. The president chastised E[rastus] Snow for not attending to the cows yesterday causing the president to lose his spyglass, it being Brother Snow's turn to drive the cows according to his own voluntary agreement. At a little before 11 o'clock Porter Rockwell, Thomas Brown and Joseph Mathews started back to hunt the spy glass . . .

About 4 Porter and the others returned having found the spy glass, which was a source of joy to all the brethren.

[May 8, 1847. Saturday.] Morning cold but fine. Started out at nine o'clock and traveled till one P.M., distance 7 1/2 miles, course a little West of N.W. The prairie on both sides the river are literally black with buffalo, and to try to say as to what number we have seen this morning would be folly. I should imagine that at a moderate calculation, we have seen over fifty thousand . . .

It is with some difficulty that the horsemen can drive them away from the track as fast as the wagons come up . . . I have counted the revolutions of a wagon wheel to tell the exact distance we have travelled . . . I found the wheel 14 feet 8 inches in circumference, not varying one eighth of an inch. I then calculated how many revolutions it would require for 1 mile and found it precisely 360 not varying one fraction which somewhat astonished me. I have counted the whole revolutions during the days travel and find it to be a little over 11 1/4 miles, (20 revolutions over.) The overplus I shall add to the next days travel. According to my previous calculations we were 285 miles from winter quarters this morning before we started. After traveling 10 miles placed a small Cedar post in the ground with these words wrote on it with a pencil. "From Winter Quarters 295 miles, May 8, 47. Camp all well. W Clayton." Some have past the days travel at 13 and some 14 miles, which serves to convince more strongly that the dis-

---

[47] Earlier in the day Brigham Young and Heber Kimball discovered that some of the cows had moved off toward a nearby buffalo herd.

tances are overrated. I have repeatedly suggested a plan of fixing machinery to a wagon wheel to tell the exact distance we travel in a day, and many begin to be sanguine for carrying it into effect, and I hope it will done . . . Two calves have been killed and brought to Camp, and multitudes would be killed if the pres[iden]t did not prohibit the brethren from killing them only as we need the meat. Truly the "Lords Cattle upon the thousand hills are numerous."

[May 9, 1847. Sunday.] . . . Soon as the camp was formed, I went about 3/4 of a mile below to the river and washed my socks, towel and handkerchief as well as I could in cold water without soap. I then stripped my cloths off and washed from head to foot, which has made me feel much more comfortable for I was covered with dust. After washing and putting on clean clothing I sat down on the banks of the river and gave way to a long train of solemn reflections respecting many things, especially in regard to my family and their welfare for time and eternity. I shall not write my thoughts down here, inasmuch as I expect this journal will have to pass through other hands besides my own or that of my family, but if I can carry my plans into operation, they will be wrote, in a manner that my family will each get their portion, whether before my death or after it matters not.

The day is very warm and the wind has moved to the west. According to my calculations, we are now 300 miles from Winter Quarters, lacking a few rods. I got a small board and wrote on it "From Winter Quarters 300 miles, May 9, 1847. Pioneer Camp all well. Distance according to the reckoning of W Clayton." This was nailed on a post and in the evening I went and set it up about 300 yards from here on a bend of the river. Spent the afternoon reading and writing in the Elder Kimball's journal. At 3 P.M. a meeting was called and the Camp addressed by several. President Young took tea with Elder Kimball, and afterwards they started out together, with one or two others to look at the country ahead of us . . .

[May 10, 1847. Monday.] The morning fine but cool. The wind nearly ceased. Last night I dreamed that I was in company with the camp which was stopping beside a considerable river of deep water. Our horses and cattle were tied to stakes all around the camp to the distance of a quarter of a mile, some good timber

313

thinly scattered around. I thought President Young, Kimball and several others started up the river in a flat boat without stating their object, leaving the brethren to guard the camp, cattle &c. in their absence. When they had been gone sometime I thought a large herd of buffalo came on full gallop right amongst our horses and cattle, causing them to break their ropes and fly in every direction. The brethren seemed thunderstruck and did not know what to do. Seeing a small skiff in the river I sprang into it and a paddle lying in it I commenced rowing in pursuit of the President. It seemed as though I literally flew through the water passing everything on the way like a railway carriage. In a few minutes I overtook the brethren in the flat boat, took the skiff and threw it on shore and to my astonishment I saw that the skiff was made only of barks and cracked all over and it seemed impossible to put it in the water without sinking it. The paddle with which I had rowed proved to be a very large feather and I had another feather in my left hand with which I steered the skiff. When I got into the flat boat I made known what had passed in the camp but the brethren seemed in no ways alarmed. I awoke and behold it was all a dream. Dr. Richards is going to deposit a letter in a stick of wood prepared for the purpose near this place in such a manner that the next company will discover it. He fixed it on a long pole and being assisted by President Young and others raised it and fixed it firm in the ground . . .

[May 11, 1847. Tuesday.] . . . We have seen few buffalo today, but there are signs of thousands having wintered in the neighborhood. The country looks beautiful, soil rich, only lacking timber. After the camp was formed, it being half a mile to water, the brethren dug two wells and about 4 feet deep found plenty of good water. One of the wells is reported to run a pail full a minute. Brother Appleton Harmon is working at the machinery for the wagon to tell the distance we travel and expects to have it in operation tomorrow, which will save me the trouble of counting as I have done during the last 4 days . . .

[May 12, 1847. Wednesday.] Morning cool, weather fine. Brother Appleton Harmon has completed the machinery on the wagon so far that I shall only have to count the number of miles instead of the revolution of the wagon wheel . . .

[May 13, 1847. Thursday.] . . . Some feelings are manifest this morning between Brothers Thomas Tanner and Aaron Farr, on account of the former taking the latter prisoner and putting him under a guard part of the night. Perhaps Aaron was a little out of order in conversing loud after the horn blew for prayers, but I think Brother Tanner's angry spirit more blameable . . .

[May 14, 1847. Friday.] . . . I discovered that Brother Appleton Harmon is trying to have it understood that he invented the machinery to tell the distance we travel which makes me think less of him than I formerly did. He is not the inventor of it by a long way but he has made the machinery after being told how to do it. What little souls work.

[May 16, 1847. Sunday.] . . . About noon today Brother Appleton Harmon completed the machinery on the wagon called a 'roadometer' by adding a wheel to revolve once in ten miles, showing each mile and also each quarter mile we travel, and then casing the whole over so as to secure it from the weather. We are now prepared to tell accurately the distance we travel from day to day, which will supercede the idea of guessing, and be a satisfaction not only to this Camp, but to all who hereafter travel this way. I have prepared another board to put up here, on which the distance from winter quarters is marked at 356 3/4 miles. I have also wrote on it that the last 70 miles are measured, and we shall continue to measure and put up guide posts as often as circumstances will permit through the journey. The whole machinery consists of a shaft about 18 inches long placed on gudgeons, one in the axle tree of the wagon near which are 6 arms placed at equal distances around it, and in which a cog works which is fastened on the hub of the wagon wheel turning the shaft once round at every 6 revolutions of the wagon wheel. The upper gudgeon plays in a piece of wood nailed to the wagon box and near this gudgeon on the shaft a screw is cut. The shaft lays at an angle of about 45 degrees. In this screw a wheel of 60 cogs works on an axle fixed in the side of the wagon and which makes one revolution each mile. In the shaft on which this wheel runs 4 cogs are cut on the fore part which plays in another wheel of 40 cogs which shows the miles and quarters to 10 miles. The whole is cased over and occupies a space of about 18 inches long

315

15 inches high and 3 inches thick.[48]

. . . After supper Elder Whipple made me a present of half a candle made from buffalo tallow by the light of which I continue this journal. Although as may be expected the buffalo are generally poorer at this season of the year yet Brother Whipple has obtained sufficient to make 2 candles from his portion of meat received yesterday morning. The candle burns very clear and pleasant. The tallow smells sweet and rich. I imagine it has a more pleasant smell than the tallow of domestic cattle.

[May 17, 1847. Monday.] The morning very cold and chilly, wind N.W. Dr. Richards left another letter on the camp ground for the benefit of the next company. The letter is secured from the weather by a wooden case and placed so that the brethren can hardly miss finding it . . .

[May 18, 1847. Tuesday.] The morning fine and very pleasant. At 7 o'clock the President called the Captains of tens to his wagons and gave them a pretty severe lecture. He referred to some who had left meat on the ground, and would not use it because it was not hind quarter. Some would murmur because a fore quarter of meat was alloted to them &c. which is not right, for God has given us a commandment that we should not waste meat, nor take life unless it is needful, but he can see a disposition in this camp to slaughter everything before them, yea if all the buffalo and game there is on our route were brought together to the camp, there are some would never cease untill they had destroyed the whole. Some men will shoot as much as thirty times at a rabbit if they did not kill it, and are continually wasting their ammunition, but when they have used all they have got, they may have the pleasure of carrying their empty guns to the mountains and back, for he will not furnish them. We have now meat enough to last some time if we will take proper care of it. As the

---

[48] This measuring device was not unique to the Mormon pioneers. Appleton Harmon, who remained at the Platte River ferry while Clayton and the pioneers moved on to Fort Bridger, noted in his diary on July 10, 1847: "The company altogether bought about $100 worth of goods of Mr. H. Quelling, a Quaker, he had a roadameter on one of his wagons" (in Maybelle Harmon Anderson, ed., *Appleton Harmon Goes West* [Berkeley: Gillick Press, 1946]). Odometers were also used in Europe at this time (Norman E. Wright, "I Have a Question," *Ensign* 11 [August 1981]:30–31).

horsemen, there are none with the exception of Brothers Kimball and Wilford Woodruff and Benson, that ever take the trouble to look out a good road for the wagons, but all they seem to care about is to wait till their breakfast is cooked for them and when they have eaten it, they mount their horses and scatter away, and if an antelope comes across the track, the whole of us must be stopped perhaps half an hour while they try to creep up near enough to kill it, but when we come to a bad place on the route all the interest they have is to get across the best they can and leave myself and one or two others to pick out a crossing place and guide the Camp all the time. Such things are not right, and he wants them to cease and all take an interest in the welfare of the Camp, be united, and receive the meat as a blessing from God and not as a stink offering from the devil. It is not necessary to preach to the Elders in this camp, they know what is right as well as he does, and he will not preach to them all the time. Let the Captains do the best they know how and teach their men to do likewise." The meeting dispersed, the meat was taken care of and at a quarter past 8 we started out again, and traveled 3/4 miles nearly a west course over a very hard prairie, and good travelling, and then arrived at a nice stream, Rattlesnake creek, about 20 or 25 feet wide, a foot or 18 inches deep and a very strong current . . .

. . . After encampment was formed, went with Elder Orson Pratt to Dr. Richards wagon to enter into arrangements for making a map of our route. The doctor wants me to do it assisted by Elder Pratt's observations. He handed me Fremonts map and I retired to my wagon to commence operations but soon found that the map does not agree with my scale nor Elder Pratts calculations. I then proposed to Elder Pratt to wait until we get through the journey and take all the necessary data and then make a new one instead of making our route on Fremonts. The subject is left here till morning. After supper I took my candle and finished this day's journal . . .

[May 19, 1847. Wednesday.] . . . When Elder Kimball went ahead this morning to search out a road he went up the creek about a mile and around over the bluffs to find if possible a better road than the one close to the river. While he was searching about a mile north from the river he went down into a deep hol-

317

low surrounded by high bluffs and as he was riding along at the bottom he turned his head to the left and saw 2 very large wolves at about 5 rods distance gazing at him. One of them he said was nearly as large as a 2 year old steer. When he saw these he looked around on the other side and saw several others about the same distance from him very large ones and all gazing fiercely at him. This startled him considerably and more especially when he reflected that he had no arms. He made a noise to try to scare them away but they still stood and he concluded to move away as soon as he could. They did not follow him and he saw a dead carcass near which satisfied him that he had interrupted their repast. On mentioning this circumstance to President Young they named the creek Wolf Creek . . .

[May 20, 1847. Thursday.] The morning fair but cloudy, light wind from N.W. and cold. At 1/4 before 8 we started out again but had not traveled over 1/4 mile before the roadometer gave way on account of the rain yesterday having caused the wood to swell and stick fast. One of the cogs in the small wheel broke. We stopped about 1/2 hour and Appleton Harmon took it to pieces and put it up again without the small wheel. I had to count each mile after this. 3/4 of a mile from where we camped we crossed a creek 8 feet wide and 2 1/2 feet deep . . . Opposite to where we are halted, we can see a ravine running up the bluffs and at the foot a flat bottom of about 15 acres. At the farther side of this bottom is a grove of trees not yet in leaf. Brother Brown thinks they are ash and that the place is what is called Ash Hollow and on Fremonts map Ash Creek. We all felt anxious to ascertain the fact whether this is Ash Hollow or not for if it is the Oregon trail strikes the river at this place and if it can be ascertained that such is the fact we then have a better privilege of testing Fremonts distances to Laramie. We have already discovered that his map is not altogether correct in several respects and particularly in showing the windings of the river and the distance of the bluffs from it. I suggested the propriety of some persons going over in the boat and Brother John Brown suggested it to President Young. The boat was soon hauled by the brethren to the river and O[rson] Pratt, A[masa] Lyman, Luke Johnson and J[ohn] Brown started to row over but the current was so exceedingly strong the oars had no effect. John Brown then jumped into the river which was about 2 1/2 feet deep and dragged the boat over the others assisting with the oars. After some hard labor they arrived on the opposite shore and went to the hollow. They soon found the Oregon trail and ascertained that this is Ash Hollow, Brother Brown having traveled on that road to near Laramie last season with the Mississippi company and knew the place perfectly well . . .

[May 21, 1847. Friday.] The morning very fine and pleasant though tolerably cold. I put up a guide board at this place with the following inscriptions on it: From Winter Quarters 409 miles. From the junction of the North and South Forks 93 1/4 miles. From Cedar Bluffs south side the river 36 1/2 miles. Ash Hollow south side the river 8 miles. Camp of Pioneers May 21, 1847. According to Fremont this place is 132 miles from Laramie. The bluffs opposite are named Castle bluffs . . . Presidents Young and Kimball rode forward to pick the road and near this place they saw a nest of wolves, caught and killed two with sticks . . . Elder Kimball proposed tonight that I should leave a number of pages for so much of his journal as I am behind in copying and start from the present and keep it up daily. He furnished me a candle and I wrote the journal of this days travel by candle light in his journal leaving 56 pages blank . . .

[May 22, 1847. Saturday.] . . . A while after we halted, Porter Rockwell came in and said he had been on the high bluff about a mile N.W. of us, and had seen the rock called Chimney rock from it, which appeared a long distance off. We have been in hopes to come in sight of it today and feel anxious in order to ascertain more certainly the correctness of Fremonts distances. In order to satisfy myself, although my feet were blistered and very sore, I determined to take my telescope and go on the bluff to ascertain for myself whether the noted rock could be seen or not. At half past 12 I started out alone. I found the distance to the foot of the bluff a good mile, the ascent gradual. From the foot the bluff looks very high and rough, many huge rocks having broke from the summit from time to time and rolled down a long distance. I found the ascent very steep and lengthy in comparison to its appearance from Camp. When I arrived on the top I found a nice slightly arched surface of about a quarter of an acre in extent, but barren and very little grass on it. Huge comparatively smooth rocks peeped through the surface on one of which I wrote

319

with red chalk: "Wm. Clayton, May 22, 1847." . . . At the distance, I should judge of about 20 miles, I could see "Chimney Rock" very plain with the naked eye, which from here very much resembles the large factory chimneys in England, although I could not see the form of its base. The rock lay about due west from here . . . The romantic bluffs on the north and the lightning playing in the S.E. all tended to fill my mind with pleasant reflections, on the goodness and majesty of the Creator and governor of the universe and the beauty of the works of his hands. At 1/4 to 6 we formed our encampment in a circle within 1/4 of a mile of the banks of the river having travelled this afternoon, 8 1/4 miles and through the day 15 1/2, making the distance from winter quarters 440 miles in 5 weeks and 3 1/2 days. The feed on the lower bench of the prairie is tolerable good, while the higher land is quite bare. We have noticed today a great many petrified bones, some very large . . . The evening was spent very joyfully by most of the brethren, it being very pleasant and moonlight. A number danced till the bugle sounded for bed time at 9 o'clock. A mock trial was also prosecuted in the case of the camp vs. James Davenport for blockading the highway and turning ladies out of their course. Jackson Redding acted as the presiding judge. Elder [Edson?] Whipple attorney for defendant and Luke Johnson attorney for the people. We have many such trials in the Camp which are amusing enough and tend among other things to pass away the time cheerfully during leisure moments . . .

[May 23, 1847. Sunday.] The morning very fine and pleasant. Brother Egan commenced washing very early on the banks of the river. He kindly volunteered to wash my dirty clothing which I accepted as a favor. After breakfast President Young, Elders Kimball, Richards, Pratt, Woodruff, Smith and Benson and Lyman walked out to view Bluff Ruins and returned at half past 11. A while ago I went out a little distance to view an adder which Geo[rge] Billings had discovered. It was a dark brown color about 18 inches long and 3/4 inch thick through the body. They are represented as very poisonous. About 11 o'clock Nathaniel Fairbanks came into camp having been bitten in the leg by a rattlesnake. He went on the bluffs with Aaron Farr and Brother Rolf and as they jumped off from the bluff the snake bit him the others having jumped over him farther. He said that in 2 minutes after

320

he was bitten his tongue began to prick and feel numb. When he got to camp his tongue and hands pricked and felt numb as a person feels their feet sometimes when they are said to be asleep. The brethren immediately applied some tobacco juice and leaves, also turpentine, and bound tobacco on his leg which was considerably swollen. We laid hands on him and Luke Johnson administered a dose of Lobelia[49] in number six, after he had taken a strong drink of Alcohol and water. The Lobellia soon vomited him powerfully. He complains much of sickness at his stomach and dimness in his eyes. He appears to be in much pain . . . P.M. At 12 o'clock the Camp were called together for meeting, and after singing and prayer addressed by Erastus Snow. Followed by President Young. The latter said there was many items of doctrine which he often felt like teaching to the brethren, but as to administering sealing ordinances &c. this is no time nor place for them, they belong to the house of God, and when we get located we shall have opportunity to build a house &c. He expressed himself satisfied with the conduct of the Camp in general. He is pleased to see so much union, and disposition to obey council among the brethren, and hoped and prayed that it may continue and increase. He wants the brethren to seek after knowledge and be faithful, acknowledge God in all things but never take his name in vain nor use profane language. If all the knowledge in this camp were put together and brother Joseph was here in our midst, he could comprehend the whole of it and wind it around his little finger, say nothing of the knowledge of Angels, and above that, the knowledge of the Gods.[50] There is much for us to learn and a faithful man who desires eternal glory will seek after knowledge all the time, and his ideas are never suffered to rust but are always bright. He will not throw away the knowledge of small things because they are familiar, but grasp all he can and keep doing so, and by retaining many small things he will thus gain a large pile &c.

---

[49] An herbal plant, also called Indian Tobacco, used as an emetic.

[50] In keeping with the scientific empiricism that pervaded the nineteenth century, the Mormon leaders were optimistic that they could comprehend the workings of an orderly universe. At the same time, they believed that the universe was operated by a transcendent God, whose powers they could only discover through a process of revelation.

He expressed his feelings warmly towards all the brethren and prayed them to be faithful, diligent and upright, for we are now sowing seed, the fruit of which will be plucked in after days whether good or bad. George A. Smith made a few remarks, also several others of the brethren. The President then stated that on Sunday next he wants the brethren to understand that there will be meeting at 11 o'clock and the sacrament administered, and he wants the brethren to attend, all that can and not ramble off and fatigue themselves, but use the Sabbath as a day of rest. He enjoined it upon Bishops T[arlton] Lewis, S[hadrach] Roundy, J[ohn] S. Higbee and A[ddison] Everett to see that the proper necessaries were prepared for the sacrament. The meeting was then dismissed. A while after meeting I walked out with Elder Kimball a piece from the Camp. We sat down and I read him my journal of the last four days with which he seemed well pleased. We then kneeled down together and poured out our souls to God for ourselves, the Camp and our dear families in winter quarters. While we were engaged in prayer the wind rose suddenly from the N.W. a heavy cloud having been gathering from the W. all the afternoon. A sudden gust struck Elder Kimball's hat and carried it off. After we got through his hat was nowhere in sight, but following the direction of the wind we soon saw it at a distance on the bottom of the prairie still flying swiftly. We both ran and chased it about 3/4 of a mile and caught it a little from the river. While we were out together I remarked that the buffalo gnat bit us very severely. Elder Kimball said they bit him very bad last evening. Their bite is very poisonous, and although they are extremely small they punish a person very much with an itching, aching pain like a mosquitoe bite. About 5 o'clock the wind blew a perfect gale and continued till 7 when it commenced to rain very heavy, large drops descending, accompanied with hail, which however did not continue very long, but the wind continued near all night. The lightning and thunder continued some time but not very severe. We saw the necessity of having good stout bows to our wagons, and the covers well fastened down, for the very stoutest seemed in danger of being torn to pieces and the wagons blown over. When the wind commenced blowing so strongly it turned very cold and long before dark I went to bed to keep warm. Brother Fairbanks seems considerably better. This evening President Young, Kimball and Benson laid hands on him and he seemed much better afterwards.

[May 24, 1847. Monday.] . . . About half past 5 we discovered a party of Indians on the opposite side the river moving west. When we formed our encampment they crossed over the river. Some of the brethren went to meet them carrying a white flag with them. When the Indians saw the flag, some of them began to sing, and their chief held up a U.S. flag. It was soon ascertained that their object was to obtain something to eat. A number of them came to the camp and were conducted around by Colonels [Stephen] Markham and [Albert P.] Rockwood. They were shown a 6 and 15 shooter also the cannon and the gunners went through the evolutions a number of times which seemed to please them much. They are all well dressed and very noble looking. Some having good clean blankets, others nice robes, artfully ornamented with beads and paintings. All had many ornaments on their clothing and ears, some had nice painted shells suspended from the ear. All appeared to be well armed with muskets. Their mocasons were indeed clean and beautiful. One had a pair of mocasons of a clear white, ornamented with beads &c. They fit very tight to the foot. For cleaness and neatness they will vie with the most tasteful whites. They are 35 in number, about half squaws and children. They are Sioux and have two recommends certifying as to their friendship &c. The brethren contributed something to eat which was sent to them . . . After the Indians had viewed the camp they returned to their horses and the rest of the party who have camped on the bank of the river about a quarter of a mile west of us. Elder Sherwood returned with them and soon after came back accompanied by the chief and his squaw who signified a wish to abide with our camp tonight. The brethren fixed up a tent for them to sleep under. Porter Rockwell made them some coffee, and they were furnished with some victuals. The old chief amused himself very much by looking at the moon through a telescope for as much as twenty minutes. Brother Fairbanks is much better this evening. Last night Luke Johnson discovered a very large petrified bone in the neighborhood of the bluffs as much as 2 feet wide but he could not ascertain the length of it. After laboring sometime ineffectually to dig it up, he broke off two pieces and brought them to camp. They are very white

323

and hard. It is now 11 o'clock. I have been writing in Elder Kimballs journal since dark and have but little chance to write as much as I want in my own and his both but I feel determined to do all I can to keep a journal of this expedition which will be interesting to my children in after days and perhaps to many of the Saints. The evening is very fine but cool and I retire to rest with the feeling "God bless my dear family."

[May 25, 1847. Tuesday.] The morning fine and very pleasant. Most of the Indians, men, women and children came early to camp on their ponies and marched round, mostly trying to obtain something to eat. Several little barters were made with them for mocasins, skins &c. John S. Higbee traded ponies with one of them. They have some good ponies and some inferior ones, but both male and females are neatly dressed and very tidy. They look cheerful and pleased to witness the Camp &c. At 20 minutes past 8 we proceeded onward. After we started, the Indians left us and went over the river . . .

[May 28, 1847. Friday.] The morning cool, damp, cloudy and some rain. Wind N.E. At about 8 o'clock the brethren were called together and the question asked shall we go on in the rain or wait until it is fair. All agreed to stay till it was fair. I went to writing in Hebers journal and wrote till near 11 o'clock. Elder Kimball came to the next wagon where some of the boys were playing Cards. He told them his views and disaprobation of their spending time, gaming, and dancing, and mock trials &c. and especially the profane language frequently uttered by some. He reasoned with them on the subject and showed them that it would lead from bad to worse if persisted in untill the consequences would become serious. He exhorted them to be more sober and wise. It growing fair we started out at 11 o'clock, our first four miles being N.N.W. in consequence of a bend in the river . . .

[May 29, 1847. Saturday.] The morning cold, wet and cloudy, with wind from N.E. We shall not travel unless it grows fair and better weather. I spent the morning writing in Elder Kimballs journal but felt very unwell having taken cold yesterday and been sick all night. About 10 o'clock, the weather looked a little better and at half past 10 the bugle sounded as a signal for the teams to be got together. After the teams were harnessed the brethren were called together to the boat in the circle.[51] President Young taking his station in the boat, ordered each captain of ten to lead out their respective companies and get all their men together. He then called on the clerk to call over the names of the Camp to see if all were present. Joseph Hancock and Andrew Gibbons were reported to be absent hunting. Brothers Elijah Newman and Nathaniel Fairbanks were confined to their wagons but answered to their names the remainder all present. President Young then addressed the meeting in substance as follows:

"I remarked last Sunday that I had not felt much like preaching to the brethren on this mission. This morning I feel like preaching a little, and shall take for my text, 'That as to pursuing our journey with this company, with the spirit they possess, I am about to revolt against it.' This is the text I feel like preaching on this morning, consequently I am in no hurry. In the first place, before we left Winter Quarters, it was told to the brethren, and many knew it by experience, that we had to leave our homes, our houses our lands and our all because we believed in the gospel as revealed to the Saints in these last days. The rise of the persecutions against the Church, was in consequence of the doctrines of eternal truth taught by Joseph. Many knew this by experience. Some lost their husbands, some lost their wives, and some their children through persecution, and yet we have not been disposed to forsake the truth, and turn and mingle with the gentiles, except a few who have turned aside, and gone away from us, and we have learned in a measure, the difference between a professor of religion, and a possessor of religion. Before we left Winter Quarters, it was told to the brethren that we were going to look out a home for the saints where they would be free from persecution by the gentiles, where we could dwell in peace and serve God according to the Holy priesthood, where we could build up the kingdom, so that the nations would begin to flock to our standard. I have said many things to the brethren, about the strictness of their walk and conduct, when we left the gentiles, and told them that we would have to walk uprightly or the law would be put in force &c. Many have left and turned aside through fear, but no good, upright, honest man will fear. The gospel does not

---

[51] The "boat" appears to refer to a position from which speakers would address a congregation.

bind a good man down, and deprive him of his rights and privileges. It does not prevent him from enjoying the fruits of his labors. It does not rob him of blessings. It does not stop his increase. It does not diminish his kingdom, but it is calculated to enlarge his kingdom as well as to enlarge his heart. It is calculated to give him privileges, and power, and honor, and exaltation, and everything which his heart can desire in righteousness all the days of his life, and then, when he gets exalted into the eternal world, he can still turn round and say it hath not entered into the heart of man to conceive the glory and honor and blessings which God hath in store for those that love and serve Him. I want the brethren to understand, and comprehend the principles of eternal life, and to watch the spirits, be wide awake and not be overcome by the adversary. You can see the fruits of the spirit, but you cannot see the spirit itself with the natural eye, you behold it not. You can see the result of yielding to the evil spirit and what it will lead you to, but you do not see the spirit itself, nor its operations only by the spirit thats in you. Nobody has told me what has been going on in the Camp, but I have known it all the while. I have been watching its movement, its influence, its effects, and I know the result if it is not put a stop to. I want you to understand that inasmuch as we are beyond the power of the gentiles, where the devil has tabernacles in the priests and the people, but we are beyond their reach, we are beyond their power, we are beyond their grasp, and what has the devil now to work upon? Upon the spirits of men in this camp, and if you do not open your hearts so that the spirit of God can enter your hearts, and teach you the right way, I know that you are a ruined people. I know that you will be destroyed, and that without remedy; and unless there is a change and a different course of conduct, a different spirit to what is now in this Camp I go no further. I am in no hurry. Give me the man of prayer, give me the man of faith, give me the man of meditation, a sober-minded man, and I would far rather go amongst the savages, with six or eight such men, than to trust myself with the whole of this camp with the spirit they now possess. Here is an opportunity for every man to prove himself, to know whether he will pray and remember his God, without being asked to do it every day; to know whether he will have confidence enough to ask of God that he may receive, without my telling him to do it. If this camp was composed of men who had newly received the gospel, men who had not received the priesthood, men who had not been through the ordinances in the Temple and who had not had years of experience, enough to have learned the influence of the spirits and the difference between a good and an evil spirit, I should feel, like preaching to them and watching over them, and teaching them all the time, day by day. But here are the Elders of Israel, men who have had years of experience, men who have had the priesthood for years, and have they got faith enough to rise up and stop a mean, low, grovelling, covetous, quarrelsome spirit? No they have not, nor would they try to stop it unless I rise up in the power of God and put it down. I don't mean to bow down to the spirit thats in this camp, and which is rankling in the bosoms of the brethren, and which will lead to knock downs, and perhaps to the use of the knife to cut each other's throats if it is not put a stop to. I don't mean to bow down to the spirit which causes the brethren to quarrel and when I wake up in the morning the first thing I hear is some of the brethren jawing each other and quarrelling because a horse has got loose in the night. I have let the brethren dance, and fiddle, and act the nigger night after night to see what they will do, and what extremes they would go to, if suffered to go as they would but I don't love to see it. The brethren say they want a little exercise to pass away time, but if you can't tire yourselves bad enough with a days journey without dancing every night, carry your guns on your shoulders, and walk, carry your wood to Camp instead of lounging and laying sleeping in your wagons, increasing the load untill your teams are tired to death and ready to drop into the earth. Help your teams over mud holes and bad places instead of lounging in your wagons and that will give you exercise enough without dancing. Well, they will play cards, they will play checkers, they will play dominoes, and if they had the privilege and were where they could get whiskey, they would be drunk half their time, and in one week they would quarrel, get to high words and draw their knives to kill each other. This is what such a course of things would lead to. Don't you know it? Yes. Well then why don't you try to put it down? I have played cards once in my life since I became a Mormon to see what kind of a spirit would attend it, and I was so well satisfied that I would rather see the dirtiest thing you could find on the earth, than a pack of cards in your hands. You never read of gambling, playing

327

cards, checkers, Dominoes &c. in the scriptures, but you do read of men praising the Lord in the dance, but who ever read of praising the Lord in a game at cards? If any man had sense enough to play a game at Cards, or dance a little without wanting to keep it up all the time, but exercise a little, and then quit it and think no more of it, it would do well enough. But you want to keep it up till midnight and every night, and all the time. You don't know how to control your selves. Last winter when we had our seasons of recreation in the council house, I went forth in the dance frequently, but did my mind run on it? No! To be sure when I was dancing, my mind was on the dance, but the moment I stoppt in the middle or the end of a tune, my mind was engaged in prayer and praise to my heavenly father, and whatever I engage in my mind is on it while engaged in it, but the moment I am done with it, my mind is drawn up to my God.

The devils which inhabit the gentiles priests are here. The tabernacles are not here, we are out of their power, we are beyond their grasp, we are beyond the reach of their persecutions, but the devils are here, and the first thing you'll know if you don't open your eyes, and your hearts, they will cause divisions in our Camp, and perhaps war, as they did the Lamanites, as you read in the book of Mormon.

Do we suppose that we are going to look out a home for the saints, a resting place, a place of peace, where they can build up the Kingdom and bid the nations welcome, with a low, mean, dirty, trifling Covetous, wicked spirit dwelling in our bosoms? It is vain! vain! Some of you are very fond of passing jokes, and will carry your jokes very far. But will you take a joke? If you don't want to take a joke, don't give a joke to your brethren. Joking, nonsense, profane language, trifling conversation and loud laughter do not belong to us. Suppose the Angels were witnessing the hoe down the other evening, and listening to the haw, haw's, the other evening would they not be ashamed of it. I am ashamed of it. I have not given a joke to any man on this journey nor felt like it; neither have I insulted any mans feelings, but I have hollowed pretty loud and spoke sharp to the brethren when I have seen their awkwardness at coming into Camp. The revelations in the bible, in the book of Mormon, and doctrine and covenants teaches us to be sober; and let me ask you Elders that have been through the ordinances in the Temple, what were your covenants there?

I want you should remember them. When I laugh I see my folly, and nothingness, and weakness, and am ashamed of myself. I think meaner and worse of myself than any man can think of me; but I delight in God, and in his commandments, and delight to meditate on him and to serve him and I mean that every thing in me shall be subject to him, and I delight in serving him. Now let every man repent of his weaknesses, of his follies, of his meanness, and every kind of wickedness, and stop your swearing and your profane language for it is in this camp, and, I know it, and have known it. I have said nothing about it, but I now tell you, if you don't stop it, you shall be cursed by the Almighty, and shall dwindle away and be damned. Such things shall not be suffered in this Camp. You shall honor God, and confess his name or else you shall suffer the penalty. Most of this Camp belongs to the church, nearly all; and I would say to you brethren and to the Elders of Israel, if you are faithful, you will yet be sent to preach this gospel to the nations of the earth and bid all welcome whether they believe the Gospel or not, and this kingdom will reign over many who do not belong to the Church, over thousands who do not believe in the gospel. Bye and bye, every knee shall bow, and every tongue confess and acknowledge and reverence, and honor the name of God and His priesthood and observe the laws of the Kingdom whether they belong to the Church and obey the gospel or not, and I mean that every man in this camp shall do it. That is what the scripture means, by every Knee shall bow &c. and you cannot make anything else out of it.

I understand there are several in this Camp who do not belong to the church. I am the man who will stand up for them and protect them in all their rights. And they shall not trample on our rights nor on the priesthood. They shall reverance and acknowledge the name of God and His priesthood, and if they set up their heads and seek to introduce iniquity into this Camp, and to trample on the priesthood, I swear to them, they shall never go back to tell the tale. I will leave them where they will be safe. If they want to retreat they can now have the privilege, and any man who chooses to go back rather than abide the law of God can now have the privilege of doing so before we go any further.

Here are the Elders of Israel who have the priesthood, who have got to preach the gospel, who have to gather the nations of the earth, who have to build up the Kingdom, so that the nations

329

can come to it, they will stoop to dance as niggers. I don't mean this as debasing the negroes, by any means; they will hoe down all, turn summersets, dance on their knees, and haw, haw, out loud, they will play cards, they will play checkers, and Dominoes, they will use profane language, they will swear. Suppose when you go to preach the people should ask you what you did when you went on this mission to seek out a home for the whole church, what was your course of conduct. Did you dance? Yes. Did you hoe down all? Yes. Did you play cards? Yes. Did you play checkers? Yes. Did you use profane language? Yes. Did you swear? Yes. Did you quarrel with each other and threaten each other? Why Yes. How would you feel? What would you say for yourselves? Would you not want to go and hide up? Your mouths would be stopt and you would want to creep away in disgrace. I am one of the last to ask my brethren to enter into solemn covenants, but if they will not enter into a covenant to put away their iniquity and turn to the Lord and serve him, and acknowledge and honor his name I want them to take their wagons and retreat back, for I shall go no further under such a state of things. If we don't repent and quit our wickedness we will have more hinderances than we have had, and worse storms to encounter. I want the brethren to be ready for meeting tomorrow at the time appointed, instead of rambling off, and hiding in their wagons to play cards &c. I think it will be good for us to have a fast meeting tomorrow and a prayer meeting to humble ourselves and turn to the Lord and he will forgive us." He then called upon all the High Priests to step forth in a line in front of the wagon, and then the bishops to step in front of the High Priests, which being done he counted them and found their number to be 4 bishops and 15 high priests. He then called upon all the seventies to form a line in the rear of the High Priests. On being counted, they were ascertained to number 78. Next he called on the Elders to form a line in the rear of the wagon. They were 8 in number. There were also 8 of the quorum of the Twelve. He then asked the brethren of the quorum of the Twelve, "if they were willing to covenant to turn to the Lord with all their hearts, to repent of all their follies, to cease from all their evils and serve God according to his laws." If they were willing, to manifest it by holding up their right hand. Every man held up his hand in token that he covenanted. He then put the same question to the High Priests and Bishops, next to the seventies, and then to the Elders, and lastly to the other brethren. All covenanted with uplifted hands without a dissenting voice. He then addressed those who are not members of the Church and told them they should be protected in their rights and privileges while they would conduct themselves well, and not seek to trample on the priesthood nor blaspheme the name of God &c. He then referred to the conduct of Benjamin Rolfe's two younger brothers, in joining with the Higbees and John C. Bennett in sowing discord and strife among the saints in Nauvoo[52] and remarked that there will be no more Bennett scrapes suffered here. He spoke highly of Benjamin Rolfe's conduct although not a member of the Church, and also referred to the esteem in which his father and mother were held by the saints generally.

He then very tenderly blessed the brethren and prayed that God would enable them to fulfill their covenants and withdrew to give opportunity for others to speak if they felt like it.

Elder Kimball arose to say that he agreed with all that President Young had said. He receive[s] it as the word of the Lord to him, and it is the word of the Lord to this camp if they will receive it. He has been watching the motion of things, and the conduct of the brethren for some time and has seen what it would lead to. He has said little but thought a great deal. It has made him shudder when he has seen the Elders of Israel, descend to the lowest, dirtiest things imaginable, the tail end of everything, but what has passed this morning will make it an everlasting blessing to the brethren, if they will repent and be faithful and keep their covenant. He never can rest satisfied untill his family are liberated from the gentiles and their corruptions and established in a land where they can plant and reap the fruits of their labors, but he has never had the privilege of eating the fruits of his labors yet, neither has his family, but when this is done he can sleep in peace if necessary but not till then. If we will serve the Lord, and remember his name to call upon him, and be faithful we shall not one of us be left under the sod, but shall be

---

[52] At Joseph Smith's trial for ordering the destruction of the *Nauvoo Expositor*, P. T. Rolfe witnessed that on Monday night, June 10, 1844, Marshall John P. Green and a company of men did destroy the press (*HC* 6:489). Rolfe was later listed by Willard Richards among the mob that killed Joseph Smith at Carthage, Illinois (ibid., 7:146). Samuel and Benjamin Rolfe were both carpenters on the Nauvoo temple (ibid., 326).

permitted to return and meet our families in peace and enjoy their society again, but if this camp continues the course of conduct they have done, the judgments of God will overtake us. He hopes the brethren will take heed to what President Young has said and let it sink deep in their hearts.

Elder Pratt wanted to add a word to what has been said. Much good advice has been given to teach us how we may spend our time profitably by prayer, and meditation &c. But there is another idea which he wants to add. There are many books in the Camp and worlds of knowledge before us which we have not obtained, and if the brethren would devote all their leisure time to seeking after knowledge, they would never need to say they had nothing with which to pass away their time. "If we could spend 23 hours out of the 24 in gaining knowledge and only sleep one hour of 24 all the days of our life, there would still be worlds of knowledge in store for us yet to learn." He knows it is difficult to bring our minds to diligent and constant studies, in pursuit of knowledge, all at once, but by steady practice and perseverance we shall become habituated to it, and it will become a pleasure to us. He would recommend to the brethren, besides prayer, and obedience to seek after knowledge continually, and it will help us to overcome our follies and nonsense. We shall have no time for it.

Elder Woodruff said he remembered the time when the camp went up to Missouri to redeem Zion, when Brother Joseph stood upon a wagon wheel and told the brethren that the decree had passed and could not be revoked, and the destroying Angel would visit the Camp and we should die like sheep with the rot, after he had repeatedly warned the brethren of their evil conduct and what it would lead to, but they still continued in their course. It was not long before the destroying Angel did visit the Camp and the brethren began to fall as Brother Joseph had said. We buried 18 in a short time and a more sorrowful time I never saw.[53] There are 9 here who were in that Camp and they all recollect the circumstance well and will never forget it. He has been thinking while the president was speaking, that if he was one who had played cards or checkers, he would take every pack of cards and

[53] Possibly cholera.

every checker board and burn them up so that they would no longer be in the way to tempt us.

Col. Markham acknowledged that he had done wrong in many things. He had always indulged himself before he came into the church, with every thing he desired; he knows he has done wrong on this journey; he knows his mind has become darkened since he left Winter Quarters. He hopes the brethren will forgive him, and he will pray to God to forgive him and try to do better. While he was speaking he was very much affected indeed and wept like a child. Many of the brethren felt much affected, and all seemed to realize for the first time the excess to which they had yielded, and the awful consequence of such things if persisted in. Many were in tears and felt humbled. President Young returned to the boat as Brother Markham closed his remarks, and said in reply, that he knew the brethren would forgive him, and the Lord will forgive us all, if we turn to Him with all our hearts and cease to do evil.

The meeting was then dismissed each man retiring to his wagon, and being half past 1 o'clock we again pursued our journey in peace, all reflecting on what has passed today, and many expressing their gratitude for what has transpired. It seemed as though we were just commencing on this important mission, and all realizing the responsibility resting upon us, to conduct ourselves in such a manner that the journey may be an everlasting blessing to us, instead of an everlasting disgrace. No loud laughter was heard, no swearing, no quarrelling, no profane language, no hard speeches to man or beast, and it truly seemed as though the cloud had burst, and we had emerged into a new element, a new atmosphere, and a new society . . .

[May 30, 1847. Sunday.] The morning fair and somewhat more pleasant, although there is yet appearance for more rain. I felt quite unwell through the night and also this morning, having severe pain in my bowels. At 9 o'clock most of the brethren retired a little South of the camp and had a prayer meeting and as many as choose to, expressed their feelings. At a little before 12 they met again in the same spot to partake of the sacrament. Soon afterwards all the members of the council of F[ifty] or Kingdom of God in the Camp except Brother Thomas Bullock, went onto the bluffs and selecting a small, circular, level spot, surrounded by bluffs, and out of sight, we clothed ourselves in the priestly

333

garments and offered up prayer to God, for ourselves, this Camp and all pertaining to it, the brethren in the army, our families and all the Saints, President Young being mouth. We all felt well and glad for this privilege. The names of those present, members of the above council are, Brigham Young, Heber C. Kimball, Willard Richards, Orson Pratt, George A. Smith, Wilford Woodruff, Amasa Lyman, Ezra T. Benson, Phineas H. Young, John Pack, Charles Shumway, Shadrack Roundy, Albert P. Rockwood, Erastus Snow, myself, Albert Carrington and Porter Rockwell. The two latter having no clothing with them stood guard at a little distance from us to prevent interruption. When we started for the bluffs, there was a heavy, black thunder cloud rising from the South west, and to all appearance, it might rain any minute, but the brethren believed it would not rain till we got through and if it did we chose rather to take a wetting than to be disappointed of the privilege. It kept off remarkably till we got through, and got our cloths on, but soon after began to rain and after we got to Camp it rained considerable accompanied by strong wind. I never noticed the brethren so still and sober on a Sunday since we started as today. There is no jesting, nor laughing, nor nonsense. All appear to be sober and feel to remember their covenant, which makes things look far more pleasant than they have done heretofore. I spent most of the afternoon in Elder Kimball's wagon with Elder Kimball, President Young, Lorenzo and Phineas Young. Read the minutes of President Youngs discourse yesterday. About 5 o'clock President Young, Kimball, Benson and others walked out together to the bluffs. They invited me to go with them but I was so afflicted with Cramps I could scarcely walk, and after drinking a cup of tea prepared by Ellen Sanders I went to my wagon and retired to bed early . . .

[May 31, 1847. Monday.] The morning fine but cool. I feel quite unwell yet, and have been sick all night. At a quarter past 8 we proceeded onward, found good level traveling, the day cool and pleasant. We soon struck a wagon trail which evidently leads direct to Fort Laramie . . .

A while after we camped, Presidents Young and Kimball went to the bluffs and again saw the Black hills in the distance. They bowed before the Lord and offered up their prayers together.

The month of May has passed over, and we have been permitted to proceed so far on our journey, being 531 1/4 miles from our families in Winter Quarters, the Camp generally enjoying good health and in good spirits; and although some things have passed which have merited chastisement we have the privilege at the closing of the month of seeing a better feeling, a more noble spirit, and a more general desire to do right than we have before witnessed.

I feel to humble myself and give God thanks for his continued mercies to me and my brethren and may His spirit fill our hearts, and may his angels administer comfort, health, peace and prosperity to all our families and all the saints henceforth and forever. Amen.

[June 1, 1847. Tuesday.] The morning very fine, warm and pleasant. All is still and quiet as a "summer's morning," the Camp well and in good spirits and a feeling of peace, union and brotherly love seems to dwell in every breast. My mind revolves back upon bygone days and then to the present, and I truly feel thankful to my God for his mercies to me and for the privilege I now daily enjoy. The idea of dwelling with my family in a land of peace, in the midst of the saints of God is better felt than described, but the mild, still, scenery of this morning puts me in mind of it. At 9 o'clock we pursued our journey, the stream we passed over is called by Grosclaude the "Raw Hide."[54] Elder Kimball let me have his horse to ride. I went in company with George A. Smith who was on foot carrying his gun in fulfillment of President Young's prophecy at the Pawnee Mission station. The wagons went on till half past 11 and then halted for noon. We were about a mile a head of them. The distance they travelled was 4 1/2 miles. At half past 1 started out again and travelled til a little after 4 and saw Fort Laramie about 4 miles to the South West. Elder Kimball and President Young then came up to where Brother Woodruff and I were looking out for feed, and we started on, President Young having stopped the wagons, and went to the ford opposite to the Fort. It was finally concluded to form our

---

[54] Justin Grosclaude was a Swiss fur trapper familiar with Indian languages who volunteered to guide the Mormons over the Rocky Mountains in 1847 to the springs of "Yellow Stone" (Morgan, 186).

encampment here on the banks of the river. Several men soon came down from the Fort which is about 2 miles from here and made themselves known as a part of the Mississippi company from Pueblo.[55] They have been here two weeks. It caused us much joy to meet with brethren in this wild region of country and also because we should have some news from the brethren in the army . . .

The brethren seemed pleased to meet us. Brother [Robert] Crow reports deaths, in the Pubelo detachment since Brothers [John] Tippets and [Thomas] Woolsey left viz. Melcher Oyler, Arnold Stevens and []. They also state that Soloman Tindall was on the point of death. The other portion of the Battalion they had not heard from.[56] The Pueblo brethren are expected to receive their pay and start for this point, at latest by this date, and will probably be here in about 2 weeks . . .

[June 2, 1847. Wednesday.] The morning pleasant. About 9 o'clock started over the river in company with the Twelve and

---

[55] A contingent of forty-three Saints in nineteen wagons from Mississippi and Illinois joined an Indian trader named Jim Clyman on the trail west. On August 4, 1846, they camped at Pueblo, Colorado, where they spent the following winter. This Mississippi/Illinois group was joined by men in the Mormon Battalion who had fallen ill. The so-called Sick Detachment and the "Mississippi Saints" from Pueblo joined up with the main pioneer company on June 2, 1847, at Fort Laramie, Wyoming. This company's members from Pueblo brought with them the idea of building houses of adobe—bricks of dried mud—a procedure which saved timber in some of the early construction in Salt Lake City (Morgan, 184–86).

[56] While the main Camp of Israel holed up at Winter Quarters, just north of Omaha, and the Sick Detachment and Mississippi Saints joined in Pueblo, Colorado, the Mormon Battalion had reached southern California in late January 1847. When gold was discovered in California in January 1848, members of the Mormon Battalion were working at John A. Sutter's mill. Among them was Addison Pratt, whose journal recorded that Sutter "employed fifty six Mormon boys and all the Indians he could get." Pratt observed that "there were strong accusations against [Sam] Brannan, by the Brooklyn company, that he had devised ways and means whereby he had swindled them out of their property by a pretense that he was collecting for the church . . . Brannan had entered into a league" with two men of the Mormon Battalion, on Mormon Island, near Sutter's Mill, "to make all that dug there pay them thirty percent of all that they should find there." Four of the battalion members in California carried the news of the discovery of gold, scooped in Brannan's *California Star* newspaper, to Salt Lake City and eastward (ibid., 184–88, 216; Arrington, *Great Basin Kingdom*, 64; Morgan, 186 and 216; S. George Ellsworth, ed., *The Journals of Addison Pratt* [Salt Lake City: University of Utah Press, 1990], 334–36, 543; compare also Journal 2, "Nauvoo, Illinois," n136, and Journal 4, "Pioneer Trek West," n63).

others to view the Fort and also learn something in regard to our journey &c. Elder Pratt measured the distance across the River at this spot and found it to be 108 yards. The water is deep in the channel and the current runs about 4 miles an hour. After crossing we went up to the remains of an old Fort called "Fort Platte" which is near the banks of the river, and the outside walls still standing, but the inside is in ruins, having been burned up. The walls are built of "daubies" or spanish brick, being large pieces of tempered clay dried in the sun and apparently laid one on another without mortar or cement. The dimensions of this Fort outside is from East to West 144 feet and from North to South 103 feet. There is a large door fronting to the South which has led to the dwellings which have been 14 in number, built in the form of a parallelogram, leaving a large space in the center. The space occupied by the dwellings is not quite half of the whole Fort. Fronting to the east is another large door which enters to a large open space 98-3/4 feet by 47 feet where it is supposed they have used for keeping horses &c. At the N.W. corner is a tower projecting out from the line of the walls 6 feet each way or in other words it is twelve feet square with port holes for cannon. At the N.E. corner has been another projection extending eastward 29.6 feet and is 19-1/2 feet wide. The walls are 11 feet high and 30 inches thick.

We took the dimensions of this with a tape line and then proceeded to "Fort Laramie"[57] about 2 miles further west. This latter fort was first built of wood about 13 years since and named Fort William, but being destroyed was afterwards built 7 years ago with "daubies" and named John. It stands on the bank of the Laramie Fork a stream 41 yards wide . . . We tarried a little while with the Mississipppi brethren who have camped close by the Fort, and then went inside . . . We went across the Square to the trading house which lays on the North Side of the Western entrance. The trader opened his store and President Young entered into conversation with him. They trade solely with the Sioux. The Crows come here for nothing but to steal. A few weeks ago a party came down and stole twenty-five horses, all that they had at

---

[57] In 1846 Lillburn Boggs went through Fort Laramie with the Russell party on the way to California (Bernard DeVoto, *The Year of Decision: 1846* [Boston: Houghton Mifflin, 1989], 124–25, 378, 459, 463).

the Fort, although they were within 300 yards of the Fort at the time and a guard round them. The Sioux will not steal on their own land. A pair of Moccasins worth a dollar, a lariette a dollar, a pound of tobacco a dollar and a half and a gallon of whiskey $32. They have no sugar, Coffee nor spices as their spring stores have not yet arrived. They have lately sent to Fort Pierre 600 bales of Robes with 10 robes in each bale. Their wagons have been gone 45 days &c. There are about [] souls at this fort, mostly French, half-breeds and a few Sioux Indians. Elder Pratt measured the river and found it 41 Yards. He also took the latitude which was 42 [degrees] 12'13" . . .

[June 3, 1847. Thursday.] The morning cold with strong S.E. wind. The first division commenced ferrying over the river at 5 o'clock and took a wagon over every fifteen minutes. After breakfast I went over and wrote a letter for Elder Kimball to James Brown at Pueblo, then walked up to a high bluff on the N.W. to view the country, but not being able to see far from it I went to another over a mile farther N.W. Although this last was very high I could see nothing but a succession of high ranges of bluffs as far as I could see, except the narrow space through which the river winds its course. Seeing some heavy thunder clouds rising very rapidly from the N.W. I returned to camp and arrived just before the rain commenced. Elders A[masa] Lyman, Thomas Woolsey, John H. Tippets and Roswell Stevens started at 1/4 past 11 on horses and mules for Pueblo. President Young, Kimball, Richards and Pratt accompanied them to the Laramie Fork, and then held a council, kneeled down and dedicated them to God and blessed them. The four then forded the river and went on their journey, the others returned to Camp. At half past 1 it commenced raining heavy accompanied with hail, lightning and very loud thunder, which lasted till half past 3 o'clock. During the storm the horses were mostly secured in the old Fort. The ferrying ceased till it was fair again, and about 5 the first division were all over. The boat was then manned by the second division John S. Higbee Captain. They averaged a wagon across in 11 minutes 10 minutes and one in 10 minutes 20 secs. The quickest trip made by the first division was 13 minutes. About 7 o'clock it commenced raining again from the S.E. and rained heavy, consequently the brethren quit ferrying, leaving 3 companies of about 15 wagons on the other side. All the wagons would have been got over today if it had not been stormy.

There is a report come in that there are 2,000 wagons on the road to Oregon but a little distance behind, but we are satisfied the report is magnified. There are 18 wagons camped about 3 miles below and one of the men who has come to the fort says that they have counted over 500 wagons. They have lost 4 horses by the Caw[58] Indians . . .

[June 6, 1847. Sunday.] At 11 o'clock, four Missourians came up mounted, being part of a company a little behind. Some of these are recognized by the brethren, and they seem a little afraid and not fond of our company. They say the old settlers have all fled from Shariton[59] Missouri only 2 tavern keepers, and I feel to wish that their fears may follow them even to Oregon. At half past 11 just as the brethren again assembled for meeting it commenced raining heavy, accompanied by lightning and heavy thunder which caused the meeting to break up abruptly. During the storm the Missouri company passed by us, having 19 wagons and 2 carriages. Most of their wagons have 5 yoke of cattle to each and few less than 4. They have many cows, horses and young Cattle with them . . . At half past 2 the Camp began to move forward . . . the wagons came to a halt in a body of timber and brushwood at 4 o'clock and halted while the brethren on horseback viz. Elders Young, Kimball and Woodruff went ahead to look for a camping ground. They returned at 20 minutes to 5 and the Camp proceeded on. Having proceeded a quarter of a mile we passed the camp of the 19 wagons close by the timber a little South of the road. Several of the men came to look at the roadometer having heard from some of the brethren that we had one. They expressed a wish to each other to see inside and looked upon it as a curiosity. I paid no attention to them inasmuch as they did not address themselves to me. At a quarter past 5 we formed our encampment in an oblong circle, at the foot of a low bluff on the west and close by water having traveled 5 miles. The feed here is very good and plentiful. Wind strong from the west.

[58] Perhaps a reference to the Crow Indians.
[59] Sheridan?

Road very crooked, mostly a South West and west course. Plenty of timber all along and the soil looks good on the low lands.

One of the men in the company of the 19 wagons told G. A. Smith that he had broke his carriage spring and seemed much troubled to know what to do to get along. He asked George if there was any man in our company who could fix it. George told him there was. After we were camped Burr Frost set up his forge and welded the spring ready to put on before dark . . .

[June 7, 1847. Monday.] Morning fine. Elder Orson Pratt gave me some instructions on the use of the sextant and showed me how to take an observation. He has promised to learn me to take observations and calculate Latitude and Longitude and I intend to improve the opportunity. At half past 6 the Missouri Company passed through again. And at 10 minutes past 7 we commenced our onward course. Dr. Richards left a letter in a guide board 30 1/4 miles to Ft. John. I walked about 5 miles mostly in company with Elder Pratt, conversing on astronomy and philosophical subjects. Elder Kimball then let me have his horse to ride. We traveled till 11 o'clock and then halted to feed on the West bank of a small stream and spring of clear water, having traveled 7 3/4 miles, mostly a N.N.W. course. The road more even and good traveling. Soon after we halted another Company of Missourians passed us having 13 wagons and mostly 4 yoke of Oxen to each. They say they are from Andrew Co. Mo . . .

[June 11, 1847. Friday.] Arose at 4 o'clock to try and get some more fish. Morning fine and warm, but caught only 4. I procured a sample of the stone coal from G. A. Smith. It looks good. This place reminds me of England. The calm, still morning with the warbling of many birds, the rich grass, good streams, and plenty of timber make it pleasant. At 25 minutes to 8 we again continued our journey along the banks of the river, which appears somewhat wider here than at Laramie . . .

[June 12, 1847. Saturday.] . . . At a quarter to 12 we halted after crossing another large ravine, having travelled 7 1/4 miles, over a sandy, barren prarie . . . During the halt Brother [Albert] Rockwood called upon the brethren to help fix another ravine immediately west of us, many turned out and it was soon done. James Case and S[tephen] Markham went to the river opposite here to see if it could be forded. They waded their horses over and found the water about 4 feet 6 deep in the channel and the current very swift and of course it could not be forded with loads in the wagons, but the loading would have to be ferried in the Boat. They made a report of this kind on their return to Camp and about the same time Brother Chessley came down from the brethren ahead and reported their progress and the nature of the crossing place &c. A number of the brethren, in company with Elder Kimball and Chessley went to the river opposite the Camp to decide whether to cross here or go on. Brothers Markham and Case again went over, but it was finally concluded to go up to the other ferry . . . The brethren concluded that a raft would be of no use on account of the swiftness of the current. The Missouri company offered to pay them well if they would carry their company over in the Boat and a contract was made to do so for $1.50 per load, the brethren to receive their pay in flour at $2.50 per hundred. They Commenced soon after, and this evening finished their work, and received their pay mostly in flour, a little meal and some bacon. They have made $34 with the cutter all in provisions which is a great blessing to the Camp inasmuch as a number of the brethren have had no bread stuff for some days. During the afternoon yesterday one of men of the Missouri company undertook to swim across the river with his cloths on. When he reached the current he became frightened and began to moan. Some of our men went to him with the cutter and arrived in time to save his life. The Missouri company seem to feel well toward us and express their joy at having got across the river so soon . . .

[June 13, 1847. Sunday.] The morning fine and pleasant. At 9 o'clock the brethren assembled in the circle for prayer and after they had spent some time Elder Kimball arose and addressed them exhorting them to be watchful, and humble to remember their covenants and above all things avoid every thing that would lead to division &c. He made use of the similitude of the potter and the clay to show that every man had the privilege of being exhalted to honor and glory if he did not mar in the hands of the potter, would continue passive &c. His remarks were very touching and appropriate to our circumstances. President Young followed next on the "liberty of the gospel" showing that it guarantees all the fullness of liberty to every man which will tend to

341

his salvation and increase, but does not give us liberty to break the laws of God, to wander off to the mountains and get lost, nor to kill the works of Gods hands to waste it &c. He was followed by Elder Pratt on the subject of our avoiding all excesses of folly of every description, inasmuch as it disqualifies from the society of just men and angels. He exhorted the brethren to be watchful and to seek after wisdom and knowledge. The meeting dismissed at half past 12 and a company were then dispatched to get poles to lash the wagons together to prevent their rolling over when crossing. Another company were sent over the river to build a raft to cross over provisions &c . . .

[June 14, 1847. Monday.] Morning cloudy and cool. At 4 o'clock the first division Commenced ferrying their goods over the river in the Cutter and some time afterwards commenced taking the wagons across on a raft which proved to be very slow work. The second division also began to take their goods over on a raft but the current was so strong they only took two loads over in it and then quit. The second division then got a rope stretched across the river from shore to shore and lashing 2 wagons fast together to keep them from rolling over they dragged them over by the roap, letting them drift with the current to save breaking the rope. When the wagons struck on the sand on the other side the upper one keeled over, and finally rolled over the other one, breaking the bows considerably and losing Iron &c. in the wagon to the amount of $30 belonging to John Pack . . . The plan of taking one wagon at a time on a raft is the safest, no accident having happened with it and the wagons get over dry, but it is very slow and would take us 3 or 4 days to get all the wagons across . . .

[June 15, 1847. Tuesday.] The morning fine but very windy. The brethren continued ferrying wagons over on the raft and also built 2 other rafts. The wind being so high they could not get along very fast . . . We have learned from a Missourian that there is a large company of emigrants coming up on the North side of the Platte above Grand Island. These are doubtless some of our brethren, and if so they will probably reach up with us before we get through.

The day continued windy and some inclined to storm, but they succeeded in getting near 20 wagons over before night . . .

[June 18, 1847. Friday.] Morning very cold and windy. The brethren continued working at the new boat, others continued ferrying the Missourians Wagons over . . . The president preached a short sermon for the benefit of the young elders. He represented them as being continually grasping at things ahead of them which belong to others instead of seeking to bring up those which are behind them. He said the way for young elders to enlarge their dominion and power is to go to the world and preach and then they can get a train and bring it up to the house of the Lord with them &c. The letter of instructions was then read and approved by the brethren and the council was then dismissed . . .

[June 20, 1847. Sunday.] Morning fine, mosquitoes very bad. Two more oxen found almost buried in the mud and all hands appeared wishful to leave this place and at a quarter past 5 o'clock we moved out . . . Elder Kimball states that when he and Elder Benson were riding ahead last evening to look out a camping ground they came within a quarter of a mile of this place but were not near enough to discover the water. A while before they arrived here as they were riding slowly along they saw 6 men suddenly spring up from the grass to the left of the road. The men were clothed in Blankets some white and some blue, and had every appearance of being Indians, and the brethren thought they were Indians. The six mounted their horses and started on in a direction parallel with the road. The brethren also kept on their course. In a little while one of the supposed Indians left the rest and rode towards the brethren and motioned with his hand for them to go back. They however kept on and paid no attention to his motion. When he saw them still coming he wheeled round and joined the others who all put spur to their horses and were soon out of sight behind a higher piece of land. Soon as they were out of sight Elder Kimball and Benson spurred their horses and rode to the ridge, and as they arrived there they discovered a camp of the Missourians about a quarter of a mile to the left of the road, and the six Indians were just entering the camp. The brethren were now satisfied that these Indians were Missourians and had taken this plan to keep us back from this good camp ground. It is considered as an old Missouri trick and an insult to the camp, and if they undertake to play Indian again, it is more

343

than likely they will meet with Indian treatment.[60] Their camp left here a little before we arrived this morning and it is now President Youngs intentions to press on a little faster and crowd them up a little . . .

I would here remark that it is the order of our traveling for each company of 10 to go forward in their turn. The first 10 in the first division taking the lead one day, then on the second day it falls in the rear of the first division and the second 10 takes the lead, and continues till each company of ten have taken the lead one day a piece. Then the first division falls in the rear of the second division which also begins by companies of ten to take the lead on the road as stated above and when each ten have had their day the second division again falls in the rear of the first which continues in the same order. Thus every man has his equal privilege of traveling one with another . . .

[June 21, 1847. Monday.] . . . President Young, Kimball and others went to view the north side of Devil's Gate and returning reported that the Devils would not let them pass, or meaning that it was impossible to go through the Gateway, so called. We proceeded on a little further and at 25 minutes to 7 formed our encampment on the bank of the river having traveled this afternoon 7 3/4 miles and during the day 15 1/4. The feed here is good and plentiful and a little Cedar can be obtained at the foot of one of the rocky ridges about a quarter of a mile back for fuel. After we had camped I went back to view the "Devils Gate" where the river runs between two high rocky ridges for he distance of about 200 yards. The rock on the east side is perpendicular and was found by a Barometrical measurements by Elder Pratt to be 399 feet 4 1/2 inches high . . .

[June 23, 1847. Wednesday.] Morning fine and warm. After breakfast I went to the top of the high bluff expecting to get a good view of the country west but was disappointed in consequence of the many ridges or bluffs but a little distance beyond us. At 7 o'clock the camp moved forward and immediately after

---

[60]Clayton's phrase, to "play Indian," anticipates the 1857 Mountain Meadows Massacre when Mormons dressed as Indians killed 120 Missouri and Arkansas emigrants (Richard D. Poll et al., eds., *Utah's History* [Provo, UT: Brigham Young University Press, 1978], 170–71).

saw a graveyard on the left of the road with a board stuck up these words written on it: Matilda Crowley. B. July 16, 1830, and D. July 7, 1846. On reflecting afterwards that some of the numerous emigrants who had probably started with a view to spend the remainder of their days in the wild Oregon, had fallen by the way and their remains had to be left by their friends far from the place of destination, I felt a renewed anxiety that the Lord will kindly preserve the lives of all my family, that they may be permitted to gather to the future home of the Saints, enjoy the society of the people of God for many years to come and when their days are numbered that their remains may be deposited at the feet of the servants of God, rather than be left far away in a wild country and oh, Lord, grant this sincere desire of thy servant in the name of thy Son Jesus. Amen. After traveling 1 1/2 miles we crossed a very shoal stream of clear, cold water about 5 feet wide. There is [little] grass here but a number of Bitter Cotton Wood trees growing on its banks. There being no name on the map to this creek it was named "Bitter Cotton Wood Creek" to designate it in our future travel . . . We continued on the banks of the river till 20 minutes past 6 at which time we formed our encampment having traveled this afternoon 8 1/2 miles and during the day [19]. As usual there is plenty of grass on the river banks but no wood. There are some dry buffalo chips and wild sage which answer tolerably well for cooking. The land over which we have travelled except in the several places above mentioned, is perfectly barren except wild sage which abounds but there is scarce a spear of grass to be seen. These granite ridges continue from the Rock Independence to this place, mostly on the North side the river. Here they receed from the river a few miles and then cease. There are two of the Missouri companies camped, one about half a mile and the other a mile west of us, as we are given to understand we have got a long distance to travel without grass or water. It is stated that a man from one of these companies left his company a few days ago and went ahead to examine the route &c. On their arrival here they found him in one of these rocky hills hid up for fear of Indians. He reports that he has been to the "Pass"[61] and that we shall find water about 14 miles from here. He has come

---

61 South Pass.

from the Pass in two nights and hid up in the day time to avoid Indians, but has seen none. He says it is not over 28 miles to the "Pass" from here.

After we camped Burr Frost set up his forge and set some wagon tire and repaired the wheels of the wagon for one of the Missourians . . .

[June 26, 1847. Saturday.] . . . Elder Pratt has gone ahead with the barometer to try to find the culminating point or highest dividing ridge of the South Pass as we are evidently at the east foot of the pass. Fremont represents that he did not discover the highest point on account of the ascent being so gradual that they were beyond it before they were aware of it, although in company with a man who has traveled it back and forth for seventeen years . . . At 20 minutes past 2 we moved onward, ascending again on pretty high land where we found good traveling. The latitude at our noon halt was 42 [degrees] 22' 42". After traveling seven miles this afternoon we arrived on a level spot of lower land and some grass, and inasmuch as we have found no stream as laid down on Freemont's map since leaving the Sweet Water, neither is there much appearance of any for some miles farther, the wagons halted while President Young and some others went over the ridge to the north to look for a camp ground as some of the brethren said the Sweet Water was close by . . . Elders Kimball, Pratt and some others are some miles ahead and not having returned at dark, a number of the brethren were sent to meet them. They soon returned in company with Elder Kimball who reported that he had been on as much as six miles to where the head waters of the Atlantic divide from those of the Pacific, that Elder Pratt was camped there with a small party of men direct from Oregon and bound for the U.S. It is now a certainty that we are yet two miles short of the dividing ridge of the South Pass by the road. This ridge divides the headwaters of the Atlantic from those of the Pacific and although not the highest land we have traveled over, it may with propriety be said to be the summit of the South Pass. The Wind River mountains appear very high from this place but on the south there is very little appearance of mountains, Table Rock itself appearing but a little elevated.

[June 27, 1847. Sunday.] Morning fine but cold. The ox teams started at 5 minutes to 8 and the remainder shortly after. We soon

met 8 of the Oregon men on their way back, having over 20
horses and the mules with them mostly laden with packs of robes,
skins &c. Several of the brethren sent letters back by them . . .
One of the Oregon men is returning with us today and then intends to wait for the next companies and act as a pilot for them.
His name is "Harris" and appears to be extensively known in
Oregon and the subject of much dispute on account of having
found out a new route to Oregon, much South of the old one.[62]
He appears to be a man of intelligence and well acquainted with
the western country. He presented a file of the Oregon papers,
commencing with February 11th 1847 and five following numbers
for our perusal during the day. He also presented a number of the
California "Star" published at Yerba Buena by Samuel Brannan
and edited by E. P. Jones.[63] I had the privilege of perusing several of these papers during the day but found little interesting
news. Mr. Harris says he is well acquainted with the Bear River
Valley and the regions around the salt Lake. From his description
which is very discouraging we have little chance to hope for even
a moderate good country anywhere in those regions. He speaks of
the whole region as being Sandy and destitute of timber and veg-
etation except the wild Sage. He gives the most favorable account
of a Small region under the Bear River mountains called the
Cach valley where they have practised caching their robes &c. to
hide them from the Indians . . . Mr. Harris has described a valley 40 miles above the mouth of the Bear River and 30 miles
below the Bear Springs which might answer our purpose pretty

---

[62] Major Moses ("Black") Harris was a trapper who had travelled the Great
Basin for twenty-five years and had piloted emigrants to Oregon in 1844. According to Orson Pratt, Harris had travelled around the lake and discovered no outlet (*Latter-day Saints' Millenial Star* 12 [April 15, 1850]: 129; [May 15, 1859]: 146).
He advised the Saints that the Great Salt Lake Valley had inadequate timber to
sustain a colony. See Unruh, 40.

[63] While in New York, Samuel Brannan had published the Mormon
newspaper, *The Prophet*, later the *New York Messenger*. Brannan chartered the ship
Brooklyn, and with his press aboard sailed with seventy men, sixty-eight women,
and one hundred children, mostly Latter-day Saints, around Cape Horn to Yerba
Buena, the early Spanish settlement that would later be renamed San Francisco.
They left on February 4, 1846, the same day the first pioneer wagons crossed the
Mississippi River from Nauvoo. In San Francisco, Brannan founded the *California
Star*, which reported the ongoing gold rush (Conway B. Sonne, *Ships, Saints, and
Mariners: A Maritime Encyclopedia of Mormon Migration, 1830-1890* [Salt Lake City:
University of Utah Press, 1987], 32-33; Morgan, 216).

well if the report is true. It is about 30 miles long and 15 miles wide, and tolerably well timbered. We generally feel that we shall know best by going ourselves for the reports of travellers are so contradictory, it is impossible to know which is truth without going to prove it.

It is 3 years today since our brethren Joseph and Hyrum were taken from us and it was a general feeling to spend the day in fasting and prayer, but the gentile companies being close in our rear and feed scarce it was considered necessary to keep ahead for the benifit of our teams, but many minds have reverted back to the scenes at Carthage Jail, and it is a gratification that we have so far prospered in our endeavors to get from under the grasp of our enemies.

[June 28, 1847. Monday.] Morning fine but cool. Many of the brethren are trading with Mr. Harris for pants, Jackets, shirts &c. made of Buckskins and also the skins themselves. He sells them high. The skins at 1.50 and 2 dollars, a pair of Pants 3 dollars &c. He will take rifles, powder, lead, caps or calico and domestic shirts in exchange but puts his own price on both sides and it is difficult to obtain even a fair trade.

At half past 7 we proceeded on our journey. Mr. Harris waiting for the other companies. After traveling 6 miles the road forks, one continuing a west course, the other taking a southwest course. We took the left hand road, which leads to California . . . after travelling a little over a mile we were met by Elder G. A. Smith who introduced us to Mr. [Jim] Bridger of "Bridgers Fort" on his way to Fort John in company with two of his men.[64] Mr. Bridger

---

[64] Considered the most widely travelled man in the West, Jim Bridger (1804–81) was a fur trapper and trader who visited the Great Salt Lake in 1824. He also found a way through the South Pass across the Rocky Mountains and explored the Yellowstone geysers. In 1843 while the Mormons resided in Nauvoo, he built Fort Bridger in southwestern Wyoming to trade with travelers on the Oregon Trail. Upon meeting Brigham Young along the trail, Bridger described the route into the Great Salt Lake Valley and warned him about the "abusive" Ute Indians. The following winter when the Saints ran low on food, he sent cattle into Utah for which they later paid him with profits from gold rush traffic. Later Bridger fell out with Brigham Young: in 1853 Young accused him of supplying liquor and arms to hostile Indians and sent a band of men to destroy his fort. Young paid him for part of the damage, but Bridger demanded his fort back. When Bridger set up a profitable ferry business across the Green River in Wyoming, Young asked for half of the profits and a ten percent surcharge on the rest. Bridger scouted for the U.S. Army

being informed that we had designed to call at his place to make some inquiries about the country &c. he said if we would turn off the road here and camp he would stay with us till morning. A camping place being selected we turned off from the road about a quarter of a mile and formed our encampment near the "Sandy" at 6 o'clock, having traveled this afternoon 1 3/4 miles, exclusive of allowance for leaving the road and during the day 15 1/4 miles. We have pretty good feed here enough to fill the teams well.

A while after we camped the Twelve and several others went to Mr. Bridger to make some enquiries, concerning our future route, the country &c. It was impossible to form a correct idea of either, from the very imperfect and irregular way he gave his descriptions, but the general items are in substance as follows:

"We will find better grass as we proceed further on. His business is to Fort Laramie. His traders have gone their with robes, skins &c. to fill a contract, but having started later than they intended the men at Laramie have taken advantage of the delay, and he is going to see to the business himself. There is no blacksmith's shop at his Fort at present; there was one but it was destroyed. There have been near a hundred wagons gone on the Hastings route through Webers Fork.[65] They crossed the Black

against the Mormons in 1857 during the "Mormon War." Nicknamed "Old Gabe" and "Blanket Chief" by the Crows, Bridger was illiterate, but he was known as a good story-teller. During his life, Bridger had in turn three Indian wives. See Morgan, 192-93; Stanley P. Hirshon, *The Lion of the Lord* (New York: Alfred A. Knopf, 1969), 142-44, 170.

[65] The Hastings route was named for Lansford W. Hastings, an Ohio lawyer who promoted emigration to California in the 1840s. After traveling through Oregon and California in 1842-43, he wrote *The Emigrants' Guide to Oregon and California*. In 1845, while promoting his book in New York, he met the Mormon publisher Sam Brannan. They both anticipated a large westward migration, including many Mormons. The *Nauvoo Neighbor* published extracts from Hastings's book, along with sections of Fremont's unpublished journals. Hastings urged Brigham Young to go to Upper California, the land between the Wasatch Mountains and the Pacific Ocean. On August 18, 1845, Hastings and nine companions traveled westward from Independence. At Fort Laramie he picked up Jim Bridger, who guided him through the precipitous Wind River Mountains in Wyoming, away from hostile Indians. After an exceptionally snowless trip across the Great Basin and the Sierra, Hastings reached Sutter's Fort in California on Christmas Day 1845. The next spring he returned to Fort Bridger to take wagonloads of immigrants to California by way of a new short-cut through the Weber Canyon, explored by John C. Fremont. Although Hastings was able to negotiate the difficult and unfamiliar terrain, the ill-fated Donner-Reed party, which had tried to follow him with wagons, was seriously delayed crossing the

Fork and go a little South of West from his place and pass under the mountains which cross Green river. The Green river runs over an extent of country of 400 miles. It is impossible for wagons to follow down Green river, neither can it be followed with Boats. Some have gone down with Canoes, but had great difficulty getting back, on account of rapid current and rough channel. Can't pass the mountains close to the river even with horses. For some distance beyond this chain of mountains the country is level, and beyond that it is hard black rock, which looks as if it was glazed when the sun shines on it, and so hard and sharp it will cut a horses feet to pieces. When we get below the mountain the Green River falls into a level country for some distance, after which it winds through a moutainous country, perfectly barren to the Gulf of California.

From Bridger's fort to the Salt Lake, Hastings said was about one hundred miles. He has been through 50 times but can form no correct idea of the distance. Mr. Hastings route leaves the Oregon route at his place. We can pass the mountains further south, but in some places we would meet with heavy bodies of timber and would have to cut our way through. In the Bear River Valley there is Oak timber, sugar trees, Cotton wood and pine. There is not an abundance of sugar maple but plenty of splendid pine as he ever saw. There is no timber on the Utah Lake only on the streams which empty into it. In the Outlet of the Utah Lake into the Salt Lake there are three streams empties which are well timbered. In the vallies South East of the Salt Lake there is an abundance of Blue grass and red and white Clover. The Outlet of the Utah Lake does not form a large river, neither a rapid current, but the water is muddy and low banks.

Some of his men have been round the Salt Lake in Canoes. They went out hunting and had their horses stole by the Indians. They then went round the Lake in Canoes hunting Beaver and were three months going round it. They said it was 550 miles round it. The Utah tribe of Indians inhabit around the Utah

---

Sierra. The Donner party had cleared a trail into the Great Salt Lake Valley which the Mormons would successfully follow the next year. See Lavender, *The Great West*, 250, 253–54, 267–70; Morgan, 161–73; Arrington, *Brigham Young*, 124, 172–73; Newell G. Bringhurst, *Brigham Young and the Expanding American Frontier* (Boston: Little Brown, 1986), 75, 95; Unruh, 288; Poll, 79–90, 123.

Lake and are a bad people if they catch a man alone they are sure
to rob and abuse him, if they don't kill him, but parties of men
are in no danger. They are mostly armed with guns.

There was a man opened a farm in the Bear River valley.[66]
The Soil is good and likely to produce corn were it not for the
excessive cold nights, which he thinks would prevent the growth
of Corn. There is a good Country South of the Utah Lake or
South East of the great Basin. There are three large Rivers which
enter into the Sevier Lake unknown to travellers. There is also
a splendid range of country on the North side of the California
mountains, calculated to produce every kind of grain and fruit,
and there are several places where a man might pass from it over
the mountains to the California settlements in one day. There is
a vast abundance of timber and plenty of Coal. There is also
plenty of coal in this region near the mountains. North of the
California mountains there is Walnut, Oak, Ash, Hickory, and
various kinds of good timber on and in the neighborhood of
the mountains and streams South East of the great Basin. There
can be a wagon road made through to it and no lack of water.
The great desert extends from the Salt Lake to the Gulf of California which is perfectly barren. He supposes it to have been
an arm of the sea. The three rivers before mentioned are South
West of the desert. There is a tribe of Indians in that country who
are unknown to either travellers or geographers. They make farms
and raise abundance of grain of various kinds. He can buy any
quantity of the very best of wheat there. This country lies South
East of the Salt Lake. There is one mountain in that region and
the country adjoining it, which he considers if ever there was a
promised land that must be it. There is a kind of Cedar grows on
it which bears fruit something like Juniper berries, of a yellow
color about the size of an ordinary plum. The Indians grind the
fruit and it makes the best kind of meal. He could easily gather a
hundred bushels off from one tree. He has lived on them and
used to pick his hat full in a very short time. There are a great
many little streams head in this mountain and many good springs.
It is about 20 days travel with horses from the Salt Lake, but the
country to it is bad to get through and over a great part of it,

---

66 Probably Miles Goodyear. See July 10, 1847.

nothing for animals to subsist on. He supposes there might be access to it from Texas.

On one of the Rivers there is a splendid Copper mine, a whole mountain of it. It also abounds with gold and silver and has a good quick silver mine. There is Iron, coal &c. The land is good and the Soil rich. All the vallies abound with bitter Simons and grapes which will make the best kind of wines.

He never saw any grapes on the Utah Lake, but there are plenty of cherries and berries of several kinds. He thinks the Utah Lake is the best country in the vicinity of the Salt Lake, and the country is still better the further South we go untill we meet the desert which is upwards of 200 miles South from the Utah Lake. There is plenty of timber on all the streams and mountains, and abundance of fish in the streams. There is timber all around the Utah Lake and plenty of good grass, not much of the wild sage only in small patches. Wild Flax grows in most of the vallies and they are the richest land. He passed through that country a year ago last summer, in the month of July, and they generally had one or two showers every day, sometimes a very heavy thunder shower, but not accompanied by strong wind.

By following under the mountain south of the Utah Lake we find another River which enters into another Lake about 50 miles South of the Utah Lake.

We shall find plenty of water from here to Bridger's Fort except after we cross Green River and travel 5 miles beyond it, we shall have to travel 18 or 20 miles without water but there is plenty of grass.

After crossing Green River we follow down it 4 or 5 miles to the old Station then cross over to a stream which heads in the mountains west. The station is more than half way from here to his place. We shall have no stream to ferry between here and the Fort except Green River.

The Indians South of the Utah Lake and this side the desert raise corn, wheat and other kinds of grain and produce in abundance. The Utahs abound more on the west of the mountains near the Salt Lake than on the East side ten to one, but we have no need to fear them for we can drive the whole of them in 24 hours, but he would not kill them, he would make slaves of them. The Indians south of the Utah Lake raise as good corn, wheat, and pumpkins as was ever raised in old Kentucky.

He knows of a lead mine between the mountains and Laramie, on a timbered creek near the Horse Shoe Creek. He has found lead there and thinks there is considerable silver in it. It can be found in a cave on the side of mountain not far from the road."

Such was the information we obtained from Mr. Bridger, but we shall know more about things and have a better understanding when we have seen the country ourselves. Supper had been provided for Mr. Bridger and his men and the latter having eat the council dismissed, Mr. B[ridger] going with President Young to supper, the remainder retiring to their wagons conversing over the subject touched upon. The evening was very fine and musquitoes numerous . . .

[June 30, 1847. Wednesday.] . . . At half past 11 we arrived on the banks of Green River, having traveled 8 miles, and formed our encampment in a line under the shade of the Cotton wood timber. This river is about 16 to 18 rods wide and altogether too deep to be forded. Its banks are well lined with Cotton wood but none large enough to make a canoe. There are also many patches of wild apple trees and rose bushes abound bearing pretty roses. This river is 338-1/2 miles from Fort John or Laramie. There is a narrow strip of land which might answer for farming on each bank of the river. The grass grows good and plentiful but still not so much as has been represented. After dinner the brethren commenced making two rafts one for each division and a while afterwards Elder Samuel Brannan arrived, having come from the Pacific to meet us, obtain council &c.[67] He is accompanied by "Smith" of the firm of Jackson, Heaton & Bonney, bogus makers of Nauvoo.[68] There is another young man in company with them.

---

[67] Brannan had crossed the Sierra to persuade the twelve apostles to settle the emigrants in California, but Brigham Young reaffirmed that they were heading for the valley of the Great Salt Lake. See Morgan, 193.

[68] The United States government did not print any currency following the failure of the oversupplied "Continentals," issued by the Continental Congress to finance the Revolutionary War, until it printed "Greenbacks" to pay for the Civil War. During this interim period, numerous private bank notes circulated as agreements to exchange them for the face value of gold or silver. Since so many diverse bills were circulating, counterfeit money was easy to pass. The *History of the Church* refers to bogus-makers, or counterfeiters, on January 24, 1846, in Nauvoo and again on the trail to Winter Quarters. Bill Hickman, an aid to Brigham Young, destroyed a counterfeit press in Winter Quarters one night. See *HC* 7: 574, 609; Hope A. Hilton, *"Wild Bill" Hickman and the Mormon Frontier* (Salt Lake City:

They have come by way of Fort Hall and brought several files of the California Star with them. They had 11 deaths on board their ship during their voyage over, the others I understand are doing well, raising grain &c. Towards evening a storm blew up from the west and although we had no rain we had tremendous wind. The first division finished their raft before dark. There is a slough a little down the river where some of the brethren have caught some very nice fish, but the musquitoes are so very troublesome it is difficult abiding out of doors . . .

[July 4, 1847. Sunday.] . . . Some of the brethren assembled for meeting in the circle. At half after 2 P. M. the brethren returned from the ferry accompanied by 12 of the Pueblo brethren from the army. They have got their discharge and by riding hard overtaken us. They feel well and on arriving in camp gave three cheers after which President Young moved that we give glory to God which was done by hosannas. William Walker was with them . . .

[July 7, 1847. Wednesday.] . . . "Bridger's Fort" is composed of two double Log houses about 40 feet long each and joined by a pen for horses about 10 feet high, constructed by placing poles upright in the ground, close together, which is all the appearance of a Fort in sight. There are several Indian Lodges close by and a full crop of young children playing around the door. These Indians are said to be of the Snake tribe, the Utahs inhabiting beyond the mountains. The latitude of Fort Bridger is 41 [degrees] 19' 13" and its height above the level of the sea according to Elder Pratts observations is 6,665 feet. It is doubtless a very cold region and little calculated for farming purposes. To the West is a pretty high mountain, which appears well covered with timber. The country all around looks bleak and cold.

[July 8, 1847. Thursday.] . . . It was decided for Thomas Williams and S[amuel] Brannan to return from here and meet Captain [James] Browns company from Pueblo. Inasmuch as the brethren have not received their discharge nor their pay from the United States, Brother Brannan goes to tender his services as pilot, to conduct a company of 15 or 20 to San Francisco if they feel disposed to go their and try to get their pay . . .

Signature Books, 1988), 20. For a discussion of coinage, see Journal 6, "Polygamy Mission to England," n22.

[July 10, 1847. Saturday.] . . . A little further, the brethren had to dig a place considerably to make a pass between the mountains. Presidents Young and Kimball labored hard with a number of others and in about a half an hour made a good road. At 20 miles from Fort Bridger passed another spring, and a little further after arriving on the bottom land the road turns near south through a beautiful low bottom filled with grass . . . After halting an hour and a half we proceeded again and after traveling 3 1/2 miles began to ascend the dividing ridge between the Colorado waters and the great basin . . . After camping Mr. Miles Good[year][69] came into camp. He is the man who is making a farm in the Bear River valley. He says it is yet 75 miles to his place, although we are now within two miles of Bear River. His report of the valley is more favorable than some we have heard, but we have an idea he is anxious to have us make a road to his place through selfish motives. Elder Orson Pratt has found a beautiful spring of clear, sweet, cold water about a hundred yards S.W. from the camp. Water excellent.

[July 11, 1847. Sunday.] Morning fine with ice a quarter of an inch thick on the water pails. Walked on the mountain East with Presidents Young and Kimball, from whence we had a pleasing view of the surrounding valley, which is about 10 miles wide. Abundance of timber on the mountains South and South West and beyond that plenty of snow. After having prayers we again

---

[69] Miles Goodyear (1817–49) travelled west from Connecticut in 1842 to become Utah's first American resident. On the way to Oregon he left his wagon train, lived among Indian tribes and mountain men, married an Indian woman, and in 1846 built a fort at the confluence of the Weber and the Ogden Rivers at the site of present-day Ogden, Utah. "Fort Buenaventura," a trading post about forty miles from where the Mormons would build Salt Lake City, had log buildings, vegetable gardens, and corralled herds of horses, cattle, and goats. It was meant to be a "half way house" between Independence, Missouri, and the Oregon and California territories, a station "where the companies may stop and refresh themselves and obtain . . . supplies" along the lines of Fort Laramie. Returning from Sutter's Fort in 1847, Goodyear passed the remains of the Donner Party along the Sierra; and, as Clayton here notes, met the Mormons on the trail near the Bear River. He influenced the choice the camp made the following day, July 11, to seek out the Donner Party route at the Bear River. In late 1847, overland emigrants began using the Greenwood (or Sublette) Cutoff, bypassing both Forts Buenaventura and Bridger. When some of their number defected to Goodyear's post on the Weber late in 1847, the Mormons bought him out for $1,950.00. See Morgan, 130–35, 147–49, 175, 194, 204, 208–10; Unruh, 205–206, 253.

descended and at the foot discovered a very strong Sulphur spring. The surface of the water covered with flour of sulphur and where it oozes from the rock perfectly black. The water in the creek shows sulphur very evident and smells bad . . . There are some in camp who are getting discouraged about the looks of the country, but thinking minds are not much disappointed and we have no doubt of finding a place where the Saints can live, which is all we ought to ask or expect. It is evident the country grows better as we proceed west, and vegitation so more plentiful and looks richer.

After dark a meeting was called to decide which of the two roads we shall take from here. It was voted to take the right hand or northern road, but the private feelings of all the twelve was that the other would be best. But such matters are left to the choice of the camp so that none may have room to murmer at the Twelve hereafter.

[July 12, 1847. Monday.] Morning cloudy and cool. We pursued our journey at a quarter past 7. At 1 1/4 miles rose a very steep low hill narrow but very steep on both sides. 1/2 a mile farther crossed the Bear River a very rapid stream about 6 rods wide and 2 feet deep, bottom full of large cobblestones, water clear banks lined with willows and a little timber, good grass, many strawberry vines and the soil looks pretty good. About 1/2 mile beyond the ford proceed over another ridge again, descended into and travelled up a beautiful narrow bottom covered with grass and fertile but no timber. 4 3/4 miles beyond Bear River passed a small spring of good clear cold water. At ten minutes before 12, halted for noon in the same narrow bottom near a ridge of high rough rocks to the right having travelled 9 3/4 miles. There is scarcely any wagon track too be seen only a few wagons of Hastings company having come this route. The balance went the other road and many of them perished in the snow it being late in the season and much time was lost quarreling who would improve the roads &c[70] . . .

---

[70] Clayton refers to the Donner-Reed party, which had tried to follow Hastings. When he realized how difficult it was for a large wagon train to navigate his cutoff, Hastings left the Donner party a note in a cleft stick along the trail cautioning them to go another way. See n65. Clayton records a similar method of leaving messages along the trail in his entries of May 10 and May 17, 1847.

[July 13, 1847. Tuesday.] A while before noon Elder Kimball and Howard Egan arrived from the company back. A meeting was called but suddenly dispersed by a thunder shower. After the rain ceased, Elder Kimball proposed that a company start from the camp with Elder Pratt to proceed on to the Weber River Canyon and ascertain if we can pass through safely if not to try and find a pass over the mountains. He reported that President Young is a little better this morning, but last evening was insensible and raving. Col. [Albert] Rockwood is also very sick and quite deranged. A company of 22 wagons, mostly Ox teams started on soon after dinner in company with Elder Pratt and soon after, Elders Kimball and Egan returned to the back company. The day has been very hot and sultry, and musquitoes are very troublesome.

[July 14, 1847. Wednesday.]. . . those who are gone on to look out and make a road . . . total, 23 wagons and 42 men.

[July 16, 1847. Friday.] This morning we have had two pleasant showers accompanied by pretty loud thunder. At 1/4 to 9 we proceeded onward passing through a narrow ravine between very high mountains. After traveling 1 1/4 mile passed a deep ravine where most of the teams had to double to get up. 1/2 mile further crossed the creek and found the crossing place very bad. . . . the mountains seem to increase in height, and come so near together in some places, as to leave merely room enough for a crooked road . . . As we halted O. P. Rockwell came up from Elder Pratt's company. He reports that it is about 25 or 30 miles to the canyon. They have found the road leading over the mountains to avoid the canyon and expect to be on top today at noon.[71] . . . for several miles there are many patches or groves of the wild currant, Hop vines, Elder and Black Birch. Willows are abundant and high. The currants are yet green and taste most like a gooseberry, thick rind and rather bitter . . .

In some places we had to pass close to the foot of high perpendicular red mountains of rock supposed to be from 600 to 1000 feet high . . . There is a very singular echo in this ravine, the rattling of wagons resembles carpenters hammering at boards

---

[71] At this point the pioneers pick up the trail left by the Donner party in the fall of 1846 (Poll, 123). See also notes 65, 69, 70, 73, and 74.

inside the highest rocks. The report of a rifle resembles a sharp crack of thunder and echoes from rock to rock for some time. The lowing of cattle and braying of mules seems to be answered beyond the mountains. Music especially brass instruments have a very pleasing effect and resemble a person standing inside the rock imitating every note. The echo the high rocks on the north high mountains on the south with the narrow ravine for a road form a scenery at once romantic and more interesting than I have ever witnessed. Soon after we camped I walked up the highest mountain on the south. The ascent is so steep that there is scarce a place to be found to place the foot flat and firm and the visitor is every moment if he makes the least slip or stumbles, [in danger] of being precip[it]ated down to the bottom, and once overbalanced, there is no possibility of stopping himself till he gets to the bottom, in which case he would doubtless be dashed to pieces. After resting about half a dozen times I arrived at the top and found the ascent equally steep all the way up. In many places I had to go on my hands and feet to keep from falling backwards. From this mountain I could see the red fork of Webers River about a mile west of the Camp, looking back I could see the road we had come for several miles, but in every other direction nothing but ranges of mountains still as much higher than the one I was on as it is above the creek. The scenery is truly wild and melancholy . . .

[July 17, 1847. Saturday.] Arose to behold a fine pleasant morning my health much better. This is my thirty second birthday being now 33 years old.[72] My mind naturally reverts back to my family and my heart is filled with blessings on their heads more than my tongue is able to express. The richest blessings that ever were bestowed upon the head of woman or child could not be more than I desire for them, whatever be my lot . . . In the afternoon Elders [Heber] Kimball, [Willard] Richards, [Ezra T.] Benson and others went onto a mountain to clothe and pray for President Young who continues very sick. On returning they rolled down many large rocks from the top of the mountain to witness the velocity of their descent &c. Some would roll over half a mile and frequently broke to pieces.

---

[72] Clayton turned thirty-three years old just before entering the Great Salt Lake Valley.

John Nixon found and brought to camp a very singular kind of thistle which I have never seen before nor recollect ever reading of the like . . . but the great curiosity of this thistle is a perfect resemblence of a snake coil round and round the crown as if in the act of guarding it against foes . . . The body of the snake is formed of the same kind of substance with the thistle itself, and has a very singular appearance. It seems that 2 of the great enemies of mankind have combined, the most bitter and destructive guarding the more innocent. The serpent tempted the woman causing her to sin, in consequence of which the earth was cursed, and decreed to produce thorns and thistles &c. but this is the first time I ever saw the snake guard the thistle . . .

[July 18, 1847. Sunday.] This morning the Camp was called together and addressed by Elder Kimball. He reports President Young as being a very sick man. He proposed to the brethren that instead of their scattering off, some hunting, some fishing, and some climbing mountains &c. that they should meet together and pray and exhort each other, that the Lord may turn away sickness from our midst and from our president that we may proceed on our journey. It was decided to assemble at 10 o'clock and at the sound of the bugle the brethren met in a small grove of shrubbery which they have made for the purpose opposite the wagons. During the meeting, Elder Kimball proposed to the brethren that all the camp, except President Young's and 8 or 10 other wagons with brethren enough to take care of him &c proceed on tomorrow and go through, find a good place, begin to plant potatoes &c as we have little time to spare. The proposition was acceded to by unanimous vote and after a number had expressed their feelings the meeting adjourned till 2 o'clock at which time they again assembled and listened to remarks from a number of the brethren. Elder Kimball again gave much good instruction and prophecied good things concerning the camp. The Bishops brake bread and the sacrament was administered. Good feelings seem to prevail and the brethren desire to do right. A number yet continue sick, but we expect all will soon recover. The day is very hot with very little air moving. Elder Kimball consented for me to go on tomorrow with the company that goes ahead.

[July 19, 1847. Monday.] Morning fine and warm, President Young considerably better. At 1/4 to 8 we started onward leaving

359

President Young and Kimball's wagons and several others. We found the road very rough on account of loose rocks and cobble stones. After traveling 2 1/4 miles we forded the river and found it about 18 inches deep, but forded without difficulty. Soon after we were over, Elder Snow came up and said the camp were requested to halt awhile till Dr. Richards came. One of his oxen is missing and he wished to go on. We concluded to move on a little to where the road should turn off between the mountains to avoid the canyon. Elder Pratt went 3 miles out of his road and had to return again. 3/4 of a mile from the ford we found the place to make the cutoff and there halted awhile. I put a guide board up at this place marked as follows: Pratts Pass to avoid canyon. To Fort Bridger 74 1/4 miles. Brother Pack, having charge of the company, concluded to move on slowly and be making our way up the mountains. We accordingly started and after traveling a mile from the forks began to ascend and wind around the mountains. We found the road exceedingly rough and crooked and very dangerous on wagons. 3 1/2 miles from the forks of the road the brethren made a bridge over a small creek over which we crossed having passed a number of springs near the road. 2 1/4 miles farther we arrived on the summit of the dividing ridge and put a guide board up 80 miles to Fort Bridger. At this place Elders Kimball, Woodruff, G. A. Smith and H. Egan rode up to view the road &c. The descent is not very steep but exceedingly dangerous to wagons being mostly on the side hill over large cobble stones causing the wagons to slide very badly . . .

[July 20, 1847. Tuesday.] . . . One of Brother [Robert] Crows men returned from Elder [Orson] Pratts company and reported that their camp is about 9 miles from here. He is hunting stray cattle. He says the road is very rough from here and about a mile beyond where they are camped the road begins to ascend over a high range of mountains. Elder Pratt has been to the top but cannot see the Salt Lake from there. Their company is gone on. I walked ahead of the camp near four miles and picked many gooseberries nearly ripe. They are very plentiful on this bottom. The brethren spent much time cutting brush wood and improving the road. After traveling 4 miles, halted about half an hour to water teams and eat dinner. The road over which we have traveled is through an uneven gap between high mountains and is exceeding rough and crooked. Not a place to be met with scarcely where there would be room to camp for the dense willow groves all along the bottom. We then proceeded on and travelled over the same kind of rough road till a little after 5 o'clock then encamped on a ridge having traveled today 7 1/4 miles . . . We have passed through some small patches today where a few house logs might be cut, but this is truly a wild looking place . . .

[July 22, 1847. Thursday.] . . . It is evident that the emigrants who passed this way last year must have spent a great deal of time cutting a road through the thickly set timber and heavy brush wood. It is reported that the[y] spent 16 days in making a road through from Weber river here which is 35 miles but as the men "did not work quarter of their time" much less would have sufficed . . . [73] Brother Stephen Markham says a good road can soon be made down the Kanion by digging a little and cutting through the bushes some ten or fifteen rods. A number of men went to work immediately to make the road which will be much better than to attempt crossing the hill, and will be sooner done.

Agreeable to President Young's instructions, Elder Pratt accompanied by George A. Smith, John Brown, Joseph Mathews, John Pack, O. P. Rockwell and J[esse] C. Little started on this morning on horses to seek out a suitable place to plant some potatoes, turnips &c. so as to preserve the seed at least.

While the brethren were cutting the road I followed the old one to the top of the hill[74] and on arriving there was much cheered by a handsome view of the great Salt Lake laying as I should judge, from 25 to 30 miles to the west of us, and at 11 o'clock I sat down to contemplate and view the surrounding scenery. There is an extensive, beautiful, level looking valley from here to the Lake which I should judge from the numerous deep green patches must be fertile and rich. The valley extends to the South probably 50 miles where it is again surrounded by high mountains. To

---

[73] The Donner Party spent fourteen days the previous year clearing a wagon road between Henefer and the Great Salt Lake Valley, which enabled the Mormons to cover the same ground in only three days. The Mormons followed the Donner tracks completely except for a short by-pass around Donner Hill (Poll, 88).

[74] While the pioneers cut a road around Donner Hill, Clayton climbed up the Donner Road to the top of the hill from which he could view the Great Salt Lake, as well as the northern and southern dimensions of the Great Salt Lake Valley.

the South West across the valley at about 20 to 25 miles distance is a high mountain extending from the South end of the valley to about opposite this place where it ceases abruptly leaving a pleasant view of the dark waters of the Lake. Standing on the Lake and about due west there are two mountains and far in the distance another one which I suppose is on the other side the Lake, probably from 80 to 60 miles distance. To the North West is another mountain at the base of which is a long ridge of what I should consider to be rock salt from its white and shini[n]g appearance. The Lake does not show at this distance a very extensive surface, but its dark blue shade resembling the calm sea looks very handsome. The intervening valley appears to be well supplied with streams, creeks and Lakes some of the latter are evidently salt. There is but little timber in sight anywhere, and that is mostly on the banks of creeks and streams of water which is about the only objection which could be raised in my estimation to this being one of the most beautiful vallies and pleasant places for a home for the Saints which could be found . . . In some places may be seen a grove of small fir or Cedar or Pine, and in the vallies some Cotton wood and other small timber . . . There is no prospect for building log houses without spending a vast amount of time and labor, but we can make Spanish brick . . . or we can build lodges as the Pawnee Indians do in their villages. For my own part I am happily disappointed in the appearance of the valley of the salt Lake, and if the land be as rich as it has the appearance of being, I have no fears but the saints can live here and do well while we will do right.

When I commune with my own heart and ask myself whether I would choose to dwell here in this wild looking country amongst the Saints surrounded by friends, though poor, enjoying the privileges and blessings of the ever lasting priesthood with God for our King and father, or, dwell amongst the gentiles with all their wealth and good things of the earth, to be eternally mobbed, harassed, hunted, our best men murdered and every good mans life continually in danger the soft whisper echos loud and reverberates back in tones of stern tho' quiet determination. Give me the quiet wilderness and my family to associate with, surrounded by the saints and adieu, adieu to the Gentile world till God says return and avenge you of your enemies. If I had my family with me, oh, happy could I be for I dread nothing so much as the journey back again, and when I think of the many dangers from accident which families travelling this road are continually liable to and especially this last mountain road from Weber River it makes me almost shudder to think of it and I could almost envy those who have got safe through, having their families with them, yet they will doubtless have a hard time of it the coming winter . . . Many signs of Deer antelope and Bears but not many have been seen here. There have been fresh Buffalo signs seen a few days travel back, but those animals evidently stay out in this region unless some come to winter. The ground seems literally alive with the very large black crickets crawling round, up grass and bushes. They look loathsome but are said to be excellent for fattening hogs which would feed on them voraciously. The bears evidently live mostly on them at this season of the year . . . We are now 5 1/4 miles from the mouth of this Kanion making the whole distance of rough mountain road from the Weber River to the mouth of the Kanion on this side a little less than 35 miles and decidedly the worst piece of road on the whole journey . . . There are many Rattlesnakes of a large size on this valley and it is supposed they have dens in the mountains . . . The grass looks rich and good. A while after we camped Elder Pratt and company returned and reported that they had been about 15 miles north from here and this region is as suitable a place to put in our seeds as they have seen . . .

A council was held at the Dr. [Willard Richards] Wagon and decided to move early tomorrow to the place designated, also, to send two men back to the president and company to report progress &c. then to commence forthwith and plow and plant about 10 with potatoes this week if possible, and thus continue till the seed is secured. John Pack and Joseph Mathews were selected to return to President Youngs company. The evening was fine and pleasant and the night feels much warmer than in the ravines of the mountain.

[July 23, 1847. Friday] This morning Elders [John] Pack and [Joseph] Mathews started to meet the president and at the same time the camp moved on to the final location. We traveled two miles and then formed our encampment on the banks of the creek in an oblong circle.[75] The grass here appears even richer and

---

[75] This final encampment was on the east bank of City Creek near the present-day intersection of Fourth South and Main streets in Salt Lake City (Poll, 124).

thicker on the ground than where we left this morning. The soil looks indeed rich, black and a little sandy. The grass is about 4 feet high and very thick on the ground and well mixed with rushes. If we stay here three weeks and our teams have any rest they will be in good order to return. Soon as the camp was formed a meeting was called and the brethren addressed by Elder [Willard] Richards, mostly on the necessity and propriety of working faithfully and dilligently to get potatoes, turnips &c. in the ground. Elder Pratt reported their mission yesterday, and after some remarks the meeting was dismissed. At the opening the brethren united in prayer and asked the Lord to send rain on the land &c. The brethren immediately rigged 3 plows and went to plowing a little North East of the Camp. Another party went with spades &c. to make a dam on one of the creeks so as to thro[w] the water at pleasure on the field, designing to irrigate the land in case rain should not come sufficient. This land is beautifully situated for irrigation being many nice streams descending from the mountains which can be turned in every dir[ectio]n so as to water any portion of the lands at pleasure. The afternoon heavy clouds began to collect in the [S]outh West and at 5 o'clock we had a light shower with thunder. We had some rain for about 2 hours . . . their has been three plows going near all day. At night the camp were called together and a[dd]ressed by Elder Richards on a subject which seemed a little unwelcome to many from the way it was handled. It was a sermon of s[al]t from end to end, some felt a little insulted but all passed off well and jokingly. Some of the thinking brethren attributed it to the Dr's [Willard Richards] being inspired warmly or in other words pretty [] . . .

[July 24, 1847. Saturday.] . . . At a quarter to 12 Presidents Young and Kimball arrived and the wagons also began to arrive at the same time. The president seems much better and the sick generally are getting better. Most of the brethren express themselves well pleased with the place,[76] but some complain because there is no timber. There appears to be a unanimous agreement in regard to the richness of the soil and the good prospect of

---

[76] By the time Brigham Young spoke his famous words, "This is the right place," Orson Pratt had guided the arriving pioneers to a location which Pratt had dedicated as the future home of the Saints, and in the two days prior to Young's arrival the pioneers had begun irrigating, plowing, and planting (ibid.).

sustaining and fatt[en]ing stock with little trouble. The only objection is a lack of timber and rain. The latter God will send in its season if the Saints are faithful and I think yesterday was a proof that He listens to, and answers the prayers of the Saints . . . Elder Kimball says that it is contemplated to send out an exploring party to start on Monday and proceed north to the Bear river and Cach vallies. They design taking several wagons with them and Presidents Young and Kimball accompanies the expedition. Another company is to start at the same time and go west to the Lake, then south to the Utah lake and return down this valley.

[July 25, 1847. Sunday.] Morning fine and pleasant. At ten o'clock a meeting was held in the camp and the brethren addressed successively by Elder G[eorge] A. Smith, H[eber] C. Kimball and E[zra] T. Benson mostly expressing their feeling of gratification for the prospects of this country, each being highly satisfied with the soil &c. Elder Kimball referred especially to the manifold blessings we have been favored with during the journey. Not a man, woman, or child has died on the journey, nor even an horse, mule, ox, cow or chicken has died during the whole journey. Many exhortations were given to the brethren to be faithful, obey the council of those in authority and we shall be blessed and prosperous. At 1 P.M. by request of Elder Kimball, the following persons viz. Howard Egan, Hans C. Hanson, Jackson Redding, Carlos Murray, Thomas Cloward, George Billings, Philo Johnson, Charles Harper, Edson Whipple, W[illia]m A. King, Hosea Cushing, Robert Byard, Orson K. Whitney and Horace Whitney assembled themselves in a willow grove adjacent to the camps, when Elder Kimball addressed them in substance as follows, (the whole reported by Horace Whitney).

"Most of you here present have become adopted into my family,[77] except a very few (calling them by name) and Horace, who

---

[77] Here Heber C. Kimball promises temporal and spiritual blessings to those "adopted" into his lineage. The practice by which pioneer families became part of the heritage of high-ranking Mormons echoed the familiar doctrine of the adoption of new converts into the lineage of Abraham and provided a place for everyone in an extended family structure. See Gordon Irving, "The Law of Adoption: One Phase of the Mormon Concept of Salvation, 1830-1900," *Brigham Young University Studies*, 14 (Spring 1974): 291-314; Lawrence Foster, *Religion and Sexuality: Three American Communal Experiments of the Nineteenth Century* (New York: Oxford University Press, 1981), 195-99.

has become connected with my family by marriage, but I do not care for that, you are all the same to me, and your interest is my interest, for what's mine is yours, and what's yours is your own. If I have the privilege of building a house, I want you to help me, and I will help you. Horace will want to build a house for some of his father's family, if they should come up, and there is plenty of timber in the hills. When my family comes up, we may conclude to settle somewhere else, if so, there will be plenty to buy us out, if we shall have made any improvements. I want you all to be prudent and take care of your horses, cattle and everything entrusted to your care. It would be a good plan (and probably will be done) for those who stay here, to go back on the 'Sweet Water,'[78] and kill buffalo &c. for winter consumption. We shall go tomorrow, if Brigham is well enough, in search of a better location, (if, indeed, such can be found) if not, we shall remain here. There should be an enclosure made for the purpose of keeping the horses and cattle in nights, for there are plenty of Indians in the vicinity. I should advise you to keep the Sabbath day holy whether others do or not. I want you to put all the seed into the ground, that you think will come to maturity. I am satisfied that buckwheat will do as well here as any other seed we can sow. I want also some peach stones, and apple seeds to be planted forthwith. Brother Byard and Hans I would like to have immediately engage in making garments of buck skins, Brother Cloward in making shoes and Brother Johnson in making hats as soon as practicable. If you wish to go hunting, fishing, or to see the country, select a week day and not the Lord's day for that purpose. Do not let us get giddy and high-minded as the nephites did of old, but strive to work righteousness in the beginning, inasmuch as we have reached the promised land. If it is advisable to work in a family capacity, we will do so and if in a church capacity, we should be equally willing to do that. I am going out on a scout with the brethren, and I shall probably want one or two of you to go with me, and also one or two wagons. I am not going to take anything back with me to Winter Quarters, only what is actually

---

[78] The Sweetwater is an east-west river in Wyoming which led explorers to the South Pass across the Continental Divide to the regions west of the Rockies. After following the Platte River through Nebraska and Wyoming, the Oregon and Mormon trails follow the Sweetwater River to the South Pass.

necessary even some of my cloths I shall leave behind. I shall leave Bishop Whipple with you, he is quite a steady and economical man, and as such I recommend him to you. I want every man to be as industrious as possible while I am gone, and get into the ground all the turnips, cabbage, and other seeds you can. In case a storm of snow should come on it would be advisable to drive all the cattle among the willows, where they can remain untill the snow goes off. I want you all to work together, untill such time shall come when every man will have his inheritance set off to him. I feel towards you as a father towards his children and I want you to banish all peevishness from your midst and accommodate yourselves as much as possible to each others wishes. I have it to say that my boys have been faithful to their various duties on this journey and other people have noticed it, and expressed their opinions, that they never saw such an attentive set of men in their lives, and I consider that their conduct is worthy of imitation. I want you to be sober and prayerful and remember me and my family in your prayers." A number of other good ideas were advanced by Brother Heber and then we closed the meeting by prayer.

At 2 P.M. the brethren again assembled within the camp and were successively addressed by Elders Woodruff, O. Pratt and W. Richards sustaining the ideas advanced by the other brethren this morning. Some remarks followed from Lorenzo Young, John Pack and others and the meeting was dismissed. It is contemplation to send some wagons back to light up and assist the next company over these rough roads. It is now certain that there is considerable timber in the ravines and valleys between the mountains, several large bodies have been seen by the brethren since our arrival. There is a mountain lying North East from here on which is considerable large timber. It is supposed to be about 10 miles distance. The northern expedition is given up for the present on account of President Youngs health. A company intend to go tomorrow to the Lake and survey that region. If they go, they will probably be gone a day or two.

[July 26, 1847. Monday.] . . . About 10 o'clock, President Young sent me a horse with instructions to join him and some others going on a short exploring expedition. I immediately started and found the company consisted of President Young, Elders

[Heber] Kimball, [Wilford] Woodruff, G[eorge] A. Smith, [Ezra T.] Benson, [Willard] Richards and [Albert] Carrington. We took a course northward passing by the land where the brethren are plowing and planting. The land indeed looks rich and light. About three-quarters of a mile north of the camp we arrived on a beautiful table of land, level and nicely sloping to the west. Here we halted to view it and the more we viewed the better we were satisfied that it is as handsome a place for a city as can be imagined . . . We passed on and began to ascend the mountains, president signifying a wish to ascend a high peak, to the north of us. After some hard toil and time we succeeded in gaining the summit, leaving our horses about two-thirds the way up. President Young felt pretty well fatigued when he got up. Some of the brethren feel like naming this "Ensign Peak." From this place, we had a good view of the Salt Lake, and could see that the waters extend for a great many miles to the north of us . . . We arrived at the big spring about 4 o'clock and making our horses fast we went down to where it boils out of the rock . . .

[July 27, 1847. Tuesday.] . . . Two of the Utah Indians came to camp early this A.M. to trade. 2 ponies were bought off them for a rifle and musket. These two are but of moderate size, pleasing countenances and dressed in skins. At half past 8 Amasa Lyman, Rodney Badger, Roswell Stevens, and Brother [Samuel] Brannan arrived in Camp. They report that the Pueblo company will be in tomorrow or the day after. The brethren are still busy plowing and planting. Bur Frost has his forge up and quite a number of plows have been rigged up by the assistance of the Carpenters . . . During the afternoon two more Indians came in to trade. Some of the brethren are making unwise trades giving 20 charges of powder and balls for a buck skin, while the usual price is three charges. This is wrong.

[July 28, 1847. Wednesday.] Morning fine and warm. Several of the Indians have remained in the Camp over night. They seem very peacable and gentle, and anxious to trade. The brethren are making a saw pit to saw lumber for a skiff . . . At half past 3 President Young and company returned. They have been at the Salt Lake and report it to be about 25 miles distance. No water after they leave the river except salt water. The lake is very clear and the water heavy, so much so that a man cannot possibily sink. Even where not more than four foot deep and they tried to fall down on their knees but could not touch the bottom. They can sit or lay in the water perfectly easy without touching the bottom. One of the brethren lay down on the water and another got on him but could not sink him. They suppose the water will yield 35 per cent of pure salt . . .

At 8 o'clock the brethren were called together and addressed by President Young on various subjects, pointing out items of law which would be put in force here, his feelings towards the gentiles &c. He said they intended to divide the City into blocks of 10 acres each with 8 lots in a block of 1 1/4 acres each. The streets to be wide. No house will be permitted to be built on the corners of the streets neither petty shops. Each house will have to be built so many feet back from the street and all the houses parallel with each other. The fronts to be beautified with fruit trees &c. No filth will be allowed to stand in the City, but the water will be conducted through in such a manner as to carry all the filth off to the river Jordan. No man will be suffered to cut up his lot and sell a part to speculate out of his brethren. Each man must keep his lot whole for the Lord has given it to us without price. The temple lot will be 40 acres and adorned with trees, ponds &c. The whole subject was interesting to the brethren and the items will probably be given more fully hereafter. The Twelve were appointed a committee to lay off the City &c.

[July 29, 1847. Thursday.] . . . At 3 o'clock the Pueblo brethren came in sight. The soldiers appearing in military order, many of them mounted. They have 29 wagons in the company and one carriage.

Presidents Young, Kimball and the Twelve went to meet the brethren and met them in the Kanion. They report that they have very heavy rain there, the water rising in the creek three feet in a very short time, caused by the rush from the mountains. The brethren arrived at the lower camp at half past, and marched in headed by the fifes and side drum. They have camped a little west of the other camp. The brethren are represented as feeling well and cheerful. At 5 o'clock the Twelve returned here and an hour later went over north to the mountains, I suppose to hold a council.

369

[July 30, 1847. Friday.] Day warm. Twelve held a council with the officers of the Battalion, then rode up to the hot spring. Evening a general meeting of the camp and addressed by President Young. He told his feelings concerning the soldiers, they have saved the people by going when required &c. He rejoices that they are here. He expressed his feelings warmly towards the brethren, and also told his feelings towards the gentiles. The meeting was opened by Hosannas three times[79] and closed by requesting the Battalion to build a bower[y][80] tomorrow on the temple lot where we can assemble for meetings &c.

[July 31, 1847. Saturday.] This morning the brethren commenced making the bower[y] on the Temple lot a little south west from our camp. They will make it about 40 feet long and 28 feet wide. Walked with Presidents Young, Kimball, Richards and others to the mississippi Camp. Brother Thomas Richardson is very sick and several others of the soldiers. Soloman Tindal is yet alive but looks feeble. Elder Kimball conversed sometime with Captain James Brown.[81] There are from 20 to 30 of the Utah Indians here and some squaws trading with the brethren. They are generally of low stature, pleasing countenance but poorly clad. While we were there a dispute arose between two of the young men and they went to fighting very fiercely . . . In the evening I walked down to the Pueblo camp and there learned the following particulars.

These Indians who are now here are of the Shoshones, about 15 or 20 in number and several women among them. There were 4 or 5 of the Utahs here this morning when the Shoshones [came]

---

[79] This ritualized form of shouting "hosannas" three times ("save, we pray" in Hebrew, signifying "praise to God") was performed at the dedication of the Kirtland, Ohio, temple in 1836, a time when several participants reported unusual visionary experiences. See *HC* 2:428.

[80] The Bowery was an open air meeting place covered with tree branches and leaves.

[81] Formerly an officer in the Nauvoo Legion, Captain James Brown led a sick detachment of the Mormon Battalion to Pueblo, Colorado, in the winter of 1846. The next year Brown, Sam Brannan, and a group of explorers rode north of the newly settled Salt Lake City to the Bear River and Cache Valley. Later that year he rode to California to collect his pay for service in the U.S. Army and bought some property north of Salt Lake City to become Brownsville. Brown built toll bridges across the Weber and Ogden rivers. In 1876 Brigham Young sent Brown to visit the Mormon villages formed by members assigned in the mission to colonize southern Utah. Brown recruited volunteers for this colonization effort (Morgan, 186, 204, 208, 247).

up, one of the Utahs had stole[n] a horse from one of the Shoshones and the latter party saw him with the horse here. He had traded the horse for a rifle but was unwilling either to give up the horse or rifle, hence the quarrel spoken of above. When the old man separated them the thief went down and hid himself in the camp below. Soon after he saw another horse walking by which he knew to belong to the Shoshones. He sprang on his own horse and drove the other one before him towards the mountains on the southeast as hard as he could ride. The Shoshones being informed of it four of them started in pursuit and as he got in between the mountains they closed on him. One of the pursuers shot him dead while another one shot his horse. They returned and made this report to the others of the tribe at the camp at the same time exhibiting fresh blood on one of the rifles. They appear to be much excited and continually on the watch. When the men returned they sat down and made a meal of some of these large crickets. They appear to be crisped over the fire which is all the cooking required. Many of the brethren have traded muskets and rifles for horses, an ordinary musket will buy a pretty good horse.

They appear to be displeased because we have traded with the Utahs and say they own this land, that the Utahs have come over the line &c. They signified by signs that they wanted to sell us the land for powder and lead. The Shoshones are poorer clad than the Utahs of the two, about the same in stature and there are many pleasing countenances among them.

Col. [Stephen] Markham reports that there are 3 lots of land already broke. One lot of 35 acres of which 2/3 is already planted with buck wheat, corn, Oats &c. One lot of 8 acres which is all planted with corn, potatoes, beans &c. And a Garden of 10 acres, four acres of which is sown with garden seed. He says there are about three acres of corn already up about two inches above the ground and some beans and potatoes up too. This is the result of 8 days labor, besides making a road to the timber, hauling and sawing timber for a boat, making and repairing plows &c. There have been 13 plows and 3 Harrows[82] worked during the week.

[August 1, 1847. Sunday.] We have had another cool, windy night. At 10 A.M. the brethren assembled for meeting under the

---

[82] A harrow is a cultivation tool that uses teeth or discs to break up the soil.

Bower[y] on the Temple Lot, all the members of the quorum of the Twelve being present except President Young who is quite sick again. After the meeting had been opened by singing and prayer by Elder G[eorge] A. Smith, Elder Heber Kimball arose and made some remarks to the following effect as reported by Brother Bullock:

"I would enquire whether there is a guard out around our cattle if not let one be placed immediately. The Indians left here very suddenly this morning and we don't know their object. If we don't take good care of what we have, we will not have any more. It is all in the world we shall ever have, for 'to him that receiveth I will give more.' We are the sons of God and He will do with us as we would do to our children, and inasmuch as I am faithful in taking care of my neighbors Goods, I shall be entitled to the same from them, for we are commanded to do unto others, as we want others to do to us. Every penurious man who takes advantage of others will come down to poverty. If we have to follow the steps of our saviour we have to follow and experience the same things; you will have to feel for men so as to know how to sympathize with them, and then you can feel for them. I feel for this people and grow more feeling for them every day. Our father in heaven is more tender to us than any mother to her little child. If I am faithful to serve others, others will be willing to serve me."

O. Pratt requested the prayers of the Saints in his behalf, "It is with peculiar feelings I arise before so many of the saints in this uncultivated region and inhabited by Savages. My mind is full of reflection on the scenes through which we have passed and being brought through the deserts of sage to this distant region. Gods ways are not as our ways. It is not wisdom that the saints should always foresee the difficulties they have to encounter for then they would not be trials. We expected some revolutions to take place, and behold they are revealed in the Book of Mormon and Doctrine and Covenants, for we are to congregate among the remnants of Joseph.[83] We did think our wives and children would be built up among the strongholds of the gentiles, we thought we should be as missionaries to them. Jehovah had different purposes, he designed

---

[83] A Mormon term for Native Americans, considered to be descendants of migrant Hebrews of the tribe of Joseph whose ancient records formed the Book of Mormon.

that this people should be brought out almost as an entire people. The Book of Mormon never would have been fulfilled if the Saints had not left the gentiles as a people, for when the gentiles rejected the gospel it was to be taken among the Lamanites.[84] So long as the Gospel, the Priesthood and the main body of the people remained with them the fulness of the gospel was not taken away from the gentiles, and this movement is one of the greatest that has taken place among this people. I feel thankful as one of the Twelve for the privilege of coming out as one of the pioneers to this glorious valley where we can build up a City to the Lord. For a many years I have not read that good old book, but I remember the predictions in it, and some that are now very nearly fulfilled by us. Isaiah says (Chapter 62) speaking of the City of Zion, It shall be a City sought out, and shall not be called forsaken &c. Many in this congregation know what is meant by the garments of salvation and the robe of righteousness. Righteousness and praise shall spring forth before all the nations of the earth and they will not hold their peace. There are many of you that feel you can cry day and night to the people, in the cause of righteousness until it shall triumph. 'For as a young man marries a virgin' &c. this belongs and refers to us. 'I will no longer give thy [corn to be meat for] thine enemy.' This has not been fulfilled heretofore but will be, the corn that we toil to raise from the earth, it shall not be given to our enemies, they that gather it shall eat it, and they shall drink it in the courts of his holiness. This wine is to be drunk in the courts of the Lords house. We have gathered out the stones out of the road and thousands will yet fulfil this prophecy. It has reference to the latter times, that was to dawn upon the world in the last dispensation. 'Thou shalt be called sought out, a City not forsaken.' If ever there was a place sought out it is this, we have enquired diligently and have found it. This cannot refer to Jerusalem, but to this very place, point and spot that the pioneers have found, where a city shall be built unto the Lord, where righteousness will reign, and iniquity not be allowed. Isaiah and Joel both spake very plainly on this subject. 'It shall come to pass in the last days that the house of the Lord shall be established'

---

[84] Another Mormon reference to Native Americans, the Lamanites defeated their more civilized and spiritual brethren, the Nephites, in a final battle in 421 A.D., which closes the Book of Mormon record.

&c. In what part of the earth could it be established more than in this place, where this congregation is gathered. In the midst of the spires of the mountains, we have found a place large enough to gather a few thousands of the saints. You may travel Europe, Asia, Africa and America but you cannot find a place higher, where any people can raise crops and sustain themselves. The house of the Lord will be established on the tops of the mountains when we shall have once reared here. The experience of the saints proves that there was no house of the Lord, and we can say travel over this earth but you cannot find the house of the Lord. The Lord must give the pattern of the building and order it, and give directions to His servants. The Lord wants a house built precisely to the pattern that he gives and He is bound to speak to and bless and make them his own children in that house and I verily believe I shall see it, and see thousands come flocking to the house to learn the way of salvation, and I want to see the time that I shall see thousands raising their voices on this consecrated land. There are many testimonies in the prophets all bearing upon this subject. Joseph in the Book of Doctrines and Covenants speaks of this very subject, and it appears there will be some sinners in Zion who will be afraid, and a devouring fire will rest upon every dwelling place in Zion. 'He that walketh righteously' &c. 'He shall dwell on high, bread shall be given him, his water shall be sure.' Isaiah was on the eastern continent when he spoke this and was speaking of a very distant place. It will be pretty difficult to get a ship of war up to this place. When we get used to this healthy climate, the people will not say, "I am sick," but will be able to smite the gentiles. They will grow up strong and will not be in jeopardy from sickness. The wilderness shall become as a fruitful field and a fruitful field as a forest." We know the time will come that the great Jehovah will cause springs of water to gush out of the desert lands and we shall see the lands [cursed] that the Gentiles have defiled. Isaiah speaks of the heritage of Jacob being in a high place. This is about 4000 feet above the level of the sea, and the high mountains will still catch the hail and we be in a low place. We will not feel discouraged but will feel full of vigor and circumscribe all things to the very heavens, for this is what we desire above all things. Let us endeavor to covenant in our hearts, that we will serve the Lord that we will keep His commandments and obey His councel. I wish that all of us should be faithful and as President Young said the other evening, 'every man is expected to do his duty.' The Lord will be with us still shield, guard and defend us by day, and be our refuge by night, and our salvation. I feel to say in the name of the Lord Jesus Christ, you shall be blest, if you keep the commandments of God. Amen."

Elder Kimball hopes the brethren will be attentive to what they hear for if you bring an evil upon this people, you will bring destruction upon yourself. If you do things according to cou[n]cil and they are wrong, the consequences will fall on the heads of those who councilled you, so don't be troubled. I don't want to be wrapt in the skins of some men who have taken a course that has brought destruction upon themselves and others, and they will have to answer for it. I am a man that would not speak to a man's daughter to marry her untill I have first spoke to her father and mother also, and then it is done by common consent, but I preach the truth every word of it.

President Young instructed the Battalion last evening, and councilled them for their comfort, and the counsel is for the brethren to keep their guns, and their powder, and their balls and lead, and not let the Indians have it, for they will shoot down our cattle. "They stole guns yesterday and had them under their blankets and if you don't attend to this you are heating a kettle of boiling water to scald your own feet. If you listen to council you will let them alone, and let them eat the crickets, there's plenty of them. I understand they offered to sell the land and if we were to buy it of them the Utahs would want pay for it too. The land belongs to our Father in heaven and we calculate to plow and plant it, and no man will have power to sell his inheritance, for he can't remove it it belongs to the Lord. I am glad I am come to a place where I feel free. I am satisfied and we are in a goodly land. My family is back, my teams are helping on several families and leaving ours. If my family was here I would not go over that road again. I believe in Brother Joseph, religion, and which he said was a key that would save every man or woman, and that it is for every man to mind his own business and let other peoples business alone. We will have a farm, and cultivate them, and plant vineyards, and if we are faithful five years will not pass away before we are better off than we ever were in Nauvoo. If we had brought our families along, everybody else would have come and we have got to lose another year. We could not bring all the

375

soldiers families for the same reason that we did not bring our own families. I thank the Lord that there are so many of the soldiers here, if they had tarried in winter quarters there would have been many more deaths among them. We brought many of these pioneers to save their lives, many of them were very sick, and were carried out of their beds and put into the wagons. They have mostly recovered their health, and we have been prosperous and have been permitted to arrive here alive, there has not one died on the journey nor an ox nor horse, nor anything except one of Brother [Robert] Crows oxen which was poisoned. We lost several horses by accident. And we shall be prosperous on our journey back again if we are faithful, those of us who go, and we shall see and enjoy the society of our families again. We will one day have a house built here and have the forts, and go into the house and administer for our dead.

Elder [Willard] Richards then read an order from Lieut. [] Cook of the Mormon Battalion on the Pacific, after which Elder [Thomas] Bullock read a letter from Jefferson Hunt to James Brown dated July 6, 1847, after which and a few other remarks, the meeting was dismissed.

At 25 minutes past 2 the congregation assembled and opened by singing and prayer by Elder Woodruff. Bread and water were then administered by the bishops after which Elder Richards, after a few preliminary remarks read the "word and will of the Lord," as given in Winter Quarters.[85] Elder Kimball made some remarks and the brethren manifested that they received and would obey the revelation by uplifted hand. He was followed by remarks by Elder Amasa Lyman, mostly sustaining the positions taken by the previous speakers.

Elder Kimball again rose to lay before the brethren some items of business, whereupon it was decided that the three companies form into one camp and labor together. That the officers be a committee to form the corral. That the corral be formed tomorrow. That horses and mules be tied near the camp at nights. That we build houses instead of living [in] wagons this winter. That we go to work immediately putting up houses. That we work

---

[85] On January 14, 1847, Brigham Young had announced "The Word and the Will of the Lord," giving instructions for the westward emigration. Clayton does not record this event at the time. See Arrington, *Great Basin Kingdom*, 22; D&C 136.

unitedly. That the houses form a stockade or fort to keep out the Indians, that our women and children be not abused, and that we let the Indians alone.

Colonel [Albert] Rockwood remarked that a Log house 16 by 15 would cost forty dollars and one of adobes half as much. Capt [James] Brown was in favor of setting men to work building both log and adobie houses to hasten the work. Capt. Lewis said that inasmuch as timber is scarce, and we have spades and shovels and tools enough as many as can be used he is in favor of building adobie houses and save the timber.

Lieutenant [Ira] Willis said, you can put up an adobe house before a man could get the Logs for a log house. Adobe houses are healthy and are the best for equinoctial gales. Elder [Samuel] Brannan has a man in California who will take 3 men, make adobes for a 30 foot house, build the house and put a family in it in a week. His printing office was put up in 14 days and a paper printed.[86]

Elder Richards said we want brick made and lime burned. If wood is put into houses it will be a waste of it. We want all the timber to make floors and roofs. We want the walls up and we are men enough to put them up in a few days, and have the white squaws protected. It was voted to put up a stockade of adobie houses.

Samuel Gould and James Drum reported themselves as lime burners.

Sylvester H. Earl, Joel J. Terrill, Ralph Douglas and Joseph Hancock reported themselves as brick makers. Elder Kimball then remarked that those who intend to send ox teams back to Winter Quarters must be ready a week from tomorrow morning, if the cattles feet are too tender have them shod, or have new shoes in the wagons. Those oxen to rest and be released from plowing &c. Don't get the Indians round here. I want you to have nothing to do with them. After a few remarks on general items, the meeting dismissed.

[August 2, 1847. Monday.] We have had another cool night but morning fine. The other companies commenced moving their wagons up and we also moved a little further east. During the

---

[86] *The California Star.*

day the whole camp was formed in an oblong circle. About noon Ezra T. Benson and several others started back to meet the next company.[87] They carried a letter, the following being a copy of the same:

"Pioneer camp. Valley of the Great Salt Lake, August 2, 1847. To Genl. Charles C. Rich and the Presidents and Officers of the emigrating company. Beloved Brethren.

We have delegated our beloved Brother Ezra T. Benson and escort to communicate to you by express the cheering intelligence that we have arrived in the most beautiful valley of the great Salt Lake, that every soul who left Winter Quarters with us is alive, and almost every one enjoying good health. That portion of the Battalion that was at Pueblo is here with us, together with the Mississippi company that accompanied them and they are generally well. We number about 450 souls and we know of no one, but what is pleased with our situation. We have commenced the survey of a city this morning. We feel that the time is fast approaching when those teams that are going to Winter Quarters this fall should be on the way. Every individual here would be glad to tarry if their friends were here, but as many of the Battalion as well as the Pioneers, have not their families here, and do not expect that they are in your camp, we wish to learn by express from you the situation of your camp as speedily as possible, that we may be prepared to counsel and act in the whole matter. We want you should send us the name of every individual in your camp, or in other words, a copy of your camp roll, including the names, number of wagons, Horses, mules, Oxen, Cows &c. the health of your camp, your location, prospects, &c. If your teams are worn out if your camp is sick and not able to take care of themselves, if

---

[87] About 16,000 Saints had left Nauvoo between February and May 1846 for the Missouri River Valley locations at Kanesville, Iowa and Winter Quarters, Nebraska. The logistics of road conditions and supplies together with the task of recruiting a 500-man battalion to join the U.S. Army influenced Brigham Young to postpone completing the pioneer trek until the following year. Initial pioneer companies of 1,600 departed Winter Quarters, Nebraska, from April 5, 1847, and arrived at the Great Salt Lake Valley as early as July 22. An escort company returned to Winter Quarters to direct succeeding migrations. The second company of 3,000 left on May 26 and arrived on September 20, 1848, at harvest time. Subsequent companies travelled at the rate of 3,000–4,000 persons each year until most all of the 16,000 Mormon refugees had arrived at Great Salt Lake City (Arrington, *Great Basin Kingdom*, 21, 22, 47, 50, 78, 79, 97).

you are short of teamsters, or any other circumstance impedes your progress, we want to know it immediately, for we have help for you; and if your teams are in good plight, and will be able to return to Winter Quarters this season, or any portion of them, we want to know it. We also want the mail, which will include all letters and papers and packages belonging to our camp, general and particular. Should circumstances permit, we would gladly meet you some distance from this, but our time is very much occupied, notwithstanding, we think you will see us before you see our valley. Let all the brethren and sisters cheer up their hearts, and know assuredly that God has heard and answered their prayers, and ours, and led us to a goodly land, and our souls are satisfied therewith. Brother Benson can give you many particulars, that will be gratifying and cheering to you which [we] have not time to write, and we feel to bless all the saints. In behalf of the council. Willard Richards, Clerk. Brigham Young, President."

This morning Elders [Orson] Pratt and [Henry] Sherwood commenced surveying the city to lay it off in lots but finally concluded to wait untill the chain could be tested by a standard pole which will have to be gotten from the mountains. Some of the brethren are preparing to make molds for adobies. In the evening Elder Kimballs teams returned from the mountains with some good house logs and poles for measuring &c. The day has been very warm but the nights begin to be very cool. The north east winds seem to prevail here at this season and coming from the mountains of snow are cold when the sun is down. After dark President Young sent for me to his wagon and told his calculations about our starting back. He wants me to start with the ox teams next Monday so as to have a better privilege of taking the distances &c. He calculates the horse teams to start two weeks later, and if the first company arrives at Grand Island before the other comes up to wait for them there, kill and dry buffalo &c. He wants the roadometer, fixed this week and Elder Kimball has selected W[illia]m King to do the work.

[August 3, 1847. Tuesday.] Morning fine but cool. Elder [Albert] Carrington starts for the mountains to look for limestone. During the day I went and bathed at Bullocks bathing place in one of the warm sulphur springs. I found the effects very refreshing

379

and benificial. Spent most of the day making a table of distances &c. The day very hot . . .

[August 7, 1847. Saturday.] . . . This morning 15 of the brethren commenced building a dam a little above the camp, so as to bring the water around and inside the Camp. They finished early in the afternoon, and we have now a pleasant little stream of cold water running on each side the wagons all around the camp . . .

In the evening many of the brethren went and were baptized on the dam by Elder Kimball for remission of sins. Elders Pratt, Woodruff, and Smith attending to confirmation. I went and was baptised amongst the rest. It has been recommended for all the camp to be baptized and this evening they have commenced it.[88]

[August 8, 1847. Sunday.] Morning cloudy with strong northeast wind. The brethren have resumed baptizing, and a number have obeyed the ordinance both male and female. At 10 a meeting was held in the bowery and instructions given to the brethren. A sacrament was administered and 110 of the brethren selected to make adobies. Wrote a letter for Heber to C. Martin and others.

[August 9, 1847. Monday.] At 11 S[am] Brannan, Capt. James Brown and several others started for San Francisco. Elder J[esse] C. Little accompanies them to Fort Hall. I spent three hours taking observations with the thermometer with Elder Pratt to ascertain the height of land on the creek above the City, Ensign Peak &c. The Twelve had decided on a name for this place and a caption for all letters and documents issued from this place, which is as follows: Salt Lake City, Great Basin, North America.

[August 10, 1847. Tuesday.] This morning, President Young and Kimball have gone to the adobie yard to commence building some houses in that region. They have already got many good logs on the ground. Col. [Stephen] Markham reports that in addition to the plowing done week before last they have plowed about 30 acres which is mostly planted, making a total of about

---

[88] Rebaptisms were practiced in the Latter-day Saint community for the purpose of renewing covenants. See Brigham's Young's advice on second baptisms in *Journal of Discourses*, 26 vols. (Liverpool: Latter-day Saints' Book Depot, 1855–86), 1:324, 2:8, 4:44.

80 acres. The plowing ceased last week and the brethren are now making adobies, hawling logs &c. Elder [Henry] Sherwood continues surveying the City. [Thomas] Tanner and [Burr] Frost are setting wagon tire and have set 52 today. The brethren who went to the Lake on Monday to boil down salt have returned this evening and report that they have found a bed of beautiful salt ready to load onto wagons. It lays between two Sand bars and is about 6 inches thick. They suppose they can easily load ten wagons without boiling. I have received from Elder Kimball a pair of buckskin pants, as a present I suppose, but as I have on similar occasions been branded with the idea of receiving a great many kindnesses without consideration, I will for this once state a little particular on the other side of the question. I acknowledge that I have had the privilege of riding in a wagon and sleeping in it, of having my victual cooked, and some meat and milk, and occasionally a little tea or coffee furnished. My flour I furnished myself. I have had no team to take care of. Howard Egan has done most of my washing untill a month ago in consideration of the privilege of copying from my journal, using my desk ink &c. The balance of my washing I have hired. Now what have I done for Brother Kimball? Am I justly indebted on this journey? Answer I have wrote in his journal 124 pages of close matter, on an average 600 words in a page, which if paid at the price of recording deeds in Illinois would amount to over $110. I have collected the matter myself, besides writing letters &c. This has been for his especial benefit. I have kept an account of the distance we have travelled for over 800 miles of the journey, attended to the measurement of the road, kept the distances from creek to creek and from one encampment to another. Put up a guide board every 10 miles from Fort John to this place with the assistance of Philo Johnson. I have mapped some for Dr. Richards and keeping my own journal forms the whole benifit to be derived by my family by this mission. I have yet considerable to write in Elder Kimballs journal before I return. I am expected to keep a table of distances of the whole route returning from here to Winter Quarters, and make a map when I get through and this for public benefit. Now how much am I considered to be in debt, and how often will it be said that I was furnished by others with victuals clothing &c. that I might enjoy this journey as a mission of pleasure. I have spent

most of this day calculating the height of this spot above the level of the sea for Elder Pratt.

[August 11, 1847. Wednesday.] Early this morning a large company of the Utah Indians came to visit the camp and it was with difficulty they could be kept outside the wagons. There are few of them who have any clothing on except the breech clout[89] and are mostly of low stature. They have scarce anything to trade and not many women and children with them. They are camped about 3 miles north of west and supposed to be going north hunting. One of them was detected stealing some clothing which lay on the bushes to dry, but was made to leave it. When they found they were not permitted inside the circle they soon moved off to their camp.

The brethren have commenced laying the adobie wall today which will be 27 inches thick and nine feet high. The adobes are 18 inches long, 9 inches broad and 4-1/2 inches thick.

The brethren in camp have finished the skiff and launched her in the creek to soak . . .

[August 12, 1847. Thursday.] . . . The soldiers are getting dissatisfied at being kept here so long from their families and yesterday several of them left the camp secretly to go to Winter Quarters and this morning others are gone, but it is probable that President Young knows nothing of it yet although about a dozen are allready gone and others are preparing to follow them.

On Tuesday President Young laid a foundation of 4 houses, Elder Kimball 4, Col. Markham 1, Dr. Richards 1, and Lorenzo Young 2, and today Dr. Richards has laid the foundation of another, George A. Smith 2 and Wilford Woodruff 2, making a total of 17 houses mostly 14 feet wide and from 12 to 17 long. Elder Kimball has his house 4 logs high.

[August 13, 1847. Friday.] Spent the day mostly writing. The brethren have got 130 bushels of salt with 24 days labor.

[August 14, 1847. Saturday.] Started at 20 minutes to 9 in company with a number of others for the Salt Lake. We arrived at 3 o'clock and estimated the distance 22 miles. We all bathed in

[89] An archaic form of the word cloth.

it and found the reports of those who had previously bathed in no ways exaggerated. We returned back to the river where we arrived at 11 o'clock at the beginning of a light thunder shower. There is no pure fresh water between the river and the Lake.

[August 15, 1847. Sunday.] President Young preached on the death of little children &c . . .

[August 16, 1847. Monday.] . . . After dark Elder Kimball called a number of us together in the tent and each one present selected a lot for himself and family. I had previously selected Lots 1, 7 and 8 on Block 95, but President Young broke into our arrangements and wished 7 and 8 reserved, consequently I made choice of Lots 1, 2 and 3 on block 95.

[August 17, 1847. Tuesday.] Started out at 10 minutes past 8 and found the distance to the mouth of the Kanyon 5 miles the difference arising from making a road across instead of following the first one. 1 3/4 miles further arrived at where the company had camped for the night and found them all ready to start only waiting for President Young to arrive and give some instructions, but he sent word he should not come, and we started forward. Elders Kimball and Richards soon overtook the company, gave some instructions, then returned and the company moved on. On arriving at Birch Spring we encamped for the night having traveled 13 1/2 miles.

There is considerable danger of cattle miring near the spring and several have already had to be pulled out. This company consists of 71 men with 33 wagons. After camping the brethren were called together by Cap[tain] Roundy for the purpose of organizing. He briefly stated the manner of the organization of the camp when we left Winter Quarters and it was unanimously voted to organize after the same pattern which was done as follows:

1st Division
1st 10

Joseph Skeen, Captn
Artemas Johnson
James Cazier
Geo[rge] Cummings
Tho[ma]s Richardson
6 Wagons

W[illia]m Burt
James Dunn
Joseph Shipley
Samuel Badham
Roswel Stevens

2nd 10

Zebedee Coltrin, Captn.   William Bird
Chester Loveland   Josiah Curtis
Lorenzo Babcok   John S. Eldridge
Samuel H. Marble   Horace Thornton
Geo[rge] Scholes
5 Wagons

3rd 10

Francis Boggs, Captain   Geo[rge] Wardle
Sylvester H. Earl   Seeley Owens
Almon M. Williams   Clark Stillman.
5 Wagons.

Tunis Rappleyee, Captn of first division. James Cazier Capn of Guard in 1st Division.

2nd Division
1st 10

R. Jackson Redding, Captain   Robert Biard
W[illia]m. Carpenter   Benj[amin] W. Rolfe
Henry W. Sanderson   Tho[ma]s Cloward
Bailey Jacobs   Lisbon Lamb
John Pack   W[illia]m Clayton
5 Wagons

2nd 10

John H. Tippets, Capn   Lyman Stevens
Francis T. Whitney   Lyman Curtis
James Stewart   John S. Gleason
Cha[rle]s A. Burke   Myron Tanner
W[illia]m McLellan   Rufus Allen
Norman Taylor
5 Wagons.

The soldiers were numbered with the 2nd division viz.

3rd 10

Allen Cumpton, Captn   Franklin Allen
John Bybee   David Garner
J[onathon] Averett   Harmon D. Persons
John G. Smith   Solomon Tindal
384 Philip Garner   Charles Hopkins

Barnabas Lake
4 Wagons

4th 10

Andrew J. Shoop, Captn	Albert Clark
Francillo Durfee	James Hendrickson
Erastus Bingham	John Calvert
Loren Kenney	Daniel Miller
Benj[amin] Roberts	Luther W. Glazier
Jarvis Johnson	Tho[ma]s Bingham

3 Wagons.

John Gleason, Captain of Guard.

Those who have horses to ride were then numbered and their duty pointed out, which is, To lead the way and fix the road where it needs it, Look out camping places, Drive the loose cattle, and hunt for the camp. Their names are as follows, John Pack, Capt, Samuel Badham, Francillo Durfee, Benjamin Roberts, Thomas Bingham, James Hendrickson, John Eldridge, R. I. Redding, Seeley Owens, Barnabas Lake, W[illia]m Bird, Daniel Miller, James Cazier . . .

[August 20, 1847. Friday.] Morning very cold. Started out at 7 and traveled til 12 1/2, the day being cool then rested and waited an hour. At half past 1 proceeded again and arrived at "Cache" or "Reddings" Cave at 5 o'clock having travelled 20 1/2 miles, but it was near 7 o'clock before the company arrived.

[August 21, 1847. Saturday.] Started at half past 7 and travelled till 12 then waited an hour. We found Bear River not over 15 inches deep. We camped on Sulphur Creek at 5 o'clock having traveled 16 1/2 miles and after camping I went with the brethren to fill their tar Buckets at the Oil spring. We followed a wagon trail made by a part of Hastings company last year about a mile and found the spring situated in a ravine a little to the left of the road just at the edge of a high bench of land. The ground is black over with the oil for several rods but it is baked hard by exposure to the sun. It is difficult to get the clear oil most of it being filled with dust and gravel. It smells much like British oil and is said to do well for greasing wagons . . .

[August 23, 1847. Monday.] We started early this morning and arrived at Fort Bridger at 1 o'clock. We found the grass pretty

385

much eat off and only stayed an hour and a half while some of the brethren traded some, then went on 8 miles farther and camped on a stream 2 rods wide, having traveled 21 1/2 miles, the day very cool . . .

[August 26, 1847. Thursday.] Started at 8 o'clock and went on to the Big Sandy and before the majority of the company arrived [Ezra T.] Benson and escort came up with letters from the companies. They say there are 9 companies between here and the Platte with 566 wagons and about 5000 head of stock. They report the companies well and getting along tolerably fast, some they expect we shall meet within three days. After eating they proceeded on. After sundown a large party of mounted Indians came up and camped on the opposite side the river. They have been on the sweet water hunting and are said to be of the Shoshone tribe.

[August 27, 1847. Friday.] Many of the brethren traded Sugar, Powder, Lead &c. to the Indians for robes and skins and meat. We started soon after 7 and traveled to the crossing of the Big Sandy then after halting an hour continued to the little Sandy making 25 1/4 miles today, but it was 9 o'clock before some of the wagons arrived . . .

[August 29, 1847. Sunday.] It was decided to remain here today to rest the teams, but our ten obtained leave to go on to Sweet Water, expecting to meet the company, and after reading the letter of instructions from the council to this camp my wagon proceeded on slowly. At the "Springs" we saw an aged Indian Squaw near the road, dwelling in a shelter composed merely of wild sage and apparently dependent on passing emigrants for subsistence. She is doubtless left to perish on account of age and infirmity but it is likely she will live some time on what she receives from those who pass by. When we arrived near the summit of the dividing ridge or south pass two Indians rode towards us and motioned for us to stop. Not seeing the other wagons coming after we stopped to wait for the wagons and the Indians soon arrived. They made signs that a large party of them were over the mountain north and they wanted to "swap." While they were conversing a number more rode over the ridge and soon after a still larger number. About this time the wagons came in sight and when the brethren saw so many Indians they were alarmed. John Pack rode back to the main camp to get some of the brethren to come up, but J[ackson] R[edding][90] said he should "not budge a foot." The brethren behind were much alarmed, some expecting to be scalped and one W. Carr ran and hid himself in the sage bushes. No one returned with John Pack but Norman Taylor and the wagons proceeded towards us. In the meantime, after learning the object for which the Indians sought us, that none of them were armed except two, and by a certificate that the first visitor was a Shoshone chief, Brother [Lisbon] Lamb and myself signified that we would trade with them and soon some of them returned with antelope, buck and Elk Skins and robes to trade. I traded some balls and a little powder for 1 robe 1 Elk Skin 2 Buck skins and 9 antelope skins and a pair of mocassins. Lamb bought 5 antelope skins.

While we were trading, the other wagons arrived and also commenced trading. The Indians about 60 in number, about 20 of them boys, all mounted seemed highly pleased to trade with us which we did mostly through the chief. By request of the chief I gave him a certificate stating that he appeared friendly and wanted to trade with the whites &c. The chief gave us a very strong invitation to go to their camp to trade and made signs that they would feed us well and we should sleep with them. I answered him by signs that we should camp when we arrived where the road crossed the sweet water but they were very anxious to have us then turn off the road and camp. After we started the chief came up and wanted to swap a good mule for my spy glass but I refused. I had let him look through it and he seemed very wishful to try it. When they saw we were determined to go on they left us, and returned to their camp while we pursued our journey to the first crossing of Sweet water where we arrived and camped at 6 o'clock, having traveled 14 miles . . .

[September 5, 1847. Sunday.] There being alkali springs near we concluded to go on to Independence Rock at which place we arrived about 3 o'clock having traveled 112 1/2 miles. Soon after

---

[90] As captain of Clayton's group of ten wagons, Jackson Redding was responsible to decide whether to accelerate their pace or to propose trading with the Indians.

we camped [Lisbon] Lamb and Jacob Cloward went to Chase some Buffalo and succeeded in killing one. I walked over the rock and had some solemn meditations and felt to humble myself and call upon the Lord for myself and family, for this company, the Twelve and all the companies on the road. Experience has taught me many maxims of late and I am intent to profit by them. Be not hasty to promise, lest thy promise be considered worthless. Make not many promises without reflection lest thou fail to fulfil them and it damp the confidence of thy friend, then be assured that thy friends will despise thy promises and have no dependence on them. Seek not to speculate out of a good brother . . .

[September 11, 1847. Saturday.] Got up at 12 o'clock and stood guard till daylight. The morning very fine and pleasant. Three of the brethren arrived from the camp back and said that during night before last the Indians had stole 16 or 17 of their horses and they were in pursuit of them . . . There are many buffalo round here also and although we have plenty of meat the brethren continue to kill them . . .

[September 12, 1847. Sunday.] . . . Our bread stuff is now out and we have to live solely on meat the balance of the journey. John Pack has got flour enough to last him through. We have all messed together untill ours was eat up, and now John Pack proposes for each man to mess by himself. He has concealed his flour and beans together with tea, coffee, sugar &c. and cooks after the rest have gone to bed. Such things seem worthy of remembrance for a time to come . . .

[September 14, 1847. Tuesday.] Started at 9 o'clock and traveled till about 5 then camped on the Platte River, having traveled 24 1/4 miles. In consequence of some things which have passed and some which at present exist I have concluded to go on as fast as circumstances will permit to Winter quarters and I intend to start tomorrow. Some have opposed it, but not with a good grace, however, I have no fears that the council will censure me when they know the cause, if they do, I will bear the censure in preference to what I now bear. Before dark Luke Johnson, William A. Empey and Appleton Harmon came up from Laramie, having learned that wagons were near from an Indian. They say that a party of Sioux Warriors have got the brethrens horses 17 in number on the Raw Hide about 18 miles north. They say that about 50 armed men might go and probably get them, but not fewer. The Sioux are at war with the Crows and Pawnees and reports say that there is a large party of the Pawnees a little down the river . . .

[September 18, 1847. Saturday.] Last night, John Packs gray horse was stole from his wagon. He lays it to the brethren ahead and with Norton Jacobs and Joseph Hancock has heaped a pretty long string of severe abusive language on them, which I consider to be premature, unjustifiable and wicked. Two frenchmen came to the camp and said they were camped below on a trading excursion among the Sioux. Inasmuch as some of the brethren wanted to trade with them it was concluded to move down opposite to them. We accordingly traveled 4 1/4 miles then again camped on the banks of the river, and the brethren bought a number of buffalo robes &c. Norton Jacobs bought 5 robes for 7 common calico shirts.

[September 19, 1847. Sunday.] The traders say they will move down the river today to where there are plenty of buffalo. Our camp also traveled 10 3/4 miles and camped a little below chimney Rock. There are many herds of buffalo around and Lewis Barney killed one which will give us a little fresh meat . . .

[September 21, 1847. Tuesday.] . . . P.M. went over the river and had a good feast on buffalo ribs with the frenchmen. The victuals were cooked by a squaw but looked much cleaner than [when] our men cook it . . .

[September 23, 1847. Thursday.] Today J[ackson] Redding and [Henry] Sanderson went back to see if they could see the other wagons. They returned at night and said the company were within a few miles having been detained at Laramie to recover their horses most of which they got. They state that news has come to the Fort by a Sioux Indian that the Twelve and their company had all their horses stole at the Pacific springs during a snow storm. The Sioux stole them supposing them to belong to the Shoshones. The man that brought the news stole 17 but lost 8 in the mountains the remainder he brought to Laramie and the brethren there knew some of them and demanded them. He gave them up, at least all they could prove and 4 of the brethren started

389

with them to meet the Twelve. The Indian says there were nine of them who stole the horses.

[September 25, 1847. Saturday.] . . . During the afternoon Joseph Hancock killed a Buffalo cow, and Captain [Tunis] Rappleyee sent a wagon to fetch the meat to camp. When it arrived John Pack took the hind quarters and the best meat off the rest of the cow, together with all the tallow, then sent for Rappleyee to take what he had left and divide it amongst the company. When Rappleyee saw what he had done he felt angry and Pack and he had some high words on the subject. Brother Pack's conduct has caused many unpleasant feelings against him among the brethren. He takes all the tallow he can lay his hands on, and all the best meat and has now got more than will serve him home while many of the rest have scarce any and that off the poorest pieces. He has got plenty of flour meal, beans, tea, coffee, sugar &c. while most of the camp are destitute of everything but meat, and while he continues to take the tallow and best of the meat there will be hard feelings against him. He has disgraced himself in the estimation of many within the past few days. I don't think I can ever forget him for his treatment to me, but I cherish no malice nor feelings of revenge, but I hope and pray that I may forever have wisdom to keep from under his power.

There have been 6 or 8 Buffalo killed by the camp, and it is intended to stay here tomorrow and try to get meat to last us through as it is not likely we shall have another privilege as good as this. Most of the camp now begin to feel that it is necessary for us to make our way home as fast as possible to save our teams and escape the cold rain and snowstorms.

[September 28, 1847. Tuesday.] . . . We have seen more buffalo today than I ever saw in one day, supposed to be not less than 200,000 . . .

[September 30, 1847. Thursday.] This day we traveled only 16 1/4 miles, then camped a quarter of a mile East of Rattlesnake Creek on the banks of the river. In this creek there is still a very heavy current of water running. It appears that some of the brethren left their fires burning this morning and the prairie has caught fire and is still burning furiously.

[October 3, 1847. Sunday.] . . . Considerable anxiety and feeling has originated in the breasts of two or three brethren in consequence of a rumor being circulated which deeply concerns one individual but it is not known who . . .

[October 8, 1847. Friday.] Just as we started this morning, 12 or 15 Indians were seen running over the river towards us. They soon came up to the wagons which were some scattered and although they shook hands they showed savage hostility. Four of the oxen were not yet yoked up, these they drove off from the wagons which now began to draw together. They soon satisfied us that they were bent on robbing us and without ceremony took Jack Reddings horse from behind the wagon. [Lisbon] Lamb went to take it from them and seized the lariette which another immediately cut with his knife. Lamb then got on the horse but no sooner on than two Indians pulled him off and marched off with the horse. They stole Jack Reddings knife out of its sheath and one from John Peacock. They also tried to get Jack off the horse he was riding but he kept his seat. They tried Skeens horse but he kicked one of them over. The Indians then tried to get the men out of their wagons so that they might get in and plunder, but every man kept in his wagon to guard it and we concluded to turn about and go back to the company. We accordingly started and the Indians turned back towards the timber with the horse four Oxen, two knives and a sack of salt. After travelling back about 6 miles we met the company, told the story and bore their slang and insults without saying much, but not without thinking a great deal. The whole company were then formed in two lines. All the arms loaded and each man that could raise a gun was ordered to walk beside the wagons, the horsemen to go ahead. We then proceeded on and when we came opposite to w[h]ere we met with the Indians the horsemen went down and found the oxen where we left them. They brought them up and we travelled til dark, then camped near the river, having traveled 5 1/4 miles from last night exclusive of the distance we went back. A strong guard was placed round the cattle and camp and kept up through the night.

Many hard speeches have passed among the brethren, such as damned hyprocrites, damned liars, mutineers &c. and most of those who started ahead are ordered to travel in the rear all the time. This savage, tyrannical conduct was one thing which induced

391

some to leave and undertake to go through alone and more peaceably, and it will still leave feelings of revenge and hatred which will require some time to cover up. Young [Lorenzo] Babcock shook his fist in Zebedee Coltrins face and damned him, said he could whip him. For my part, I shall be glad when I get in more peaceable society, and I think I shall not easily be caught in such a scrape again.

[October 9, 1847. Saturday.] We have had no disturbance from Indians. We started at 6 o'clock and went on 5 miles to get better feed. We then halted for breakfast. The remainder of the days travel was mostly over Dog towns. A United States soldier came up to the wagons and went with us a few miles. He says there are 90 of them on the Island, surveying and looking out a place to build a Fort. We traveled 17 1/4 miles today then camped near a low bench of land where is plenty of grass and water, and willows for fuel. A number of the soldiers came over to camp. They say the Pawnees are perfectly enraged and savage and that the worst band of between 4 and 500 are on the north side the Platte about 40 miles below . . .

[October 14, 1847. Thursday.] Much time was lost this morning in hunting for a place to cross the river. It was finally concluded to cross a mile higher up and we proceeded to the place. While going up we saw a company of horsemen and two wagons on the other side of the river, which we soon recognized to be our brethren from Winter quarters. All the wagons got over safe and camped on the hill having traveled 2 miles. The company is a part of the old police going to meet the next company. We were gladdened with the news they bring from Winter quarters.. .

[October 16, 1847. Saturday.] The night has been very stormy, there being strong wind, rain and very cold. We made an early start and by noon arrived at the mission station. We found the Pawnees busy gathering corn, probably near a thousand of men, women and children. They soon began to come to the wagons and their chiefs made inquiries by signs about the Chirrarots or Sioux. Some of the brethren gave them to understand that the Sioux were within 5 days of them. The chief immediately gave the word to the rest and in half an hour the squaws had loaded their corn on ponies and mules and then began to march towards the river. They show great fear of the Sioux. They were very anxious to have us camp with them tonight but we kept moving on. One of the wagons was upset crossing a ravine. Several of the brethren traded for corn. At 3 o'clock we arrived and turned out the teams on Beaver River having traveled 17 1/4 miles. Soon after we arrived some of the Indians came up having followed with corn to trade. They have conducted themselves peaceably so far, but they are not to be trusted. In consequence of their following us, it was the feeling of most of the brethren to go on a few miles after dark. At 1/4 to 4 we started on and travelled til half past 8 being 6 1/2 miles, then camped beside the Lakes. Evening very fine and pleasant. We have travelled 23 3/4 miles today . . .

[October 21, 1847. Thursday.] This morning Brother [William] Empey, [Lisbon] Lamb and myself started early accompanied by 6 horsemen and arrived in Winter Quarters a little before noon. I found my family all well except Moroni who is very sick and his mother is some sick. Their circumstances are not good, but in other respects they have been prospered for which I thank my God. There has been much sickness here and many deaths during the fall, and many are now suffering for lack of some of the comforts of life. We have been prospered on our journey home and have arrived in 9 weeks and 3 days, including a week's delay waiting for the Twelve and killing buffalo. Our health has been remarkably good, but we have lacked provisions, many of us having nothing but dry buffalo meat. I have succeeded in measuring the whole distance from the City of the Great Salt Lake to this place except a few miles between Horse Creek and the A La Bonte river which was taken from the measurement going up. I find the whole distance to be 1032 miles and am now prepared to make a complete travelers guide from here to the Salt Lake, having been careful in taking the distance from creek to creek, over bluffs, mountains &c. It has required much time and care and I have continually labored under disadvantages in consequence of the companys feeling no interest in it. The health of my family has encouraged me for all that is past and my secret gratitude shall ascend to Heaven for the unbounded kindness and mercies which the Almighty has continually poured upon them in my absence.

[October 31, 1847. Sunday.] I have spent the past week fixing the houses, making window sash &c. and have been once up to the farm. Our health continues good, and Moroni is improving, but I find it impossible to get a little sugar for the sick and several other little necessaries which are much needed. My situation is gloomy but I am in hopes it will soon improve. Elder Amasa Lyman got in from the company of the Twelve on Thursday evening and says they are yet a hundred miles back, and their teams wore [down]. Some of the men are sick and the whole lack provisions. A company left here yesterday morning with teams and provisions for their help. The Twelve and company arrived in Winter Quarters this afternoon which cheered the hearts of the saints much.

[November 27, 1847. Saturday.] During the last 4 weeks I have spent part of the time writing and part attending on my family. Gloomy prospects seem to thicken around my family and it requires a constant effort to keep pace with crowding scenes of suffering and sorrow. I have killed an old Ox of Church property to sustain us. We have had 2 rain storms which beat into the houses and wet every thing. James has been very sick for 3 weeks past and now is low indeed, in fact but small hopes for his recovery. I have got a mission to England as soon as I can arrange to go.

[November 29, 1847. Monday.] This day James was buried. His age is 23 years 6 months and 5 days.

[November 30, 1847. Tuesday.] Paid for lumber for the coffin in cordage and paid for digging the grave in cash.

[December 3, 1847. Friday.] Spent the evening at Elder Joseph Fieldings.

[December 5, 1847. Sunday.] W[illiam] Pitt got home from Missouri. We met at my house and played some.

[December 6, 1847. Monday.] Wrote a letter to father informing him of the death of James, and requesting John[91] to come.[92]

---

[91] James and John were William Clayton's brothers.
[92] The last four pages of Clayton's journal are a ledger of distances travelled over the route from Winter Quarters, Nebraska, to the Great Salt Lake.

1 8 5 2

A*s camp historian for a seventy-nine-
member expedition, William Clayton
visits the territorial capital at Fillmore and other settlements in southern
Utah. The expedition explores farming and mining possibilities, identifies
timber sources, records distances, appoints town officers, and meets with the
Pahvant Ute Indians.*

[April 21, 1852. Wednesday.] Started from G[reat] S[alt] L[ake]
City in company with W[illia]m Pitt, W[illiam] Glover and Barnet
Rigby at 7 o clock, A.M. morning cloudy. On Big Kanyon Creek
met Cha[rle]s C. Rich and a few others returning from California. He brings a very favorable report of the prosperity of the
settlement where Elder Amasa Lyman is. They have purchased a
splendid district of country on the Colorado 20 miles long by 12
miles wide for $75,500. Have paid about $24,000 and could now
sell a small strip off one end for sufficient to pay the balance.
Elder Rich appears in good spirits.[1] We had several showers during

---

[1] In 1851 a group of five hundred Mormons led by apostles Amasa Lyman
and Charles C. Rich bought and settled the land where San Bernardino, California,
now stands. Lyman was Clayton's friend and for a brief time was his

the day. Camped at 4 o clock at the Hot Springs near the foot of Utah Mountain having travelled 21 1/2 [?] miles. The evening was very cold and stormy.

[April 22, 1852. Thursday.] Heavy showers of rain and hail, accompanied by thunder most of the night. This morning is very cold. Heavy showers constantly falling attended by very strong winds. At 9 o clock the weather was more favorable and we continued our journey. The road [round] the point of the mountain although considerable digging has been done is yet very rough, and appears dangerous. We got over safe and it immediately after commenced raining heavy and continu[ed] some time. We arrived at E[dwar]d Robinson, at noon very cold and wet. He pressed us to stop and warm and gave us plenty of good beer. We tarried with him one hour and then went on to Battle Creek,[2] where we found Geo[rge] Wardle Edwin Rushton and W[illia]m Dunn waiting for us having travelled [] miles.

[April 23, 1852. Friday.] Ground covered with hail, and still raining and hailing very heavy. 9 o clock it cleared off and we continued our journey. Arrived at Provo at noon, and camped a little west of the fort.[3] I went up to L[ucius] N. Scovils to deliver him a copy of the census returns. Afterwards saw Bishop

---

father-in-law. In 1866, when Clayton was fifty-two, he married Lyman's daughter, seventeen-year-old Maria Louisa Lyman (Clayton's eighth plural wife). Five years later, after Lyman was excommunicated for apostasy, Maria Louisa left Clayton, taking their young son with her. She soon remarried and had two more children. San Bernardino represented the largest Mormon colonizing attempt in California and ultimately failed (Eugene E. Campbell, "Early Colonization Patterns," in Richard D. Poll et al., eds., *Utah's History* [Provo, UT: Brigham Young University Press, 1978], 145).

[2] Later renamed Pleasant Grove.

[3] Fort Utah, colonized in 1849 by thirty-three families under the leadership of John H. Higbee, sent to the site on the Provo River by Brigham Young who commissioned them for "fishing, farming and teaching the Indians in cultivating the earth and teaching them civilization." This colony was incorporated as Provo, Utah, future home of Brigham Young University. See Dale L. Morgan, *The Great Salt Lake* (Albuquerque: University of New Mexico Press, 1947), 222; Campbell, 138–39.

The Mormons colonized in a quasi-military fashion, organizing into companies, as they had as pioneers. They shaped their settlements around "forts" which served as communal centers as well as protection against the Indians (Leonard J. Arrington, *Great Basin Kingdom: Economic History of the Latter-day Saints 1830–1900* [Lincoln: University of Nebraska Press, 1958], 89).

Blackburn. This town looks dirty. The houses look miserable, and many young men idling in the Streets. It seems there is not much energy here, and there seems to be little spirit of accommodation or friendship among people. Evening the Band played at Josh Worthens, and then danced a few cotillons.

[April 24, 1852. Saturday.] This A.M. weather more favorable. Gave George Bean a copy of the delinquent Tax list for Utah County.[4] Started out at 9 o clock and went on to Springville. Stopped at David Andersons. After dinner had a severe Snow storm. At 5 o clock P.M. President Young and 19 Waggons arrived and camped at this place a little West of the Fort. Evening the band went to the camp and played some,. then adjourned to the school house and the Company spent the evening dancing.

[April 25, 1852. Sunday.] This morning is very fine and pleasant. The president holds a meeting in the school house. G. A. Smith arrived at 9 o clock.

Springville is one of the most handsome locations we have seen on the route.[5] The land is beautifully situated, plenty of water. The houses all look clean and neat, and the hand of industry is clearly manifested throughout the village. We left this place at 2 o clock, and proceeded on. At 6 1/2 miles arrived at Spanish Fork, a stream about 2 rods wide with a swift current. The land here seems but poorly calculated for farming, being very sandy. There are several houses built and farms opened. There is abundance of Timber on the creek at the mouth of the Kanyon. 5 1/2 miles further we arrived at Payson, on the Petete nete[6] at half past 5 and camped a little west of the fort on the south bank of the creek. There are about 20 families here, and considerable farms opened. The land looks better here than at the Spanish Fork, though pretty sandy. After camping President Young,

---

[4] Clayton had just been appointed territorial auditor. He gave the delinquent tax list to George Bean, the probate judge for Utah County.

[5] Springville was one of a line of settlements, including Spanish Fork and Payson, built in 1850–52, utilizing "every mountain spring and so spaced that the outlying farms and pasture lands of each community could touch the next and all the settlers could rally to meet external dangers or unusual internal challenges" (Campbell, 139).

[6] A stream named after a Ute chief named Peteetneet, whose band had lived in the Utah Valley (Morgan, 131).

Kimball and others went up to visit Walker[7] who is camped about half a mile east. President Young presented him with considerable flour and potatoes and held quite a lengthy conversation with him.

[April 26, 1852. Monday.] Morning fine but cloudy. The camp started on at 1/4 to 8 o clock all well. Elijah B. Ward's horse cannot be found, he thinks one of Walkers Indians has stole him. After travelling 6 1/4 miles arrived at Summit Creek where Benj[ami]n F. Johnson and three other families are located. This creek runs on high land at the commencement of the dividing ridge between Utah and Juab Vallies, and is near the dividing line of Utah and Juab counties.[8] The scenery is pleasant and make a handsome settlement.

At 6 1/2 miles further arrived at the Pungent Spring. This spring is about 9 feet in diameter, circular and lays on the west side of the road. The Indians say it has no bottom and it is said they sometimes worship it. The water dont look very clear. At 12 1/4 o clock we arrived a Clover Creek having travelled 16 3/4 miles. On this creek brother Andrew Love John A. Wolf and two other families have lately located, and have commenced to open farms. It is a pleasant place, but little water. Directly opposite on the East is the "Mount Nebo", so named by W. W. Phelps, and is supposed to be the highest of the mountains in this range.[9] At 2 o clock we continued our journey [and?] arrived at Nephi City at 1/4 past 4 having travelled since [the] noon halt 8 miles. At this City Joseph L. Haywood resides, and about 20 other families. It is located on Salt Creek, and is a pleasant situation. At this place we leave the Little Salt Lake road, and pass up Salt creek Kanyon on the San Pete road. It is 89 1/3 miles from Salt Lake City. Bishop Heywood had a load of wood waiting for the use of the camp, as there is some in the immediate vicinity. He greeted us

<hr>

[7] A Ute Indian chief whose name was anglicized from Wahkara, meaning "yellow." Known to John C. Fremont and Brigham Young, Chief Walker agreed to be baptized into the church in 1850 (S. Lyman Tyler, "The Indians in Utah Territory," in Poll, 361; Morgan, 40–41).

[8] The Mormons settled Utah County in 1849, Juab County in 1851 (Arrington, 84).

[9] In the Old Testament, Mount Nebo was the summit of Mount Pisgah, the mountain from which Moses surveyed the Promised Land (Deut. 34:1).

kindly and appeared pleased to see the company. There apppears to be a good feeling prevailing here.

At dusk the Camp was called together at the presidents quarters and proceeded to organize by appointing the following officers viz.

Brigham Young. President of Camp
Heber C. Kimball, 1st Councillor
George A. Smith   2nd Councillor
W[illia]m Clayton   Historian
Daniel H. Wells   Captain of Camp
James Ferguson   Captain of Guard
S. M. Blair and John Kay   Chaplains
W[illia]m Pitt, Cap[tai]n   Marshall Music
W. M. Andrews   Surgeon
Orson Pratt and Albert Carrington   Topographical Engineers.
Jacob F. Hutchinson. Dancing Master.
Elijah B. Ward and Miles Weaver   Indian interpreters.
George S. Clark and Josh L. Robinson, Bishops
W[illia]m W. Major, Artist.
Samuel L. Sprague and E. G. Williams   Botanists.
George A. Smith, Orson Pratt, Albert Carrington, Zerubabel Snow, and Morgan Phelps, Geologists and minerologist.
Wilford Woodruff, Phonographical Reporter

The names of the individuals who compose the camp are as follows viz.

President Brigham Young
   Susan Young
   Joseph A. Young
President Heber C. Kimball
   Mary Ann Kimball
   David H. Kimball
Dan[ie]l H. Wells   Martha Wells
George A. Smith Sen[io]r   Geo[rge] A. Smith Jr
Wilford Woodruff   Clarissa Woodruff
Wilford Woodruff Jr   W[illia]m Clayton
Seth M. Blair   Cornelia Jane Blair
Loren Farr   Olive Ann Farr
Joseph B. Noble   Mary Ann Noble
Elizabeth Noble   Jacob F. Hutchinson
Zerubabel Snow   Mary Augusta Snow

James Ferguson   Jane Ferguson
James Bean   Elizabeth Bean
W[illia]m D. Huntington   Caroline Huntington
Orson Pratt   Albert Carrington
Hiram B. Clawson   W[illia]m W. Major
Albert P. Rockwood   Samuel L. Sprague
W[illia]m Pitt   W[illia]m Glover
George Wardle   W[illia]m Dunn
Barnet Rigby   Edwin Rushton
Joseph L. Robinson   George L. Clark
W. M. Andrews   Ezra G. Williams
Joel Ricks   Ira S. Miles
Franklin B. Wooley   Hopkins C. Pender.
Morgan Phelps   George Barber.
Jesse Sleet   Nathan Tanner
James Beck   W[illia]m Fotheringham
Josh S. Scofield   Samuel Moore
Cristopher Merkley   Stephen Moore
W[illia]m Miles   Francis M. Pomroy.
George Chase   Andrew Moffet.
Tho[ma]s Treat   Jehiel McConnel[l]
Alanson Eldredge   John Eldredge
Charles Ford   Edw[ar]d Stevenson
John Kay   James M. Barlow
Elijah B. Ward   Miles Weaver.
Lot Smith   W[illia]m Robinson
Levi Savage Sen[io]r   Levi Savage Jr
John Witbeck

Making a total of 64 men 11 women, 3 Boys and 1 Girl.[10]

Captain Wells then instructed the men that every man own-
ing horses or mules will be expected to see that they are safe or
tied up at dusk every night, and also to see to them at day break
every morning. He remarked that those who ride on horses have
hitherto gone ahead on the road regardless of the wagons, whether
they were in difficulty or not. Wants a part of the horsemen to go
in front of the train to examine the road, warn the company of all
difficulties or bad places, and otherwise aid the camp as circumstances may direct. 2 or 3 horsemen ought to ride in company

---

[10] Here follows a list of wagon teams comprised of thirty wagons, sixty-nine
horses, and twelve mules.

with the train to act as messengers in case of necessity. The balance of the horsemen to guard the rear and be ready to assist any wagon which might need assistance. The horsemen are also expected to examine every camping ground when the train leaves to see that nothing is left behind or lost. When men go after their horses in a morning he wants every man to bring all the horses or mules belonging to the camp which he finds on his road, and not to bring his own and leave his neighbors horse behind. Wants horsemen and all having horses not to hopple their horses in camp, but to take them to the herd ground before they do it. Wants horsemen to be careful and not ride on the wind side of the wagons so as to drive dust into them &c.

After organization the guard was detailed and President Young went over to the school house and preached to the citizens. This is one of the most pleasant places on this rout and the industry and energy of those who reside here is almost without a parallel. On the 25th September 1851 the first stick of Timber was hauled on the ground by George Bradley. There are some 20 good houses, a school house, a good carrol for cattle, a large amount of land fenced and broke, besides 6 good bridges built over the creek up the Salt creek Kanyon. Every man appears to be busily employed and the good spirit seems to prevail.

[April 27, 1852. Tuesday.] We left Nephi City at 7 1/2 o clock and proceeded up the Kanyon in a due east direction. The Kanyon is no [way] difficult since the bridges were made, and the camp proceeded without accident or hindrance. After traveling 6 miles we arrived at the road to the Salt cave. Many of the brethren went to see it. It lays about a quarter of a mile from the road at the foot of the mountain. The cave is a hole about 20 feet deep and about 4 feet in diameter at the bottom. The whole side of the mountain appears like a solid mass of salt, but the specimens are generally obtained near the bottom of the cave. The salt is almost as hard as rock and of a reddish color. 3 miles beyond this we arrived at the entrance of San Pete Valley[11] and

---

[11] The Sanpete (originally Sanpitch) Valley was first settled in November 1849, a critical period in which Brigham Young, competing with the lure of the gold fields of California, sent colonists to cultivate the high desert valleys south of Salt Lake City (Morgan, 222; Campbell, 140).

travelled till 12 1/2 o clock when we halted for noon on the bottom land near a small creek, having travelled 14 1/3 miles.

At 2 o clock we proceeded onward. We found the bottom land generally soft and heavy travelling. At 4 o clock we crossed the San Pete River, a stream about 25 feet wide, and a very swift current. At 5 1/4 P.M. we camped in Canal Creek, a small stream four feet wide, having travelled during the day 26 3/4 miles, camp all well and in good spirits. Weather cloudy.

[April 28, 1852. Wednesday.] Morning cloudy. Started at 7 1/2 o clock, found good roads but some rough. After travelling 6 3/4 miles arrived at "Pine creek" late Willow creek were Brother Isaac Behunin has lately located alone. We changed the name of the creek in consequence of there being several other creeks of the same name on the road. At 11 o clock we arrived at the City of Manti and encamped on the square near where President Brigham Young's house is to be built, having travelled 13 3/4 miles.[12] To the liberty Pole of this City from G.S.L. City is 130 1/4 miles by the Odometer. This city is located at the foot of the mountains on the East side of the valley and is a pleasant situation. The land does not look rich, though it produces good crops of wheat. The place appears to be in a flourishing condition, and the inhabitants seem kind and prosperous. Soon after our arrival President Young Kimball and others went to visit Arapene[13] who is laying very sick. They laid hands on him and blessed him. At 5 P.M. the people met in the School House, and were addressed by Elder O. Pratt on general subjects, and was followed by Presidents Young and Kimball.

In the evening the company and many of the citizens met and joined in the dance till 12 o clock.

[April 29, 1852. Thursday.] This morning we are surrounded by deep, heavy mud. It has rained heavy near all the night, and the morning is cold and unpleasant. The camp moved out to drier ground. After noon we had another cold storm. It was concluded

---

[12] Isaac Morley led 225 colonists to settle Manti in the Sanpete Valley near the hunting territory of Ute Chief Walker. See n7 above. Brigham Young hoped that the Mormons might teach the Utes the practice of agriculture. In 1877 Manti became the site of the second temple built in the west (Campbell, 139–40).

[13] Brother of Chief Walker.

not to leave here on account of the storms and badness of the roads. Arapene is considerable better.

[April 30, 1852. Friday.] Morning fine and more pleasant. President Young gave Isaac Morley a license to trade with the Indians, and he associated with him. Murray Brown, Alfred Billings, Augustus E. Dodge, Jefferson Patten and Jerome Kempton as clerks and assistants.

News has been brought to camp this A.M. that Joseph Worthen has been shot at Provo by a gentile, and that he is dead.

Arapene is much better and is now considered out of danger. At half past 9 the camp again moved forward. Found the roads very heavy. We travelled to Big Pine Creek a distance of 11 miles and at 1 1/2 o clock halted for noon. At 3 o clock continued our journey taking near a North West course and at 6 o clock camped on [Greas?] Wood creek, a small stream about 3 feet wide. There is scarce any feed for the horses, no wood, and the water is unpleasant.

We have been joined by the following brethren and teams from the City of Manti viz.

Dimick B. Huntington	1 Wagon	2 Horses
W[illia]m P. McIntyre.		
Isaac Morley.		
John O. Warner.	1 Wagon	2 Horses
John Lowry Sen[io]r	1 " "	2 " "
James P. Brown		
W[illia]m W. Potter	1 " "	2 " "
Albert Petty.		1 " "
Nelson Higgins		1 " "
Augustus E. Dodge	1 " "	1 " "
Daniel B. Funk		2 " "
Gad Yale		2 " "
John Lawson	1 " "	1 " "
R. Wilson Glenn		1 " "

A total of 14 men 6 Wagons and 17 Horses. In addition also Nathan Tanner has traded for a Pony, which now makes a total in the Camp as follows, viz. 78 Men, 3 Boys, 11 Women, 36 Wagons, 87 Horses and 12 Mules. The camp are all healthy and in good spirits. The evening is fine and pleasant and all is well.

[May 1, 1852. Saturday.] In consequence of the feed being very poor at this place it was thought best to start before breakfast and go to better feed. The camp accordingly moved on at 6 o clock and travelled till half past 8 distance 8 1/2 miles then halted in tolerable good, grass for breakfast, but being near a mile to water. Morning fine but windy. At 10 o clock we proceeded on and after travelling 1 1/4 miles furthur, we arrived on the banks of the severe River,[14] about 11 miles above the old ford. This stream is about 6 rods wide, about 3 feet deep in the channel and the current very swift. Immediately on our arrival the horsemen forded in various places to find the best place to ford, which being decided on, a number of men were carried across on horses, who commenced digging down the bank, to make a road to go out. While crossing Elijah B. Wards horse stumbled in the channel, and threw both him and W[illia]m Fotheringham, who was crossing with him over its head into the stream. Fortunately they went far enough over the horses head to be out of his way, and although Brother Ward struck his head on the rocks at the bottom of the river, they were soon seen swimming towards the shore. They lost a spade and the horses bridle but sustained no farther damage. After working about an hour and a half the bank was considered passable and E. G. Williams started across with his buggy. President Young then led the way, and the camp followed. When Judge Snow's[15] carriage had got about half way across, his hind axle broke off, the wheel fell into the river and let the corner of the carriage into the water. He had to take his horses off, and two of the brethren carried Sister Snow to the shore. A rope was then attached to the wagon and it was dragged across. All the rest got over without difficulty, and after fixing Judge Snows wagon, at 20 minutes to 1 the camp proceeded forward, President Young taking the lead to break a new road. The wind blew very strong and the country was sandy and very heavy travelling. After travelling 6 1/6 miles we arrived at the old Ford amidst rain and very strong wind. It is considered that this will be a better road than the old one from San Pete to Filmore City, and some shorter but

---

[14] The Sevier River.
[15] Zerubbabel Snow was appointed by President Millard Fillmore to be associate justice of the new Utah Territory, created January 27, 1851 (Campbell, 208-9).

it is pretty rough and very crooked. After watering the teams we again proceeded onwards in a south direction and at half past 6 camped in a very pretty place on fall creek, at the foot of the mountain, having travelled during the day 28 miles. This camping place is about 3 miles out of the direct road, but will no doubt be resorted to by those that pass through this region on account of the scarcity of water. This creek is in what is called Lake valley. After we got camped it commenced snowing very heavy, and the evening was cold and very unpleasant.

[May 2, 1852. Sunday.] This morning the ground is covered with snow. After breakfast a company of men started on foot to improve the road up the Kanyon. At 8 o clock the camp proceeded forward, and travelled very slow. The roads are rough and have many rocks laying in places, many of which were removed by the men on foot. Snow fell heavy untill noon when it cleared off some. After travelling 14 1/4 miles we arrived at Cedar springs and halted for noon at 1/4 past 1 P.M.

At 1/4 past 3 the camp moved on, and soon after the snow again began to fall heavy, and continued untill we arrived at Filmore City[16] a distance of 10 1/4 miles from Cedar springs, and by the road we have travelled 202 1/3 miles from G.S.L. City. We arrived here at half past 6 o clock and camped inside this fort. Filmore City is built on the West banks of [] or Chalk creek a stream about 12 feet wide with a very swift current. There is abundance of large Cedar growing almost in every direction through the upper side of the valley, and apparently plenty of Pine Timber in the mountains. This is a very extensive valley far larger than any other we have seen. It is named "Pauvan" or as the Indians have it "Pawante", and will evidently afford facilities for a heavy settlement, not only here, but in various parts of the valley.[17] There are about 25 families now located here, and their houses are built in the form of a square fort. It is a pleasant place to live, and will doubtless become thickley settled. There is a band of the Pawante Indians here. They are good looking and have the character of being very peaceable. The chief [came] into

---

[16] Capital of Utah, 1851–56 (Arrington, 163).
[17] The Pahvant valley, settled in 1851, was named after the indigenous Pahvant Ute Indians (Morgan, 39; Arrington, 84).

camp and made some complaints. Says the brethren dont feed them enough, and that they take advantage of them in trading.

The camp are all health and in good spirits, and the people here appear kind and hospitable, though poor on account of having but lately located here.

[May 3, 1852. Monday.] Morning fine and pleasant. Judge Snow organized the U.S. Supreme Court for this county at 10 o clock A.M. Dr. Sprague has attended on and given medicine to a sick family who live about a mile down the creek names not known. The husband, wife, and 2 children are sick with the bilious fever. He also gave medicine to one of the Indians who is sick. The Bishops went round the camp to collect some bread for the Indians. They received enough to give them quite a feast. P.M. the weather turned cold and looks like for more storms. At 4 o clock the saints assembled in the school house, and were addressed by [].

[May 4, 1852. Tuesday.] Morning fine and pleasant. This A.M. President Young gave a certificate to the chief of the Parvante Indians, in the following words, viz.

"To all whom it may concern.

This may certify that we have had a talk with Canosha,[18] the chief of the Parvante Indians, and we find him and his Band friendly to white people; they have invariable manifested a friendly and peaceable disposition towards those who have located in Parvan valley, and are anxious to cultivate the kind feelings of all who settle in their neighborhood. I therefore recommend him to the sympathies and charitable feelings of all to whom he may present this certificate.

Filmore City   Brigham Young.
May 4th 1852.["]19

This certificate was given to the chief at his earnest solicitation, and when the substance of it was interpreted to him, he seemed well pleased with it.

A company of men was selected at this place to go in search of a lead mine, discovered by Elijah B. Ward sometime ago, some

---

[18] Kanosh, chief of the Pahvants in central Utah, was known for his peaceful ways, in contrast to the more warlike Walker (Morgan, 41).

[19] Clayton's quotation marks along the left hand side of Brigham Young's letter in the original holograph have been eliminated for readability.

distance North West from here; also to continue the search farther South West for a silver mine spoken of by the Indians, and
also to explore and make all the discoveries they can on the in
route and finally meet us at [Parowan]. The names of those who
leave the camp for this expedition are as follows. Albert Carrington. Elijah B. Ward, Lot Smith, John Kay, Samuel Moore,
Daniel B. Funk, Augustus E. Dodge, Thomas Treat, Stephen
Moore, John Witbeck and Cristopher Merkley.

They are accompanied by [William] H. Dame and Noah W.
Bartholomew from Filmore City. They go well armed, with about
15 days provisions. The President appointed Samuel P. Hoyt to
superintend the Public works in this place. Noah W. Bartholomew
is the Bishop and will receive and disburse the tithing received
here.[20]

At half past 11 the Camp left Filmore City for Little Salt
Lake, leaving Orson Pratt with brother Garners Wagon, and two
other wagons to follow tomorrow. Brother Pratt stays to get an
observation of an eclipse of one of Jupiters satellites, in order to
determine the Longitude of Filmore City. The Camp travelled 11
1/2 miles and then halted for night on Corn Creek. At the same
time the wagons left, the exploring company also took their departure. Late at night Robert S. Burton, W[illia]m Taylor and
Cha[u]ncey W. West arrived at Filmore with the Mail,[21] having
come from G.S.L. City in 2 1/2 days. They report peace and
good news at headquarters. During the night Elder Pratt succeeded in getting an observation as he expected but the time was
unfavorable on account of the planet Jupiter being too near the
neighborhood of the moon.

[May 5, 1852. Wednesday.] The Mail left Filmore at half
past 5 and Elder Pratt and those with him at a quarter past 6.
They arrived at the Camp at 8 o clock. The mail was opened on
its arrival at half past 7 and the papers and letters distributed to

---

[20] In 1850, a General Tithing Office and Bishop's Storehouse were established
in Salt Lake to collect tithes, or one-tenth portions, of the produce of each individual member. These tithes were used to serve the entire church. Local and district
tithing storehouses were set up throughout Mormon settlements. Contributions of
animals and produce were a form of cooperative saving which financed the
economic growth of Utah (Arrington, 133).

[21] The carrying of mail qualified as "tithing labor" during the 1850s
(Arrington, 142; see also Journal 6, "Polygamy Mission to England," n12).

their owners. At 1/4 past 9 the camp proceeded onwards, weather fine but cool, and the roads good, Travelled [26?] 1/2 miles and encamped on Pine Creek in Prospect Valley.

After the horses were attended to the brethren and sisters were called together, when Cap[tai]n D[aniel] H. Wells read some letters, received from Elder John M. Bernhisel who is at the City of Washington. From the tenor of his letters the excitement caused by the malicious reports of Judges Brochus and Baundebury is much abated,[22] and the news contained in his letters is good and satisfactory. James Ferguson traded again with one of the Parvante Indians for an Indian child. A[lbert] P. Rockwood had traded for one previous. These Indians appear anxious to trade children for guns, but it is supposed the children are taken from the Piutes or Pah Utes.[23]

Prospect Valley is one of the nicest valleys we have seen. It is small, but the land is rich and beautifully adorned with large Cedar, which is scattered from end to end in large groves. The mountains appear well supplied with timber, and the only lack is water. There appears to be only one small stream about 3 feet wide, but it is considered to be sufficient for 20 or 25 families both for home use and for purposes of irrigation.

[May 6, 1852. Thursday.] This morning left Pine Creek a little before 8 o clock. One of Ira S. Mile's horses and Dr. Andrew's horse was missing and some of the horsemen remained to help hunt them up. After travelling about 2 miles, the road begins to wind over a succession of steep hills and hollows, and is very crooked for about 6 miles. After that it descends gradually for about 4 or 5 miles further then enters the Bever River Valley. We arrived on the banks of the Bever river at 1 o clock and encamped for the night, there being no water nearer than about 20 miles ahead, having travelled 21 1/2 miles. Dr. Andrews and I. S. Miles found their horses and arrived in camp soon after we stopped.

---

[22] Lemuel E. Bradbury and Perry E. Brocchus, both non-Mormons, had been appointed by President Fillmore as chief justice and associate justice of Utah Territory. They had sent complaints to Washington, D.C., because the Mormons had held elections prior to their arrival and Brigham Young had publicly insulted them (Eugene E. Campbell, *Establishing Zion: The Mormon Church in the American West, 1847–1868* [Salt Lake City: Signature Books, 1988], 210–15).

[23] Paiute Indians.

This is another pretty valley. The land is dark and rich, grass abundant, and the Cedar groves are truly beautiful. Bever river is about 20 feet wide; water clear, current swift, and abounds with trout. This will make a good place for a settlement. The day has been warm and pleasant. Soon after 6 o clock, John L. Smith and his cousin arrived from Parvaun[24] having started out to meet us. The[y] report that the brethren are making preparation for us, and constantly Cooking for our arrival. About 9 o clock another Brother arrived from Parowan. His crossing the creek frightened the horses which were all tied to stakes near the wagons and caused a stampede. A number of horses broke loose, and for a short time there was considerable excitement.

[May 7, 1852. Friday.] The camp proceeded on at half past 7. After travelling 3 1/2 miles crossed the summit of the dividing ridge between Bever and Parowan Vallies.[25] The road after this is very crooked and over hills and hollows for a few miles. When leaving the ridges the road is rocky and unpleasant travelling. We arrived at Red Creek at 3 P.M. and there stopped to feed. At 4 started for Parowan City and arrived there at 5 1/2 o clock. The horses were sent back to Red Creek to feed a distance of 4 1/2 miles.

This City or Fort is 296 1/2 miles from G.S.L. City by way of San Pete. It is located on a pleasant elevation about half a mile from the foot of the mountains on the East side of the Valley. It is well picketed around the Fort, and each lot is divided off and enclosed by a good board fence. All the lots are adorned with young firs and other varieties of trees and shrubbery. There is a general carrol in the centre of the Fort, and each family have a small carrol attached to the larger one. The houses generally look neat and clean, and the whole place has a pleasant appearance. The citizens appear very hospitable and kind.

[May 8, 1852. Saturday.] At 10 A.M. a meeting was held in the new council House, and the saints received instruction from

---

[24] Clayton may be referring to Parowan.

[25] The Parowan settlement, begun in 1851 in the Little Salt Lake Valley, had iron mines which were important for the development of Utah. The 447 colonists, led by George A. Smith, left Provo in December 1850 with the responsibility to plant crops so succeeding immigrants could open up the local iron deposits. See Arrington, 87; Ward J. Roylance, *Utah: A Guide to the State* (Salt Lake City: Utah: A Guide to the State Foundation, 1982), 634.

several. The evening was occupied in dancing. The council House is about 44 by 21 feet in the clear, having spacious recess on each side.

[May 9, 1852. Sunday.] Meetings were held in the council house and the brethren were edified on various subjects.

[May 10, 1852. Monday.] The company proceeded to Coal Creek settlement a distance of eighteen miles. Bishop Lewis and several others accompanied us the Bishop to gather up the Church cattle, and forward them to G.S.L. City.[26]

This Fort is also a pleasant [location]. They have got a field fenced in, about 2 miles long and a mile wide, besides another field on the east and one on the west of the Fort. The whole enclosed by a ditch and posts and poles, making a good and secure fence. The Cedar is abound around this valley. The mountains are of various colors, but the most abundant is a deep red, which has a very imposing appearance. The land is also a kind of red sand. There is plenty of water, but very muddy.

[May 11, 1852. Tuesday.] This A.M. a company was selected to start back with the church cattle. They started in good season with 40 Oxen, 4 Cows, and 5 young heifers.

At 10 A.M. a meeting was held and the saints addressed on various subjects. At 4 o clock P.M. another meeting was held to organize a company for the manufacture of Iron.

[May 12, 1852. Wednesday.] Started early on our return and arrived at Parowan at 1 o clock amid a heavy shower of rain. The exploring company who left the camp at Filmore arrived here this morning. They did not find either the lead or silver mine, but received good evidence of the existence of the latter. The[y] report a very beautiful valley west of this place, called Bever Valley. Much larger than G.S.L. Valley, and well supplied with water and Cedar. They report it as being splendid for grazing.

At 4 o clock a meeting was held in the council House, to organize and arrange matters pertaining to this branch of the church. There was present President Brigham Young and Heber C. Kimball of the first presidency. Of the quorum of the Twelve

[26] An example of tithing remitted to the General Tithing Office.

Orson Pratt, Wilford Woodruff, and George A. Smith. After singing the meeting was opened by Elder Orson Pratt, after which President Kimball addressed the audience for some time.

The following persons were then nominated and appointed by unanimous vote to the offices attached to their names as follows,

John C. L. Smith, President of this stake
John Steele, his first counsellor.
Henry Lund his second counsellor
Elisha H. Groves a member of the High Council
Mathen [?] Carwithers [?] a member of do
Richard Harrison, member of High Council
Joseph Chatterly, member of do
John Easton, member of do
James S. Little, member of do
William H. Dame, member of do
John D. Lee, member of do
Lamiel West, member of do
Elijah Newman, member of do
Francis J. Whitney, member of do
Joel H. Johnson, member of do

Philip Clingensmith was nominated and appointed Bishop of Cedar City.

Tarlton Lewis was confirmed as Bishop of Parowan City.

The brethren above mentioned were then ordained to their respective offices by Elders Orson Pratt, Wilford Woodruff, and George A. Smith, after which President Kimball continued his remarks, and gave much salutary instruction and concluded by blessing the brethren and the people here in the name of the Lord.

Brother James Ferguson then read an Epistle from the first presidency to the saints of Parowan and vicinity, showing them what was required of them, and what would be for the present eternal salvation. After it was read the saints voted unanimously to abide by the council therein set forth, and it was left with them for their future guidance and comfort.

President Young then made some remarks, said the former officers of this stake had done well; but it was necessary that men who preside as officers in the Church should be men of experience and judgement.

James Lewis was then nominated and appointed clerk of the High Council.

President Young then organized the High Council according to order and gave them instructions. He concluded by blessing the people in the name of the Lord and after singing the meeting dismissed. At 4 o clock also, Judge Z. Snow, proceeded to organize the U.S. Court for the Third Judicial District of Utah Territory. Joseph L. Heywood U.S. Marshall by his deputy James A. Little was duly sworn. James Lewis was sworn as clerk of said court. Seth M. Blair, District Attorney Wm. H. Dame and Wm Leany Bailiffs John Topham, Crier. All of the foregoing officers of Court were duly sworn in open Court. The district Attorney then applied for a summons of 17 Grand Jurors which was granted by the Court, and the Jurors were forthwith selected and placed under charge of Bailiff Wm H. Dame, when the court adjourned till tomorrow 8 o clock A.M.

The evening was spent by many by dancing in the Council House till midnight.

[May 13, 1852. Thursday.] Morning fine and pleasant. Last evening a number of the Wagons and men belonging to the Camp went on to Red Creek in order to obtain better feed. This morning the balance of the company began to leave at 7 o clock. The first 18 miles we travelled at a brisk speed, except halting half an hour on Red Creek. The balance of the road being considerable rough we travelled slow and arrived on Beaver creek at 5 o clock P.M. making the distance travelled today as p[e]r Odometer 35 miles. Judge Snow remains at Parowan today to attend the business of Court. We have had several showers during the day and the evening is quite cool.

[May 14, 1852. Friday.] Morning cloudy and quite cool. The camp started this morning at a quarter after 7 and travelled on to Dry Creek a distance of 13 1/2 miles and at a quarter to 11 o clock halted for noon. Previous to our arriving here we had a heavy storm of hail and rain which made the air quite chilly. This creek has now plenty of water, but it is not usually the case. The banks are steep on both sides. Plenty of grass around and the neighborhood abounds with Cedar or rather Juniper. During the noon halt we had another heavy hail storm.

We started again at 1 o clock P.M. Immediately on crossing

the creek we ascend a very steep hill for about a quarter of a mile. We travelled on, amidst storms of hail and snow till 5 o clock when we camped for the night at the crossing of Cove Creek. This is a pleasant place to camp, with the exception of water, which we have to fetch from springs about a mile up the creek. Feed is pretty good and Juniper abundant. The evening was more favorable. The storms had ceased but the wind blew some, and it was pretty cold. The distance we travelled this day is 27 1/2 miles, mostly in the midst of heavy storms.

[May 15, 1852. Saturday.] Started at 1/4 past 7 and travelled slow. The morning fine and pleasant. On arriving at the foot of the ridge called Baker's Pass, the President lead off on a new road to avoid the steep ridges. We made about 5 miles of new road, but it is gradually descending all the way until after we arrive about a mile from the entrance into Paroan Valley, when we ascend a small ridge but no [way] difficult, or hard on teams.

At 20 minutes to 2 P.M. we arrived and halted on Corn Creek, having travelled 21 1/4 miles. A number of the Pauvan Indians were here to beg, and wanted to trade a female child for a gun and two blankets, but none of the brethren appeared disposed to give as much. Francis M. Pomroy was waiting for us here. He says the herd of cattle arrived here yesterday at 2 P.M. and have gone onto Filmore. At 4 o clock started on again. Built a bridge across meadow creek a little east of the old crossing place. At a quarter to 8 o clock arrived at Filmore City and encamped in the Fort, having travelled during the day 33 3/4 miles. Weather warm and pleasant. 2 horses gave out and all the teams seem pretty well tired. We found the brethren appointed to come from G.S.L. City to work on the State House all here. They have been engaged the week past in working a road to the Timber.

[May 16, 1852. Sunday.] Morning fine. The saints met in the Fort at 10 o clock and were addressed by Elder Orson Pratt, Elder W. Woodruff followed.

At 2 o clock D. B. Huntington talked to the Indians who live in this neighborhood. He told them to quite stealing from the Mormons and go to work as Mormons do. He told them to cease killing Indians told them the doctrine of baptism hinted at the resurrection, and told them that God made the land for Mormons as well as them. He advised them to cease trading children to the

413

Spaniards, but if the[y] will trade children let the Mormons have them that they may be taught to read and write and be clothed like Mormons are. If they will go to work as Mormons do, in a while they will have cattle and houses and wagons as the Mormons have.

Canosha their chief replied, that he heard what has been said and it is good and they will do it. They will not Rile any more, nor steal from the Mormons but will go to work. He says, when they see the Mormons eat cattle and they are hungry it is hard work to keep from Killing them, but they will Kill no more. They appeared pleased with the conversation.

Journal Six
Polygamy Mission
to England

1852-1853

*F*ollowing *the official announcement of the Mormon doctrine of plural marriage, William Clayton, then thirty-eight, is sent back to England to explain and defend the long-denied controversial practice.*

[August 28, 1852. Saturday.] At a special conference of the Church of Latter Day Saints, held in the Tabernacle in Great Salt Lake City Utah Territory, on Saturday the 28th of August, 1852, I received an appointment to take a mission to England to preach the gospel and sustain the Revelation on Celestial Marriage, given by our beloved Prophet July 12 1843.[1] This is a privilege which

---

[1] On the next day of the conference, August 29, Apostle Orson Pratt announced the doctrine of plural marriage publicly for the first time. In 1851 after federal officials had arrived to administer the new territorial government of Utah, it was no longer possible for Mormons to continue disguising their practice of polygamy. Utah's representative in Congress, John M. Bernhisel, had on August 14 advised Brigham Young against publicity, "for the public mind is exceedingly sensitive on that subject, not at all prepared to receive it, and its effect would be decidedly injurious" (Richard S. Van Wagoner, *Mormon Polygamy: A History* [Salt Lake City: Signature Books, 1986], 83). But after the announcement, Young minimized the opposition, saying, "[only] a small portion of the world is opposed to [it]," and prophesied that "It will sail over, and ride triumphantly above all the prejudices and priest-craft of the day; it will be fostered and believed in by the more

I have desired for years, in as much as when I left England in the year 1840 I had then a mission appointed to me to Birmingham, which I never fulfilled, and I have often felt a deep desire to bear my testimony once more in my native country.[2]

I felt this appointment to be a great favor, and believe it will prove an everlasting blessing to me and my family . . .

All the . . . Elders accepted their appointments, and the nominations was sanctioned by the unanimous vote of the Conference. After which the day was spent in giving instructions by Elder Orson Pratt, President Young and others.[3] Monday the 13th of September was appointed as the day for those to start who have to cross the plains and pass through the United States, that they may be enabled to get over the plains before the cold winter weather sets in.

I spent the time thus alloted for the brethren to prepare for the journey, in settling business in the Tithing Office, giving instructions to the Clerks, and in making preparations for our journey across the plains.

Brothers W[illia]m Glover, Thomas M. Treat and myself agreeing to fit up a team and wagon and travel together. Brother Treat furnished a span of Horses and half the harness. Brother Glover furnished the other half of the harness, wagon cover and part of the provisions, and I furnished the wagon and the balance of the provisions. It was with the greatest difficulty I could get anything done at the Public works, or even get a little clothing or groceries to take over the plains. Brother Enock Reece kindly gave me a piece of Bacon. And Brother Willis charged me double price for

---

intelligent portions of the world, as one of the best doctrines ever proclaimed to any people" (*Deseret News*, September 14, 1852). He had acknowledged his own plural marriages over a year earlier: on February 4, 1851, he told the territorial legislature that he had more than one wife (Van Wagoner, 82).

[2] Clayton had left his mission in England in 1840 to join his family in emigrating to Nauvoo, Illinois (Journal 1, "England and Emigration," July 7, September 5, 1840).

[3] Pratt's words at this conference indicate that both the knowledge and practice of plural marriage had extended beyond the church leadership: "We shall have to break up new ground. It is widely known, however, to the congregation before me that the Latter-day Saints have embraced the doctrine of plural wives, as a part of their religious faith" (*Journal of Discourses*, 26 vols. [London: Latter-day Saints Book Depot, 1854–86], 1:54). See also Max H. Parkin, "The Nature and Cause of Internal and External Conflict of the Mormons in Ohio Between 1830 and 1838," M.A. thesis, Brigham Young University, 1966, 162–63.

baking our crackers, because he had to take his pay in flour at the Tithing Office price. But although my outfit was of the poorest kind, I felt determined not to complain, but do the best I could.

On Saturday the 11th of September the Brethren all met in the Tabernacle to receive their blessings; the Seventies being blest by the Presidents of Seventies, and the body of the Tabernacle, and the High Priests were blessed and set apart for their respective missions, by the Twelve Apostles in the vestry. I was blessed by Orson Pratt, George A. Smith and Franklin D. Richards; Orson being mouth.

[September 15, 1852. Wednesday.] This day was finally set for all the company to meet on Kanyon Creek, over the first mountain. Several Wagons have started previously, but not untill today was there a general move. I left my family and affairs in charge of my brother Thomas and Mathew Clayton[4] who both pledged themselves to do the best they could in my absence, and at 10 o'clock A.M. parted with my family and bade them farewell. It was about 3 o'clock before we got the wagon loaded and left Brother Glover's house. On passing President Youngs house we met him starting out in his carriage, I asked him what he wanted I should do when I got to England. He said, What do you want to do? I replied; If I had my own way I would go and visit all the branches of the Church and bear my testimony to them. Well, said he, go and do it, and you shall be blessed in it. We then bid farewell, and we proceeded on our way for the mountains. Towards night it rained heavy which made the roads soft and muddy, and the first mountain was difficult to get up.

It was 8 o'clock at night when we arrived in the camp at the foot of the first mountain, being then 12 miles from the City. We fixed up the wagon as well as we could and retired for the night being pretty well fatigued.

---

[4] Into the care of his twenty-year-old brother, Thomas, and his relative, Matthew Clayton, William Clayton placed his thirteen children and four wives: Jane was no longer with him, and Diantha had died, leaving Ruth, Margaret, Alice, and Augusta. Ruth gave birth to a fourteenth child (her eighth) on November 11, 1852. Clayton left his family in economic need, "very poorly situated for clothing &c" (Clayton to Brigham Young, October 4, 1852, archives, historical department, Church of Jesus Christ of Latter-day Saints, Salt Lake City; hereafter LDS archives).

[September 16, 1852. Thursday.] The camp moved forward at 8 o'clock and travelled over the second mountain without accident or delay. We went about 2 miles down Kanyon Creek, and camped for the night having travelled 12 miles. I walked all the way and waded the streams, preferring to walk rather than ride over the rough roads. The grass is very poor and scarce being all fed off by the companies which have lately passed. We have met many of the Saints on their way to the Valley. They appear in good spirits and their teams generally are in good condition. We were informed that as Edward Stevenson was ascending the first mountain, his mules ran away, and broke his carriage and carriage springs so bad, that he had to return to the City for repairs. This evening, not withstanding the heavy rains the Brethren were called to go to Elder Orson Pratt's wagon and the camp was organized for the journey, by appointing the following officers viz.

Orson Pratt ----------------President of the Camp

Daniel Spencer--------------Captain of the Camp

John Brown and Benjamin Brown ---Councillors
                                to Captain Spencer

Orson Spencer-----------------------------Chaplain

W[illia]m Clayton ----------------------------Clerk

Horace S. Eldredge---------Sergeant of the guard

William Pitt --------------------------------Trumpter

John Brown and Charles Smith-----------Pioneers
        to ride ahead and select camping grounds

There are yet a number of men and wagons which have not joined the main camp. Some 5 or 6 wagons have gone on ahead; and several have not yet arrived from the City . . . The total number of Elders in Camp, on missions as appointed by vote of Conference is 73,[5] Men on their own business 10, 1 woman and 2 children, 29 Wagons, 69 Horses and 19 Mules.

[September 17, 1852. Friday.] This morning the weather is cloudy and very cold, so much so, that it froze the towels stiff,

[5] Of the seventy-three elders, thirty-nine were headed toward Britain.

while the brethren washed themselves in the creek. The camp started at 7 o'clock and traveled 8 1/2 miles, and again encamped soon after noon on the East branch of Kanyon Creek at the foot of the steep hill 32 1/2 miles from the City, I traveled the distance again on foot. While we were forming our encampment, Elder Wrigley, (late president of the Saint Louis Branch) and company, arrived and halted to exchange greetings. We find that many of them are out of bread stuff, and if they had many days to travel, must suffer from hunger. With this company I met my natural Sister Dinah Ann, whom I had not seen for near seven years. We neither of us knew each other, but met accidently, on her enquiring if W[illia]m Clayton was in the company. It may be supposed we felt glad to see each other. She told me that Mrs. Wrigley had treated her very unkindly, having to carry a heavy child on foot, while Mrs. Wrigley took her ease riding in the wagon. But she is near the end of her journey, and will be made welcome by many warm friends. She states that my brother Joseph is with one of the company on his way to the Valley. When they arrive in Salt Lake City I shall have the satisfaction of knowing that my brothers and sisters who are living are in the Vallies of the mountains, except Sister Ellen[6] who is yet in St Louis.

The afternoon was fine, but towards night the weather became cloudy and we had some rain. About sun down another company of the Saints arrived and camped close to us on the opposite side of the creek. They are also mostly destitute of bread stuff and suffering some.

This morning Aaron F. Farr, Alfred B. Lambson, Darwin Richardson and Jesse Turpin, left the camp by permission; with Mr. Livingston to go on to Fort Bridger, in order that Brother Lambson can shoe Mr. Livingstons mules, before the balance of the company arrive there.

This evening for the first time the camp was called together for prayer. After singing the Chaplain called upon Elder John S. Fullmer, who offered up prayers for the camp, the presidency &c. It was also considered wisdom to commence guarding the camp and our teams through the night, in order to get the brethren accustomed to camp duties before we get into the Indian Country.

---

[6] Dinah Ann Clayton was seventeen; Joseph Clayton was thirteen; and Ellen Clayton was thirty.

The sergeant of the guard, H[orace] S. Eldredge, accordingly appointed five watches of 2 men to each watch for the night, to commence guard at 7 o'clock. The first watch to stand 3 hours and the other four watch 2 hours each. It is decided to continue this order of guarding during the journey over the plains, increasing or diminishing the number for each watch according to circumstances. Agreeably with this resolution a guard was set at 7 o'clock, and after spending some time conversing round the fires the camp retired to rest for the night.

[September 18, 1852. Saturday.] The morning cloudy and very cold. It rained heavy near all the night . . .

A very singular incident transpired this morning, which I will here record. The circumstances occurred with Chauncy G. Webbs team as they were ascending the hill near where we camped last night. I will record the event in nearly his own words, which is as follows:

"As we were rising a sharp, but short hill, a ring which fastened the stretchers to the tongue of the wagon gave way, and our lead horses being under good speed, drew the lines from the driver, and started off on a fast gallop. They had not proceeded but a few yards, when the whipple trees, from some unseen cause, were instantly detached from the traces.[7] The fastings were hooks secured by steel springs. The horses ran about 80 yards and stopped without injuring either themselves or the harness. There was something also very remarkable about the above mentioned ring, for we had passed over the first and second mountains with perfect apparent safety, and on examination, the ring had the appearance of having been broken for some length of time, being broken in two pieces, and both divisions being thoroughly rusted with a very small exception. This scenery was witnessed by a number of individuals."

This circumstance caused the hearts of the brethren to rejoice, and all who were acquainted with it could see that the angel of the Lord freed the horses from the whipple trees; because being

---

[7] When the mechanism for pulling the wagon broke (the stretcher frame attached to the horses' collars separated from the wagon tongue), the horses risked injury because they were still attached to the guidance system (by harness straps or traces fastened to the wooden bar called a whipple tree). Fortunately, the whipple tree detached from the harness traces, freeing the horses.

fastened by steel springs, it was utterly impossible for them to become unloosed by accident; and the fact that the four became unhooked at the same instant, proves beyond a doubt that some unseen power was present to perform such an act so speedily. The circumstance of the broken ring, is also another evidence of the interposition of an unseen power, for it had sustained the draught over the two large mountains; and when after the lead horses ran away, the brethren took hold to assist the wagon up the hill, the ring instantly broke in two pieces.

This is not the only instance that the brethren have had, that the Angel of the Lord guards us by night, and by day, and the hearts of the brethren are made to rejoice continually. It would scarcely be possible to find the same number of men traveling together, who manifest a better Spirit, than has hitherto been manifested in this camp. Every man seems to be full of the spirit of his mission, and as far as can be discovered, no one has any other object in view, but to go and fulfil the duties for which he has been called and set apart. There is no murmuring about home; no wondering how families are situated; in fact wives and children are rarely mentioned, only in prayer night and morning, and even then they are sometimes forgot. There is no complaints of hardships, not withstanding the stormy weather we have had daily. Every man's mind seems to centre in the field of his labors, and generally the leisure hours are spent in reading and profit-able conversation, although sometimes jokes are passed, and per-haps there is more loud laughter than is profitable or proper. The chaplain has commenced to call upon each man in his turn to offer up prayers, and the most prominent supplication is that we may have wisdom to fulfil our mission with honor and dignity. The blessing of the Lord have thus far attended us, and we can truly say, all is well. For my own part I never felt a more earnest desire to do my duty and magnify my calling than I do on this mission, and I earnestly pray that the Lord will enable me to do it that it may be a blessing to me in time and to all eternity.[8]

[September 19, 1852. Sunday.] Morning fine and clear, but very cold. The water in the pails was froze over. At 7 o clock camp was called together, and after singing I offered up prayers

---

[8] In this world and in the next.

with the Brethren. Elder [Orson] Hyde and his company started on their journey towards the Valley. The Brethren spent the morning in cleaning theirselves, and regulating their wagons for the journey. About 10 o'clock, part of Henry [W.] Miller's company, which was the 20th company organized, passed us; they having passed many of the other companies on the road. He gives us some encouragement concerning feed for our teams, but as a general thing he reports it very scarce near the road. At 11 o'clock the brethren were called together, and, after singing and prayer Elder Orson Pratt read the new translation of the first and second Chapters of the book of Genesis, and also the Revelation on Celestial Marriage, given to the Prophet Joseph July 12, 1843, giving many explanations and much instruction on various passages and points of doctrine contained therein, all of which will be highly beneficial to the Elders during the present mission.

At 12 o'clock Amos M. Musser and Joseph M. Simmonds arrived in Camp from the City, bringing the document for which we were waiting viz, the "Deseret News extra"[9] and the Licenses and passports for the Brethren. This caused our hearts to rejoice, as we can now proceed on our journey without delay. The afternoon was spent mostly in reading the extra News and social conversation. At 7 o'clock the brethren were called together and the duties of the day were concluded by prayer from Benjamin Brown. The evening fine and pleasant, and the spirit of peace surrounds the camp.

[September 20, 1852. Monday.] Morning fine and frosty. At quarter to 7 prayer was offered up by Charles Smith, and soon after Brothers Mussers and Simmonds started back for the City, bearing a number of letters for different persons. At a quarter to 8 the camp moved forward, travelling slowly on account of rough road. At half past 11 we halted an hour and fed the animals grain, then continued our journey till 5 o'clock, and camped on Yellow Creek, having traveled 26 miles. During the day we have met many small companies of the saints, travelling to the Valley.[10]

---

[9] The September 14, 1852, issue printed the doctrine of plural marriage which had been announced to the general church membership on August 29.

[10] About 10,000 emigrants came to Utah in 1852, the peak year from 1847–60 (John D. Unruh, Jr., *The Plains Across: The Overland Emigrants and the Trans-Mississippi West, 1840–60* [Urbana: University of Illinois Press, 1982], 85).

At night Brother David Grants horse was very sick, supposed to be caused by letting him drink freely of water after feeding him wheat.

8 o'clock the camp was called together and the throne of grace addressed by Thomas Jeremy, after which the Brethren cast lots for their places in the train, so as to avoid confusion and unpleasant feelings when travelling . . . Evening fine and cold. This evening I composed a song in relation to our present mission, to the tune of "My Heart and Lute."

[September 21, 1852. Tuesday.] Morning clear and very cold. At half past 7 o'clock the camp was called together and prayer offered by Richard Cook. At 8 oclock we continued our travells, all well and in good spirits. At half past 11 we halted on Sulphur Creek for one hour to feed. At this place there was a company of 8 or 10 men with about eight thousand sheep, bound for California. It is their intention to winter in the Valley, and proceed to their destination next spring. Their sheep look well. They started from the States with ten thousand, but they traded off the old ones, and they have also lost some by the way. The wool from such a number of sheep will be something like 10 tons, and will in all probability be left amongst the saints, and made into clothing. Thus we see that the Lord will often cause the enemies of his people to bless them, although it may grieve them to do so.

After resting an hour, we proceeded onward, the wind blowing strong, which raised vast clouds of dust and made it unpleasant travelling. About half past 4 o'clock we formed our encampment near the Copperas or Soda Spring, having traveled 25 1/4 miles.

We have again passed many companies of our brethren bound for the Valley. Their teams generally look well, and the Saints appear quite cheerful and glad to be so near the end of their journey.

In traveling through the large, rough sage brush, to get wood for a fire I burst my shoes, which is very unfortunate as I shall have to wear them to the States.[11] Some of the brethren let their

---

[11] Clayton is re-entering the United States from what had been Mexican territory when the Mormons left Nauvoo in 1846 (see Introduction, n87). In 1848, by the treaty of Guadalupe Hidalgo, Mexico ceded California and New Mexico (which included present-day Utah) to the United States. Although Utah became a territory of the United States as part of the Compromise of 1850, it would not be

fires spread amongst the sage brush, which was soon burning rapidly. Fortunately, the wind which was blowing strong carried the fire from the wagons, and after some hard fighting the fire was stayed without doing any damage. At 7 o'clock the camp was called together by the trumpeter, and prayer offered up by John Brown. Evening calm and pleasant.

[September 22, 1852. Wednesday.] . . . On arriving at Fort Bridger we halted to feed the animals and eat a little ourselves. Here we found all the brethren who had gone on before us. They were waiting anxiously for our arrival, and immediately made preparations to fall in with the company. We rested here an hour and a half, during which time many of the Brethren made purchases of Buffalo Robes, Moccasins &c. and then traveled on till 4 oclock. We formed our encampment on Blacks Fork, having travelled 21 1/4 miles. As usual we have passed a great many of the emigrating brethren, moving steadily towards the home of the saints in the vallies of the mountains. At half past 6 the brethren assembled, and Elder Preston Thomas called upon our Father in Heaven, for His blessings upon us, and for the Saints in general . . . After the meeting was dismissed, it rained heavy and finally changed to a cold snow storm.

. . . We journeyed till a quarter past 4 P.M. and again camped on Blacks Fork, about 2 miles above the road, having travelled 20 miles. A little before dark, Brother Charles Decker came into camp, having come from Fort Laramie with the United States mail in eight days[12] . . .

---

granted statehood until 1896. From March 1849 to the spring of 1851, a provisional state government called the "State of Deseret" served as the effective government. Upon receiving territorial status, the "State of Deseret" became officially designated as Utah. In the unfulfilled expectation of being granted statehood, the shadow legislature of the "State of Deseret" continued to meet until 1870 (Leonard J. Arrington, *Great Basin Kingdom: Economic History of the Latter-day Saints, 1830–1900* [Lincoln: University of Nebraska Press, 1958], 50, 437).

[12] The first mail connecting Salt Lake City to the East was carried in 1847 by emigrant trains and occasional private expresses. Beginning in 1850, the U.S. Post Office contracted with Samuel H. Woodson to deliver mail monthly between Independence, Missouri, and Salt Lake City along the "Oregon Trail," up the Platte River and through South Pass. Feramorz Little of Salt Lake City held a subcontract with Woodson between Salt Lake and Fort Laramie, the nearest settlement, to which Clayton refers in this entry. By 1856 the Brigham Young Express and Carrying Company, known as the "Y.X. Company," held the mail

At 7 o'clock the Brethren assembled, and joined in prayer with Elder Aaron F. Farr. The night was cold and windy and the atmosphere betokens more snow. After prayer I wrote a letter to President Willard Richards giving him a history of our travels thus far. I also wrote a letter to my family. These kept me up till midnight and the air being damp and chilly, I took a severe cold.

[September 24, 1852. Friday.] . . . On arriving on the banks of Green River we halted an hour to feed and eat dinner, the weather some more favorable but cloudy. We then continued our journey, fording the river at the general ford. The water runs very swift which makes it hard to ford and especially as we have to ford up stream. On the left bank of the river we saw Dimick B. Huntington encamped. He is here to trade with the Indians this winter and also is one of a company, chartered by the Legislature of Utah to build a Bridge across Green River.[13]

We went on about 5 miles beyond the Ford, and at half past 4 formed our encampment on the Big Sandy, having traveled 26 miles. We have passed companies of the brethren bound for the Valley, most of the day. Their teams do not look quite so well as those who are farther advanced on the journey, but they have generally plenty of team on each wagon; and in fact the companies this year, appear to be far better supplied with team than any other companies which have ever emigrated to Salt Lake Valley.

After the camp was formed it was reported that Elder Moses Thurston had had the misfortune to break the iron straps which fastened his wagon tongue to the axle tree, while travelling somewhere on Green River. He also has not yet arrived in Camp, and as there is a Blacksmiths Shop near Green River ford, it is supposed he has gone there to have his wagon repaired. A fire was

contract to Independence. The stations they operated were subsequently maintained by the Pony Express (LeRoy R. Hafen, *The Overland Mail 1849-1869: Promoter of Settlement, Precursor of Railroads* [New York: A.M.S. Press, 1969; reprinted from 1926 ed.], 53-62; Arrington, 162-65).

[13] The Mormons had established ferries across the North Platte and Bear rivers, and also the Green River in southwestern Wyoming. It was thought prudent to supplement difficult ferry crossings with bridges, such as the one planned at the Green. However, ferry crossings served as an important source of income. In 1853 the Utah territorial legislature allocated ten per cent of ferry proceeds to be paid to the Perpetual Emigrating Company. Thus emigrants to California and Oregon helped support Mormon emigration to Utah (Arrington, 69, 105-106).

made on the highest land for a guide to him in case he should come in the night.

At 7 o'clock the brethren assembled and joined in prayer with Elder Horace S. Eldredge. The night was fine and clear.

[September 26, 1852. Sunday.] Morning clear and frosty. At 7 o'clock the Brethren met for prayers, and joined in supplication of the Father of mercies, with Elder Moses Daily, after which the order of the day was a general time of washing, shaving, changing clothing &c. I took a Good wash in the river and felt much refreshed after changing all my clothing. I then went to work to fetch up the camp journal for the week past, having merely kept minutes in a memorandum book, and having little opportunity to write in the evening while the weather has been so very cold.

At half after 10 A.M. the trumpeter called the brethren together for public worship. The chaplain, Orson Spencer,[14] after the meeting was opened by Singing and prayer, addressed the brethren, advising them to cherish a kind feeling towards each other, and towards our animals. And also when we get abroad in the world, not to ridicule men because of their peculiar notions and ignorance, but rather to manifest a feeling of sympathy and charity for them, knowing that they are all the children of our Father in heaven, and our brethren. He thinks we will have more influence over them, by manifesting and cherishing a spirit of kindness toward them, than we shall by taking any other course.

He was followed by Elder Daniel Spencer, who agreed with the sentiments Brother Orson had advanced, and also strongly recommended the brethren not to indulge in trifling conversation, and loud laughter; but to cultivate a prayerful spirit, and devote our spare time to reading and gaining intelligence, and by this means be preparing for the mission before us . . .

It was considered best inasmuch as the weather is favorable, to go on this afternoon some 8 or 10 miles to the Little Sandy. Accordingly this afternoon at 1 P.M. we resumed our travels, but on arriving at the Little Sandy, we found it entirely destitute of

---

[14] Orson Spencer (1802–55) had served as president of the British mission from 1847 to 1849. In 1850 he became the first chancellor of the newly formed University of Deseret, the forerunner of the University of Utah. He was also a member of the Council of Fifty. Spencer traveled with Clayton to England and then unsuccessfully tried to introduce Mormonism to Prussia (a separate kingdom from 1701–1871).

grass for miles, and no prospect for camping. After counseling on the subject it was concluded to water the teams, fill our vessels with water and then proceed on till we found grass for the animals, and then stop whether there was water or not. This plan was followed accordingly and we were soon moving onward again. The whole country is barren, and destitute of grass, the places where grass is usually found being all eat off, by the vast emigration which has passed during the season. We traveled on, to the "Dry Sandy," expecting to halt there for the night, but the ground being white with alkali, it was considered decidedly unsafe to risk the teams overnight in its neighborhood, and we again traveled onward, and at half past 9 at night encamped on the "Pacific Creek" about two miles below the crossing having travelled 26 miles. The day has been fine and pleasant, and the night clear but cold. After feeding the animals and cooking a hasty supper, the brethren retired to rest without assembling for prayers; all being fatigued and glad to lay down to refresh themselves by the balmy influence of sleep.

[September 27, 1852. Monday.] . . . At the Pacific Springs we passed a large company of the Saints encamped, and preparing to travel onward. At this place also is a portion of the company who are taking the machinery for the manufacture of sugar.[15] The cattle belonging to this company are poor indeed; many of them can scarce stand on their feet and it appears to be with the greatest difficulty they can move along. Their loads generally are very heavy, but as Brother Joseph Horn is gone in to the City to procure more team, they will no doubt meet help in a few days. Brother Alonzo Le Baron says that this company generally are living on 4 ounces of flour each per day; and if they are not met soon with both team and provisions they will undoubtedly suffer. The gloomy, downcast countenances of both men and women, shows that they feel this a very severe hardship, and they

---

[15] Apostle John Taylor purchased the machinery for the Deseret Sugar Manufactory, the first sugar beet factory in America, to be located in Salt Lake City. It was carried from Liverpool on the *Rockaway* with thirty Mormon passengers, arriving April 25 in New Orleans. Fifty-two wagons containing machinery left the Missouri River on July 6 of that year and arrived in Salt Lake on October 8. Among the thirty Mormons who had sailed on the *Rockaway* was L. John Nuttall, whose excerpts from Clayton's writings form an appendix to this volume.

427

are evidently nearly discouraged. The worn out condition of the teams proves that the teamsters do not understand the nature of cattle. If this company had been under the charge of an Old Yankee farmer the cattle would doubtless have been in a much better condition. Inexperienced Englishmen or Frenchmen are not the men to drive teams across the plains as heavily loaded as these are.

A part of the company, say 6 or 8 men with 12 of the most heavily laden wagons, are back on the Sweet Water about 20 miles from the Pacific Springs, upwards of sixty head of their cattle having been scattered in a snow storm, and they cannot move untill their cattle are found. This appears to be the last company of saints on the route, and it is evident that unless a strong re-inforcement of team soon comes to their assistance, they must suffer with the cold, and will have difficulty to get to the valley before the snows of winter meets them. The machinery which they are taking along, is far beyond the expectations of anyone who has heard of it, and if the Brethren will raise the Beets, we are independent of Gentile Merchants for sugar, molasses or spirits, inasmuch as a large distillery is included with the sugar manufactory, by which can be made the best article of spirituous Liquors, equal to the best made in France or elsewhere. The hearts of the Saints will be made to rejoice when this company arrives in the Valley; and may God speed them on their way.

At half past 1 o'clock P.M. we formed our encampment on the banks of the Sweet Water, about 3 miles below the upper crossing, having travelled 20 miles by the road, and 2 miles out of the way to find grass for the teams, which is very plentiful and good. The day has been warm and pleasant. I walked most of the way and on the South Pass picked up a number of pebbles as a matter of curiosity. The afternoon was spent by most of the brethren in reading and conversation; some went hunting ducks and geese, and others were cleaning and putting their Rifles in order, as we expect to see Buffalo in a few days, and some of the Brethren have got no meat of any kind. I went out in the afternoon with my gun to get a duck, but was not fortunate enough to get any. In fact I only saw one or two during the time I was out. I noticed quantities of wagon tire and iron and parts of wagons scattered in every direction in this place. It [has] evidently been a place much frequented as a camping ground. At 7 o'clock the camp was called together, and prayer was offered up by Elder Osmyn M. Deuel, after which the evening was very pleasantly spent in conversation on times that are passed. Elder Orson Pratt read me a portion of an article he is preparing for the press on Celestial Marriage.[16] It is truly an able work, and invaluable to the Elders.

[September 28, 1852. Tuesday.] Morning fine and frosty. Soon after day break, a large head of cattle was discovered about a mile down the river from our camp. They are doubtless the missing cattle belonging to the Sugar company. At a quarter to 8 o'clock the Brethren assembled as usual, and Elder Williams Camp offered up prayers. We then proceded on our journey, and on arriving at the "Branch of Sweet Water," found the men and wagons belong to the sugar Company camped there. They had found a few of their cattle, and were glad to learn that we had discovered the remainder. The place where they camp is perfectly filthy. Many dead bodies of horses and cattle laying around, and the whole ground is literally covered with filth . . .

At half past 7 the brethren assembled . . .

President Orson Pratt spoke in favor of the suggestions of the Chaplain, and advised the brethren to improve the opportunity while we cross the plains, to get all the information we can. It was finally moved and carried *viva voce*,[17] that the doctrine of the Resurrection be the subject to commence with, and the following Brethren expressed their views in regard to it viz. Charles Smith, Jesse Turpin, George Mayer, James Park, David Wilkin, Edward Stevenson, and Edward Bunker. The views of these Brethren seemed to differ very materially on the subject, and there was very little or no light manifested by any one. It appears that the great difference in the views, is in regard to what is commonly called the baby resurrection, which idea is, that instead of the bodies being raised out of the ground &c. we shall again be born of a woman, as we were when we came into this world. Brother

---

[16] Orson Pratt prepared this article for *The Seer*, a new magazine he would begin publishing in Washington, D.C., later that year (1852). The periodical would primarily treat the subject of plural marriage and run until August 1854. See Richard S. Van Wagoner and Steven C. Walker, *A Book of Mormons* (Salt Lake City: Signature Books, 1982), 214.

[17] By word of mouth.

James Park agreed very strongly in favor of this kind of doctrine. This was a matter of astonishment to me, as I had never before heard of such a doctrine to understand it.[18]

[September 29, 1852. Wednesday.] . . . At 7 o'clock we assembled for prayers, and joined with Elder William Glover who was appointed to lead this evening, after which on being called upon I gave my views in relation to the subject under consideration last evening. I remarked that I considered, that as the keys of the Resurrection are not yet given, it is useless for us to endeavor to pry into things which are not yet revealed. And as we are not sent to preach the Resurrection, only as far as revealed, we might spend our time more profitably by studying and conversing on subjects which we understand, and which we will have to defend before the world. It was then voted that the subject be discontinued. Elder Orson Spencer, John S. Fullmer, David Wilkin, Jesse Haven and Orson Pratt made remarks on the doctrine of the resurrection, and also, as to whether Adam was created directly out of the dust of the earth, or he imbibed the principles of mortality by eating the fruits of the earth. Very warm feelings were exhibited by some of the speakers, especially Elders David Wilkin and President Pratt. Brother Wilkin's language in reference to my remarks I considered insulting, and beneath an Elder in Israel, and Brother Pratt considered that there is as much or

---

[18] Clayton's October 4, 1852, letter to Brigham Young (noted in his October 8 entry) reports on discussions regarding "baby resurrection"—resurrection by literal rebirth through a woman. This notion was related to the speculation that Adam came to earth with a resurrected body instead of being formed from the "dust of the earth." Clayton and Orson Pratt agree that "baby resurrection" is an erroneous doctrine; like Brigham Young, Clayton believes that Adam "came here with a resurrected body and became mortal by eating the fruits of the earth," although Clayton does not articulate Young's position that Adam was God. He considers Pratt's discourse on the pre-existence written for *The Seer* "one of the best works ever [to be] published by this Church . . . beyond refutation."

Clayton ends his letter with an earnest reflection to Young which is ironic in light of the difficulties which would befall him later on this mission: "I feel well, my spirits are free and buoyant," and then confides that in the past two years he has "often feared that I should lose my senses, with the care and anxiety of mind, in relation to the business which was put upon me; no man on earth knows what I have felt, for I cannot let things go at loose ends and feel satisfied as some men can." Clayton then refers to a previous confession "as I told you in your office, I left my follies in the City," presumably Salt Lake City. Without identifying the follies, he assures Young, "I dont intend to ever take these up again."

more revealed in regard to the resurrection than on any other doctrine, and he had felt anxious to hear the views of the Elders in relation to it, that we might be able to set each other right in relation to it. The views of the brethren seem to be greatly at variance in relation to this matter.

[September 30, 1852. Thursday.] Morning fine and pleasant. The Brethren all around the camp are expressing their feeling in regard to last night's discussion. The prevailing sentiment appears to be, that it will be more profitable to drop it, than to continue it any longer, inasmuch as there appears to be no light given, but rather tends to create a wider difference in opinion.

. . . Soon after we started this morning father Rhodes wounded an Antelope, which was chased and finally killed by Washington L. Jolley. This evening the brethren kindly divided it amongst the camp, and it was indeed a treat.

At a quarter past 6 the brethren assembled for prayer and joined with Elder W[illia]m Pitt. Brother Erick G. M. Hougan being quite unwell, desired the brethren to administer to him. Elders Orson Pratt, Orson Spencer and Horace S. Eldredge laid hands on him and Elder Pratt rebuked his sickness.

Elder Pratt then delivered a discourse on the doctrine of the Resurrection. He advises the Elders never to advance an idea before the world, which we cannot substantiate by revelation; and also to respect each others views and sentiments however much we may differ in opinion; inasmuch as it is but reasonable to suppose that every brother entertains his opinions honestly; and if we know anyone to be in error, and cannot convince him of his error by sound argument and revelation, not to ridicule him for his opinion, but treat him with respect . . .

His whole discourse was interesting and profitable, and was delivered in a meek and kind spirit. I have no opportunity to take full minutes, on account of having to write in the camp journal every night, besides generally having to do my share in getting wood and preparing for supper. The evening was mild and pleasant.

[October 1, 1852. Friday.] Morning cloudy and wet, but about 7 o'clock cleared off, and was more pleasant. At 20 minutes to 8 the Camp was called together for prayers, when the Chaplain called on Elder James Pace to officiate. We then continued our

431

travels, and the roads being good we moved on at a brisk speed, untill 11 o'clock, when we halted at Independence Rock to feed. At Devil's Gate we passed a small Fort, lately erected by a Frenchman for a trading post, to trade with the Indians and emigrants. He has a great number of cattle, which must be difficult to winter here as this country is very bleak and cold, and liable to deep snows in the winter season.

The Fort is composed of a good hewed log-house, and a strong yard for his stock, other sides being about 8 feet high, also built of hewed logs . . .

[October 2, 1852. Saturday.] Morning cloudy, cold and disagreeable, with about 2 inches of snow on the ground. The feed being so poor, and no fuel to be got, but sage brush, which was too wet to burn, it was concluded to roll on without waiting to attempt to cook breakfast; accordingly after prayers by Elder Orson Pratt, at 7 o'clock we started onward. The roads were muddy and very heavy travelling. Near the Willow Spring we met a mule team and carriage with two men, supposed to be the U.S. Judge and new Secretary, on their way to the Valley, but we could not learn anything from them in relation to their business or destination.[19] A few miles further we discovered four Buffalo within a quarter of a mile of the road. These being the first we have seen for a certainty on this trip, although some of the company say they saw one, or two on the Sweet Water.

A. B. Lambson, Moses Cluff, Edw[ar]d Stevenson and A[londus] D. L. Buckland gave chase and succeeded in killing one, which however proved to be a very poor Bull. After crossing the Alkali Swamp, and travelling a few miles, we took the new road to the Platte River, and at half past 2 encamped on its banks, one mile from where the road joins it, and 9 miles above the Upper Ferry, having traveled 25 miles.

The feed on the opposite side of the river was ascertained to be good, (some of the men going over on horseback for that

---

[19] Following the nationally publicized Brocchus federal report in 1851 which denounced Mormons as traitorous and immoral, President Millard Fillmore appointed Lazarus Reid as territorial chief justice; Benjamin Ferris, territorial secretary; and Leonidas Shaver, territorial associate justice in Utah. See Eugene E. Campbell, *Establishing Zion: The Mormon Church in the American West, 1847–1869* (Salt Lake City: Signature Books, 1988), 217–21; Journal 5, "Visit to Utah Settlements," n22.

purpose), much better than any we have had on the whole route. There being also plenty of timber on the opposite side and more on this, the brethren tried in various places to find a place to ford the wagons over, but the water was too deep. The brethren however carried wood over on their horses, and some also took a wagon box off and fetched over a load of wood sufficient for fuel for a number of them. The horses were taken over by the guard, who also took their blankets to stay with the Animals overnight, the whole night guard going over at the same time.

At half past 6 the camp assembled, and prayer was offered up by Elder Jesse Turpin, after which Elder Orson Pratt read to the Elders an article or treatise on Celestial marriage, and the pre-existence of man, which he is compiling for publication, and although not near finished it is truly an able and interesting document.[20] Evening pleasant.

[October 3, 1852. Sunday.] Morning foggy and very chilly, but about 10 o'clock it cleared off fine and pleasant, and the brethren were called together for public worship. The chaplain Orson Spencer addressed the meeting for an hour and a half on the doctrine of our father Adam coming to this earth in the morning of creation with a resurrected body &c. He read extracts from the New translation of the 1st and 2nd Chapters of the Book of Genesis, and the Prophecy of Enoch to maintain his position. He was listened to with great attention. He was followed by Elder Orson Pratt on the same subject, who read more copiously from the above mentioned works, followed by deep and reasonable remarks. He takes the literal reading of the scriptures for his guide, and maintains that God took the dust of the earth and moulded a body into which he put the spirit of man just as we have generally understood from the scriptures; while Brother Spencer endeavors to substantiate the position taken by President Young viz. that Adam came to this earth with a resurrected body, and became

---

[20] Pratt, the ranking church leader on this trip, developed his articles for *The Seer* along the trail. He discussed his material with the missionaries, preparing them to preach plural marriage in England. Also in *The Seer*, Pratt developed Smith's notion of man existing in the mind of God before birth, an idea that evolved into a doctrine of man's preexistence. See Blake T. Ostler, "The Idea of Preexistence in Mormon Thought," in Gary James Bergera, ed., *Line Upon Line: Essays on Mormon Doctrine* (Salt Lake City: Signature Books, 1987), 127–44.

mortal by eating the fruits of the earth which was earthy. The subject was finally left in much difficulty and obscurity as it has been from the beginning. The Brethren are evidently getting tired of arguing on a subject in regards to which so little is known, or satisfaction desired; and on which there is so great a difference of opinion.[21] Elder Pratt advised the Brethren to pray to God for a knowledge of the true principles and it appears evident that when ever the question is decided, it will have to be by revelation from God.

At a quarter past 3 the brethren assembled again, and after singing and prayer Elders Charles Smith, George Mayer, Jesse Haven and James P. Pack expressed their views on the subject of the morning's discourses, without however bringing any new light in regard to it. The knowledge of the truth in relation to the whole matter, is in the bosom of God, and when He sees fit to Give the key, it will be plain and easy to be understood; like all other true principles emanating from him, will cause the hearts of his servants to rejoice. Truly we are shortsighted beings, and are constantly dependent on him for all the light and good we enjoy. In the midst of all the discussions, notwithstanding the difference of opinion, a good feeling has generally been manifested and the soul and only object of the Brethren is evidently to arrive at a knowledge of true principles.

This afternoon Aaron F. Farr, John Brown and John C. Hall have started out with pack mules to try to kill an Elk, as many signs have been noticed where they have been recently. They intend to stay from camp overnight, and join us again at the Upper Platte Ferry. The evening was cloudy with some rain; the brethren singing in different parts of the camp. At a quarter to 8 the brethren who started to hunt Elk, returned to camp in consequence of the appearance of rain. They succeeded in killing a black tailed Deer, which they brought into camp. At 8 o'clock the weather became fine and mild.

---

[21] Orson Pratt disagreed with Brigham Young over the teaching that Adam was God as he here disputes with Orson Spencer. This issue is anticipated in the September 29 entry. On Adam-God, see Journal 3, "Nauvoo Temple," n39, and David John Buerger, "The Adam-God Doctrine," *Dialogue: A Journal of Mormon Thought* 15 (Spring 1982): 14–58; on Pratt's conflicts with Young, see Gary James Bergera, "The Orson Pratt/Brigham Young Controversies," *Dialogue: A Journal of Mormon Thought* 13 (Summer 1980): 7–58.

[October 4, 1852. Monday.] After prayer by Elder George Mayer, we resumed our journey at a quarter to 8 o'clock. I started out on foot. Brother [Thomas] Treat showed a low disposition because Brother [William] Pitt had cooked us some cakes for breakfast at the request of Brother [William] Glover. He threw them down wrathfully in Brother Pitt's presence. In fact of late he is generally unwilling to cook himself, and is angry if anyone else does it. He is truly a disagreeable man to travel with . . .

[October 5, 1852. Tuesday.] This morning after prayers by W[illia]m A. Empey the camp started at a quarter to 8 o'clock. The roads are much improved since yesterday and we had fair travelling. About 3 miles above Deer Creek, we came upon a large party of Cheyenne Indians, and one or two Lodges of Crows with them. They are here on their Buffalo hunt, and have their Squaws and Papooses with them, and a great many horses. Many of them came over the river to us, (they being camped on the north side) and appear very friendly. They are generally a tall, robust set of men, and appear clean when compared with many tribes of Indians. In fact they are the noblest set of Indians I have ever seen, and have generally pleasing countenances. At a quarter past 12 we halted for noon on Deer Creek. Brother Williams Camp's horse was taken very sick, which prolonged the noon halt to near two o'clock, at which time we resumed our onward course, taking the road through the Black Hills. At 4 o'clock, we encamped on the "Fourche Boise," having travelled 24 miles. Brother Camp's horse is yet quite sick.

We found here a small party of the Chayenne Indians, several of whom came into camp. Some of the Brethren tried to trade with them, but they appear indifferent about trading, unless they are offered more than full value for their robes or ponies. On account of their being camped so near us, it was thought wisdom to increase the guard to 6 men on each watch, instead of 4, which was accordingly done.

At a quarter to 7 met for evening service, and after singing and prayer by Elder Leonard I. Smith, the following brethren spoke their feelings on various subjects, bearing testimony to the truth viz. Nathan T. Porter, John Perry, Jesse Turpin, Washington L. Jolley, Jacob F. Secrist, and Nathan T. Porter. The best of feelings prevailed and peace surrounds the camp.

[October 6, 1852. Wednesday.] The camp being together, prayer was offered by Elder Isaac Allred, and at a quarter to 8 we continued our journey. After travelling about 6 miles, Brother John McDonald had the misfortune to break his hind axle while descending a very steep hill. The linchpin by some means worked out, and the wheel coming off, let all the weight of the load on the axle which struck on its point to the ground. This caused us to halt at a quarter after 11 on the "A La Prele." He contrived to bring his wagon into camp, and in an hour and a half from the time we halted, he had his axle spliced and we again proceeded onward.

We travelled till half past 4 then camped on the "A La Bonte" about 2 miles below the crossing having travelled 26 miles. The day has been very windy, towards night the roads were very dusty indeed.

At half past 6 the brethren assembled for prayers and joined with Elder Moses Clough, after which Captain Daniel Spencer proposed, that inasmuch as many of the Brethren would want to purchase feed for their animals, and perhaps other things at Fort Laramie, and as they will be more likely to take advantage of us, if every man goes to purchase for himself, we appoint a committee to do our trading for us, which was agreed to by unanimous vote.

On motion Horace S. Eldredge was appointed said committee. John Brown was also appointed to assist Brother Eldredge in the business.

Captain Spencer then recommended the brethren to leave their names, together with the amount, they wished to purchase with me, as clerk, either tomorrow or by Friday morning.

A[ndrew] L. Lamoreaux offered as a motion that W[illia]m Pitt be excused from guarding as he is constantly wanted in camp as trumpeter. The motion passed by unanimous vote.

There is quite a joke in this motion, which I will relate. There has been considerable murmuring for sometime because some of the camp officers are exempted from guard duties. The principle complaint has been against John Brown and Horace S. Eldredge as they consider that these Brethren have no extra duties more than any other man in camp. The motion to excuse Brother Pitt was merely got up to agitate the question, so that they could have the privilege of politely expressing their feelings in regard to Brother Eldredge and Brown, but instead of the question being brought up in regard to Brother Pitt the motion to excuse Brother Pitt from guarding passed without a dissenting voice, or a word said against it, and thus they failed to accomplish their object and made the matter worse than it was before.

The Captain of the guard H[orace] S. Eldredge then advised the brethren to be vigilant when on guard in the night, and to have their arms and ammunition with them so that in case of necessity they would be ready at a moment's warning. He also cautioned them against keeping caps on their guns to avoid accidents. The night was very windy with some rain, and in fact there was every appearance for a very stormy night. Camp all well.

[October 7, 1852. Thursday.] . . . Half past seven the Camp was called together and prayer offered by Elder John Robinson, after which Elder Orson Spencer made some remarks, advising the brethren to keep a good spirit, and not to be backward to express their feelings in our meetings, as it must be much easier to speak here among the Elders of Israel, where the spirit of God reigns, than amongst the Gentiles where the spirit of darkness has dominion.

Remarks were then made by Chauncy G. Webb, Williams Camp, Sylvester H. Earl, Joseph Mille[r], and John Brown, each testifying of their faith in the work and their determination to fill their missions with honor and dignity. The Brethren spoke by the spirit of God, and it was as good a meeting, if not better than any we have had on the road.

[October 8, 1852. Friday.] The camp assembled about the usual hour and joined in prayer with Elder George C. Riser, then resumed our travels. On arriving at the warm springs we halted an hour for noon, then we proceded on until half past 3 and camped on the North Fork of the Platte River, 7 1/4 miles above Fort Laramie, having traveled 22 1/4 miles.

Brothers Orson Pratt, John Brown and David Wilkin took the prairie road from warm Springs, and went direct to Fort Laramie, to make inquiries concerning prospect for our purchasing flour, grain, meat &c.

About 3 miles above this place there is a new Fort, apparently lately erected, also a Blacksmith Shop. A number of white men are residing there no doubt to trade and work for emigrants as well as Indians. From them we learned that our chances to buy grain and bread stuff, at the Fort, (Laramie) is poor. They say that flour is $9.50 per 100 lbs, and corn from 6 to 8 dollars per bushel.

There are about 40 Lodges of Sioux Indians within 4 miles from our camp, about 30 of which are on the other side opposite to us. Many of them came over to camp. They appear friendly and peaceable, although one of them was caught stealing an ax, but it was taken from him without any difficulty.

At half past 6, the camp assembled for prayers and joined with Elder Samuel I. Burgess; after which those who intend to purchase flour and grain at Laramie reported the amount to me which kept me busy until late at night.

For several days I have been writing a letter to President Young whenever I could get a little opportunity, informing him of our travels thus far. At this place I finished it, and also one to my family which I shall mail at the Fort.

[October 9, 1852. Saturday.] This morning we had prayers as usual after which we proceded on our journey taking the road over the Bluffs to Fort Laramie, at which place we arrived at 10 o'clock and halted to do our trading. Elder John Brown had already made arrangements with Lieut[enant] R. B. Barnett, the commanding Officer for 20 lbs of flour each person, for the whole company. This was all the law authorized him to let us have, but as there are many who need none, this amount will be abundant supply for those who are in want.

I got an order of Lieut[enant] Barnett, for 1700 lbs of Flour, and some Bacon, and immediately went and drew the whole amount from the commissary.

I had then to divide it amongst the brethren according to the money they paid me and in the operation had to make up some money myself, as the brethren paid me five franc pieces at 95 cents each, and the commissary would only take them at 90 cents each. Sovereigns were also counted to me at $4.85 and I could only get $4.80 for them.[22] Many of the brethren bought Pork,

---

[22] Foreign coins, such as the British gold sovereign and the French franc, were frequently used in the new American nation. Earlier England had limited the supply of money to the American colonies in order to force them to trade solely with England using bills of exchange, which were not accepted anywhere else. The

Bacon, Hams, Apples, Peaches, rice &c. themselves, independent of the general purchase. Flour was $10.50 for a hundred pounds, Pork 12 1/2 cents per lb, Hams and Bacon 16 cents, dried apples 16 cents, and dried Peaches 12 1/2 cents per lb. The flour was damaged some, having been wet. Hams and bacon 16 cents a pound, dry apples 16 cents a pound, and dried peaches 12 1/2 cents a pound. All the other articles were good, and the prices we had to pay was merely first cost and carriage.

Brother [William] Glover and myself had our feelings much hurt by [] Brother Treat's conduct. Our grain for all the horses was all consumed, and for some days past we have been trying to make arrangements to purchase here. But whenever we would begin to talk to Brother Treat on the subject, the only answer we could get was, "I know my own business."

W[illia]m Pitt and W[illia]m Glover and Washington L. Jolley sold their worn down horses for $30 each, and Jesse Turpin sold his poor, blind horse for $12. These animals had become lame and very poor, and were of but little use. It is considered that they are well Sold, as no one believes that any of them, would be able to go through the journey.

At 12 o'clock having concluded our trading, we again proceeded onward, and travelled about 14 miles down the river, taking the South Side, then camped at 4 o'clock on the banks of the Platte, having traveled about 21 1/4 miles.

There are two trading stations between Fort Laramie and this point, and upwards of 120 Lodges of Indians in the neighborhood. At the lower trading house we noticed a stack of wheat in the sheaf. Wheat is offered at $4 per bushel, Sugar and Coffee 50 cents per lb, tea $2.50 per lb. Four of the brethren suceeded in trading each a worn down horse with the Indians for a good pony each; the Indians following the camp and appearing very anxious to trade, which was indeed unexpected by the brethren. This again convinces us that the Lord is with us and favors us every

---

colonies, and later the young nation, used any foreign coins they could get: English pounds, French francs, Spanish dollars (which were cut into "pieces of eight," two "bits" of which equalled a quarter of a dollar). The U. S. started to mint coins in 1792 but included foreign coins as part of the monetary system until 1857, when they were removed from circulation. These coins were valued according to the amount of gold or silver they contained. For a discussion of paper currency, see Journal 4, "Pioneer Trek West," n68.

day for it seems unreasonable to suppose that the Indians would have traded for such animals as they have, unless they were impelled by a superior power.

At half past 6 o'clock P.M. the brethren met on call of the Cornet, and prayer was offered up by Elder W[illia]m Woodward. The evening was spent by the following brethren speaking their feelings, bearing testimony viz. Samuel Glasgow, Leonard J. Smith, George Mayer, Dan Jones, Spicer Crandel, Edward Bunker, Millen Atwood, and Daniel A. Miller. The best of feelings prevailed, prophecies were delivered and all is well.

[October 10, 1852. Sunday.] The morning being cloudy, and some appearance of stormy weather, and it being the general opinion, that our teams fail as much or nearly so, when laying bye as when travelling unless they are fed on grain; it was considered wisdom to travel today while the road is dry and good and the weather fair . . .

Thus another week has passed away and this camp has been blessed beyond our expectations, everything appears to work in our favor, and the kindness and care of our Father in heaven, is daily and hourly realized by the brethren; and we feel to give him praise and gratitude of our hearts continually.

The same good spirit prevails over the minds of the brethren, as has been hitherto manifested, and the faith and joy in the mission, appears to increase in the minds of the brethren as the distance between us and our destination is lessened. Scarcely a jar, or cross word is heard in the camp, but the motto is, Our mission before Us. May this spirit increase daily. Even so, Amen.

[October 11, 1852. Monday.] This morning the ground is white with snow, the weather cloudy and cold, and the snow falling pretty freely. At 8 o'clock we assembled for prayer and joined with Elder Erick G. McHougan. A few of the brethren appear to think this snow storm is sent as a scourge for our travelling on yesterday, but such an idea cannot be substantiated, as it is well known that the storms we endured are light indeed, when compared with storms which have been a few days ahead of us all the time. There are but few however, who have such feelings, and is to be hoped they will soon think different . . .

While passing Scotts Bluff, many of the brethren through a curiosity to visit them, turned off the road and soon found themselves surrounded by a truly picturesque scenery. They had to descend into deep pits and climb steep precipices until they were well tired and glad to get to their wagons to rest. They represent the scenery as truly grand, and well worth a traveler's labor to visit, but all represent the passage through as very laborious. In the evening the brethren were called together and prayer offered up by Elder Orson Pratt. The evening being chilly and the air damp, it was voted not to prolong the meeting and it was accordingly closed.

[October 12, 1852. Tuesday.] Morning fine but frosty and cold. The camp assembled for prayers at half after 8 and joined with Elder William Walker. After prayers we continued our journey and travelled till a quarter past 1, then halted one hour to feed. This morning we passed a couple of men on mules, driving 5 yoke of Oxen before them. They state they have been down the river to meet a train of goods, destined for the second trading house, east of Laramie; but 25 yoke of the cattle they took down to assist the train, broke away in a Stampede and cannot be found. Soon after 2 o'clock we proceeded on again, and travelled until half past 4, then camped on the banks of the river, having travelled about 26 miles during the day.

A while before we camped, we passed 2 carriages belonging to the train before referred to. The owners of the carriages had several Sioux Squaws and Papooses with them. They report that a party of Pawnees fell on a small band of Sioux, and killed several of the men, besides stealing some 17 horses. They are taking the Squaws and children to Fort Laramie.

At half past 6 the camp assembed at the call of the trumpet . . .

[October 13, 1852. Wednesday.] The Morning fine and pleasant. It has been suggested this morning that it will be wisdom to start a little earlier in the day, and camp sooner at night, to give a better opportunity to get through camp duties before dark, and also have the guard set sooner, as the evenings are growing longer, and it now becomes necessary to have 6 watches each night instead of five as heretofore. Accordingly at half past 7 the brethren joined in prayer with Elder Moses Thurston, and immediately after started forward. We journeyed till 11 o'clock then halted near an hour to feed; after which we traveled until 4 P.M. and

441

once more camped on the banks of the river, the day's journey being about 25 miles. The roads have generally been sandy and very heavy travelling, but the feed so far has been good.

Soon after we stopped, the mail from Independence arrived, and halted near us for a few hours, designing to go on about 11 miles further tonight. The mail carrier States that one of the U.S. Judges for Utah, supposed to be the chief Justice, is in company with him, but is so much afraid of the cold that it is uncertain whether he will dare to go further than Fort Laramie this season.

The other Judge, (Reed of New York) came 12 miles above Fort Kearney, and then became so much alarmed on account of Indians, that they had to take him back and leave him at Fort Kearney.

At half past 6 the brethren were called together, and after prayer by Elder Joseph Millet, the evening was spent in preaching by Elders John McDonald, Samuel Glasgow, Jesse Haven, Darwin Richardson, David Wilkin, Jesse Turpin, John Brown, George Mayer, Edward Stevenson and Benjamin Brown. The subject under consideration was the question, Will those who are raised to a Telestial and Terrestrial glory ever be exalted to a Celestial glory? The vision given to the Prophet Joseph Smith and Sidney Rigdon being taken as ground work for arguments for and against the doctrine. Elder Jesse Haven, who introduced the subject, maintained the opinion that they never can be exalted to a Celestial glory; the other Brethren spoke earnestly in favor of the contrary, and argued that the work of redemption never can be complete on any other principle. President Orson Pratt was asked to offer some remarks on the subject, but he begged to be excused as the matter has not been in his mind lately, he being otherwise engaged.

The brethren appeared to be anxious to learn truth, and have manifested a very good feeling throughout the meeting.

[October 14, 1852. Thursday.] After prayer by Elder Noah T. Guyman we took an early start and traveled 24 miles, then encamped for the night about 1 mile west of Ash Hollow. We have had considerable sandy road, and consequently travelled slow.

During the noon halt Brother George Percy and several others killed a Buffalo; which not withstanding its being very old, proved quite a treat for supper. A few miles back we passed a train of 17 wagons, apparently heavily loaded, on their way to one of the trading houses east of Laramie. It is said that they are laden principally with corn, but ask seven dollars per bushel for it. We have noticed large herds of Buffalo on the north side of the river, but very few on this side. This is probably in consequence of so many persons travelling on this side. There has not a day past since we left Fort Laramie, but we have passed either Indians, trading establishments, or men from the States traveling up the river.

After prayer by Elder Daniel Toner, the brethren as usual spent the evening in endeavoring to enlighten each others minds, and in searching after truth. The doctrine contained in the vision talk[ed] over last evening, was again brought up by the Chaplain Elder Orson Spencer, who gave his views in short in regard to it. He considers that the distinctions between the Telestial, Terrestrial and Celestial glories, will forever be maintained, notwithstanding the inhabitants of the two former may advance in knowledge, wisdom, power &c. He was followed by Elder Jesse Haven, after which President Orson Pratt delivered a very interesting discourse on that and other subjects, after which the meeting was closed. The evening fine and pleasant.

[October 15, 1852. Friday.] This morning after prayer by Elder Jacob Houtz, we took an early start and proceeded up Ash Hollow, on the road leading to the nearest point on the South Fork of the Platte River. The road for about 3 miles up Ash Hollow was very sandy, and the ascent up the Bluffs is very steep indeed. After that the road is rolling and good. Numerous large herds of Buffalo were grazing on both sides of the road as far as we could see. We arrived on the banks of the "South Fork" at half past 12 and halted for noon; some of the teams appearing much tired and ready to give out. Elder David Grant's horse which he was driving loose, having completely failed, ran off with a herd of Buffalo, and he had a hard chase to catch him again.

The buffalo on both sides the "South Fork" are very numerous, the ground being literally black with them as far as we could see; in consequence of which, and the teams requiring rest as

443

well as a number of the brethren having no meat, the camp voted unanimously to lay bye tomorrow and [en]deavor to get a supply of meat to last to the Missouri River.

After halting an hour myself and most of the footmen started to wade across. We found it laborious work on account of the quick sand, and we were glad to get over. The teams and wagons started soon after and all got across safe. On the East bank we found a company of Frenchmen with 5 very heavily loaded wagons, some of them having upwards of 4 tons in. They say they are going to Deer Creek to trade with the Indians who are already there, and others whom they expect to meet there viz. Sioux, Shoshones, Crows and Arrapahoes. They also state that they intend to build a firm and substantial Bridge, over the North Fork of the Platte River 5 miles above Deer Creek.

We journeyed on down the South Fork, untill a quarter past 4, then encamped for the night having traveled 28 miles. Elder John Brown killed a Buffalo on the west side of the river, and several of the brethren went with horses and mules to fetch in the meat. They got back to camp at 7 o'clock.

During the evening, after prayer by Elder James Park, the brethren continued to express their views on the doctrine under consideration last evening and the evening previous. The following brethren occupied the evening viz. James Park, John Perry, Charles Smith, George Mayer, Millen Atwood and Sylvester H. Earl. President Orson Pratt then advised the brethren when they attempted to reason on the person of God, to be careful not to indulge in levity, nor to speak of God irreverently. He brought forth proofs sufficient from revelations already given to satisfy any reasonable mind, that the Gods do not eternally progress in knowledge, or wisdom, but shewed that when they arrive at a fulness they have learned all there is to learn. He then referred to the peace and union and the desire after knowledge there is in this camp; and also demonstrated that the Lord is pleased to see us search after the mysteries of his kingdom, for this is eternal life to know God and Jesus Christ whom He has sent. He further showed that there is no difference in opinion between him and President Young in regard to the Gods progressing in knowledge, but the apparent difference arises from our not taking time to connect the ideas.[23] When President Young speaks by the power of the spirit there is frequently such a flood of revelation that he has not time to explain every particular, and unless we have the spirit of God resting upon us, it is easy to get wrong ideas.

Jesse Turpin offered some remarks on the subject and kind of conversation followed amongst several of the brethren. It is evident that the Elders generally are diligently searching after knowledge and God is bestowing it upon them. The camp is abundantly blessed every day.

[October 16, 1852. Saturday.] The brethren assembled for prayers as usual and joined with Elder Thomas Jeremy; after which Captain Daniel Spencer called for the minds of the brethren in relation to staying here tomorrow also, and keeping the Sabbath. It appears to be the prevailing feeling, that it will be better for our teams, to travel a few hours, and get to fresh feed, accordingly it was voted that we start at the usual hour in the morning and travel till 11 o'clock; then halt on the first good feed we come to and spend the afternoon in public worship, at which time President Orson Pratt intends to deliver a discourse, to prove the God we worship is the same God that is worshipped by millions of other worlds besides ours.

The meeting was then dismissed to be assembled at the sound of the Cornet, either before or after dark this evening according to circumstances.

A number of the brethren then started out to hunt Buffalo; while the remainder spent the forenoon, in washing, repairing their clothing and reading. The Buffalo which Elder John Brown killed last evening was distributed, and the brethren went to jerking it for the journey. About noon others were brought into camp which were disposed of in the same way. There has been 5 Cows and 2 Calves killed during the day, which

---

[23] In spite of his attempts to appear to be in agreement with Brigham Young, Pratt's theological differences with Young on this point remained distinct. From the premise that God knows all things past, present, and future, Pratt concluded that God (the Gods) are no longer acquiring knowledge. Brigham Young saw God and God's children as forever progressing. See Gary James Bergera, "Grey Matters: Does God Progress in Knowledge?" *Dialogue: A Journal of Mormon Thought* 15 (Spring 1982): 1:179–81. See also Bergera, "Orson Pratt/Brigham Young Controversies."

will be an abundant supply for the whole camp, if it is all brought in and properly taken care of . . .

At half past 10 o'clock, the brethren being all gone to rest except the guard, the horses took a stampede, the whole band galloping close past the wagons, and going off in a near west course. A scene of excitement now ensued, such as is rarely witnessed except in similar occasions. Every man was on the alert in less than a minute and immediate pursuit given. Fortunately some of the hindmost of the horses were caught by the Lariettes, and on these the brethren pursued the others. The general fear was that it was the Indians that had caused the Stampede, and if so it was impossible to estimate the danger we were placed in, the night being very dark. Indians might be concealed all around the camp, and we not know it. Elder Edward Martin, who was one of the guard on duty at the time, stated that he had observed a strange horse come towards our animals up the river bank, and had gone within ten rods of it, to assure himself of the fact; and that when he got that near it the horse started, and its sudden movement caused something to jingle like a cow bell, at which the whole band took fright and galloped off, the strange horse running in amongst them, causing the jingling sound before mentioned which increased the fright of our animals.

Within twenty minutes after the Stampede, the brethren began to return to camp, one or two at a time, always bringing some of the animals with them. At a quarter past 1 the whole company had returned with all the animals, having the strange horse with them also. This horse had full equipment on it, viz. Saddle, Bridle and Martingales[24]: also 2 good blankets, shot pouch, powder horn &c. There was a tin cup tied to the pummel of the saddle, which sounded something like a cow bell when the horse moved, and this was no doubt the cause of the nights trouble and alarm. When the horses were brought back to camp, those which were considered the most likely to run, some of them hobbled, and some tied down to stakes; yet notwithstanding this precaution, they started again twice before morning but were soon secured.

When animals are frightened in the night on the plains, so as to cause them to Stampede, it appears that they will sometimes

[24] A martingale is a part of the harness used to hold down the horse's head.

be days and even weeks before they forget it; and every sound whether unusual, or sounds to which they have become familiar causes them to startle, and appears to fill them with fear. Perhaps the smell of fresh meat tends to increase their fright.

[October 17, 1852. Sunday.] This morning all is well, and quiet reigns in the camp, but the excitements of last night is uppermost in all our thoughts. At 8 o'clock the camp was called together and prayer offered up by Elder Elias Gardner. Immediately afterwards we journeyed onward till half past 12, then encamped for the day, having traveled about 15 miles.

After partaking of some dinner at 3 o'clock we assembled for public worship. The meeting was opened with prayer by Elder Daniel Spencer, after which President Orson Pratt delivered a very interesting discourse on the nature and character of the God we worship. Showing that he is the same God who is worshippped by all the millions of worlds besides this. That it is not the person of God we worship, but the attributes or properties which constitute the Godhead. He also proved that there is a substance which fills all the elements of eternity called the Holy Spirit, separate from the personage of the Holy Spirit. He referred to many passages in the Bible, Book of Covenants, and modern revelations, to sustain his arguments. The discourse was highly interesting and full of instructive matter.

At half past 7 o'clock, at the first sound of the cornet to call the camp together for prayers, the horses took another Stampede, but the guard being on the alert, and those in camp being speedily on the ground, most of the animals were prevented from getting away, and those which did run were soon surrounded and brought back. Thus far the mercy of the Lord has preserved the brethren from any accident, although they have been in great danger when the horses have taken fright of being trampled down by them, but none have suffered only from extra labor and excitement.

A while after the foregoing scene, the animals were again startled by the howling of a wolf, but were calmed before they would break away. The brethren on guard were advised to keep up a continual conversation amongst the animals, which they did and sometimes sang hymns, and it is thought that this tended to allay the excitement as the animals were afterwards peaceable till morning . . .

447

[October 18, 1852. Monday.] After prayer by the Chaplain Orson Spencer at 8 o'clock we moved forward. We passed a company of four wagons and several horsemen with about four thousand sheep on their way to Fort Laramie to winter, designing to proceed to California in the spring. Many of their sheep appeared to be very lame with travelling.

We traveled about 22 miles, and at 3 o'clock again camped on the banks of the South Fork. Some of our animals appear ready to give out, and all are failing in a greater or less degree. At 6 o'clock we met for prayers, and joined with Elder Nathan T. Porter. All is peace in the camp.

[October 19, 1852. Tuesday.] Every thing has been still and peaceful the past night, and the horses appear to have got over their fright. After prayers by Washington L. Jolley, we resumed our journey at half past 7 o'clock. The road soon leaves the river and passes over the Bluffs for near 20 miles. We nooned at a small creek near the road, then continued on till a quarter past 4 when we formed our encampment on the banks of the main Platte, having travelled about 27 miles. Some of the teams did not get into camp till near dark. At half past 6 we assembled for prayers and joined with Elder B. T. Mitchell after which Captain Daniel Spencer stated that some of the brethen thought that we are driving faster than our teams can bear, and they seem to think we shall have to leave many of our horses on the road unless we travel slower. He also stated that many of the brethren are near out of feed, and went to make some arrangements in regard to purchasing more before we get to Kearney . . . One or two of the brethren appear to think that if we travel a less distance each day our teams would recruit[25] on the prairie grass; but the general opinion is that there is little if any nourishment in this prairie grass, and unless we can get more substantial feed our teams will fail, even if we don't travel at all.

All appear to think it wisdom not to travel out of a walk, and by starting earlier in a morning it is believed we can average 20 or 25 miles a day, and not injure the teams anymore than to lay still. It was finally voted unanimously 1st that we travel on a

[25] To recruit is a rare term meaning to regain one's energy.

walk, and not let the animals trot, the number of hours to be travelled each day to be decided by the Captain and Pilot.

2nd that we start each morning by 7 o'clock.

3rd that the Trumpeter call up the Camp each morning at 5 o'clock. The meeting was then closed.

[October 20, 1852. Wednesday.] The brethren were up this morning near two hours before sunrise, and after prayer by Elder Canute Peterson, at 10 minutes before 7 we moved away, and travelled on a walk. The teams generally appear as well as usual. We halted an hour and half for noon, then journeyed till a quarter after 4 and camped on the banks of the Platte, having traveled about 22 miles. Brother Williams Camp is again considerably behind, but he would not start this morning untill near an hour after the rest had left. He appears very obstinate and determined to have his own way let the consequence be as it may. It appears he has taken offence at some remarks made last night, in relation to his having loaded his team down with Buffalo meat &c. and is unwilling on that account to travel in company with us.

Captain Spencer voluntarily offered him the use of strange horse, to enable him to keep in company with the other wagons, but this offer he refused to accept, and said he preferred to be left rather than travel with the company. This makes the brethren generally feel bad, as no one wishes nor is willing to leave him in the road; but he appears determined to be left or otherwise detain the camp unnecessarily. The brethren have offered to take part of his load, or otherwise help him all they can; but he refuses every offer of assistance which has been tendered to him, and appears very wilful.

We passed today 2 carriages with some merchants on their way to Fort Laramie where they intend to winter, and then proceed to Salt Lake with their merchandise in the spring. We are informed that Judge Reed is in company with them, all bound for Salt Lake next spring.

Soon after 6 o'clock the camp assembled as usual for public worship . . .

Elder Dan Jones asked the question, whether the spirit we receive is a personage, or merely the elements of light and truth, the particles of the substance which fill the immensity of space &c. Elder Preston Thomas spoke in reply and illustrated his ideas, 449 by relating the operations of [the] spirit on himself. While he was speaking two fires were noticed, west of us. The farthest one was supposed to originate from the grass taking fire where we camped last night, as it was observed to burst out and spread after we left this A.M. The other is supposed to be Brother Camp's fire as he has not yet arrived among us. Elder John Mayer travelled in company with him this afternoon, and left him a little while before we stopped to overtake the camp supposing that Brother Camp was immediately after him; but it appears that as soon as Brother Mayer left him he has turned off the road and camped alone.

These facts being related to the brethren by Elder Horace S. Eldredge, a council was held to decide what is best to be done. The brethren are still willing to help Brother Camp all they can; and none wish to have him behind, if he can be prevailed upon to go along with us. Elder Orson Pratt proposed that a committee be appointed to wait on Brother Camp immediately, to ascertain his feelings, make propositions to assist him, and endeavor to encourage him to go along with us, because if he breaks off from the company he will lose great blessings and get into darkness. This was put to vote and passed unanimously. Preston Thomas and Capt[ai]n Daniel Spencer were selected by unanimous vote, to be the committee, and they proceeded forthwith to fulfil their mission. They however returned unsuccessful, not being able to find where he was camped.

[October 21, 1852. Thursday.] This morning Capt[ai]n Daniel Spencer took the strange horse which came into camp last Saturday evening, up to Elder Williams Camp to assist him on his way. It is believed that he is now feeling better and will go on cheerfully.

After prayer by Elder John A. Hunt, at 20 minutes past 7 we continued our journey. The morning being cool, the teams walked at a good speed. Last night the U.S. Mail from Fort Laramie tarried a little above us, and went on again early this morning . . .

[October 22, 1852. Friday.] This morning the Camp assembled for prayer at a quarter past 7 and joined with Elder Samuel Glasgow. We then continued our travels. We had travelled but a short time before we met a United States Officer, with several men in company on their way to Fort Laramie. They stated that the mail carrier told them that we were burning all the grass off as we travelled down the river, which they considered very wrong, as there are teams passing constantly to and from Fort Laramie, which require the grass for subsistence. We corrected the statement and told them there was no truth in the report. In fact we have only known of the fire breaking out from our fires once during the whole journey. The report however appears to have created considerable excitement at Fort Kearney, but we have hopes that Messrs. Kinkead and [Cogswell] will correct the statement.

After halting an hour for noon, we journeyed on, and soon passed a train of 13 heavily laden wagons, bound for Fort Laramie to Winter, but we are told their final destination is Salt Lake City.

The teamsters report that the Pawnees have followed them, and stole 2 mules and 3 oxen which they recovered back by pursuing the thieves to Fort Kearney. At half past 4 we camped at little above Grand Island, having travelled about 21 miles. The teams have generally travelled well, but many are failing daily. Brother [Andrew L.] Lamoreaux left his horse about two miles back.

At half past 6 we assembled for worship and after prayer by Elder James Pace it was voted that Elder Horace S. Eldredge proceed tomorrow in advance of the train, to ascertain the prospect to purchase grain, flour &c. at the Fort. Also that Captain Daniel Spencer report the [stray] horse to the Commander of the Fort, and if it is not claimed, then to say no more about it, but to take it along with us.

The Sergeant of the guard cautioned the brethren to be vigilant when on guard duty, as we are now liable to have our animals stole by the Pawnees. The evening was then spent in discussing the operation of the Holy Spirit. The subject was introduced by Elder Dan Jones this evening, and remarks followed by Elders Orson Spencer, George Mayer, Chauncy G. Webb, J[oh]n L. Fullmer and Orson Pratt.

[October 23, 1852. Saturday.] This morning we joined in prayer with Elder John C. Hall, then continued our journey to Fort Kearney, where we arrived a little before noon. The company went to work to purchase flour, corn, fruit and groceries. Brother H[orace] S. Eldredge had endeavored to make the necessary arrangements, but none could be made to benefit the Camp.

451

Captain Wharton, the commanding officer, would only let us have 2 barrels of flour for the whole company, alleging that he has received no stores from Government, and dare not spare more. We got the 400 lbs at 6 1/2 cents per lb, and weighed out 6 lbs to each person for the time being. We got all the rice, dried apples, Peaches and groceries we wanted. Several of the brethren sold their worn out horses, and got for them all they were worth in money. After we got through trading at half past 3 we journeyed on, and camped on the banks of the Platte, having travelled today about 15 miles.

The camp is well suppl[i]ed with horse feed, but had to give $3.50 per Bushel for shelled corn. Brother [Thomas M.] Treat bought 4 bushels of Corn, although he had intimated that he had no money. One of his horses is very poor indeed and it will require kind treatment to get him to the Missouri River. Brother Treat is a hard teamster and very unkind to his team. But we cannot say anything to him. I had the good fortune to get $10 for my double barrel shotgun while at the Fort. This is all the money I have for the remainder of the journey. It is generally believed that we can get to the Missouri River, in about 8 days. Should we be longer than that, many will lack bread stuff.

Soon after we camped, 5 or 6 Indians came down from the Fort and camped on the island near by us. They have four of the Pawnees imprisoned in the Fort, and are now in pursuit of their chief. They have robbed a man, who was on his way to California, and shamefully abused his wife, which was the cause of their arrest. The soldiers anticipate a fight if the chief is taken, and they say the whole tribe are now on their way up to try to rescue the prisoners.

The question was then proposed, Shall we travel tomorrow, or shall we lay by to keep the Sabbath? Three of the brethren reasoned in favor of laying bye, saying that we are commanded to keep the Sabbath day holy; and also that it has been experienced that the Saints generally lose time by travelling on the Sabbath, others reasoned in favor of travelling tomorrow, alleging as a reason, that to us every day is a Sabbath; that we have only got feed for eight days, if we lay bye we consume the feed without shortening the journey; that our horses are far more liable to Stampede when we stay two nights in a place; that we are in more danger from Indians than we have been on any other part of the road;

that we are daily liable to stormy weather, which would injure our teams much worse than to travel a hundred miles in good weather, and that President Young travels on the Sabbath when on a journey and circumstances require it &c. The question was finally put to a vote, and it was decided in favor of travelling tomorrow by an overwhelming majority; three brethren viz. Preston Thomas, John S. Fullmer and Jesse Haven voting in opposition. It was then voted that the distance we travel each day shall be left to the judgement of the Captain and Pilot as usual. The remainder of the evening was spent in exhortation by several of the Elders, the best of feelings evidently prevailing.

[October 24, 1852. Sunday.] Morning cloudy with appearance for rain. This morning Brother Daniel A. Miller offered to sell the Stampede horse to Brother Camp for $60 to help him forward on the journey. Or, he offered also to furnish a team for the balance of the journey, if Brother Camp would feed them well, and pay $25 for the use of them. Brother Camp finally bought the horse for $55 with the privilege of giving his note for the amount untill he can obtain the money. It is now expected that he can travel as fast as any one in the company.

After prayer by Elder John Brown, we started at half past 7, and travelled along slowly, the weather looking some more favorable. Soon after our noon halt we passed 5 wagons loaded with stores for the Sutler[26] at Fort Kearney. They say they passed large bands of Pawnees, both last night and this morning, on their way down the river; and that the Indians have fired the grass below. Last evening we noticed the reflection of fire in the clouds eastward, but it seemed to be a considerable distance from us. To day the atmosphere is thick with smoke, which is quite unpleasant. At half past 4 o'clock on arriving at a point where the roads run close to the river we formed our encampment having traveled about 25 miles.

Not long after we camped we noticed that the prairie was burning not far below us, and was coming very fast towards us, so much so that it soon became evident we had got to do some-

---

[26] Sutlers were civilian merchants who monopolized the sale of provisions to military post troops. Overland immigrants often obtained supplies from their stores (Unruh, 216).

thing for our safety. Many offered their opinions as the best course to be pursued, but that which appeared to be the best and safest was to set what is termed back fire, that is to set the grass on fire close to us, so that the grass may burn off immediately around before it gets much head way. Before the minds of the brethren were fully made up what to do, we could plainly hear the roar of the raging element, and the fire was approaching so rapidly that not another moment was to be lost. The whole camp was then in motion and such a scene of bustle and excitement as issued for a few minutes is rarely witnessed. While some ran with fire below the wagons to get the grass burning, another party ran and drove the animals over to the island opposite; others were backing the wagons across the road to within a few feet of the river bank moving bedclothing, harness[es], provisions, and cooking utensils into and under the wagons, and then drenching the wagons, wagon covers and bedding with water, some throwing on their hot tea and coffee and anything they could get to prevent their taking fire from the sparks, or intense heat of the flames. All this, altho' done in far less time than it takes it to be written, was scarce accomplished before the full tide of the warring element was on us. A death like silence ensued for about a minute and the brethren stood with deep anxiety imprinted in their countenances close by their wagons, ready at a moments notice in case a wagon took fire to back it into the river, altho' the banks are about 10 feet deep. For a short time the smoke was so thick that it was scarc[e]ly possible to breathe. On came the roaring element, resembling in sound the distant thunder, and moving direct towards the waggons at a fearful speed. The sight was indeed grand and awful when within about 3 rods of the wagons, the fire which we had started met it; a sudden puff of wind sprung up from the north East, and drove the vast blaze in a South West direction and away from the wagons. The fire deadened along the whole line of wagons in a very few seconds, the involuntary exclamation, we are safe, burst from the lips of many at the same instant. The fire had passed and we men miraculously preserved. The speed at which the fire ran was variously estimated at from 3 to 10 miles an hour; it appeared to me to move as fast as a horse could trot, for in a very few minutes after it had passed us, we could see it burning far away southwest.

We had just commenced cooking supper when the bustle commenced, and cooking things, plates, cups &c. were scattered in every direction, and left to the mercy of the flames generally. While the fire was passing, the animals stood in the river beside the island watching the roaring flames as if panic-stricken and rivited to the spot.

The excitement lasted for about an hour, and through the mercy of God we escaped, I had almost said without a hair of our heads being singed, but there were some who had their eyebrows scorched, and all felt it much too hot to be pleasant. It was indeed a providential thing our camping where we did, the space between the river bank and the road being barely wide enough for a wagon to stand, being only about 8 feet. The brethren also plainly saw the power of God manifested in our behalf in the wind striking the fire from us, when only about three rods distant; for it appeared at the moment that there was no chance for us but to jump into the river; and a true feeling of gratitude filled the hearts of the brethren for this manifestation of his preserving care over us.

After the excitement had subsided, a deep anxiety was again felt for Brother Camp, as it was ascertained that his wagon had not yet come up, and the fire was still raging above us to the West, South West and south for many miles. While we again set to work to prepare for supper, two of the brethren went back on the road to see if they could find him, and to learn if he had escaped. They went back about three miles and found him secure on a sand bar. They pleaded with him faithfully to have him harness up and go with him to camp; but he said his horses were tired and must rest. They then offered to put their horses to his wagon and take it along, and he drive his horses loose; but he said he had not had his supper, and did not want to move without it. They then told him that its not safe for him to stay there alone, as the Pawnees are both above and below us, but all was to no purpose, and the brethren had no alternative but either to stay with him, or to return without him. He appeared so wilful and obstinate that they finally returned to camp and made their report. He, however, soon after harnessed up and came to the camp.

A large patch of grass, which lay on the north side of the road above the camp, by some means escaped the fire and the animals were driven back to it and left in charge of the night guard. After

455

supper the brethren assembled for prayers and joined with Elder C[hauncey] G. Webb. Elder Orson Spencer then addressed the brethren, referring in a spirited manner to the mercies of our heavenly Father towards us; the high and holy calling with which we are called, the power and blessings promised to us if we are faithful &c. He was followed for a short time by Elder Andrew L. Lamoreaux after which the meeting adjourned.

There was some thunder and lightning, immediately after the fire, and the heavens betokened rain. A little before midnight it began to rain heavy, and continued to do so the remainder of the night. When we went to bed we found the blankets, quilts and all our bedding, pretty well soaked with water, and I felt satisfied they would not have been burned even if the fire touched the wagons. We were cold and uncomfortable.

[October 26, 1852. Tuesday.] Morning fair, but the weather looks quite unsettled . . .

About dusk we noticed the prairie burning very rapidly a few miles East of us. I started on the road to ascertain on which side of the river the fire was coming, but it was sometime before I could satisfy myself. Others came down the river on the same errand, and we finally became convinced that the fire was on the north side of the river, and of course we were in no danger.

Evening prayers was offered by Daniel Daniels . . . The Sergeant of the guard, exhorted the brethren to be dilligent while on duty, and earnestly recommended that we encamp in a more compact form. It was voted that we form our camp in a line hereafter, and have the wagons placed close together.

The meeting was then dismissed; and about the same time two soldiers came into camp to stay with us overnight. They have been down the river to hunt some stray cattle, and are on their way to their quarters at Fort Kearney. They say there are about 5000 Pawnees about 10 miles below here, on their way to Fort Kearney. They say the Pawnees don't steal, but they walk up and take what they want without leave or license.

Our wagons this night were very much scattered some being as much as 200 yards from the others, which causes more trouble in guarding, and would be very hard in case of an attack from Indians. We are now in close proximity to them and it appears that more caution ought to be observed the nearer we get to them, but it appears the brethren are less cautious than usual.

[October 27, 1852. Wednesday.] The night has passed off peacefully. The fire on the north side of the river passed us about 10 o'clock, and although it must have been over a mile distant from us, the roar of the raging element was heard for about four hours, like the rumbling of distant thunder. The heavens were so much illuminated by it most of the night, that the brethren could see to read quite easy without any other light. The sight was indeed awfully grand. The atmosphere this A.M. is quite cool and cloudy with every appearance of another storm. The brethren were astir early, and at half past 6 prayer was offered up by President Orson Pratt. We then continued our travel at a more rapid pace than we have done for several days; in fact the footmen needed to walk fast to keep warm. We soon began to meet straggling Indians on their way up the river, and the further we travelled the more we met in number together, untill about 9 o'clock, when the great mass of the band came in view. The plain appeared alive with them for miles; the warriors old and young, carrying their bows and arrows, or guns; the women loaded with packs and Papooses, and their animals heavily packed with their domestic implements, lodge poles &c. Such a scene of shaking hands and "how-de-do's," as is rarely witnessed was the order of the day. Many of the warriors inquired (by signs) how far it was to the Buffalo herds. Our replies appeared to give them great satisfaction. We passed the whole band without one unpleasant circumstance transpiring, much to our joy and gratitude. Very many of the old, middle aged and young warriors are blind of the right eye, supposed to be caused by the bow string bounding, when accidently drawn too tight. There were a number of very aged men and women in the company, some evidently, totally blind, notwithstanding which they had to work their way without any guide or help; in fact the oldest females appeared to carry the heaviest packs. By far the greatest number, the men especially, are very much marked with the small pox; and the whole tribe are very much inferior to the Sioux, Shayennes or Shoshones both in stature and general appearance. We noticed quite a number of half-breed children among them. They are truly a race to be pitied.

457

At a quarter past 11 we halted a little while to feed and then continued to travel till after 3 o'clock when we camped on the banks of the Platte river having travelled about 27 miles. The whole surface of country as far as we have travelled since Sunday, and as far as we can see on both sides of the river is burned off, except small patches of grass occasionally between the road and the river, leaving travellers few choices of camping grounds. The weather is cloudy and very cold. A snow storm is feared, but the Brethren pray and exercise faith that we may be spared a storm until we are safely off the plains.

Many animals have failed fast since the heavy rain, but our God who has blessed us thus far can sustain them the remainder of the journey. Half past 6 o'clock the camp assembled and prayer was offered up by Elder Charles Smith. On account of the cold, the meeting then adjourned.

[October 28, 1852. Thursday.] About 5 o'clock this morning several Indians passed the camp, on their way up the river. The sight of them in the dark, caused another Stampede among our animals, and the first thought of the guard was that the Indians had run the horses off. The whole camp was quickly in pursuit and one or two Indians, then in camp, were seized as hostages untill the animals were recovered. This set them to yelling loudly to their companions which tended to increase the excitement, and they were again liberated, but strictly watched. After about an hour's chase, the animals were all recovered and brought back to camp. We then prepared and eat a hasty breakfast, and after prayer by Elder David Wilkin, pursued our journey. The morning was very cold, and at 9 o'clock snow began to fall very thick. The atmosphere betokened a very stormy day, and after travelling two hours in the snow storm, we turned off the road at 11 o'clock, and pitched our camp near an island, pretty thickly covered with Cedar trees. The animals were driven across to the island, which afforded them good shelter, and proved to be a good place for feed. The snow fell thick all day, and in consequence of the cold and wet, we retired to rest without meeting for prayer. The whole of the guard detailed for the night, took their blankets and Buffalo Robes, and went over to the island to sleep (when not on duty). They made up a large fire, which made them far more comfortable than they would have been in their wagons. The distance we travelled today was 13 miles. These cold storms are causing many of the horses to fail fast. The government mules are also getting very poor and weak. One of Brother Treat's horses appears as tho' he cannot endure much longer, and I have to go on foot near all the time.

[October 29, 1852. Friday.] This morning the snow is all gone, yet the weather is cold. The camp being called together, prayer was offered by Elder Benjamin Brown, and at half past 8 o'clock we pursued our way. The day was cloudy with strong wind; and the grass is burned off the whole surface of county as far as can be seen. We traveled 19 miles, myself on foot near all the way, then camped in a hollow in the Bluffs some 4 or 5 miles from the river. The snow lays quite thick in patches. Grass is scarce, and wood for fuel has to be carried about a quarter of a mile.

After supper the camp assembled, and I being called upon officiated as mouth. After which as we are now within two or three days travel of the Missouri River, Elias Gardner, Alondus D. L. Buckland, Noah T. Guyman, Ira Saby and Aaron F. Farr, petitioned to go ahead of the company, as their teams are in good order. The matter was discussed by several, and it was finally decided by unanimous vote, that those Brethren get to the River as soon as they can, and endeavor to make arrangements for a Ferry-boat so that we may not be delayed when we arrived at the river.

President Orson Pratt then arose to make some remarks, and stated that on his arrival in Washington City, he designs publishing a monthly periodical, to be called the "Seer." The price will be one dollar per annum. He requested the Brethren to stir up the minds of the people abroad, and endeavor to get as many subscribers as possible. He then gave the Brethren some parting instructions and advice, and among other things said, that he believes the Lord will do more for us, who are going on this mission, than we ever before realized. It is our privilege to hold communion with the heavens. It is the privilege of every man in this company to attain to direct revelation and prophecy; to receive revelations with the same certainty that the Holy Ghost revealed things to Joseph, or Brigham or Peter. He don't wish to be understood that we are to receive revelations to govern the Church, that

459

belongs to the presidency; but to know our duties daily; to know the faith and standing of the Churches over which we preside, and to know things that are immediately going to transpire. It is the privilege of the brethren to prophecy to the world, and to work all kinds of miracles that will be for the good of the Kingdom &c.

He spoke at some length and felt to bless the Brethren with all his heart. The camp felt highly pleased with his remarks and peace prevailed.

[October 30, 1852. Saturday.] The morning cloudy but warm. At half past 6 the camp started forward, those who petitioned to go "a-head" started at a good pace. I kept up with these wagons for a number of miles on foot, Sometimes going across to save travelling round a large bend in the road. I also rode a short distance with Aaron F. Farr. The roads were soft and muddy caused by the melting of the snow, and they are indeed crooked enough, generally following the highest ridges.

We travelled till 11 o'clock then halted 3/4 of an hour to let the animals graze and rest a little. After eating some dinner I started on foot again the wagons following soon after. I could easily keep a long distance before the wagons, by crossing over deep ravines, instead of following round by the road. We travelled till a quarter to 7 but could still find no suitable place to camp, for altho' we could find small patches of grass, it was in places where there was no wood, and sometimes no water. The night was so dark that we had frequently to feel carefully with our feet to assure ourselves that we were on the road, and at a quarter to 7, it was concluded to halt untill the moon rose. David Wilkin stopped soon after dark and we could see his light a long way in the rear from where we were halted. We eat a little cracker, the brethren giving me some, as Treats wagon had not yet arrived. At 8 o'clock, the moon having risen, we started onward. I went before the wagons on foot about half a mile, and from the edge of the Bluffs saw plainly the fire of the brethren who started ahead this morning. I called back as loud as I could and gave them notice and we were soon camped with these brethren. Our wagon did not arrive till late, but I was invited to eat supper with Aaron F. Farr. Several of the teams have about given out, having traveled 35 miles during the day, which is too much for weak teams but there was no chance to stop sooner and find a suitable place to camp. Brothers McDonald and Camp and Mr. Vanderhoff did not come to the main camp, but as we are considered out of all danger from Indians, and they preferring to travel slow, no anxiety was felt on their account. The night was beautifully clear and pleasant.

[October 31, 1852. Sunday.] A[londus] D. L. Buckland and company started on again at 2 o'clock this morning. After prayers, at about 8 o'clock the camp again moved forward. I proceeded onward to Salt Creek on foot, a distance of 18 miles where I arrived about 1 o'clock with two other brethren. We waded the stream which is about 4 rods wide, the water being cold and the bottom rough with sharp stones. We found some fire and wood which the other brethren left, and sat by the fires waiting for the wagons, which arrived at 2 o'clock and then halted to feed and eat dinner. Near all the teams had to be helped up the bank which is steep and teams are very weak. Brother Treat did not arrive till near an hour after the others came up. After cooking and eating a little dinner the footmen started on again, and the wagons started at half past 4. We expected to be able to find a new road which was made last season, and which is said to be shorter than the old road by about 15 miles, but the night being dark we passed it without noticing it. I walked in company with Andrew L. Lamoreaux, who had much to say in regard to the hard treatment he had received from Dr. Willard Richards. We went on till half past 8 and then camped on the high Prairie, having travelled 28 miles during the day. Brother Treat did not arrive till near midnight and the night being frosty I suffered much from cold. When the wagon did arrive we made our bed down on the grass and were soon sound asleep. It is very doubtful whether Brother Treats horse will get to the Missouri River, for he fails fast. The government mules have given out and the wagon was left. Brother Miller will send for it from Kanesville. Many of the animals are nearly too weak to walk.

[November 1, 1852. Monday.] This morning we started at 4 o'clock, and after travelling 12 miles, arrived at the Forks of the road, one of which leads to Bethlehem, the other to Fort Kearney. We halted for breakfast and also to ascertain who intended going on each route. President Orson Pratt, John Brown, W[illia]m A. Empey, Edw[ar]d Stevenson, John Hart and Thomas Jeremy, and

461

those who travelled with them in the same wagons, decided to take the Fort Kearney road, and the others decided to go to Bethlehem. Accordingly after halting an hour, the brethren separated, and each party went on their separate ways. This of course was virtually a breaking up of camp, and many of the brethren felt a little sorrowful to part from those with whom they had thus journeyed across the plains; but realizing the necessity and propriety of it, all went on their way rejoicing; each and all full determined to get to the scene of their labors as soon as possible, and where they are to work with all their might to fulfill their mission with dignity and honor; so that when they are called home, they may return to the valley of the mountains with clean hands and pure hearts. This feeling strongly possessed my heart, and having a constant fear of my own failings, I felt to pray that God will preserve me, that I may do a good work in his kingdom. Brother Treat's horse grows weaker all the time, and as we could get no satisfaction from him whether he would try to keep up with the camp, I started on foot carrying my cloak and a Buffalo robe with me to sleep on in case he did not arrive. I was permitted to put them in the other wagons after carrying them over a mile. I walked on slowly and on arriving at the first creek 5 miles from the forks of the road I sat down to wait for the wagon. Several other wagons with weak team afterwards came up and halted on the same creek, and finally Brother Treat came, bringing the wagon with one horse. His other one fell down, completely exhausted while descending the hill a little [piece] back.

We cooked and eat some dinner, and I prevailed on William Walter to put his extra horse along with Brother Treat's and take the wagon along to camp. After resting awhile we proceeded on 4 miles further, when we found the other brethren camped on a small creek, in a low bottom land. We arrived here at 3 o'clock and was truly glad to get with the main camp again.

Brother Treat stopped back at the creek 4 miles back, to try to get his horse along to camp. Just at dusk he came into camp for help. He said he had got him to the slough about 2 miles back, but there he fell down, and he wanted help to lift him up again. Several brethren volunteered to go with him. They got the horse on his feet but had to leave him as he was to weak to walk until he had time to rest.

In the evening I tried to get some assurance from the Brethren that our wagon will be taken to the Missouri River tomorrow. Daniel D. McArthur opposed the idea of our having any help, and although he could have spared a horse for that distance (being only 16 miles), and he knew that our wagon was our only dependence for means to take us on, yet he said we might leave the wagon and all our things he should not help us. I felt this very unkind treatment indeed, for I saw that it would please him if we had to lose the wagon and all we had. After much persuasion and pleading Brother Moses Daley agreed to let W[illia]m Walker have a horse to work with his to the river, and we then felt that we should get our things through. Brother Treat absolutely refused to let his well horse work in the wagon anymore, and acted so stubborn and wrathful that we were glad to let him have his own way.

It really appears hard to keep the spirit of union till we get through, altho' but 16 miles to go.

[November 2, 1852. Tuesday.] This morning we started at 4 o'clock, I going ahead on foot. I arrived at the Missouri River opposite Platteville about 9 o'clock. I followed the track of the other wagons, which had taken this road by accident instead of the Bethlehem road, and it was fortunate they did so as there is no Ferry at the latter place. Brothers Farr, Buckland &c. had got their wagons over and were camped in the timber on the opposite side. At 10 o'clock our wagons began to arrive, and soon after the Brethren brought the ferry boat over, and we commenced crossing two wagons at a time. I went over with the second load. We could not get the Ferry boat nearer the dry sand than about 5 or 6 rods, which we had to wade, being some of the way over two feet deep. I of course got well wet. Before night all the wagons were safe across, except McDonalds, Camps, and McVanderhoffs. Arrangements were made to ferry them over if they came this way.

After all the wagons were over we started on and went about 2 miles through timber, and then camped for the night. After supper the brethren assembled for prayers, after which Elder Orson Spencer addressed the Brethren for sometime, as from here we shall scatter through the States, and probably not see each other again until we arrive in England.

[November 3, 1852. Wednesday.] This morning Brother [William] Glover sold our wagon to Daniel A. Miller for $35.00 which was a good price, and we felt it quite a relief to get it disposed off. He also agreed to carry our trunks and bedding up to Kanesville. We gave him our cooking things and all we did not want to take any further. After breakfast Brother Glover and myself gave the parting hand to the two Spencers and others who are going down the river. We felt truly sorrowful to part from their society. Although we had both resolved not to travel any further with Brother Treat in consequence of his disagreeable conduct, yet we felt deeply grieved to part from him. We however started on foot for Kanesville. The roads were very muddy and tiresome traveling. We called at Brother David Gamuts to get a little dinner, and although it was very poor, and we had informed Sister Gamut that we were missionaries &c. she received 50 cents for what little we eat. We then travelled on slowly and arrived at Brother A[lmon] W. Babbits in Kanesville at 4 o'clock P.M. having walked 18 miles in the mud. Brother Babbit told us we should be welcome at his house as long as we tarried in Kanesville, and there we took our things.

Thus our journey across the plains was safely ended and we were once more securely sheltered in the house of a friend. The brethren realize sensibly that the kind mercies of our father in heaven have followed us by night and by day during our journey from Salt Lake City till the time we separated this morning . . .

The brethren have endeavored to live faithful and humble before him continually . . . And may the same spirit and power, continue with every man during his mission while abroad in the world: may the power of the Most High attend all their labors; and when they shall testify of the truth before the saints and the world, may the spirit of God bear witness with them, that all the honest in heart may be constrained to embrace the truth and continue in it, that thousands may see the salvation of God through their instrumentality; and when they are called home may every man return with clean hands and a pure heart; and may we all have just cause to rejoice in time and eternity, that we had a part in this mission. And when we have done with this world, may we all with our families be crowned with eternal lives in the world to come. Amen.

[November 4, 1852. Thursday.] We ascertained today that we cannot get a conveyance to Fort Des moines until next Monday, the regular day for the Stage to leave. We had of course to content ourselves here the best way we could Spend the time till then, visiting some but mostly at Brother Babbits. Edw[ar]d Martin, Jos[eph] Park and W[illia]m Taylor are here also, trying to sell their team and wagon, to help them on their journey, but they cannot sell unless [at] a great sacrifice. All believe that horses and wagons will be in great demand, but the spirit of speculation reigns predominant not only among the world but with the Saints also. The brethren will not buy unless they can assure themselves of a handsome profit, altho' they know these Elders need the means, to help them on their mission.

We are credibly informed that there are already upwards of 700 wagons belonging to imigrants in the neighborhood of Kanesville, and more daily arriving. These design wintering here, so as to be ready to start across the plains for the gold mines at the first opening of spring. There are also some family of saints gathering here to winter, to be ready to go on to the Valley amongst the first companies. These emigrants have caused an advance in the price of grain and provisions, and the Kanesville merchants appear to be doing a good business.

I learned that Father [Alpheus] Cutler is living somewhere down the river. George W. Harris is living here in Kanesville. Both are waiting for the time to come when the saints shall go back to Jackson County, Missouri, to build up Zion. They say it is useless to go over the mountains, and have to come back to Missouri again.

The doctrine of Baneemyism[27] appear to have a many advocates here. The system has Charles B. Thompson as its leader. They are bitterly opposed to President Young and call him the beast. They say Joseph lived and died a Prophet of God, and that all the Revelations which came through him to the day of his martyrdom are true, and binding upon this generation. They preach much against the plurality doctrine, and teach that it is got up by the Twelve to gratify their lusts. How will they get along with the Revelation of July 12, 1843[?] I saw [Libeus] T.

---

[27] See entry for November 28, 1852.

Coons, Joseph W. Coolidge, Luke Johnson, Dustin Amy and others of the old Saints, but could find none who were willing to offer the least assistance for our mission. There is a great difference between the Spirit of the Saints here, and those at Salt Lake City.

[November 8, 1852. Monday.] On going to the Stage Office this morning we learned that the Stage will not start today, in consequence of one of the horses being sick. From this fact we became satisfied that it is uncertain when it will go. Perrigrine Sessions and John S. Fullmer being in the same situation with Brother Glover and myself, we finally concluded to hire a passage to Fort Des moines, in a common covered lumber wagon with a Brother Stevens, who has offered to take us for $4. each, and will be ready to start tomorrow morning.

[November 9, 1852. Tuesday.] This morning we bid farewell to Brother Babbits family and took our departure. I left my Spy glass at Brother Babbits in consequence of its being so heavy. About 9 o'clock myself, W[illia]m Glover, P[eregrine] G. Sessions, and John L. Fullmer got aboard Mr. Steven's wagon which was made tolerably comfortable. Soon after Edw[ar]d Martin, James Park and W[illia]m Taylor, having disposed of their wagon, packed their horses and started for St. Josephs on foot, driving their horses before them. Samuel Glasgow, Edward Bunker and John Robinson started with the team and wagon with which they crossed the plains. Andrew L. Lamoreaux, John Percy and John Mayer engaged passage with an ox team; and Richard Cook and [Osmyn] M. Deuel took the stage, which also started this morning. All these Brethren started for Fort Des moines about the same time we did.

[November 10, 1852. Wednesday.] After breakfast we started on again, the day was very unpropitious . . . On arriving at the body of timber where we expected to find the Stage Stand, we had great difficulty to find the road, and had to scrape the snow with our feet frequently to assure ourselves that we were right. At a quarter past 7 we arrived at Mr. Hamlin's, the Stage House having traveled 40 miles. We found Brothers Glasgow, Bunker and Robinson already here, and the others arrived soon after. The latter part of the day and the night was very cold, and we were indeed glad to get standing around a comfortable fire. The accommodations were very poor, being only about 4 seats for the whole of us, and as to bed, we had to sleep on the floor in our own Buffalo Robes &c.

[November 11, 1852. Thursday.] Morning very cold . . . We started on again and travelled till a little after dark, when we arrived at a Mr. Moores, the next stage stand, and was soon enjoying the warmth of a good fire, and a first rate supper.

The evening passed as pleasantly as could be expected, considering our crowded situation. The brethren advised the stage driver to fix up a sled and take his passengers along with him, and learning there was a "jumper" which he could have and which needed but little repairs, he finally concluded to make the attempt in the morning. The distance we traveled today was 30 miles.

[November 12, 1852. Friday.] We started this morning at 8 o'clock and found the roads very hard travelling. We soon lost sight of the other brethren, and did not see them again until we arrived at Fort Des moines. We found that we could not get to the Fort today without doing injustice to the team; accordingly we stopped early at a Mr. Millers having traveled 20 miles. We soon found that several of the family were afflicted with the mumps, which alarmed Brother Sessions and Fullmer considerable. I felt no alarm as I have had them. The Brethren took each a pile of [asafoetide],[28] to prevent their taking the disease.

[November 13, 1852. Saturday.] . . . We arrived at Fort Des moines at 1 P.M. distance 12 miles, and found the other brethren here. After taking dinner at the Stage Hotel, I went to inquire for Brother Lamoreaux's brother, in order to learn if we could get a place to stay with the brethren till Monday morning, as the Stage does not run on Sundays . . . I then . . . went with him, was introduced to Sister Buzzard who said we should be welcome to stay with them . . . We had considerable conversation with Brother [Philip L.] and Sister Buzzard. She appears strong in the faith and wants to gather to the Valley, but he appears to have little inclination to go. We preached to them and advised to go to the valley as soon as they possibly could. After supper we went to a

---

[28] Asafetida is a strong-smelling gum resin obtained from parsley roots, which is used in folk medicine to repel disease.

Tavern to sleep as Brother Buzzard could not accommodate us on account of having a woman boarder in the only spare room.

[November 14, 1852. Sunday.] This morning the weather is fine and pleasant. After breakfast Brother Buzzard took Elders Glover, Fullmer, and myself to visit Amos B. Fuller according to a promise made yesterday. Brother Fuller married Elias Smith's sister. He lives on his own farm about 2 miles out of Town. He has a good house, barn, stables &c. and altogether he considers his property worth some $4,000. We found Brother Cook there. We soon saw that Brother Fuller has no faith in the authorities of the Church, and he thinks like some others that it is all nonsense to go to the Valley, to have to travel back again to Missouri in a few years. He is evidently drunk all the time, and the effects of strong drinks are plainly visible in his countenance. He cannot keep his eyes still a moment, and it is doubtful about his living long unless he speedily change his course of life. His wife looks melancholy and has every appearance of a heartboken woman. We took dinner with them, and then returned to Brother Fullers. With all Brother Fullers wealth we could not prevail upon him to help us on our mission.

I spent the evening writing a letter to my family which I design finishing in St. Louis.

Brother Buzzard gave me $2. besides paying for our sleeping at the Hotel.

[November 15, 1852. Monday.] This morning we were called up at a quarter past 3, and on going over to the Stage Office were joined by some of the other brethren. At 4 o'clock we started out being six of us in company; viz., myself, Elder W[illia]m Glover, Richard Cook, John S. Fullmer, John Perry and John Mayer. We had expected that the passengers would cross the Des moines River in a skiff, but none could be found, although it is very bad to ford we had to risk. We however got safe over and proceeded on. The first 3 miles of the road is through timber and very rough indeed. At the request of the Stage driver we walked it, which was very unpleasant in the dark. While passing over this road, one of the thoro'-braces[29] broke, but

---

[29] Pairs of leather straps that support a horse-drawn wagon and serve as springs.

we got along to the stage house without trouble, distance 8 miles. Here we took breakfast and after changing horses and driver proceeded on again. The day was very cold and roads rough. We rarely went above a walk. We arrived at Pella at 6 o'clock P.M. and there was informed we would have to stay over night and wait for the next stage as this hack must be repaired. We have travelled only 39 miles instead of going to Fairfield which is 16 miles further. We were not sorry to stay here, for it was snowing very fast, and was very cold. However we told the stage driver we wished to go on because if we had desired to stay, we would have to run the risk of the next stage being full; but as it was, and our demanding to go on, the next stage is bound by law to take us whether there are other passengers or not. We had very good entertainment, and felt much better by a warm stove than to be riding in a cold hack all night.

[November 16, 1852. Tuesday.] This morning we found the proprietor of the Des moine Stage Hotel had arrived. He had followed us for a trunk which had been put on the Stage by mistake. It was fortunate for us he did arrive, for he immediately went and engaged a sled to take us to Oskaloosa, otherwise we should have had to wait till night for the other Hack. We started at 8 o'clock, and had a fine sleigh ride to Oskaloosa where we arrived at half past 11. Here we learned that the other stage left this morning, taking the mail &c. in an open wagon, as the roads are so very bad they dare not trust the Hack. We had no alternative but to stay till morning, and we accordingly put up at the "Oskaloosa House" a place which will be long remembered by us. I consider this Hotel under its present manager a disgrace to civilization. We had to stay in what is called a bar room, but its filthy appearance makes it much more like a hog pen. There was only one short bench and a broken chair for seats. Half the time we were near froze for they were too lazy to let us have coal for a fire; and a set of loafers and rowdies being constantly passing in and out, the place was disagreeable in the extreme. The table was miserably furnished and we were fortunate if we got half enough to eat. The beds were about equal to all the rest, and it is truly the most miserable place to be called an Hotel I was ever in, in my life.

[November 17, 1852. Wednesday.] The stage which ought to have left here at 8 o'clock A.M. did not arrive till noon, and then of course we had to wait dinner, after which we settled our bills, having to pay just as much for our miserable fare as we have in other places for the best accommodation. At 1 P.M. we got on board the hack, glad to leave Oscaloosa and her comforts; but we soon found we had not bettered our condition much. The Hack was only calculated for 4 persons, and there being 6 of us, we were very much cramped indeed. We found the roads dreadful rough, and were in continual danger of being upset. The road had been badly cut up in wet weather, and the hard frost had made them rough enough. Sometimes the wheels would slide into the deep ruts, inspite of all the efforts of the driver, and while the wheels on one side would be rolling on the hubs, on the other side they would sometimes not touch the ground for a rod at a time. After traveling 12 miles we stopped to change horses. Brother Fullmer determined not to go any further, on account of being so crowded. He was sure we should be upset if we undertook to travel in the night, so many of us in that small Hack, and he should wait for the next stage.

After putting on fresh horses and a new driver, we proceeded on in the same tossing, tumbling manner. After traveling 8 miles, being then going through a large body of timber the driver ran the Hack against the end of a large log about 18 inches through, which brought us up standing. On attempting to turn the horses a little so as to pass it, he broke the wagon pole square off, close to the axle. This was a little after 9 o'clock, the night being dark and very cold. The snow of course relieved the darkness a little. After a long tirade of bitter oaths and blasphemy, the driver started in search of a common lumber wagon, in which to take us on. I suppose if he had not had the mail along, we might have tarried where we were or gone on foot just as we pleased, at least we understood so from what he said. After we had set two hours in the cold, he returned with an open wagon, into which we moved ourselves and luggage and started on again. We traveled in this situation all night, changing horses and driver once in the meantime, and such a jolting, and shaking as we took over the frozen rough ground I never wish to endure again . . .

During the evening the Democrats held a "Torchlight" procession, headed by a band of music, and being saluted by the firing of cannon. This was done in honor of the election of Mr. [Franklin] Pierce to the Presidential chair of the United States.[30]

[November 19, 1852. Friday.] On being called up this morning at 5 o'clock to proceed on, we found Brother Fullmer ready to go with us, having travelled all night, and but just arrived. He informed us that soon after he started from the Tavern where we left him, they were upset off a bridge into a ditch but fortunately no one was hurt. The horses ran a considerable distance, but these stages are so constructed, that in case they do turn over, the body of the carriage and hind wheels detach themselves from the fore wheels, and when the horses run as in this case, they take nothing but the fore wheels with them . . .

[November 20, 1852. Saturday.] We arrived at Keokuk at 4 o'clock A.M. almost frozed, very tired and sleepy. We went to the Wharf and found a Boat laying there, expecting to Start for St. Louis in a few hours. We got our things on board the Boat (Kate Kearney) and after washing felt some refreshed.

. . . The Stage fare from Fort Des moines to Keokuk is 9 dollars and the average time of travel 3 days, distance 180 miles.

It took us 5 days and 2 whole nights. At every stage stand, it is the practice to change horses and driver both. The men being hired to run it from stand to stand with their own teams, for a certain price, which I believe is $12. per month and all expenses paid. Thus the traveler is continually under the care of a new driver some of whom are indeed foul-mouthed, wicked men, which make it very disagreeable for travellers.

The river is full of floating ice, and it is probable that navigation to this point will soon be closed. We started at daybreak down the river, taking a cabin passage which cost us 5 Dollars each. We were however well repayed by the privilege of laying down and taking a refreshing nap.

[November 21, 1852. Sunday.] We arrived at St. Louis at noon, and went to my sister Ellen Howard's, where Brother Glover and myself were kindly received and made welcome. Elder Orson Pratt is here and has been preaching on the plurality doctrine, and also read the revelation. I understand quite a number have

---

[30] Franklin Pierce was the fourteenth president of the United States, 1853–57.

sent in their resignation in consequence.[31] There are a number of the Elders here to get means to go on. A collection was taken for the purpose of assisting the Elders which amounted to forty dollars, which will probably afford the brethren some two dollars each. In the evening I went to meeting, but soon returned again feeling very weary and sleepy.

[November 22, 1852. Monday.] Got up before daylight, and finished the letter I commenced at Fort Des moines; then took it to the Post Office, where I also received a long letter from my family and a line from Brother Thomas Bullock, which gave me much joy. Augusta's sister Clarry called to see me, but was too mad and fiery to hold any conversation.[32] Her husband came afterwards, and threatened to kill me on the spot. He was ordered out of the house, but he stood in the street opposite for sometime foaming and threatening dreadfully.

[November 26, 1852. Friday.] We have spent the week visiting friends and trying to obtain means, to help us onward . . .

We then went back to my brother in law's to take our luggage to the Boat. He gave me $10. which, with what I have already will pay my passage to Pittsburgh. I bid them goodbye, and also at the same time parted with my brother in law Aaron F. Farr probably for years.

At 4 o'clock we went on board the steam Boat St. Clair, Captain Cochran, and soon after left the wharf for Pittsburgh. W[illia]m Walker was also along with us on the same Boat.

I learned that my brothers Davids[33] widow has made a perfect waste of the "Guides"[34] I left. She is keeping a Gentile boardinghouse and has no more faith in the Church than the gentiles themselves. A new edition of the guide has been printed by

---

[31] In addition to defections at home, nearly 2,000 British Mormons would leave the church in the first six months that polygamy was preached. See Introduction, n111.

[32] This was probably Augusta Braddock's sister. A native of Bedfordshire, England, Augusta was Clayton's sixth wife, whom he married October 5, 1850, when she was just seventeen (James B. Allen, *Trials of Discipleship: The Story of William Clayton, A Mormon* [Urbana: University of Illinois Press, 1987], 204). Her relatives were probably angry at Clayton for marrying her.

[33] At thirty-four, David was William Clayton's next youngest brother.

[34] Clayton's *The Latter-Day Saints' Emigrants' Guide*, published in St. Louis in 1848.

Fisher and Bennet, which they are selling at 50 cents each. I offered to sell them the copyright, but they considered themselves perfectly safe without it. I had not the money to secure it myself, and had to leave it to do as they saw proper. I intend however, if all right, to print it in England, and as near all the emigration will herefoth come through England, I am in hopes to spoil their speculation.

[November 28, 1852. Sunday.] Brother Glover has had some conversation today with a Baneemyite. He was able to show the folly of his faith in such a doctrine; but like all other apostates he cherished his errors, although he cannot sustain them either by reason or revelation. They believe that all the Revelations which were given through the Prophet Joseph to the day of his death are true and binding upon this generation. They are decidedly opposed to the plurality; (what will they do with the revelation of July 12, 1843?). They believe that the President Brigham Young, and the Patriarch are the two horns of the beast. They believe in three orders of Priesthood; and that Baneemy is the man to gather the armies of Israel and redeem Zion, or Jackson County, Missouri. Charles B. Thompson is evidently Baneemy altho' they say it has not been told who Baneemy is. They are going to have a grand convocation about Christmas, and all the members are required to bring their tithes and offerings, and also a report of all their property and effects to the agent C. B. Thompson &c.

There are two quaker priests on the Boat; and a certain Cap-[tai]n Bennett, formerly a sea-captain, together with some others, proposed that we have a sermon this evening by one of the quaker brethren. Application was made to the Captain who gave his consent. Accordingly after supper the passengers assembled in the after part of the cabin and we had a sermon from the text, The kingdom of heaven is like unto three measures of meal &c. The whole sermon was a complete tirade of spiritualization and nonsense, and being delivered in the "good old tone" or rather sung, it was all we could do to maintain our gravity. Brother Glover thought he could confound the preacher without an effort, and exclaimed, "Well, I used to think I knew nothing, but now I begin to think I know something."

Cap[tai]n Bennett tried hard to get a privilege for me to preach but it could not be granted, being a "Mormon."

473

[December 1, 1852. Wednesday.] Last night at midnight, we arrived at Cincinnatti, and this morning as the Boat will not leave till near night, we went through the Town to see if we could find any of the Saints; but not having the address of anyone, we could find none. I however bought me a vest, pantaloons and stock for $1.50. Brother Glover also bought himself a vest and cravat.

Cincinnatti is a very pretty place. The streets are wide and clean; most of them adorned with shade trees. The buildings are generally large and handsome, many of them having marble steps in front. It appears a great place for business.

Brother Charles A. Harper joined us here, and at 4 P.M. we went on board and started on.

We saw Brother Daniel [Toner] here. He has been very unfortunate, having lost his money about $70. which was stole from him on the Boat. His clothing is taken on to Pittsburgh by the Boat on which he came from St. Louis. It appears he had gone on shore somewhere while the Boat stopped, and although he was told she would leave again soon he said he did not believe it, they had lied so much before in the same way. The consequence was the Boat started before he got back and he was left.

He has sent out to Pittsburgh for his cloths, and intends to turn about and go to Texas to sell some property he has there, and thus procure another outfit for his mission.

[December 5, 1852. Sunday.] On our way up the river we passed under the Wheeling Suspension Bridge,[35] one of the curiosities of modern times, but it being dark we had no opportunity of satisfying our curiousity by examining it. This afternoon we arrived at the foot of the Beaver Shoals. The water is falling some and we found it difficult to get over. We stuck on the sand bars a number of times, and had as often to back down again. During the attempt to get over the machinery of the [larboard][36] Engine broke which hindered two hours to repair it, and brought us to dusk in the evening. Another attempt was made to cross the bar, as unsuccessful as the rest, and the Captain finally headed her down stream, and tied up at the foot of the rapids till day light. We were then in sight of Beaver Town, at which place

---

[35] At Wheeling, West Virginia.
[36] Nautical term for left, usually expressed as "port."

Brother Glover and myself intend to leave the boat on a visit to his Father in law.

[December 6, 1852. Monday.] Some of the other passengers being as anxious to get on shore as we were, at 4 o'clock this morning we got some of the hands to set us on shore in the yawl.[37] After a toilsome journey, we arrived at Beaver Town at 6 o'clock. Altho' we had but a little over two miles to walk, the exertions to get up the long steep banks of the river, and having my trunk and other things to carry we felt pretty tired. From this place Brothers Walker and Harper, took the cars at half past 7 for Pittsburgh. We had to wait till 2 o'clock for the Youngstown Packet and after taking some bread and cheese and beer, we spent the time till 2 in walking round the town &c.

At 3 P.M. we went on board the Packet, "Lake Erie," and proceeded for Youngstown. A great part of this route is up the Beaver river occasionally entering a Canal, opposite the falls, to be raised by the Locks, which are very numerous. The distance to Youngstown from Beaver is called 50 miles. This was about the stillest, and easiest, travelling we have had on the whole journey, and we were enabled to take a very comfortable nights rest on the Packet.

. . . I walked round visiting several of the coal pits, which are numerous here. I was shocked to hear little children who can scarcely talk plain, curse and swear bitterly. Mrs. Cowan say it is very common here, and children are taught to swear and blaspheme by their parents.

I think the people of the United States, especially the laboring classes, boatmen &c. are the most wicked and blasphemous people I ever was near in my life. The daily language we here wherever we travel is truly shocking and disgusting.

[December 8, 1852. Wednesday.] This morning we were up at 4 o'clock . . .

We arrived at Salem at 12 o'clock, and after taking dinner at the Hotel, proceeded to the Railroad Station. We had not to wait long here, as the cars arrived soon after we got there. We got 'aboard' and at 1 o'clock started [] 'Railroad' for Pittsburgh. This

---

[37] A yawl is a small boat with oars that carries a ship's passengers across shallow water to shore.

is the first ride I have had on a Railroad since I left England in 1840, and I confess I did not feel very easy under the severe jolting of the cars, for sometime. The cars here are very large. They will hold about 60 persons. They are very handsomely built, being ornamented and finished off in a very costly style. The average weight of the empty cars is from 7 to 8 tons. They are placed on 8 wheels four under the fore part of the car and four under the hind part.

The distance to Pittsburgh is 68 miles from Salem. We arrived there at half past 4 o'clock. On arriving here our first inquiry was for the Philadelphia Railroad Station, and on ascertaining its locality, took a carriage and went thither. As the cars do not start till 3 in the morning we put up at a Dutch Tavern close by . . .

[December 9, 1852. Thursday.] We started on the Railroad for Philladelphia at 3 o'clock this morning, paying $9. fare. For the first time in my life I crossed the Alleghany mountains. The Railroad runs over this range of mountains; the cars being drawn up on the west side, up 4 steep and lengthy inclines by stationary Engines; and let down 5 similar inclines on the East side by similar means. At 10 o'clock we arrived at the Railroad Hotel, at the East foot of the mountains, where we were allowed half an hour for a very scanty breakfast, and for which we had to pay the moderate sum of fifty cents each. After the half hour was expired we proceeded on again, till 4 o'clock, then stopped for dinner. We choose this time to go to an opposition tavern, where we had a comfortable dinner for 25 cents. After resting 40 minutes we puffed forward again, and at half past 9 were safely landed in Philladelphia, having traveled today 350 miles which is the greatest distance we have ever traveled in one day.

Captain J[oh]n W. Bennett, our old Steam Boat acquaintance came to Philladelphia. In the same train, and by him we were escorted on foot to the York House, at the foot of Fulton St. where we put up for the night.

[December 10, 1852. Friday.] This morning I went with Elder Glover to the Reading Railroad station, on which he started at half past 7 to see his Father's folks who live 80 miles up the country . . . I met Joseph Risley, and stopped to converse a little with him. Brother Glover expected to have got about 25 dollars of Brother Risley but he made excuse saying he could not receive his money till January. He however gave me 5 dollars and I started on. At dusk I arrived in Recklesstown 4 miles, and on enquiring for Brother Robins' found a young man who was going by there with a wagon load of empty barrels. He asked me to ride, and I accordingly piled myself up among the barrels as well as I could. On arriving at Brother Robins' I was kindly received and made welcome. I found Elder Jesse Haven here, on the same errand with myself, viz. to get a little help, and I felt as tho' Brother Haven was disappointed to see me there. Two other brethren came in to spend the evening and we preached to them till 10 o'clock. Brother Robbins gave us a $20. bill, and one of the other Brethren a 5 dollar bill, the other 1 dollar to be divided between us. There does not appear to be much of the spirit of Mormonism here, altho' Brother Robins says he intends going to the Valley in the Spring.

[December 11, 1852. Saturday.] This morning Brother Robbins showed us his furniture which he designs taking to the Valley. His parlour and sitting room are elegantly fitted up with rich sofas, chairs, stands, tables &c. and very handsomely carpeted. He has a very large, fine house, with barns, stables, graineries &c. all as comfortable as this world can afford. He has two extensive farms, and is well situated in regard to earthly comforts, and has means enough to do much good if he will use it wisely.

At 10 o'clock myself and Elder Haven were taken by one of the brethren in Brother Robbins' carriage to Bordentown. On our way we stopped at Recklesstown and I conversed some with Elder W. I. Appleby's father-in law. They had heard all kinds of bad reports, such as Sister Appleby being unhappy and wishing to come back, Brother Appleby striking his son &c. I gave the old gentlemen the right version of the story, and he appeared much pleased. He wept tears of joy, and said he should like to go to the Valley, but his wife is very much opposed to it.

We arrived in Bordentown, just as the Cars came up, and had barely time to get aboard before we were off again. We arrived at Philadelphia at 1 P.M. and went up to Brother Osgenthorpe's to dinner. Here a letter was put into my hands, from three of the brethren who are living at Wallingford, Connecticut, stating that if one of the Elders would go there they would do all they could to help him. After an hours deliberation, seeing that Brother Haven

477

did not wish to go I concluded to go myself and immediately made preparations for the journey, by getting my trunk to the Boat &c. I had to wait several hours for the Boat to start, and the day being damp I was very uncomfortable and cold. At half past 5 the Boat started across the river, and I was soon seated in the cars on my way to New York. The fare was three Dollars. I arrived in New York at half past 9 o'clock, and it being to late to find the presiding Elders, I put up at the Jersey Hotel, foot of Courtland Street. The distance from Philladelphia to New York is 96 miles.

I have thus arrived in this place only one day later than I appointed to get here when crossing, the plains, and considering the little encouragement we have met with among the brethren, I feel that I have been abundantly prospered on the journey.

[December 12, 1852. Sunday.] After breakfast I went to Brother [] Hicks the presiding Elder of the New York Branch. I was very coolly received by Brother Hicks which I find has been the case with all the brethren. I found several of the Elders here, and from them learned that there are 16 of them here and that they have engaged a passage in the Packet Ship, "American Union," bound for Liverpool and advertised to sail tomorrow; fare with sea [stores] $22.50.

Inasmuch as the cars do not run on Sundays, and the brethren had appointed a meeting at one of the Saints' houses, I went with them to meeting; but after waiting two hours, and only about 3 of the saints coming, we dismissed till 2 o'clock. In the meantime I went with Elder John McDonald to look at the "American Union." We went on board and looked through her, but I do not like her appearance. The Brethren will be much crowded, and have to endure the society of all kinds of spirits.

We returned, and after partaking of a little dinner at an eating house, again went to meeting. Elders Perrigrine Sessions and George C. Riser had arrived in the meantime, and were with us during the afternoon. A number of the brethren bore their testimony, myself among the rest. We had a pleasant interview.

After meeting I went back to the Jersey Hotel to prepare for my journey to Wallingford.

POLYGAMY MISSION TO ENGLAND

[December 13, 1852. Monday.] Started before breakfast to the Railroad station, corner of Canal and Broadway,[38] and took my fare for New Haven. At half past 7 we started, and arrived at New Haven 70 miles at half past 11. On arriving here I learned that no train leaves for Wallingford till 3 P.M. I went to an eating house and took a little breakfast, then walked around the town in the cold till the time for the train to leave. New Haven is a pleasant place and has a fine harbor. I noticed that a great many of the business men are named Hotchkiss, and I suppose are relatives of Horace R. Hotchkiss who in connection with Gilles and Tuttle owned much of old Commerce.

At 5 P.M. started again on the cars, and arrived in Wallingford at half past 3. Distance 12 miles. I enquired for the New England Knife Factory, and there found Brothers John Barnes, George S[a]lsby and Samuel Wells, formerly of Sheffield, Yorkshire. They immediately left their work and accompanied me to Brother Doolittle's, the presiding Elder's, where I was gladly received. I soon learned that the brethren here are very much scattered, and as I cannot stay longer than tomorrow on account of the ship being expected to sail on Wednesday we could not get notice to but a few of them for a meeting. However after Ten, the brethren went round to notify those in the neighborhood, and at 7 o'clock, there were 7 brethren and 1 sister to hear what I had to say. I commenced talking to them and continued till 1 o'clock. The brethren amongst them gave me $26. and Brother Wells and Barns presented me with a knife each, of their own make. I administered to 3 of them, for restoration to health.

The three Sheffield brethren are determined to go to the Valley in the spring, but Brother Doolittle has not much faith in going. He told me that the Lord had shown him in a dream that he need not go to the Valley; he was better here &c. I told him it was a trick of the Devil to try to destroy him, and advised him by all means to go to the Valley as soon as possible. At 2 o'clock we retired to bed much fatigued.

---

[38] After the completion of Grand Central Station, which was designed and constructed 1907–13, trains from New York to New Haven would have left from Park Avenue and 42nd Street.

[December 14, 1852. Tuesday.] After breakfast I laid hands on Elder Doolittle, his wife and daughter, and at half past 8 started for the cars, Brother Doolittle accompanying me. We had to travel 2 miles to the station, and being rather late had to run a good portion of the way. We however arrived in time, and bidding the Brethren good-bye, in a few minutes we were rapidly running for New York. I arrived in New York at 2 o'clock P.M. and commenced searching for Elder Glover, but could hear nothing of him. I slept again at the Jersey Hotel.

[December 15, 1852. Wednesday.] After breakfast, went down to the American Union, and there found several others of the Elders who had just arrived. They were also dissatisfied with the crowded state of the "American Union," and had partially concluded to go on board the Packet Ship "Columbia," advertised to sail tomorrow.

We went to see this ship, and liking her appearance immediately went and engaged passage at $22.50 each including sea [stores]. The agent Jacob Wilson guarantying also to hire a cook for the company which we learned to be a [swap]. This Jacob Wilson is a thoro' land shark, and evidently lives by swindling emigrants.

In the evening Elder Glover and myself, amused ourselves by a visit to Barnum's Museum. Here we witnessed the frolics of the living Sea Tiger, a great curiosity. We also witnessed the Theatrical performance of the celebrated Miss Mestayer, one of the greatest stars now shining. From here I again went to the Jersey Hotel to sleep.

[December 16, 1852. Thursday.] Started early this morning and got our luggage to the shipping agents Office, where we got our [stores] put up and also purchased many little notions extra for our comfort such as are not included in the agents sea [stores]; Oysters, Oranges, Lemons, Soda Powders &c.

At half past 11 o'clock we were taken on board in a steamer, and then towed a piece up the river where we anchored till morning. The following are the names of the brethren who have taken passage on board this ship (Columbia, Capn. Bryer) viz., myself, W[illia]m Glover, W[illia]m Walker, W[illia]m Woodward, Jesse Haven, Levi E. Riter, John A. Hunt and Leonard J. Smith. There are 20 of the brethren altogether who have taken passage on the "American Union," and as the two ships expect both to sail tomorrow, the Captains are inclined to run a race, and see which arrived in Liverpool first.

[December 17, 1852. Friday.] The steamer arrived this morning at 8 o'clock, Brother Richard Cook having engaged passage on this ship, came on board with her. The Sailors were also brought on board, most of them drunk, and several with their faces badly bruised. When the hands were mustered to answer to their names, it was found that there are only about 6 good sailors on board, the remainder being all raw hands, and of the poorest and weakest kind. I never saw a meaner looking crew. One of the old sailors said he should not Stop, for if we encountered a gale with such a crew the ship would surely be lost.

It appears the seamen are employed by the proprietors of the line, (The Black Bale) and the captain being employed or hired also, he knows nothing of the qualifications of his hands untill they are brought on board, hence he is frequently imposed upon. In this case our Captain (Bryer) and the passengers were cruelly imposed upon. His chief mate (Maples) was also a new hand and an entire stranger to the Captain.

At 8 o'clock the steamer commenced towing us up the river and at noon being then off Sandy Hook and in open sea she left us. The Sails were unfurled and we fairly entered on our voyage. Most of us were soon sick and vomiting, myself being one of the worst. We had a fair wind, which caused the vessel to rock very bad, and I was glad to keep my birth. Eight of us occupied one State Room ourselves, and Brother Cook was in the next with other immigrants.

[December 18, 1852. Saturday.] We had a stiff aft breeze, and altho' making good headway, the vessel rocked very bad. In the evening we organized for prayers by appointing Elder Levi E. Riter Chaplain. He called upon Elder Glover who closed the duties of the day by prayer.

[December 20, 1852. Monday.] Today I felt much better, and ate some, which is the first I have eat since I came on board the ship. We have still a good, fair breeze, and are sailing fine. In the evening after singing, prayer was offered up by Elder Jesse Haven.

[December 23, 1852. Thursday.] The wind has continued favorable. This day it has increased, and towards night we had a gale. The sea washed the decks considerable. We met in our state room and most of us offered up prayers, that the Lord would control the elements. I prophecied that we should all be landed safe in Liverpool, to accomplish the work we are sent to perform.

[December 28, 1852. Tuesday.] This day the atmosphere looks very stormy. Heavy, black clouds gathering in the North West, and white vapors flying into their surface with rapid speed. The Captain says we are going to have a terrific gale. The mate says he never knew the Barometer so low as it is today. He does not understand the meaning of it, but apprehends a dreadful time. The wind has been blowing fresh from the S.W. all day, till between 3 and 4 o'clock P.M. when it shifted to the N.W. All the sails were close secured, except just sufficient to give her headway to steer with. At 4 o'clock the gale commenced, and increased in force for several hours. We united in prayer, and nearly all of us put up our petitions to him who controls the elements by the word of his power. 6 o'clock P.M. I was standing at the cabin doorway, reflecting that it was time to make the door fast, as the wind was blowing exceeding strong, and the ship flying before it over the mountain waves, at a rapid speed. While standing here a vast wave dashed over the bulwarks, burying me for an instant in the briny element. The force of the water broke the door from its hinges, and dashing it on the deck, also broke about half of one side of the frame off. The cabin was then about a foot deep in water. The mate immediately sent the carpenter and some of the hands down to nail the door fast, which was done, and a lot of pieces of boards were nailed over it to strengthen it.

I felt very uncomfortable, being thoroughly drenched with water and chilled with cold. The brethren who occupied the upper births went to bed, but the one in which Brother Glover and myself slept being the lower one, and running parallel with the side of the ship, the water washed up into it, every time the ship rolled, wetting it so that we felt no disposition to go to bed.

10 o'clock the gale seemed to be at the heighth of its fury. The moon once in a while be visible showed that the clouds were hurled past with fearful rapidity, and everything betokened the most awful danger. The Captain governed the helm himself, and

mates and all hands were obliged to screen themselves from the fury of the tempest by taking shelter in the wheel House. It was impossible to stand on deck as the waves were continually sweeping over the vessel, and nothing could be done but to keep her fair before the wind, and steer her so as to ride over the foaming, mountain waves, and keep her out of the trough of the sea. About this time most of the passengers were gone to bed and I was standing along near the cabin door. A heavy sea, more furious than usual, dashed over the bulwarks, and again dashed down the door, pouring its flood into the cabin and again burying me completely over. It was sometime before I could get any help to fasten up the doorway. None of the passengers seemed disposed to come to my assistance, and it appeared that the Carpenter and hands did not feel disposed to risk coming to our assistance. However after half an hours delay, they came down and again secured the part of the door that was left, in its places and nailed pieces of board across more firmly than before. I also put two strong props against it on the inside to support it.

The births and cabin now looked awful indeed, the water for sometime being near two feet deep, and the scuttle holes, by some means, being nearly choked up it lessened very slowly. Our bottom chests of provisions were deep in the water, which sometimes washed completely over them saturating our crackers &c. with the sea salt water. The passengers in the after part of the cabin, most of whom were Irish, were very much frightened and instead of the vulgar oaths and blasphemy which in ordinary times constantly saluted our ears, we could frequently hear their groans and petitions to God for mercy.

For ourselves, we felt to trust in the promises of God, and altho' I realized we were in the greatest possible danger, I never felt calmer in my life, nor a greater asssurance in the mercies of our heavenly father that he would bring us through safe and unhurt. Being the only person now up in the cabin, I sat me down on a bail of cotton to watch the door and keep my feet out of the water.

[December 29, 1852. Wednesday.] About 4 o'clock this morning the door was again burst open by the force of the waves. Two large casks filled with barrel heads had broke from their lashings, and were hurled by the water on deck from side to side of the ship

483

like a sledge hammer. One of these had struck the door and broke it down. The gale appeared to be somewhat abating, and as I could get no help to fasten up the doorway again it had to take its chance. I had slept none all night and felt very weary and uncomfortable. To get myself warm I commenced bailing the water out of the cabin, and continued at intervals until 6 o'clock, when several of the brethren and other passengers came to my help. The gale was evidently abating, but the ship looked gloomy enough. The empty barrels and barrel heads were floating from side to side of the deck. The sides of the ship were pretty well shattered. The force of the barrels had knocked the plank off her sides for 8 or 10 feet in length, and from 2 to 3 feet high. Through these holes the seas were continually washing in and out of the ship, rendering it dangerous for any person to attempt to go outside of the cabin door.

8 o'clock. The water is all bailed out of the cabins, and the countenances of the passengers begin to brighten up. The Captain and mates consider that we are now in the utmost danger, as the wind has abated considerable and the tremendous swell of the sea, is liable to break away the masts, or founder the ship between the mountain waves. However we were mercifully preserved, and did not lose as much as a spar or [sail], neither was there a sail damaged. The Captain says he has been on the sea 20 years but he never witnessed such a gale before. Twice we were fairly in the trough of the sea, with mountain waves running on each side, when it appeared impossible to avoid being engulfed and sunk by them; but the Lord bore up the vessel and caused her to ride nobly on their angry bosom without any material accident. The Captain and all hands, regard our preservation as a miracle, and we feel to give glory and gratitude to our Father in Heaven, for this manifestation of his preserving care over us.

On examining our provision chests, we found most of our bread, and our sugar &c. completely saturated, but as we have thus far made rapid progress to our destination we had no fears but that we should have plenty. The Captain informs us that we were taken about 70 miles out of our course, in consequence of the ship drifting before the wind; but this is a trifle when we consider the terrible gale we have passed through. The Brethren fully realized the hand of God in our preservation and deliverance.

[January 1, 1853. Saturday.] The weather has continued favorable; we have had a good, fair wind and have progressed well. Today we have frequent showers. At 11 o'clock passed the Brig Eugenia, in Longitude 10" 26" bound for Greenwich. At 12 M., passed the meridian of "Cape Clara" being one degree of 70 miles south of it.

In the evening we joined in prayer with Elder William Glover. This evening the Irish passengers have exhibited their joy on our near approach to land, by singing and getting drunk. A regular Irish row was the consequence, with swearing and fighting, with women screaming and threatening closed the scene. Truly the wicked soon forget the mercies of God, and those prayerful feelings, instigated by the fear of death, vanish as a light vapor when the danger is past.

[January 2, 1853. Sunday.] Morning clear and beautiful. We were cheered by the sight of land on the Irish Coast, a place called Waterford, being plainly visible from the larbo[a]rd. At 11 o'clock we passed "Tuscur Light House." In the afternoon the wind increased and blew very strong, accompanied with frequent storms, which on account of our being so near land placed us in considerable danger. At 11 P.M. we passed Hollyhead Light House, which is on the Welsh coast, the wind blowing very strong. We sailed about 20 miles below this place, and then backing sail lay too until morning. All gave thanks for our safe Journey.

[January 3, 1853. Monday.] This morning at 1 o'clock a Pilot came on board, but we had to wait for the tide. The ship draws 21 feet of water, and it was unsafe to attempt crossing the bars in low water.

At 9 o'clock we sailed on untill 11 and again lay to for the tide. Soon after noon a steamer came to tow us in, but the wind being fair, we sailed without her, untill we arrived near the mouth of the river. The Steamer then towed us up the river, and at 6 o'clock we anchored opposite to Princess Dock, all safe, in good health and truly thankful to God that we are thus safely on the shores of England. Thus have we been wafted across the bosom of the Ocean, through gales and storms, with a wretched crew, in the short period of 15 days and 8 hours sailing time that is from Sandy Hook to Hollyhead, which considering the weather we have encountered is a very short time.

We learn from the Pilot, that the American Union and Constellation which both sailed from New York the same day we did, have neither of them arrived, nor been heard from.

The Pilot says that during the past two months, there has been a continual succession of gales and stormy weather, such as was never known in the memory of the oldest man living. Many vessels have been wrecked, and a great many lives lost. A great many ships which had left Port, have had to return either dismasted or otherwise so seriously damaged that they dare proceed no further. Great destruction of property on the coasts, and in fact the awful disasters which have befallen the shipping is truly sickening.

We feel more abundantly thankful that we have been preserved, when we hear of the terrible shipwrecks and disasters which have befallen a great many other vessels; and from all we can learn we passed through the severest portion of the worst gale. We felt considerable anxiety for the Brethren on the "American Union", yet had a firm faith that the same infinite power which has preserved us will also preserve them.

[January 4, 1853. Tuesday.] The steamer came along side this morning, and we immediately transferred our luggage to her decks. We were soon after taken on shore, and our luggage to the "searching house." We felt to rejoice to place our feet on the streets of Liverpool, after such an uncomfortable time spent on the sea. Our State room floor had never been dry from the time we began to sail untill we landed, and my boots having ripped my feet were constantly wet and cold.

While the custom House Officers were searching our luggage, Elders Samuel W. Richards,[39] Willard Snow, John E. Forsgren and Vincent Shurtliff came to see us. We were heartily welcomed by them, and Brother Shurtliff tarried to conduct us to our lodging house. There is a company of near 300 Danish Saints now laying on board the ship opposite, ready to sail for New Orleans under charge of Elder Forsgren.

---

[39] Samuel W. Richards (1824–1909) worked as a carpenter on the Nauvoo Temple and was an officer in the Nauvoo Legion. When the temple was closed in 1846, he joined the British mission and served as president of the European mission from 1852 to 1854.

After the Officers had got through with us, we proceeded to Brother Cowley's Temperance Coffee House in Great Cross Hall Street, where we took up our abode for the time being. After eating dinner we went to the Bath House where we took a glorious scrubbing for about an hour. This with a change of clothing refreshed us very much. In the evening we went to the Office in Wilton Street, and spent a season with Brother S[amuel] W. Richards, taking some bread and cheese and Port Wine; after which we returned to Brother Cowley's and were soon comfortable in a warm bed.

[January 5, 1853. Wednesday.] Spent the day looking around the town and purchasing a few articles which we were much in want of. I purchased a pair of Boots and 2 pairs of socks, which Brother Shurtliff kindly paid for. He appears to have plenty of gold. In the evening I had a visit from Elder Willard Snow. He returns to Denmark.

[January 6, 1853. Thursday.] Today we went down to the docks, and soon learned that the "American Union" is coming up the river. At noon we saw her being in tow of one of the Steam tugs. At 3 o'clock the brethren landed, all safe and well, and according to their report having had much better voyage than we had, altho' two days longer on the sea.

In the evening we went to the Office and received our appointments and papers. Elder Glover being appointed to be president over the Sheffield branch in place of John Albiston, who goes to Leeds, and myself to the Pastoral charge of the Sheffield and Lincolnshire Conferences. I borrowed two pounds of Brother Samuel and also got a Book of Mormon, Hymn Book and Pearl of great price.[40] He made Brother Glover and myself a present of each a Book of Doctrine and Covenants. We then left the Office designing to proceed to our destination tomorrow. Evening went to visit Wombwells Managerie.[41]

---

[40] Along with the Book of Mormon and Doctrine and Covenants, the Pearl of Great Price is one of the unique Mormon scriptures.

[41] "Captain" George Wombwell's Menagerie was a well known travelling collection of wild animals brought mostly from Asia and Africa. Visiting such menageries was a popular entertainment in mid-nineteenth-century Europe. Some wild animal exhibitions later became part of circuses and others developed into zoos

[January 7, 1853. Friday.] Brother Glover and myself started on the Railway for Preston, where we arrived soon after 10 o'clock. We left our luggage at the Station, and went to visit old Cock Pit, and various other places, with which I was formerly familiarly acquainted. We took dinner at a Tavern, and then hired a hack and went to visit Bashal's Factory. We went through the Mill from end to end. Some of the old Reelers, who were there when I left were indeed glad to see me; one of them Elizabeth Beck a Baptist, ran at me, put her arms around my neck, and embraced me like a long lost child would its parent.

We then went to Charnock Moss and paid a visit to the old house where I was born and raised. Many solemn thoughts passed through my mind while thus viewing the scenes of my childhood. We then returned to Preston. I visited Mr. James Fielding, having a letter of introduction to him from Brother Joseph Fielding in the Valley. We had some conversation together, but I found him as bitter against Mormonism as ever. We went to Brother John Mellen's to tea. He appears to have settled down to stay in Preston and manifests but little desire to gather with the Saints. While here we were visited by John Halsal, who appears much the same as when we left him twelve years ago.

[January 8, 1853. Saturday.] Started for Manchester. I had some letters for several of the Saints here, which I was requested to deliver personally. After seeing our luggage safe at the Sheffield Station, we started to find the persons to whom the letters were addressed. We found them all removed, and after hunting sometime I left Brother Glover to go to dinner with the residing Elder, agreeing to meet at the Railroad station at half past 4. I then continued my search but as unsuccessful as ever, until the time appointed to meet at the Railroad, and hurried off then as fast as I could. Unfortunately, I was about 2 minutes too late. The cars were just starting out as I got there. I then concluded to take lodgings till morning and then follow Brother Glover by the first train. I found a place to stay, which I afterwards learned to my sorrow was the house of an Apostate Mormon; and through him I have passed through the most unpleasant, and bitterest period of

(Earl C. May, *The Circus from Rome to Ringling* [New York: Duffield & Green, 1932]). Clayton frequently visited such animal exhibitions.

my life. On getting set down, being wet with perspiration through walking so much with my heavy cloak on, I began to chill and was soon taken very sick indeed with cold on my lungs.

[January (23?), 1853. Sunday.] . . . on the revelation. He is a fine man and a good speaker. His heart is in the work and he enjoys the spirit to a good degree.[42]

[January 24, 1853. Monday.] Spent the day visiting among the saints. Evening met the Priests and Teachers at the room and gave them a lecture on the duties of their offices, counselling them to visit all the members in their several districts to know their standing, that those who will not be faithful may be rooted out. Then gave them instructions in regard to the Revelation and explanations on various subjects.[43] Elder Glover followed on the same subject. The brethren expressed themselves much edified, and appear determined to do their duty to the letter. After meeting went to supper to teacher George Lees.

[January 25, 1853. Tuesday.] Took dinner at Brother [] Wharton's. Brother and Sister Winfield came to spend the afternoon with Brother Glover. I went alone to visit the new Barracks. Then to Brother Whiteleys to Tea, and after Brother Whiteley came from work, we went together in the Omnibus to Attercliffe 2 miles; where I preached on the plurality doctrine. There are but few saints at this place, but they appear very attentive. Brothers Whiteley, Perks and several others bore testimony after me, Brother Watts, a druggist, got up to oppose the doctrine, and in answer to the question, said he wished to be cut off from the church; and the brethren and sisters raised their hands against him to cut him off from the Church. He has for sometime been an unfaithful member, and has been a grief to the saints. He opposed Elder Glover a week ago, and then called to be cut off from the Church, but mercy was exercised towards him, as the Brethren wished to save him if possible. Returned to Sheffield on foot.

---

[42] The holographic journal pages covering the dates between January 8 and 24 appear to have been removed from the original record. The remaining entries resume in mid-sentence just prior to January 24.

[43] By this time Clayton had arrived in Sheffield and began to explain and defend the revelation on plural marriage.

[January 26, 1853. Wednesday.] Went to dinner to Brother Betz's and spent two hours with them. Then went to Brother Memmet's to inquire for letters. I found [one] from President Samuel W. Richards containing intimations of an accusation being brought me, concerning my situation the night I arrived in Sheffield.[44] I concluded to go to Liverpool at once and meet the accusation face to face. It was then 20 minutes past 2 o'clock. I went to Sister Whartons to change my Shirt and then to the Railroad depot, as fast as I could go, Brother Memmet accompanying me. We got there just before the train started and at five minutes to 3 I was on my way to Liverpool. On arriving at Manchester at 5 o'clock I had to wait till half past 6 for a third class train as I had not much money. I arrived in Liverpool about half past 8 and went direct to Wilton Street; but found to my sorrow that Brother Samuel had gone to a tea party and would not be home till after midnight. I then went to Brother Cowleys and after taking a little supper went to bed.

[January 27, 1853. Thursday.] After breakfast went to Wilton Street and had an interview with President Richards. I found that the report had been painted in the blackest colors, and I have reason to believe that the Apostate, with whom I boarded in Manchester has used much dilligence in his endeavors to injure

---

[44] After receiving Richards's letter and reading notice of his suspension from church activity (see February 2 entry), Clayton explained the charge of adultery against him in a letter to Thomas Bullock. When Clayton stopped at Manchester to deliver letters and missed the train to Sheffield, he said that he stopped at the house of an (unnamed) apostate Mormon where he remained for ten days confined to bed with an illness. Although Clayton tried to avoid talking about the sensitive doctrine of plural marriage to this family, the host raised the issue in a volatile argument. Clayton wrote: "This scoundrel to be revenged on the doctrine of plurality, made use of arguments which I used to show him that it was scriptural, as though I had acknowledged that I had more wives than one, and has trumped up a malisious set of lies and told them to some of the brethren in Manchester." Some British Saints "uncautiously believed his wicked statements," Clayton recalled, and Samuel Richards, the mission president in Liverpool, "evidently give some credit to the report." To complicate matters, Clayton "took a glass of gin to stimulate me for the task" of explaining his late arrival at his mission assignment. "Unfortunate act," he observed. "The weakness of my body, and being so long without food, caused it to take hold of me," so when he arrived, the brethren "could see that I had had something to drink very plain." Clayton lamented that "the effects of the gin almost made me crazy." Since "I have indulged to much in times past," he realized, President Richards would "naturally conclude[] that the report must be true" (Clayton to Bullock, February 5, 1853, LDS archives).

me. Brother Spencer was present during the interview and both seem very much grieved, and doubtless they believe the reports. The mail arrived from Salt Lake yesterday, and the news is good. I received a note from Brother [Thomas] Bullock stating that my family were writing in full, but there are no letters for me in the office. After conversing a while Brother Samuel requested me to call again at 5 o'clock, and I left to do so. Brothers Charles A. Harper, John C. Hall, Erick G. M. Hougan and Canute Peterson have arrived safe across the sea and are preparing to go their several fields of labor. I spent the day walking along the dock and looking at the shipping. At 5 o'clock I went to see President Richards again and found that his mind is still the same. He advised me not to act in a public capacity nor preach for a week or two, untill the excitement and prejudice has subsided. I promised I would not do it, and left him my licenses as a guarantee. He gave me two sovereigns to pay my expenses, and I bid him good-bye with a heavy heart, seeing plainly that the devil is determined to destroy me if possible. In the evening I went to Wombwell's Menagerie to pass away the time, then went to rest at Brother [] Cowleys after paying him 4/6 for my board, two nights and one day.

[January 28, 1853. Friday.] Started on the railroad at a quarter to 7. The morning being cold and frosty. Arrived at Manchester at 9 o'clock and there had to wait near 5 hours for a third class train. Took breakfast at a Temperance Coffee House, then waited at the Station in the cold till a quarter to 2 o'clock, at which time the train started for Sheffield. I arrived at Sheffield at 4 o'clock and went direct to Brother Barraclough's where I lodged and took tea. Brother Glover has not yet returned from his weeks mission. After tea I started to go to Brother Memmets to see if there were any letters for me from home. I met him on the way and learned that no letters have arrived. I then went and spent the evening at the circus to pass away a lonely hour.

[January 29, 1853. Saturday.] Spent several hours with Sister Plant formerly from Manchester and took dinner with her. Then went to Brother Wharton's and took tea and shaved there. At 8 o'clock went to meet the officers of the Church at their room. I there made a statement of the circumstances which has lead to the unpleasant feelings now existing, my object in going to

491

Liverpool &c. and asked, inasmuch as any one's feelings had been injured that they would forgive it. Brother Glover arrived while I was speaking and made some remarks on the subject. The brethren voted unanimously to forgive all that is past, and also to write the facts to the office at Liverpool The brethren appear to feel very well towards me.

[February 1, 1853. Tuesday.] At Brother [] Barracloughs all day reading and writing in the Camp journal. Wrote a letter to Mr. Satterthwaite at Preston, concerning the affairs of my father. Evening attended meeting at Brother Barracloughs, and was pleased to hear the faithful testimony of the Saints.

[February 2, 1853. Wednesday.] Went to take my clothes to Sister Whartons to get them washed. Afterwards writing in the Camp Journal. Evening went to visit the old Manor house and the remains of the ancient castle of the Dukes of Norfolk. It is truly a very ancient building. Those parts which are yet standing, although inhabited, appear as though they might fall down any minute; the walls being crooked, and the roofs of the houses having sunk in very much. The walls which are of thin stone have apparently been about four feet thick, and the action to the wind and rain, together with their vast age, have worn deep holes all over the walls, and it is truly in a dilapidated state. In this Castle Mary, queen of Scots was imprisoned twelve years, commencing in the year 1569, and from here she was taken to Lincolnshire where she was condemned and executed. The owner of this Castle being one who passed sentence of death upon her. Here also the celebrated Cardinal Wolsey was imprisoned 18 days after he lost the favor of his King.

The stone which formed the building where the unfortunate queen was imprisoned, has been moved by a gentleman to his new castle, about a mile south of the old site, and they are there laid up into a building as a matter of curiosity and relic of the olden times.

In 1647 this Castle was destroyed by a resolution passed by the house of commons, and all that remains of it, are some old buildings, some vaults, and part of a tower on the South West corner which is used as a deposit for ashes and all kinds of filth.

At night I went with Brother Barraclough to visit Brother Fisher and family. Sister Allen was also there. They had heard many false reports concerning our customs in the Valley, such as taking a man's wife from him and giving her to another, without her consent; and taking young women and giving them to men contrary to their feelings &c.[45] I explained the true principles to them, and showed them that such reports are false. Spent an hour and a half teaching them and they appeared to feel much better, and fully satisfied in regard to the plurality. On returning to Brother Barraclough's I was astonished to see a notice in the Star of the 5th inst. that I was suspended from office.[46] Truly I feel this hard, especially when it is done to gratify the envy and jealousy of certain individuals who have believed the slanderous reports of a wicked apostate. However, I feel to bear it calmly, knowing that it will be right in the end.

[February 3, 1853. Thursday.] At Brother Barraclough's all day fetching up this journal by copying from the camp journal. At 4 o'clock went to visit the Cholera Monument. This monument was erected in remembrance of the awful scourge by the Cholera in the year 1832, when some hundreds of the inhabitants of Sheffield fell victims to its ravages. It is erected on a beautiful peace of elevated ground on the South-east part of the town. The monument is of cut stone of a triangular form, and is supported at its base by three wings at its base, branching out from the points of the triangle. About half way up, there are the representation of three females one on each side of the triangle in a standing position, their hands clasped in an attitude of prayer. They are fixed in riches and are apparently cut in the marble. The whole is surrounded by an iron railing which is kept lock[ed]. The monument is of plain work, and bears no inscription on it. Underneath lay the bodies of those who fell by that dread scourge. Previously the spot of ground has been a stone quarry, and the bodies of the dead were hauled promiscuously into the vase pit which was finally covered up, and the present monument erected. On the east and

---

[45] See Journal 3, "Nauvoo Temple," December 21, 1845, and n32.

[46] The notice of suspension reads: "Notice. — Elder William Clayton, by late appointment Pastor of the Sheffield and Lincolnshire Conferences, is suspended from acting in any official capacity in the Church of Jesus Christ of Latter-day Saints. S. W. Richards, President of said Church in the British Isles" (*Latter-Day Saints' Millennial Star* 15 [February 5, 1853]: 96). Clayton's suspension was brief. He was reinstated the following week by a letter from Samuel Richards received on February 12.

north is a beautiful park, and a walk around it for enjoyment in the pleasant summer season and where people may recreate free of charge. The lands on which the monument and Park stands were given by the late Duke of Norfolk.

Evening went and took tea with Brother Walters, and visited some with him.

[February 4, 1853. Friday.] Went to visit Sister Womack, who is some better, a little wine apparently nourishing her. Took dinner with them and watched Brother Womack put some pocket knives together. It is astonishing to see the number of times such small things have to go through the workmens hands. Returned in a snow storm, very cold and spent the afternoon and took tea with Brother Newsham.

[February 6, 1853. Sunday.] Wrote a long letter to Thomas Bullock, giving him the history of my travels from the 3rd of January, untill the time I was suspended, the cause for which it was done &c. The remainder of the day I was writing in this journal. In the evening a number of the Brethren called, and I felt well while instructing them on the principles of eternal life.

[February 7, 1853. Monday.] After breakfast Brother Glover and myself went up to Brother Memmets where I received a very consoling letter from President S. W. Richards as follows: "15 Wilton Street, Liverpool, February 5th, 1853."

Dear Brother William. Your letter of the 30th ult. came duly to hand which gave me great satisfaction, and which should have been replied to sooner, only I have been obliged to lay bye nearly all the correspondence of the office for a few days, while fitting the ship "Jersey" with saints, for sea. They sailed this morning about 7 o'clock, and today I resume the office correspondence trusting you will not feel neglected as you might perhaps have justly felt under other circumstances.

I have received a line from the Sheffield Council noticing their satisfaction in the interview you had with them; which causes me to feel that the spirit of God was there and approbated it.

Altho' the most of the Presidents letter, will appear in the next week's "Star," yet I take pleasure in forwarding it for your perusal and satisfaction. You state that Brother Bullock informed you, that your family were writing you by the same mail but no letters were received here address[ed] to you.

I have received a letter from Elder Carn in Germany, stating that he has been expelled from the free city of Hamburg, by a special decree of the Senate, for no other reason but that of propagating his religious views. He has taken refuge in another part of the country, to watch the movements of things for a time. I understand he left the City before the time expired allowed to him, and without the interference of authority, so that he will have the privilege of returning again when he may deem it prudent. He fully exonerates the American Counsul, who interfered in his behalf without effect.

A brief line from O[rson] Spencer, Berlin, February 7th informs me that upon obtaining an interview, or an investigation before the President of the King's Police, he and Elder Houtz were required to leave the Kingdom of Prussia the next morning at 8 o'clock under penalty of Banishment. Upon asking permission to remain 1 or 2 days as visitors and close a little business it was denied them; not a moment was granted past the hour of eight o'clock; they therefore left at that time and are expected in Liverpool on the 7th inst.

Such demonstrations as these need but one little comment to show the condition of the powers that be when protestant governments can do such things, without the fear of shame or rebuke from powers professedly more liberal.

Please excuse my brevity at this time, as I purpose you shall hear from me again soon, and accept the constant and prayerful regard of your Brother and Servant in Christ, S. W. Richards."

The following is a copy of that portion of President Youngs letter of October 29, 1852, which is not inserted into the Star. viz. "So soon as our indebtedness shall become liquidated so that Dr. [] Bernhisel will not have to draw upon the funds at the Liverpool Office, (which we hope may not be long) we wish you to devote the Tithing fund, and all of the profits of the Office, that can be spared, to the replenishing of the Perpetual Emigrating Funds, and payment of money which you may have borrowed. We send you the enclosed list of names to assist, if it be in your power. I wish that you would send a few pieces of bolts of good crumb cloth, as we very much need it to preserve Carpets in some of our rooms, which you know are in constant use.

Brother William Clayton as you will observe by the minutes of Conference is appointed on a mission to England; he is now with the rest of the missionaries on his way and will probably arrive early in the winter. Brother William has always been closely tied up to business; and previous to his coming from England travelled but very little outside of his native country. It is therefore my wish, as it is his desire that he be permitted to visit the Conferences in England and the adjacent countries.[47] In this capacity of a travelling Elder, he may prove a very useful auxiliary and be the means of accomplishing a great work which his eminent qualifications and abilities so well enable him to perform and realize the just expectations of his friends as reasonably inspired by the superior advantages which he has enjoyed to obtain intelligence, and the well known capacity and strength of mind which he unquestionably possesses.

I wish for you to get the Fustian[48] sent for in my former communication providing you can get a good, first rate article; if not, I would prefer that you save the money and not make any purchases."

This letter gave me much joy and comfort, and inspired me with fresh energy to be faithful and do the will of God, that the anticipations of my Brethren in regard to me may be fully realized, and that I may be the means of doing a good work during my stay in this country. And may the Lord enable me to do it, for I have no other object and desire but to do this thing.

After reading the letters, we went to Brother Wharton's and then separated. I went with Sister Atkinson to "California" to visit Sister Hartley. She had forgot the directions, and after travelling up hill and down for about an hour, and inquiring directions in vain for Sister Hartley we returned to town without making our intended visit. We called at Sister White's and took dinner. Sister White is a very talkative woman, and has much fault to find with others. Her youngest child is very sick, and at her request I administered to it, but she has little faith. I then

---

[47] After repenting of his "follies" and sharing the anxieties of his responsibilities, Clayton had requested in his October 4, 1852, letter to Brigham Young that he "should not be confined to any particular location in England, but may have the privilege to visit the branches" (LDS archives).

[48] A coarse cotton cloth, once hand-woven at Manchester.

returned to brother Barraclough's and felt too tired to visit anymore today.

[February 8, 1853. Tuesday.] This forenoon I commenced writing in this journal again. At noon went to Brother Pickering's to dinner. He was not at home. I find Sister Pickering to be a very nice woman, of a mild, quiet disposition and evidently a good saint. After spending about 2 hours I returned home and continued writing till evening. Then attended prayer meeting at Brother Barracloughs. I spoke to the saints sometime on the subject of faith, and exhorted the saints to arouse themselves, and keep the commandments of God, that they may realize the fulness of his blessings. Elder Glover followed and spoke well. The saints bare a good testimony, the spirit of God was with us, and the saints acknowledge it to be the best meeting they have been at for a long time.

[February 9, 1853. Wednesday.] This morning we went to Brother Walters to breakfast, then to Sister Wharton's to take our clothing to be washed. From there we went to Brother Abram Hunt's to dinner, and I preached to them on the principles of eternal lives for upwards of an hour. We then took a walk to the old Manor House, and returned to Thomas Leas to tea, where we spent an hour and a half. We then went to the Circus and spent the evening.

Sister Perks related a dream, which sustains the feelings Brother Glover and myself both have in relation to Elder Roper and John Memmet. They are both in opposition to us and will injure us and destroy our influence as far as they can.

[February 10, 1853. Thursday.] Spent the day writing in this journal. Evening Elder Glover and myself attended the prayer meeting at Brother Barracloughs. I spoke sometime on the principle of faith, and exhorted the saints to faithfulness and diligence. Elder Glover also spoke some on the subject of obedience &c. The meeting was a good one, and all the Saints felt well.

[February 12, 1853. Saturday.] A.M. writing in this journal. Last evening I received a leter from S[amuel] W. Richards restoring me to my labors again, and expressing his very kind feelings and confidence; and also saying that he will publish the facts of his confidence, as far as he has published his disaprobation of

497

the past. I am firmly convinced that Brother Samuel believes the false and exaggerated reports of J. V. Long and others, and my only course is to let time tell the secret who is right, and who is wrong.

Brother Hain called to see Elder Glover and reports that the Branch in Rotherham are in a very low state. Their case will be attended to.

Brother John Memmet called with Elder E. Sutherland who has arrived from London today; we had some conversation together. He says the work is prospering in London. Three of the Elders have lately held a discussion each, with as many popular ministers. The Priests cannot bring anything against the doctrine of plurality only slanderous reports.

Elders Glover and Hains have started for Pilley. Elder Sutherland and myself went to Brother Whartons where we took supper and spent the evening with them. Brothers Winfield and James Goodwin spent the evening with us.

[February 15, 1853. Tuesday.] This morning Elder Glover and myself went with Elder Sutherland to the Wicker Station. He and Elder Haines go to Doncaster. I purchased a book of Plays to send to the Deseret Theatrical Association. Afterwards writing in this journal. Elders T. J. Schofield and Western called to see me. Brother Western is in trouble, having lost his employment and sold his furniture to go to the Valley on strength of Brother Warehams promises. Brother Wareham has now declined going or helping Brother Western in any way, and Brother Wareham is in [great] distress in consequence of it.

When Elder Glover returned in the evening he informed me, that he had been to visit Brother Wareham in company with Elder Western. He was informed that Brother Wareham "was too sick to see him." He however obtained the loan of 28 pounds for Elder Western. This was done by Sister Wareham, who is represented as a good Saint, and is deeply grieved on account of her husbands conduct.

In the evening we went to the Theater, and saw the plays of "Belphego[o] or the Mountebank" and the Lady of Lyons, both good plays, and the leading parts were admirabl[y] sustained by Mr. Charles Dillion and wife, who are evidently performers of the first class.

Sister Womack is represented as being only just alive, and is given up as past recovery by the Doctor.

[February 17, 1853. Thursday.] A.M. at home writing in this journal. After dinner Elder Glover returned from Liverpool, and informed that Elder Richards has agreed to send the $100. to Mr. Kinkead by his Uncle Levi who leaves next month. This is a source of comfort to us, and moves a heavy burthen from our minds. He also brings assurance of the confidence and kind feelings towards me of Elders Richards and Spencer. Also a proof sheet of No. 9 Star which notices my restoration to my labors. The same Star also notices the arrival of Elders Edward Martin, W[illia]m Taylor and James Parks in Liverpool in the 8th inst. being 40 days from New Orleans. The brethren have now all arrived except Elders A. L. Lamoreaux, W[illia]m Pitt and Daniel [Toner].

Orson Spencer expects to go to Washington to labor in connexion with Elder Orson Pratt. We went to Sister Whartons to tea, and tarried a season there; then went to the Theater to spend the evening, to be out of the way, and relieve our minds a little.

[February 19, 1853. Saturday.] I wrote a letter to President S[amuel] W. Richards, one to John [C.] Armstrong, and one to George Tipler. The latter was to get information concerning matters and addresses pertaining to the Lincolnshire Conference.

Sister Hall called to get counsel in relation to her going to Liverpool to emigrate. Her daughter has wrote for her to go. We advised her to be still untill she heard from President Richards. Sister Hall's husband is a very drunken man, and abuses her shamefully.

P.M. Elders Sutherland and Schofield called, and we counselled together on the propriety of giving a course of lectures in Sheffield. We finally agreed to do so, and immediately drew up a bill for a notice of the same, designing to get a number of copies printed and distributed through the Town.

Elder Sutherland says that five of the brethren in Doncaster are ready to pay 10/6 each towards hiring a large room there. We design giving a course of lectures in that place also, and in all the principal branches of this conference as fast as the way opens. He says the brethren where he has been this week begin to feel better, and we have a very good prospect for work enough soon.

I received a letter from President S. W. Richards requesting the Sheffield Conference to subscribe 10 pounds towards assisting the Elders off, who are going on foreign missions. Went to visit Sister Plant, Brothers Newsham and Wharton, and returned home at 8 o'clock very unwell. Sent Elder Richards' letter by Elder Glover to be read to the Council. When the brethren heard the letter they cheerfully reponded to the call and seem disposed to do all they can towards raising the amount. They are also ready to assist us in defraying the expenses of the Lectures, such as printing hand bills &c.

[February 20, 1853. Sunday.] A.M. Went to meeting in company with Elders Glover and Sutherland. There were but a very few present. Several of the resident Elders addressed the saints. Went to Elder Whartons to dinner and attended meeting again in the Afternoon. Elder Glover addressed the Saints for some length of time.

Took Tea at Brother W[illia]m Memmet's, then again went to meeting. I addressed the Congregation and proved to them, that even if we were deceived in regard to the administering of the angel &c. we were still better off than the sectarians in every sense of the word. I bore testimony to them of the truths of the Gospel, and the mission of Presidents Joseph Smith and Brigham Young. The saints appeared highly rejoiced. Elder Glover made some remarks also and all seemed to feel well.

We went to supper to Brother Wilbraham's Skyhill, and at 9 o'clock returned home.

Elders Peck and Thomas Lea returned from the Rotherham Branch and brought 13 shillings which the Saints have donated for the Elders according to Elder S. W. Richards request.

[February 21, 1853. Monday.] Got the matter for the hand-bills to the printing office; then wrote a letter to President S. W. Richards. Went to George Lea's to dinner, with Elder Glover, Sutherland, and Schofield. We there met Elder Haines and wife and sister Camel. We spent a few hours very pleasantly together, then returned and sent notices to the Doncaster district of Elder Sutherlands intended visit this week.

In the evening myself and Elder Sutherland went to hear the band play. Elder Glover tarried at home and had an interview with Brother and Sister Wareham. Brother Wareham has decided to go to work and sell his property, which is worth about 600 pounds and start for the Valley with the next company. He has also agreed to take Elder Schofield and wife along with him. If he will do this it will be his salvation, and if he don't do it he will be ruined for he is literally surrounded by fiends in human shape who seek his overthrow.

Elder Glover had also a long interview with Elders Roper, Memmett and Wharton. The two former confessed their feelings in humble terms and have promised to sustain us in all our movements for the building up of the Kingdom; and Elder Roper has agreed to take part in the lectures. They have both agreed to do all they can and say they are determined to do as we tell them.

This is truly a relief to us, for these two brethren have stood in opposition to us (in feeling) ever since we came here. We feel now that every obstacle is removed, and the Lord has wrought every thing round to our hearts desire. We could not have been more blest in regard to these matters, even if we had had the privilege of asking the Lord for them, face to face; and to his name be all the praise and glory forever and ever.

[February 22, 1853. Friday.] Sister Newsham called to give me 1/6 to pay my fair to Chesterfield. And may the Lord bless her with means to do as her heart desires; Yea Oh Lord abundantly bless all thy Saints who bless thy servants, and may all they do be increased to them an hundred fold.

In the afternoon went to see Elder Schofield, to make arrangements to meet at the Railroad Station. Not finding him at home, Elder Glover, Sutherland and myself went to Brother Morris' to tea. Here I waited for Elder Schofield as long as I dare; then went to his house, and learned he had been gone to the Station about half an hour previous. I hurried after as fast as I could but was too late for the train, and had to wait till morning. I truly felt disappointed and mortified, in being this defeated in my expected visit to Chesterfield. Elder Schofield said he did not know where Brother Morris lived. And being engaged with Brother Wareham in getting ready to go to the Valley I felt to excuse him.

[February 23, 1853. Wednesday.] I was up this morning early, and after taking a little breakfast went to the Station. At a quarter to 8 the train started and at half past 9 arrived at Chesterfield. Elder Schofield was waiting for me. We went to Elder Is[aac]

Allen's where I was very warmly received by both Brother and Sister Allen. They expressed deep sorrow at the way I have been treated; but are truly rejoiced to see me amongst them again.

From here we went to Elder McDuff's in Brampton, where Elder Schofield left me while we went to Brother Shorts on business. I took dinner at Sister McDuff's and spent the afternoon preaching to a number of the Sisters, who came together to hear something of the plurality doctrine. I find the same wicked reports have been circulated here, as in other places, viz. that when they arrive at the Valley the husband and wife are separated, and daughters taken from their parents and given to whoever the authorities think proper regardless of their feelings. I took pleasure in correcting the reports, and taught them the true principle, which seemed to cheer them much.

About 4 o'clock we were visited by a very heavy snow storm from the north accompanied by high wind. For a short time the atmosphere was dark as approaching night. It was such a storm as is rarely witnessed. Elder Schofield arrived soon after, having been in the storm from its commencement. After tea, we returned to Chesterfield, and took the Railroad to Clay Cross Station 4 miles. We had a mile to walk from the station, but the night was clear, although the snow made it unpleasant walking. On arriving at the Clay Cross meeting room, we found most of the Saints assembled and services commenced. There are only some 16 or 18 Saints in this branch. Elder Schofield bore a farewell testimony to them for sometime. I also bore my testimony and exhorted the saints to be faithful. A good feeling prevailed. This branch subscribed 1 pound towards helping the Elders on foreign missions.

After meeting was over we returned to one of the brethren's houses to supper. I talked to them and instructed them on the Revelation and other principles till near midnight, when we went into Sister White's, next door, and went to bed, both much pleased with the good feeling of the saints and the kind and faithful spirit manifested by them.

[February 24, 1853. Thursday.] After taking breakfast at Sister White's, we started on foot across the country for Bolsover. On our way we passed Wingfield Church, a very ancient edifice, of rather small dimensions. We stopped to view the figure of a man in full armor, cut in stone, and laying on its back with hands clasped, as was the customary position in olden times when laying in state. The figure represents one of the heroes of the crusades, and bears the marks of time in many respects. It is laid in a niche in the south wall of the Church, and is quite an ancient curiosity.

I was informed that this Church was one of the rendezvous of the celebrated Robin Hood and his archer band, and that the surrounding country was the scene of many of his famous exploits. The scenery is indeed beautiful, the high hills on every side, once covered with dense forests of timber, now laid off in rich fields and farms; the rolling appearance of the country with deep secluded vales on every hand makes it look like enchanted ground. The head quarters of the noted free booter, (Sherwood Forest) is 12 miles from here, and doubtless the whole of this region has been the scene of stirring and thrilling events as history relates.

A piece further we passed through Sutton Park, a splendid enclosure of about 500 acres; beautifully adorned with stately timber, and nice lakes of water. The residence of the present owner Esquire Arkwright, lays on a beautiful eminence on the eastern part of the Park, and commands a fine view of Bolsover castle and surrounding country. The mansion or Hall is a large building, built in the most costly and stylish fashion, and the owner who is a bachelor is represented as being immensely wealthy; the family having in three generations rose from abject poverty, to unbounded wealth, but from causes which ought to be a sting in the hearts of the family forever. The tale runs thus. The grandfather of the present Esquire was a poor cobbler (I believe) living near this neighborhood. Close by him resided an ingenious man, also a poor laborer, and with whom Arkwright was on the most intimate terms. This man had spent years in constructing a model of a spinning jenny to supercede the spinning by hand as was then the only method known. He had completed his task to his own satisfaction, and felt encouraged to hope that this achievement would raise him from his poverty, and place him in comfortable circumstances. His intimacy with old Arkwright caused him to show the latter his model, and explained the nature and purpose of the invention. Arkwright saw the importance of the invention at once, and immediately his avaricious propensities

503

prompted him to lay plans to get possession of the model, by any means. An opportunity soon served his purpose. He made occasion to send the poor inventor on an errand some miles from home, and the dupe to earn a trifle scrupulously started on his errand. As soon as the man was out of sight, old Arkwright went to the man's house, and told the wife that her husband had sent him for the model for a short time, as he was at his (Arkwrights) house, and wanted it for some purpose. The wife unsuspectingly fetched the model and handed it to the villain, who, now secure of his prize returned home in triumph and without loss of time took the necessary steps to secure a patent in his own name as the original inventor. When the poor fellow returned home, and learned from his wife what the villain Arkwright had done, he became nearly distracted. He saw his brightest prospects blasted, and his hopes for years plundered from him, and himself left as an unknown miserable slave while his treacherous neighbor enjoyed the honor and benefit of all his toils. He fell upon his innocent wife, and nearly killed her in his frenzy. What became of him afterwards is not stated.

Arkwright secured the patent, and by the help of friends, was enabled in course of time to erect a small factory, where the spinning jenny was introduced and put into successful operation. He rose to affluence as if by miracle, and it is said that the present Esquire don't know what he is worth.[49] About half a mile north west of the mansion is a beautiful, level spot of land, which is marked out as the spot where Oliver Cromwell planted his cannon, while endeavoring to destroy the famed Bolsover Castle. His army occupied the Park, which is some two miles from the castle, while its defenders occupied the steep hills, adjacent to and surrounding the Castle, forming an impenetrable barrier to the

---

[49] Industrialized cloth-making took place in two phases. Mechanized looms began to draw weavers out of their homes in the 1830s, several decades after spinners went from home to factory. In 1767, Richard Arkwright pioneered the use of the spinning jenny, a machine which made it possible to spin more than one thread at a time. A recent biographer of the family recounts two persistent legends about the origins of the jenny: one casts Arkwright as an illiterate barber in Preston who heard about a Chinese machine from a sailor; the other, which Clayton repeats here, is that Arkwright stole the invention from a poor carpenter (R. S. Fitton, *The Arkwrights* [Manchester: Manchester University Press, 1989], reviewed in *The Economist*, February 4, 1989). Contrary to Clayton's rendition, Arkwright never secured a patent for the invention.

usurpers' farther progress. After an unsucessful attempt for a number of days, he departed elsewhere without effecting the destruction of the castle, or subduing the owner or his tenants. See history of O[liver] Cromwell.[50]

We arrived at Bolsover about 5 o'clock, and called at Brother Stocks' where we took tea. Here we learned that the saints of Bolsover have given notice to quit their meeting room because the Landlord charges 1/6 per week for it. The rent is low indeed, but for some cause or other they are about 15 shillings in arrears already although Brother Gaskin owns a number of houses and is building more. He is probably worth from 150 pounds to 200 pounds, but is so penurious, he is unwilling to pay more than an equal share with the poorest member. He quietly satisfies his conscience by paying 8 pence a month, and appears to care nothing whether the room is given up or not.

When meeting time arrived we both went to the room, and both addressed the saints; the principle topic being to exhort them to faithfulness, and by no means to part with their present place of meeting for the paltry sum of 1/6 per week. I think the saints will arouse themselves and act more wisely. We returned to Brother Gaskins' where we stayed overnight.

[February 25, 1853. Friday.] After breakfast we went to visit the castle which is truly an object of interest. It is owned by the Duke of Portland, who, after the attack made on it by Cromwell, left it, and built a new mansion at a place called Welback, his present residence. The Castle buildings are about 100 yards square, the south side forming the front or grand entrance. On this side are very large, stately rooms, one of which is probably 100 feet by 30, but all in an unfinished state, never having been roofed. Over the main entrance, inside is the Portland Arms, beautifully carved in stone, they are of the blood Royal, as their arms indicate. The outside is of finely chiseled stone work, and presents a grand appearance. This part of the Castle was erected in the year 1630 one part of which was expressly designed to accommodate the King who frequently visited this Castle.

---

[50] Oliver Cromwell (1589–1658) was a Puritan revolutionary against the king. He ruled England from 1653–58 as a virtual dictator but refused the title of King.

The west end is the Castle proper or tower, a square building 5 stories high ornamented with cupolas and bears a truly strong and ancient appearance. This is the only habited part, and is now occupied by the Reverend Mr. Gray the minister of Bolsover Church who has possession of the whole premises for the nominal rent of 5 pounds a year. The east end was originally designed for riding rooms and places of amusement, but now converted into stables for horses. The west is enclosed by a wall, thick enough for a Coach and horses to travel on it. The space within the walls is beautifully laid off with shubbery and gravel walks, and the whole, though unfinished has a truly grand and imposing appearance. Under the buildings which form the south side, have formerly been numerous cellars, now mostly filled up with earth and ruins; one of these I noticed has from its peculiar position evidently been an under ground prison.

The south wall bears the marks of Cromwells balls in several places. One ball has struck the side of the grand entrance, and split a piece off the stone work. Another has cut its way through the corner of a projecting turret; and a third has made its way through the wall under one of the large windows, leaving a rough hole about 4 inches in diameter. It is said that if Cromwell had known that his shot had ever struck it, he would never have left it, until he had levelled it with the ground. The Castle stands on the brink of a very steep hill, and being surrounded by a strong wall is impregnable except from the East, where the town of Bolsover stands. On the East part of town is the fortification, said to be thrown up by the Duke of Portlands troops in one night. It is formed by a ditch about 12 feet wide, and an embankment about 8 feet high on the side nearest the town. From this embankment on the east, there are watch towers still standing on the hill side south of the castle walls and outside them, all along the western side of the Castle.

The whole works show great strength and are a monument of troublesome times.

After dinner we started on foot to Stavely a distance of 4 miles. The roads were very muddy and slippery. We arrived at Stavely at 3 o'clock and stopped at Brother Ottaway's. The Saints here are poor and few in number, several of whom have been turned out of employment because they are "Mormons."

After tea Elder Schofield and myself walked out together. He informed me that Elder [] Wheelock is one who has tried to injure my character deeply. At this I was astonished, as I have not seen Elder Wheelock for many years, much less ever given him any cause for such treatment. However as the revelations came from Elder Schofield of Brother Wheelocks conduct I am not much astonished. The following are amongst some of them: He has taught that he was a priviledged person by the presidency. He has given washings and anointings to individuals as preparatory to their endowments. He made great promises to the saints to secure their being sent to the Valley this season, by which means he received large sums of money for himself, and departed from England without fulfilling no promise. He collected 300 pounds in one conference and 200 pounds in another to pay his expenses to the valley when one sister had made him a present of a thousand pound by her will. He was seen in the half guinea boxes of the theater, with a lady on each side, and a fashionable quizzing glass like a gentleman, when the poor Saints were subscribing of their hard earnings to send him home. One of the sisters has testified in counsel that he taught her he was a privileged character and had connexions with her. Has promised several young women to take them to the Valley and marry them &c.

How true these reports are I know not. Elder Schofield says the whole and more of a similar character can be proved if necessary. It is not my business, and I shall not interfere with neither speak of it to his injury.

Attended meeting when Elder Schofield preached and I followed with testimony; several ranter preachers were present, and the saints were made to rejoice. Though few in number, they appear faithful. We returned to Brother Ottaways where we tarried over-night.

[February 26, 1853. Saturday.] We started early this morning, and walked to Chesterfield 4 miles. The morning was very stormy, snow fell thick and we were both near wet through. On arriving at Elder Isaac Allen's I received 3 letters; one from Elder Twelves of Lincolnshire, one from the Liverpool Office, and one from Elder John C. Armstrong. By the first named letter I learned that Elder Twelves will wait for me at the Boston Railroad Station

507

today, but not receiving his letter sooner I shall necessarily dissapoint him.

After dinner I took the 2 o'clock train for Sheffield, Elder Schofield staying till 6 o'clock, to transact some private business. Half past 3 I arrived in Sheffield both wet and fatigued; yet well satisfied with my week's work.

After resting awhile and changing my clothes, Elder Glover and myself went to Brother Morris's where we spent the evening very pleasantly in the company with Brother and Sister Wharton's and Morris's.

Whenever I have travelled this week I have met with the most cordial reception. The Saints universally rejoice to see me, and I feel blest in instructing them. Truly the Lord has over-ruled everything for my good, and I feel lead to praise him continually.

[February 27, 1853. Sunday.] A.M. at home preparing for the evening's lecture. Afternoon attended meeting and spoke to the saints a short time. Went to Brother Morris's to tea, and at 6 o'clock returned to the room, and delivered a lecture on the Restoration of the Jews, and Apostacy of the Gentiles, according to previous notice given in the hand bills. The room was well filled, and many strangers were present. I never saw better attention than was given during the whole lecture, which was an hour and three quarters long. I felt great liberty while speaking, and the saints remarked afterwards that the time I was speaking did not appear to them more than 1/2 an hour.

We again went to Brother Morris's to supper. News has been received today that Elders Cook, Deuel, and Long have been mobbed at Cambridge. A company of ruffians having assembled during meeting, extinguished many of the lights, creating a general sense of confusion and excitement. The brethren escaped without personal harm, although their hats were crushed on their heads. When they applied to the magistrates for redress, the magistrates began to question them on the doctrine, and the brethren commenced preaching to them. The result was, they were soon stopped and the case dismissed from court.

[February 28, 1853. Monday.] Went to make arrangements with Elder John Memmet to send the 10 pounds to Liverpool. I left the money I had with him to forward this evening. Then went to Brother Hansons to select cloth for a pair of Pantaloons which the saints have subscribed for me according to Elder Glovers request yesterday. I got a good piece of black Kerseymere[51] at 1/6 per yard. Brother Hanson also presented Elder Glover and myself with a good pattern for a pair of pantaloons each for every day.

Went to Elder Camall's to dinner, where we met Elder Schofield and wife, Elder Haine and wife, Elder Sutherland and others and had a pleasant interview for a few hours. After dinner we went to visit Sister Womack, calling at Brother Morris's to leave the cloth, on the way. We found sister some better, but she is so weak, and so far gone with consumption that she cannot recover unless by miracle. After administering to her, we returned to visit Sister Hopkins who we found much better. After taking tea with Brother Hopkins, we repaired to the Baths, where Elder Glover baptized five brethren and sisters for remission of sins. These baths have a very filthy appearance, and I felt to advise the brethren not to use them any more. The water looks dirty, and the room is also very dirty. Moreover there is no convenience for changing clothing.

There are good baths at Upper Thorpe, kept clean, with good accommodation, but the Saints have patronized these because they are kept by one of the brethren. He appears however to be too indolent to keep them clean. Sister Atkinson was taken very sick, after being baptized, being troubled with wind on her stomach. We laid hands on her, and administered some Cayenne which soon gave her relief.

We then went to Brother Wharton to supper, and spent the evening in conversation, till near midnight. We both felt to caution Sisters Wharton and Morris about going abroad so much; and have both resolved to avoid being seen travelling through streets with them, lest scandal should ensue, and evil appearance be made to grow out of it.

[March 1, 1853. Tuesday.] Brother Warham called this A.M. stating that he has effected the sale of his 8 houses for 70 pounds each and his business will be closed on Friday.

---

[51] Named for the village Kersey in Suffolk, England, kerseymere is a woolen cloth used for men's suits.

I wrote a long letter to my family and also one to President S[amuel] W. Richards.

Evening Elder Glover and myself clothed ourselves in order, and offered up our prayers that the Lord will enable us to accomplish a great work &c. Afterwards I had a farewell interview with Elder Thomas J. Schofield, as it will probably be the last time I shall see him until we meet in the valley.

I have purchased another Book of Plays to send to the Valley by Brother Schofield.

[March 2, 1853. Wednesday.] At home writing the last week's journal in this book. The day is very stormy, and snow is falling fast.

Elder Glover returned about 3 o'clock, having been to baptize Mrs. Potter.

About the same time Sisters Hartley and Schofield called to pay us a visit. Sister Hartley is taking a course to bring disgrace on the cause. She is scarce ever at home, and we feel to give her a rebuke that she may learn better.

Elder Glover and myself went to administer to Brother Perks who is sick. He felt relieved instantly. We then went to Brother Henry Morris's and spent the evening. Brother Morris has made me a pair of every day Pantaloons gratis, and he and his wife have both treated us with the greatest kindness.

Spent the forenoon writing a letter for Elder Glover to his family. Then went to visit Sister Potter where we took dinner. Afterwards went to visit Elder Roper's family and Brother Morris. Evening preparing to go to Lincolnshire.[52]

---

[52] Clayton's "Polygamy Mission to England" journal ends here abruptly. The following month Clayton sailed back to America.

APPENDICES

Extracts from
William Clayton's [Private] Book —

KEYS

*J*oseph Smith began presenting the *following "keys of the mysteries of the kingdom" to his twelve apostles prior to their August 8, 1839, mission to England. William Clayton, who remained in England another year, subsequently copied these discourses along with others he evidently recorded from the prophet in 1840–41. In 1880 L. John Nuttall, secretary to the First Presidency of the LDS church, made extracts from Clayton's account. Nuttall wrote on the inside front cover, "L. John Nuttall his Book 1880," and entitled the work as above.*

O ye Twelve[1] and all saints profit by this important key that in all your trials, troubles, temptations, afflictions, bonds, imprisonments, and death, see to it that you do not betray heaven, that you do not betray Jesus Christ, that you do not betray your brethren, that you do not betray the revelations of God, neither in the Bible, Book of Mormon or Doctrine and Covenants or any *other that ever was or ever will be given and revealed unto men in this world, or in the world to come,* yea in all your kickings and flounderings see to it

---

[1] Apostles.

that you do not this thing, lest innocent blood be found in your skirts, and you go down to hell. *All other sins are not to be compared to sins against the Holy Ghost and proving a traitor to thy brethren.*[2]

A final key delivered by Joseph Smith in the following language:

I will give you one of the keys of the mysteries of the kingdom, it is an eternal principle that has existed with God from all eternity: that, that man who rises up to condemn others, finding fault with the church, saying that they are out of the way, while he himself is righteous, then know assuredly that that man is in the high road to apostacy and if he does not repent will apostatize as God lives. The principle is as correct as the one that Jesus put forth in saying that he who seeketh after a sign is an adulterous person; and that principle is eternal, undeviating and firm as the pillars of heaven: for whenever you see a man seeking after a sign, you may set it down that he is an adulterous man.[3]

A key by Joseph Smith Dec
1840 W[illiam C[layton][4]

If an Angel or spirit appears offer him your hand; if he is a spirit from God he will stand still and not offer you his hand. If from the Devil he will either shrink back from you or offer his hand, which if he does you will feel nothing, but be deceived.

---

[2] Still in England when Joseph Smith spoke these words, Clayton evidently copied this first paragraph selectively from Wilford Woodruff's journal entry for July 2, 1839, leaving out an earlier key. See Scott G. Kenney, ed., *Wilford Woodruff's Journal*, 9 vols. (Midvale, UT: Signature Books, 1983), 1:342–44. The italicized lines were added by Clayton, perhaps copied from another source; they are replicated with minor word differences in Joseph Smith, Jr., et al., *History of the Church of Jesus Christ of Latter-day Saints*, ed. B. H. Roberts, 2d ed. rev., 7 vols. (Salt Lake City: Deseret Book, 1963), 3:384; hereafter *HC*.

[3] Willard Richards apparently copied this paragraph in England from another diarist, possibly Wilford Woodruff or John Taylor, who heard Joseph Smith speak these words. Smith delivered the discourse on July 2, 1839 (*HC* 3:385; Andrew F. Ehat and Lyndon W. Cook, eds., *The Words of Joseph Smith* [Provo, UT: Religious Studies Center, Brigham Young University, 1980], 413).

[4] Clayton arrived in Nauvoo, Illinois, on November 24, 1840. His journal entry for that date is apparently retrospective and must have been written sometime after December since it includes references to 1841. Clayton mentions that he had heard Joseph Smith speak twice.

A good spirit will not deceive. Angels are beings who have bodies and appear to men in the form of man.

By Joseph, Jany. 5th, 1841 at the
organization of a school of instruction.[5]
Description of Paul — He is about 5 foot high; very dark hair; dark complection; dark skin; large Roman nose; sharp face; small black eyes, penetrating as eternity; round shoulders; a whining voice, except when elevated and then it almost resembles the roaring of a Lion. He was a good orator, but Doctor Bennett[6] is a superior orator, and like Paul is active and diligent, always employing himself in doing good to his fellow men.

By Joseph, January 5th, 1841
Answer to the question, was the
Priesthood of Melchizedeck taken
away when Moses died.
All priesthood is Melchizedeck; but there are different portions or degrees of it. That portion which brought Moses to speak with God face to face was taken away; but that which brought the ministry of angels remained. All the Prophets had the Melchizedeck Priesthood and was ordained by God himself.

The world and earth are not synonymous terms. The world is the human family. This earth was organized or formed out of other planets which were broke up and remodelled and made into the one on which we live. The elements are eternal. That which has a beginning will surely have an end. Take a ring, it is without a beginning or end; cut it for a beginning place, and at the same time you have an ending place.

A key, every principle proceeding from God is eternal, and any principle which is not eternal is of the Devil. The sun has no beginning or end; the rays which proceed from himself have no

---

[5] The journal of William P. McIntire, one of Joseph Smith's scribes, records weekly meetings of this school from the day it was organized. He identifies it as a lyceum. See William P. McIntire, "Minute Book," March 30, 1841, reproduced in Ehat and Cook, 68.

[6] See discussion of Dr. John C. Bennett in Journal 1, "England and Emigration," n85.

515

bounds, consequently are eternal. So it is with God. If the soul of man had a beginning it will surely have an end. In the translation, "without form and void" it should read "empty and desolate." The word "created" should be formed or organized.[7]

Observations on the Sectarian God

That which is without body or parts is nothing. There is no other God in heaven but that God who has flesh and bones. John 5 — 26, "As the father hath life in himself, even so hath he given the son to have life in himself." God the father took life unto himself precisely as Jesus did. The first step in the salvation of men is the laws of eternal and self-existent principles. Spirits are eternal. At the first organization in heaven we were all present and saw the Savior chosen and appointed, and the plan of salvation made and we sanctioned it. We came to this earth that we might have a body and present it pure before God in the Celestial Kingdom. The great principle of happiness consists in having a body. The Devil has no body, and herein is his punishment. He is pleased when he can obtain the tabernacle of man and when cast out by the Savior he asked to go into the herd of swine showing that he would prefer a swines body to having none.[8] All beings who have bodies have power over those who have not. The devil has no power over us only as we permit him; the moment we revolt at anything which comes from God the Devil takes power.

This earth will be rolled back into the presence of God and crowned with Celestial Glory.

Remarks by Joseph, May 16th, 1841.[9]

There are three independent principles — the spirit of God, the spirit of man, and the spirit of the devil. All men have power to resist the devil. They who have tabernacles have power over those

---

[7] These ideas of uncreated matter reflect contemporary science, although the sun is now recognized to have a beginning and a projected end. See also Journal 2, "Nauvoo, Illinois," n27.

[8] See Mark 5:11-13; Luke 8:32-33.

[9] Clayton frequently kept concurrent journals. In his "England and Emigration" journal for this date he cites an address by Smith on eternal judgment and says "See Record," possibly the following entry.

who have not. The doctrine of eternal judgment Acts 2 — 41 Peter preached repent and be baptized in the name of Jesus Christ for the remission of sins, &c; but in Acts 3 — 19 he says "Repent and be converted that your sins may be blotted out when the time of redemption shall come and he shall send Jesus" &c. Remission of sins by baptism was not to be preached to murderers. All the priests in christendom might pray for a murderer on the scaffold forever, but could not avail so much as a gnat towards their forgiveness. There is no forgiveness for murderers. They will have to wait until the time of redemption shall come and that in hell. Peter had the keys of eternal judgment and he saw David in hell and knew for what reason, and that David would have to remain there until the resurrection at the coming of Christ. Romans 9 all election that can be found in the scripture is according to the flesh and pertaining to the priesthood.

By Joseph.[10]

Everlasting covenant was made between three personages before the organization of this earth and relates to their dispensation of things to men on the earth. These personages according to Abraham's record are called God the first, the Creator; God the second, the Redeemer; and God the third, the Witness or Testator.

Priesthood.[11]

The priesthood was first given to Adam; he obtained the first presidency and held the keys of it from generation to generation; he obtained it in the creation before the world was formed as in Gen. 1 — 26, 28, he had dominion given him over every living creature. He is Michael the Archangel spoken of in the scriptures.

---

[10] Although L. John Nuttall does not date this entry, William P. McIntire includes a similar discussion in his "Minute Book," dated March 9, 1841 (Ehat and Cook, 64).

[11] The last three discourses, on "the priesthood," "the sower," and untitled, were probably initially recorded by John Taylor before August 8, 1839, since Taylor left on that date for a mission to England and his initials appear twice in this discourse. Clayton could have copied this discourse from the diaries of John Taylor or from Willard Richards, whose "Pocket Companion" also includes it. See Ehat and Cook, 8-12.

Then to Noah who is Gabriel, he stands next in authority to Adam in the priesthood. He was called of God to this office, and was the father of all living in his day and to him was given the dominion. These men held keys first on earth and then in heaven. The priesthood is an everlasting principle and existed with God from eternity, and will to eternity, without beginning of days or end of years. The keys have to be brought from heaven whenever the gospel is sent. When they are revealed from heaven it is by Adam's authority. Daniel 7 speaks of the Ancient of Days, he means the oldest man our Father Adam, Michael. He will call his children together and hold a council with them to prepare them for the coming of the Son of man. He (Adam) is the father of the human family and presides over the spirits of all men, and all that have had the keys must stand before him in this great council. This may take place before some of us leave this stage of action. The Son of man stands before him and there is given him glory and dominion. Adam delivers up his stewardship to Christ, that which was delivered to him as holding the keys of the Universe, but retains his standing as head of the human family.

The spirit of man is not a created being, it existed from eternity and will exist to eternity. Anything created cannot be eternal. Air, earth, water, all these had their existence in an elementary state from eternity. Our Savior speaks of children and says "their angels always stand before my father."

The Father called all spirits before him at the creation of man and organized them — he (Adam) is the head and was told to multiply. The keys were given to him; he will have to give an account of his stewardship and they to him. The priesthood is everlasting. The Savior, Moses and Elias, gave the keys to Peter, James and John on the mount, when they were transfigured before him. The priesthood is everlasting without beginning of days or end of years, without Father, Mother &c. If there is no change of ordinances, there is no change of priesthood. Whenever the ordinances of the Gospel are administered there is the priesthood. How have we come at priesthood in the last days — they came down in regular succession. Peter, James and John had it given to them and they gave it up. Christ is the great High Priest. Adam next. Paul speaks of the church coming "to an innumerable company of angels, to God the judge of all: the spirits of just men made perfect, to Jesus the mediator of the new covenant" &c. Heb. 12—23. I saw Adam in the valley of Adam-ondi-ahman,[12] he called together his children and blessed them with a Patriarchal blessing. The Lord appeared in their midst and he (Adam) blessed them all and foretold what should befall them to the latest generation. See D.C. Sec. 3−28, 29.[13] This is why Abraham blessed his posterity. He wanted to bring them into the presence of God; they looked for a city &c. Moses sought to bring the children of Israel into the presence of God through the power of the priesthood; but he could not. In the first ages of the world they tried to establish the same thing, and then were Elias raised up who tried to restore these very glories but did not obtain them. (Enoch did for himself and those that were with him but not for the world, J. T.[14]) They prophesied of a day when this glory would be revealed. Paul spoke of the dispensation of the fullness of times when God would gather together all things in one &c. Those men to whom these keys have been given will have to be there (I.E. when Adam shall again assemble his children of the priesthood and Christ be in their midst the ancient of days come &c. &c. J. T.) and they without us could not be made perfect. These men are in heaven but their children are on earth, their bowels yearn over us. God sends down man for this reason Matt. 13−41 and the son of man shall send forth his Angels &c. All these authorative characters will come down and join hand in hand in bringing about this work. The Kingdom of heaven is like a grain of mustard seed. The mustard seed is small but brings forth a large tree. The fowls are the Angels, the Book of Mormon perhaps, Thus Angels come down combined together to gather their children and gather them. We cannot be made perfect without them nor they without us; when these are done, the Son of man will descend, the Ancient of Days sit. We may come to an innumerable company of angels, have communion with and receive instruction from. Paul had these things, we may and have the fowls of the heaven lodge in the branches. The horn made war with the Saints, overcame them &c. until the Ancient of Days come and judgment was given to the Saints of the Most High from the Ancient of Days; the time came that the Saints

---

12 See discussion of Adam-ondi-Ahman in Introduction, n18.
13 Doctrine and Covenants.
14 Probably John Taylor.

possessed the kingdom. It not only makes us ministers here but in eternity. Salvation cannot come without revelation; it is in vain for any one to minister without it. No man is a minister of Jesus Christ without being a prophet. No man can be the minister of Jesus Christ except he has the testimony of Jesus, and this is the spirit of prophecy. Whenever salvation has been administered it has been by testimony. Men at the present time testify of heaven and hell and have never seen either, and I will say that no man knows these things without this. Men profess to prophecy. I will prophecy that the signs of the coming of the Son of man are already commenced, one pestilence will desolate after another. We shall soon have war and bloodshed, the moon will be turned to blood. I testify of these things and that the coming of the Son of man is nigh, even at your very doors. If our souls and our bodies are not looking forth for the coming of the Son of man and after we are dead if we are not looking forth we shall be among those who are calling for the rocks to fall upon us &c. The hearts of the children will have to be turned to the fathers and the fathers to the children living or dead to prepare them for the coming of the Son of Man. If Elijah did not come the whole earth would be smitten. There will be here and there a stake &c. Some may have cried peace but the saints and the world will have little peace from henceforth. Let this not hinder us from going to the Stake; for God has told us to flee not or we shall be scattered, one here another there.

There your children shall be blessed and you in the midst of friends where you may be blessed &c. The Gospel net gathers in of every kind. I prophesy that the man who tarries after he has had an opportunity of going will be affected by the Devil. Wars are at hand we must not delay but we are not required to sacrifice. We ought to have the building up of Zion as our greatest object. When wars come we shall have to flee to Zion, the cry is to make haste. The last revelation says ye shall not have time to have gone over the earth until these things come. I will come as did the cholera, war and fires, burning, earthquakes, one pestilence after another &c. until the Ancient of Days come, then judgment will be given to the Saints.

Whatever you may hear about me or Kirtland take no notice of, for if it be a place of refuge the Devil will use his greatest efforts to trap the saints. You must make yourselves acquainted with those men who like Daniel pray three times a day, to the hour of the Lord. Look to the Presidency &c. Every man who is afraid, covetous &c. will be taken in a snare. The time is soon coming when no man will have any peace but in Zion and her Stakes. I saw men hunting the lives of their own sons and brother murdering brother, women killing their daughters and daughters seeking the lives of their mothers. I saw armies arrayed against armies. I saw blood, desolation and fires &c. The Son of Man has said that the mother shall be arrayed against the daughter and the daughter against the mother &c. &c., these things are at our doors, they will follow the saints of God from city to city. Satan will rage; the spirit of the Devil is now enraged &c. I know not how soon these things will take place, and with a view of them shall I cry peace, No! I will lift up my voice and testify of them. How long you will have good crops and the famine be kept I do not know. When the fig trees leave know then that the summer is nigh at hand. We may look for angels &c., but we are to try the spirits and prove them. It is often the case that men make a mistake in regard to these things. God has so ordained that when he has communicated no vision to be taken but what you see by the seeing of the eye, or what you hear by the hearing of the ear. When you see a vision &c. pray for the interpretation, if you get not this shut it up. There must be certainty. An open vision will manifest which is more important. Lying spirits are going forth in the earth. There will be great manifestations of spirits false and true &c. Being born again comes by the Spirit of God through ordinances. An Angel of God never has wings. Some will say that they have seen a spirit, that he offered them his hand but they did not touch it; this is a lie for it is contrary to the plan of God. A spirit cannot come but in glory. An Angel has flesh and bones we [see] not their glory. The Devil may appear as an angel of light. Ask God to reveal it; if it be of the Devil he will flee from you, if of God he will manifest himself or make it manifest. We may come to Jesus, he will know all about it. If he comes to a little child he will adopt himself to the language and capacity of a little child. There is no gold nor silver &c. it is false all is plain in heaven. Every spirit and vision or singing is not of God. The Devil is an orator &c; he is powerful, he took our Savior to a pinnacle of the Temple and kept him in the wilderness for forty days. The gift of discerning spirits will be given to the presiding Elder, pray for him &c. Speak not in the gift of tongues without understanding it, or without interpretation. The Devil can speak in tongues. The adversary will come with his work, he can tempt all classes, can speak in English or Dutch. Let no one speak in tongues unless he interpret except by the consent of one who is placed to preside, then he may discern or interpret, or another may. Let us seek for the glory of Abraham, Noah, Adam, the Apostles, have communion with these things and then we shall be among that number when Christ comes.

Behold a sower went forth
to sow &c.

Our Savior is the sower — the people are the world — the harvest is the end of the world — the reapers are the angels. The end of the world is not come consequently the harvest cannot come without angels. The Son of man is to send forth his angels. The Son of man says that the Saints shall judge the world and angels. God has revealed himself. When they come up before God they will be asked, did this angel perform this or that, that he was sent to do, if not they will be judged — the world judged.

Some fell among thorns &c. God sows — the enemy comes and sows parties, division, heresies, shall we kill them. No, not till harvest, the end of the world. The Son of God will do as he ever has done from the beginning — send forth his angels. If the reapers do not come the wheat cannot be saved. Nothing but kingdom being restored can save the world. Like unto a treasure hid in a field, this figure is a representation of the kingdom in the last days. Michael, Adam, Noah, I am Gabriel, well says I who are you, I am Peter the angel flying through the midst of heaven. Moroni delivered the Book of Mormon.

The Pearl of great price is the inheritance prepared for the Saints — sell all you have get purchase &c. What is the end of the world, the destruction of the wicked, the angels have begun to be revealed, they shall bind up the testimony. Like unto a Merchant man buying goodly pearls; a net that gathers of every kind; the wheat gathered into the barn; the tares left on the field to be burned. The net gathers in of every kind. Those who hold keys

were more concerned about their children than themselves it happens to be our lot to live in a day when this place.[15]

It is the privilege of the children of God to come to God and get revelation. John 14 ch. 1. Let not your hearts be troubled &c. There are a great many mansions in my father's house, I am going to prepare one for you rather better than common. It is the privilege of the sons of God to inherit the same mansion &c. When any person receives a vision of heaven he sees things that he never thought of before. If we should tell of different glories as Paul did—in my father's house there are many mansions—every man that receives the gospel receives that inheritance that the Apostles did. Everyone that hath seen me hath seen my Father. He that believeth—any person that believes the works I do shall he do also, and greater works. The Father could not be glorified in the Son on any other principle than we coming to God asking, receiving, heavens open, visions &c. They are done away because of unbelief. I will pray the Father and he shall send you another comforter to abide with you forever reach to things within the vail. Know that you are sealed, if you get it it will stand by you forever; how is it to be obtained? Keep my commandments and I will pray &c. It is a privilege to receive the Son of Man himself, he dwelleth with you and shall be in you. I will not have you comfortless. His spirit shall be in you. I will come to you, abide with you forever, seal you up to eternal life. Yet a little while and you shall see me no more but ye see me. He that hath my commandments and keepeth them he it is that loveth me &c. I will manifest myself to him; if he does not he has not told the truth. I will put promise in your hearts that will not leave you, that will seal you up. We may come to the general assembly and church of the first born spirits of just men made perfect; unto Christ. The innumerable company of Angels are those that have been resurrected from the dead. The spirits of just men made perfect are those without bodies. It is our privilege to pray for and obtain these things. How wilt thou manifest thyself unto us and not to the world evidently knowing that it would be so that he would manifest himself. There was no cholera, no mobs, before this came. I told them that rejoice in mobs that they should have

---

[15] The following discourse, the third and last in this series recorded before August 8, 1839, is untitled.

them. They have since come in torrents, they did not receive the testimonys of the Son of God. If a man love me he will keep my words and my Father will love him, and we both me and my Father will take our abode with him. There are certain characters that walked with God — saw him, conversed about heaven &c; but the comforter that I will send (not the other comforter) shall teach you all things — who? He that loveth me &c. This shall bring all things to your remembrance whatsoever thing I have said unto you; he shall teach you until you come to me and my Father. God is not a respecter of persons; we all have the same privilege come to God, weary him until he blesses you &c. all are entitled to the same blessings — Jesus, revelations just men, Angels &c., &c. not laying again the doctrine of Christ go on unto perfection. Obtain that holy Spirit of promise when you can be sealed to eternal life.

B.

An Interesting

JOURNAL

Seven *years after William Clayton died, his family published "An Interesting Journal, by William Clayton" in* The Juvenile Instructor, *21 (January 15–Oct. 15, 1886), 2–20:23–311, published by the LDS church in Salt Lake City. The following appendix contains issues 2–10, the portion derived from the original handwritten narrative presently filed in LDS archives as "William Clayton's Journal, etc." It recounts the early history of the Mormon church, with primary focus on the construction of the Nauvoo temple. The narrative ends shortly after Joseph Smith's death.*

The Latter-day Saints were expelled from the State of Missouri, under the exterminating order of Governor Boggs in the Fall and Winter of the year of our Lord, one thousand eight hundred and thirty-eight. Having been plundered of all their property, they settled in this place — then called Commerce but subsequently named Nauvoo; while they were in a stripped and destitute condition. Nearly all of the Saints were sick, and many of them died in consequence of exposure and the lack of the necessaries of life. There were then but two or three houses in the place; and, therefore, the majority of the people dwelt in tents and in the open air, exposed to all the rigors of an inclement season.

In September, 1839, the Apostles started the second time for England. They, themselves, were ill and they left their families in sickness and poverty. The Apostles who took this trying journey at that time were Brigham Young, Heber C. Kimball, Parley P. Pratt, Orson Pratt, John Taylor, Wilford Woodruff and George A. Smith. Elder Richards was already in Great Britain; and he was ordained to the Apostleship when the others of the Twelve reached their destination.

During the Winter and Spring of 1839, nearly all of the Saints moved into Nauvoo, the only exceptions being some few families who scattered about among the people of the State of Illinois.

As soon as the health of the brethren would in anywise permit, they began the work of putting up log cabins for shelter. In the course of the season the majority were made tolerably comfortable in this respect, though many still suffered greatly for want of food.

The spot of land on which the Saints located was very wet and consequently very unhealthy; but by the blessing of God the health of the Saints improved, and they learned the necessary course of life in this trying region, and were able to improve the character of the soil which they cultivated.

Before even this state of comfort was achieved, the authorities began to talk upon the subject of building a temple, wherein to administer the ordinances of God's house. Several councils were held and a place selected whereon the temple was contemplated to be built. The matter was laid before the conference on the 6th of October, in the year 1840; and the Church voted to commence the work immediately. On this day the conference appointed a committee of three, viz: Alpheus Cutler, Elias Higbee and Reynolds Cahoon, to carry the business into operation and to oversee the work.

During conference President Joseph Smith explained to the Saints the law of tithing and the plan upon which the building of the temple was to be conducted.

Several plans for a temple were made and submitted by various individuals, but the only one which was satisfactory to the Prophet was the one drawn and presented by William Weeks.

On the twelfth day of the same month, the brethren commenced the opening of a quarry from which to obtain stone for the building. Brother Elisha Everett was the man who struck the first blow on the works. He has continued in this labor from that time on until the present, and has proved himself a faithful worker and a worthy man.

The committee contracted with Daniel H. Wells, Esq., for the land whereon to build the temple; and on the nineteenth day of January, in the year 1841, the Lord, through His servant Joseph gave a revelation approving the selection of a temple site and commanding the erection of the sacred structure upon that spot.

In the month of February, 1841, Elder Alpheus Cutler, assisted by Elder Cahoon and others, laid out the foundation of the temple. On the eighteenth day of that month the brethren began to dig the cellar. As it was the wish of President Joseph that the corner stones of the temple should be laid on the sixth day of the next April, the Corners for the foundation were first excavated; and about the first day of March the cellar walls were commenced.

On February 22nd the committee organized the city into Wards and called upon the brethren to come forward and labor every tenth day. By this means they were enabled to rush on the work so rapidly that by the sixth day of April the walls were sufficiently high at the corners to admit of the laying of the corner stones. And notwithstanding the extreme poverty of the Church, the labor moved so quickly and the prospects seemed very cheering and pleasing.

I will now extract from the Times and Seasons of April 15, 1841, as follows:

"At an early hour on the sixth inst. the several companies constituting the Nauvoo Legion, with two volunteer companies from Iowa Territory, making sixteen companies in all, assembled at their several places of rendezvous, and were conducted in due order to the ground assigned for general review. The appearance, order and movements of the Legion were chaste, grand and imposing, and reflect great credit upon the taste, skill and tact of the men comprising said Legion, especially the chief officer of the day, Major General Bennett. We doubt whether the like can be presented in any city in the western country.

"At half past 7 o'clock, a.m. the fire of artillery announced the arrival of Brigadier Generals Law and Smith at the front of their respective cohorts; and at 8 o'clock Major General Bennett was conducted to his post under the discharge of cannon and took command of the Legion.

527

"At half past 9 o'clock, a.m. Lieutenant General Smith with his guard, staff and field officers arrived at the ground and were presented with a beautiful silk national flag by the ladies of Nauvoo, which was respectfully received and hailed by the firing of cannon, and borne off by Colonel Robinson, the cornet, to the appropriate position in the line; after which the lieutenant general, with his suite, passed the lines in review. At 12, m. the procession arrived upon the temple ground, inclosing the same in a hollow square, with Lieutenant General Smith, Major General Bennet, Brigadier Generals Law and Smith, their respective staffs, guard, field officers, distinguished visitors, choir, band, etc., in the center and the ladies and gentlemen citizens surrounding the interior. The superior officers, together with the banner, architects, principal speaker, etc., were duly conducted to the stand at the principal corner stone, and the religious services were commenced by singing from page 65 of the new hymn book."

President Sidney Rigdon addressed the assemblage at some length, after which a hymn was sung under page 205, and the closing prayer was offered.

"The architects then, by the direction of the First Presidency, lowered the first (S.-E. corner) stone to its place, and President Joseph Smith pronounced the benediction as follows:

" 'This principal corner stone, in representation of the First Presidency, is now duly laid in honor of the great God; and may it there remain until the whole fabric is completed; and may the same be accomplished speedily, that the Saints may have a place to worship God, and the Son of Man have where to lay His head.'

"President Sidney Rigdon then pronounced the following:

'May the persons employed in the erection of this house be preserved from all harm while engaged in its construction, till the whole is completed; in the name of the Father, and of the Son and of the Holy Ghost; even so. Amen.'

"Adjourned for one hour.

"Assembled according to adjournment and proceeded to lay the remaining corner stones according to previous order.

"The second (S.-W.corner) stone, by the direction of the President of the High Priesthood, with his Council and President Marks, was lowered to its place, when the President of the High Priesthood pronounced the following:

528

"The second corner stone of the temple now building by the Church of Jesus Christ of Latter-day Saints, in honor to the great God, is duly laid, and may the same unanimity that has been manifested on this occasion continue till the whole is completed; that peace may rest upon it to the laying of the top stone thereof, and the turning of the key thereof; that the Saints may participate in the blessings of Israel's God within its walls, and the glory of God rest upon the same. Amen.

"The third (N.-W. corner) stone, superintended by the High Council, as representatives of the Twelve (they being in Europe), was then lowered to its place, with the benediction of Elias Higbee as follows:

" 'The third corner stone, in representation of the Twelve, is now duly laid; and as they are, in some measure, the support of the Church, so may this stone be a firm support to the corner, that the whole may be completed as before proposed, and according to the order of the priesthood.'

"The fourth (N.-E. corner) stone, superintended by the Bishops, was then lowered to its place, and Bishop Whitney pronounced the following:

" 'The fourth and last corner stone, expressive of the Lesser Priesthood, is now duly laid; and may the blessings before pronounced, with all others desirable, rest upon the same forever. Amen' "

After the corner stones were laid and the conference was over, the work upon the temple seemed to progress more rapidly. There were about eighteen stone cutters engaged to dress the rock for the building. Up to this time the work performed was nearly all done by tenth days' labor. But after this the Saints began to bring in some provisions, property and money; and the committee was enabled to employ a number of stone cutters and keep them constantly at work. The tithing labor also increased through the continued immigration of Saints from abroad.

When the Winter season set in toward the close of the year 1841, the walls on the south side were built up to the water table, a part of which also was laid. On the north side the walls were only about two feet high. In this state the structure remained until the Spring of 1842.

During all this time there had been no general tithing record opened. The money and other property contributed had all been paid over to the committee, and receipts were issued to the several donors. Elias Higbee kept the books and work accounts, and generally wrote the receipts for tithing. This branch of the business occupied nearly the whole of his time. Elders Cahoon and Cutler hired the laborers, superintended the work and kept an oversight of the entire business.

On the 25th day of September, 1841, Elders Alpheus Cutler and Peter Haws, started for the pine country to obtain lumber for the Temple and Nauvoo House. They took with them, Tarleton Lewis, Jabez Durfee, Hardin Wilson, Wm. L. Cutler, Horace Owens, Octavious Pauket, Blakely B. Anderson, James M. Flack, Nathaniel Child, Brother Child's wife and daughter, and Peter W. Conover. These brethren spent the Winter in the pine forests, and toiled diligently in their appointed work. They suffered some because of the cold in that northern region, but they made good progress. By the following July, they had succeeded in making up and bringing to Nauvoo a large raft of first-rate pine timber. By this means the prospect of the work was much brightened.

On the 13th day of December, 1841, the Prophet Joseph appointed Apostle Willard Richards to be recorder for the temple and scribe for the private office of the President.

The recorder opened his office in the counting room of President Joseph's new brick store on Water Street, and he immediately began to record the tithings on the Book of the Law of the Lord,[1] page 27. The first record was made under the date of

---

[1] Begun in 1841, "The Book of the Law of the Lord" is a large, leatherbound, 500 plus-page record book of donations—primarily for the construction of the Nauvoo Temple—minutes of meetings, and Joseph Smith's journal entries, some of which were used in compiling the *History of the Church*. The first entry in this book is Joseph Smith's "proclamation to the kings of the earth" (D&C 124). The scribes for this record book include William Clayton, Thomas Bullock, Willard Richards, and Robert B. Thompson. On June 29, 1842, Willard Richards, the temple recorder, transferred this book to Clayton, as related in this appendix. Clayton wrote about 370 pages of donation records (September 12, 1842, to May 4, 1844) and about sixty pages of manuscript documents. "The Book of the Law of the Lord" is housed in the archives of the First Presidency of the Church of Jesus Christ of Latter-day Saints, Salt Lake City, Utah. See discussion and excerpts of this book in Scott H. Faulring, ed., *An American Prophet's Record: The Diaries and Journals of Joseph Smith* (Salt Lake City: Signature Books in association with Smith Research Associates, 1987), 242–43; James B. Allen, *Trials of Discipleship: The Story of William Clayton, A Mormon* (Urbana: University of Illinois Press, 1987), 118; Dean C. Jessee, ed., *The Personal Writings of Joseph Smith* (Salt Lake City: Deseret Book, 1984), 531–34, 691; and

December 1, 1841. It was one gold sovereign, valued at $5.00, to the credit of John Sanders, late from Cumberland, on the borders of Scotland, Europe.

A short time previous to this Joseph had been appointed "Sole Trustee-in-Trust for the Church of Jesus Christ of Latter-day Saints;" and, consequently, it became his prerogative to receive all the donations for the Church and the temple. Late in the evening of the 11th of December, the Trustee-in-Trust instructed Brigham Young, president of the quorum of the Twelve Apostles, to visit the members of the building committee and inform them more fully regarding their duties — to notify them not to accept any more tithes and consecrations, except such as were received from him. On the morning of the 13th, this message was delivered by Brigham to the committee in the presence of Elders Kimball, Woodruff and Willard Richards.

When this order was understood by the Saints, the business of the recorder increased rapidly, and having many important matters crowding upon him, he found it necessary to appoint Saturday of each week as the time for receiving and recording the tithings of the brethren. He published a notice under date of January 12, 1842, informing the Saints of this regulation; and it was subsequently carried into effect. But the business increased so rapidly that he could not keep pace with the work. He therefore counseled with his brethren of the Twelve; and, having received permission from President Joseph, he called Elder William Clayton, lately from England, to assist him. Elder Clayton accordingly entered the recorder's office on the 10th day of February, 1842, and continued therein from that time forward.

I will now copy an extract from the revelation of January 19, 1841, concerning a baptismal font:

"For there is not a place found on earth that he may come and restore again that which was lost unto you, or which he hath taken away, even the fullness of the Priesthood:

"For a baptismal font there is not upon the earth, that they, my saints, may be baptized for those who are dead;

Andrew F. Ehat and Lyndon W. Cook, eds., *The Words of Joseph Smith* (Provo, UT: Brigham Young University, 1981), 91, 406.

"For this ordinance belongeth to my house, and cannot be acceptable to me, only in the days of your poverty, wherein ye are not able to build a house unto me.

"But I command you, all ye my saints, to build a house unto me; and I grant unto you a sufficient time to build a house unto me, and during this time your baptisms shall be acceptable unto me." (Doc. and Cov. Sec cxxix. 28,29,30,31).

In conformity with the foregoing item of law, in the Summer and Fall of the year 1841, the brethren entered into measures to build a baptismal font in the cellar floor near the east end of the temple. President Joseph approved and accepted a draft for the font, made by Brother William Weeks; and on the 18th day of August of that year, Elder Weeks began to labor on the construction of the font with his own hands. He labored six days and then committed the work to the carpenters. On the 11th day of August, Brother Weeks began carving the oxen, twelve in number, upon which the font was to stand. After carving for six days, he consigned this branch to Brother Elijah Fordham, the principal carver, who continued until they were finished. They were completed about two months after their commencement.

At 5 o'clock in the evening, the 8th day of November, 1841, the font was dedicated by Joseph Smith the Prophet. After the dedication Brother Reuben McBride was the first person baptized, under the direction of the President.

Brother Samuel Rolfe, who was seriously afflicted with a felon upon one of his hands, was present. President Joseph instructed him to wash in the font and told him that the hand would be healed. The doctors had told him that he could not recover before Spring, and had advised him to have his hand cut. He dipped his hand in the font, and within a week he was perfectly healed.

After this time baptisms were continued in the font, and many Saints realized great blessings both spiritually and bodily.

I will here state that on the 25th day of September, 1841, a deposit was made in the south-east corner stone of the temple.

It was late in the Spring of 1842, when work was opened upon the walls, and little was done until Brother William W. Player came in June. He had just arrived from England and had come with the full intention of working on the temple. He began to labor about the 8th day of June; and he spent some time in regulating the stone work already set which had not been done very well. About the 11th of the same month he set the first plinth[2] on the south-west corner of the south side.

During the Summer he lost two weeks of work, having to wait for Elder Cahoon's sons' plinths, which they were cutting, they playing in the stone shop much of their time.

The work progressed but slowly during this season, as there was but one crane; but the delay arose through the stones not being cut fast enough. By the Fall, however, Brother Player had got all the rock-work laid around as high as the window sills, together with all the window sills including that of the large east Venetian window. He had also two courses of pilaster stones[3] on the plinths all around.

During the greater part of the time in the Fall, and especially toward the season when the work ceased. When Winter set in, brother Player was very sick. He nearly lost the use of his hands and feet, and several times he fell, through weakness while on his way home. He considered that his sickness was caused by the change of climate and by his having drunk bad water while coming up the river.

On May 11, 1842, General John C. Bennett was cut off from the Church for adultery and other wicked conduct. He soon after turned to be a very bitter enemy of the Church, generally, and of President Joseph, especially. He labored hard to create excitement and bring a mob upon the Church.

On the 14th day of May, a report came into the city that Ex-Governor Boggs, of Missouri, had been shot; and, upon the morning following, the report seemed confirmed. The Quincy Whig published an article in which the Prophet was charged with being accessory to the assassination of Boggs. Soon after this time, John C. Bennett left Nauvoo, and taking advantage of the shooting, he used every effort to criminate President Joseph.

On the 8th day of August following, the sheriff of Quincy came with a writ and arrested the President at the gate of his own premises. Joseph immediately took out a writ of habeas corpus from the Municipal court of the city of Nauvoo. The sheriffs were

---

[2] A square stone at the base of a column.
[3] A rectangular support that partially projects from a wall and appears as a column.

unwilling to listen to it; but, fearing to attempt taking him away by force, they agreed to leave him in the hands of the city marshal, while they went to consult Governor Carlin upon the subject. On the 11th, the sheriffs returned, but the Prophet had concluded to keep out of their reach; and, consequently, they could not find him. The sheriff tarried in Nauvoo several days, frequently uttering heavy threats to be executed if the President failed to give himself up, but the officer finally concluded to leave the city. The President remained secure at Brother Sayers' of the north of the city, about a mile from the corporation, where he was visited frequently by Sister Emma and his brethren. As soon as it was satisfactorily ascertained that the sheriff had gone away, Joseph returned home and remained in the city, but not coming out before the public.

Many rumors were constantly in circulation concerning the threats of the Governor and the Missourians; and considerable excitement was manifested throughout the country. Governor Carlin offered a reward for the apprehension of the President, as, also, for O. P. Rockwell who was charged as being the principal in the assassination of Boggs.

On Saturday the 3rd day of September, the sheriff (Pitman) came again, with another writ, and entered the house while the Prophet was at dinner; but Joseph succeeded in getting away undiscovered. At night he went to Brother Edward Hunter's house, and remained there for some time, in perfect security. After the officers returned to Quincy, the President came home; but yet kept himself close and out of sight.

On Friday, October 7th, several reports came to Nauvoo, showing Governor Carlin's determination to have Joseph taken to Missouri. The Prophet concluded that it would be wisdom to be still more careful, and in order the more effectually to secure himself from the grasp of the enemy, he left the city that same evening, accompanied by John Taylor, Wilson Law and John D. Parker. They traveled all night up the country to the north, and went to the house of Elder John Taylor's father, where Joseph stayed for some time. By these means, the plans of his enemies were completely frustrated, and the officers gave up the chase. He was, however, at any time liable to be arrested both by virtue of the writ and the proclamation offering a reward of $200 for his capture.

On Monday, December 26th, he suffered himself to be arrested by Wilson Law, in the proclamation, and on the following morning started for Springfield, accompanied by about sixteen of the brethren. His object was to stand trial before Judge Pope on habeas corpus. This was consented to, at the suggestion of Mr. Butterfield, U.S. District Attorney, who had been consulted in relation to the matter and had expressed assurance that the President would be acquitted.

The company arrived at Springfield on Friday the 30th, and on the following morning application was made for a writ of habeas corpus from the U.S. District Court. The writ was granted and Monday morning, January 2, 1843, was appointed as the time to try the validity of the arrest. On Monday the company repaired to the court; but Mr. Lamborn, the State's attorney, pleaded that he was not ready for trial, and the case was postponed until Wednesday. Accordingly, on Wednesday at 9 a.m. the trial was opened. Its result was the release and discharge of Joseph both from the writ and proclamation.

This was a source of great rejoicing to the brethren; and, on our return to Nauvoo, it gave gladness to the whole Church. The Saints regarded this as another interposition of the Almighty in behalf of His persecuted people; and great joy prevailed to see our Prophet once more freed from his enemies.

During all these troubles and excitement the Saints did not cease in the least their exertions to build the temple. The work continued to move on with the usual vigor.

Several circumstances pertaining to the temple occurred during this time, which I now proceed to notice:

Willard Richards, the recorder, having in the early part of June obtained permission from the President to go to the East to get his family, made preparations to depart upon this journey. On the 29th of June he transferred the "Law of the Lord" and books belonging to the temple to the care and charge of William Clayton. One or two days later Elder Richards started away.

About nine o'clock on the evening of Saturday, September 3rd, the President was at Bishop N. K. Whitney's but was about to leave that place to go to Edward Hunter's. He called William Clayton to him and said:

"Brother Clayton, I want you to take care of the records and papers; and from this time I appoint you Temple Recorder; and when revelations are to be transcribed, you shall write them."

This was done because Elder Richards had more work than he could attend to, he being engaged upon the Church History, which the President was anxious should progress as fast as possible.

While President Joseph was concealed at Father Taylor's, Elder Cahoon and some others went to visit him. He gave them many glorious instructions, and in his conversation requested Brother Cahoon, as soon as he should return home, to call upon the Saints to put a temporary floor in the temple, that we might be enabled to hold our meetings within its sacred walls.

Accordingly, On Sunday, the 23rd day of October, the committee laid before the Saints the President's request and called upon them to begin work on the morrow to accomplish this object.

On the following day the brethren began their labor on this temporary floor; and on Friday, the 28th, the floor was laid and seats were fixed ready for meeting.

On Sunday, the 30th, the Saints held the first meeting in the temple, and were addressed by Elder John Taylor, one of the Twelve Apostles. It was expected that the President would be there himself; but he was sick and unable to attend.

This movement added a new stimulus to the work; and the hearts of all the Saints seemed to be filled with joy and gratitude for this privilege.

The Prophet, before he went up the river, had called upon the members of the Temple Committee to come together to have a settlement.

On Saturday, October 1st, they met at the President's house, he being sick. The recorder and Bishop N. K. Whitney were present.

Some reports had been circulated to the effect that the committee was not making a righteous disposition of property consecrated to the building of the temple, and there appeared to be some dissatisfaction among the laborers on account to these reports.

After carefully examining the books and making inquiry into the entire proceeding of the committee, President Joseph expressed himself as being perfectly satisfied with the committee and its work.

The books were balanced between the Trustee-in-Trust and the committee, and also each individual account was carefully examined.

The wages of the Trustee-in-Trust, the members of the committee and the recorder were also fixed by the President; and it was agreed that each should receive two dollars per day for his services.

The President remarked that he was amenable to the State for the faithful discharge of his duties as Trustee-in-Trust, and that the Temple Committee was accountable to him and to no other authority; and that no notice must be taken of any complaint unless it were properly brought to him, when he would make things right if any change were needed.

The parties separated perfectly satisfied, and the President said that he would have a notice published stating that he had examined the accounts and was satisfied. This notice appeared in the Times and Seasons of October 15th, 1842.

At this council it was also agreed that the recorder's office should be removed to the Committee House near the temple for the better accommodation of the business.

Accordingly the committee built a small brick office for the recorder; and on Wednesday, November 2nd, the recorder moved his records, books, papers, etc., to the new office and began business there forthwith.

Brother James Whitehead was called into the office on the 11th of June to assist in keeping the books; and from this time forward the business continued to increase and contributions came in plentifully.

After the work ceased upon the walls of the temple, in the Fall of 1842, the rock-cutters continued their labor with the intention of having a goodly number of the stones ready for the Spring.

Some time in the month of November a feeling against the committee arose among the stone-cutters, who finally presented a charge to the First Presidency against Elders Cahoon and Higbee for oppressive and unchristian conduct, and against the committee for an unequal distribution of provisions, iron, steel, tools, etc.; also alleging that favors were shown by the committee to the sons of its members.

The trial began about 11 o'clock in the day and continued until 9 at night. Henry G. Sherwood made a plea on the side of

Justice and the Patriarch Hyrum on the side of Mercy. The decision was given by the President. He decided that the members of the committee should retain their standing and gave much good instruction to all parties correcting the errors of each in kindness. The decision was marked by judgment and wisdom and cannot fail to produce a good effect.

On Sunday, May 21, 1843, President Joseph preached in the temple from the first chapter of Peter's second epistle. In the afternoon of that day the ordinance of partaking of bread and water, as the sacrament, was administered to the Saints for the first time in this temple.

The work on the building was delayed considerable this Spring, on account of the necessity for fixing runways for the crane.

Brother Player had been sick during the entire Winter, and he continued in a very feeble state until the time when he commenced again to lay the stone on the walls, which was on the 21st day of April, 1843.

From this time the work progressed steadily but slowly. There was no other hindrance until the next Winter set in, which was rather early, and at which time the walls were up as high as the arches of the first tier of windows all around. In this state the building was left through the Winter and until the Spring of 1844.

Early in the morning on the 8th day of June, 1843, Elder Elias Higbee, one of the temple committee, died after an illness of only five days. His death was unexpected and deeply lamented by all his brethren. He had proved himself a worthy man, and was much respected by all who knew him.

After this event several applications were made by men to be appointed to fill the vacant place of Elder Higbee. Elder Jared Carter was very anxious to have the appointment and, for some cause or other, claimed it as his right. But the Spirit whispered that it would not be wisdom to appoint him. After some delay and consultation on the subject, the Patriarch Hyrum Smith was appointed by the Trustee-in Trust, with the consent of the other committee; and on the morning of the 23rd day of October, 1843, he entered upon the duties of his office, amidst the greetings and good feelings of the workers universally.

On the 6th day of October, 1843, the special conference was held in the temple. This was the first time a conference was held in the building.

At this conference charges were again preferred against the temple committee, and a public investigation was entered into; and it was again voted that the members of the committee should be retained in their standing.

On this occasion the President proposed to the people to place under bonds all agents who were sent out to collect funds for the temple and Nauvoo House. He showed that some of the Elders, when they were away, received contributions to the temple; but as they sometimes devoted a portion of the money in other channels, they did not make proper returns at Nauvoo and the account did not, therefore, accurately balance.

He stated that the Twelve Apostles were now about to go East to raise means for the temple and also for the Nauvoo House. He suggested that they give bonds to the amount of two thousand dollars each; and that this rule be enforced upon all the Elders from this time forward. An action was taken by the Conference and it was decided by unanimous vote to carry this proposition into effect. The Twelve gave bonds in the required amount previous to their going East, which bonds were filed in the office of the Trustee-in-Trust.

Thus the Twelve were the first agents who were ever placed under bonds, when sent to collect funds for the Church. The wisdom of this order was soon manifest; for, although it was well understood and universally believed that the Twelve would invariable make correct returns, there were others who might not be so careful or scrupulous. And, inasmuch as members of this first quorum were required to give bonds, no other man could justly complain if he were brought under the same rule.

At this conference the Saints again voted to renew their exertions and double their diligence in order that the temple might be speedily finished.

During this conference, also, Elder Sidney Rigdon was tried for his fellowship, charged with a long course of conduct which rendered him unworthy of a place in the Church. President Joseph told the Saints that he had carried Elder Rigdon long enough and that he should do so no more. But nothwithstanding this, the Patriarch Hyrum pleaded for mercy in Sidney's behalf; and the conference voted to Sustain Elder Rigdon in his position as counsellor to the First Presidency.

Some time in the Winter or Spring of the year 1844, the Patriarch Hyrum made a proclamation to the women of the Church, asking them to subscribe in money one cent each per week, for the purpose of buying the glass and nails for the temple. He represented to them that by this means he would be able to meet all the requirements in this regard. He also gave a promise that all the sisters who would comply with this call should have the first privilege of seats in the temple when it was finished.

He opened a record of these conributions, which he kept, with the aid of Sister Mercy R. Thompson, until his death.

Afterwards Brother Cutler was appointed to receive these offerings, assisted by Sister Thompson. There was soon a great anxiety manifest among the sisters to pay their portion and nearly all paid a year's subscription in advance. Since that time many have given the donation for the second year; and there has been already realized nearly two thousand dollars which will do much towards accomplishing the desired object. These contributions yet continue to come in each day.

Early in the Spring of 1844, the committee commenced the construction of a second crane in order to expedite the work, and the labor having all been performed with but one crane up to this time. During the month of March the new crane was rigged and immediately after the April conference Brother Player again began work on the walls. It was on the 11th of the month when he resumed this labor.

Soon after this time there was a considerable excitement raised in this county especially, and also in the counties adjoining, by apostates who threatened destruction and extermination to the whole Church. Among these apostates were:

William Law, Wilson Law, Robert D. Foster, Francis M. Higbee, Chauncy L. Higbee.

These men conspired with others who had been citizens of Nauvoo to bring on a mob.

The names of the principal persons in this business were:

Joseph H. Jackson, Austin Cowles (an apostate), John M. Finch, William H. Rolloson, William H. I. Marr, Silvester Emmons, Alexander Simpson, S. M. Marr, John Egle, Henry O. Norton, Augustine Spencer, Charles Ivins, P. T. Rolfe, William I. Higbee, James Blakeslee.

In order to effect their purposes the more speedily the apostates obtained a printing press; and on Friday, June 7th, the first number of a paper called the Nauvoo Expositor was issued. The paper was full of the most libellous and slanderous matter against the President, imaginable, and was designed as an engine to bring destruction upon the city.

On the 10th, the city council passed a resolution ordering the press to be abated as a nuisance, which was done the same evening.

The following day there was great excitement concerning the destruction of the press; and Foster and the Higbees threatened vengeance. Some of them said that in a few weeks there should not be left one stone of the temple standing upon another.

On the 12th, a number of writs, or rather one writ for a number of the brethren, was brought in and served by a constable of the name of Bettisworth. Among the number were Joseph and Hyrum.

Joseph immediately procured a writ of habeas corpus from the municipal court; and after a lengthy examination was discharged.

This constable returned and stated that he had been resisted. The mob took advantage of the circumstance to fan the flame of excitement and threatened terrible vengeance. They also went to the Morley settlement and branches around, demanded the arms of the brethren and ordered them to leave their homes within a few days.

The excitement continued to increase and the enemy circulated all manner of inflamatory reports and also sent messages to the governor, which had the effect of bringing him to Carthage, where he arrived about the 21st.

The governor immediately sent a messenger with a letter, requesting those named in the writ to go to Carthage for trial. An answer was sent explaining the reasons why they had not gone.

On the following evening the governor sent in a posse of about thirty men, bearing a letter in which he made use of severe threats, and said that if the prisoners did not appear at Carthage on the morrow, he should take it as a resistance to the law and should immediately call in force sufficient to take them, even if it required all the militia of the State.

On receiving this information the President and one or two others concluded to leave the city and go over to Iowa in the night.

541

During the day following some of the brethren, with Sister Emma Smith, despatched messengers to request the President and those with him to come and give themselves up, fearing that the city would be destroyed and the people massacred if they did not do it.

About five o'clock, p.m., the little party returned and concluded to surrender, although it was contrary to the President's feelings to do so.

On Monday the 24th, the prisoners started for Carthage: but within about four miles of the place they were met by a messenger from the governor with an order for the State arms. The company immediately returned to collect the arms, which took some time.

About six o'clock the company started again and went through to Carthage. While there a great many threats were offered and they suffered considerable abuse from the mob. They however succeeded in obtaining a pledge from the governor, in the name of the State, for their safety before they went out.

About two days after they arrived in Carthage they were thrust in jail without lawful process.

On the afternoon of the 27th, the governor disbanded his troops except his body-guard; and, leaving the brethren in jail under charge of the Carthage Greys, some of their bitterest enemies, he came out to Nauvoo and made a harsh address to the people.

When he left Carthage a body of men collected from Nauvoo and started for Carthage, and when within a few miles they stopped to black their faces. They proceeded through the woods to the north side of Carthage; then, leaving the woods, they went to the jail, and the doors being open, they rushed up stairs with their rifles and muskets and commenced firing into the room. The brethren defended themselves as well as they could; but, having no arms, they were soon over-powered. Hyrum was shot through the head and fell backwards dead. John Taylor had four balls shot into him. Joseph jumped through the window and was immediately surrounded by the mob. They raised him up and set him against the well-curb; but as yet it appears he had not been hit with a ball. However, four of the mob immediately drew up their guns and shot him dead. This was all the work of about two minutes. The mob then fled as fast as possible. A messenger was dispatched to bring the news to Nauvoo, but was met by the governor and taken back for fear the whole city would rush out and desolate the country.

The painful news reached the city the following morning, which filled the hearts of the Saints with the most intense gloom and sorrow.

On the 28th, at half past two, p.m., the bodies were brought to the city in two wagons and were taken to the mansion to be prepared for burial.

On the following day the Saints were permitted to go and see them; and at night they were secretly buried near the mansion.

The foregoing is but a mere sketch of the massacre, designed to show the date of the martyrdom and also the means by which it was brought about.

During this excitement the works on the temple ceased for about two weeks. All the hands having to watch and stand on guard night and day.

The works were suspended about the 20th of June. On the second sabbath after the murder, the subject of the temple was brought into consideration, and the Church voted to commence work again and finish it as speedily as possible.

On the 8th of July the laborers resumed their work, although the committee had not so much as a bushel of meal, nor a pound of flour, nor a pound of meat to feed the hands with; but all seemed determined to go to work and trust in God for the means.

At this time the majority of the quorum of the Twelve were away in the East. Only P. P. Pratt, John Taylor and W. Richards were here. Elder Taylor was very sick and for some time in a dangerous state, through the wounds he received at Carthage. He had four balls shot into him and another ball struck his watch and broke it to pieces. To this small shield he may truly be said to owe his life; for but for that the ball doubtless would have gone through his heart. Dr. Richards was not hurt, although he was in the room where Hyrum was killed all the time the firing continued.

This sorrowful circumstance had a tendency to cement the hearts of the Saints more closely than ever. No threats were offered, no disposition for revenge; all concluded to leave the case in the hands of the governor, who had pledged himself that the murderers should be brought to justice; and if he failed, the Saints were willing to leave it in the hands of God.

On Friday, the 5th of July, a large raft of pine lumber, containing 87,732 feet, was landed at the city for the temple. The brethren turned out liberally with their teams to haul it to the temple, where it was secured in a few days.

In a few days afterwards another raft, of 67,952 feet was received and hauled to the temple. This gladdened the hearts of the Saints.

Soon after this period the Saints were again made to sorrow on account of the death of Brother Samuel H. Smith, which took place on Tuesday evening, the 30th of July, after a very short illness; this being the third death in the family within five weeks.

There is now only one brother left of the family, viz: William. He was in the East during the progress of the afflicting events.

About the middle of July, the sisters of the branches of La Harpe and Macedonia sent work to the temple committee and stated their anxiety to see this building progress still more rapidly.

They proposed if the committee would build another crane, they would furnish the means to build it with, and seemed wishful to go ahead with immediately. The committee and recorder councilled on the subject and it was decided to comply with the wishes of the sisters.

Sister Clark, wife of Raymond Clark, was authorized to collect the contributions. She immediately started, and returned on the 29th with money and other property, amounting in the whole to $194, which was more than sufficient to build a new crane.

The committee immediately set the carpenters to work, and on the 3rd of August the crane was put in operation under the management of Joshua Armstrong, the setter, and Horace Owens to back up, and W. W. Dryer, Wm. Austin and Archibald Hill to attend to the crane.

They commenced work on the north side and very soon satisfied the Saints of the utility of the movement. The works now progressed rapidly.

On the 4th of August, Elder Rigdon returned from Pittsburg and laid a plan to draw away the minds of the Saints by proposing or instructing the Saints that they must now choose a guardian, intimating that he himself was the proper person.

Fortunately, on Tuesday, the 6th of August, five of the Twelve returned home, viz: Brigham Young, Heber C. Kimball, Lyman

Wight, Orson Pratt and Wilford Woodruff. This event appeared very providential. They were just in time to frustrate Elder Rigdon's plans. This they did effectually.

On Thursday, the 8th, the Church voted to sustain the Twelve as the proper authority to govern the Church. The result was the open apostasy of Elder Rigdon and some others, who immediately left for Pittsburg.

After this event the Saints seemed more and more united, and a better feeling prevailed. The works of the temple moved on with astonishing rapidity, and on the 23rd of September the first capital was put up.

The stone weighed about two tons and when the stone was at its hight, and the men were attempting to draw it to the wall, the crane gave way at the foot of the wing or angle, which circumstance caused considerable danger. By great care the stone was safely landed and set without any further accident.

On Wednesday, the 25th, as the brethren were beginning to raise one of the capitals, having neglected to fasten the guys, the crane fell over with a tremendous crash, breaking it considerably. As soon as it was perceived that the crane was falling, the hands fled to get out of the way. One of the brethren, Thomas Jaap, running directly in the course of the falling crane, barely escaped being killed. The crane struck the ground and was within a foot of striking his head. This circumstance hindered the workmen some; but in a few days the crane was mended, reared and the brethren again went to work on it.

About this time, Ira T. Miles came down from Lyman Wight's company, who were then in the north, having left the city, as was supposed, through cowardice, as they expected we should be routed and the city destroyed.

About the same time, Jacob Morris came down from the same company and stated that Miles had come with the intention of setting fire to the lumber, that the building might be hindered, as Lyman Wight had said the temple never would be built.

Whether this was the intention of Brother Miles or not we could not learn satisfactorily. However, enough was known to induce the authorities of the Church to advise the committee to have some of the old police guard the lumber and the temple night and day. The police have continued to guard it to this time. There has since that been many threats thrown out from the

545

Rigdonites and other sources that the temple never should be built, and no doubt an attempt would have been made to set fire to it if it had not been well guarded all the time.

The workmen continued raising the capitals until December, when on the 6th of that month, the last one was safely deposited in its place; which was a source of great joy to the Saints. Many fears had been entertained that Brother Player would not be able to finish them before Winter set in, but it seemed as though the Lord held up the weather until this important piece of work was accomplished. About two hours after the capital was set it commenced snowing very briskly, and at night the ground was covered about four inches, and it froze very keenly.

There were then twelve of the capitals without the trumpet stones; and they remained in this state until the following Spring.

The cost of each of the capitals was about $300. The first and last of the capitals were cut by Charles Lambert and Harvey Stanley.

I will further say that when the hands were raising the last capital, and had got it about half-way up, one of the block shives in the tackle broke and rendered it impossible in the situation either to raise or lower the stone. This circumstance presented a great difficulty, but after some consultation the hands fastened the rope below the tackle, so that it could not slip, and left the stone suspended while they took down the blocks, put in a new shive and fixed the blocks again.

The stone was then raised without further difficulty, and was set precisely at twenty minutes before one o'clock. This was the heaviest stone among the whole number.

After the death of President Joseph and Patriarch Hyrum, Joseph having been sole Trustee-in-Trust, when the Twelve returned home they held a council and appointed Newel K. Whitney and George Miller, the two presiding bishops, Trustees-in-Trust. This was on the 9th of August; and a few days afterwards, the trustees entered upon the duties of their office.

In the early part of December the trustees and Twelve held a council to talk on the propriety of employing a suitable number of carpenters this Winter to prepare the timber works for the temple, so as to have it all ready when the stone work is finished. It was decided to employ fifteen persons as steady carpenters; and the architect was authorized to select such men as he may have confidence in — men who are well qualified to do the work that is wanted.

It was also concluded to fix up a shop in the temple for the carpenters to work in. Accordingly the south side of the lower story of the temple was weather-boarded around. A very good shop was made by this means, which was completed on the following Saturday; and on Monday, the 16th, the men selected went to work in their new shop. Their names are as follows:

Truman O. Angell, William Felshaw, William F. Cahoon, Joseph T. Schofield, Samuel Rolfe, Zimri H. Baxter, Adison Everett, John Stiles, Hugh Riding, Miles Romney, Jabez Durfee, Stephen Longstroth, Benjamin Rolfe, Nicholas T. Silcock and William Carmichael. Hiram Mace, Wandel Mace and Gideon Gibbs were appointed to attend the saw-mill and Daniel Avery to turn grindstone for the carpenters, keep the shop clean and take care of strangers who might visit the building.

During the early part of January, 1845, the High Priest quorum entered into an investigation of the propriety of building a hall for their accommodation. On the 26th, President Young and some others of the quorum of the Twelve attended the meeting of the quorum, when the subject was again discussed. President Young made some remarks on the subject and concluded by advising them, instead of building a hall, to go to work and finish the upper room of the temple, and by this means they would soon have room to attend to the ordinances and save much expense.

A vote was taken on accepting President Young's proposition, which was carried without a dissenting voice. The brethren immediately commenced bringing in their donations to the bishops for that purpose. This matter served as a new stimulus among the saints to use every exertion to finish the temple as speedily as possible.

On Wednesday, the 12th of March, Brother William W. Player commenced work again on the walls. He got one stone up just as the bell rung for dinner.

On Friday, the 14th, there was a man killed on the stone quarry by a stone falling on his head while the brethren were blasting rocks. This is the only accident of any moment that has ever happened on the temple or any of the works connected with it.

On Thursday, the 27th of March, 1845, Brother Player put up the last trumpet stone, at about three o'clock, p.m. He also laid the first stringer for the large upper Venetian window in the east side.

On Monday, April 21st, Brother Player put up the first star in the architrave.[4] At half past two o'clock, p.m., he notified me that they were about to begin to raise it. I immediately went to the east end of the temple. On my way I met Elder Heber C. Kimball, one of the Twelve, and we went and sat down together on Brother Cutler's fence, opposite where the stone stood.

We entered into conversation together on various matters, chiefly pertaining to our spiritual interest. We watched the slow upward progress of the star with great pleasure. At precisely a quarter before three o'clock, it was properly set in its place; and the instant it was set, Brothers Edward Miller and Elisha Everett sprung for the top; but Brother Miller being a little the smartest he was on first and stood erect, viewing with pride the surrounding scenery. After he got down brother Everett also mounted the stone and stood on it for some time. The top of the star is fifty-five feet above the ground.

The first star was put up on Joseph's corner, being the first one north of the south-east corner.

On the morning of Tuesday, the 29th of April, the first upper circular window was finished setting by Brother Player.

On Friday, May 16th, a little after two o'clock, p.m., having been notified, I went on the temple and sat down on the top of the south-west corner stairway, on the highest part of the stone work. I then watched Brother Player set the last star, being on the west end and the second one from the south-west corner. It was set exactly at three o'clock, p.m. At this time the carpenters were very busy raising the timbers for the upper floor of the temple, having them all framed and quite a large amount was already upon the walls and body of the building.

On Monday, the 19th of May, while I was sitting on the temple, Brother Stephen H. Goddard met with an accident which was very near proving fatal. He was standing on the wall on the north side of the temple assisting some others to take down one of the scaffolding poles. By some accident the foot of the pole slipped and struck him on the left side of the head. He fell head foremost,

[4] A beam resting on the tops of columns.

being stunned by the blow. Fortunately they had just got two joists in the floor and he fell across them which prevented him from going down into the cellar, a distance of about sixty-two feet. And in all probability, if he had fallen down he would have been killed. The brethren raised him up and on examination found that he had received a cut on the upper corner of his left eye. His face was also much bruised. He bled profusely. I laid hands on him with two other brethren and he went home. He suffered considerable pain until evening, when it ceased, and in two days afterwards he was at work again, as usual.

On Friday, the 23rd, all the stone on the outside of the wall was laid, except the south-east corner stone. This progress was a great rejoicing to the Saints.

The Rigdonites have prophecied that the walls would never be built; but through the blessing of God we have lived to see the prediction come to naught.

On Saturday the 24th, at a quarter before six o'clock a.m., was the time appointed for the laying of the capstone of the temple. Quite a number of the Saints had assembled to witness the interesting ceremony. There were present, of the quorum of the Twelve; President Brigham Young, Heber C. Kimball, John Taylor, Willard Richards, Amasa Lyman, George A. Smith, John E. Page, Orson Hyde, and Orson Pratt; also Newel K. Whitney, and George Miller, Trustees-in-Trust; Alpheus Cutler and Raymond Cahoon, building committee; William Clayton, temple recorder; John Smith, Patriarch and president of the Stake, and Charles C. Rich his counselor. Of the High Council William Huntington, Sr., Aaron Johnson, George W. Harris, James Allred, David Fullmer, William Weeks, architect, and William W. Phelps.

A few minutes before six, the band came up and arranged themselves on the platform in a circle a little back from the corner.

The names of the band who were present are as follows: William Pitt, leader, Stephen Hales, William F. Cahoon, Robert T. Burton, John Kay, James Smithies, Daniel F. Cahoon, Andrew Cahoon, Charles H. Hales, Martin H. Peck, J. T. Hutchinson, James Standing, William D. Huntington. Charles Smith and Charles C. Robbins, also William H. Kimball, Color bearer.

At six o'clock the band played "The Nightingale;" and afterwards while the people were collecting, they played another tune.

549

At eight minutes after six Brother William W. Player commenced spreading his mortar, perfect silence prevailing.

President Young stood on the wall immediately north of the corner stone, with Elder Heber C. Kimball at his right hand.

When the mortar was spread, the stone was lifted to its place by President Brigham Young, William W. Player, Tarlton Lewis, Elisha Everett, John Hill, Edward Miller, Charles W. Patten, Samuel Hodge, Hans C. Hanson, and Thomas Jaap.

President Young then stepped on the stone, and taking a large pestle began beating it to its place. He finished laying the stone with the assistance and direction of Brother Player precisely at twenty-two minutes after six o'clock.

The band then struck up the "Capstone March," composed and arranged by William Pitt, the leader, for the occasion.

President Young then spoke to the congregation, instructing them with regard to shouting the "Hossannah."

He then said, "The last stone is laid upon the temple, and I pray the Almighty in the name of Jesus to defend us in this place, and sustain us until the temple is finished and have all got our endowments."[5]

The whole congregation then, following the motion of President Young, shouted as loud as possible; "Hossannah, hossannah, hossannah, to God and the Lamb! Amen, amen and amen!"

This was repeated a second and third time.

The President concluded by saying; "So let it be, thou Lord Almighty!"

He continued and said: "This is the seventh day of the week, or the Jewish Sabbath. It is the day on which the Almighty finished His work and rested from His labors. We have now

---

[5] It was the great frame of hewn stone just completed that impressed John Greenleaf Whittier to reflect upon the Nauvoo Temple as a significant physical mark left by Joseph Smith: "Joseph Smith has left his track on the great pathway of life. He has incorporated himself with the enduring stone of the great Nauvoo Temple . . . with its huge walls of hewn stone . . . their massive caps carved into the likeness of enormous human faces, resting themselves upon crescent moons, with a giant profile of a face within the curve. It stands upon the highest elevation of the most beautiful city of the west" (cited in William Mulder and A. Russell Mortensen, eds., *Among the Mormons: Historic Accounts by Contemporary Observers* [New York: Alfred A. Knopf, 1958], 159).

finished the walls of the temple, and we may rest to day from our labors."

He said he would take it upon him to dismiss the workmen for the day; and requested the people to hallow the day, and spend it giving thanks to God.

He then dismissed the congregation, and in company with the brethren of the Twelve retired to the place of their retreat, where they can be safe from arrest by constables, and other officers who are prowling around the city from Carthage.

The people began to move away, but the band continued playing. John Kay also went on the corner stone and sang a song composed by Elder William W. Phelps, called the "Capstone Song." The morning was very cold and chilly. The Saints seemed highly interested and pleased with the morning's performance. According to the request of President Young all works were suspended and the day was kept as a holiday.

A few minutes after the Twelve left the temple a constable came up with a summons for several of the brethren, but he could not find them. He had also a summons for Daniel Avery, and we had notified Avery of it and he was counseled to keep out of the way; but contrary to counsel he unwisely went and made himself known to the officer, who immediately served the process upon him. For this piece of conduct, and others as bad, a council of the Twelve and trustees dismissed him for the work and took Jesse P. Harmon, one of the old police in his stead.

On Wednesday the 28th day of May the first "bent" of the attic story of the temple was raised by the carpenters, and up to this time they continued to raise the timber works with pleasing rapidity.

Thus the work of this temple has progressed from the beginning to the present time without any serious accident except in the incident which happened at the stone quarry. The blessing of God has attended the whole progress of the work, and it has advance beyond our most sanguine expectations. Our enemies have threatened all the time, and for the last two years we have had very little cessation from writs and other efforts of the enemy to prevent our finishing it. Many prophecies have been uttered against it; but the Saints have invariably pursued a steady course of perseverance. As the building has progressed, the Saints have increased their donations and tithings; and this Spring

551

has exceeded all past times for liberality and donations from the brethren.

This being Saturday, the 31st of May, 1845, I will now say the circuit court of this county (Hancock) has been in session the past two weeks. Nearly the whole of the time has been occupied in that trial of Jacob C. Davis, senator for this county, Thomas C. Sharp, Editor of the Warsaw Signal, Levi Grover, before Richard M. Young, for the murder of Generals Joseph and Hyrum Smith on the 27th of June 1844. The verdict was brought in yesterday had returned "Not guilty."

Thus the whole State of Illinois has made itself guilty of shedding the blood of the Prophets by acquitting those who committed the horrid deed, and it is now left to God to take vengeance in His own way in His own time.

On the 16th of December, 1840, the State of Illinois granted us a liberal charter. The principal officers of the State being as follows: Thomas Carlin, governor, William Wilson, chief justice; Samuel D. Lockwood, Thomas C. Brown, Walter B. Scates, associate justices. These men formed the council of revision.

On the 21st of January, 1845, the State took away all our chartered rights and left us entirely destitute of protection.

The council of revision then stood as follows: Thomas Ford, governor; William Wilson, chief justice; and Samuel H. Treat, Richard M. Young, James Shields, Jesse B. Thomas, and John D. Caton.

President Joseph Smith, first President and sole Trustee-in-Trust for the Church of Jesus Christ of Latter-day Saints, together with Hyrum Smith his councilor and Patriarch to the whole church, was martyred on the 27th of June, 1844.

They died firm in the faith and favor of God and universally respected and beloved by all the Saints. Their death was universally lamented, and their names will ever be held sacred by all the faithful in time and to all eternity.

William Law, who was appointed councilor in the stead of Hyrum when the latter was ordained a Patriarch, apostasized in the Spring or early in the year of 1844. And was a principal agent in causing the massacre of the President and Patriarch.

Sidney Rigdon, the other councilor, was rejected by the Saints in September last, for endeavoring to deceive the people and lead them to ruin. He has since denied the Church and organized a new one under another title, and from evidence before us has sought diligently to bring trouble and destruction upon the Saints of Nauvoo.[6]

---

[6] The material published from "William Clayton's Journal, Etc." ends here. In the following issue of the *Juvenile Instructor* 21 (June 15, 1886): 12, the editor acknowledges a gap of more than one year and explains that "we cannot, at present, obtain the manuscript covering the remainder of 1845 and the whole of 1846." What follows is a revised form of Clayton's journal of the pioneer trek west, beginning with January 1, 1847, at Winter Quarters, Nebraska, and extending to April 27, 1847, part way to the Great Salt Lake Valley. The editors of the *Juvenile Instructor* do not explain that they have amalgamated these two sources under the series entitled, "An Interesting Journal."

TESTIMONY

*I*n an 1874 signed affidavit, William *Clayton described his introduction to plural marriage in Nauvoo, Illinois, thirty years before. This statement was included with others in an article written by LDS assistant church historian Andrew Jenson, entitled "Plural Marriage," published at Salt Lake City in the* Historical Record 6 (May 1887): 224-26.

WILLIAM CLAYTON'S TESTIMONY

The following statement was sworn to before John T. Caine, a notary public, in Salt Lake City, Feb. 16, 1874:

"Inasmuch as it may be interesting to future generations of the members of the Church of Jesus Christ of Latter-day Saints to learn something of the first teachings of the principle of plural marriage by President Joseph Smith, the Prophet, Seer, Revelator and Translator of said Church, I will give a short relation of facts which occurred with my personal knowledge, and also matters related to me by President Joseph Smith.

"I was employed as a clerk in President Joseph Smith's office, under Elder Willard Richards, and commenced to labor in the office on the 10th day of February, 1842. I continued to labor with Elder Richards until he went east to fetch his wife to Nauvoo.

"After Elder Richards started east I was necessarily thrown constantly into the company of President Smith, having to attend to his public and private business, receiving and recording tithings and donations, attending to land and other matters of business. During this period I necessarily became well acquainted with Emma Smith, the wife of the Prophet Joseph, and also with the children Julia M. (an adopted daughter), Joseph, Frederick and Alexander, very much of the business being transacted at the residence of the Prophet.

"On the 7th of October, 1842, in the presence of Bishop Newel K. Whitney and his wife Elizabeth Ann, President Joseph Smith appointed me Temple Recorder, and also his private clerk, placing all records, books, papers, etc., in my care, and requiring me to take charge of and preserve them, his closing words being, 'When I have any revelations to write, you are the one to write them.'

"During this period the Prophet Joseph frequently visited my house in my company, and became well acquainted with my wife Ruth, to whom I had been married five years. One day in the month of February, 1843, date not remembered, the Prophet invited me to walk with him. During our walk, he said he had learned that there was a sister back in England, to whom I was very much attached.[1] I replied there was, but nothing further than an attachment such as a brother and sister in the Church might rightfully entertain for each other. He then said, 'Why don't you send for her?' I replied, 'In the first place, I have no authority to send for her, and if I had, I have not the means to pay expenses.' To this he answered, 'I give you authority to send for her,[2] and I will

---

[1] The sister in England was probably Sarah Crooks. Crooks emigrated to Nauvoo, but on August 16, 1843, she married another man, William Cook (Lyndon W. Cook, ed., *Civil Marriages in Nauvoo and Some Outlying Areas* [Provo, UT: Lyndon W. Cook, 1980]; Journal 2, "Nauvoo, Illinois," June 28, 1844).

[2] In 1842 Smith reputedly justified his own proposal of plural marriage to a reluctant Nancy Rigdon with a similar appeal to authority: "That which is wrong under one circumstance, may be, and often is, right under another . . . Whatever God requires is right, no matter what it is, although we may not see the reason thereof till long after the events transpire" (quoted in Joseph Smith, Jr., et al., *History of the Church of Jesus Christ of Latter-day Saints*, ed. B. H. Roberts, 2d ed. rev.,

furnish you with means,' which he did. This was the first time the Prophet Joseph talked with me on the subject of plural marriage. He informed me that the doctrine and principle was right in the sight of our Heavenly Father, and that it was a doctrine which pertained to celestial order and glory. After giving me lengthy instructions and informations concerning the doctrine of celestial or plural marriage, he concluded his remarks by the words 'It is your privilege to have all the wives you want.' After this introduction, our conversations on the subject of plural marriage were very frequent, and he appeared to take particular pains to inform and instruct me in respect to the principle. He also informed me that he had other wives living besides his first wife Emma, and in particular gave me to understand that Eliza R. Snow, Louisa Beman, Desdemona W. Fullmer and others were his lawful wives in the sight of Heaven.

On the 27th of April, 1843, the Prophet Joseph Smith married to me Margaret Moon, for time and eternity, at the residence of Elder Heber C. Kimball: and on the 22nd of July, 1843, he married to me according to the order of the Church, my first wife Ruth.

"On the 1st day of May, 1843, I officiated in the office of an Elder by marrying Lucy Walker to the Prophet Joseph Smith, at his own residence.

"During this period the Prophet Joseph took several other wives. Amongst the number I well remember Eliza Partridge, Emily Partridge, Sarah Ann Whitney, Helen Kimball and Flora Woodworth. These all, he acknowledged to me, were his lawful, wedded wives, according to the celestial order. His wife Emma was cognizant of the fact of some, if not all, of these being his wives, and she generally treated them very kindly.

"On the morning of the 12th of July, 1843, Joseph and Hyrum Smith came into the office in the upper story of the 'brick store,' on the bank of the Mississipppi River. They were talking on the subject of plural marriage. Hyrum said to Joseph, 'If you will write the revelation on celestial marriage, I will take and read it to Emma, and I believe I can convince her of its truth, and you will hereafter have peace.' Joseph smiled and remarked, 'You do

7 vols. [Salt Lake City: Deseret Book, 1963], 5:134-36; Richard S. Van Wagoner, *Mormon Polygamy: A History* [Salt Lake City: Signature Books, 1986], 30-31, 234n8).

not know Emma as well as I do.' Hyrum repeated his opinion and further remarked, 'The doctrine is so plain, I can convince any reasonable man or woman of its truth, purity or heavenly origin,' or words to their effect. Joseph then said, 'Well, I will write the revelation and we will see.' He then requested me to get paper and prepare to write. Hyrum very urgently requested Joseph to write the revelation by means of the Urim and Thummim[3] but Joseph, in reply, said he did not need to, for the knew the revelation perfectly from beginning to end.

"Joseph and Hyrum then sat down and Joseph commenced to dictate the revelation on celestial marriage, and I wrote it, sentence by sentence, as he dictated. After the whole was written, Joseph asked me to read it through, slowly and carefully, which I did, and he pronounced it correct. He then remarked that there was much more that he could write, on the same subject, but what was written was sufficient for the present.

"Hyrum then took the revelation to read to Emma. Joseph remained with me in the office until Hyrum returned. When he came back, Joseph asked him how he had succeeded. Hyrum replied that he had never received a more severe talking to in his life, that Emma was very bitter and full of resentment and anger.

"Joseph quietly remarked, 'I told you you did not know Emma as well as I did.' Joseph then put the revelation in his pocket, and they both left the office.

"The revelation was read to several of the authorities during the day. Towards evening Bishop Newel K. Whitney asked Joseph if he had any objections to his taking a copy of the revelation; Joseph replied that he had not, and handed it to him. It was carefully copied the following day by Joseph C. Kingsbury. Two or three days after the revelation was written Joseph related to me and several others that Emma had so teased, and urgently entreated him for the privilege of destroying it, that he became so weary of her teasing, and to get rid of her annoyance, he told her she might destroy it and she had done so, but he had consented to her wish in this matter to pacify her, realizing that he knew the revelation perfectly, and could rewrite it at any time if necessary.

[3] See Journal 2, "Nauvoo, Illinois," n7.

"The copy made by Joseph C. Kingsbury is a true and correct copy of the original in every respect. The copy was carefully preserved by Bishop Whitney, and but few knew of its existence until the temporary location of the Camps of Israel at Winter quarters, on the Missouri River, in 1846.

"After the revelation on celestial marriage was written Joseph continued his instructions, privately, on the doctrine to myself and others and during the last year of his life we were scarcely ever together, alone, but he was talking on the subject, and explaining that doctrine and principles connected with it. He appeared to enjoy great liberty and freedom in his teachings, and also to find great relief in having a few to whom he could unbosom his feelings on that great and glorious subject.

"From him I learned that the doctrine of plural and celestial marriage is the most holy and important doctrine ever revealed to man on the earth, and that without obedience to that principle no man can ever attain to the fulness of exaltation in celestial glory.

(Signed) WILLIAM CLAYTON.

"Salt Lake City, February 16th, 1874."

INDEX

—role in Nauvoo land business, xxi–xxii

—plural marriage: discussion with Clayton, xxii–xxiii, xxviiin42; encouraged Clayton in, 94, 113, 115, 122, 556–57; limitation to two sisters, xxviii, 120; proposal to Nancy Rigdon, 556n2; revelation, 110; visit to Benjamin Johnson, 102n23

—plural wives: Almera and Delcena Johnson, 95n5, 102n23; Desdemona Fullmer, boarded with Clayton, 101, 125, 557; Eliza Partridge, 101, 105–106, 117, 557; Emily Partridge, 101n21, 117, 122n59, 557; Eliza R. Snow, xxvii, 118, 557; Fanny Alger, relationship with, xxv; Flora Woodworth, 100, 118–19, 557; Helen Kimball, 557; Louisa Beaman, first recorded plural wife, xxv, 103n25, 557; Lucy Walker, 100, 279, 557; Maria and Sarah Lawrence, 107; Patty Sessions, 195–96; Sarah Ann Whitney, 120, 199n2, 557

—property: asserts right to temple property, 100; deeds city lots and *Maid of Iowa* to Emma Smith, 110; estate settlement, 136–37, 142n103

—protective clothing and assassination, 224

—on record-keeping, xix

—on the resurrection, 99, 104

—revelations of. *See* Doctrine and Covenants; Revelations: instances of

—trial of alleged murderers of, 552

—U.S. presidential campaign, xxxiii, 125

—visions, 54, 55, 67, 86

Smith, Joseph, III, 196n167

Smith, Lucy Mack, 202n4

—and property, 136

—revelation of, 169–70

Smith, Samuel H., 136, 138

—death of, 140, 544

—an initial member of Mormon church, xii

Smith, William

—correspondence with Brigham Young, 170–72

—disfellowshipped and excommunicated, 184, 187

—marriages of, 174

—Nauvoo land business, xxii, 81

—opposition to Quorum of Twelve, 152, 166, 187

—and the *Prophet*, 166n136

Snow, Zerubbabel, 404

Socialists, American, 26, 263n

Son, the. *See* Jesus

Soul of Man, 516

South Pass

—Jim Bridger explores 348n

—Clayton crosses, 346, 428

—divides waters of two oceans, 345–46

—Orson Pratt measures, 346

Spencer, Orson

—on Adam, 433

—on afterlife kingdoms, 443

—biographical note, 426

—expelled from Prussia, 495

Spirit

—of man, 518

—relative to matter, 103–4

Spirits, discernment of good and evil, 326–27, 522

Stout, Hosea

—Lieutenant-Colonel in self-defense battalion, 289–90

—threatens Clayton, 295

Strang, James J., church of, 196

Sugarbeet factory, first in America, 427–28

Sun, without beginning or end, 515

Sweetwater River, 366

Tax issues, xxin, 100n19, 106, 113–14

Taylor, John

—arrival in England, 5

—bought machinery for sugarbeet factory, 427n

—at Carthage jail, 137, 542

—"keys of the mysteries" recorded, liv, 514n3, 517n11, 519n14

—speaks in tongues, 21

About the Editor

George D. Smith, a native of New York City, was trained in political science at Stanford University and holds a master's degree in business administration from New York University. He worked in the banking and investment industries before co-founding Signature Books in 1981.

His essays have appeared in *Dialogue: A Journal of Mormon Thought, Sunstone*, the *John Whitmer Historical Association Journal*, the *Journal of Mormon History*, and *Free Inquiry*. Besides *An Intimate Chronicle: The Journals of William Clayton*, Smith has edited *Faithful History: Essays on Writing Mormon History* and *Religion, Feminism, and Freedom of Conscience: A Mormon/Humanist Dialogue*. He formed Smith Research Associates in 1987 to encourage historical research and writing and has co-published the journals of significant Mormons, including Joseph Smith, Heber C. Kimball, John Henry Smith, Rudger Clawson, and others.

Smith lives in San Francisco, is married to Camilla Miner, and is the father of five children.